Children's Literature Review

Guide to Gale Literary Criticism Series

When you need to review criticism of literary works, these are the Gale series to use:

If the author's death date is: **You should turn to:**

After Dec. 31, 1959
(or author is still living)

CONTEMPORARY LITERARY CRITICISM

for example: Jorge Luis Borges, Anthony Burgess,
       William Faulkner, Mary Gordon,
       Ernest Hemingway, Iris Murdoch

1900 through 1959

TWENTIETH-CENTURY LITERARY CRITICISM

for example: Willa Cather, F. Scott Fitzgerald
       Henry James, Mark Twain, Virginia Woolf

1800 through 1899

NINETEENTH-CENTURY LITERATURE CRITICISM

for example: Fedor Dostoevski, George Sand,
       Gerard Manley Hopkins, Emily Dickinson

1400 through 1799

LITERATURE CRITICISM FROM 1400 TO 1800
(excluding Shakespeare)

for example: Anne Bradstreet, Pierre Corneille,
       Daniel Defoe, Alexander Pope,
       Jonathan Swift, Phillis Wheatley

SHAKESPEAREAN CRITICISM

Shakespeare plays and poetry

Gale also publishes related criticism series:

CONTEMPORARY ISSUES CRITICISM

Presents criticism on contemporary authors writing
on current issues. Topics covered include the social
sciences, philosophy, economics, natural science, law,
and related areas.

CHILDREN'S LITERATURE REVIEW

Covers authors of all eras. Presents criticism on
authors and author/illustrators who write for the
preschool to junior-high audience.

volume 6

Children's Literature Review

Excerpts from Reviews,
Criticism, and Commentary
on Books for Children

Guest Essay, "The Children's Book World Today,"
by Zena Sutherland

Gerard J. Senick
Editor

Gale Research Company
Book Tower
Detroit, Michigan 48226

STAFF

Gerard J. Senick, *Editor*

Jeanne A. Gough, Susan Miller Harig, and Melissa Reiff Hug, *Assistant Editors*

Sharon R. Gunton, *Contributing Editor*

Robert J. Elster, *Production Supervisor*
Lizbeth A. Purdy, *Production Coordinator*
Denise Michlewicz, *Assistant Production Coordinator*
Eric Berger, Michael S. Corey, Paula J. DiSante, Maureen Duffy,
Serita Lanette Lockard, Amy Marcaccio, Janet S. Mullane, Yvonne Huette Robinson, *Editorial Assistants*

Victoria B. Cariappa, Jeannine Schiffman Davidson, Karen Rae Forsyth, Robert J. Hill, James A. MacEachern, Leslie Kyle Schell,
Mary Spirito, Margaret Stewart, Valerie Webster, *Research Assistants*

Linda M. Pugliese, *Manuscript Coordinator*
Donna Craft, *Assistant Manuscript Coordinator*
Colleen M. Crane, Maureen A. Puhl, Rosetta Irene Simms, *Manuscript Assistants*

L. Elizabeth Hardin, *Permissions Supervisor*
Filomena Sgambati, *Permissions Coordinator*
Janice M. Mach, *Assistant Permissions Coordinator*
Patricia A. Seefelt, *Assistant Permissions Coordinator, Illustrations*
Susan D. Nobles, *Senior Permissions Assistant*
Margaret A. Chamberlain and Joan B. Weber, *Permissions Assistants*
Sandra C. Davis and Virgie T. Leavens, *Permissions Clerks*
Margaret Mary Missar and Audrey B. Wharton, *Photo Research*

Arthur Chartow, *Art Director*

Copyright © 1984 by Gale Research Company

Library of Congress Catalog Card Number 75-34953
ISBN 0-8103-0331-0
ISSN 0362-4145

CONTENTS

Preface   7

A Partial List of Authors Who Will Appear in Future Volumes   9

Acknowledgments   11

Guest Essay, "The Children's Book World Today," by Zena Sutherland   13

Appendix   265

Cumulative Index to Authors   273

Cumulative Index to Titles   279

Cumulative Index to Nationalities   293

Authors Included in Volume 6

PREFACE

Walter de la Mare wrote that "only the rarest kind of best of anything can be good enough for the young." The editors of *Children's Literature Review* enthusiastically endorse this belief. Accordingly, *CLR* has been designed and published to assist those who select reading materials for children in making wise choices. As a collection of critical opinion on children's literature, *CLR* also provides a record of scholarship for researchers.

Each biannual volume contains selected excerpts from published criticism on the literary works of approximately twenty-five authors and author/illustrators who create books for children from preschool to junior high age. The author list for each volume of *CLR* is compiled to represent a variety of genres—including picture books, fiction, nonfiction, poetry, and drama—and is international in scope. Since the majority of authors covered by *CLR* are living and continue to write, it is necessary to update their entries periodically. Future volumes of *CLR* will include criticism on the works of authors covered in earlier volumes and the entire careers of authors new to the series.

Organization of the Book

An author section consists of the following elements: author heading, bio-critical introduction, author's commentary and general commentary (when available), title entries, and bibliographical citations.

- The *author heading* consists of the name under which the author is most frequently published and his or her birth and death dates. If an author writes consistently under a pseudonym, the pseudonym will be listed in the author heading and the real name given in parentheses on the first line of the bio-critical introduction.

- The *bio-critical introduction* contains background information designed to introduce the reader to an author. The introduction begins with a phrase describing the author's nationality and the genres in which he or she writes. The text of the introduction presents an overview in two to four paragraphs of the author's themes and styles, biographical facts, a summary of the critical response to the author's works, and major awards and prizes. Where applicable, the introductions include references to other biographical and critical reference books published by Gale Research Company. These books include *Contemporary Authors, Contemporary Literary Criticism, Something about the Author, Yesterday's Authors of Books for Children,* and past volumes of *CLR*. When available, a photograph of the author accompanies the introduction.

- The *author's commentary* presents background material written by the author being profiled. This commentary may cover a specific work or several works, or discuss the reasons why an author writes.

- *General commentary* consists of critical excerpts from articles that consider more than one work by the author being profiled.

- *Title entries* consist of critical excerpts on the author's individual works, arranged chronologically. They generally include two to six reviews per title, depending on the stature of the book and the amount of criticism it has generated. In some cases not every title published by the author is represented. The editors select titles which reflect the author's variety of genres and subjects as well as his or her most important books. Thus, the reader is provided with a record of the author's literary development. An effort is made to reprint criticism from sources which represent the full scope of each title's publication history—from the year of its initial publication to current references. Titles by authors being profiled in *CLR* are highlighted in boldface within the text for easier access by researchers.

All title entry headings include publication information on the work being reviewed. Title headings list the work's title as it appeared in its country of origin. If the work's U.S. title differs from the original title, the U.S. title follows in brackets. The work's first publication date is listed in parentheses following the brackets. When a work first published in the U.S. has been published in Great Britain under an alternate title, this information follows the publication date.

Illustrations are featured, when available, within the title entries of authors who illustrate their own works. An effort has been made to select illustrations which are mentioned in the criticism and to place each one as close as possible to its critical reference. Each illustration is accompanied by a caption identifying the work in which it originally appeared. An acknowledgments section giving credit to copyright holders of illustrations follows the preface.

• A complete *bibliographical citation* designed to facilitate the location of the original article or book follows each piece of criticism. An asterisk following a citation indicates that the essay or book contains information on more than one author.

Each volume of *CLR* includes a guest essay following the acknowledgments section. Guest essays are original pieces written specifically for *CLR* by prominent critics on subjects of their choice. Volume 6 contains Zena Sutherland's "The Children's Book World Today" as its guest essay. The editors are honored to feature Mrs. Sutherland in this volume.

Each volume of *CLR* contains cumulative indexes to authors and titles; *CLR* volumes 1-5 contain a cumulative index to critics. Starting with volume 3, each volume includes an appendix which lists the sources from which material has been reprinted in the volume. It does not, however, list every book or periodical consulted during the preparation of the volume.

New Features

Selected excerpts are now prefaced by *explanatory notes* as an additional aid to users. These notes provide information on the critic or the work of criticism to enhance the usefulness of the excerpt.

A cumulative nationality index accompanies cumulative indexes to authors and titles beginning with volume 6. Author names are arranged alphabetically under their respective nationalities and are followed by the volume number(s) in which they appear.

Acknowledgments

The editors wish to thank the copyright holders of the excerpts included in this volume, the permissions managers of many book and magazine publishing companies, Jeri Yaryan for her assistance in locating copyright holders, and Henrietta Epstein and Erik Dal for their editorial assistance. We are also grateful to the staffs of the Kresge Library at Wayne State University, the libraries of the University of Michigan, and the Detroit Public Library as well as to research clerks Kevin J. Campbell, Kathleen E. Carroll, Barbara H. Goldman, Tracy N. Jordan, Donna J. Morgan, and Winifred F. Powers.

Suggestions Are Welcome

If readers wish to suggest authors they are particularly anxious to have covered in upcoming volumes, or if they have other suggestions, they are cordially invited to write the editors.

A Partial List of Authors Who Will Appear in Future Volumes

Abbott, Jacob 1803-1879
Adams, Adrienne 1906-
Adams, Harriet S(tratemeyer)
  1893?-1982
Adkins, Jan 1944-
Adler, Irving 1913-
Adoff, Arnold 1935-
Aesop 620?BC-564?BC
Aliki 1929-
Anderson, C(larence) W(illiam)
  1891-1971
Asimov, Isaac 1920-
Avery, Gillian 1926-
Avi 1937-
Bailey, Carolyn Sherwin 1875-1961
Ballantyne, R(obert) M(ichael)
  1825-1894
Banner, Angela 1923-
Bannerman, Helen 1863-1946
Barrie, (Sir) J(ames) M(atthew)
  1860-1937
Baum, L(yman) Frank 1856-1919
Baumann, Hans 1914-
BB 1905-
Behn, Harry 1898-1973
Belpré, Pura 1899-1982
Benary-Isbert, Margot 1889-1979
Benchley, Nathaniel 1915-1981
Bennett, John 1865-1956
Berenstain, Stan(ley) 1923- and
  Jan(ice) 1923-
Berger, Melvin 1927-
Berna, Paul 1910-
Beskow, Elsa 1874-1953
Bianco, Margery Williams 1881-1944
Bishop, Claire Huchet
Blos, Joan W(insor) 1928-
Blyton, Enid 1897-1968
Bond, Nancy 1945-
Bonham, Frank 1914-
Branley, Franklyn M(ansfield) 1915-
Brazil, Angela 1869-1947
Breinburg, Petronella 1927-
Briggs, Raymond 1934-
Bright, Robert 1902-
Brink, Carol Ryrie 1895-1981
Brooke, L(eonard) Leslie 1862-1940
Brooks, Gwendolyn 1917-
Brown, Marcia 1918-
Brown, Margaret Wise 1910-1952
Bruna, Dick 1927-
Buff, Mary 1890-1970 and Conrad
  1886-1975
Bulla, Clyde Robert 1914-
Burch, Robert 1925-
Burchard, Peter 1921-
Burgess, (Frank) Gelett 1866-1951
Burgess, Thornton W(aldo) 1874-1965
Burnett, Frances Hodgson 1849-1924

Burningham, John 1936-
Burton, Virginia Lee 1909-1968
Busch, Wilhelm 1832-1908
Butterworth, Oliver 1915-
Carle, Eric 1929-
Carlson, Natalie Savage 1906-
Carrick, Donald 1929- and Carol 1935-
Charlip, Remy 1929-
Chönz, Selina
Christopher, Matt(hew) 1917-
Chukovsky, Kornei 1882-1969
Clark, Ann Nolan 1896-
Clarke, Pauline 1921-
Cleaver, Elizabeth 1939-
Cohen, Barbara 1932-
Colby, C(arroll) B(urleigh) 1904-1977
Colman, Hila
Cone, Molly 1918-
Conford, Ellen 1942-
Coolidge, Olivia 1908-
Coolidge, Susan 1835-1905
Cooney, Barbara 1917-
Cox, Palmer 1840-1924
Cresswell, Helen 1934-
Crews, Donald 1938-
Crompton, Richmal 1890-1969
Cunningham, Julia 1916-
Curry, Jane L(ouise) 1932-
Dalgliesh, Alice 1893-1979
Danziger, Paula 1944-
Daugherty, James 1889-1974
d'Aulaire, Ingri 1904-1980 and Edgar
  Parin 1898-
d'Aulnoy, Countess Marie 1650-1705
de la Mare, Walter 1873-1956
de Regniers, Beatrice Schenk 1914-
Dillon, Eilís 1920-
Dodge, Mary Mapes 1831-1905
Duvoisin, Roger 1904-1980
Eager, Edward 1911-1964
Edgeworth, Maria 1767-1849
Edmonds, Walter D(umaux) 1903-
Epstein, Sam(uel) 1909- and Beryl 1910-
Ets, Marie Hall 1893-
Ewing, Juliana Horatia 1841-1885
Farber, Norma 1909-
Farjeon, Eleanor 1881-1965
Farmer, Penelope 1939-
Fatio, Louise 1904-
Field, Eugene 1850-1895
Field, Rachel 1894-1942
Fisher, Dorothy Canfield 1879-1958
Fisher, Leonard Everett 1924-
Flack, Marjorie 1897-1958
Forbes, Esther 1891-1967
Foster, Genevieve 1893-1979
Freeman, Don 1908-1978
Fujikawa, Gyo
Fyleman, Rose 1877-1957

Garfield, Leon 1921-
Garis, Howard R(oger) 1873-1962
Garner, Alan 1935-
Gates, Doris 1901-
Giff, Patricia Reilly 1935-
Godden, Rumer 1907-
Goodall, John S(trickland) 1908-
Goodrich, Samuel G(riswold) 1793-1860
Gorey, Edward 1925-
Graham, Lorenz B(ell) 1902-
Gramatky, Hardie 1907-1979
Greene, Constance C(larke) 1924-
Grimm, Jacob 1785-1863 and Wilhelm
  1786-1859
Gruelle, Johnny 1880-1938
Guillot, René 1900-1969
Hader, Elmer 1889-1973 and Berta
  1891?-1976
Hale, Lucretia Peabody 1820-1900
Harnett, Cynthia 1893-1981
Harris, Christie 1907-
Harris, Joel Chandler 1848-1908
Haywood, Carolyn 1898-
Hoban, Tana
Hoff, Syd(ney) 1912-
Hoffman, Heinrich 1809-1894
Holling, Holling C(lancy) 1900-1973
Howe, James 1946- and Deborah
  1946-1978
Hughes, Langston 1902-1967
Hunter, Mollie 1922-
Ipcar, Dahlov 1917-
Isadora, Rachel
Iwasaki, Chihiro 1918-
Jackson, Jesse 1908-1983
Janosch 1931-
Jeschke, Susan 1942-
Johnson, James Weldon 1871-1938
Jordan, June 1936-
Judson, Clara Ingram 1879-1960
Juster, Norton 1929-
Keith, Harold 1903-
Kelly, Eric P(hilbrook) 1884-1960
Kennedy, Richard 1932-
Kent, Jack 1920-
Kettelkamp, Larry 1933-
King, Clive 1924-
Kipling, Rudyard 1865-1936
Kjelgaard, Jim 1910-1959
Kraus, Robert 1925-
Krauss, Ruth 1911-
Krüss, James 1926-
La Farge, Oliver 1901-1963
La Fontaine, Jean de 1621-1695
Lagerlöf, Selma 1858-1940
Langton, Jane 1922-
Lavine, Sigmund A(rnold) 1908-
Leaf, Munro 1905-1976
Lenski, Lois 1893-1974

Lent, Blair 1930-
Levy, Elizabeth 1942-
Lewis, Elizabeth Foreman 1892-1958
Lightner, A(lice) M. 1904-
Lindsay, Norman 1879-1969
Lionni, Leo 1910-
Lively, Penelope 1933-
Livingston, Myra Cohn 1926-
Lofting, Hugh 1866-1947
Lunn, Janet 1928-
MacDonald, George 1824-1905
Mahy, Margaret 1936-
Mann, Peggy
Marshall, James 1942-
Martin, Patricia Miles 1899-
Mayer, Mercer 1943- and Marianna
   1945-
Mayne, William 1928-
McCloskey, Robert 1914-
McCord, David 1897-
McDermott, Gerald 1941-
McKillip, Patricia A(nne) 1948-
McNeer, May 1902- and Lynd Ward
   1905-
Meader, Stephen W(arren) 1892-1977
Means, Florence Crannell 1891-1980
Meigs, Cornelia 1884-1973
Merriam, Eve 1916-
Merrill, Jean 1923-
Miles, Betty 1928-
Milne, Lorus 1912- and Margery 1915-
Minarik, Else Holmelund 1920-
Mizumura, Kazue
Mohr, Nicholasa 1935-
Molesworth, Mary Louisa 1842-1921
Montgomery, L(ucy) M(aud) 1874-1942
Morey, Walt(er) 1907-
Mukerji, Dhan Gopal 1890-1936
Munari, Bruno 1907-
Neville, Emily Cheney 1919-
Newfeld, Frank 1928-
Nic Leodhas, Sorche 1898-1969
Nichols, Ruth 1948-

North, Sterling 1906-1974
Oakley, Graham 1929-
Olney, Ross R(obert) 1929-
Olsen, Ib Spang 1921-
Ormondroyd, Edward 1925-
Ottley, Reginald
Oxenbury, Helen 1938-
Parish, Peggy 1927-
Paterson, Katherine 1932-
Pearce, A(nn) Philippa 1920-
Pease, Howard 1894-1974
Peck, Robert Newton 1928-
Peet, Bill 1915-
Perl, Lila
Perrault, Charles 1628-1703
Petersham, Maud 1890-1971 and Miska
   1888-1960
Pfeffer, Susan Beth 1948-
Picard, Barbara Leonie 1917-
Politi, Leo 1908-
Prelutsky, Jack
Price, Christine 1928-1980
Provensen, Alice 1918- and Martin
   1916-
Pyle, Howard 1853-1911
Ransome, Arthur 1884-1967
Rawls, Wilson 1913-
Richards, Laura E(lizabeth) 1850-1943
Richler, Mordecai 1931-
Robertson, Keith 1914-
Rockwell, Anne 1934- and Harlow
Rodgers, Mary 1931-
Rollins, Charlemae Hill 1897-1979
Rounds, Glen 1906-
Sandoz, Mari 1896-1966
Sawyer, Ruth 1880-1970
Scott, Jack Denton 1915-
Selden, George 1929-
Seredy, Kate 1899-1975
Seton, Ernest Thompson 1860-1946
Sharp, Margery 1905-
Sidney, Margaret 1844-1924
Silverstein, Alvin 1933- and Virginia
   1937-

Simon, Seymour 1931-
Sinclair, Catherine 1880-1864
Skurzynski, Gloria 1930-
Slobodkin, Louis 1903-1975
Snyder, Zilpha Keatley 1927-
Spence, Eleanor 1928-
Sperry, Armstrong W. 1897-1976
Spykman, E(lizabeth) C. 1896-1965
Spyri, Johanna 1827-1901
Steele, William O(wen) 1917-1979
Stevenson, Robert Louis 1850-1894
Stolz, Mary 1920-
Stratemeyer, Edward L. 1862-1930
Streatfeild, Noel 1897-
Sutcliff, Rosemary 1920-
Taylor, Sydney 1904?-1978
Taylor, Theodore 1924-
Ter Haar, Jaap 1922-
Thomas, Ianthe
Titus, Eve 1922-
Trease, Geoffrey 1909-
Tresselt, Alvin 1916-
Treviño, Elizabeth Borton de 1904-
Tudor, Tasha 1915-
Turkle, Brinton 1915-
Udry, Janice May 1928-
Unnerstad, Edith 1900-
Uttley, Alison 1884-1976
Vining, Elizabeth Gray 1902-
Waber, Bernard 1924-
Wahl, Jan 1933-
Watanabe, Shigeo 1928-
Westall, Robert 1929-
Wiese, Kurt 1887-1974
Wilkinson, Brenda 1946-
Williams, Jay 1914-1978
Yates, Elizabeth 1905-
Yonge, Charlotte M(ary) 1823-1901
Zaffo, George J.
Zemach, Harve 1933-1974 and Margot
   1931-
Zion, Gene 1913-1975

Readers are cordially invited to suggest additional authors to the editors.

ACKNOWLEDGMENTS

are made to the following publishers, authors, and artists for their kind permission to reproduce copyrighted material.

Casterman Publishers. Illustration by Hergé from *The Crab with the Golden Claws* by Hergé. Art © by Casterman, Tournai. Text © by Methuen, London; Little, Brown, Boston./ Illustration by Hergé from *King Ottokar's Sceptre* by Hergé. Art © by Casterman, Tournai. Text © by Methuen, London; Little, Brown, Boston./ Illustration by Hergé from *Red Rackham's Treasure* by Hergé. Art © by Casterman, Tournai. Text © by Methuen, London; Little, Brown, Boston./ Illustration by Hergé from *The Seven Crystal Balls* by Hergé. Art © by Casterman, Tournai. Text © by Methuen, London; Little, Brown, Boston./ Illustration by Hergé from *Tintin in Tibet* by Hergé. Art © by Casterman, Tournai. Text © by Methuen, London; Little, Brown, Boston. All reproduced by permission of Casterman Publishers.

Delacorte Press. Illustration by Jan Pieńkowski excerpted from the book *Robot* by Jan Pieńkowski. Copyright © 1981 by Jan Pieńkowski. Used by permission of Delacorte Press.

Elsevier-Dutton Publishing Co., Inc. Illustration by Steven Kellogg from *Can I Keep Him?* by Steven Kellogg. © 1971 by Steven Kellogg./ Illustration by Steven Kellogg from *The Island of the Skog* by Steven Kellogg. © 1973 by Steven Kellogg./ Illustration by Steven Kellogg from *The Mystery of the Missing Red Mitten* by Steven Kellogg. © 1974 by Steven Kellogg./ Illustration by Steven Kellogg from *Pinkerton, Behave!* by Steven Kellogg. © 1976 by Steven Kellogg./ Illustration by Steven Kellogg from *The Mysterious Tadpole* by Steven Kellogg. © 1977 by Steven Kellogg./ Illustration by Steven Kellogg from *A Rose for Pinkerton* by Steven Kellogg. © 1981 by Steven Kellogg. All reproduced by permission of the publisher, Dial Books for Young Readers, a Division of E.P. Dutton, Inc./ Illustration by Jan Pieńkowski from *Haunted House* by Jan Pieńkowski. © 1979 by Jan Pieńkowski. Reproduced by permission of the publisher, E.P. Dutton, Inc.

Harcourt Brace Jovanovich, Inc. Illustration by Yoshiko Uchida from *The Magic Listening Cap* by Yoshiko Uchida. Copyright 1955 by Yoshiko Uchida. Reproduced by permission of Harcourt Brace Jovanovich, Inc.

Harper & Row, Publishers, Inc. Illustration by Ludwig Bemelmans from *The High World* by Ludwig Bemelmans. Copyright, 1950, by the Curtis Publishing Company. Copyright, 1954, by Ludwig Bemelmans. Used by arrangement with International Creative Management, Inc., New York./ Illustration by Ludwig Bemelmans from *Parsley* by Ludwig Bemelmans. Copyright 1953, 1955 by Ludwig Bemelmans. Reprinted by permission of Harper & Row, Publishers, Inc.

Holt, Rinehart and Winston, Publishers. Illustration by Evaline Ness from *Sam, Bangs and Moonshine* by Evaline Ness. Copyright © 1966 by Evaline Ness. Reprinted by permission of Holt, Rinehart and Winston, Publishers.

Merrimack Publishing Corporation. Illustration by Kate Greenaway from *Kate Greenaway's Book of Games* by Kate Greenaway. Reproduced by permission of Merrimack Publishing Corporation, a Division of B. Shackman & Co., Inc.

Charles Scribner's Sons. Illustration by Evaline Ness from *Josefina February* by Evaline Ness. Copyright © 1963 by Evaline Ness./ Illustration by Evaline Ness from *Exactly Alike* by Evaline Ness. Copyright © 1964 by Evaline Ness./ Illustration by Evaline Ness from *A Double Discovery* by Evaline Ness. Copyright © 1965 by Evaline Ness. All reprinted with permission of Charles Scribner's Sons./ Illustration by Evaline Ness from *Long, Broad and Quickeye* adapted by Evaline Ness. Illustrations copyright © 1969 by Evaline Ness. Used with permission of the author.

Viking Penguin Inc. Illustration by Ludwig Bemelmans from *The Castle Number Nine* by Ludwig Bemelmans. Copyright 1934 by Ludwig Bemelmans. Reproduced by permission of Madeleine Bemelmans and Barbara Bemelmans Marciano./ Illustration by Ludwig Bemelmans from *Hansi* by Ludwig Bemelmans. Copyright 1934 by Ludwig Bemelmans./ Illustration by Ludwig Bemelmans from *The Golden Basket* by Ludwig Bemelmans. Copyright 1936 by Ludwig Bemelmans./ Illustration by Ludwig Bemelmans from *Madeline's Rescue* by Ludwig Bemelmans. Copyright 1951, 1953 by Ludwig Bemelmans./ Illustration by Ludwig Bemelmans from *Madeline in London* by Ludwig Bemelmans. Copyright © 1961 by Ludwig Bemelmans. All reproduced by permission of Viking Penguin Inc./ Illustration by Ludwig Bemelmans from *Madeline* by Ludwig Bemelmans. Copyright 1939 by Ludwig Bemelmans; copyright renewed 1967 by Madeleine Bemelmans and Barbara Marciano. Reprinted by permission of Viking Penguin Inc.

GUEST ESSAY

The Children's Book World Today
by Zena Sutherland

Just as our children study history in part to increase their understanding of how the past prepares for and impinges on the present, so we must look backward to fully understand what is happening in the children's book world today—to know what is going on not only in the books that are published, but also in the publishing industry from which the books emanate and in the libraries through which they are made accessible to children.

In the first quarter of this century, when publishing houses set up their first separate children's book departments, leading children's librarians were instrumental in initiating the reviewing of children's books, in publicizing children's book awards, and in filling the new editorial posts that were being created. Then, as now, the bulk of sales of children's books were to school and public libraries, so that the major efforts of promotion managers and advertising budgets were directed toward this market rather than toward sales to individual buyers in bookstores.

It was also during the first half of the century that authors and, to an even greater extent, illustrators from other countries enriched the stream of books that were being published in increasing numbers by the versatility and variety of their creative work. This phenomenon was particularly true in the production of picture books, a segment of children's book publication in which the United States became and remained preeminent.

When, in the 1960s, federal legislation made monies available to libraries, they were able to expand their book buying, and publishers were quick to respond with expanded production programs, both in the quantity of books published and in the size of print runs. Everybody was a beneficiary, not least the children who were the ultimate consumers. When the golden flow stopped, libraries were forced to cut their book budgets and publishers were forced to cut both their seasonal lists of new titles and the backlists of older titles. As production costs and overhead costs mounted in a spiralling economy, the prices of children's books rose. All of these problems were exacerbated in the late 1970s and the 1980s as the gloomy economic situation, with its combined recession and inflation, made further inroads on libraries and publishing houses.

Among the repercussive results of financial attrition have been mergers within the publishing industry and takeovers by monolithic businesses that were not publishing companies. These moves have sometimes resulted in the detriment of the quality or quantity of books published; in the demise of children's book departments; in increased efforts to urge bookstore owners to expand and publicize children's books; in the shrinkage of space allotted to coverage of children's books in some magazines and newspapers; in higher prices of both hardbound and paperback books; in the growing market for paperback books; and in the growing importance of those books that might gain for publishers and authors the lucrative benefits of sales of subsidiary rights. Oddly, the numbers of books published each year have held up well.

Perhaps the oddity of this sign of apparent stability can be explained by the fact that, because of all the economic pressures, the market has become more competitive; while every children's book department feels a modicum of nervousness about untried authors, it also has high hopes that a new author may turn out to be an asset. In the past, many editors felt they could publish some books that they knew would not have large sales but that deserved publishing; now, even if they would like to publish books they love but that have little promise of having popular appeal, they seldom can afford this luxury, if they can afford it at all. Indeed, one of the visible publishing phenomena of the 1980s has been the enthusiasm with which any innovatory, successful book has been imitated.

For several reasons, one of the changes observable in the 1980s is the decrease in the number of translated books that were first published in other languages in other countries. The economy itself is one factor; another is that many of the books from other countries have always had small sales, and small sales today are frightening. Another consideration is that federal legislation has made it possible for British publishers, whose books may or may not be adapted for readers in the United States, to distribute their books directly in this country; still another is the fact that fewer publishers, in all countries, are as ready to make contractual arrangements for joint publication, a venture that (because it increases the size of the print run) brings down the cost and therefore the price of the book.

So book prices are high, although they haven't increased any more than other goods and products when viewed on a percentage basis. Since reading proficiency and voluntary reading have not been flourishing in our society, many adults and children are more willing to spend what entertainment money they have on other (equally high-priced and often less durable) competitors for leisure time, such as electronic games, film cassettes, comic books, and toy books. Most children prefer, when they spend their own money, to purchase paperback books rather than hardcover books. Many fine titles that were originally published as hardbound books are reprinted in paperback editions, although original paperbacks tend, with exceptions, to be of inferior literary quality.

Of the many observable trends in the children's books published today, one of the most prominent is the teenage romance. One after another, paperback publishers have brought out new lines of romantic stories (some publishers have more than one series of books), usually pedestrian in quality, that are written to formula; indeed, some paperback houses have printed guidelines that instruct and limit authors as to subjects and themes, ages of protagonists, taboos and limitations, and even number of words to be used in manuscripts.

There has been the same kind of imitative frenzy in another trend, the choose-your-own adventure (or romance, or mystery detection) book, in which readers, at various points in the story, choose between alternatives and are directed to certain pages in the volume. Almost every publisher has produced some (some have produced many) toy books, books that have pop-ups or paste-ins or pull-tabs or other movable parts; occasionally these are used as integral parts of the forward progress of a text, but for the most part they are as peripherally ornamental as they are fragile.

The changes just discussed are fairly recent, and many of them have to do with format; many of them seem to be induced by the profit motive rather than to be published for the sake of giving children good books. This is not to say that popular appeal, or the potential for popular appeal, should not be considered by all the adults—authors, artists, editors, parents, teachers, librarians, and reviewers—who are instrumental in creating books for children and disseminating them, but that many of these books or semi-books seem to have been produced with no regard for literary quality or intrinsic worth.

There are other trends today that are long-term trends and that have to do with more substantive issues, issues that affect the contents of today's books. As has always been true of children's books, contemporary books reflect not only their producers' concerns about societal issues, but also the concepts that our society has of children, of what children's needs and concerns are, and of what children ought to know or learn. In today's world there are currents and crosscurrents of social forces, reform movements, protest groups, educational theories, technological advances, and expanding frontiers of scientific understanding. All of them can be observed in children's books today, and their inclusion has changed the content and approach in many books and created controversy about many.

In the earlier years of the century, there existed a large body of taboos as well as certain expectations of what a children's book should and ought to be. Few books challenged, for example, the concept of the wise and kind parent or pictured parents who had weaknesses or showed hostility or favoritism. Most of the families in children's books were white, most were middle-class; fathers went to work and mothers stayed at home wearing an apron and baking cookies. Grandparents, usually pictured as inactive and doting, were present in some of the books but they seldom became senile or died. There were few children who suffered from physical or emotional disabilities, even fewer who were members of minority groups. Girls, like their mothers, gravitated toward the kitchen; boys were given active roles and prospects for a broad range of careers. There were boys' adventure tales and sport stories; there were girls' love stories; the few career stories for girls showed them primarily in those few professions that were deemed acceptable for women: teachers, secretaries, and nurses. Nurses proliferated in series that almost invariably included the thawing of a strict supervisor after the student nurse had performed some extraordinary feat of nursing, and almost invariably ended with the eyes of the heroine meeting those of the handsome young doctor across a candle-lit room at a capping ceremony. Formula writing, stereotypical characters.

Of course there were exceptions. There have always been fine books published in every age; in a country where so many children's books have been published annually, there are fine books every year. Unfortunately, they are not in the majority, although (despite the series books, mediocre romances, and toy books) there are probably more good books published in this decade than in previous decades. The changes in contemporary books are marked and sometimes remarkable, but there continues to be a wide range of quality in books on every subject and of every genre.

One of the more encouraging trends, for example, has been an increase in the quality of native fantasy. For many years the best English-language fiction available to children in the United States and Canada came from Great Britain, beginning with such older classics as Lewis Carroll's *Alice's Adventures in Wonderland* and the stories about the Bastable children by Edith Nesbit to such writers as Pamela Travers, Philippa Pearce, Lucy Boston, and Alan Garner. Save for the stories of Oz by Lyman Frank Baum, there was little produced in America that was of lasting value.

Today such writers as Lloyd Alexander, E.B. White, Susan Cooper, and Ursula Le Guin have produced a steady stream of innovative and beautifully polished fantasy.

In the realm of nonfiction, there has been improvement in almost every aspect of books for children. Editors have been more selective in screening the credentials of authors to establish their qualifications to write about special subjects. More informational books have full indexes, notes on sources, and more-than-token bibliographies than in the past. There is more attention paid to the use of appropriate reading level and concepts in judging the comprehension level of the intended audience. Aware that the television generation is being exposed to programs that expand their interests, editors have encouraged authors to provide material to meet those interests at all levels, so that there are mathematics books, computer books, ecology books, and so on, for younger children as well as for older readers. Biographies are more candid, more comprehensive, and less likely to create an idealized but wooden figure; there are more biographies of women, more biographies of members of minority groups; more biographies about men and women whose achievements span almost every field of endeavor.

The new diversity in biographical writing is a clear indication of some of the changes in our society; with the growth of the feminist movement, the burgeoning of ethnic protest groups and the civil rights movement, more informational books reflect these developments in our society. Nowhere, however, are such developments as well as the changes in life styles, sexual mores, increasing concern about the old and the disabled, and the growing body of knowledge about the importance of early childhood or about children's emotional needs and developmental stages more often mirrored than in contemporary realistic fiction.

The fact that realistic fiction reflects deep concerns and problems has led to use of the term "problem novel." It is true that many children's novels are concerned with such problems as premarital pregnancy, drugs, divorce, intra-family tensions, dissatisfaction with school or with a teacher, death, illness, and other situations or relationships that cloud the lives of children as well as adults. There are adults who object to the inclusion of these things in books for young readers, who feel that children should be protected or who feel that such books set poor examples. Other adults feel (with equal sincerity and conviction) that such books are more true to life, that they help prepare children for encountering problems, and that little in children's realistic fiction is not already familiar to them through newspapers, magazines, radio, and television, both in the programming of the latter and in the reporting of the news. This conflict has led to an increasing number of attempts on the part of censorious groups and individuals to have certain books removed from library shelves and to some extent has led to self-censorship on the part of book clubs that are publishing reprints of books they consider controversial.

The aspects of controversy that receive the most publicity are those concerned with sexual patterns, the use of what is considered coarse language, and parent-child relationships in the main, although in the 1980s there has been an upsurge of protest about "secular humanism" from the several national organizations that have been dubbed "The New Right." These groups have given most of their attention to textbooks for children and young people but are also concerned about trade books. Not all the pressure comes from this group, however; there is protest from those who feel that a book should convey messages that propound ethnic equality (or positive images of the elderly or the disabled) and from those who feel that a subject should be handled in another manner, or covered only for an older age group. We have always had protest; the difference today is that it is more highly organized, more strident, and often more successful.

Despite the protest and the censorship, books flourish. Never before has there been so much available for young children: picture books, wordless books, concept books, alphabet and counting books, and single story editions of folktales, often beautifully illustrated. The range of illustrative styles and techniques is impressive, with the work of new artists like Chris Van Allsburg, Michael Hague, and Susan Jeffers adding to the continuing contributions of established artists like Maurice Sendak, Arnold Lobel, and John Burningham.

New authors, too, are adding prestige to the world of children's literature; the versatile and polished writing of Lois Lowry, the sensitive stories about handicapped children by Jan Slepian, the strong and perceptive novels by Robert Cormier and Robert Westall have received acclaim from reviewers and have delighted readers. Fine collections of folklore appear in a steady, quiet stream, as do poetry anthologies and volumes by individual poets.

Interest in poetry has been stimulated by the establishment of an award for the body of a poet's work, given annually by the National Council of Teachers of English. An award is given each year by the International Reading Association for the best first or second book by a new author; the first Scott O'Dell Award for Historical Fiction, an award established by O'Dell, was given for the first time for a book published in 1983. Such awards, as well as those given annually by children's librarians in Canada, Great Britain, and the United States, have encouraged authors and illustrators and have contributed to public awareness of children's books.

Those who have felt that children's literature is part of the mainstream of literature, and especially those who have felt for some time that writing for children has surpassed that of adult books in quality, must be gratified by the current spate of books about children's literature and by the growing insistence on the need for scholarly criticism. With all its problems, the world of children's books is doing very nicely, thank you. The books pour out of presses, varied and often exciting; children buy them and borrow them and exchange them and love them. Even in the computer age, we may feel some confidence that books will continue to give children information and pleasure, and will help them to understand themselves and the world in which they live.

Zena Sutherland is an American author, editor, critic, educator, librarian, and lecturer. She began editing *Bulletin of the Center for Children's Books* in 1958. Mrs. Sutherland succeeded May Hill Arbuthnot as the author of the *Children and Books* series (fourth edition, 1972; fifth edition, 1977; sixth edition, 1981). From 1972 to 1977 she was the contributing editor for children's books at *Saturday Review* and in 1977 she became the children's book review editor of the *Chicago Tribune.* She was appointed to the first National Book Award committee in 1969 and chaired the 1975 Newbery-Caldecott Award committee. In 1981, Mrs. Sutherland was honored by the publication of *Celebrating Children's Books: Essays on Children's Literature in Honor of Zena Sutherland* and the establishment of The Zena Sutherland Lectureship at The University of Chicago.

Hans Christian Andersen

1805-1875

Danish author of fairy tales, poet, playwright, and novelist.

Andersen is perhaps the foremost writer of fairy tales in literary history. He expanded the scope of the genre by creating original stories that draw from a wealth of folklore, personal experience, and boundless imagination. Before Andersen, most fairy tales were retold folk tales set down by scholars to preserve their historical and cultural value. Andersen used their structure to transform his life, ideas, and ideals into allegories about human nature. He directed these works to children, writing in a conversational language they could understand and enjoy. "I seize an idea for older people," he wrote, "and then tell it to the young ones, while remembering that father and mother are listening and must have something to think about." Many critics believe that Andersen's genius lies in the fact that he never really grew up. He saw nature, events, people, and objects the way a child sees them: with curiosity, close inspection, and imagination. He infused his subjects with traits never before attributed to them. His plants and animals, for example, possess the innocence and simplicity of children, while inanimate objects become symbols of greed, pride, envy, and other imperfections. The children who appear in his tales are often secondary, but the stories contain some of the most memorable child characters in literature, such as The Little Match Girl, Kay and Gerda in "The Snow Queen," and Karen in "The Red Shoes." Andersen's tales are usually regarded as works of sheer poetry, to be read as autobiography, philosophy, or pure story by children of any age.

Andersen is considered the first prominent Danish writer of proletarian origin. His life is often viewed as a romantic success story, but Andersen's early years were filled with poverty and suffering. Andersen pursued recognition with unyielding confidence and dedication. He hoped initially to succeed as a performer, but eventually decided to devote himself to creating serious literature. In 1835, when his first pamphlet of *Eventyr*, or "Wonder Stories," was published, Andersen was well-known in Denmark for his travel books, plays, and a novel, *The Improvisatore*. His collection included only four stories, three of which were retellings of tales he knew from childhood. Critical reaction to the tales was generally negative. They were seen as unsuitable for children because they lacked didacticism, and too unsophisticated for adults because of their colloquial style. The tales were, however, praised by such figures as Hans Christian Ørsted, the discoverer of electromagnetism. Ørsted claimed that if *The Improvisatore* made Andersen famous, the tales would make him immortal. At first Andersen agreed with his detractors and tried to ignore the tales. He called them *smaating*, or trifles, but was drawn to them when he realized they were the perfect outlet for his message to the world. He also discovered that the tales commanded his greatest audience and could bring him the international fame he sought.

Andersen published nearly two hundred tales throughout his career. Many of them are at least somewhat based on incidents and periods in his life, such as "The Steadfast Tin Soldier," "The Little Mermaid," and "The Swineherd," which examine his unrequited loves in varying degrees of melancholy

and satire. Perhaps "The Ugly Duckling" is the autobiographical tale best known by children. Just as the snubbed signet becomes a beautiful swan, so Andersen became the pride of Denmark and its international literary representative. Not all of Andersen's tales end happily, however. He reflects the hardships he knew as a child as well as strongly moralistic and religious attitudes: Andersen had a childlike faith in God, and he viewed death as a reward. The inclusion of these elements causes some reviewers to insist that Andersen's stories are maudlin and sentimental, as well as too disturbing for young readers. However, Andersen's underlying cosmic view is positive, and he often invests his tales with a mischievous sense of humor which is occasionally lost in translation. He is usually recognized today as a consummate storyteller who distilled his vision of humanity into a simple format that can be universally appreciated. Edmund Gosse wrote, "It will probably be centuries before Europe sees again a man in whom the same qualities of imagination are blended."

(See also *Yesterday's Authors of Books for Children*, Vol. 1.)

[Due to the large amount of available criticism on Andersen, this entry is composed exclusively of general commentary in English and in English translation. It centers on Andersen's collections of fairy tales and his literary reputation as their author. Additional general commentary and criticism on individual tales will appear in future volumes.]

AUTHOR'S COMMENTARY

A few months only after the publication of "**The Improvisatore**" I brought out the first part of my "**Wonder Stories**," but the critics would not vouchsafe to me any encouragement.... The "Monthly Review" never deigned to mention them at all, and in "Dannora," another critical journal, I was advised not to waste my time in writing wonder stories. I lacked the usual form of that kind of poetry; I would not study models, said they—and so I gave up writing them; and in this alternation of feeling between gayety and ill-humor I wrote my next novel, "**O. T.**" I felt just at the time a strong mental impulse to write, and I believed that I had found my true element in novel-writing. (p. 135)

In my book "**In the Hartz Mountains**" one finds properly my first wonder story, in the section "**Brunswick**," where it appears as a bit of irony in the drama "**Three Days in the Life of a Looking-glass;**" in the same book one also finds the first suggestion of "**The Little Mermaid;**" the description of the Elves belongs quite to this class of writing. Only a few months after the "**Improvisatore**" appeared, in 1835, I brought out my first volume of "**Wonder Stories**," which at that time was not so very much thought of. One monthly critical journal even complained that an author who had taken such a step forward in the "**Improvisatore**," should immediately fall back with anything so childish as the tales. I reaped a harvest of blame, precisely where people ought to have acknowledged the advantage of my mind producing something in a new direction. Several of my friends, whose judgment was of value to me, counseled me entirely to abstain from writing tales, as these were a something for which I had no talent. Others were of opinion that I had better, first of all, study the French fairy tale. (pp. 202-03)

I would willingly have discontinued writing them, but they forced themselves from me.

In the volume which I first published, I had, like Musäus, but in my own manner, related old stories, which I had heard as a child. The tone in which they still sounded in my ears seemed a very natural one to me, but I knew very well that the learned critics would censure the style of talk, so, to quiet them I called them "**Wonder Stories told for Children**," although my intention was that they should be for both young and old. The volume concluded with one which was original, "**Little Ida's Flowers**," and seemed to have given the greatest pleasure, although it bore a tolerably near affinity to a story of Hoffman's, and I had already given it in substance in my "**Foot Journey**." In my increasing disposition for children's stories, I therefore followed my own impulse, and invented them mostly myself. In the following year a new volume came out, and soon after that a third, in which the longest story, "**The Little Mermaid**," was my own invention. This story, in an especial manner, created an interest which was only increased by the following volumes. One of these came out every Christmas, and before long no Christmas-tree could exist without my stories. (pp. 203-04)

In order that the reader might be placed in the proper point of view, with regard to the manner in which I told the stories, I had called my first volume "**Stories told for Children**." I had written my narrative down upon paper, exactly in the language, and with the expressions in which I had myself related them, by word of mouth, to the little ones, and I had arrived at the conviction that people of different ages were equally amused with them. The children made themselves merry for the most part over what might be called the actors; older people, on the contrary, were interested in the deeper meaning. The stories furnished reading for children and grown people, and that assuredly is a difficult task for those who will write children's stories. They met with open doors and open hearts in Denmark; everybody read them. I now removed the words, "told for children," from my title, and published three volumes of "**New Stories**," all of which were of my own invention, and were received in my own country with the greatest favor. I could not wish it greater; I felt a real anxiety in consequence, a fear of not being able to justify afterward such an honorable award of praise.

A refreshing sunshine streamed into my heart; I felt courage and joy, and was filled with a living desire of still more and more developing my powers in this direction,—of studying more thoroughly this class of writing, and of observing still more attentively the rich wells of nature out of which I must create it. If attention be paid to the order in which my stories are written, it certainly will be seen that there is in them a gradual progression, a clearer working out of the idea, a greater discretion in the use of agency, and, if I may so speak, a more healthy tone and a more natural freshness may be perceived.

As one step by step toils up a steep hill, I had at home climbed upward, and now beheld myself recognized and honored, appointed a distinct place in the literature of my country. This recognition and kindness at home atoned for all the hard words that the critics had spoken. Within me was clear sunshine; there came a sense of rest, a feeling that all, even the bitter in my life, had been needful for my development and my fortune. (pp. 204-05)

Hans Christian Andersen, in his The Story of My Life *(originally published in part as his* Mit Livs Eventyr, *1859), Hurd and Houghton, 1871, 569 p.*

GENERAL COMMENTARY

[There] has lately come into our hands the autobiography of Hans Christian Andersen, "**The True Story of my Life**," and this has revealed to us so curious an instance of intellectual cultivation, or rather of genius exerting itself without any cultivation at all, and has reflected back so strong a light, so vivid and so explanatory, on all his works, that what we formerly read with a very mitigated admiration, with more of censure than of praise, has been invested with quite a novel and peculiar interest. Moreover, certain tales for children have also fallen into our hands, some of which are admirable. We prophesy them an immortality in the nursery—which is not the worst immortality a man can win—and doubt not but that they have already been read by children, or told to children, in every language of Europe. (p. 388)

When Andersen writes *for* childhood or *of* childhood, he is singularly felicitous—fanciful, tender, and true to nature. This alone were sufficient to separate him from the crowd of common writers. (p. 389)

He ought to have been exclusively the poet of children and of childhood. He ought never to have seen, or dreamed, of an Apollo six feet high, looking sublime, and sending forth dreadful arrows from the far-resounding bow; he should have looked only to that "child upon the cloud," or rather, he should have seen his little muse as she walks upon the earth—we have her in Gainsborough's picture—with her tattered petticoat, and her bare feet, and her broken pitcher, but looking withal with such a sweet, sad contentedness upon the world, that surely, one thinks, she must have filled that pitcher and drawn the water which she carries—without, however, knowing anything of the matter—from the very well where Truth lies hidden. (pp. 389-90)

"Works of Hans Christian Andersen," in Blackwood's Edinburgh Magazine, *Vol. LXII, No. CCCLXXXIV, October, 1847, pp. 387-406.*

[Andersen] is quite unrivalled for power in rivetting the attention of children by his fascinating little stories. He himself says that "children are most amused with new expressions, and being spoken to in an unusual manner." This, however, would by no means explain satisfactorily the secret of his power of charming them. We rather would attribute it to the soul of goodness that shines in such a transparent manner through all that he writes. Children are acute critics in these matters. They can intuitively distinguish between tinsel and pure gold—between simulated sensibility and goodness, and the genuine thing. Then his style is so genial, so winning; his words are so happily chosen, that every sentence is a picture instinct with life. Yes, Andersen is the prince of fairy lore and story-telling, in the estimation of children of every growth. (p. 609)

"Hans Christian Andersen, His Life and Writings," in The Dublin University Magazine, *Vol. XLV, No. CCLXIX, May, 1855, pp. 605-23.*

It is by [Andersen's fairy tales] that he is most known, and by them that he will be chiefly known in the future. . . .

[They] seem to us the finest ever written. The class of literature to which they belong is probably the most ancient in the world, dating from the golden age, when men spoke in allegories and fables, and beguiled their leisure hours in relating wild and imaginative stories. Alike, the most savage and the most civilized of nations have their fairylore. . . .

Andersen, however, is the master of the school, the very sovereign of the whole realm of fairy-land. We doubt whether his poetry is near so poetical as his tales; certainly it cannot exhibit their creative imagination—the poem proper demanding a severity of treatment wholly at variance with the latitude of the fairy story. To us they read like children's poetry—little prose poems, full of nature and simplicity.

The wildest and most extravagant has a certain completeness of conception, and a wonderful finish of execution—the perfection of art, because it is art concealed. They seem to gush from his brain like brooks, to grow from his heart like flowers. No matter what may be their object, whether to inculcate a moral, or to riot in the world of imagination—whether dealing with mortals like ourselves, or with fairies and angels, and the personifications of abstract qualities—they are alike excellent, and alike beautiful. (p. 433)

R. H. Stoddard, "Hans Christian Andersen," in The National Magazine, *New York, Vol. VII, November, 1855, pp. 428-33.*

[According to Elias Bredsdorff, who is considered the foremost contemporary Andersen scholar, Georg Brandes "may be said to have been the first scholar altogether who realised that Andersen's tales gave him an important and unique place in world literature and who saw that the tales themselves merited serious critical discussion." The following essay by Brandes is generally recognized as one of the most important examples of Andersen scholarship.]

To replace the accepted written language with the free, unrestrained language of familiar conversation, to exchange the more rigid form of expression of grown people for such as a child uses and understands, becomes the true goal of the author as soon as he embraces the resolution to tell nursery stories for children. He has the bold intention to employ oral speech in a printed work, he will not write but speak, and he will gladly write as a school-child writes, if he can thus avoid speaking as a book speaks. The written word is poor and insufficient, the oral has a host of allies in the expression of the mouth that imitates the object to which the discourse relates, in the movement of the hand that describes it, in the length or shortness of the tone of the voice, in its sharp or gentle, grave or droll character, in the entire play of the features, and in the whole bearing. The nearer to a state of nature the being addressed, the greater aids to comprehension are these auxiliaries. Whoever tells a story to a child, involuntarily accompanies the narrative with many gestures and grimaces, for the child sees the story quite as much as it hears it, paying heed, almost in the same way as the dog, rather to the tender or irritated intonation, than to whether the words express friendliness or wrath. Whoever, therefore, addresses himself in writing to a child must have at his command the changeful cadence, the sudden pauses, the descriptive gesticulations, the awe-inspiring mien, the smile which betrays the happy turn of affairs, the jest, the caress, and the appeal to rouse the flagging attention—all these he must endeavor to weave into his diction, and as he cannot directly sing, paint, or dance the occurrences to the child, he must imprison within his prose the song, the picture, and the pantomimic movements, that they may lie there like forces in bonds, and rise up in their might as soon as the book is opened. In the first place, no circumlocution; everything must be spoken fresh from the lips of the narrator, aye, more than spoken, growled, buzzed, and blown as from a trumpet: "There came a soldier marching along the high-road—*one, two! one, two!*" "And the carved trumpeters blew, 'Trateratra! there is the little boy! Trateratra!' "—"Listen how it is drumming on the burdock-leaves, 'rum-dum-dum! rum-dum-dum!' said the Father Snail." At one time he begins, as in **"The Daisy,"** with a "Now you shall hear!" which at once arrests the attention; and again he jests after the fashion of a child: "So the soldier cut the witch's head off. There she lay!" We can hear the laughter of the child that follows this brief, not very sympathetic, yet extremely clear presentation of the destruction of an imposter. Often he breaks into a sentimental tone, as for instance: "The sun shone on the Flax, and the rainclouds moistened it, and this was just as good for it as it is for little children when they are washed, and afterward get a kiss from their mother; they became much prettier, and so did the Flax." That at this passage a pause should be made in the narrative, in order to give the child the kiss mentioned in the text, is something to which every mother will agree, and which seems to be a matter of course; the kiss is really given in the book. This regard for the young reader may be carried still farther, inasmuch as the poet, by virtue of his ready sympathy, so wholly identifies himself with the child and enters so fully into the sphere of its conceptions, into its mode of contemplation, indeed, into the range of its purely bodily vision, that a sentence like the following may readily flow from his pen: "The biggest leaf here in the country is certainly the burdock-leaf. Put one in front of your waist, and it is just like an apron, and if you lay it upon your head, it is almost as good as an umbrella, for it is quite remarkably large." These are words which a child, and every child, can understand.

Happy, indeed, is Andersen! What author has such a public as he? . . . [No] one can boast of so fresh and eager a circle of readers as Andersen is sure of finding. His stories are numbered among the books which we have deciphered syllable by syllable, and which we still read to-day. There are some among them whose letters even now, seem to us larger, whose words appear to have more value than all others, because we first made their acquaintance letter by letter and word by word. And what a delight it must have been for Andersen to see in his dreams this swarm of children's faces by the thousands about his lamp, this throng of blooming, rosy-cheeked little curly-pates, as in the clouds of a Catholic altar-piece, flaxen-haired Danish boys, tender English babies, black-eyed Hindoo maidens,—rich and poor, spelling, reading, listening, in all lands, in all tongues. . . . Such devout believers, such an attentive, such an indefatigable public, none other has. None other either has such a reverend one, for even old age is not so reverend and sacred as childhood. (pp. 2-5)

[It] is only needful to study the imagination of the audience, in order to become acquainted with that of the author. The starting-point for this art is the child's play that makes everything out of everything; in conformity with this, the sportive mood of the artist transforms playthings into natural creations, into supernatural beings, into heroes, and, *vice versa*, uses everything natural and everything supernatural—heroes, sprites, and fairies—for playthings, that is to say, for artistic means which through each artistic combination are remodelled and freshly stamped. The nerve and sinew of the art is the imagination of the child, which invests everything with a soul, and endows everything with personality; thus, a piece of household furniture is as readily animated with life as a plant, a flower as well as a bird or a cat, and the animal in the same manner as the doll, the portrait, the cloud, the sunbeam, the wind, and the seasons. Even the leap-frog, made of the breastbone of a goose, becomes thus for the child a living whole, a thinking being endowed with a will. The prototype of such poesy is the dream of a child, in which the childish conceptions shift more rapidly and with still bolder transformations than in play; therefore, the poet (as in **"Little Ida's Flowers," "Ole Shut Eye," "Little Tuk," "The Elder-Tree Mother"**) likes to seek refuge in dreams as in an arsenal; therefore, it is, when he busies his fancy with childish dreams, such as fill and trouble the mind of childhood, there often come to his his wittiest inspirations, as, for instance, when little Hjalmar hears in his dream the lamentation of the crooked letters that had tumbled down in his copy-book: " 'See, this is how you should hold yourselves,' said the Copy. 'Look, sloping in this way, with a powerful swing!' 'Oh, we should be very glad to do that,' replied Hjalmar's letters, 'but we cannot; we are too weakly.' 'Then you must take medicine,' said Ole Shut Eye. 'Oh no,' cried they; and they immediately stood up so gracefully that it was beautiful to behold." This is the way a child dreams, and this is the way a poet depicts to us the dream of a child. The soul of this poetry, however, is neither the dream nor the play; it is a peculiar, ever-childlike, yet at the same time a more than childlike faculty, not only for putting one thing in the place of another (thus, for making constant exchange, or for causing one thing to live in another, thus for animating all things), but also a faculty for being swiftly and readily reminded by one thing of another, for regaining one thing in another, for generalizing, for moulding an image into a symbol, for exalting a dream into a myth, and through an artistic process, for transforming single fictitious traits into a focus for the whole of life. Such a fancy does not penetrate far into the innermost recesses of things; it occupies itself with trifles; it sees ugly

faults, not great ones; it strikes, but not deeply; it wounds, but not dangerously; it flutters around like a winged butterfly from spot to spot, lingering about the most dissimilar places, and, like a wise insect, it spins its delicate web from many starting-points, until it is united in one complete whole. What it produces is neither a picture of the soul nor a direct human representation; but it is a work that with all its artistic perfection was already indicated by the unlovely and confusing arabesques in "The Foot Journey to Amager." Now while the nursery story, through its contents, reminds us of the ancient myths (**"The Elder-Tree Mother," "The Snow Queen"**), of the folk-lore tale, on whose foundation it constructs itself at times, of proverbs and fables of antiquity, indeed, sometimes of the parables of the New Testament (the buckwheat is punished as well as the fig-tree); while it is continually united by an idea, it may, so far as its form is concerned, be compared with the fantastic Pompeian decorative paintings, in which peculiarly conventional plants, animated flowers, doves, peacocks, and human forms are entwined together and blend into one another. A form that for any one else would be a circuitous route to the goal, a hindrance and a disguise, becomes for Andersen a mask behind which alone he feels truly free, truly happy and secure. His child-like genius, like the well-known child forms of antiquity, plays with the mask, elicits laughter, awakens delight and terror. Thus the nursery story's mode of expression, which with all its frankness is masked, becomes the natural, indeed, the classic cadence of his voice, that but very rarely becomes overstrained or out of tune. The only disturbing occurrence is that now and then a draught of whey is obtained instead of the pure milk of the nursery story, that the tone occasionally becomes too sentimental and sickly sweet (**"Poor John," "The Poor Bird," "Poor Thumbling"**), which, however, is rarely the case in materials taken from folk-lore tales, as **"The Tinder-Box," "Little Claus and Big Claus,"** etc., where the naïve joviality, freshness, and roughness of the narrative, which announces crimes and murders without the slightest sympathetic or tearful phrase, stand Andersen in good stead, and invest his figures with increased sturdiness. Less classic, on the other hand, is the tone of the lyric effusions interwoven with some of the nursery stories, in which the poet, in a stirring, pathetic prose gives a bird's-eye view of some great period of history (**"The Thorny Path of Honor," "The Swan's Nest"**). In these stories there seems to me to be a certain wild flight of fancy, a certain forced inspiration in the prevailing tone, wholly disproportionate to the not very significant thought of the contents; for thought and diction are like a pair of lovers. Thought may be somewhat larger, somewhat loftier, than diction, even as the man is taller than the woman; in the opposite case there is something unlovely in the relation. With the few exceptions just indicated, the narrative style of Andersen's nursery stories is a model of its kind. (pp. 5-8)

In order to be understood by such youthful readers as those to whom he addressed himself, he was obliged to use the simplest possible words, to return to the simplest possible conceptions, to avoid everything abstract, to supply the place of indirect with direct language; but in thus seeking simplicity, he finds poetic beauty, and in attaining the childlike he proves that this childlike spirit is essential to true poetry. . . . (p. 13)

He loves the child because his affectionate heart draws him to the little ones, the weak and helpless ones to whom it is allowable to speak with compassion, with tender sympathy, and because when he devotes such sentiments to a hero,—as in **"Only a Fiddler,"**—he is derided for it. . . . But when he dedicates them to a child, he finds the natural resting-place for his mood. It is owing to his genuine democratic feeling for the lowly and neglected that Andersen, himself a child of the people, continually introduces into his nursery stories (as Dickens, in his novels), forms from the poorer classes of society, "simple folk," yet endowed with the true nobility of the soul. As examples of this may be mentioned the washerwoman in "**Little Tuk**" and in "**Good-for-Nothing**," the old maid in "**From a Window in Vartou**," the watchman and his wife in "**The Old Street-Lamp**," the poor apprentice boy in "**Under the Willow-Tree**," and the poor tutor in "**Everything in its Right Place**." The poor are as defenseless as the child. Furthermore, Andersen loves the child, because he is able to portray it, not so much in the direct psychologic way of the romance,—he is by no means a direct psychologist,—as indirectly, by transporting himself with a bound into the child's world, and he acts as though no other course were possible. . . . He seldom introduces the child into his nursery stories as taking part in the action and conversation. He does it most frequently in the charming little collection "**A Picture-Book without Pictures**," where more than anywhere else he permits the child to speak with the entire simplicity of its nature. In such brief, naïve child-utterances as those cited in it there is much pleasure and entertainment. . . . In his nursery stories we find sundry illustrations of the fact, as in the charming words of the child in "**The Old House**," when it gives the man the pewter soldiers that he might not be "so very, very lonely," and a few kind answers in "**Little Ida's Flowers**." Yet his child forms are comparatively rare. The most noteworthy ones are little Hjalmar, little Tuk, Kay and Gerda, the unhappy, vain Karen in "**The Red Shoes**," a dismal but well-written story, the little girl with the matches and the little girl in "**A Great Sorrow**," finally Ib and Christine, the children in "**Under the Willow-Tree**." Besides these real children there are some ideal ones, the little fairy-like Thumbling and the little wild robber-maiden, undoubtedly Andersen's freshest child creation, the masterly portrayal of whose wild nature forms a most felicitous contrast to the many good, fair-haired and tame children of fiction. We see her before us as she really is, fantastic and true, her and her reindeer, whose neck she "tickles every evening with her sharp knife." (pp. 23-5)

[Sympathy] with child-nature led to sympathy with the animal which is doubly a child, and to sympathy with the plants, the clouds, the winds, which are doubly nature. What attracts Andersen to the impersonal being is the impersonal element in his own nature, what leads him to the wholly unconscious is merely the direct consequence of his sympathy. The child, young though it may be, is born old; each child is a whole generation older than its father, a civilization of ages has stamped its inherited impress on the little four-year-old child of the metropolis. How many conflicts, how many endeavors, how many sorrows have refined the countenance of such a child, making the features sensitive and precocious! It is different with animals. Look at the swan, the hen, the cat! They eat, sleep, live, and dream undisturbed, as in ages gone by. The child already begins to display evil instincts. We, who are seeking what is unconscious, what is naïve, are glad to descend the ladder that leads to the regions where there is no more guilt, no more crime, where responsibility, repentance, restless striving and passion cease, where nothing of an evil nature exists except through a substitution of which we are but partially conscious, and which therefore, robs our sympathy of half its sting. An author like Andersen, who has so great a repugnance to beholding what is cruel and coarse in its nakedness, who is so deeply impressed by anything of the kind that he dare not relate it, but recoils a hundred times in his

works from some wanton or outrageous deed with the maidenly expression, "We cannot bear to think of it!" Such an author feels content and at home in a world where everything that appears like egotism, violence, coarseness, vileness, and persecution, can only be called so in a figurative way. It is highly characteristic that almost all the animals which appear in Andersen's nursery stories are tame animals, domestic animals. This is, in the first place, a symptom of the same gentle and idyllic tendency which results in making almost all Andersen's children so well-behaved. It is, furthermore, a proof of his fidelity to nature, in consequence of which he is so reluctant to describe anything, with which he is not thoroughly familiar. It is finally an interesting phenomenon with reference to the use he makes of the animals, for domestic animals are no longer the pure product of nature; they remind us, through ideal association, of much that is human; and, moreover, through long intercourse with humanity and long education they have acquired something human, which in a high degree supports and furthers the effort to personify them. These cats and hens, these ducks and turkeys, these storks and swans, these mice and that unmentionable insect "with maiden's blood in its body," offer many props to the nursery story. They hold direct intercourse with human beings; all that they lack is articulate speech, and there are human beings with articulate speech who are unworthy of it, and do not deserve their speech. Let us, therefore, give the animals the power of speech, and harbor them in our midst.

On the almost exclusive limitation to the domestic animal, a double characteristic of this nursery story depends. First of all, the significant result that Andersen's animals, whatever else they may be, are never beastly, never brutal. Their sole faults are that they are stupid, shallow, and old-fogyish. Andersen does not depict the animal in the human being, but the human in the animal. In the second place, there is a certain freshness of tone about them, a certain fullness of feeling, certain strong and bold, enthusiastic, and vigorous outbursts which are never found in the quarters of the domestic animal. Many beautiful, many humorous and entertaining things are spoken of in these stories, but a companion piece to the fable of the wolf and the dog—the wolf who observed the traces of the chain on the neck of the dog and preferred his own freedom to the protection afforded the house dog—will not be found in them. The wild nightingale, in whom poetry is personified, is a tame and loyal bird. . . . Take even the swan, that noble, royal bird in the masterly story, "**The Ugly Duckling**," which for the sake of its cat and its hen alone cannot be sufficiently admired,—how does it end? Alas! as a domestic animal. This is one of the points where it becomes difficult to pardon the great author. O poet! we feel tempted to exclaim, since it was in your power to grasp such a thought, to conceive and execute such a poem, how could you, with your inspiration, your pride, have the heart to permit the swan to end thus! Let him die if needs must be! That would be tragic and great. Let him spread his wings and impetuously soar through the air, rejoicing in his beauty and his strength! let him sink down on the bosom of some solitary and beautiful forest lake! That is free and delightful. Anything would be better than this conclusion: "Into the garden came little children, who threw bread and corn into the water. And they ran to their father and mother, and bread and cake were thrown into the water; and they all said, 'The new one is the most beautiful of all! so young and handsome!' and the old swans bowed their heads before him." Let them bow, but let us not forget that there is something which is worth more than the recognition of all the old swans and geese and ducks, worth more than receiving bread-crumbs and cake as a garden bird,—the power of silently gliding over the waters, and free flight!

Andersen prefers the bird to the four-footed animal. More birds than mammals find place with him; for the bird is gentler than the four-footed beast, is nearer to the plant. The nightingale is his emblem, the swan his ideal, the stork his declared favorite. It is natural that the stork, that remarkable bird which brings children into the world,—the stork, that droll, long-legged, wandering, beloved, yearningly expected and joyfully greeted bird, should become his idolized symbol and frontispiece.

Yet plants are preferred by him to birds. Of all organic beings, plants are those which appear most frequently in the nursery story. For in the vegetable world alone are peace and harmony found to reign. Plants, too, resemble a child, but a child who is perpetually asleep. There is no unrest in this domain, no action, no sorrow, and no care. Here life is a calm, regular growth, and death but a painless fading away. Here the easily excited, lively poetic sympathy suffers less than anywhere else. Here there is nothing to jar and assail the delicate nerves of the poet. Here he is at home; here he paints his Arabian Nights' Entertainments beneath a burdock leaf. Every grade of emotion may be experienced in the realm of plants,—melancholy at the sight of the felled trunk, fulness of strength at the sight of the swelling buds, anxiety at the fragrance of the strong jasmine. Many thoughts may flit through our brain as we follow the history of the development of the flax, or the brief honor of the fir-tree on Christmas evening; but we feel as absolutely free as though we were dealing with comedy, for the image is so fleeting that it vanishes the moment we attempt to render it permanent. Sympathy and agitation gently touch our minds, but they do not ruffle us, they neither rouse nor oppress us. A poem about a plant sets free twofold the sympathy to which it lays claim; once because we know that the poem is pure fiction, and again because we know the plant to be merely a symbol. (pp. 25-9)

Yet a step farther, and the fancy of the poet appropriates all inanimate objects, colonizes and annexes everything, large and small, an old house and an old clothes-press (**"The Shepherdess and the Chimney Sweep"**), the top and the ball, the darning needle and the false collar, and the great dough men with bitter almonds for their hearts. After it has grasped the physiognomy of the inanimate, his fancy identifies itself with the formless all, sails with the moon across the sky, whistles and tells stories like the wind, looks on the snow, on sleep, night, death, and the dream as persons.

The determining element in this poetic mind was, then, sympathy with all that is childlike, and, through the representation of such deep-seated, elementary, and constant spiritual conditions as those of the child, the productions of this imagination are raised above the waves of time, spread beyond the boundaries of their native land and become the common property of the divers classes of society. The time when genius was looked upon as a meteor fallen from the skies, has long since passed away; now it is known that genius, as all else that comes from nature, has its antecedents and its conditions, that it holds relations of general dependence with its epoch, is an organ for the ideas of the age. Sympathy for the child is only a phenomenon of the love of nature. In society, in science, in poetry and in art, nature and the child had become objects of veneration; in the realms of poetry, art, science, and society, there takes place a reciprocal action. If there arise, therefore, a poet whose affections are attracted to the child, whose fancy is

allured by the animal, by plants, and by nature, he dares follow his impulses, he gains courage to give utterance to his talent, because a hundred thousand mute voices about him strengthen him in his calling, because the tide he believes himself to be stemming, rocks him gently as it bears him onward to his goal. (pp. 29-30)

There are two kinds of naïveté. One is that of the heart, the other that of the understanding; the former is frank, free, simple, and touching, the latter has a distorted appearance, is jocose, full of ready wit, and subtile. The one evokes tears, the other a smile; the former has its beauty, the latter its charm; the former characterizes the good child, the latter the *enfant terrible;* and Andersen is the poet of the former. . . . [His] naïveté is that of innocence which takes it for granted that its Garden of Eden is the whole world, and consequently puts the whole world to shame without being aware that it is doing so, and at the same time with so appropriate a choice of words that it assumes the appearance of a mask. (p. 32)

The most marked trait in Andersen's mode of viewing life, is that which gives the ascendency to the heart, and this trait is genuinely Danish. Full of feeling itself, this method of contemplation takes every opportunity to exalt the beauty and significance of the emotions. It overleaps the will (the whole destiny of the Flax, in the story of its life, comes from without), does combat with the critique of the pure reason as with something pernicious, the work of the Devil, the witch's mirror, replaces pedantic science with the most admirable and witty side-thrusts (**"The Bell," "A Leaf From the Sky"**), describes the senses as a tempter, or passes them over as unmentionable things, pursues and denounces hardheartedness, glorifies and commends goodness of heart, violently dethrones coarseness and narrowness, exalts innocence and decorum, and thus "puts everything in its right place." The key-note of its earnestness is the ethic-religious feeling coupled with the hatred felt by geniality for narrowness, and its humorous satire is capricious, calm, in thorough harmony with the idyllic spirit of the poet. Its satire has only the sting of a gnat, but it stings in the tenderest places. (pp. 33-4)

A genius, born in an age whose every influence opposes his development, is either hopelessly crushed or goes to ruin like any inferior talent. An Andersen born in Denmark in 1705, instead of 1805, would have been a most unfortunate and thoroughly insignificant individual, perhaps even a maniac. A genius born at a period when everything unites to come to its aid, produces classic, genial creations. Now, this first harmony between a poet and his era (in a measure also, his country) corresponds to a second one between the individual faculties of genius, and to a third one between genius and its peculiar type of art. The nature of genius is an organically connected whole; its weakness in one direction is the condition of its strength in another; the development of this faculty causes that one to be checked in its growth, and it is impossible to alter any single particular without disturbing the entire machinery. We may wish that one quality or another was different than it is, but we can readily comprehend that any decided change is out of the question. We may wish our poet had stronger personality, a more manly temperament, and more mental equilibrium; but we have no difficulty in understanding that the lack of defined personality, and the incompleteness of the character whose acquaintance we make in **"The Story of my Life,"** stand in the most intimate relationship with the nature of his endowments. A less receptive mind would not be so susceptible to poetic impressions, a harder one would not unite so much flexibility with its more rigid attitude, one more susceptible to criticism and philosophy would not be so naïve.

Since then, the moral attributes are requisite to the intellectual, so, too, they are mutually contingent one upon the other. An overflowing lyric sentiment, an exalted sensibility, cannot exist with the experience and method of a man of the world, for experience chills and hardens. A lightly vaulting fancy that hops and soars like a bird, does not admit of being united with the logically measured crescendo and decrescendo of dramatic action. An observation by no means inclined to be cold-blooded cannot possibly penetrate psychologically to the heart of things; a childlike, easily quivering hand cannot dissect a villain. If, therefore, we place genius of this kind face to face with sundry defined and well-known types of art, we can determine beforehand precisely what its relations with each of them will be.

The romance is a species of poetic creation which demands of the mind that would accomplish anything remarkable in it, not only imagination and sentiment, but the keen understanding, and the cool, calm power of observation of the man of the world; that is the reason why it is not altogether suited to Andersen, although it is not wholly remote from his talent. In the entire scenery, the background of nature, the picturesque effect of the costumes, he is successful; but where psychological insight is concerned, traces of his weakness may be detected. He will take part for and against his characters; his men are not manly enough, his women not sufficiently feminine. I know no poet whose mind is more devoid of sexual distinctions, whose talent is less of a nature to betray a defined sex, than Andersen's. Therefore his strength lies in portraying children, in whom the conscious sense of sex in not yet prominent. The whole secret lies in the fact that he is exclusively what he is,— not a man of learning, not a thinker, not a standard-bearer, not a champion, as many of our great writers have been, but simply a poet. A poet is a man who is at the same time a woman. Andersen sees most forcibly in man and in woman that which is elementary, that which is common to humanity, rather than that which is peculiar and interesting. I have not forgotten how well he has described the deep feeling of a mother in **"The Story of a Mother,"** or how tenderly he has told the story of the spiritual life of a woman in **"The Little Sea-Maid."** I simply recognize the fact that what he has represented is not the complicated spiritual conditions of life and of romance, but the element of life; he rings changes on single, pure tones, which amid the confused harmonies and disharmonies of life, appear neither so pure nor so distinct as in his books. Upon entering into the service of the nursery story all sentiments undergo a process of simplification, purification, and transformation. The character of man is farthest removed from the comprehension of the poet of childhood, and I can only recall a single passage in his stories in which a delicate psychological characteristic of a feminine soul may be encountered, and even this appears so innocently that we feel inclined to ask if it did not write itself. It occurs in the story of the new porcelain figures, **"The Shepherdess and the Chimney-Sweep."** (pp. 35-7)

A more profound, more mercilessly true, more self-evident analysis of a certain kind of feminine enthusiasm and its energy when it undertakes to act boldly without regard to consequences, and without looking backwards, can be found, I think, in the works of no other Danish writer. (pp. 37-8)

The drama is a species of poetic production that requires the faculty for differentiating an idea and distributing it among many characters; it requires an understanding of conscious action, a logic power to guide this, an eye to the situation, a passion for becoming absorbed and overwhelmed in the inexhaustible study of individual, many-sided characters. Therefore it is that the drama is still farther removed from the genius of Andersen than the romance, and that his lack of capacity for the dramatic style increases with mathematical exactness in the same ratio as each variety of dramatic art is removed from the nursery story, and consequently from his gifts. He naturally succeeds best with the nursery-story comedy; although, to be sure, it possesses little more of comedy than the name. . . . In the comedy of special situations he is happy with respect to the poetic execution of single scenes (**"The King's Dream"**), but singularly unfortunate in the execution of the idea as a whole (**"The Pearl of Good Fortune"**). The comedy proper is not poorly suited to his gifts. Certain of his nursery stories are, indeed, veritable Holberg comedies; **"The Happy Family"** is a Holberg character-comedy, and **"It is Quite True"** possesses a decided Holberg plot. In stories of this kind character delineation comes easier to him than in the grave drama, for in them he walks directly in the footsteps of Holberg, so strikingly does his talent accord in a single direction with that of this early Northern dramatist. Andersen is, as I have already remarked, no direct psychologist; he is rather a biologist than an especially well-informed student of human nature. His predilection is for describing man through animals or plants, and seeing him develop from the rudiments of his nature. All art contains an answer to the question, What is man? Inquire of Andersen how he defines man, and he will reply, Man is a swan hatched in the ''duck-yard'' of Nature. (pp. 38-9)

In lyric poetry Andersen has met with foreign success—even Chamisso has translated some of his songs; yet I am always loathe to see him lay aside his bright colored, realistic prose dress, that is so true to nature, in order to veil himself in the more uniform mantle of verse. His prose has fancy, unrestrained sentiment, rhythm, and melody. Why, then, cross the brook to find water? His poems, too, are frequently distinguished by a peaceful and childlike spirit, a warm and gentle sentiment. We see that the result of his attempts in the different regions of poetry proceeds quite directly, like the unknown x in mathematics, from the nature of his talents on one side, and the nature of the kind of poetic creation he has chosen on the other.

Thus the nursery story remains his sole individual creation, and for it he requires no patent, since no one is likely to rob him of it. In Andersen's day it was a common thing to attempt to classify all kinds of poetic creations with their varieties in an æsthetic system, according to the method of Hegel; and Hegel's Danish disciple, Heiberg, projected a complicated system in which the rank of the comedy, the tragedy, the romance, the nursery story, etc., was definitely fixed, while to Heiberg's own art-form an especially high rank was accorded. It is, however, in a certain measure pedantic to speak of general classes of art. Every creative artist thoroughly individualizes his own species of art. The form which he has used, no other has it in his power to use. So it is with the nursery story, whose theory Andersen made no attempt to describe, whose place in the system there has been no effort to establish, and which I, for one, should take good care not to define. (pp. 40-1)

Georg Brandes, ''Hans Christian Andersen'' (1869), in his Eminent Authors of the Nineteenth Century: Literary Portraits, *translated by Rasmus B. Anderson (copyright © 1886 by Thomas Y. Crowell & Co.; reprinted by permission of Harper & Row, Publish-*

ers, Inc.; *originally published as* Det moderne Gjen-
nembruds Maend: Em Raekke Portraeter, *1883),
Thomas Y. Crowell Co., Inc., 1886 (and reprinted
in* Creative Spirits of the Nineteenth Century *by Georg
Brandes, translated by Rasmus B. Anderson, Thomas
Y. Crowell Company, 1923, pp. 1-53).*

[*Horace E. Scudder is considered Andersen's American champion.
As editor of* Riverside Monthly Magazine for Young People, *he
arranged a contract between Andersen and Riverside's publishers.
Hurd and Houghton. Although Andersen's works sold well in
America, he never received any money for them until Scudder
intervened. Their agreement specified that Andersen's stories
would be sent in advance of their publication in Denmark and
Germany; several of the later tales were published in America
before their Danish publication. Scudder and Andersen carried on
an amicable professional correspondence for many years, although
they never met. Scudder also translated many of Andersen's fairy
tales and his autobiography,* The Story of My Life.]

[Andersen] has made the most unique contribution not only to
the literature which children read, but to that which is illustrative of childhood. He attained his eminence sheerly by the
exhibition of a power which resulted from his information by
the spirit of childhood. He was not only an interpreter of childhood; he was the first child who made a real contribution to
literature. The work by which he is best known is nothing more
nor less than an artistic creation of precisely the order which
is common among children.

It is customary to speak of his best known short stories as fairy
tales; wonder-stories is in some respects a more exact description, but the name has hardly a native sound. Andersen himself
classed his stories under the two heads of *historier* and *eventyr;*
the *historier* corresponds well enough with its English mate,
being the history of human action, or, since it is a short history,
the story; the *eventyr,* more nearly allied perhaps to the German
abenteuer than to the English *adventure,* presumes an element
of strangeness causing wonder, while it does not necessarily
demand the machinery of the supernatural. When we speak of
fairy tales, we have before our minds the existence, for artistic
purposes, of a spiritual world peopled with beings that exercise
themselves in human affairs, and are endowed in the main with
human attributes, though possessed of certain ethereal advantages, and generally under orders from some superior power,
often dimly understood as fate; the Italians, indeed, call the
fairy *fata.* In a rough way we include under the title of fairies
all the terrible and grotesque shapes as well, and this world of
spiritual beings is made to consist of giants, ogres, brownies,
pixies, nisses, gnomes, elves, and whatever other creatures
have found in it a local habitation and name. The fairy itself
is generally represented as very diminutive, the result, apparently, of an attempted compromise between the imagination
and the senses, by which the existence of fairies for certain
purposes is conceded on condition they shall be made so small
that the senses may be excused from recognizing them.

The belief in fairies gave rise to the genuine fairy tale, which
is now an acknowledged classic, and the gradual elimination
of this belief from the civilized mind has been attended with
some awkwardness. These creations of fancy—if we must so
dismiss them—had secured a somewhat positive recognition
in literature before it was finally discovered that they came out
of the unseen and therefore could have no life. Once received
into literature they could not well be ignored, but the understanding, which appears to serve as special police in such cases,
now has order to admit no new-comers unless they answer to
one of three classes: either they must be direct descendants of
the fairies of literature, having certain marks about them to
indicate their parentage, or they must be teachers of morality
thus disguised, or they may be mere masqueraders; one thing
is certain, they must spring from no belief in fairy life, but be
one and all referred to some sufficient cause,—a dream, a moral
lesson, a chemical experiment. But it is found that literature
has its own sympathies, not always compassed by the mere
understanding, and the consequence is that the sham fairies in
the sham fairy tales never really get into literature at all, but
disappear in limbo; while every now and then a genuine fairy,
born of a genuine, poetic belief, secures a place in spite of the
vigilance of the guard. (pp. 51-2)

By a tacit agreement fairy tales have come to be consigned to
the nursery; the old tools of superstition have become the child's
toys, and when a writer comes forward, now, bringing new
fairy tales, it is almost always with an apology, not for tres-
passing upon ground already occupied, but for indulging in
what is no longer belief, but make-belief. "My story," he is
apt to say, "is not true; we none of us believe it, and I shall
give you good evidence before I am done that least of all do
I believe it. I shall probably explain it by referring it to a
strange dream, or shall justify it by the excellent lesson it is
to teach. I adopt the fairy form as suited to the imagination of
children; it is a childish thing, and I am half ashamed, as a
grown person, to be found engaged in such nonsense." Out
of this way of regarding fairy tales has come that peculiar
monstrosity of the times, the scientific fairy tale, which is
nothing short of an insult to a whole race of innocent beings.
It may be accepted as a foregone conclusion that with a disbelief
in fairies the genuine fairy tale has died, and that it is better
to content ourselves with those stories which sprang from actual
belief, telling them over to successive generations of children,
than to seek to extend the literature by any ingenuity of modern
skepticism. There they are, the fairy tales without authorship,
as imperishable as nursery ditties; scholarly collections of them
may be made, but they will have their true preservation, not
as specimens in a museum of literary curiosities, but as children's toys. Like the sleeping princess in the wood, the fairy
tale may be hedged about with bristling notes and thickets of
commentaries, but the child will pass straight to the beauty,
and awaken for his own delight the old charmed life.

It is worth noting, then, that just when historical criticism,
under the impulse of the Grimms, was ordering and accounting
for these fragile creations,—a sure mark that they were ceasing
to exist as living forms in literature,—Hans Christian Andersen
should have come forward as master in a new order of stories,
which may be regarded as the true literary successor to the old
order of fairy tales, answering the demands of a spirit which
rejects the pale ghost of the scientific or moral or jocular or
pedantic fairy tale. Andersen, indeed, has invented fairy tales
purely such, and has given form and enduring substance to
traditional stories current in Scandinavia; but it is not upon
such work that his real fame rests, and it is certain that while
he will be mentioned in the biographical dictionaries as the
writer of novels, poems, romances, dramas, sketches of travel,
and an autobiography, he will be known and read as the author
of certain short stories, of which the charm at first glance seems
to be in the sudden discovery of life and humor in what are
ordinarily regarded as inanimate objects, or what are somewhat
compassionately called dumb animals. When we have read and
studied the stories further, and perceived their ingenuity and
wit and humane philosophy, we can after all give no better
account of their charm than just this, that they disclose the
possible or fancied parallel to human life carried on by what

our senses tell us has no life, or our reason assures us has no rational power.

The life which Andersen sets before us is in fact a dramatic representation upon an imaginary stage, with puppets that are not pulled by strings, but have their own muscular and nervous economy. The life which he displays is not a travesty of human life, it is human life repeated in miniature under conditions which give a charming and unexpected variety. By some transmigration, souls have passed into tin-soldiers, balls, tops, beetles, money-pigs, coins, shoes, leap-frogs, matches, and even such attenuated individualities as darning-needles; and when, informing these apparently dead or stupid bodies, they begin to make manifestations, it is always in perfect consistency with the ordinary conditions of the bodies they occupy, though the several objects become by this endowment of souls suddenly expanded in their capacity. Perhaps in nothing is Andersen's delicacy of artistic feeling better shown than in the manner in which he deals with his animated creations when they are brought into direct relations with human beings. The absurdity which the bald understanding perceives is dexterously suppressed by a reduction of all the factors to one common term. (pp. 52-3)

The use of speaking animals in story was no discovery of Andersen's, and yet in the distinction between his wonder-story and the well-known fable lies an explanation of the charm which attaches to his work. The end of every fable is *hæc fabula docet,* and it was for this palpable end that the fable was created. The lion, the fox, the mouse, the dog, are in a very limited way true to the accepted nature of the animal which they represent, and their intercourse with each other is governed by the ordinary rules of animal life, but the actions and words are distinctly illustrative of some morality. The fable is an animated proverb. The animals are made to act and speak in accordance with some intended lesson, and have this for the reason of their being. The lesson is first; the characters, created afterward, are, for purposes of the teacher, disguised as animals; very little of the animal appears, but very much of the lesson. The art which invented the fable was a modest handmaid to morality. In Andersen's stories, however, the spring is not in the didactic but in the imaginative. He sees the beetle in the imperial stable stretching out his thin legs to be shod with golden shoes like the emperor's favorite horse, and the personality of the beetle determines the movement of the story throughout; egotism, pride at being proud, jealousy, and unbounded self-conceit are the furniture of this beetle's soul, and his adventures one by one disclose his character. It there a lesson in all this? Precisely as there is a lesson in any picture of human life where the same traits are sketched. The beetle, after all his adventures, some of them ignominious but none expelling his self-conceit, finds himself again in the emperor's stable, having solved the problem why the emperor's horse had golden shoes. "They were given to the horse on my account," he says, and adds, "the world is not so bad after all, but one must know how to take things as they come." There is in this and other of Andersen's stories a singular shrewdness, as of a very keen observer of life, singular because at first blush the author seems to be a sentimentalist. The satires, like **The Emperor's New Clothes** and **The Swiftest Runners,** mark this characteristic of shrewd observation very cleverly. Perhaps, after all, we are stating most simply the distinction between his story and the fable when we say that humor is a prominent element in the one and absent in the other; and to say that there is humor is to say that there is real life.

It is frequently said that Andersen's stories accomplish their purpose of amusing children by being childish, yet it is impossible for a mature person to read them without detecting repeatedly the marks of experience. There is a subtle undercurrent of wisdom that has nothing to do with childishness, and the child who is entertained returns to the same story afterward to find a deeper significance than it was possible for him to apprehend at the first reading. The forms and the incident are in consonance with childish experience, but the spirit which moves through the story comes from a mind that has seen and felt the analogue of the story in some broader or coarser form. The story of **The Ugly Duckling** is an inimitable presentation of Andersen's own tearful and finally triumphant life; yet no child who reads the story has its sympathy for a moment withdrawn from the duckling and transferred to a human being. Andersen's nice sense of artistic limitations saves him from making the older thought obtrude itself upon the notice of children, and his power of placing himself at the same angle of vision with children is remarkably shown in one instance, where, in **Little Klaus and Big Klaus,** death is treated as a mere incident in the story, a surprise but not a terror.

The naïveté which is so conspicuous an element in Andersen's stories was an expression of his own singularly artless nature. He was a child all his life; his was a condition of almost arrested development. He was obedient to the demands of his spiritual nature, and these led him into a fresh field of fancy and imagination. What separates him and gives him a distinct place in literature is, as I have said, that he was the first child who had contributed to literature. (pp. 54-5)

Now that Andersen has told his stories, it seems an easy thing to do, and we have plenty of stories written for children that attempt the same thing, sometimes also with moderate success; for Andersen's discovery was after all but the simple application to literature of a faculty which has always been exercised. The likeness that things inanimate have to things animate is constantly forced upon us; it remained for Andersen to pursue the comparison further, and, letting types loose from their antitypes, to give them independent existence. The result has been a surprise in literature and a genuine addition to literary forms. It is possible to follow in his steps, now that he has shown us the way, but it is no less evident that the success which he attained was due not merely to his happy discovery of a latent property, but to the nice feeling and strict obedience to laws of art with which he made use of his discovery. Andersen's genius enabled him to see the soul in a darning-needle, and he perceived also the limitations of the life he was to portray, so that while he was often on the edge of absurdity he did not lose his balance. Especially is it to be noted that these stories, which we regard as giving an opportunity for invention when the series of old-fashioned fairy tales had been closed, show clearly the coming in of that temper in novel-writing which is eager to describe things as they are. Within the narrow limits of his miniature story, Andersen moves us by the same impulse as the modern novelist who depends for his material upon what he has actually seen and heard, and for his inspiration upon the power to penetrate the heart of things; so that the old fairy tale finds its successor in this new realistic wonder-story, just as the old romance gives place to the new novel. In both, as in the corresponding development of poetry and painting, is found a deeper sense of life and a finer perception of the intrinsic value of common forms.

This, then, may be taken as the peculiar contribution of Andersen: that he, appearing at a time when childhood had been laid open to view as a real and indestructible part of human life, was the interpreter to the world of that creative power which is significant of childhood. The child spoke through him, and disclosed some secrets of life; childhood in men heard the speech, and recognized it as an echo of their own half-forgotten voices. The literature of this kind which he produced has become a distinct and new form. It already has its imitations, and people are said to write in the vein of Andersen. Such work, and Andersen's in particular, presents itself to us under two aspects: as literature in which conceptions of childhood are embodied, and as literature which feeds and stimulates the imagination of children. But this is precisely the way in which a large body of current literature must be regarded. (pp. 55-6)

> *Horace E. Scudder, "Hans Christian Andersen"* (1875), in his Childhood in Literature and Art *(Copyright, 1894, by Horace E. Scudder. Reprinted by permission of Houghton Mifflin Company), Houghton Mifflin, 1894 (and reprinted as "Of Classics and Golden Ages: Hans Christian Andersen," in* Children and Literature: Views and Reviews, *edited by Virginia Haviland, Scott, Foresman and Company, 1973, pp. 50-6).*

Andersen's best literary productions remain his **"Märchen."** . . . Their rapid and universal circulation may be largely ascribed to the fact that from the beginning he made it clear to himself that he wrote for a definite public,—for children. Thus the choice of the simplest and most *naïve* themes, as well as a simple treatment and language, were a necessity. Together with this, however, the poet could give the reins to his fancy; for a child's imagination is also boundless, and believes everything that is not beyond the pale of its horizon. In order to find the right key for children's tales, Andersen had merely to follow the dictates of his own childlike soul. Therefore he succeeded in attaining to a cheerful, gentle, optimistic view of life which corresponded to the nature of every unspoiled, healthy, and therefore sanguine child. He does not assume the presumptuous, pedagogic tone into which many writers for the young are apt to fall, and yet he works more healthily upon the mind of the child, more educationally, and more ennoblingly than all instructive moralizing. The high, artistic finish in the form of his stories, and their complete harmony of treatment and matter, bring the result that every grown-up person reads these charming tales with delight, though their author did not write them for this public. He lets the creatures of his imagination feel, speak, think, and act exactly as their nature requires; we will only indicate the stork who described Egypt, the cockchafer in **"Little Thumb,"** the darning-needle, the tin soldier. (p. 167)

> *Leopold Katscher, "Hans Christian Andersen," in* The International Review *(copyright, 1881. A. S. Barnes & Co.), Vol. X, February, 1881, pp. 153-68.*

Hans Christian Andersen was a unique figure in Danish literature, and a solitary phenomenon in the literature of the world. Superficial critics have compared him with the Brothers Grimm; they might with equal propriety have compared him with Voltaire or with the man in the moon. Jacob and Wilhelm Grimm were scientific collectors of folk-lore, and rendered as faithfully as possible the simple language of the peasants from whose lips they gathered their stories. It was the ethnological and philological value of the fairy-tale which stimulated their zeal; its poetic value was of quite secondary significance. With

Andersen the case was exactly the reverse. He was as innocent of scientific intention as the hen who finds a diamond on a dunghill is of mineralogy. It was the poetic phase alone of the fairy-tale which attracted him; and what is more, he saw poetic possibilities where no one before him had ever discovered them. By the alchemy of genius (which seems so perfectly simple until you try it yourself) he transformed the common neglected nonsense of the nursery into rare poetic treasure. (p. 155)

In another species of fairy-tale, which Andersen may be said to have invented, incident seems to be secondary to the moral purpose, which is yet so artfully hidden that it requires a certain maturity of intellect to detect it. In this field Andersen has done his noblest work and earned his immortality. Who can read that marvellous little tale, **"The Ugly Duckling,"** without perceiving that it is a subtle, most exquisite revenge the poet is taking upon the humdrum Philistine world, which despised and humiliated him, before he lifted his wings and flew away with the swans, who knew him as their brother? And yet, as a child, I remember reading this tale with ever fresh delight, though I never for a moment suspected its moral. The hens and the ducks and the geese were all so vividly individualized, and the incidents were so familiar to my own experience, that I demanded nothing more for my entertainment. Likewise in **"The Goloshes of Fortune"** there is a wealth of amusing adventures, all within the reach of a child's comprehension, which more than suffices to fascinate the reader who fails to penetrate beneath the surface. The delightful satire, which is especially applicable to Danish society, is undoubtedly lost to nine out of ten of the author's foreign readers, but so prodigal is he both of humorous and pathetic meaning, that every one is charmed with what he finds, without suspecting how much he has missed. **"The Little Mermaid"** belongs to the same order of stories, though the pathos here predominates, and the resemblance to De la Motte Fouqué's "Undine" is rather too striking. But the gem of the whole collection, I am inclined to think, is **"The Emperor's New Clothes,"** which in subtlety of intention and universality of application rises above age and nationality. Respect for the world's opinion and the tyranny of fashion have never been satirized with more exquisite humor than in the figure of the emperor who walks through the streets of his capital in *robe de nuit,* followed by a procession of courtiers, who all go into ecstasies over the splendor of his attire.

It was not only in the choice of his theme that Andersen was original. He also created his style, though he borrowed much of it from the nursery. "It was perfectly wonderful," "You would scarcely have believed it," "One would have supposed that there was something the matter in the poultry-yard, but there was nothing at all the matter"—such beginnings are not what we expect to meet in dignified literature. They lack the conventional style and deportment. No one but Andersen has ever dared to employ them. As Dr. Brandes has said in his charming essay on Andersen [see excerpt above], no one has ever attempted, before him, to transfer the vivid mimicry and gesticulation which accompany a nursery tale to the printed page. If you tell a child about a horse, you don't say that it neighed, but you imitate the sound; and the child's laughter or fascinated attention compensates you for your loss of dignity. The more successfully you crow, roar, grunt, and mew, the more vividly you call up the image and demeanor of the animal you wish to represent, and the more impressed is your juvenile audience. Now, Andersen does all these things in print: a truly wonderful feat. Every variation in the pitch of the voice—I am almost tempted to say every change of expression in the story-teller's features—is contained in the text. He does not write his story, he tells it; and all the children of the whole wide world sit about him and listen with eager, wide-eyed wonder to his marvellous improvisations. (pp. 156-59)

We all have a dim recollection of how the world looked from the nursery window; but no book has preserved so vivid and accurate a negative of that marvellous panorama as Andersen's **"Wonder Tales for Children."** . . . All the jumbled, distorted proportions of things (like the reflection of a landscape in a crystal ball) is capitally reproduced. The fantastically person-ifying fancy of childhood, where does it have more delightful play? The radiance of an enchanted fairy realm that bursts like an iridescent soap-bubble at the touch of the finger of reason, where does it linger in more alluring beauty than in **"Ole Luköie"** (**"The Sandman"**), **"The Little Mermaid,"** or **"The Ice-Maiden"?** There is a bloom, an indefinable, dewy fresh-ness about the grass, the flowers, the very light, and the chil-dren's sweet faces. And so vivid—so marvellously vivid—as it all is. (p. 171)

You feel with what beautiful zest it was written; how childishly the author himself relished it. The illusion is therefore perfect. The big child who played with his puppet theatre until after he was grown up is quite visible in every line. He is as much absorbed in the story as any of his hearers. He is all in the game with the intense engrossment of a lad I knew, who, while playing Robinson Crusoe, ate snails with relish for oysters.

Throughout the first series of **"Wonder Tales"** there is a capital air of make-believe, which imposes upon you most delight-fully, and makes you accept the most incredible doings, as you accept them in a dream, as the most natural thing in the world. In the later series, where the didactic tale becomes more fre-quent (**"The Pine Tree," "The Wind's Tale," "The Buck-wheat"**), there is an occasional forced note. The story-teller becomes a benevolent, moralizing uncle, who takes the child upon his knee, in order to instruct while entertaining it. But he is no more in the game. (p. 173)

[Andersen's] life was indeed as marvellous as any of his tales. A gleam of light from the wonderland in which he dwelt seems to have fallen upon his cradle and to have illuminated his whole career. It was certainly in this illumination that he himself saw it, as the opening sentence of his autobiography proves: "My life is a lovely fairy-tale, happy and full of incidents."

The softness, the sweetness, the juvenile innocence of Danish romanticism found their happiest expression in him; but also the superficiality, the lack of steel in the will, the lyrical vague-ness and irresponsibility. If he did not invent a new literary form he at all events enriched and dignified an old one, and revealed in it a world of unsuspected beauty. He was great in little things, and little in great things. He had a heart of gold, a silver tongue, and the spine of a mollusk. Like a flaw in a diamond, a curious plebeian streak cut straight across his na-ture. With all his virtues he lacked that higher self-esteem which we call nobility. (pp. 177-78)

> *Hjalmar Hjorth Boyesen, "Hans Christian Ander-sen," in his* Essays On Scandinavian Literature *(copyright, 1895 by Charles Scribner's Sons), Charles Scribner's Sons, 1895, pp. 155-78.*

[*The first extensive biography of Andersen was written by Robert Nisbet Bain, an Englishman, who published his work ten years before the first Danish biography of Andersen.*]

Little as he suspected it, Andersen . . . laid the foundations of his future fame [with his fairy tales]. At last, though he himself would never admit as much, he had discovered his own peculiar domain in literature, where none will dare to dispute his sway. The very limitations of his fancy, its exces-sive delicacy, flightiness, and instability, its trick of perpetually hovering around a thousand objects without fastening on any, its superficiality, which made him but an indifferent dramatist, and not much more than a second-rate novelist, were in their proper element among the ever-shifting phantasmagoria of fairyland. He had, too, a child's imagination, which personifies and vivifies everything, whether it be a plant, a flower, a bird, a cat, a doll, or clouds, sunbeams, winds, and the seasons of the year. The determining quality of Andersen's art, therefore, was sympathy with the childlike in the widest sense—with children first of all, and then with everything that most nearly resembles children; with animals, for instance, who may be regarded as children who are never anything but children; and with plants, who are also like children, but children who are always sleeping. Nay, even his defects, mental and moral, that sensitive shrinking from all that is disgusting or distressing, that disinclination to look the uglier facts of life fairly in the face, defects that are responsible for so much of the indefi-niteness and mawkish sentiment of his novels and plays, do but lend an additional charm to his fairy tales, and make them suitable above all others for children. What is mawkishness elsewhere here becomes simply sweetness. Hence it is that all, or nearly all, the children in his fairy tales are good children, and all the animals friendly domestic animals, who may some-times be stupid and snobbish, but are never savage or brutal. Finally—and here we hit upon the real secret of Andersen's unique art as a teller of fairy tales—he possessed the rare gift of fashioning, or rather evoking supernatural beings of every sort and kind, . . . who are always true to the characters he gives them. It is impossible not to believe in Andersen's fan-tastic creations; he had as keen an eye for the oddities of the elfin race as Dickens had for the oddities of human nature. Andersen is the only story-teller who has succeeded in in-venting fairy tales which are as fresh, natural, and spontaneous as a genuine *märchen*. All other workers in this field are either mere collectors, like Grimm and Asbjörnsen, or clever adap-tors, like Madam d'Aulnoy. Andersen also drew largely from the common stock, and such little masterpieces as **"The Tinder Box"** and **"The Wild Swans"** are living instances of the in-imitable skill with which he could transform a good old story into a new one, and even improve it in the process; but he is at his best when he is original—he never wrote anything finer than **"The Shadow"** or **"The Little Mermaid."** (pp. 140-42)

> *R. Nisbet Bain, in his* Hans Christian Andersen: A Biography, *Dodd, Mead & Company, 1895, 461 p.*

[Andersen] was of the opinion that a man's whole future fortune might turn on a game he played as a child. Such a fine ap-preciation of small things—such an aptitude for detail—would be a very dangerous possession for a man of letters did it not run in double harness with a capacity for nice discrimination. Fortunately in Andersen's case it did. He never fell into the fallacy of supposing that, because the important happenings of life are often externally trivial, therefore all externally trivial happenings are important. His eye was true with regard to salient points, and his tales are never overburdened. Some of them—the shorter fairy-tales, in particular—are plain to bare-ness. But they grip. Moreover, it must be remembered he was a master of style. He could, in a few happy words, clutch a new truth from a commonplace, and he had an inexhaustible fund of simile and metaphor, of which he made free use, but which never led him into the error of tediousness. There is nothing final to be said about his style: it eludes hard-and-fast definition. Perhaps the best adjective to apply to it is ''happy.'' He had the good fortune to think some very happy thoughts about men and things, and the almost better fortune to express some very ordinary ones happily. (p. 126)

In these days of prolific Christmas literature for children, we are well accustomed to the animation of the inanimate; when Andersen wrote talking was not considered part of a darning-needle's mission. His undertaking was a dangerous one, with more than the usual number of possibilities of straying into the by-ways of bathos. With less genius some of his stories might have drifted into sheer nonsense (as many of his disciples have demonstrated in treating similar themes), but he was a man of genius, and he was not afraid. He succeeded signally. (p. 127)

> Shirley Knapton, ''Hans Andersen: An Appreciation,'' in The Bookman, *London, Vol. XXV, No. 147, December, 1903, pp. 121-28.*

Things have been said about most men, great or little, in our fevered time, so exaggerated, so local and so lacking balance, whether of experience or of the fear of posterity, that contemporary opinion should not be allowed by its misfortunes to weigh them down. But a man has a quality of his own when he is so made that even his contemporaries do him justice, and that was the case with Hans Christian Andersen. I will bargain that if our letters survive five hundred years, this excellent writer will quietly survive. . . . And next it is the business of one who praises so much to ask in what the excellence of this writer consists. It is threefold: in the first place, he always said what he thought; in the second place, he was full of all sorts of ways of saying it; and, in the third place, he said only what he had to say.

To say what one thinks, that is, to tell the truth, is so exceedingly rare that one may almost call it a grace in a man. Just those same manifold strings which pull contemporary criticism hither and thither, and which have made me suggest above that contemporary criticism commonly belittles a man in the long run, just those same strings pull at every writer to make him conform to what he knows to be false in his time. But some men—with limitations, it is true, and only by choosing a particular framework—manage to tell the truth all their lives; those men, if they have other literary qualities, are secure of the future.

And this leads me to the second point, which is that Andersen could not only tell the truth but tell it in twenty different ways, and of a hundred different things. Now this character has been much exaggerated among literary men in importance, because literary men, perceiving it to be the differentiation which marks out the great writer from the little, think it to be the main criterion of letters. It is not the main criterion; but it is a permanent necessity in great writing. There is no great writing without this multiplicity, which is sometimes called imagination, sometimes experience, and sometimes judgment, but which is in its essence a proper survey of the innumerable world. This quality it is which makes the great writers create what are called ''characters''; and whether we recognise those ''characters'' as portraits drawn from the real world (they are such in Balzac), or as figments (they are such in Dickens), or as heroines and heroes (they are such in Shakespeare and in Homer, if you will excuse me), yet that they exist and live in the pages of the writer means that he had in him that quality of

contemplation which corresponds in our limited human nature to the creative power.

Lastly, I say that Andersen said what he had to say and no more. This quality in writers is not restraint—a futile word dear to those who cannot write—it is rather a sort of chastity in the pen. The writer of this kind is one who unconsciously does not add; if any one were to ask him why he should not add an ornament or anything supposititious, he would be bewildered and perhaps might answer: ''Why should I?'' The instinct behind it is that which produces all terseness, all exactitude, and all economy in style.

Andersen, then, had all those three things which make a great writer, and a very great writer he is.

Note that he chose his framework, or, at any rate, that he was persuaded to it. He could not have been so complete had he not addressed himself to children, and it is his glory that he is read in childhood. There is no child but can read Hans Christian Andersen, and I at least have come across no man who, having read him in childhood, does not continue to read him throughout life. He wrote nothing that was not for the enlivening or the sustenance or the guiding of the human soul; he wrote nothing that suggested questions only. If one may speak of him in terms a trifle antiquated (or rather for the moment old-fashioned), he was instinct with charity, and therefore he is still full of life. (pp. 150-52)

> Hilaire Belloc, ''Hans Christian Andersen,'' in his On Anything *(reprinted by permission of A D Peters & Co Ltd), E. P. Dutton & Co., 1910 (and reprinted by Books for Libraries Press, 1969; distributed by Arno Press, Inc.), pp. 149-53.*

In very few of Andersen's stories is there any deliberate effort to choose the bright side of things, or even to ensure a happy ending, unless it occurs naturally. With that he was not in the least concerned, and he was not always concerned with the story itself; many of his best tales are just pictorial impressions. What then is the secret of his appeal to children? I think it is that he was, most essentially, a poet, and that the poet's and the child's mind are a great deal closer than many of us suppose.

He wrote of the world about him and of the things in it, as colored by his own vision. He didn't choose those things; they were there, and he saw no reason to exclude or disguise them. In this world as he saw it there were drunken old washerwomen, mothers who abandoned their children, dark ruinous houses with neglected and unhappy old people living in them; there was ingratitude, poverty and death, hypocrisy and a great deal of foolish talk, which none than he knew better how to satirize. But there was also faith, charity and humour, love and happy respected old age; there were enchanted forests, trees that dreamed and birds and beasts who talked, and there was at times, if only for his eyes, a great and shining spiritual light that fell on all these things alike and made one as beautiful as another.

''You must not look at it from the sorrowful side,'' says the little boy. ''To me it all appears remarkably pretty. . . .''

This is not priggishness; still less is it the conventional optimism which, by insisting so much on the ''happy ending,'' also postulates a possible unhappy ending. To Andersen all endings were happy; they were as they should be. Old people die, but would you have them go on living forever? Wicked Inge is punished for her pride, but her soul, after long suffering, turns into the little bird that ''flew straight into the sun''; the little Match Girl starved, but she had the vision of eternal life, and the happiest moment of the little Fir Tree is when it bursts into deathless flame.

He had the child mind, which does not conceive of sadness as does the older mind. It is all relative. He was not sorry for this sort of thing at all. What he was really sorry for were the stupid people, the mean and the snobbish and the little-minded, who are blind to beauty though it walks beside them and who can never see life—or death—as the real adventure that it is; the huckster and the Emperor and the Portuguese duck. These he satirizes again and again, but his satire is always kindly; it could not be otherwise.

There has been no writer for children with such amazing range and variety as Andersen. "Tell me a story!" cries the little boy in the **"Elder Tree Mother."** And the stories begin to come out of the teapot. Each is different from the next; each is as spontaneous as though it were the only story he really wanted to write. He gave of his best unsparingly, and to choose among them were an almost hopeless task.

Everything in his world is animate, has personality and expression; the old streetlamp, the china ornaments, the toys, the poker and the darning-needle, no less than the daisy, the farmyard fowl and the family of snails. This is truly a child's world as a child might conceive it. Everything has its own philosophy, everything moves and acts in its proper way. The soul of the flower is as real as the soul of the poet. The old cupboard creaks; it has a voice and wants to tell us something. Listen, and you will hear the knives and forks chattering in the table drawer. No sooner are the family a-bed than the tulips and hyacinths jump out of their flowerpots and begin to dance. Everything has a story to tell. And before us, turning those magic pages, there arises surely the most wonderful tapestry that any single human mind has conceived.

I remember a print, seen in childhood, of a well-known poet surrounded by all the creations of his genius. Enormous, indeed, would be the canvas that could contain all the figures to which Hans Andersen gave being and life.

The story of **"Waldemar Daa and His Daughters"** produces very much the same atmosphere as "Wuthering Heights" or Balzac's "Quest of the Absolute"; against a majestic background of storm and ruin the characters move inexorably to their doom. It has the feeling of some old romantic landscape, blackened with age. Here in a few pages is the tragic story of a whole generation. In **"The Marsh King's Daughter,"** with its rare fantasy and rarer spiritual beauty, is a great conception, but no greater in degree than **"Anne Lisbeth," "The Angel"** or **"The Child in the Grave."** Even the humblest things take somehow an element of greatness; he gave nobility to whatever he touched. And if there is one motif that stands out more than any other in his writing, that recurs again and again, it is that expressed most clearly in the words of the angel to the child:

"The good and the beautiful shall not be forgotten; it shall live on in legend and in song." (pp. 31-4)

Margery Williams Bianco, "The Stories of Hans Andersen," in The Horn Book Magazine *(copyrighted, 1927, by The Horn Book, Inc., Boston), Vol. III, No. 2, May, 1927, pp. 29-34.*

This writer, who shaped his stories for children first of all, had humour, poetry, knowledge of the world, a clear sense of form. . . . He is a great writer because he has created a world that we can move in and live in, and Tolstoy and Balzac could do no more. "'But that is superb,' said the Princess, as she went away, 'I have never heard a finer composition. Listen! run in and ask what the instrument costs.' 'He wants a hundred kisses from the Princess,' said the maid of honour who had gone to ask. 'I think he is crazy,' said the Princess, and she went away; but when she had gone a little way she stood still. 'One must encourage art,' she said. 'I am the Emperor's daughter! Tell him he can have ten kisses, like yesterday, and he can take the rest from my maid of honour.' 'Oh, but we hate to,' said the maids of honour. That's all nonsense,' said the Princess, 'if I can allow myself to be kissed, you can too.'" In that little talk we have society girls of all seasons. All imposters are in the pair who set up their loom to weave the Emperor's clothes out of nothing. All people who hold offices are in the Cat and the Hen who were the inmates of the house to which the poor Ugly Duckling came. . . . We get no profounder sense of evil even from those who have made a cult of their knowledge of it than we get from a view of the Witch's dwelling as the Little Mermaid came to it. . . .

Andersen's stories have in them a heroism that far transcends the military virtues—they have the sort of heroism that one finds in the lives of the saints—indeed the story of the Little Mermaid and of the Princess who wove shirts for her swan-brothers out of the churchyard nettles reminds one of stories about the saints. And what heroic virtue was in this man who made out of his memories stories which have such humor, such poetry, such keen and such kindly observation, and over and over again, such perfection of form. (p. 988)

Padraic Colum, "Hans Christian Andersen," in The Saturday Review of Literature *(© 1927 Saturday Review Magazine Co.; reprinted by permission), Vol. III, No. 52, July 23, 1927, pp. 987-88.*

[*Elias Bredsdorff has written that "the only acceptable book in English before 1930 was a translation from Danish, Elith Reumert's* Hans Christian Andersen the Man." *Reumert was an actor and lecturer who traveled around the world speaking about Andersen.*]

Andersen appeals to the child within us as no other writer, before or after him, has done. And, thank God, we have all kept something of the child within us, however old and wise we may have grown. Andersen's writings, therefore, have an everlasting message to the whole of mankind, to the old and young of all nations. (p. vi)

Elith Reumert, in his Hans Andersen the Man *(originally published as H. C. Andersen som han var, 1927), translated by Jessie Brochner, Methuen & Company, Limited, 1927 (and reprinted by Tower Books, 1971), 192 p.*

[*H. Topsøe-Jensen spent much of his career analyzing the accuracy of Andersen's memoirs and the contents of his letters. Bredsdorff says that "Topsøe-Jensen's studies of Andersen as an autobiographer are among the pillars of contemporary Andersen research." Paul Rubow published* H. C. Andersen Eventyr *in 1927, a discussion of the literary genres in Andersen's fairy tales which is considered a forerunner of later works in the field.*]

[Andersen's] art was distinctly an art of moods, born of momentary inspiration. Many of his best fairy tales were, as he tells us in **"The Bell,"** lying dormant in his mind "like a seed that only needed a breath, a sunbeam, a drop of wormwood, in order to blossom." But this did not prevent him from laboring with his manuscripts. He went over them again and again, with all the care of a skilled craftsman, until he had attained a finish that was at once perfect art and pure nature. (p. 205)

Hans Christian Andersen's name will for ever be bound up with his Book of Fairy Tales—Denmark's only contribution to world literature. The spirit of the fairy tale was present in everything he wrote, no matter what its form, and within the domain of the fairy tale itself he found his own particular field in which no one can dispute his supremacy. (p. 206)

Both [*A Picture Book without Pictures* and the *Fairy Tales*] have in common the important rôle played by the narrator with his constant marginal notes. This is a characteristic of Andersen's literary method so significant that it may perhaps contain the clue to why he was never quite at home either in the purely subjective lyric or in the purely objective drama. Both necessarily presuppose the absence of any narrator, any mediator between the subject matter and the audience. On the other hand, the presence of the narrator is a fundamental requisite of the fairy tale, and it was the harmony between the author's mentality and this special form of composition that gave his fairy tales their immediate success and lasting world fame. (p. 209)

He felt that the great creative writer must necessarily turn against all forms of imitation in literary art. In literature, as in the conception of life, the future must break with the past. Terseness, clarity, richness—these should be the characteristics of the literature of the future. But as human character is the one fixed quantity in a shifting world, and the content of living literature is the emotions of the human heart, so its essence must always be the same, even though the external form changes.

Andersen felt that in his fairy tales he was working for the literature of the future. In **"The Gardener and the Family,"** one of the stories which he especially recommends to the notice of his listeners, he has in a few words defined his position in the world of letters. He writes: "What no other gardener had thought of planting in the flower garden, he set in the kind of soil that each should have, and in shade or in sunshine as every kind required. He tended it in love, and it grew in magnificence." (pp. 209-10)

> *Helge Topsøe-Jensen and Paul V. Rubow, "Hans Christian Andersen the Writer," in* The American Scandinavian Review *(copyright 1930 by The American-Scandinavian Foundation; reprinted by permission of* Scandinavian Review*), Vol. XVIII, No. 4, April, 1930, pp. 204-12.*

[Andersen's] stories rivalled those which, elaborated by entire peoples, have come to us down the ages.

Fairy tales such as those which underpin a few of Andersen's and were rivalled by his original tales of crowned birds, dreaming fir-trees, and constant nightingales, are but the detritus of the great nature myths. . . . Like the blocks from which they have become detached in the course of centuries, they symbolize, with representations of the actions of living beings, particularly human beings, or imaginary extra-human creatures—eloquent animals and things behaving like men—the operations of natural forces and the psyche's nameless powers. And only twice in modern times have individuals, from out their own imaginations, produced nature myths with the magic and the vitality of those which have come to us down the ages, and thus in single lifetimes paralleled the long careers of races. One of these individuals was, as we have said, the grotesque daddy-long-legs. The poetry, wit, and exquisite freshness of the detail in his fairy stories make half of those in the collections of the brothers Grimm seem wooden. The other historical mythmaker was Shakespeare. His infinitely glamorous nature myth is "A Midsummer Night's Dream."

In what manner Andersen's deepest wisdom, his personal experience of the profound powers of the psyche, their life, struggles, and goals of release and perfection, and also his acute social criticism, transformed itself into original and humorous mythological symbols couched in the language of the people, we do not know: any more than we know how Shakespeare came to compose his fairy comedy. We do not, for instance, know whether Andersen found his images in dreams or in waking fantasies. We merely surmise his stories were not allegories; or even fables—though they have their archly didactic side. They possess all the earmarks of direct poetic experience: the inimitable force and freshness of ideas not mentally worked up and not quite susceptible of rational analysis. Quantities of the details too have this unfathomable poetic quality: for example, the famous picture of the stork "tiptoeing on his red legs, jabbering Egyptian, a language his mother had taught him." This alone is certain, that by an infallible instinct their author took these gay and melancholy, brilliant and deeply moving little tales directly to one of their predestined audiences. Long before he wrote them down, Andersen recounted them to children—his friends' and acquaintances'—with appropriate gestures and grimaces which enchanted his hearers and later became the rhetoric of his narratives. The child, of course, is much closer to the pan-psychic, marvelous world of sentient darning-needles and tops and of reasoning field mice than is the rationalistic adult. And the stories, as has been said, contain all that satisfies the child. They convey the feeling of life, the sense of the familiar, and portray human relations, in especial those of adults and children. They are filled with surprises, with sense-impressions, with beauty, wonder, mystery, magic, adventure, action, success, humor, and poetic justice. They are rhythmic and repetitive, and sincerely emotive despite their occasional sentimentalities, and full of appeal to the imagination. Besides, children have this in common with the embodiments of the human psyche which figure in these immortal tales under the names Thumbelina and the little mermaid, the soldier and the sister of the swan-fraternity: the determination of growth and the persuasion that "ripeness is all."

And Andersen had intense sympathy for these little manikins; he gracefully adjusted his tales to their understandings, and represented the natural world from their angle of vision. "To the water's edge," he says in a characteristic passage, "the bank was covered with great wild rhubarb leaves so high that little children could stand upright under the biggest of them." No wonder no author has ever had a greater audience of children. None ever has placed better material within their grasp. But while he addressed children, he very subtly and poetically expressed mature experience. The humbug of society, the self-interest which controls judgment, the cowardice and fear of acting otherwise than the world which keeps men from speaking the truth—wherever has it more lightly and deftly been expressed than in **"The Emperor's New Clothes"**? The deadliness of rationalism and mechanistic science, the life-bestowal of all which holds us in bondage to nature—where more succinctly than in **"The Nightingale"**? The fact that what happens in life doesn't matter quite so much as the way in which we accept what happens—where has it been put less pedantically than in **"The Steadfast Tin Soldier"**? Or the truths that grandeur alone recognizes grandeur, and that ugly ducklings become swans only through struggle with the world and by doing something for themselves,—where have they been put more penetratingly than in the most enchanting of all his enchanting tales?

Indeed . . . we cannot help wondering whether any story-teller other than Andersen ever has represented equally significant material in compasses as diminutive as theirs. We cannot help finding even their interpretations of human nature more acceptable than those in most naturalistic novels. Andersen archly comprehends its inexplicable incoherency, as where, in **"Big Claus and Little Claus,"** he lets the bully who has the small man in a bag and is about to kill him, think, as he passes a church and hears singing within it, that "it might be a good thing to go in and hear a little hymn before going any further." Above all, through his myths we again feel the struggles, deaths, and births of the basic forces of the human soul: their self-expenditure in fruitless yearning, their travail to free themselves from the webs of circumstance; their ability to endure endless winter and to transform and spiritualize themselves and reawaken from subterranean slumbers and fly and sing. And to do so is to grasp anew the mystery, wonder, and meaning of life. (pp. 10-11)

> *Paul Rosenfeld, "The Ugly Duckling," in* The Saturday Review of Literature *(© 1938, copyright renewed © 1965, Saturday Review Magazine Co.; reprinted by permission), Vol. XVIII, No. 3, May 14, 1938, pp. 10-11.*

[The] great beauty and enduring value of Hans Andersen's *Fairy Tales* is that they show life as it is, birth at the beginning and death at the end, and a whimsical mixture of laughter and tears in between. I do not understand why it should be thought right or necessary to shield a child from the knowledge that death is the inevitable, the logical, the adventurous end to living. I think he should know that none of us understands what comes afterwards, but that it is necessary to create, out of one's life, something worthy of survival. This idea must grow by slow and comfortable degrees, and I know of few things that show the way more simply and sweetly than Hans Andersen's stories. He does not twist things away from their natural direction in order to bring about a happy ending, and I think that children feel the dignity and tranquillity of his rounded episodes. Tragedy, in Andersen's tales, is never shocking; he is gentle and patient in teaching children that life does not always have a happy face, and his sense of proportion is so delicate that he never overburdens his readers with sadness. The persuasive feeling of quiet confidence and conviction of the rightness of things as they happen flows steadily through Hans Andersen's *Fairy Tales*. . . . (pp. 176-77)

> *Annis Duff, "A Brief for Fairy Tales," in her* "Bequest of Wings": A Family's Pleasures with Books *(copyright 1944 by Annis Duff; copyright renewed © 1972 by Annis Duff; reprinted by permission of Viking Penguin Inc.), The Viking Press, 1944, pp. 170-80.**

The Grimm brothers were the first men to attempt to record folk tales exactly as they were told by the folk themselves without concessions to bourgeois prudery or cultured literary canon, an example which, in the case of prudery, at least, has not been followed, I am sorry to say, by their translators.

Hans Andersen, so far as I know, was the first man to take the fairy tale as a literary form and invent new ones deliberately. Some of his stories are, like those of Perrault, a reworking of folk material—**"The Wild Swans,"** for example, is based on two stories in the Grimm collection, "The Six Swans," and "The Twelve Brothers"—but his best tales, like **"The Snow Queen,"** or **"The Hardy Tin Soldier,"** or **"The Ice Maiden"** are not only new in material but as unmistakably Andersen's as if they were modern novels.

Compared with the Grimm tales, they have the virtues and the defects of a conscious literary art. To begin with, they tend to be parables rather than myths.

> "Little Kay was blue with cold—nay almost black—but he did not know it, for the Snow Queen had kissed away the icy shiverings, and his heart was little better than a lump of ice. He went about dragging some sharp flat pieces of ice which he placed in all sorts of patterns, trying to make something out of them, just as when we at home have little tablets of wood, with which we make patterns and call them a 'Chinese puzzle.'

> "Kay's patterns were most ingenious, because they were the 'Ice Puzzles of Reason.' In his eyes they were excellent and of the greatest importance: this was because of the grain of glass still in his eye. He made many patterns forming words, but he never could find the right way to place them for one particular word, a word he was most anxious to make. It was 'Eternity.' The Snow Queen had said to him that if he could find out this word he should be his own master, and she would give him the whole world and a new pair of skates. But he could not discover it."

Such a passage could never occur in a folk tale. Firstly, because the human situation with which it is concerned is an historical one created by Descartes, Newton, and their successors, and, secondly, because no folk tale would analyze its own symbols and explain that the game with the ice-splinters was the game of reason. Further, the promised reward, "the whole world and a new pair of skates" has not only a surprise and a subtlety of which the folk tale is incapable, but, also a uniqueness by which one can identify its author.

It is rarely possible, therefore, to retell an Andersen story in other words than his; after the tough and cheerful adventurers of the folk tales, one may be irritated with the Sensitive-Plantishness and rather namby-pamby Christianity of some of Andersen's heroes, but one puts up with them for the sake of the wit and sharpness of his social observation and the interest of his minor characters. One remembers the old lady with the painted flowers in her hat and the robber's daughter in **"The Snow Queen"** as individuals in a way that one fails to remember any of the hundreds of witches and young girls in the folk tales. The difference may be most clearly seen by a comparison of stories about inanimate objects.

> "Soon . . . they came to a little brook, and, as there was no bridge or foot-plank, they did not know how they were to get over it. The straw hit on a good idea, and said: 'I will lay myself straight across, and then you can walk over on me as a bridge.' The straw therefore stretched itself from one bank to the other, and the coal, who was of an impetuous disposition, tripped quite boldly onto the newly built bridge. But when she had reached the middle, and heard the water rushing beneath her, she was, after all, afraid, and stood still, and ventured no further. The straw, however, began to burn, broke

in two pieces, and fell into the stream. The coal slipped after her, hissed when she got into the water, and breathed her last. The bean, who had prudently stayed behind on the shore, could not but laugh at the event, was unable to stop, and laughed so heartily that she burst. It would have been all over with her, likewise, if, by good fortune, a tailor who was traveling in search of work, had not sat down to rest by the brook. As he had a compassionate heart, he pulled out his needle and thread and sewed her together. The bean thanked him most prettily, but, as the tailor used black thread, all beans since then have a black seam.''

So Grimm. The fantasy is built upon a factual question. ''Why do beans have a black seam?'' The characterization of the straw, the coal, and the bean does not extend beyond the minimum required by their respective physical qualities. The whole interest lies in the incidents.

Andersen's story, **''The Darning Needle,''** on the other hand, presupposes no question about its protagonist.

''The darning needle kept her proud behavior and did not lose her good humor. And things of many kinds swam over her, chips and straws and pieces of old newspapers.

'''Only look how they sail!' said the darning needle. 'They don't know what is under them! . . . See, there goes a chip thinking of nothing in the world but of himself—of a chip! There's a straw going by now. How he turns! how he twirls about! Don't think only of yourself, you might easily run up against a stone. There swims a bit of newspaper. What's written upon it has long been forgotten, and yet it gives itself airs. I sit quietly and patiently here. I know who I am and I shall remain what I am.'

''One day something lay close beside her that glittered splendidly; then the darning needle believed that it was a diamond; but it was a bit of broken bottle; and because it shone, the darning needle spoke to it, introducing herself as a breastpin.

'''I suppose you are a diamond?' she observed.

'''Why, yes, something of that kind.'

''And then each believed the other to be a very valuable thing; and they began speaking about the world, and how very conceited it was.

'''I have been in a lady's box,' said the darning needle, 'and this lady was a cook. She had five fingers on each hand, and I never saw anything so conceited as those five fingers. And yet they were only there that they might take me out of the box and put me back into it.'

'''Were they of good birth?' asked the bit of bottle.

'''No, indeed, but very haughty. . . . There was nothing but bragging among them, and therefore I went away.'

'''And now we sit here and glitter!' said the bit of bottle.''

Here the action is subordinate to the actors, providing them with a suitable occasion to display their characters which are individual, i.e., one can easily imagine another Darning Needle and another Bit of Bottle who would say quite different things. Inanimate objects are not being treated anthropomorphically, as in Grimm; on the contrary, human beings have been transmuted into inanimate objects in order that they may be judged without prejudice, with the same objective vision that Swift tries for through changes of size. The difference is one that distinguishes all primitive literature, primitive, that is, in attitude, not in technique, from modern. (pp. 204-07)

W. H. Auden, ''Grimm and Andersen'' (1952; copyright 1952 by W. H. Auden; reprinted by permission of Random House, Inc.), in his Forewords and Afterwords, *edited by Edward Mendelson, Random House, 1973, pp. 198-208.*

Among the writers of fairy tales, Hans Christian Andersen . . . ranks foremost. These are the three simple reasons why the inventions and retellings of Hans Christian Andersen are welcomed by everybody: he brought back to life a lost sense of innocence, wonder and happiness. (p. 9)

Sean O'Faolain, ''For the Child—And for the Wise Man,'' in The New York Times (© *1955 by The New York Times Company; reprinted by permission), March 27, 1955, pp. 9, 67-8, 76.*

Hans Andersen's countryman Kai Munk has remarked that there are two kinds of writing: writing of entertainment, which is ephemeral, and writing of existence, which has a life of its own and can be very entertaining as well. It would seem that a fairy tale must of necessity belong to the first, but Andersen's Tales are writing of existence, and potent existence at that; for all their fantasy, they are life, universal, eternal; for all their lightness of touch, they are serious. (pp. 7-8)

People who have not read Andersen may ask, with him, what there was in these little tales that has placed them where they are. Why these? What is it that makes them so different from Perrault or Grimm? The answer is ''everything.''

To begin with, they have a perfection of form that none of the others achieved. . . . Each story has the essence of a poem, and a poem is not prose broken into short lines, but a distilling of thought and meaning into a distinct form, so disciplined and finely made, so knit in rhythm, that one word out of place, one word too much, jars the whole. In Andersen we are never jarred and it is this that gives the Tales their extraordinary swiftness—too often lost in translation—so that they are over almost before we have had time to take them in, and we have had the magical feeling of flying. The children, he remarked, always had their mouths a little open when he had finished; that is the feeling we have too.

But they were not written swiftly, were not the happy accidents that some people think them; anyone who has studied the original manuscripts from the first short draft of a story, through all its stages of crossings out, rewritings and alterations in Andersen's small spiky handwriting, the cuttings and pastings together, until the last draft was ready for the printer, can see how each word was weighed, and what careful pruning was done, what discipline was there. Even the discipline was skillful; Andersen never let it kill the life in his style.

That life is his hallmark. A sentence from one of Hans Andersen's Tales is utterly different from a sentence by anyone else. (pp. 145-46)

In the Bible we are told that God formed Man out of the dust of earth and breathed into his nostrils . . . and Man became a living soul. Without irreverence it might be said that Hans Andersen did something like that too; he formed his stories of the dust of earth: a daisy, an old street lamp, a darning needle, a beetle, and made them live. His breath was unique; it was an alchemy of wisdom, poetry, humor, and innocence.

He was adult, a philosopher, and a lovable man; his stories are parables and have meanings that sound on and on—sometimes over our heads—after their last word is read. He was a poet and knew the whole gamut of feeling from ecstasy to black melancholy and horror. People call him sentimental; in a way he was, but in the first meaning of the word, which is not "excess of feeling" but an abounding in feeling and reflection. He was a child; children have this godlike power of giving personality to things that have none, not only toys, but sticks and stones, banister knobs and footstools, cabbages; it dies in them as they grow up, but Andersen never lost this power. "It often seems to me," he wrote, "as if every hoarding, every little flower is saying to me: 'Look at me, just for a moment, and then my story will go right into you.'" "Right into you," that is the clue. The daisy, the street lamp, the beetle—they are suddenly breathing and alive. (pp. 147-48)

All the stories have [an] economy, [a] startlingly quick effect. None of them, except *The Snow Queen*, which is almost a novel, is long; Andersen is verbose and boring in his novels and autobiography, but these are his poems—for that is what he always was, a poet. (p. 150)

Stories as vividly horrid as *The Girl Who Trod on a Loaf*, as sad as *The Shadow*, should perhaps be kept away from children altogether, but to expunge parts of them, to tell them in another way, is to destroy them, and that is desecration, not too strong a word; and almost always it is safe to trust to the children. Andersen's *The Little Mermaid* has terrible parts, the story is one of the saddest on earth, but it is also one of the very best loved.

In pictures and statues of Andersen, tiny children are shown listening to the stories. This is sentimentally false; the stories were not meant for tiny children. In Andersen's time, very little children were kept in the nursery when visitors came to the house; it was not until they were eight or nine years old that they were allowed to go down to the drawing-room or in to dessert to meet Mr. Hans Andersen and perhaps hear his Tales. Even then they did not understand the whole; they were not meant to; all Andersen wanted was that they should love them; presently, as they grew up, they would understand; to stop and explain—as conscientious mothers do—is to spoil the rhythm, the whole feeling. Let the children wonder; these are wonder tales. (pp. 151-52)

"It is easy," Andersen was to say of the Tales. "It is just as you would talk to a child. Anyone can tell them." Time has made it very plain that no one can tell them but Hans Andersen. (p. 154)

Rumer Godden, in her Hans Christian Andersen: A Great Life in Brief *(copyright © 1954 by Rumer Godden; reprinted by permission of Alfred A. Knopf, Inc.), Knopf, 1955, 206 p.*

Any account of Andersen's fairy-tales must inevitably, I suppose, start from the verity that, being in so many ways a child himself, he was just the boy to write children's stories. A useful addition to this can be made by an approach only slightly more sophisticated: Andersen is a real gift for the school which finds in art a re-enactment of personal conflicts and obsessions. Seen from this angle, '**The Swineherd**' becomes a symbolical attack on the triviality of the women who laughed at his huge head, straggling hair and stork-like legs, and ends, with the phrase 'I am come to despise thee', in a symbolical rejection. Again, the heroine of '**The Little Mermaid**' possessed, quite irrelevantly from the story's point of view, a beautiful voice, and in an attempt to win her Prince suffered her tongue being cut out; it is hard to forget that Andersen was unhappily in love with Jenny Lind. And we all know who the Ugly Duckling was and what it went through before 'it realized its happiness in all the splendour that surrounded it.' Hidden and neglected merit finally revealed and rewarded is perhaps the central theme of the stories, and it is here, of course, that their obsessional origin ties up with their appeal to children. It took a man like Andersen to remember, or to re-evoke, childhood's dreadful impatience with the unregarding world and to dramatize it in terms that childhood can understand. To read of the immense care he lavished on his tales, to remember how scrupulously he preserves the repetitive element that children love, and how boldly he anthropomorphizes trees, needles and firetongs, makes it tempting to believe that he knew exactly what he was doing, that he was consciously offering up his own prolonged childhood. And yet he seems to have regarded the whole business as a sideline; the tales were written as a diversion from the serious concerns of a novelist and poet, or else to raise money, and although good at entertaining children there is little evidence that he was fond of them. Was he perhaps secretly ashamed and frightened of being childish? He need not have been. It made him an insufferable companion, but how many great writers have been any better? (pp. 28-9)

Kingsley Amis, "Stork, Stork, Long-Legged Stork" (1955), in his What Became of Jane Austen? and Other Questions *(copyright © 1970 by Kingsley Amis; reprinted by permission of Harcourt Brace Jovanovich, Inc.; in Canada by Jonathan Cape Limited), Jonathan Cape, 1970 (and reprinted by Harcourt, 1971), pp. 25-29.*

Supposing that, by some stretch of imagination, we were called upon to choose the very prince of all story writers for children, my vote would go . . . to Hans Christian Andersen. (p. 92)

He is unexcelled because, within the slender framework of his tales, he brings in all the pageantry of the universe. It is never too much for children. You will find there not only Copenhagen and its brick houses, and its great reddish roofs and copper domes, and the golden cross of Notre-Dame that reflects the sun; Denmark with its marshes, its woods, its willows bent by the wind, its ever-present sea; Scandinavia, Iceland, snowy and frozen, but you will also find Germany, Switzerland, Spain flooded with sunshine, Portugal, Milan, Venice, Florence and Rome, Paris, city of the fine arts, city of revolutions. You will find there Egypt, Persia, China, the ocean to its very depths where the mermaids live; the sky where floats the whiteness of great wild swans.

It is a marvelous picture book that the moon makes in relating what she saw in the mountains, over the lakes, through the windows of human dwellings, in every place where her blue and melancholy light softly steals, plays and vanishes. If the present is not enough, evoke the past—Pompeian villas or the barbaric palaces of the Vikings. If reality is not enough, see magic scenes that the fairies build. If your eyes are not surfeited by nature's countless spectacles, close them; in your dreams will appear the luminous spirit of the truth, variable, ever changing, and more beautiful than the beauties of the waking day.

In these feasts of imagination, others will perhaps be capable of equalling him, but there are values he has revealed that are his very own sumptuous gift to children; enchanted scenes they will find only in him, the memory of which will charm them forever. . . . (pp. 94-5)

Andersen is unique in his capacity for entering into the very soul of beings and of things.

That animals have an intelligible language, Andersen and children know better than anyone. When the cat says to little Rudy: "Come out on the roof; put one paw here, another a little higher; come on, hoist yourself up; see how I do it, nothing is easier," little Rudy understands perfectly. And the dog that, not satisfied with barking, expresses himself also with his eyes, his tail, and his whole body speaks a language that seems quite natural to the child. That plants talk is taken for granted also. After all, why should Mother Elder and Father Willow not exchange confidences like everybody else? Leaves are very talkative; they murmur for no reason at all.

But what is rarer and finer is to see objects become animated and to hear their voices. Not only the toys, not only the porcelain dancer on the mantelpiece so full of airs and graces, not only the grotesque Chinese figure on the console who shakes his head when looking at you. This innumerable folk, that the indifferent call "things," stirs, moves, speaks and fills the air with its complaints or its songs. Everything is alive: the ray of sunshine that dances through the window, the branch of apple tree in its spring frock, the salon furniture, the gardener's tools, the kitchen utensils, the pail, the broom, the basket, the plates and even the matches, although they are a bit stiff. Of all the objects that you can imagine, there is not one that does not want to chat with its neighbors and make merry. At night, you believe there is no longer any life. On the contrary, it is the moment when silent ones feel free to speak; when the motionless ones feel their limbs itching and gambol about gaily. The arithmetic problem fidgets about on its slate, the letters grow restless in the copy book and complain at having been badly traced.

> When one is a child, and can hardly talk, one understands perfectly the language of the hens and ducks, dogs and cats. They speak to us as distinctly as father and mother. At that age we even hear grandfather's cane whinny; it has become our horse, and we see a head on it, legs and a tail. But once grown up this faculty is lost. However, there are children who keep it longer than others; we say of them that they remain big simpletons. . . .

Big simpletons or geniuses. On this latter count, let us thank Heaven that Andersen remained a child.

If others shrivel up everything they touch by analyzing and dissecting, Andersen, on the contrary, animates and vivifies. On the summit of mountains, on the highest peaks, he is hypnotized by Vertigo who tries to make him totter and fall headlong into the abyss. In the depths of the crevices lives the

Queen of the glaciers. She is asking for her victims, and you hear her voice. Andersen is never alone. He is surrounded by a multitude of little lives, by countless beings who observe and watch him. He is only one of them, perhaps a little better endowed, in the vast comedy in which thousands of actors take part. All the others, the oak, the house, the butterfly, the wave, the stick of wood, the gravestone, rejoice or suffer with him. (pp. 97-9)

When we finish reading the **Tales** we are not entirely the same as we were when we began them. We would gladly become, as Rimbaud says, *un opéra fabuleux.* The wheat that bends, what emotion makes it tremble? Where do the white clouds go that are passing over us? Do they go in light attire to some celestial festival in the palace of Prince Azur?

But of all Andersen's claims to supremacy, the finest and noblest claim is the wisdom inherent in his tales, their inner life. (p. 101)

It is this inner life that gives the **Tales** their deep quality. From it also comes that exaltation which spreads through the soul of the readers. From it comes, finally, a marked quality of serenity. (p. 104)

The teller of tales stands at his window. He listens to the swallows and the storks that have returned to Denmark for the fine summer days. He listens to his friend the wind. Or, he mingles with the crowd and listens once more to what the gingerbread merchant is relating, to what the old eel fisherman is telling. He makes use of everything. He tells them again in his own way, these stories that provoke a smile or a tear. He gives them a lyrical style, dramatic and always simple, a style of which he alone is master. He adorns them with brighter and more delicate colors; and, lending them wings, he send them to the very limits of the world. But he fills them also with intense feeling and therein, without doubt, added to all the other qualities, lies the final attainment which explains their great power.

The children are not mistaken. In these beautiful tales they find not only pleasure, but the law of their being and the feeling of the great role they have to fill. They themselves have been subjected to sorrow. They sense evil confusedly around them, in them; but this vivid suffering is only transitory and not enough to trouble their serenity. Their mission is to bring to the world a renewal of faith and hope. What would become of the human spirit if it were not refreshed by this confident young strength? The new generation arrives to make the world beautiful once more. Everything grows green again. Life finds its reasons for enduring. Andersen, imbuing his tales with an invincible belief in a better future, communes with the soul of children, harmonizes himself with their deep nature, allies himself with their mission. He upholds, with them and through them, the ideal forces which save humanity from perishing. (pp. 104-05)

Paul Hazard, "Superiority of the North over the South," in his Books, Children and Men, *translated by Marguerite Mitchell, fourth edition (copyright © The Horn Book, Inc.; all rights reserved; reprinted with permission), fourth edition, Horn Book, 1960, pp. 77-110.**

[*In his* Hans Christian Andersen, *Bo Grønbech writes, "Erik Dal is the leading expert in the field of Andersen studies." Dal is the editor of* Hans Christian Andersens Eventyr, *a critical edition of the fairy tales.*]

[Andersen] was not only Denmark's greatest writer . . . but perhaps the world's one and only—in the true sense—universal poet.

For it is his fairy-tales above all which bear witness to this; by their range in their serried ranks; by their depth in the finest of them; and by the way their immortal seed, despite all abuse, has taken root, sprouted, blossomed and borne fruit throughout the world. (p. 183)

> *Erik Dal, "Research on Hans Christian Andersen: Trends, Results and Desiderata," translated by David Hohnen, in* Orbis Litterarum, *Vol. XVII, Nos. 1 & 2, 1962, pp. 166-83.*

[In and with his fairy tales, Andersen] not only won that place among Denmark's leading poets, between Holberg and Oehlenschläger, to which he had unabashedly laid claim . . . : he won much more. He put his fellow poets in the shade. His fairy tales are Denmark's greatest contribution to world literature, and no country possesses an author who has acquired a fresher and truer immortality than Hans Christian Andersen's. His place is beside Homer, Dante, Shakespeare, Cervantes, and Goethe. (p. 190)

Edvárd Collin has given a fine picture of Andersen as a teller of fairy tales before he wrote any of them down:

> In many of the circles to which he paid daily visits were little children with whom he concerned himself; he told them stories which he had partly made up for the occasion, and partly taken from familiar fairy tales; but whether the tales he told were of his own invention or borrowed, his manner of telling them was so exclusively his own and so vivid, that the children were enchanted. He himself enjoyed having a chance to give his humor free play, his speech came in an unobstructed stream, richly provided with expressions familiar to the children and with gestures to fit. He put life into even the driest sentence; he did not say: "The children climbed up into the wagon and then they rode away," but: "Then they climbed up into the wagon, good-by, father, good-by, mother, the whip cracked, snap, snap, and away they went, hey, will you really pull there!" Those who have heard him read his fairy tales later on can only form a weak notion of the strange vitality his delivery had in the midst of a circle of children.

Here Edvárd Collin emphasizes two aspects of the style of the fairy tales: their bold use of the spoken language and their plasticity. Nothing is unclear, nothing is vague; it is all precise, exact, just as in the imagination of a child. It has the oral directness of the theater, where everything must be expressed in dialogue or action. H. C. Andersen acted before the children. The dream of the theater, which had filled him ever since he was a little fellow in Odense and which had driven him to Copenhagen, had been realized here. The new genre was created by transferring the method from private life to literary creation. (pp. 193-94)

There is no longer any doubt that Andersen was born so that he could write these fairy tales and stories: they are his contribution to world history.

Andersen complained bitterly about the lack of encouragement and approval which his first fairy tales met. One literary magazine advised him not to waste his time on fairy tales for children, and another praised the fairy tales of his old adversary, Christian Molbech, at his expense—Molbech's calm and simple manner was more tasteful. Had not Molbech himself once inquired in a review: "When will Andersen ever learn to write Danish?" He never learned; instead, he taught the Danes to write their language in a different way. (pp. 194-95)

One can, of course, point to the style, the manner of narration, as Edvárd Collin did, one can say that their imaginative plasticity combines the nursery's fresh naïveté with the theater's artful precision in a way which was only possible in innocent Denmark's cunning capital during the aesthetic Age of Gold. . . . (p. 196)

One can emphasize the fact that he saw human existence in all its manifold and vital richness simply because he had come up from below, out of the dark depths of poverty and want—more can be seen from the ground, as it were, than from the sky. And one can continue the thought: he possessed a great advantage over other poets who, although gifted with emotion and imagination, had never experienced elementary excitement—they had never gone cold and hungry, they had never trembled with mortal fear. H. C. Andersen had known these experiences, and so he had something to tell; from this reality stems his rushing *élan*, which is authentic—the dizzying tempo which takes the listener's breath away. His knowledge of reality was present at the very outset, in **The Tinderbox,** and it is the source of inspiration for all the fairy tales—**Thumbelina, The Ugly Duckling, The Little Mermaid.** Each of them is concerned with a question of life or death.

One can amuse oneself by applying a purely literary-historical yardstick to the tales. . . . In this case, one will discover that Andersen, with extraordinary sensitivity and receptivity, absorbed the early nineteenth century's whole current of international Romanticism. One will discover parallels to and connections with his fairy tales everywhere, not only in folk literature but also in conscious literary work, and above all in the German Romanticists, those worshippers of life's magical elements. . . . But in making such comparisons, one should not forget the core of the matter . . . : all these Romanticists and fairy-tale poets enthused about the mystical motifs of popular belief and superstition, they wanted to squeeze poetry out of them, but not a single member of their band could for a moment transport himself back to the world of primitive superstition— none save H. C. Andersen, who was born in its midst and preserved traces of it his whole life through. For this reason all the other fairy tales are paper work, literary decorations, while his are authentic products of experience—both those he repeats and those he invents. He is the earth's last teller of fairy tales; from the dark womb of Fyn's primitive peasant culture he came directly before the footlights of Copenhagen's Romantic theater. Since he was the last, he was also the first and the greatest. He preserved the old, primitive qualities, and added new and subtle ones to them.

He added, for example, nature poetry, depictions of landscape, which had no place in the old folk tales. The delicacy, the intensity, the splendor, and the beauty of his pictures of nature compose an essential part of the fairy tales' enchantment, but we no longer realize exactly to what extent Andersen was a revolutionary creator of new things, a rebel against literary stereotypes. In his poverty-stricken childhood he had sat for days on end, staring at a single leaf on the gooseberry bush, and he kept this ability to see wonderful worlds of beauty in what was commonplace, in what others scorned. Even in his last years he put together bouquets of grass and frostbitten meadow flowers far into the winter, he made the discovery that blooming apple-branches were still lovelier than carefully tended flowers in their beds; and in his fairy tales he reproduced real nature, the nature he had experienced as a little boy in the town and in the countryside. . . . His perception of nature had that naïve and ruthless love of truth which one finds in the unspoiled mind of a child.

The epicist was also a lyricist, and the lyricist was a psychologist besides. An extraordinary wealth of experiences, observations, and reflections is concealed within the fairy tales. . . . A drop of the heart's blood lies in each of the fairy tales [Danish critic Hans Brix says in his *H. C. Andersen and His Fairy Tales*], and that is why they remain fresh and vital; one can follow in detail the process by which all the occurrences and the moods of Andersen's existence impregnated his imagination and, in accordance with their own secret laws, were crystallized into the fairy tales' symbolic script. It is realistic literature, saturated with life and actuality; one knows this from the unflagging interest the fairy tales arouse, even though one is not always able to interpret their symbols. The reader cannot remain indifferent. The true fairy tale, like the true dream, always has the force of a dark message. (pp. 197-200)

Happiness and joy emanate from the fairy tales, they are written in a spirit of triumph; that is why the first one deals with the soldier who owns the tinderbox, and the second has Little Claus as its hero—both are fortune's darlings. What created the productive mood in which Andersen wrote the fairy tales?

It seems as though it were sheer luck, at least in the soldier's case, pure magic; but in Little Claus the truth leaks out—it is a piece of nature's magic instead; behind Little Claus's naïve and clumsy innocence there are concealed inventiveness, guile, waggishness, just as in Andersen himself. Writing the fairy tales, he had the victorious sense of advancing through all the world's difficulties and trials by means of his wit and his humor.

The genre could have turned out to be a vulgar one, a crude and forceful joke in the clownish manner of Till Eulenspiegel, and *Little Claus and Big Claus* has something of Eulenspiegel's mood. But heaven had not cut Andersen after this pattern; his laughter was not boisterous and empty, his humor was not crude and without nuances. No one has had a finer, subtler, more highly strung, more sensitive spirit than he—it is for this reason that the third tale is called *The Princess on the Pea*. Nor was this enough: in his soul there lay depths of bitterness, fear, unrest, and melancholy; his seed-leaf had sprouted amidst suffering and want, deprivation and humiliation; and there was an ineradicable trembling in his whole being as in the leaves of an aspen. All these elements lay behind his smile, and therefore his smile became so brilliant and so enchanting.

The merriment in the fairy tales and their grace—these things expressed Andersen's own triumph over the shadows. Edvard Collin has borne witness to the fact that the basic mood in his friend's life was melancholy, and under this rubric he includes his vanity, his impatience, his suspicion, his unhealthy outbursts of emotion. (pp. 205-06)

In poetic creation, in the fairy tales, there was a remedy and there was health, and liberation, triumph, and victory. There he has pressed the healing balm of humor from life's bitter herbs, there he attains a smiling equilibrium, there he tells of the ugly duckling and the shadow, of all his life's tribulations, with fairness, joy, and playful temerity.

It is for this reason that the fairy tales offer such a deep and exquisite pleasure to their readers: pain has been not forgotten but overcome.

But intelligence, *esprit,* is not the only factor in the fairy tales which delights the reader; he also rejoices at watching the imagination at work, he knows the satisfaction which arises when, like fireworks, colorful and surprising visions follow one upon the other. The child's imagination is highly developed, and that is why Andersen originally addressed himself only to little children; but he very shortly discovered that adults were equally enchanted, and then he abandoned the fiction that the fairy tales were told exclusively or principally for the young. What infinite enjoyment it must have given him to keep a whole public of large and small breathless with excitement—and, at the end, a public which embraced the entire globe! The pleasure a magician takes in swinging his wand is part of the enchantment which streams out of the fairy tales—a demonic pleasure, in Andersen's case as in E.T.A. Hoffmann's, but also an innocent one, white magic, not black. The demonic desire to perform, to draw attention, to be the center of interest, had made Andersen a scandal and a hissing from childhood on, it had branded him as being half-crazy, a monster of vanity. It was his creative and supreme imaginary life which shook the conventions of everyday existence as a lion shakes the bars of its cage. When this life had its chance to flame up unfettered in the fairy tales, then the final great symbolic figures were born, to become the common possession of all humanity; the youngest sisters and brothers of those primal figures, Tom Thumb, Little Red Ridinghood, and the Master Thief, emerged—Thumbelina, the little mermaid, the ugly duckling. (pp. 206-07)

[If] we wish to take him and his fairy tales seriously, we must ask what sort of wisdom it is he preaches.

At first glance it seems to be anything but deep. Life is a beautiful fairy tale, and there is a loving God Who arranges everything for the best. Andersen takes the practical proof of this teaching from his own life story; the hopeful dream was realized as if through a miracle.

This is the basic type of all his fairy tales: that they treat of fortune's chosen darling. It can scarcely have escaped the author that not all the children of men maintain a magical alliance with the Almighty: on the contrary, some of them lead an unhappy life, in want and poverty, frustrated and betrayed in their fondest desires. Andersen does not close his eyes to any of these unfortunates, and he has a consolation for them, for the little match girl frozen to death, for the withered cripple in the cellar beside a metropolitan street: the joys of Heaven, bliss in the arms of God. Even the little mermaid, apparently excluded, will reach this goal by a detour. Thus the books always balance; we all become favorites like the ugly duckling, although some of us do not attain happiness save through that second sandman, the one who is called "Death." (pp. 208-09)

Religion, a firm belief in an eternal bliss, is thus the foundation of the fairy tales and their optimism. However, Andersen was by no means an orthodox Christian. He resembled the picture he had given of his poor father, a seeker, a brooder, a doubter. Now and then he glorified the faith, the mystery of Christ, and the authority of the Bible, but it was more an expression of his longing than of his conviction. . . . Andersen had . . . lost the faith of his childhood, and he was also an idealist, a believer in the spirit. He never abandoned his belief in a personal God. He fought eagerly against the doctrine of hell and eternal punishment; and he had every conceivable difficulty in holding fast to his belief in the immortality of the soul—in other words, he had to fight hard to maintain the very basis of both his own existence and that of the fairy tales. (pp. 209-10)

Charles Kingsley, a Christian idealist and also a contemporary of Andersen's, has given the matter [of distorting the metaphysical urge for eternity, religious idealism, into an argument for the preservation of earthly injustice a] caustic formulation: "The Bible has become a mere police handbook, a dose of opium to make the beasts of burden patient beneath their loads." Did Andersen write his fine fairy tales so that they might be used in the same spirit? Did he have the sandman's magic lantern enchant sick children so that they would forget their pain—or forget to seek a cure for it? In principle, the two matters are very different; in practice the boundary between them often becomes blurred. Morphine is a boon for suffering humanity—a fact which, one guesses, neither Marx nor Lenin would dare dispute—but it is not a panacea; it has no use in the science of hygiene, nor can it prevent sickness; the man who tries to make it the basis of therapeutics is a charlatan, a spirit akin to those men who make an idyllic falsification of religion. Was Andersen one of their number? They were legion in that age, and one must ask oneself whether Andersen's moral and intellectual independence was sufficient to enable him to see through their sophisms. This is no vain question, for in the final analysis it concerns the content of truth in Andersen's fairy tales.

The request for a vote of confidence was made in all due order by the critical representative of the new generation, the realistic age—by Georg Brandes, who in 1869, to the very great pleasure of the old poet, wrote an excellent treatise on Andersen's fairy tales [see excerpt above]. Georg Brandes' admiration is provided with a number of question marks and reservations; he criticizes, among other things, H. C. Andersen's preference for tame and submissive domestic animals—even the nightingale, which is supposed to symbolize poetry, is a docile bird with monarchistic tendencies, and the ugly duckling ends in a castle park, where it swims around as a prisoner and is fed with cakes and crumbs from the table of the rich. "How can your enthusiasm, your pride allow you to let the swan end in this way?" Brandes cries pathetically. Let it die, tragically and magnificently, let it fly away unfettered through the air, rejoicing at its beauty and its strength, let it sink into the depths of a lonely forest lake—but spare it the approval of old swans and ducks, spare it the cakes and the crumbs!

This is indeed a very elegantly formulated criticism of Andersen's social attitudes, and no one can deny that Brandes put his finger on a sore spot. But at the same time one has a strong feeling that we no longer could formulate the accusation as Brandes did. It cannot be considered a failing on the ugly duckling's part, on the part of poetic genius, if it is too humble, if it shows too little arrogance at its strength and its beauty, if it remains among men and joins their community instead of mirroring its fascinating and tragic ego in a wilderness lake. In Brandes one detects the ghost of Romantic individualism from the nineteenth century's beginning, or else it is a sign of the superman who would appear at the century's close; it does not harm Andersen in our eyes if he fails to be demonic or autocratic. On the contrary: Brandes' enthusiasm for the wild, freedom-loving wolf seems to us to be a rather empty pose.

No, we should like to express our criticism in a different way. Has the ugly duckling, once he has succeeded in entering the paradise of the swans, forgotten his brothers in misery, all the other starved, mistreated, and hapless creatures? Did he lament only at his own misfortune, his own sufferings, did life's injustice merely consist in all the hardships he had to undergo himself, was he merely another of the world's many sentimental complainers? . . . Was Andersen . . . actually the incurable egoist, the literary hustler blinded by vanity, whom Carsten Hauch happened—quite by accident—to portray [in *Only a Fiddler*]? Does the fairy tales' optimism, their free play of humor, simply mean that, after the poet himself is in the clear, his heart no longer bleeds so readily? And, that the sandman with his magic wand . . . may take charge of the other victims?

If this had really been true in Andersen's case, then we still should not have the right to condemn him too severely, for this was the typical moral attitude of the nineteenth century's *bourgeoisie*, and one cannot require miracles of perspicacity or tolerance from Andersen. He was a child of the age of aesthetic idealism, his intellectual energy was concentrated on the theater, art, literature, poetry; and the refinement, the mastery, he and his kindred spirits achieved was dearly purchased at the cost of one-sidedness, passivity, blindness. (pp. 211-13)

However well things went for H. C. Andersen, he was never ashamed of his origins; he never went back on his childhood memories or his family's experiences.

Thus there is no doubt at all where Andersen's deepest sympathies lie: with the unpropertied, the oppressed, and the cowed, with the people—the withered cripple in a back street, the beggar girl, the drunken laundress and her boy in his broken-billed cap. To be sure, he did not demand reforms or pose problems or incite to revolution; but although he stayed quite clear of politics, his fairy tales perhaps exerted a psychological influence nonetheless, an influence which then extended itself into the sphere of action: they had a chastening, a softening, a disturbing effect upon their readers. . . . This is the influence Andersen had in Denmark, and not in Denmark alone; this is the influence he had on one generation, and on many. One thinks of the nightingale's promise to the sick emperor: that he would bring him news of happy men and of those who suffer, of the poor fisherman and the cottager's roof—that he would report whatever is otherwise kept hidden from the court and the throne. It is a program, of course, which Andersen did not realize; but the nightingale's words cannot be dismissed as exaggerations, either: attempts in this direction are to be found more than once in Andersen's works. (pp. 216-17)

> *Frederick Böök, in his* Hans Christian Andersen: A Biography, *translated by George C. Schoolfield (copyright 1962 by the University of Oklahoma Press; originally published in an expanded form as* H. C. Andersen: En levnadsteckning, *revised edition, 1955), University of Oklahoma Press, 1962, 260 p.*

[After a childhood of poverty and misfortune, the] enormous social as well as financial improvement in Andersen's circumstances meant that he was able to apply his spellbinding powers of persuasion equally to a portrayal of 'the little match-girl' as to that of the little girl who proved the truth of her claim to be a princess by suffering the discomfort of a pea beneath a whole mountain of mattresses. It is this huge range of sensitivity and experience which is probably one chief reason for his success, although it is necessary to add that his most affecting stories in whatever form have almost all grown out of the depths of his childhood memories. Similarly they have roots which go down into the folk-tales which he knew so well and into the superstitions of the simple people from the spinning-rooms of his native town. There are also clear traces of *The thousand and one nights,* harking back to his childish enjoyment of that book in the one room of the cobbler's house.

But how he has enriched everything and given it a relevance for our own time. He has brought to the plain black and white of the European fairy tale an artistry typical of the poetic sensibility of the North, its irony and its psychological subtlety. What is new here and has hardly ever been employed before, is the manner in which dead things are invested with a soul, are brought to life in a quite unforgettable way, learning to speak and to become creatures in their own right. (pp. 48-9)

Again, never before or since, has a miserable little one-legged soldier been the hero of such a beautiful and enthralling story as *The steadfast tin-soldier.* Andersen shows a splendidly developed artistry in the way he brings these things to life. . . . (p. 49)

Everything in Andersen has a soul of its own and is correspondingly capable of appealing to the reader's imagination. Only seldom are children moved to tears over Grimm's fairy tales, and then only when something particularly sad or horrible is taking place. The fairy tales always remain to a certain extent independent of the reader's experience, tales simply of what goes on in fairyland and thus impossible for ourselves. But with Andersen it is completely different. It is true that he adopts elements from old tales, but what happens to them then? What happens to the little mermaid, for instance, who to begin with is an actual figure from Nordic legend? In order to be near her beloved prince she barters her tail for a pair of human legs, but after that a great change takes place. In spite of her goodness and her obvious faery characteristics, the little princess from the sea must suffer monstrous agonies. Her happiness is paid for with pain, human happiness with human pain. With her we must walk on a thousand knives and our buried feelings are stirred up from depths far removed from those of the folk-tale, whose world of feeling is unsophisticated, and follows accepted rules among which the so-called happy and just ending to stories is one.

For the first time in fairy stories Andersen admits the tragic ending. The little tin-soldier melts in the stove, the little match-girl freezes to death in the street, and the lovelorn little mermaid vanishes in foam at the end of her life as a mortal. Nor is the effect of these tragic conclusions, which stem from Andersen's own experience of life, in any way mitigated by the superb poetry of their telling. The effect they have on a sensitive child is enormous. Thus when people talk about the dangerous influence of fairy tales on children (and people, especially in the fields of education and psychology, often do, thinking mostly of the rather horrific witches and stepmothers that are found in Grimm) it is necessary to affirm that such plainly wicked characters are common to all folk-tales and never emerge triumphant anyway. They cause a much less profound emotional disturbance in a child than the 'pure tragedy' of *The little mermaid,* to take one of the most prominent examples. (pp. 49-50)

The third important aspect of Andersen's tales is the fantasy in their poetic association with nature and with the cosmos, above all the moon, which finds its most beautiful expression in *The picture-book without pictures.* Andersen here places himself in the tradition of the great Romantics, except that his

attitude to nature is free from their brand of mysticism, being on the contrary full of intelligence and wit. (This, of course, applies less to the kind of story which has been prevalent since classical times and which, by allowing animals speech and free-will, more or less robs them of their real nature.)

In Andersen animals remain animals and plants plants, each peculiar to itself. (p. 50)

Andersen could get the subject for a story from such everyday things as a drop of water, which he observed through the recently perfected microscope, or a family of snails, simply by revealing the marvel of their real nature. In *Five peas from one pod,* for instance, a pea lodges in the crack in some roof-tiles outside a little girl's bedroom window. It germinates, grows, and blossoms, and saves the life of a child whom everyone expected to die. In other words, a small, accepted process of nature is seen in the light of its own mystery and turned into a fairy tale.

Simply by looking at the openings of these tales one can see how the countryside, the seas, and the rivers are made to become backcloths or even performers. Winds and tempests, the sun, the moon and the stars, elves, water-sprites, and mermen all push the action along, and often Death will come too. For Andersen was no escapist taking refuge in nature. He stood centrally between the age of Romanticism and the age of Technology. The one gave him his profundity, bearing him forward and enriching him, the other he greeted with enthusiasm. (pp. 50-1)

> *Bettina Hürlimann, "The Ugly Duckling," in her* Three Centuries of Children's Books in Europe, *edited and translated by Brian W. Alderson (© Oxford University Press 1967; reprinted by permission; originally published as* Europäische Kinderbücher in drei Jahrhunderten, *Atlantis Verlag, 1959), Oxford University Press, Oxford, 1967, pp. 42-52.*

It is undeniable that as Andersen went on his stories became less generally interesting. Fewer of them have any link with the older folk-lore; more of them are sketches from ordinary life with no touch of the supernatural; there is, I am afraid, more of the mawkishness which was Andersen's besetting danger, and less—almost none—of the humour of his own special brand. Exceptions, to be sure, there are: [such as] the *Beetle,* which is one of the funniest of all the stories. . . . (p. 12)

> *M. R. James, in a preface to* Forty-Two Stories *by Hans Andersen, translated by M. R. James (reprinted by permission of Faber and Faber Ltd.), Faber and Faber, 1968, pp. 11-19.*

Andersen's whole life is in his fairy stories: his love of the look of things, the look of the natural world, of animals and birds and buildings and textures and of the humblest objects used by man (he was, as the Danes called him, "God's word from the countryside"); his joy in physical comforts and the companionship of loved friends; his terror of poverty and hunger and his visceral knowledge of what it can do to the body and to the human spirit; his horror of evil and selfishness and greed and cruelty, but his clear-sighted acknowledgment of their existence, either grinning boldly in plain view or hidden behind hypocritical words and actions; his longing to believe that there is a plan, some obscure pattern or purpose beneath the seeming mindlessness of the universe, which visits the extremest miseries on innocent creatures and bestows pleasure and advantages on those who seem least to deserve them; his continual struggle with himself and his own faults, which were very often pointed out by well-meaning friends for his own good; his discovery that every honor, no matter by whom it was given, even the King himself, could not avail in the face of the fact that his physical love for women was never returned, the essence of which is distilled in **"The Little Mermaid."**

What an indictment of human society lies in many of Andersen's stories, though we are told that the Danes are maddened to discover that Andersen in translation loses much of that satirical, irreverent, even malicious wit which makes him, on his own ground, closer to Dean Swift than to Andrew Lang and without which he is no longer a Dane to the core. (pp. 38-9)

The most enchanting humor, fresh and uninhibited, plays through Andersen's tales, and if at times it takes a sly, even a sardonic turn, this turn arises not only out of Andersen's past humiliations but out of the fact that Danes are masters at intimate persiflage, the disguised swordthrust, the polite jibe; and Andersen was an artist when it came to wrapping this kind of wit in disarming innocence. . . . Andersen's egoism, his vanity, his overwhelming, his almost demonic desire to perform, to be the center of attention, had made a scandal of him since childhood, but in the fairy tales his true genius blazed up, releasing bitterness into healthy laughter, celebrating the beauty of the natural world, emanating joy and merriment woven into his level-eyed assessment of life and of human nature. Out of all this the great symbolic figures were born—the ugly duckling, Thumbelina, the little mermaid, the nightingale, the steadfast tin soldier. They take their places as if they, too, had been handed down out of the past along with Cinderella and Tom Thumb and Red Riding Hood and all the others beloved of childhood, but offer as well a moving inner life which can be understood most deeply when one understands also something of the man who created them. (p. 40)

> *Eleanor Cameron, "The Unforgettable Glimpse," in her* The Green and Burning Tree: On the Writing and Enjoyment of Children's Books *(copyright © 1962, 1964, 1966, 1969 by Eleanor Cameron; reprinted by permission of Little, Brown and Company in association with the Atlantic Monthly Press), Atlantic-Little, Brown, 1969, pp. 3-47.**

[*A poet and author of books for children, Haugaard published an English translation of Andersen's collected fairy tales in 1974. Haugaard's translation reflects Andersen's use of colloquial Danish, rather than employing the sophisticated terms found in most English-language collections. Ralph Lavender wrote, "This new translation is of our time, and it is the best we have."*]

[Andersen possessed] honesty that made it possible for him to write his fairy tales. In them you find no Swiftian bitterness, for faults and failings are portrayed with compassion. But such honesty is a god-send to those who try to negate genius by classifying geniuses as mad, childish, or perverted, in order to sanctify dull mediocrity.

That there are no purely evil characters in Andersen does not surprise us so much as the fact that there is none who is faultless. Even the nightingale has his weakness: the throne, the seat of power, attracts him; and tears in the emperor's eyes mean more to him than tears on a face in the crowd. There is no doubt that Andersen thought of himself as the nightingale; and how easy it would have been for him to make the little brown bird the epitome of all virtue, and thus enhance himself.

Few nineteenth-century writers have tried so hard to understand what was happening in their times, and how the world would

be changed by scientific progress as Andersen. He even attempted to write fairy tales about it. The most interesting is **"The Wood-Nymph,"** which takes place at the Paris Exposition of 1867. In it Andersen pits Arcadia against the world of technology; and although his sympathy is with the defeated little nymph—who has been affected, among other things, by air pollution!—the staunchest supporters of the previous age are the rats of the Parisian sewers, who miss the good old days when they and the plague ruled the city. Andersen realized that science could alleviate suffering. He expected that the machine would eliminate drudgery; but he did not envision the latter as man's liberator, for he called it "master bloodless". In **"The Muse of the Twentieth Century,"** he recorded his fear that in our era, the works of the immortal poets would be written on prison walls.

Although Andersen speculated much about the physical aspects of the future world, he did not believe that the nature of man would change. Fools would gain power and misuse it; and the clever would dance to their tune. The bad and the good would continue to exist side by side, and the saints would be martyred.

Is that a message of despair? Andersen did not think that it was; for he had faith that beyond human justice, a divine one existed. I do not share this view, however much I should like to. I belong to that generation who called themselves materialists, and yet worshipped such phantoms as paradise without free speech, and justice which was only to be ours when we learned to bow to despotism. Maybe because of this, I love Andersen's world now; and I do not mind that stupidity and evil are eternal as long as beauty and goodness cannot die either. Hope—not on a world scale, but on a personal one—is there; and when that is denied, then humour may carry the burden for us. (pp. 72-3)

> *Erik Christian Haugaard, "The Simple Truth" (copyright © 1973 Erik Christian Haugaard; reprinted by permission of the author and The Thimble Press, Lockwood Station Road, South Woodchester, Glos. GL55EQ, England), in* Signal, *No. 11, May, 1973, pp. 69-73.*

From the very beginning Hans Andersen was more than a mere anthologist. He used the folk tale as a loose framework for his early stories but often exploded its conventions, especially its stock of endings. The folk tale never follows life's unpredictable, fanciful and irreversible pattern; it corrects, compensates and inevitably contrives reassuring endings. Hans Andersen's tales, on the other hand, never try to reassure; they offer no outlet to desire, no concessions to wishful thinking, and do not redress the balance of life. He does not lead his heroes to their destination but leaves them to wander as best they can towards a goal they may never reach. In a fairy story the peasant-prince as in Grimm's *King Thrushbeard* or the outcast brother as in *Ivan the Ninny* may finally marry the princess; but Hans Andersen's swineherd refuses to do so.

> And with that he went into his Kingdom, shut the door and bolted it; but she could stand outside if she cared to and sing:
>
> Ach du lieber Augustin
> Alles ist Voek, Voek, Voek!

The tune ends on a note that echoes in the imagination with the sadness of a future beyond human control. Thus *The Swineherd* is an anti-story where real time, fluid and unpredictable, takes the place of mythical time and this is the poet's first step towards the conquest of reality.

From then on Hans Andersen tried, in one tale after another, to distinguish between the folk tale and the story and to establish their different forms: *Little Ida's Flowers, The Snow Queen, a folk tale in seven parts, The Wind tells the Story of Valdemar Daa and his Daughters, Willie Winkie, The Elder Mother.* His whole output may be seen as an exercise in the art of the narrative, in the various ways of telling a story. He invites the reader to share the exercise and participate in the story. In a single tale we find different paces in the narrative and different depths of imagination. (pp. 47-8)

In folk tales the hero sets out 'to seek his fortune'; the goal is never more definite than that and in Andersen's early stories the wanderers are aimless, too: 'Hi, there, my friend, where are you off to?' 'Out into the wide world . . .' But the meaning of these wanderings gradually emerges: the bird, the leaf and the story-teller himself are in search of a story; they set out 'into the wide world' to look for stories. Tales are to be found in the most unexpected places, in the heart of a rose or in the eye of a needle and when they are recognized, they transform the most commonplace objects into something magical. . . . How can we recognize a story? What is the gift that makes mere talk fall into place and become a story? How does a story with its characters and its pattern emerge from a jumble of words or ideas suggested by the wind, a leaf, a bird, perhaps something mentioned idly by a child, or by the story-teller himself? The answer is a sudden flash of perception about the nature of an object. The thing itself will not necessarily take first place in the story—the teapot, the tin soldier, the rose or the pea—it is more likely simply to be the thing that sparks off the story-teller's imagination, setting the creative mechanism in motion—the flowers on the balcony in *The Shadow*, the window-boxes on the roof in *The Snow Queen*. Simply to see the thing is not always enough to give birth to a story, sometimes it must be touched as well; 'Mother says that everything you look at becomes a fairy tale and that everything you touch turns into a story' says the little sick boy to his old neighbour in *Elm-Tree Mother*. Here the sensuous nature of inspiration is emphasized by the mention of 'touch'. Hans Andersen was not given to abstract visions. He was not obsessed by strange imaginary worlds like Blake or Poe, nor did he see things in a haze, emerging from mists or artistically blurred: he saw them clearly, and to make doubly sure of their real existence he went right up to them and touched them. A man becomes a poet when seeing things in their total reality, as though he had been short-sighted and had put on a pair of spectacles for the first time: 'I see everything so clearly, I feel so bright and intelligent,' says the clerk turned poet under the spell of the *Goloshes of Fortune*. It is not sufficient to see things from far, you must go as close as you can. That is the reason why so many tales begin with a gesture such as knocking at a door or opening a window which expresses a desire to go further, to penetrate more deeply. . . . (pp. 49-50)

To enter is to try to reach what is most hidden in all things and all beings, to get to know them so intimately that one becomes almost a part of them. . . . (p. 50)

Things and people, however ordinary and humble they are, have a secret which has nothing to do with their outward appearance, but which beckons and calls to us, and this gives them a kind of vibration which attracts the viewer's attention. The viewer is the child, discovering his familiar surroundings, looking and *perceiving,* not conditioned by moral and social conventions, but in terms of the emotional relationships he spontaneously creates around him. In this respect some of the games Andersen's children play are very revealing, as when they make use of a specific object without resorting to fancy or to notions picked up in books. . . . (p. 51)

This closeness of observation, this appreciation of the object from a child's-eye view is the second step towards the conquest of reality. For Hans Andersen what the world around him had to offer was not a store of conventional ideas; living people or inanimate objects affect us, certainly, in terms of the past, but this past is not so much 'history' as the story of each particular person or thing. Hans Andersen's memories are always of a particular kind: they are not primarily concerned with historical or legendary events. Unlike the Scandinavian story-teller Selma Lagerlof, whose inspiration is entirely derived from the legends of her native land, Hans Andersen does not set out to evoke an image of Denmark—except in one or two stories, and these are not his best works. In fact, even if the tales are set in a specific place and describe traditional objects, actions and customs in detail, this is never done to provide local colour. The places—countryside or town—and their inhabitants are described for their own sake—nothing more. Hans Andersen was undoubtedly a national writer, but not a folklorist. He had no particular veneration for the past—in fact he sometimes made fun of historical yearnings and staunchly supported the present day. In *The Goloshes of Fortune,* the councillor's heart 'was full of thankfulness for the happy reality of our own time' when he realized that he had awakened from his medieval nightmare. Memories are everywhere because to be is to have been, and everything in the world—living creatures and inanimate objects—remembers. Creatures and things represent nothing but themselves, however, and the past survives in the present so that a man can relive his childhood experiences whenever he pleases; all he has to do is be on the alert for signs. When a young man finds his tin soldier in the sand he does not recognize it, but he recalls a fragment of his past and for a moment the child he was lives again in him (*The Old House*). Past and present merge in each of us and time is continuous.

Hans Andersen was convinced that childhood never ends. It is not a specific experience in which the human being is confined for a given time, more or less in limbo until he finally starts to live. There was no such break for Hans Andersen between one state and the other; he rejected the need for initiation rites, and saw childhood, forever present and vigorous, continuing to develop for the whole of life. As winter contains all the seeds and the promise of spring, memory preserves childhood intact in the grown man. Thus, in *The Snow Queen*—the parable of Andersen's dearest beliefs—Kay and Gerda, hand in hand, after a long winter find the rose-trees blossoming on the roof in front of the window and their little stools side by side, just as before; the only thing that has changed, in fact, is themselves: they are both grown up; 'There they sat, the two of them, grown up and yet children—children at heart. And it was summertime, warm, delicious summertime' and the Grandmother was reading these words: 'Except ye become as little children, ye shall not enter into the Kingdom of Heaven . . .'

To be aware of the continuity of time, one must be on the look-out for certain signs. There are favourable moments and also certain messages and unexpected messengers which must be perceived. Space is peopled with organisms, invisible and unimaginable to those who will not see, but they are there, connecting creatures to creation so that the infinity of existence may be perceived. There is the angel—who has nothing in common with the angels of the 'baby Jesus' cult of Christian mythology—and the elves, and the 'daughters of the air', and those particles of light commonly known as sparks; there are, also, other less perceptible messengers: 'And more delicate even than the flame, quite invisible to the human eye, there hovered tiny beings, just as many as there had been blossoms on the flax. . . . But the little invisible beings each of them said: "No, no, the song is never over. That is what is so lovely about the whole thing. I know this and that's luckiest of them all".'

These mediating beings are therefore related to the elements air and fire. . . . The little mermaid, prisoner of an earthly love, physically and spiritually tortured, regains her freedom and plenitude of being, not by returning to the sea, but by dissolving into air and rising to the sun, because air and fire are the elements of combustion, which ensures life—and the continuity of life.

In spite of this, people die a great deal in Hans Andersen's fairy tales. His partiality for the macabre is as notorious as his unhappy endings which are so traumatic for small children. His characters die, and often more than once in the same tale. For instance the flax undergoes the pangs of death for the first time when it turns from plant into linen; then again when it is made into paper; and lastly when, as a bit of wastepaper, it is thrown into the fire. If death is an end, can this really be death? Not that we find in Hans Andersen's tales any consoling notions of an after-life. No, it is death itself which is seen as a renewal. He forces the reader to ask himself whether death is, in fact, irreversible and final; to wonder how it occurs and what visions accompany it. At the moment of death, the two basic elements air and fire—those life-giving principles which form the very texture of Hans Andersen's thought—are once again present; death comes like a revelation, a sudden flash, an ascent towards the light. This is the symbol contained in the story of *The Little Match-Seller* for whom death is the place where 'it became brighter than broad daylight'. But other characters, too, experience this splendour at the moment of vanishing: the Tin Soldier, melting in the fire with his love, the Dancer:

> . . . when the maid cleaned out the ashes next morning, she found him in the shape of a little tin heart; but all that was left of the dancer was her spangle, and that was burnt black as coal.

The little mermaid 'had no feeling of death. She saw the bright sun . . .' Death is sometimes not even mentioned because it has become synonymous with this luminosity, as in *The Snow Queen:* 'Grannie was sitting there in God's clear sunshine'. This is not rhetoric. The image represents a deeply felt, definite idea. For Hans Andersen physical death is this combustion which ensures the continuity of the species and the permanence of life. Through death the living become light and merge into the universe. . . . This cannot be seen as an orthodox adherence to the Christian faith in the immortality of the soul and in a life to come. It is rather—and quite simply—a negation of physical death: the Phoenix rising from its ashes, the bird of folk poetry whose voice 'cannot die' and the flaming paper says: 'the song is never over. That is what is so lovely about the whole thing!' For, in fact, nothing dies, not even what seems most vulnerable and transitory—childhood. There are not two distinct worlds, one for grown-ups and one for children, just as life and death are not distinct; there is only a perpetual renewal. Hans Andersen, the poet of continuity and fusion, was the meeting-place of two worlds: in him childhood and manhood merged. (pp. 51-5)

Isabelle Jan, "Hans Christian Andersen or Reality," in her On Children's Literature, *edited by Catherine*

Storr (originally published in French by Les Editions ouvrieres; reprinted by permission of Penguin Books Ltd.; copyright © 1969; translation copyright © Allen Lane, 1973), Allen Lane, 1973, pp. 45-55.

Andersen took the folk tale, in his day only recently made respectable (that is to say, worthy of notice) by Scott and the Grimms, and transmuted the form by substituting for the brutal and pagan element of arbitrary chance the more civilized concept of meaningful coincidence. The people and objects he writes about are woven into a pattern of events so real that the events themselves are like characters, which have existed and will exist for ever. His protagonists are not subjected to, but encounter these events. It follows that the people and the objects do not alter: their appearance may change, but they remain steadfastly themselves. They are not degraded. What they have in common—the Tin Soldier, the bottle neck, the dung beetle, the nightingale, and the fir tree—is that they fit into their histories like the keystone of an arch, the final clinching piece of a jigsaw. They demonstrate meaningfulness.

On one level it is quite clear that Andersen, though not an avowed Christian, saw existence in terms of Heavenly Grace: crudely, God is working out His purpose. In his stories there is a proper place for everything, and, less obvious but always implied, a use for everything. For Andersen's purpose is reassurance: "Our Lord looks after all small creatures; otherwise, very few of them would survive". All that is required is to see things as they really are. Everything makes sense: the only sin is self-delusion. Since everything in the universe is a product of every other thing, nothing is dispensable. Translate for children and this becomes: you are wanted, you are needed, you are loved (therefore you exist).

Andersen's gentleness and humour are universally recognized. That his philosophy is equally civilized is less apparent. Above all . . . Andersen can be trusted—his imagination is not only superb, it is entirely sane. It is a very rare gift to demonstrate free will and the workings of fate at one and the same time. Can any other children's writer claim such kinship with Shakespeare?

For clearly Andersen's is not a fantasy world, but a microcosm reflecting with delightful precision our everyday surroundings. Forget all about children, and fairy tales, and read them as you would read, say, short stories by T. F. Powys: but what a sharper mind and wit, what a much more universal genius Andersen has. Stopping to consider which living writer most resembles Andersen, I suggest it is Kurt Vonnegut, who, particularly in his earlier (and best) books, manipulates coincidence with the same marvellous quirky style of humour and storytelling. Andersen does not belong with the old tradition of Grimms' tales, with their baroque and Bach-like piling up of incident. He is the first modern writer for children, a perfect precursor like Mozart, combining classical poise with romantic idealism. . . . (pp. 15-16)

Alan Tucker, "Andersen Complete" (copyright © 1975 Alan Tucker; reprinted by permission of the author and The Thimble Press, Lockwood Station Road, South Woodchester, Glos. GL55EQ, England), in Signal, *No. 16, January, 1975, pp. 12-17.*

In Sweden we don't say Hans Christian, we say Andersen, that's all, for we only know one Andersen, and that is Andersen. He is the Andersen of our parents, our childhood, our manhood and our old age. . . . I can remember a little quarto volume printed in Gothic type; I remember the woodcuts, the willow tree that went with 'The Tinder Box', 'The Top and the Ball', 'The Steadfast Tin Soldier', 'Willie Winkie', 'The Snow Queen' and the rest of them. And as I read and when I had finished, my life became embittered. This horrible everyday life with its bad temper and injustice, this dreary monotonous existence in a nursery where we young plants grew up too close together and pushed and squabbled for food and privileges—I suddenly found it all unbearable, for in Andersen's world of fairy tale I had learnt of the existence of another world, a golden age of justice and pity in which parents really fondled their children and did not just pull them by the hair, in which something I had never known before threw a rosy gleam over even poverty and meekness: that gleam which is known by the now obsolete name of LOVE.

It was Orpheus that he called to mind—this poet who sang in prose so that, not only animals, plants and stones listened and were moved, but toys came to life, goblins and elves became real, those horrible schoolbooks seemed poetic; why, he squeezed the whole geography of Denmark into four pages—he was a perfect wizard!

> *August Strindberg, in an essay translated by Elias Bredsdorff, in* Hans Christian Andersen: The Story of His Life and Work, 1805-75 *by Elias Bredsdorff (copyright © 1975 by Phaidon Press Limited; reprinted with permission of Elias Bredsdorff),* Charles Scribner's Sons, 1975, p. 10.

Hans Christian Andersen wrote what he called fairy tales, what were accepted by his audience as fairy tales, but which show on almost every page how much a break had been made, with the oral as well as the written tradition. The voice of Andersen is the voice of a teller, but Andersen was a writer, a writer of the Romantic period, and so he tries to put his personal stamp on his tales, even the ancient ones he only retold, and he always considered himself his own major resource, his own necessary and sufficient inspiration. Many of his openings reveal this all too clearly:

> The Emperor of China is a Chinese, as of course
> you know, and the people he has about him are
> Chinese too.
>
> [**"The Nightingale"**]

Not just a joke, but a bad one; and if not that, pretty vividness:

> Far out at sea the water is as blue as the bluest
> cornflower, and as clear as the clearest glass;
> but it is very deep, deeper than any anchor cable
> can fathom.
>
> [**"The Little Mermaid"**]

And, if not vividness, remarks about storytelling:

> Listen! Now we are going to begin. When the
> story has ended, we shall know a lot more than
> we do now.
>
> [**"The Snow Queen"**]

He aims satiric shafts, he points his morals and adorns his tales. Of all the major reputations among authors of children's literature, Andersen's is much the hardest to understand or justify. Yet for precisely these reasons he is useful here, as a way to mark the transition from fairy tales to later children's literature, because what is wrong with his work is, almost without exception, what is wrong with all inferior children's literature and what mars even some of the masterpieces.

Since children's literature is written by adults and "for" children, authors of children's books can be strongly tempted to make the central relation be between the teller and the audience rather than the teller and the tale. The older authors of fairy tales . . . know their audience very well, but never alter anything in the tale to suit or please the audience; their respect for their materials is too great. But when children's literature was invented, the adults who wrote the tales often started contemplating the children who were to hear and read them, and they tended to get lost, because they became involved in what was essentially a false rhetoric. "The Emperor of China is a Chinese" is such a silly thing to say that it must express an essentially patronizing attitude toward the audience. The teller has an idea of a child in his head, he acts as though he knows "what children like" or "how children think," and the moment he does that his language becomes false. The tellers of fairy tales before this never thought their audience was any different from themselves, never thought of themselves as authors forced to conceive a relation to an audience. But after childhood was invented, adults inevitably began thinking about what language, what stance or tone, what materials were appropriate for children, and so we get something like the large and often subtle machinery of the Pooh books in which A. A. Milne guides his son toward an acceptance of the loss of early childhood. Even in many books which idealize children, the implicit rhetoric insists it is better to be an adult, and thereby be able to do this idealizing, than it is to be a child, who doesn't know any better than not to know that his or hers is the ideal time of life. Of course, anyone who writes a book for children will make some adjustments, but when the writer is really concerned with the tale and not the audience, the adjustments are easily made, since they will concern themselves with a simplification of vocabulary and the avoidance of prolonged abstract argument and discourse.

Andersen had certain initial advantages as a teller of fairy tales. . . . He was an only child, smaller and slighter than the others in his school, and his response to feeling an ugly duckling was to create his own small worlds, with dolls, puppets, songs, and retold stories; he became famous in Odense as a gifted lad who gave charming performances. The results of these beginnings can be seen in his lifelong love of the theatre, in his continual stance as a performer, in his love of pathos, in his evocations of the outcast who longs to be different or in a different place. Clearly, too, this early success failed to satisfy for very long. He hated Odense, for all it gave him the setting and imagery for many of his tales, and he was in Copenhagen before he was fifteen, trying to be an actor. All his apparent advantages, then, were something he wanted to exploit, to use as food for his inventiveness, his powers of mimicry, his theatricality, his desire not to be an ugly duckling. He wanted to be latter-day, to be famous as a writer and actor, but his shyness and sense of personal inadequacy kept throwing him back on his origins, on his loneliness, on his incurably provincial sense that life was better where the lights were brighter.

So Andersen is the soldier as well as the cobbler's boy in **"The Tinder Box,"** he is the little mermaid, the mole in **"Thumbelina,"** the steadfast tin soldier. Women could only admire and pity him, and their rejection in turn intensified his sense of himself as an outcast, with pathos and spurts of satiric revenge his only weapons. His stories of the figures he made out of himself gained him fame greater than any Danish writer, before or since, has achieved, and during the last thirty years of his life he could travel anywhere he wished, meet anyone he chose, and be adored. But a writer who uses personal un-happiness as an exploitable resource is artistically as well as humanly engaged in civil war, since what succeeds is also what makes miserable. Especially in his earlier years Andersen was stubborn in his belief in his talent, but there was always something compulsive about this belief, because it was designed to take him away from who and where he had been as much as to take him any place he wished to go. The result was, on the one hand, great creative energies. He wrote many plays, novels, poems, and travel books in addition to the fairy tales for which he is still known, and the complete tales make a volume of half a million words. But on the other hand he wrote quickly, even slapdash, and counted on his assumed talent to carry him through. The result is not just a good deal of inconsequential work, but many stories whose confusions and contradictions reveal his civil war, often in embarrassing ways.

"The Little Mermaid," for instance, is one of Andersen's most popular tales, which means its pathos has found a responsive echo in many who feel they are little mermaids. But it really is a chaotic, desperate piece of work, very much out of touch with itself. "You are to keep your gliding motion, no dancer will be as able to move as gracefully," the sea-witch tells the mermaid who wants to become a human being, "but at every step it will feel you are treading on a sharp-edged knife." Andersen, himself willing to suffer great pain to be near the woman he loved, apparently never saw the trouble he entailed the moment he made the mermaid want to become a human being and established conditions for her transformation. D'Aulnoy and many other writers of fairy tales have characters willing to suffer for the sake of their beloved. In most of these cases, a transformation is involved, one that assumes the natural state of the lover is human, and the unnatural state is the green snake, the white deer, or the ram. In **"The Little Mermaid,"** Andersen is driven to making the mermaid naturally inferior to the prince as a way of expressing his own sense of his social or sexual inferiority. If she is going to step "up" to the prince's class, she must no longer be a mermaid. To complicate the issue still further, since Andersen was also resentful of those who rejected him, he makes all the mermaids beautiful and the beloved prince a dense and careless man, so that one cannot imagine where the "natural" inferiority of the mermaid lies, and it seems like lunacy to suffer as she does in order to be able to dance before the prince.

All these difficulties would tear away at the story even if the prince finally were to love the mermaid, but Andersen felt driven, in addition, to have the prince reject her as Andersen himself had been. Since he could find no way to describe the appearance or the behavior of the mermaids so as to make them seem inferior to human beings, Andersen posited that mermaids have no immortal souls. He cannot say what this means, however, since the mermaids seem to lack nothing possessed by human beings except legs. The sea-witch tells the mermaid she can have a soul if a mortal will love her, which reduces "soul" to a romantic and sexual prize; worse, the mermaid has vastly more of something like a soul than does the prince. Then, since Andersen partly wants to revenge himself against the prince for rejecting the mermaid, he has the mermaid's sisters tell her she can become a mermaid again if she will kill the prince, which makes the mermaid's love into even more of an unnatural passion than it is before this. Finally, since of course the mermaid will not kill the prince, Andersen must invent a trapdoor to escape from these impossible tangles, and so he invents the daughters of the air, who "have no immortal soul either, but they can gain one by their good deeds." But the trapdoor

refuses to open, since Andersen cannot imagine why daughters of the air, any more than mermaids, should have to work for immortal souls, while human beings have them as part of their birthright. Indeed, the whole question of an immortal soul is much trickier in a story like this than Andersen realizes, and it illustrates the great good sense of earlier oral and written tellers of fairy tales in leaving out all explicit religion. To make socially inferior into sexually inferior, and to make sexually inferior into naturally inferior, is bad enough, but to make naturally inferior into religiously inferior is sheer desperation. The original longings which created the story are, I think, the reason for its continued popularity; all the snobberies and reverse snobberies that follow seem just to be ignored, at least by people I know who claim the story as one of their favorites—and they invariably first read it early in adolescence.

"Thumbelina" has the same kind of difficulty, though the surface of the story is much more clear and calm. Thumbelina, born tiny, on the pistil of a tulip, is captured by a toad who takes her away so she can be married to the toad's ugly son. Andersen must have known many stories in which such a kidnapping was threatened or achieved by giants, ogres, and dwarves. But the toads here, though indeed ugly, are not the least wicked or brutal, so that when Andersen says "She did not want to live with the horrid toad, neither did she want the toad's ugly son for a husband," he is once again confusing difference and inferiority. The toad isn't nasty at all, just a toad. James Thurber has a fable about a crow and a Baltimore oriole which employs this same situation, but Thurber's aims are far different from Andersen's. Thurber's crow may be a fool for falling in love with a Baltimore oriole, but the pretty oriole is no prize either. Andersen, though, can't avoid sanctioning Thumbelina's distaste for toads by implying that toads should stay in their place and know better than to want Thumbelina. Indeed, the same thing happens a second time when a field mouse rescues Thumbelina from the oncoming winter and very pleasantly thinks she would make a good mate for her friend the mole, who is prosperous and has a shiny dark coat. Thumbelina understandably does not care for this idea, especially since she doesn't want to live underground and prefers sunshine and song. But Andersen persists in blaming the field mouse and the mole for being a field mouse and a mole, ground and underground animals: "For their neighbor, the tiresome mole in the black velvet coat, had proposed to her"; "But she was not at all happy, for she did not care one bit for the tiresome mole." It is as though Andersen never asked what the implications were of his projecting his own feelings of being rejected onto the animal world. Stranger still is a little story called **"Sweethearts,"** which makes a class matter between a top and a ball, so both the top who wants and the ball who rejects are figures of mere silliness. Andersen was always improvising, outfitting objects and animals with his own feelings, and so seldom stopped to respect the nature of his characters.

Fortunately, some of Andersen's stories are more impersonal and therefore much better than **"The Little Mermaid"** or **"Thumbelina." "The Snow Queen"** is riddled with faults, but it shows what Andersen could do well, which was something that older tellers and writers of fairy tales had not tried to do. By the time he wrote **"The Snow Queen,"** a long, loose narrative in seven stories, he had done a lot of traveling, and everyone he met in Germany, France, England, and Italy knew he was a Dane, a man from a little-known northern country. In this tale he seems to be asking what it means to be from such a country, considered not as a place where Andersen had suffered, and not as a society, but as a climate. He opens with some little devils that go everywhere with their looking glass, "reducing the reflection of anything good and beautiful to almost nothing, while what was no good or was ugly stood out well and grew even worse." The devils take their mirror too high in the heavens, and it breaks, but that only means that its pieces, when they fall to earth, can become lodged in the eyes and hearts of people: "A few people even got a splinter of it into their hearts, and that was terrible indeed, for then their hearts became exactly like a lump of ice." Andersen knew all about ice, and when, one summer day, a bit of the glass strikes a boy named Kay in the heart, and another lodges in his eye, Andersen knows this lump of iciness can have little effect in the summertime. Come winter, though, Kay starts trying to act more grown-up; he ridicules the childish delights of his friend Gerda, and then he begins to offer clever parodies of his grandmother and to insist that a snowflake under a magnifying glass is better than one that just falls to the ground, and much better than a rose's petals.

One day Kay goes out into the square with his sled, and soon a big sleigh comes along and the driver ties up Kay's sled and carries it out of the village: "All of a sudden they flew to one side, the big sleigh stopped, and the person who was drawing it stood up. The fur coat and cap were made entirely of snow. It was a woman, tall and slender, and glittering white. It was the Snow Queen." She kisses Kay, and:

> Kay looked at her. She was so beautiful. He could not imagine a brighter or more lovely face. She didn't seem to be all ice now, as she did when she sat outside the window and beckoned to him. In his eyes she was perfect. He was not at all frightened; he told her he could do mental arithmetic even with fractions; that he knew the areas of all the countries, and the answer to "What is their population?" And she went on smiling. Then he began to suspect that he did not know so much after all. Bewildered he gazed into space. She flew away with him, flew high up onto the black cloud, while the storm howled and roared—it sounded very much like old folk tunes. They flew over woods and lakes, over sea and land; below them the cold icy wind went whistling, wolves howled, black screaming crows flew low over the glistening snow, but over it all shone the moon, large and clear, and on that Kay gazed during the long, long winter's night. By day he slept at the feet of the Snow Queen.

We have seen nothing like this before; it is grand, atmospheric writing about nature, seeking effects the teller of "The Juniper Tree" would not have needed or understood. Andersen here is finding something new for a fairy tale to do. This abduction is thrilling as well as frightening, because Andersen has pondered what it means to be a snow *queen* as well as a *snow* queen. Unlike the devils, the Snow Queen is a natural force, and therefore powerful, and to be queen of such a force is to be beautiful and perfect, so that all Kay's homage to her, his fractions and facts, is not enough. By introducing the little devils, by having them make Kay susceptible with the glass caught in his heart and eye, Andersen frees the Snow Queen of any suggestion that she is demonic or malicious; she is really only claiming her own.

Just as the author of *Beowulf,* of an earlier time but a similar latitude, knew that what lay outside the meadhalls was named

Grendel, and that what lived in the meres was Grendel's mother, so Andersen knows that even in a city snow and cold can grip and dominate, finding the victims of the imps and claiming for them a particularly northern fate. But the Snow Queen must take Kay out of Denmark, because spring and summer return there, and up to Lapland, her home. Gerda, the child who didn't want to be grown up, sets out to find him. She visits an old wizard woman who is kind to her but wants to keep Gerda for herself, which makes her like the Snow Queen except her dominion is a flower garden, not a sleigh, and that makes all the difference. Gerda keeps asking the flowers where Kay is, and they all give lovely irrelevant answers, lovely because each tells a fairy tale, irrelevant because they know nothing of Kay, and Gerda can barely understand them. That all things are bright and beautiful does not connect them, or make them know each other—the world is too large and various for that, especially in the warmer months.

But as autumn comes, Gerda sets out again, and meets a crow who tells her about a princess who has announced she will marry any young man who can come and talk to her as though he were at home. Most young men became so nervous at trying that they failed, but one lad finally appeared and said to the palace guards, "It must be boring standing on the stairs; I'm going inside." That is exactly how Kay sounded after the glass pierced his heart and eye, so Gerda goes to the palace, is sneaked in by the crow's sweetheart, only to discover the prince is not Kay. Very nice he is, as is the princess, and they listen to Gerda's tale and offer to outfit her trip north. "How good they are, human beings and animals," Gerda thinks as she tries to overcome her disappointment, and to remember that everyone she has met on her journey has been as helpful as he or she could be. So it is with the rough robber band that captures Gerda, where a woman wants to kill her but her perky daughter gets her mother drunk so Gerda can escape; so too with the Lapp woman and the Finn woman and the reindeer who guide and take her to the Snow Queen's palace. The story is long because it must be, in order to show the world, when it is not dominated by the Snow Queen, is not paradise but the world, multiple, varied, usually helpful to a distressed girl if it doesn't have to go far out of its way to do so. Gerda, seen by herself, is an awfully passive, pallid heroine, but Andersen, though he praises her highly, only offers sweetness and innocence as her virtues, and he does not pretend they light up the sky.

In the Snow Queen's palace all is cold, ordered, and dazzling; Kay drags about pieces of ice, makes shapes and words, because the Snow Queen has told him "you shall be your own master, and I will give you the whole world, and a new pair of skates" if you can spell the word "eternity." But he cannot, and it is winter now, so the Snow Queen is off in more southern regions; Kay "looked at the pieces of ice and thought and thought for all he was worth." This is satire, of course, derived from Andersen's dislike of the math and spelling taught in schools, but here it is decently muted, and the point Andersen makes is not entirely irrelevant. At least as good, surely, to have the Snow Queen set Kay the task of spelling "eternity" as it is to have Winnie-the-Pooh hunt for a backson because Christopher Robin doesn't quite know how to spell "back soon."

Then, at the climax:

> She walked into the big empty hall, caught sight of Kay, and knew him at once, and flew towards him and flung her arms around his neck,

held him tight and shouted: "Kay! darling little Kay! At last I've found you!"

But there he sat quite still, and stiff and cold. Then Gerda shed hot tears, which fell on his breasts, and penetrated right into his heart. They thawed the lump of ice, and dissolved the splinter of glass that was lodged in it. He looked at her, and she sang:

As roses bloom in the valley sweet,
So the Christ child there ye shall truly meet.

Kay burst into tears. He cried and cried so hard that his tears washed the tiny chip of glass out of his eyes. Now he knew her and exclaimed for joy.

The Savior makes a much better appearance here than the immortal soul does in **"The Little Mermaid."** Salvation is in the world, not in eternity, and we can know this by knowing the roses in the valley, which fade and are not perfect. Roses have no place in the Snow Queen's palace, no more than do hot tears and hymns, and it is Gerda's "heroism" that her persistence has allowed her to do so much with the little she has, and it is the glory of the world that it has, this way and that way, shown her the way.

The symbols and actions all work in **"The Snow Queen"** because Andersen has asked what it means to be captured by the queen of the snow, and what power can rescue what she has captured. Gerda is no Beowulf or Siegfried, and the Snow Queen cannot be killed, and it takes all the power of the spring and summer, all the determination of Gerda, plus a prince, a princess, a crow, reindeer, and two women who live up north just to release the lad with the glass in his eye and heart. Someone who lived much south of Denmark might not need to know all this, and someone who lived much north of Denmark might not be able to. But, knowing what he knows, and, for once, trusting what he knows, Andersen can release his story from the personal bondage that ties up so much of his other work. To be sure, there are the nips and barks of the satire, the idealization of the child for her innocence only, and the lengthy clumsiness of the stories of Gerda's journey, and we can see that it is always unfortunate that Andersen was a *writer* in ways earlier tellers of tales did not have to be, and in ways that Tchaikovsky and the great choreographers and dancers did not have to be either. (pp. 63-73)

It is often said of Andersen, and of many later successful storytellers for children, that they never grew up themselves and so could better speak to the young. There is perhaps truth in this, but most of the conclusions one might want to draw from this idea seem false. In Andersen's case it is demonstrable that what retarded his maturing as a person handicapped him as an author, and all his defects, by comparison with the earlier authors of fairy tales, seem the result of an inability to be calm, confident, transparently anonymous, a partaker in a tradition older than he, and wiser. (p. 73)

Roger Sale, "Written Tales: Perrault to Andersen," in his Fairy Tales and After: From Snow White to E. B. White *(copyright © 1978 by the President and Fellows of Harvard College; excerpted by permission), Cambridge, Mass.: Harvard University Press, 1978, pp. 49-75.**

Few of Andersen's tales are built around a clearly defined idea. Nevertheless, the tales as a whole do express a universal wis-

dom of life. In the multiplicity of events in his tales Andersen has put down thoughts about mankind, the world, and life in general, thoughts that have grown out of the extensive experiences and adventures of his own life.

First, Andersen makes no bones about which kind of person is worthy of respect and which is not. Those who accept the gifts life offers with gratitude are always depicted with sympathy. The person with a warm heart or the one who throws himself into life with a cheerful spirit and pays no heed to formalities will eventually defeat the scheming rationalist. The loving Gerda rescues her friend Kay from the Snow Queen's palace of cold intellect; the cheerful, singing nightingale is stronger than Death at the emperor's bedside; Simple Simon (in the tale with the same title) wins the princess. On the other hand, the self-satisfied philistine who is only interested in his own affairs and nothing more, who arrogantly judges all and sundry from his own limited experience, and who is always willing to strut in borrowed plumage (like the Beetle and the Shirt Collar), is mercilessly exposed in the fairy tales to laughter, whether directly or indirectly does not matter, for the intention is always plain. The narrow-mindedness of the philistine was an abomination to Andersen.

Second, the fairy tales contain quite precise ideas about the universe and the evaluation of its phenomena. These are far from always being explicitly expressed. Yet it is striking that no form of common universe exists for the characters of the tales. Each group of creatures lives within its own surroundings which for the individuals of that group is *the world:* they are unaware of what lies beyond. Nor is there any uniform opinion about existence concerning what is better or worse. Just as great a difference exists among the humans. The little girl with the matches has few thoughts in common with the princess on the pea; children and adults live in separate worlds.

Even the same surroundings and the same events can look fundamentally different. In the great fairy story set in Switzerland, **"The Ice Maiden,"** the characters appear on three levels: (1) the Ice Maiden and the other sinister spirits of nature who rule the great icy wastes of the glaciers, for whom humans are ridiculous insignificant creatures who in their arrogance believe that they can control the forces of nature; (2) Rudy, the young chamois hunter, his sweetheart, and their families; and (3) the domestic animals which, so to speak, see the humans from a lower level and who, by the way, think that humans are strange, illogical creations. Time upon time these three completely different views of life come into conflict; the most charming occasion being brought out in the little scene where the kitchen cat relates what it has heard the rats say about happiness. Happiness to them was to eat tallow candles and to have their bellies filled with putrified pork; while Rudy and his sweetheart had said that the greatest of happinesses was understanding each other. "Whom should we believe, the rats or the sweethearts?" is the cat's question.

The answer to this reasonable question must be that both are right, in their own ways, since the appearance of the world and its objects depends on the eyes that are doing the looking, and we humans, who are often mutually in disagreement, have no grounds on which we can claim that our view of the world is the only correct one. In the fairy tales there are countless other creatures that have other opinions and whose words have as much weight as those of the humans. This point can be seen at the conclusion of **"The Marsh King's Daughter"** which, like **"The Ice Maiden,"** also contains three levels: the trolls, the humans, and finally the stork family; the storks watch and comment on the events from their point of view. While it is the fate of the human characters that makes up the main theme of the tale, it is the storks' comments that conclude the story. The final words in "Heartbreak" state directly that what might seem unimportant to adults might be of extreme importance to children. When the pea pod in "Five Peas from one Pod" gradually turns yellow, the five peas that are inside say that the whole world is turning yellow, "and they had a perfect right to say so," adds the narrator. Different beings must inevitably have different thoughts and opinions about the world, and they have a right to have them, the small and insignificant just as much as the great. When judgment is passed in the fairy tales it is only passed on those who believe they have a monopoly of the truth: they are handled roughly.

Now to the third point: What thoughts about life as a whole are to be found in the fairy tales? Is life good or evil, just or unjust? Has it anything to offer us pitiful humans, or should we turn our backs on it?

At a first glance the tales provide self-contradictory answers to these questions. Andersen's works can both affirm the highest of expectations and shatter all illusions. Comfort can be found, for instance, in "The Traveling Companion" and "The Wild Swans," where the pious and good principal characters go through much hardship but nevertheless are finally happy—and, naturally, in "The Ugly Duckling," an inspired symbol of Andersen's own life where the most important moods, events, and, in part, characters from his strange career have been recast in other dimensions and thereby made universal in an impressive hymn of praise to life. Many of the other fairy tales contain similar reassuring thoughts: everything will take up its rightful place, the good will not be forgotten, arrogance and wickedness will suffer defeat, and, if not at once, it is because the Lord has time to wait.

But far more fairy tales depict quite a different course of events. Nearly all the short stories are about people for whom things have gone badly in life and who finally are left with their frustrated hopes, alone and disappointed—if, that is, they do not find freedom and reconciliation in death.

The bitter pessimism revealed here lay deep in Andersen's mind and is also to be felt in some of the shorter fairy tales, though nowhere so movingly as in "The Story of a Mother." One cold winter's night Death fetches a little, sick child, and the desperate mother runs out into the darkness to overtake him. She meets Night, comes to a crossroads where there is a thorn bush all frosted over, and then reaches a lake that she must cross; at each place she has to sacrifice something of herself in order to find out which way she has to go. When she finally gets to Death's great greenhouse, Death has not yet arrived and when he does he cannot, and will not, surrender the child.

A harrowing story, a monument to mother-love as well as to the mercilessness of existence. In form it is a fairy tale; mythological beings such as Death appear; natural phenomena, Night, the Thorn Bush, the Lake, are personified; the mother's sorrow makes her travel even faster than Death, for in the world of the fairy tale the soul is stronger than the body. But "The Story of a Mother" is far from being a folktale. The subject is handled with supreme imagination and brilliant mastery. We are also far from the noncommittal pleasure of "The Tinderbox" or the elegant irony in "The Shirt Collar" or the optimism of "The Ugly Duckling." "The Story of a Mother" speaks with relentless earnestness; Night, Thornbush, Lake, and Death, all show a heartrending remorselessness toward the poor mother.

For all her sacrifices she gains nothing save an awareness that perhaps it would be even worse for the child to be brought back to life. Without a strong faith in the Providence of God the reader of this terrifying story will be horror-stricken by the meaninglessness of life. (pp. 125-28)

But even though existence, in the fairy tales as well as in reality, can be brutal and unjust, and sorrows more frequent than pleasures, the reader is left in no doubt that life is worth living. One must take things as they come. Sorrows are heavy, but if we accept them as part of the pattern of life they can also bring us blessings (as shown in "The Last Pearl"). Everything depends on oneself. With open eyes and receptive mind it is possible to discover that existence is rich and beautiful, full of events, both big and small; that the world contains a multitude of people and other beings, each with his own individuality, all so different that we need never be bored if we will just look and listen. (p. 129)

The fairy tales emphasize the gospel of an open mind and immediate emotion; they speak the case for the small, overlooked creatures, and they let it be understood that existence is richer and greater than our limiting notions of good and evil, so rich as never to be exhausted.

It is plain that such a philosophy has spoken to many hearts and given much comfort to many people. It will also appeal to modern readers. But by reading the tales carefully and by drawing conclusions from what is told, the reader will be more disquieted than comforted. Even the portraits of the philistines are enough to frighten the reader: Was it not only in those days that people were like that, or are there many of that type today? Are you yourself so narrowminded? Do you dress up in borrowed plumage like so many of the philistines in the fairy tales? Do fine phrases also pour from our lips? Are we slaves of catchwords, slogans, and other simplifications of reality?

A chill runs down your spine when you see the gulf separating the characters, including the human ones, in the tales. Are people really so different? Can we not somehow become homogeneous? Are not our democratic ideals valid? Are those not due to one-eyed idealists' rejection of an inescapable reality? The fairy tales are one great rejection of any uniformalization of life and any comformalization of people. Was Andersen, as a writer, more realistic than we are?

Furthermore, is the great physical universe that we are brought up to believe in, the ultimate truth? Is it possible that things are not dead and that natural forces are not impersonal? Our knowledge of physics says one thing while the artist in Andersen claims another. Should we believe the physicist or the artist? The fairy tales say that if you live intensely with your immediate surroundings they will come to life for you, and then the great mechanism loses all interest. Does the modern reader accept such a viewpoint?

Finally, the fairy-tales' message about the riches of life: Do we understand how to accept its gifts both large and small? Are we just as open as the writer and many of his characters? Or do we go through life deaf and blind, unable to respond to the little experiences that it has to offer us? Do we have a superficial and rash relationship to our surroundings?

The fairy-tales are not a harmless and innocent reading. If you know how to read, they leave your soul disturbed. Andersen's worldly wisdom, his knowledge of people and life was far beyond the normal man's.

Andersen was a mediocre dramatist, an average poet, a good novelist, and a brilliant travel writer. But in the fairy tales he attained perfection. That it was precisely this form that suited his genius was due to an exceptional conjunction of external and internal circumstances: a special social background, a special temperament, and a special artistic talent.

The social background was his childhood in poverty in Odense. As far back as he could remember he had known legends and tales, and, what was of even greater importance, he was completely familiar with the world that was the setting of these folktales. Up to his fourteenth year he had lived among people who were unaffected by the physical view of nature that the cultured class had been brought up on. For the peasant class there was nothing unreasonable or absurd in what the tales contained. Nor was there for Andersen. A feeling for the mystery of existence was part of his makeup. Other Danish writers had composed or retold tales, but they only knew the world of the fairy tale from literature. Andersen knew it from his own experience and was able to give his narration quite another authority, a far greater credibility than his fellow writers could. His roots among the common people were a social handicap at the beginning of his career but proved in the fullness of time to be his fortune as an artist.

Andersen's psychical constitution was the second prerequisite for the writing of the tales. For a start, his ungovernable imagination made the fairy tale form more natural for him than the novel or the play. In these last two genres attention has to be paid to the practical likelihood of events. But in the fairy tale so much can happen that the improbable can become probable; true, there ought to be a certain logic behind the events, but there is far greater room for imagination.

Moreover, Andersen was born with a sensitiveness which meant that he experienced his surroundings with a far greater intensity than most people. He was, so to speak, caught up in what he saw and was able to forget himself in the phenomena of the surrounding world. Animals of all sizes became thinking, reasoning individuals to him; even so-called inanimate objects received a personality. . . . It is quite natural that animals, flowers, or toys in his fairy tales are living personalities, for that is how he experienced them in real life. When Andersen created, his observations of nature were married with human experiences and the results were characters that were animals, objects, etc., with human reactions. The Dung-beetle is a dung-beetle on the surface and a human beneath.

Of equal importance was the enormous range of his psyche. He had maintained the child's spontaneity in his reactions and its intimacy with its surroundings, while at the same time he had an adult's matter-of-fact reflection. It was this ambivalence of mind that enabled him to write for both children and adults at the same time. He was able to be on a child's terms with a tin soldier while depicting experiences that could enrich every adult.

Finally, there is the third prerequisite: his special form of artistic talent, or if you like, its limits. Andersen's difficulties lay in holding on to a large-sized composition or a detailed and varied characterization. His strength was the brief glimpse of a person, the elegant phrase, the rapidly outlined situation. The fairy tale was as if created for his episodic gifts. The genre did not permit circumstantiality, and at the same time it was so free that Andersen was able to locate his countless fragmentary observations about nature and people practically anywhere, either as a small portrait of a type or as a personal aside. He could freely jump from the animal kingdom to the world of humans, from narrating for children to reasoning for adults, from gravity to lightheartedness and back again.

Thus the fairy tale became the most direct way for him to express his expansive and capricious temperament. Here in a poetic sense he felt at home, and this perhaps explains the strange fact that here he was so inordinately painstaking with the form. The fortuitousness and negligence that often mark his poetry and his plays are never present in the fairy tales. On a number of occasions he had rewritten his plays in response to criticism from the theater's literary advisers; but no one was a better judge of how a fairy tale should be written than himself. He polished his language and gave free reign to his imagination. There is strict moderation and clear consistency in the supernatural events. . . . No fairy tale was sent to the printer until Andersen was convinced that it could not be improved. Depth of experience and clarity in expression are the hallmarks of his fairy tales. (pp. 130-33)

> *Bo Grønbech, in his* Hans Christian Andersen *(copyright 1980; reprinted with the permission of Twayne Publishers, a division of G. K. Hall & Co., Boston), Twayne, 1980, 170 p.*

Thomas G(ibbons) Aylesworth

1927-

American author of nonfiction and editor.

Aylesworth applies his background as a science teacher and lecturer to unique and mystifying topics that children want to learn about. His practical, humorous approach allows them to enjoy the excitement of such topics as the occult, monsters, and parapsychology while being reassured that many phenomena have logical explanations. Aylesworth also treats such fascinating but down-to-earth subjects as storms, earthquakes, body language, and extrasensory perception. While some critics claim that his coverage is too broad and superficial, others are pleased with his attractive choice of topics.

Perhaps his most popular book among both children and critics is *Monsters from the Movies*, which discusses early film monsters and their origins in history and legend. Critics sometimes see Aylesworth's humor here as condescending, but most find his approach entertaining and appreciate his detailed account of little-known facts. This book was so popular with younger children that Aylesworth wrote a simplified version. Aylesworth is also known for his science books, which focus on current topics of high interest such as *Search for Life*, *Geographical Disasters: Earthquakes and Volcanoes*, and *Science at the Ball Game*. The latter is welcomed for applying an otherwise unappealing subject (physics) to a more appetizing topic (sports) and providing information on both. While some critics say these books include too much surface information and several errors, many praise Aylesworth's inclusion of the philosophical responsibilities of science, his exploration of its new techniques and theories, and his stimulating conversational narratives. It is clear by the enthusiastic reception of Aylesworth's books by young readers that he knows what nonfiction topics will appeal to children and how to present them.

(See also *Something about the Author*, Vol. 4 and *Contemporary Authors*, Vols. 25-28, rev. ed.)

AUTHOR'S COMMENTARY

It's nearly 12 years since I got a telephone call that changed my hunt-and-pecking life. Up to that time I had been toiling in the gardens of rationality, writing about science and technology for youngsters. The call came from Ray Broekel, who was an editor at Addison-Wesley at the time, and he said, "Hey, Tom, how would you like to do a children's book on witchcraft for me?"

Of course I pointed out that I didn't know much about witchcraft (not having read "The Exorcist" yet), but he insisted. "Treat it like a science book," he argued. "Approach it as if it were a piece of anthropology or ethnology research."

I reminded him that kids don't buy books, grandmothers do—and that no grandmother would take the chance of scaring the socks off her innocent young grandson or granddaughter by buying a witchcraft book. But my arguments, as they say in romantic fiction, were to no avail.

"Let *us* worry about that. We're after the children's librarian market. They know what kids like, and they'll *buy* what kids like." Bless his heart, he was right.

After my debut, **"Servants of the Devil,"** came books on vampires, werewolves, dragons, ESP and even movie monsters. And, except for the occasional book on science, travel or body language, I've never (well, hardly ever) looked back.

I think I speak for my colleagues in the genre—people like Dan Cohen, Dave Knight and Nancy Garden—when I say we are not trying to terrify kids. We're trying to help them cope with subjects they are interested in anyway, by telling them blood-and-guts stories, while at the same time explaining how people came to believe in supernatural people and events.

Let's take my witchcraft book. My biggest problem when I am out speaking to kids in their schools is to explain that the book is nonfiction. They think I made the whole thing up. And when they find out I didn't, they begin to doubt my sanity when I tell them that the happenings were the truth—or at least what some people thought were the truth.

So I try to get off the hook. I tell them that probably only about 50% of the "facts" in the book are true; but the problem is that I don't know which 50% they are. The crunch is that most of the items of information presented come from reports of people who talked to witches (who may or may not have been real witches) or from people who thought they themselves were witches (and who may have been either witches or mental patients).

The question arises, "Are there such things as witches?"

The answer must be, "Of course there are." Although most of the people who were tortured and executed on charges of witchcraft were probably really not witches, there are hundreds of people, even today, who maintain that they themselves are witches. And who am I to argue?

You learn early to be careful what you say to youngsters about the occult. There was the time I went blithely through a school presentation, but forgot to point out that I was talking about the old-fashioned bad witch only. After the session, a 10-year-old girl came up to me in tears, sobbing that I had insulted her. It turned out that she thought she was a modern good witch (she showed me a pentacle in the palm of her hand), and had been tarred with the same brush I had used on the witches who worshiped the Devil.

One also quickly learns about the many problems involved in writing an occult book. The biggest one is: Whose theories do we accept? There are vast numbers of conflicting ideas on all those subjects, and a writer who has never been a witch, a vampire or a werewolf must pick and choose. One cannot prove there was a system of covens in the Middle Ages. There is no way to find out the correct spelling of the name of one of the most famous werewolves of all time, Peter Stubb—he spelled his name in at least three ways. We really do not know whether the people of the time thought of Vlad the Impaler as a vampire or a werewolf, if they thought of him at all. (pp. 80-1)

It always seems like a good idea to ease the reader's anxiety concerning certain aspects of the supernatural. That is, to tell him or her that there are logical explanations, sometimes even scientific reasons, why people used to believe in those occult creatures.

Take the witches of Salem, for instance. There is a possibility that the people in Salem had been eating bread made with rye flour that contained a mold called ergot. They came down with a disease called ergotism, and were really suffering from something remarkably akin to an LSD trip. And what if they were suffering from Tourette's Syndrome? Victims of this condition are afflicted with bouts of twitching and involuntary cursing.

Throw things like this into a book about the supernatural and you have given children a rationalization that eases the titillation. They have had a thrill—but they still should realize that the truth of the stories might not lie in the occult, but rather in reasonable explanations. (p. 81)

"Witchcraft for Kids," in Publishers Weekly *(reprinted from the February 26, 1982 issue of* Publishers Weekly, *published by R. R. Bowker Company, a Xerox company; copyright © 1982 by Xerox Corporation), Vol. 221, No. 9, February 26, 1982, pp. 80-1.*

SERVANTS OF THE DEVIL (1970)

Highly entertaining and informal in style, this anecdotal, selective survey of witchcraft offers much information. . . . Fact and fiction are seldom distinguished, but the author warns readers about this in the introduction. . . . However, particular incidents are often described in a context that makes them credible; for instance, the impression of flying reported by many witches may be accounted for by the presence of certain drugs in the potions of the day. . . . Dr. Aylesworth touches on all facets of witchcraft, ancient and modern; but for a more

systematic, formal survey, students should refer to a work like Jennings' *Black Magic, White Magic* (Dial, 1965).

Brooke Anson, in a review of "Servants of the Devil," in School Library Journal, *an appendix to* Library Journal *(reprinted from the April, 1971 issue of* School Library Journal, *published by R. R. Bowker Co./A Xerox Corporation; copyright © 1971), Vol. 17, No. 8, April, 1971, p. 112.*

"Servants of the Devil" promises to describe and illustrate "initiation, annual Sabbats, and the rituals of Devil Worship." Like Mr. Aylesworth's "Werewolves and Other Monsters," it seems culled from standard reference books on the subject and is composed in the traditionally lacklustre prose of the hack. (p. 43)

Richard Elman, "A Goulash of Ghouls," in The New York Times Book Review, *Part II (© 1971 by The New York Times Company; reprinted by permission), November 7, 1971, pp. 42-4.**

VAMPIRES, AND OTHER GHOSTS (1972)

Of course, there are no such things as vampires and ghosts. Or are there? In this cheerful and witty book, the author explores the roots of legends that lie behind Dracula and his fellow friends, zombies (the undead) and people and animal ghosts. He includes stories of some human devils whose anti-social deeds often gave rise to stories of hellish beings. This is a shivery but good-natured account, written with a view to reassuring those who fear otherworldly creatures because, of course, there are no such things. Or . . .? (pp. 58-9)

A review of "Vampires and Other Ghosts," in Publishers Weekly *(reprinted from the September 11, 1972 issue of* Publishers Weekly, *published by R. R. Bowker Company, a Xerox company; copyright © 1972 by Xerox Corporation), Vol. 202, No. 11, September 11, 1972, pp. 58-9.*

MONSTERS FROM THE MOVIES (1972)

[These] movie monsters are merely entertainingly weird. We may doubt whether Charles Laughton actually invented the phrase "the natives are restless tonight" in the film *The Island of Lost Souls,* but Aylesworth keeps us busy pondering such trivia conundrums as he traces the major categories of movie monsters—man-made, self-made, other-worldly, etc.—back to their origins in literature and folklore. . . . Whether delving into the history of alchemy and pacts with the devil or reviewing the evolution of the Frankenstein monster's makeup, the tone remains light and never slips into the ponderous self-importance so common in juvenile surveys of offbeat subjects. It's hard to imagine the kid who wouldn't enjoy spending an hour or two meeting his favorite cinema monsters in this relaxed and informative setting. (pp. 1203-04)

A review of "Monsters from the Movies," in Kirkus Reviews *(copyright © 1972 The Kirkus Service, Inc.), Vol. XL, No. 20, October 15, 1972, pp. 1203-04.*

If Boris Karloff's birthday (November 23) is celebrated at your house, a touching remembrance might be Thomas G. Aylesworth's *Monsters from the Movies.* . . . This is a handbook for dedicated monster lovers. . . . Possibly in an attempt to talk to young people in what he feels is their own quaint language, the author breaks into an informal cuteness every so often that is neither informal nor cute. His description of *Psycho* as "one of the best films about an out-and-out nut case" defies comment. However, it is the information, not the style, that will delight faithful fiend fans.

> *Karla Kuskin, in a review of "Monsters from the Movies," in* Saturday Review *(© 1972 Saturday Review Magazine Co.; reprinted by permission), Vol. LV, No. 46, November 11, 1972, p. 79.*

In a thoroughly entertaining and knowledgeable narration, the author reveals the discoveries and experiments that led to the creations of movie monsters. Even the young movie buff is familiar with Dracula, Frankenstein's monster, King Kong, and other famous creatures that have given delicious shivers to generations of cinema-goers (thanks to TV). Aylesworth has obviously studied the books, legends, and techniques that resulted in drama of the macabre. . . . (pp. 39-40)

> *A review of "Monsters from the Movies," in* Publishers Weekly *(reprinted from the December 18, 1972 issue of* Publishers Weekly, *published by R. R. Bowker Company, a Xerox company; copyright © 1972 by Xerox Corporation), Vol. 202, No. 25, December 18, 1972, pp. 39-40.*

THE ALCHEMISTS: MAGIC INTO SCIENCE   (1973)

Abandoning the tongue-in-cheek approach employed frequently in his *Servants of the devil* . . . and *Vampires and other ghosts* . . . Aylesworth gives a straightforward yet entertaining history of alchemy. He tells the stories of Merlin, Paracelsus, and Cagliostro and describes the beginnings of alchemy but focuses on the activities of a number of out-and-out frauds as well as serious alchemists whom he treats as forerunners of the modern scientist.

> *A review of "The Alchemists: Magic into Science," in* The Booklist *(reprinted by permission of the American Library Association; copyright © 1973 by the American Library Association), Vol. 69, No. 15, April 1, 1973, p. 762.*

This is a well-written account of the rogues, rascals, magicians and scientists who from ancient Egypt to contemporary times have been smitten (for a number of reasons) with the desire to change metals into precious gold. The author presents brief biographies of notorious alchemists and describes interesting situations involving them and their discoveries, including chemicals used in dyes, medicine, glass, waterproofing, sleeping potions and a pain-killing drug. The author points out that the age-old attempt to develop a little man grown in a bottle, the feverish search for the philosopher's stone and the hope of discovering an elixir of life are not such crazy ideas in the light of what modern science is accomplishing today. Each of the eight chapters is assigned an alchemic symbol. . . . The book includes a table of contents, a list of acknowledgements and information on the pictures and chapter symbols and a brief index. Recommended as supplementary science reading for advanced elementary and junior high students and as fascinating reading for interested persons of all ages.

> *A review of "The Alchemists: Magic into Science," in* Science Books *(copyright 1974 by the American Association for the Advancement of Science), Vol. X, No. 1, May, 1974, p. 68.*

ASTROLOGY AND FORETELLING THE FUTURE   (1973)

A rainy day would fly by with this fascinating book at hand. The author explains various ways of predicting the future concentrating, at first, on astrology. He tells about the influence of various planets as well as Zodiac signs and defines arcane terms such as cusps and decans. . . . Since a mystic lurks in almost every young person these days, the book should attract much interest.

> *A review of "Astrology and Foretelling the Future," in* Publishers Weekly *(reprinted from the June 4, 1973 issue of* Publishers Weekly, *published by R. R. Bowker Company, a Xerox company; copyright © 1973 by Xerox Corporation), Vol. 203, No. 23, June 4, 1973, p. 90.*

In his preface, the author says, ". . . most of the information in this volume came either from conversations with people who practice these methods of divination, or from books on the subject"; however, no sources are identified. Astrology, telling fortunes with cards, teacups, and dominoes, etc. are included, but there are large gaps in the coverage. Serious readers will object to the repeated suggestion of experimenting with the occult for fun. . . . The last chapter, which expounds Aylesworth's theory of man's attempts to know the future, is helpful, but it can't redeem this dull, superficial account.

> *Lela M. Holmes, in a review of "Astrology and Foretelling the Future," in* School Library Journal, *an appendix to* Library Journal *(reprinted from the July, 1973 issue of* School Library Journal, *published by R. R. Bowker Co./A Xerox Corporation; copyright © 1973), Vol. 20, No. 1, July, 1973, p. 137.*

ESP   (1975)

Aylesworth's early section on "who has the power" is really a not-so-subtle bid for acceptance: higher psi scores are achieved by believers and by happy people, during a full moon, and when the subject likes the experimenter. The rest of this is simply an uncritical reiteration of reported phenomena and prominent conversions. . . . Credulity fodder.

> *A review of "ESP," in* Kirkus Reviews *(copyright © 1975 The Kirkus Service, Inc.), Vol. XLIII, No. 14, July 15, 1975, p. 779.*

An exceedingly brief introduction to the emerging science of parapsychology. . . . [The] text—clearly presented for the most part but containing only 35 pages of text overall—is frustratingly skimpy (e.g., a less than two-page chapter is included on **"Psychic Research in Russia,"** a country which is the world leader in ESP research). The seventh grade and up audience for whom this is intended deserves more than a superficial coverage of an increasingly important subject.

> *Donald A. Colberg, in a review of "ESP," in* School Library Journal *(reprinted from the January, 1976 issue of* School Library Journal, *published by R. R. Bowker Co./A Xerox Corporation; copyright © 1976), Vol. 22, No. 5, January, 1976, p. 51.*

ESP is clearly defined and placed within the science called parapsychology or psi. Three accepted types are explained in detail: clairvoyance, precognition and telepathy. Psycho-kinesis or PK is included as another branch of psi and Uri Geller's demonstrations are included (but no conclusions, though). The author wants to foster an attitude of open-mindedness and the realization that many experiments are necessary before conclusions may be drawn. The presentation is balanced. . . . The style is fast paced and interesting—even when describing experiments with dice and cards. (pp. 6-7)

> *Miriam Shapiro, in a review of "ESP," in* Appraisal: Science Books for Young People *(copyright © 1976 by the Children's Science Book Review Committee), Vol. 9, No. 2, Spring, 1976, pp. 6-7.*

The topic of ESP has long been and continues to be a very controversial issue among scientists. In this very short book, Aylesworth deals with the topic in an interesting as well as scientific manner (as much as is possible). . . . The nontechnical presentation makes the book very easy to comprehend, and those technical terms which do arise are well defined in the text as well as in a glossary. One shortcoming of the book is the absence of a complete listing of studies cited. All in all, the book is well written. . . .

> *Benjamin Wallace, in a review of "ESP," in* Science Books & Films *(copyright 1976 by the American Association for the Advancement of Science), Vol. XII, No. 1, May, 1976, p. 2.*

WHO'S OUT THERE? THE SEARCH FOR EXTRATERRESTRIAL LIFE (1975)

A conservative approach to the question of life on other planets—within or beyond the solar system. Aylesworth looks for positive evidence of visits to earth by alien space creatures and finds none; looks for fossils in meteorites and finds nothing conclusive; and believes that in efforts to communicate with alien creatures, other beings (or coincidence) could have intervened. A sound and sober assessment of the situation as it now stands, this is a good complement to Engdahl's *The Planet-Girded Suns* (Atheneum, 1974) which is a history of the belief in creatures from outer space.

> *Ovide V. Fortier, in a review of "Who's Out There?" in* School Library Journal *(reprinted from the September, 1975 issue of* School Library Journal, *published by R. R. Bowker Co./A Xerox Corporation; copyright © 1975), Vol. 22, No. 1, September, 1975, p. 116.*

Exobiology has become scientifically respectable—although the recent "Chariots of the Gods" fad has not been helpful. Dr. Aylesworth has made a fairly up-to-date summary of the field, though, of course, no hardcover book stands much chance of reaching the public without becoming dated.

As an Air Force officer I have to take issue with the author on one point, and as a scientist on a few others. The Air Force did not close down Project Bluebook because it "figured the public . . . had lost interest in UFO's" . . . but because the responsible officials decided, very justly in my opinion, that the objects did not represent a threat to national security.

Dr. Aylesworth fails to mention that the speeding up of Phobos' orbit turned out to be spurious. Dry ice is not hydrated carbon dioxide . . . ; it is plain, frozen carbon dioxide, though this error may be due to bad sentence structure rather than to bad science. The conditions needed for life are covered rather conservatively by science-fiction standards. Methods of communicating with other intelligences are described in fairly standard fashion. The book is worth having for students too young for Shklovskii and Sagan's *Intelligent Life in the Universe* (Holden-Day). (pp. 614-15)

> *Harry C. Stubbs, in a review of "Who's Out There? The Search for Extraterrestrial Life," in* The Horn Book Magazine *(copyright © 1975 by The Horn Book, Inc., Boston), Vol. LI, No. 6, December, 1975, pp. 614-15.*

Writing in a very conversational tone, the author quotes numerous scientists and scientific findings concerning extraterrestrial life. The difficulty for the average reader will be the high density of facts and ideas, some of them explained only briefly. However, Aylesworth gives a comprehensive review of the arguments for and against life elsewhere with a dramatic zest which builds to the climax: we must keep on searching without fear of an "invasion."

> *Thornton Page, in a review of "Who's Out There? The Search for Extraterrestrial Life," in* Science Books & Films *(copyright 1976 by the American Association for the Advancement of Science), Vol. XI, No. 4, March, 1976, p. 196.*

MOVIE MONSTERS (1975)

If this seems familiar you might be thinking of Aylesworth's *Monsters from the Movies*. . . . What we have here is little more than an easy reading, movie-by-movie rewriting, mostly plot summaries with photos and occasional references to special effects. . . . Second generation booksploitation—a whiz to read even if you wind up thinking that going to movies is a lot more fun.

> *A review of "Movie Monsters," in* Kirkus Reviews *(copyright © 1975 The Kirkus Service, Inc.), Vol. XLIII, No. 18, September 15, 1975, p. 1069.*

Just the book for movie maniacs who thrive on the likes of Frankenstein, Dracula, and the Mummy. . . . Original black-and-white photo stills . . . from studio archives such as RKO and Universal reinforce the authenticity of the text. Trivia fans will also delight in the filmography section (James Arness is listed as a supporting actor in "The Thing"), and a name/title/subject index rounds out the coverage. A ghoulishly good complement to Aylesworth's *Monsters from the Movies* . . . and Edward Edelson's *Great Monsters of the Movies* (Doubleday, 1973).

> *Ilene F. Rockman, in a review of "Movie Monsters," in* School Library Journal *(reprinted from the January, 1976 issue of* School Library Journal, *published by R. R. Bowker Co./A Xerox Corporation; copyright © 1976), Vol. 22, No. 5, January, 1976, p. 43.*

The greatest difficulty with books proposing to summarize an era or a genre in less than 150 pages is that the subject treatment is necessarily so brief that it becomes superficial. Despite this drawback, . . . *Movie Monsters* could be useful for those in middle school and remedial students in high school who like to read about movies. *Movie Monsters* is such easy reading that some upper elementary level children might enjoy it as well.

> *Anne G. Coughlin, in a review of "Movie Monsters," in* Curriculum Review *(© 1977 Curriculum Advisory Service; reprinted by permission of the Curriculum Advisory Service, Chicago, Illinois), Vol. 16, No. 3, August, 1977, p. 205.*

THE SEARCH FOR LIFE (1975)

An utterly intriguing inquiry into the exact nature and definition of life and death and the moral issues involved. There is discussion of the various ways scientists have found to aid life and life's failings: external and internal spare parts, electrical and chemical stimulation, transfusions, and grafts. The possibilities for controlling life—sex determination, life expectancy, cloning, cryogenics—are also presented. Not as difficult as it sounds, this intellectually challenging introduction to "research with responsibility" should be a part of all well-balanced science collections.

> *Shirley A. Smith, in a review of "The Search for Life," in* School Library Journal *(reprinted from the November, 1975 issue of* School Library Journal, *published by R. R. Bowker Co./A Xerox Corporation; copyright © 1975), Vol. 22, No 3. November, 1975, p. 68.*

Updated examples (i.e. 1975 developments on Dr. Barnard's new twin-heart operations) constitute the chief difference between this and previous reports from the frontiers of medicine. Aylesworth surveys past and projected work on well-publicized, life-extending projects. . . . [Throughout] Aylesworth covers background biology, philosophical questions and ingenious devices with the same once-over lightness. Spare parts. (pp. 1240-41)

> *A review of "The Search for Life," in* Kirkus Reviews *(copyright © 1975 The Kirkus Service, Inc.), Vol. XLIII, No. 21, November, 1, 1975, pp. 1240-41.*

In a thought-provoking study Aylesworth brings together various scientific accomplishments in man's search for the secret of life. . . . Interspersed in the discussion are questions about ethical standards which need to be considered as research continues. Young readers looking for an approach to the current life-death debates will find this a helpful reference.

> *Barbara Elleman, in a review of "The Search for Life," in* The Booklist *(reprinted by permission of the American Library Association; copyright © 1975 by the American Library Association), Vol. 72, No. 7, December 1, 1975, p. 510.*

Search is a collection of interesting accounts on the subject of life and death. . . . The book is interesting, highly sensational and not very critical. The choice of material is not based on purely scientific grounds. In fact, there are many biologic errors within the book, indicating that the author may not be sufficiently familiar with some biological principles. (For example, he talks about fingernail cells that are bitten off when nervous.) He also lists 10 things a living creature must do to be called alive, and among them is the attribute of taking in oxygen—even though this is not necessary for many living cells. In addition, the uncritical presentation often leads the reader to assume progress in a given area where, in fact, little progress has been made. Yet, with all its faults, this book will be attractive to those students interested in future developments in life sciences, particularly in human physiology. It may stimulate a student to learn more about the human body and the application of physics or engineering to the design of new components.

> *L. M. Beidler, in a review of "The Search for Life," in* Science Books & Films *(copyright 1976 by the American Association for the Advancement of Science), Vol. XII, No. 1, May, 1976, p. 21.*

CARS, BOATS, TRAINS AND PLANES OF TODAY AND TOMORROW (1975)

Although Aylesworth begins by recognizing that our machines perform below capacity because of traffic jams, overcrowding and poor planning, there's an implicit assumption here that new technology alone can solve our transportation problems. Just the same, the technological specifics are scanty. The progress reviews on hovercraft and hydrofoils are the most up to date we've seen. But Stambler has far more to say about the cars of the future (see *Automobile Engines of Today and Tomorrow*, 1972, for example), and the chapters on SSTs and high speed trains are sketchy, even if the former does focus on the economic question of speed vs. high cost. Since so much of the 96 page text merely recaps news stories, price will be a factor here too.

> *A review of "Cars, Boats, Trains & Planes of Today and Tomorrow," in* Kirkus Reviews *(copyright © 1975 The Kirkus Service, Inc.), Vol. XLIII, No. 23, December 1, 1975, p. 1336.*

[*Cars, Boats, Trains and Planes of Today and Tomorrow* is a] thoughtful inquiry into transportation of the future. . . . Many questions are raised as to speeds, power resources, and costs. An extensive appendix giving important dates in the history of transportation is extremely useful and enlightening. This will be useful for raising questions, stimulating discussions, and challenging creative thinking.

> *Shirley A. Smith, in a review of "Cars, Boats, Trains and Planes of Today and Tomorrow," in* School Library Journal *(reprinted from the January, 1976 issue of* School Library Journal, *published by R. R. Bowker Co./A Xerox Corporation; copyright © 1976), Vol. 22, No. 5, January, 1976, p. 43.*

An overview of various transportation means. . . . Even though the assumption is made that engineers must come up with new ideas, technological specifics are scanty. . . . The coverage of the hydrofoil and hovercraft is especially well presented. . . . Information is presented in newspaper style, but as the future projections are meager, the book might more appropriately have been named "Cars . . . of yesterday and today."

> *Barbara Elleman, in a review of "Cars, Boats, Trains and Planes of Today and Tomorrow," in* The Booklist *(reprinted by permission of the American Library Association; copyright © 1976 by the American Library Association), Vol. 72, No. 13, March 1, 1976, p. 971.*

Cars, Boats, Trains and Planes is by no means as wide a survey of these vehicles as the title implies, but Aylesworth does provide a fine overview of a limited number of these modes of transportation, considering his space limitations. . . . The author's descriptions, particularly of the hovercraft and hydrofoil, are well done and will stimulate the reader's imagination. However, he overemphasizes the hovercraft and underemphasizes space vehicles. (pp. 106-07)

> *Jason Taylor, in a review of "Cars, Boats, Trains and Planes of Today and Tomorrow," in* Science Books & Films *(copyright 1976 by the American Association for the Advancement of Science), Vol. XII, No. 2, September, 1976, pp. 106-07.*

PALMISTRY (1976)

Your tolerance for the subject will determine your reception; Aylesworth offers some relatively straight rules of thumb (and of fingers, mounts and lines) for matching up a person's hand with his character, physical or mental state, and past and future lives. Though he admits there are frauds, his instructions imply that his formulas are to be taken seriously; for example, he cautions palm readers to avoid alarming their subjects with predictions of failure or early death, but suggests that a person be warned to save for retirement if a forked life line indicates an insecure old age. And he's not above using some "amateur psychology" in interpreting clenched, fluttery, twisting or hidden hands. . . . Ours are thrown up.

> *A review of "Palmistry," in* Kirkus Reviews *(copyright © 1976 The Kirkus Service, Inc.), Vol. XLIV, No. 6, March 15, 1976, p. 325.*

Starting with a short overview of its history, this highly readable introduction to palmistry logically and succinctly covers basic palm reading, major lines, mounts, hands, fingers, and thumbs. The author asks readers to keep an open mind about the legitimacy of palmistry's predictive powers but places the most importance on the fun of reading personalities through the palms and hands. . . . [This is a] book which should be a suitable starting point for beginning palmists.

> *Sheila M. Best, in a review of "Palmistry," in* School Library Journal *(reprinted from the May, 1976 issue of* School Library Journal, *published by R. R. Bowker Co./A Xerox Corporation; copyright © 1976), Vol. 22, No. 9, May, 1976, p. 66.*

GRAPHOLOGY: A GUIDE TO HANDWRITING ANALYSIS (1976)

Aylesworth is even more cautionary than Mann was in *The Telltale Line: The Secrets of Handwriting Analysis* . . . and initially more instructive as well when explaining the external factors that might alter or influence a subject's writing style. His samples of writing sizes, angles, and spacing seem more realistically demonstrative than Mann's, although portions describing specifics—like how T's are crossed or how small letters are formed—lack illustrated examples. There are some writing samples tossed in for readers to practice on but regretfully no accompanying analysis against which they can check their findings. The signatures of several well-known people are scrutinized and a summary of writing traits that might signal good luck for the writer are included almost as an afterthought. Somewhat faulty, but suitable for filling requests on a popular subject.

> *Denise M. Wilms, in a review of "Graphology: A Guide to Handwriting Analysis," in* Booklist *(reprinted by permission of the American Library Association; copyright © 1976 by the American Library Association), Vol. 73, No. 4, October 15, 1976, p. 316.*

Beginning with a brief discussion of the history of writing, this is a well-organized, practical guide for beginning graphologists. Aylesworth clearly believes there is validity in graphoanalysis but urges readers to use commonsense and take into consideration a subject's age, sex, and general health before analyzing a signature. Handwriting samples elucidate the text and several are included for test analyses. A section on signatures of famous people lends additional interest to this entertaining and informative introduction.

> *Sheila M. Best, in a review of "Graphology: A Guide to Handwriting Analysis," in* School Library Journal *(reprinted from the December, 1976 issue of* School Library Journal, *published by R. R. Bowker Co./A Xerox Corporation; copyright © 1976), Vol. 23, No. 4, December, 1976, p. 59.*

THE STORY OF VAMPIRES (1977)

As Aylesworth has already investigated *Vampires and Other Ghosts* [and touched on them in his *Monsters from the Movies* and *Movie Monsters*], it should come as no surprise that he hasn't much to report in this skimpy mishmash of sloppy anthropology, undifferentiated folklore, cursory film history, and harum-scarum biography. . . . At least Nancy Garden's *Vampires* (1973) does the same sort of thing more thoroughly and with some pretense to research.

> *A review of "The Story of Vampires," in* Kirkus Reviews *(copyright © 1977 The Kirkus Service, Inc.), Vol. XLV, No. 10, May 15, 1977, p. 541.*

Dr. Aylesworth is a seasoned hand at providing readable fare for the young on unearthly subjects. This book . . . is an engrossing account of Count Dracula and other fascinating figures. The author's style is engagingly light and humorous but by no means offhand. He goes into all the myths, legends and histories of real people responsible for the belief in vampires.

> *A review of "The Story of Vampires," in* Publishers Weekly *(reprinted from the May 16, 1977 issue of* Publishers Weekly, *published by R. R. Bowker Company, a Xerox company; copyright © 1977 by Xerox Corporation), Vol. 211, No. 20, May 16, 1977, p. 63.*

Librarians besieged by requests for vampire material will want to consider Aylesworth's exploration into the lore, facts, and superstitions that surround this popular issue. The straightforward presentation is firmly grounded in reality—"There is no such thing as a vampire"—but enlivened with tongue-in-cheek subtleties and probing questions such as: Where do vampires come from? What do they look like? Were there real ones? How do you avoid and get rid of the creatures? (Silver bullets, stakes through the heart, and carrying garlic are suggested remedies.) Facts from historical sources, Hollywood movies, and books are illustrated with photographs and old prints, all appealingly designed in a format bound to pull reluctant readers in.

> *Barbara Elleman, in a review of "The Story of Vampires," in* Booklist *(reprinted by permission of the American Library Association; copyright © 1977 by the American Library Association), Vol. 74, No. 1, September 1, 1977, p. 35.*

SCIENCE AT THE BALL GAME (1977)

Why must a muscle-bound weight lifter struggle to lift his barbells when a puny kid can roll the same barbell onto a cart and carry it away without any difficulty? Is a pitcher's curve ball simply a figure of speech, and why do baseball players often slide when stealing second base? Why is a football easier to catch on a high pass than on a hard, flat pass? As he answers these and many other questions pertaining to a panorama of sports, Thomas Aylesworth applies such rudiments of physics as motion, friction, gravity, and acceleration to the automatic actions of athletes. The book's concluding chapter relates the fundamental roles the lever, inclined plane, and pulley play in a number of sports. A painless way for reluctant scientists—but avid sports fans—to pick up some principles that will benefit them in both fields.

> Ellen Mandel, in a review of "Science at the Ball Game," in Booklist (reprinted by permission of the American Library Association; copyright © 1977 by the American Library Association), Vol. 74, No. 3, October 1, 1977, p. 302.

The text is clearly written and easy to follow. A prior knowledge of forces, gravity, and acceleration is required, as this is more useful as a review than as an introduction to the subject.

> Martha Barnes, in a review of "Science at the Ball Game," in School Library Journal (reprinted from the December, 1977 issue of School Library Journal, published by R. R. Bowker Co./A Xerox Corporation; copyright © 1977), Vol. 24, No. 4, December, 1977, p. 46.

This book's title does not accurately describe its content: a more appropriate title would be, *Biomechanics and Physics of Sports.*... Throughout the book the author attempts to make science simple for the layperson by employing examples of various phases of sports activities. However, his attempts at clarity and clear detail fail consistently. For example, in describing a lever, Aylesworth states, "A lever is a rigid bar, according to physicists, that is free to turn on a fixed pivot. And that could be a description of your throwing arm. The arm contains rigid bones that are free to turn on the fixed pivots of your elbow and shoulder. . . . If you want to throw a short pass, you can toss it like a bullet. However, you know without ever having read about it that if you want to throw a long pass, you have to put some arc in it." Explanations such as this one can leave a reader cold and frustrated. The combining of scientific explanations with black-and-white photographs of sports activities was apparently intended to relate science to something that interests most youngsters. Unfortunately these photographs, which comprise about one-half of the book, are frequently not clearly related to the text. Many of the author's statements about physics concepts are careless and inadequate and will not result in the reader becoming really knowledgeable. In addition, it is not clear to what age level this book is aimed. Aylesworth has tried to do too much. What was conceived as a unique and good idea has failed, and most youngsters attempting to read this book will be left with a fuzzy understanding of the concepts involved.

> Jason R. Taylor, in a review of "Science at the Ball Game," in Science Books & Films (copyright 1978 by the American Association for the Advancement of Science), Vol. XIV, No. 1, May, 1978, p. 38.

THE STORY OF WEREWOLVES (1978)

[**The Story of Werewolves**] is everything you wanted to know about werewolves and if you're afraid to ask, don't bother picking up the book. This one has *all* the facts and pictures. The chapters are laid out in a simple-to-understand style ("Where did it come from? What did it look like?") and there is a good bibliography at the end.

> A review of "The Story of Werewolves," in The Babbling Bookworm (copyright 1979 The Babbling

Bookworm Newsletter), Vol. 7, No. 1, February, 1979, p. 2.

In a companion volume to **The Story of Vampires**..., Aylesworth continues his exploration of the strange and mysterious. Stories of lycanthropy, the act of turning into a wolf, are found in Greek and Roman times, but the height of the macabre belief was in the Dark Ages in Europe. Included in this historical account are brief descriptions of the transformation process, physical characteristics, habits, and remedies for extermination of werewolves. Folktales including these quasi-beasts, comments on motion pictures made about them, and sources for explanations of the legends' growth round out a somewhat choppy text. (pp. 862, 864)

> Barbara Elleman, in a review of "The Story of Werewolves," in Booklist (reprinted by permission of the American Library Association; copyright © 1979 by the American Library Association), Vol. 75, No. 11, February 1, 1979, pp. 862, 864.

A reworking of the section on werewolves in the author's **Werewolves and Other Monsters** . . . , this uses very nearly the same text. . . . Aylesworth handles the subject with a minimum of sensationalism but the tone is occasionally patronizing. . . . *Werewolves* by Nancy Garden (1973, . . . Lippincott) covers the same material in slightly more depth. (pp. 126, 128)

> Janice F. Giles, in a review of "The Story of Werewolves," in School Library Journal (reprinted from the September, 1979 issue of School Library Journal, published by R. R. Bowker Co./A Xerox Corporation; copyright © 1979), Vol. 26, No. 1, September, 1979, pp. 126, 128.

THE STORY OF WITCHES (1979)

Mr. Aylesworth traces the early history of witches through the witches of Salem and their famous trials. He adds some new theories from scientists as to possible reasons for behavior, superstitions and so forth. All in all, a readable account for those who enjoy something a bit offbeat or for those who may be in need of researching a term paper on an interesting subject.

> A review of "The Story of Witches," in The Babbling Bookworm (copyright 1979 The Babbling Bookworm Newsletter), Vol. 7, No. 9, October, 1979, p. 6.

Although intended for a younger audience, this is nearly identical in scope to *Out of the Cauldron* by Bernice Kohn (Holt, 1971). . . . [Aylesworth's] strong descriptions of diseases such as epilepsy and Huntington's Chorea, which may have caused superstitious people to suspect bewitchment, might inspire young hypochondriacs to adopt them as their own. Nevertheless, like his other books on popular topics, this is an excellent introduction to a subject which seems to be perennially in demand.

> Ann G. Brouse, in a review of "The Story of Witches," in School Library Journal (reprinted from the April, 1980 issue of School Library Journal, published by R. R. Bowker Co./A Xerox Corporation; copyright © 1980), Vol. 26, No. 8, April, 1980, p. 103.

UNDERSTANDING BODY TALK (1979)

An intriguing discussion of "kinesics" (commonly known as body talk). . . . The readable text, using sharp bold print and easy-to-understand examples, explores cultural and sex-role conditioning and how it affects body movements; how moods and emotions can be identified by observing body language; how our need for certain kinds of space determine conversations, reactions to stress, even prejudices. Although the author explains (repeatedly) why he has chosen WASPs to represent the "typical" American, some readers may object. And since distinctive behavior of ethnic groups is described, e.g., Jewish and Italian Americans gesture more broadly than WASPs, it is sometimes hard not to perceive such characterizations as stereotypes. Despite these problems, however, this is a relevant portrayal of a rapidly evolving science, told with ease and useful both for assignments and browsing.

> *Cyrisse Jaffee, in a review of "Understanding Body Talk," in* School Library Journal *(reprinted from the May, 1979 issue of* School Library Journal, *published by R. R. Bowker Co./A Xerox Corporation; copyright © 1979), Vol. 25, No. 9, May, 1979, p. 69.*

Although communication through movements of the body is generally the focus of a discussion on kinesics, equal emphasis is given here to a new and urgent science called proxemics, "the study of how people structure space in their everyday affairs, and what effect the distance between people and their objects has on them." . . . The relationship between territorial reactions and physical expression is not always made clear, but the connection is interesting enough to lead to further reading, for which a bibliography is appended. (pp. 1359-60)

> *Betsy Hearne, in a review of "Understanding Body Talk," in* Booklist *(reprinted by permission of the American Library Association; copyright © 1979 by the American Library Association), Vol. 75, No. 17, May 1, 1979, pp. 1359-60.*

GEOLOGICAL DISASTERS: EARTHQUAKES AND VOLCANOES (1979)

Aylesworth's coverage of earthquakes is similar to that of Simon's *Danger from Below*. . . . Like Simon, he reviews major quakes, explains basic plate tectonics theory, and describes observation methods scientists hope will help accurately predict earthquakes. A section on volcanoes that seems almost an afterthought gives this a slightly wider scope, and in general there are more examples listed to support ideas (though some of this information adds mere breadth rather than depth).

> *Denise M. Wilms, in a review of "Geological Disasters: Earthquakes and Volcanoes, in* Booklist *(reprinted by permission of the American Library Association; copyright © 1979 by the American Library Association), Vol. 75, No. 20, June 15, 1979, p. 1534.*

I have a personal bias against the exploitative use of the word "disaster" in titles, but actually this book is a prosaic explanation of how earthquakes and volcanoes are caused using the theory of plate tectonics. There is one chapter devoted to describing recent earthquakes, but the writing is not sensational. Of equal interest are the preventive measures taken to quakeproof buildings in susceptible areas and the surprising accuracy of scientist's predictions. . . . All in all, the book is adequate, but I doubt that it will have the impact the series heading [Impact Books] indicates. If you own the revised edition of Rebecca B. Marcus' *The First Book of Volcanoes and Earthquakes* (Franklin Watts, 1972), it'll do nicely.

> *Mary Johnson-Lally, in a review of "Geological Disasters: Earthquakes and Volcanoes," in* Appraisal: Children's Science Books *(copyright © 1980 by the Children's Science Book Review Committee), Vol. 13, No. 2, Spring, 1980, p. 9.*

Geological Disasters: Earthquakes and Volcanoes is destined to become a very popular science book. The subject is inherently interesting and the author, who actually experienced a weak earthquake while living in El Salvador in 1976, treats the reader to the intellectual pleasures of ongoing science. With a clarity of expression rarely found, Thomas Aylesworth allows the reader to experience some of the intellectual tension of scientific debate and research. With provocative questions: "What is this strange connection between volcanoes and earthquakes?" the author skillfully engages the curiosity of the young reader. Technical vocabulary is employed very sparingly, and a glossary is provided. This book is uncommonly effective as a means of relating science to the humanities and human affairs, and could easily be used in an interdisciplinary program of studies. . . . Although the author includes a small bibliography "For Further Reading", he fails to cite the relevant articles in *Scientific American* and *National Geographic*, and no films are included in the bibliography. For most science books, these bibliographic oversights would probably not be mentioned, or even regarded as oversights. When we have a book that is as interesting and well-written as this one, however, it must be anticipated that many young readers will want much more. For this reason, a more extensive bibliography is a must for future editions. In summary, *Geological Disasters: Earthquakes and Volcanoes* is highly recommended, both for its writing style, and for its scientific content. With books of this caliber, dealing with mankind and science on a global scale, we may be somewhat optimistic about the future of our youth and our science. (pp. 9-10)

> *Clarence Truesdell, in a review of "Geological Disasters: Earthquakes and Volcanoes," in* Appraisal: Children's Science Books *(copyright © 1980 by the Children's Science Book Review Committee), Vol. 13, No. 2, Spring, 1980, pp. 9-10.*

Geological Disasters is a lucid account of two of the earth's most spectacular and destructive events. . . . This splendid, easy-to-read book would provide good supplemental reading for earth science classes or would serve as a good introduction for general audiences.

> *John D. McLeod, in a review of "Geological Disasters: Earthquakes and Volcanoes," in* Science Books & Films *(copyright 1980 by the American Association for the Advancement of Science), Vol. XV, No. 5, May, 1980, p. 261.*

STORM ALERT: UNDERSTANDING WEATHER DISASTERS (1980)

"Weather disasters" immediately conjures up images of tornadoes and hurricanes, but the author's scope is much broader, beginning with the "common" thunderstorm and ranging through landslides, avalanches, floods, droughts, and the "great cold" of the winter of 1976-1977. Deftly avoiding the pitfall of emphasis on dramatic incident, Mr. Aylesworth weaves a fascinating account of how these weather disasters occur, just what they are, and why they occur *where* they do; a surprising and thought-provoking point which is gradually borne in upon the reader, is how much more we theorize than we actually know about weather dynamics. The author also deals with the effects and study of the phenomena, human reactions, and preventative measures; the last includes lists of very practical measures to take in the event of danger. This is a well-balanced, interesting, and intelligent treatment of the subject and is highly recommended.

> *Daphne Ann Hamilton, in a review of "Storm Alert: Understanding Weather Disasters," in* Appraisal: Science Books for Young People *(copyright © 1981 by the Children's Science Book Review Committee), Vol. 14, No. 2, Spring, 1981, p. 8.*

Storm Alert is spellbinding with descriptions, explanations and anecdotes of past and recent natural disasters. . . . By knowing safety recommendations given here, it may help avoid loss of life and lessen destruction of property due to natural disasters.

> *A review of "Storm Alert: Understanding Weather Disasters," in* Science Books & Films *(copyright 1981 by the American Association for the Advancement of Science), Vol. 17, No. 1, September/October, 1981, p. 32.*

ANIMAL SUPERSTITIONS (1981)

After reading a few pages of this book, you might justifiably begin to think that if you've read one superstition about animals, you've read them all. Hundreds of superstitions about a host of different animals are described. Don't expect any logic or unifying principles in all of this. After all, the subject is superstition.

> *Elliot H. Blaustein, in a review of "Animal Superstitions," in* Children's Book Review Service *(copyright © 1981 Children's Book Review Service Inc.), Vol. 9, No. 12, Spring, 1981, p. 105.*

Animal Superstitions is a compendium of hundreds of superstitions about animals, described in a clear, concise, and often humorous way. The superstitions are grouped by animal phyla, and individual superstitions are ordered by particular kinds of animals within each phylum. This very logical organization, although easy to grasp, provides the reader with many facts but does little to develop a sense of unity about the functions of superstitions in human lives. The author takes great care to describe the characteristics of the animals in the major grouping. By contrast, he neglects to define superstitions or even to mention their ubiquity in human societies. Consequently, the book remains a series of sketchy descriptions of beliefs. . . .

> *Fred Rasmussen, in a review of "Animal Superstitions," in* Science Books & Films *(copyright 1982 by the American Association for the Advancement of Science), Vol. 17, No. 3, January/February, 1982, p. 149.*

SCIENCE LOOKS AT MYSTERIOUS MONSTERS (1982)

All of this is well-traveled territory, but for those libraries needing more information on elusive monsters, here it is. Aylesworth's offering covers a broader spectrum and has a more sedate tone than [Daniel Cohen's *Big Foot*]. Along with his inquiries into the nature of the Abominable Snowman and Bigfoot, Aylesworth looks at the Loch Ness monster and other mysterious sea and land creatures.

> *Ilene Cooper, in a review of "Science Looks at Mysterious Monsters," in* Booklist *(reprinted by permission of the American Library Association; copyright © 1982 by the American Library Association), Vol. 78, No. 22, August, 1982, p. 1520.*

No library serving children ever seems to have enough "monster" books to satisfy the demand. That fact makes this book very welcome. However, anyone expecting a scientific treatment of the subject, as indicated in the title, will be disappointed. Brief retellings of hundreds of "eyewitness" accounts of appearances of the "Abominable Snowman" or Yeti, "Bigfoot" or Sasquatch, other similar "hairy men," sea monsters, the Loch Ness monster and several other lake monsters make up the text. (p. 62)

> *Ann G. Brouse, in a review of "Science Looks at Mysterious Monsters," in* School Library Journal *(reprinted from the December, 1982 issue of* School Library Journal, *published by R. R. Bowker Co./A Xerox Corporation; copyright © 1982), Vol. 29, No. 4, December, 1982, pp. 62-3.*

Although there are a host of books available about the [monsters Aylesworth discusses, he] . . . has condensed them all in one small volume. The title, *Science Looks at Mysterious Monsters,* is accurate in that the book is merely a recounting of the many sightings and search expeditions that have occurred over the years. As none of these has produced a solid specimen, there is little scientific information to add. . . . As this is always a popular subject I am sure this book will enjoy frequent circulation, however, it is similar to other choices such as *Monsters, Mysteries and Man* by Michael Newton, (Addison-Wesley, 1979).

> *Sallie Hope Erhard, in a review of "Science Looks at Mysterious Monsters," in* Appraisal: Science Books for Young People *(copyright © 1983 by the Children's Science Book Review Committee), Vol. 16, No. 1, Winter, 1983, p. 10.*

From the cover and title of *Science Looks at Mysterious Monsters,* one might expect a book that is suited for the Halloween display in the children's section of the library. Look again. Inside, its pages contain a well-documented, serious discussion of various types of mysterious creatures. In six thoroughly researched chapters, Aylesworth discusses the Abominable Snowman, Bigfoot, Nessie, and many other legendary or documented "monsters." Using broad and brief summaries of historical sightings, scientific searches, and published accounts, the author gives a balanced and intellectually satisfying view of each credible or incredible creature. Aylesworth heaps on the facts and then challenges the reader to decide whether the creature really exists or not. This literary technique is certainly thought-provoking. . . . It is an excellent beginning point for readers with specific interest in "monsters." The only shortcoming of the book is the occasional sensation by the reader that the author is hurrying through the information. Minor criticisms aside, this book appeals to a wide variety of readers—from older children to adults. It is a nice treatment of a consistently popular topic.

> *Yvonne Heather Burry, in a review of "Science Looks at Mysterious Monsters," in* Science Books & Films *(copyright 1983 by the American Association for the Advancement of Science), Vol. 18, No. 4, March/April, 1983, p. 207.*

Ludwig Bemelmans

1898-1962

Austrian-born American author/illustrator of fiction, nonfiction, poetry, and essays, illustrator and editor.

Creator of the memorable *Madeline* series, Bemelmans captivates readers with his unique blend of gaiety and action. He expressed his love of life in humorous, gentle stories of prose or verse and in expressionistic watercolor paintings, chalk, and line drawings reminiscent of James Thurber. Bemelmans's art is noted for its vibrant color, sense of design, cartoon-like quality, use of exaggerated movement, and an anatomical and architectural primitiveness that makes the work look deceptively simple. Bemelmans claimed he had no imagination for writing, and based his books on real events and people. He traveled extensively and illustrated settings from the Austrian Tyrol, Belgium, Paris, London, Ecuador, and New York. Bemelmans's works are seen as a natural extension of his buoyant personality and his affinity with childhood.

Born in a hotel and raised in three countries, Bemelmans showed early signs of becoming cosmopolitan: he became multilingual, traveled, and met people from all walks of life. His carefree, unruly nature led to trouble, however, and occasioned his leaving Europe as a teenager. In America, he worked in the hotel business, eventually establishing himself as a successful hotelier and restauranteur. Bemelmans often painted to ease his homesickness during those early years. He took few art lessons, preferring instead to absorb all that was around him and to paint what gave him pleasure. Eventually, his work received limited recognition. When he met May Massee, children's book editor of Viking Press, she encouraged Bemelmans to create an illustrated book. *Hansi*, the story of a boy in the Austrian Tyrol, was a critical success and launched Bemelmans's career as an author/illustrator of over forty books for adults and children.

Bemelmans's books for children ranged from stories with serious overtones (*Parsley*), to fantasies (*Rosebud*), to those written for pure fun (the *Madeline* escapades). *Hansi*, *The Golden Basket*, and *The High World* are considerably longer than other books by Bemelmans and draw on his personal experiences while living in the mountains and in hotels. *Quito Express*, set in Ecuador, is unique for its use of chalk drawings as opposed to the artist's usual work in watercolor. *Madeline*, however, assures Bemelmans of lasting recognition. The charming heroine, the other little girls "in two straight lines," and the harried Miss Clavel are spotlighted in flowing verse and lively drawings. Further adventures introduce Genevieve the dog in *Madeline's Rescue* and the mischievous Pepito in *Madeline and the Bad Hat*. These and the succeeding books retain the original, popular characters and beautiful panoramic scenes, but are thought to be marred by awkward verse in the later stories.

Critical response to Bemelmans is largely favorable. He is regarded as an innovator for his use of magnificent color and comical movement, but is sometimes faulted for a lack of anatomical and architectural accuracy in his paintings. Reviewers commend the complementary union of his text and pictures, but see his prose as better constructed than some of his verse. Throughout his works, Bemelmans combined his artistic

talent with touches of spontaneous humor and perceptive insights into the world of children, attributes which make him highly respected by critics and children alike. *The Golden Basket* was a Newbery Honor Book in 1937, *Madeline* was a Caldecott Honor Book in 1940, and *Madeline's Rescue* won the Caldecott Medal in 1953. The *New York Herald Tribune* Children's Spring Book Festival Award was given to *Sunshine* in 1950 and to *Madeline and the Bad Hat* in 1957. The *New York Times* Choice for Best Illustrated Book of the Year was awarded to *Madeline's Rescue* in 1953 and to *Parsley* in 1955.

(See also *Something about the Author*, Vol. 15; *Contemporary Authors*, Vols. 73-76; and *Dictionary of Literary Biography*, Vol. 22.)

AUTHOR'S COMMENTARY

I love the gothic, the baroque. I can write at times, freely and loosely, at others, particularly when I wish to say something very definitely, some issue that is close to my heart, I write with difficulty, shoot past the mark, have a tendency to be fantastic on some points.

Knowing this, I put such things away, look at them after weeks, make them right or sidetrack them if they seem unfair or not clear to my basic design that is set within myself.

I have great affection for humble people, for old cities, little lonesome women, shop windows and animals. As a child I could never be sent out anywhere, because I never came back until late after dark, standing in front of whatever interested me and drinking it into myself.

When I think of a book, I arrange those objects of my belief and of my affection, the basic things I wish to say very clearly . . . the love for landscape, for time and place that is quiet, simple and honest and when all the sentiment that I wish to transfer to other people is so decided on, I bury it as deep as I can into the story so that no one says, ''ah! he means this or that,'' and ''there is a lovely moral in this book.'' For to the children I feel that . . . first of all . . . is owed a story. If this story is robust enough it will, to the best of my ability and endeavor, hold their interest, be liked for its own sake. Then I am as close to being satisfied as it is possible. (pp. 4-5)

Ludwig Bemelmans, in an extract from ''Ludwig Bemelmans and His Books for Children'' (copyright © 1957 by the National Council of Teachers of English; reprinted by permission of the publisher and the author), in Elementary English, *Vol. XXXVI, No. 1, January, 1957, pp. 4-5.*

GENERAL COMMENTARY

He says that he has no imagination and so has to fall back on actual persons and real events for his stories and pictures; but the increasing number of children who enjoy Ludwig Bemelmans' books would scarcely agree with him. . . . Lack of imagination is the last accusation anyone could bring against Ludwig Bemelmans.

There is considerable point to his statement, though, when one remembers that his imagination seems to exercise itself most fully on real objects and real persons. . . . For to this fun-loving artist most of the world is slightly fantastic. In his pictures the most ordinary objects become, by some process in his own mind, faintly ridiculous, and people walk, sit and talk in a fashion most disconcertingly ludicrous.

This quality, coupled with a shrewd and accurate faculty of observation, gives to his work a strange mixture of reality and fantasy which delights children and adults, too. The almost literal basis of his peculiar brand of humor can be seen clearly in some of the murals he did for the Hapsburg where, in one room, he calmly painted a pair of open windows on a blank wall. The windows look real, down to the last screw; but the wind which stirs the curtains blew out of nowhere except Mr. Bemelmans' imagination. And an old coat, painted hanging on a door, a bird-cage and a sprig of green vine are for some reason funny. In the same way an accurately observed train in his most recent children's book, **''Quito Express,''** a baby's shirt or a handful of corn become warmly amusing. (p. 1508)

[Being able to write precisely what he pleases] is the key to his whole method of doing children's books, for he has no theories on the subject. He says that he never consciously writes specifically for children, that is, it never occurs to him to write down to them. He simply writes stories that he himself likes and wants to write. Undoubtedly this gives his books a simple, direct quality which children like, just as they like his fun and amazingly tender good humor. (pp. 1509-10)

''The Humor of Ludwig Bemelmans,'' in Publishers Weekly *(reprinted from the October 22, 1938 issue of* Publishers Weekly, *published by R. R. Bowker Company; copyright © 1938 by R. R. Bowker Company), Vol. CXXXIV, No. 17, October 22, 1938, pp. 1508-10.*

Hansi, in Ludwig Bemelmans's book by that title, is a very real little boy, and no one who follows him home through the wintry streets of Innsbruck, sees him (with the help of the author's lively drawings) sitting on a school bench with two mischievous comrades, or shares with him the hushed and lovely joy of a Christmas that was kept high up in the mountains of the Austrian Tirol, but will enlarge his circle of friends and increase his understanding of human nature. (p. 200)

Ludwig Bemelmans's pictures, with their unconventional treatment of perspective, may cause an adult to query a child's ability to grasp and to enjoy them, but boys and girls whose taste has not been spoiled by too many pictures of the ''pretty-pretty'' type receive the drawings in **Hansi** and in **The Golden Basket** with delight and are in entire agreement with the seven-year-old who, after looking at **The Castle Number Nine,** announced without a moment's hesitation: ''Those are perfectly *beautiful* pictures.'' (pp. 282-83)

Anne Thaxter Eaton, ''Roundabout the Earth'' and ''Artists at Work for Children,'' in her Reading with Children *(copyright 1940 by Anne Thaxter Eaton; copyright renewed 1967 by Anne Thaxter Eaton; reprinted by permission of Viking Penguin Inc.), Viking Press, 1940, pp. 193-219, 281-309.**

The Bemelmans drawings will never be hoarded as great works of draftsmanship. They seem to the average person like the kind of thing that almost anyone could do and this is nearly true. But they contain some precious ingredients that are missing in the great mass of more skillful work. They contain delight and spontaneity and charm, a power to reveal, seemingly artlessly, a hundred and one tiny facets of humanity's maneuvers. The little sidelights of the human heart that strike the Bemelmans heart come through without stress or interruption to the beholder. (p. 49)

Henry C. Pitz, ''Ludwig Bemelmans,'' in American Artist *(copyright © 1951 by Billboard Publications, Inc.), Vol. 15, No. 5, May, 1951, pp. 48-9.*

[**Hansi** and **The Golden Basket** showed that Ludwig Bemelmans] could tell a simple story with clarity and sparkle which with his pictures made the whole book sing. (p. 263)

[These books] established Ludwig as an important writer-artist or artist-writer with a cosmopolitan genius all his own. He has written many brilliant, witty, amusing books from then to now. (p. 266)

May Massee, ''Ludwig Bemelmans,'' in The Horn Book Magazine *(copyrighted, 1954, by The Horn Book, Inc., Boston), Vol. XXX, No. 4, August, 1954, pp. 263-69.*

In spite of, or perhaps because of, . . . [the] idiosyncrasies of genius, Mr. Bemelmans has a deep understanding of his subject matter, the command of an artist over the tools of his trade, and high regard for his juvenile public. (p. 4)

Mr. Bemelmans may be quite correct in saying that he doesn't know any ordinary people well enough to write about them, but one suspects that the truth of the matter is rather in the fact that he does not see people in an ordinary way, nor does he see his relationships with people as ordinary events. All of which is another way of saying that he doesn't consider himself to be an ordinary person. (p. 6)

[Living] long and intimately with one's subject matter has contributed heavily to Bemelmans' best books. . . . [**Hansi**] is peopled with simple folk and built around human emotions and incidents which are common in many countries. A trip alone to the home of relatives; sadness of farewell to mother; the feeling of smallness which comes from solitary travel; . . . the warm good feeling which comes from finding oneself back with mother and in long familiar surroundings—all are in *Hansi*. (pp. 6-7)

In many ways, *Hansi* might be called Bemelmans' best. In it can be found little direct appeal to an adult audience. It is a story written about children, for children. . . . *Hansi*, unlike most of Mr. Bemelmans' more recent work, is a long story, and though profusely illustrated, is not to be read at one sitting.

The Golden Basket is another of Bemelmans' longer stories. It, too, draws heavily on the author's knowledge of hotels and things European. . . . Though this is a children's story, and a good one too, Mr. Bemelmans' sometimes not-so-gentle spoofing of Eighteenth Century etiquette cannot be overlooked. In fact, it is just this kind of overdrawing which is responsible for one of the most laughable episodes in the book. The Mayor of Bruges, the hotel manager, and the two young ladies find themselves very waterlogged as the result of too much politeness on the parts of the adult occupants of the boat in which they were rowing on a Bruges Canal. The hero of this incident fails to gain proper recognition. But the Mayor, a rather pompous individual, becomes a hero. All of which is most obviously a commentary on local politics in nearly any western community.

In both *Hansi* and *The Golden Basket*, Bemelmans, the artist, demonstrates his ability to capture the essence of city scenes. As with his later books, these scenes may be crowded with detail, but with essential detail. They are never cluttered. He had not, however, mastered the ability to breathe life and motion into his human beings as he now does so well in his Madelines. His people "leaned" in the right direction, but did not move across the page. They were done with more completeness of feature and detail but with less character. Nor had he forsaken his very effective prose style for what is his sometimes less effective doggerel, a matter which one may overlook. For though there are many equally capable prose story spinners, there are none who can tell a better story with brush, paint, and rather poor narrative poetry. (pp. 7-8)

All of Bemelmans' juveniles have not been equally successful. A matter which may be accounted for in part by the fact that not all of the works of any artist are equally good, in part by the fact that a low bank account, though a good source of motivation, may not permit the artist time to polish his product, and in part by an observation which Bemelmans made concerning himself [in his Caldecott acceptance speech; see excerpt below]:

> I have repeatedly stated two things that no one takes seriously, and they are that first of all I am not a writer, but a painter, and secondly that I have no imagination.

Bemelmans' own writing helps refute the supposition that he is not a writer, but an analysis of his children's books gives evidence that he may, indeed, be somewhat lacking in imagination.

Castle Number Nine is a fairly good reworking of the English household tale, *Master of All Masters*, done in a Germanic setting. The story lacks the spark of enthusiasm and originality. *Quito Express* is a humanly warm account of the train trip

accidentally taken by a very small South American Indian boy who was unable to communicate with the adults who, throughout his journey, met and attended to the child. The characters are treated with the kindness that any really sympathetic tourist would extend to those members of a culture which was alien to his, but whom the visitor was seriously attempting to understand. *Sunshine* is a modern fairy tale which, like the fairy tales of old, does not seem to have been written for young children. *Sunshine* is, illustration-wise, as gorgeously illustrated as any of Bemelmans' work.

But, of all his picture books, *Parsley* best illustrates Mr. Bemelmans' lack of imagination. By his own account the plot was not his to begin with. . . . In *Parsley*, Bemelmans can do nothing better to make life serene for the forest animals than to send the story's only human character, an inoffensive hunter, crashing to his death at the bottom of an abyss. Perhaps death to the hunter was the only solution which occurred to Bemelmans. For the hunter, who bears a striking physical resemblance to his illustrator, would otherwise have returned with Germanic tenacity for his binoculars which, as he fell, were entangled in an anthropomorphic tree.

Not only does *Parsley* lack imagination, but also the book lacks nearly everything else which Bemelmans might have done to make it more palatable to a young audience. Whatever story content does exist hangs gauntly over bleached bones of message. An illustration or two are a cut above run-of-the-mill Christmas card art. But the pictures of "New England pine furniture" and the forty-six different varieties of carefully identified wild flowers with which the book is strewn do nothing to recommend it to any reading public worthy of mention. The best that can be said for "Old Parsley" is that he must have helped replenish Bemelmans' bank account. (pp. 8-9)

In *The High World*, Bemelmans is back in the familiar mountains of Austria telling a story about people and places he knows and loves well. But since the readers of *Holiday* magazine were his first audience, *The High World* is not really a children's story. It is, however, a rather delightful account of the humor and hardship encountered when simple mountain folk find themselves facing overbearing bureaucracy. In this story Bemelmans' plot and characterization ring true, and, with just a little more careful editing of the author's sometimes belabored English, this would have been a tale well told. (pp. 9-10)

Since it is for the two "Madelines" that Bemelmans is best known in the juvenile field, it might be well to examine them for their similarities and differences. In both books the illustrations are superbly done. Their childlike quality, the minimum of elaboration, the ability to pack the illustrations with supporting detail but to leave the main theme standing in bold relief are Bemelmans at his best. The verse in one book scans no better than the verse in the other. The rhyme in one is just as hilariously contrived as it is in the other. Madeline is her same effervescent self in both books, and her eleven peers are equally anonymous as they march through both plots.

Though the similarities are great, they are not great enough to make the two books equally good. It is the disparity in strength of plot and characterization which leads to an unfavorable comparison. In *Madeline*, the plot is built upon the kinds of occurrences which must be almost common in a boarding school. Appendectomies, the temporary crises they cause, and the enviable periods of convalescence are not only fairly common to private French schools, but are known to most school age children in any community where medical science has discovered the appendix and the scalpel.

Madeline is the only character to emerge with a full enough personality to permit reader identity. The child reader, therefore, finds it easy to identify himself solely with Madeline. In *Madeline*, Miss Clavel's character is also established. She is clearly a long suffering, mild-mannered governess who seems always to understand her charges and always to be ready to rise to any emergency. The child who has read *Madeline* knows that Miss Clavel is to be trusted. He knows that, though she is not a fellow conspirator, she is a consistently benevolent adult. These, then, seem to be among the chief of *Madeline's* virtues.

By way of contrast, the plot of *Madeline's Rescue* does not, as its predecessor did, march straight-lined to a satisfying and simple conclusion. Though there are fifty-six pages, the book has earned its title by page fifteen when a nondescript dog, Genevieve, "dragged her safe from a watery grave." At this point the story ceases to be Madeline's and becomes Genevieve's. Here, too, the reader is asked to end a familiar relationship with Madeline and to identify henceforth with the dog. This might not have been too difficult had the dog at least been Madeline's. Such is not the case, for never is a clear-cut pattern of possession established and Genevieve remains, to the end, her own master. All of which lends support to the contention that it is nearly impossible for a young child to place an already fully developed leading character in a supporting role.

The episodes which follow the rescue scene provide Bemelmans with the occasion to demonstrate his superior artistic talents. Otherwise the episodes might better have been used for chapter organization in a longer book for older children.

The reader of *Madeline's Rescue* is bound to raise an eye-brow at Miss Clavel's ineptitude during the expulsion of Genevieve from school. It becomes clear that this single pillar of adult strength in the lives of the girls is not to be completely trusted in a crisis. And, without Miss Clavel, the young reader is entitled to ask, "Are there no adults who can be completely trusted?" In truth, had Miss Clavel lived up to expectation, Bemelmans would have been left with no further story line—that she did not is to be lamented.

Though Genevieve returned to the bereft girls in time to deliver herself of "enough hound to go all around," one suspects that Genevieve's return might have been more of a convenience than of undying devotion to the girls—a matter which may be all too common in the domain of pets and children, but one which children do not find particularly appealing.

These and other inadequacies of the second Madeline inevitably lead the reader to wonder why Bemelmans didn't leave well enough alone. And, when in his acceptance speech he said: "There are many problems ahead. Who are Madeline's parents? Who are the other girls, what are their names, what new disaster shall Mademoiselle Clavel rush to?" it was to be hoped that, the American Library Association and the Caldecott Award not withstanding, both Mademoiselle and Madeline would come to the next adventure with a stronger children's story than they had come with to the last.

This they most assuredly seem to have done! (pp. 9-12)

In *Bad Hat*, Madeline is once again fully in command. She is not asked to share bows with anyone, though The Bad Hat becomes a despicably delightful object of Madeline's scorn. The action in this book starts almost immediately. . . . And, through many absorbing episodes [Pepito] remains an unregenerated sinner until the natural consequences of his actions

From Madeline's Rescue, *written and illustrated by Ludwig Bemelmans.*

and Madeline's hesitating forgiveness put him on the road to reform. This is a book which should be appreciated both by those who already know and love Madeline and by those who have not yet been introduced to her childlike charm. In *Madeline and the Bad Hat*, Madeline seems a bit more sophisticated than in the first book, but none the less appealing.

Though Ludwig Bemelmans once wrote, "I always wanted to conduct an orchestra or be a surgeon . . . and if I was less lazy would still study music and try to conduct the philharmonic," the field of children's literature would have been much less rich had he chosen either as a vocation. (p. 12)

Shelton L. Root, Jr., "Ludwig Bemelmans and His Books for Children" (copyright © 1957 by the National Council of Teachers of English; reprinted by permission of the publisher and the author), in Elementary English, *Vol. XXXVI, No. 1, January, 1957, pp. 3-12.*

All the ordinary yardsticks which measure the quality of art are worse than useless when applied to Ludwig Bemelmans and his paintings. Every so often an artist of this kind comes along—a man whose lack of academic talent is so far offset by the charm and verve of his work that the critic has to invent new standards in order to begin to criticize. There's no hidden meaning, no nebulous or enigmatic title to explain what might otherwise remain aimless daubing. There is little of anatomic correctness to his people; his buildings would undoubtedly collapse if unseen carpenters weren't frantically scurrying around behind them, nailing away like mad. But they enjoy one virtue: they are sheer delight to behold. And, like the art of James Thurber, (another writer of tales for children whose art was incidental music to accompany the words) . . . Bemelmans caseins will continue to captivate viewers. . . . They are well worth studying. They have an odd ability to inspire artists of every age. (p. 106)

"Art, As Bemelmans Sees It," in Design *(copyright 1962 by Design Publishing Company), Vol. 63, No. 3, January-February, 1962, pp. 106-08.*

His books for children were sophisticated and debonair; his books for grown-ups, childlike. Children were delighted to be taken seriously; adults loved his taking them lightly. But Ludwig Bemelmans was consistent in his way—his unvarying gift was gaiety.

He painted the things he wrote about, and wrote of the things he loved. . . . But, as Bemelmans' admirers are well aware, his subject was never important. He wrote as easily as he talked, and, talking or writing, it was all a matter of style. . . .

[He] loved to recount his difficulties with **"Madeline."** "Nobody wanted to publish it. . . . They said it was too sophisticated for children. Of course, I never in my life wrote for children. I write for myself."

"Madeline's Master," in Newsweek *(copyright 1962, by Newsweek, Inc.; all rights reserved; reprinted by permission), Vol. LX, No. 16, October 15, 1962, p. 115.*

There is little doubt that Bemelmans' talent was a large and exceptional one. (p. 565)

[It] is in its approach to the child that the art of Bemelmans has its greatest strength. . . . Bemelmans depended greatly on the child artist for his inspiration. In the pictures of *Madeline's Rescue* (and in the other picture books) there is a casualness, a carefree spirit, and a childlike approach to the representation of details. It is this immediacy, simplicity, and directness of approach to the subject that beckons the child's spontaneous approval. The child feels akin to the pictures because of the "sudden" approach of the painter. Like Bemelmans, the child is also a dauber with the consequent boldness and freedom of effort. In Bemelmans the child gains an imaginative, visual communication, given with a vigorous and even an anxious manipulation of the artist's tools. The paintings say, "First a slap, then a splash, and then a quick stroke to finish up." The colors used are rich and satisfying—which renders a note of security. As a series of illustrations unfolds, it expresses to children a symbol of their rejection of academic art or that of scientific severity.

Beyond this, Bemelmans makes himself comprehensible to the child. The total effect of his painting adds to the intimacy of his words and pictures. His illustrations are full of hidden details that appeal to the child, that stimulate his curiosity, and that help to improve his span of attention. And all this is done without the hazards of over-statement of excessive complication.

And yet, despite this relationship to childlikeness, Bemelmans' illustrations are not vague and unrehearsed. He has firm aesthetic convictions. His pictures as they come to light are quite intentional and methodical in spite of their shroud of childlike naivety and comicalness.

We have undoubtedly witnessed in Bemelmans a major influence upon the art of children's picture books. To prove this, one need only page through an early *Madeline* book to henceforth instantly recognize on all occasions this unique and compelling talent. One must also say and rather regretfully, however, that the latter *Madeline* books failed to maintain the forceful promise of his earliest efforts. Thankfully this was only in the text. . . . [While] Bemelmans' visual artistry remained at a consistently high peak throughout his books, his writing, which hit its peak with *Madeline's Rescue,* fell to an embarrassingly mediocre level after 1953.

The reasons for this eclipse are probably complicated by the press of his other writing interests and perhaps even by a relaxation of effort that sometimes comes with success. It is important to say, nevertheless, that as a visual artist he was undiminished. (pp. 565-66)

Patrick Groff, "The Children's World of Ludwig Bemelmans" (copyright © 1966 by the National Council of Teachers of English; reprinted by permission of the publisher and the author), in Elementary English, *Vol. XLIII, No. 6, October, 1966, pp. 559-68.*

[It] was *Madeline* . . . that made Bemelmans famous. And with every succeeding Madeline book, Paris became more familiar to American children. Madeline falling into the Seine, Madeline grandly enjoying appendicitis, Madeline and the eleven other little girls searching for their dog, and Madeline in London—these big, handsome pictures, sketchily drawn but full of details and lovely color, have made Madeline and her creator forever beloved by children.

May Hill Arbuthnot and Zena Sutherland, "Artists and Children's Books: Ludwig Bemelmans, 1898-1962," in their Children and Books *(copyright © 1972, 1964, 1957, 1947 by Scott, Foresman and Company; reprinted by permission), fourth edition, Scott, Foresman, 1972, p. 64.*

Bemelmans' style is based on a strong sense of design and an ability to suggest movement. In *Madeline* . . . he uses the "twelve little girls" as page patterns. Wherever the twelve are placed, they are so arranged that the grouping of twelve similar shapes of capes, round hats, and thin legs forms a design on the page. His designer skills are evident also in the large full-page paintings in which he depicts monumental buildings, the panorama of a park, the zoo—all with the same humorous, free, and highly personal style.

A Bemelmans trademark is his ease in handling intricate architectural detail such as the facade of Notre Dame in Paris. He washes a color over and beyond the area in which he plans to place a building. The area of the wash is not specifically limited to or related to the structure of the building. He uses the same technique for the delineation of trees, and for the large white decorative urns in the park. This manner is very like that of the Dufy brothers in technique as well as in mood. The effect is gay and energetic, with an animated sense of design and pattern. His black-and-white pages are often audacious in their movement, as in the extreme acute angle used for Miss Clavel to run "fast and faster."

In *Madeline's Rescue* . . . Bemelmans continues in the same decorative manner, but the groupings of the twelve little girls are more variously handled. He utilizes the wide-brimmed hats, capes, and thin legs occasionally as one large shape; on one page all twelve little girls become a single blue shape, which is detailed not with his usual black line but with smaller shapes—twelve white collars, gloves, stockings, oval faces, and yellow hats. This kind of tightly knit design of smaller shapes and colors within a larger shape is illustrative of Bemelmans' awareness of design and his talent for reducing many complicated objects to a cohesive and decorative whole.

Sometimes Bemelmans forsakes elaborate background detail in favor of a solid-color ground wash. In *Madeline in London* . . . a double-page spread contains brilliantly colored birds, the girls' twelve yellow capes, and the guards' vermilion capes and white hats against a dull green ground color. On other pages (and this is more customary for Bemelmans) he fills the page from bottom to top with people, buildings, trees, fences, statues—everything his eye has recorded. As in other books, he reduces human forms into design patterns and still retains a feeling of movement. Sometimes this is accomplished by assigning the feeling of movement not only to one individual but to a whole crowd of people, who seem to move together as a river, flowing out from an urban background and becoming quite specific in the foreground.

Few artists have portrayed contemporary humanity as perceptively and sympathetically as Bemelmans, or with such pleasing spontaneity. (p. 48)

> *Donnarae MacCann and Olga Richard, "Outstanding Contemporary Illustrators: Ludwig Bemelmans (1898-1962)," in their* The Child's First Books: A Critical Study of Pictures and Texts *(copyright © 1973 by Donnarae MacCann and Olga Richard; reprinted by permission of The H. W. Wilson Company), Wilson, 1973, pp. 47-8.*

[Bemelmans] has blazed a trail for some of the most innovative of contemporary artists. His pictures have a new, cartoon-like quality, both when restricted to simple yellows and blacks and when running the gamut of riotous colors.

His pictures, too, are full of action: Miss Clavel, running "fast and faster to the scene of the disaster"; Pepito and Madeline whirling around on the ferris wheel; the gendarmes, with their hooks, rushing to fish Madeline out of the Seine. With their wild exaggeration, brilliant color, and wayward humor, they lead straight to the zany world of such popular modern illustrators as Maurice Sendak and Dr. Seuss. (p. 77)

> *Norah Smaridge, "Ludwig Bemelmans," in her* Famous Author-Illustrators for Young People *(copyright © 1973 by Norah Smaridge; reprinted by permission of Dodd, Mead and Company, Inc.), Dodd, Mead, 1973, pp. 70-7.*

Ingenious rhymes and the endless inventiveness of a superb caricaturist have established for all time Pepito the Bad Hat, Genevieve the excessively fertile bitch adopted by the school, Miss Clavel (always seen either stiffly vertical or fully extended as she runs even faster toward some anticipated disaster), and the demure individualist Madeline.

> *Margery Fisher, "Who's Who in Children's Books: Madeline," in her* Who's Who in Children's Books: A Treasury of the Familiar Characters of Childhood *(copyright © 1975 by Margery Fisher; reprinted by permission), Holt, Rinehart and Winston, 1975, Weidenfeld and Nicolson, 1975, p. 196.*

As a picturebook, [*Hansi*] is a monstrosity. Solid 9 x 12 pages of type confront similar pages with now a sketch at the top, now a colored panel part way down; for all its great size and its sixty-four pages, there are very few large-scale drawings: if Bemelmans gave any thought to the book he was making, there is no sign of it.

Still, *Hansi* is insidious. In Uncle Herman's house high in the mountains where Hansi goes for Christmas the smell of Lebkuchen spreads from cellar to roof. . . . Earlier, the little mountain train, short and fat, shares the station with a sleek streamliner from Paris and Vienna; the stationmaster, glorious in red and gold, signals the start with his baton; snow piled high on either side whispers snowballs but no, Hansi isn't to open the window. And then, quickly, Post Seppl waits at the station with his mail sleigh, Aunt Amalie, Uncle Herman, cousin Lieserl and dachshund Waldl wait at the door, and here is Hansi, "like a little sack of potatoes," mumbling, his long message muffled as much by embarrassment. . . . "If a dog is around that is a great help"—and Hansi pets Waldl, admires his tricks with Lieserl, follows her under the broad stomach of Romulus in the stable, proves to her that not even Uncle Herman can draw a pig without looking; and so, circuitously, reaches safe harbor. . . .

It is true that Bemelmans's interjections are adult observations, that he is writing not so much about a little boy named Hansi as about a little boy like Hansi, and with nostalgic affection. But he is observant—a dog *is* a great help in making friends—and he remembers well. The pictures reinforce him: however haphazard the overall scheme, individual illustrations are attentive to detail, brisk and good-humored. . . . Acknowledging Bemelmans's charm, Pitz disparages his draftsmanship [see excerpt above]—but in what does his charm consist, when setting and circumstances are removed, if not in the perpendicular of a peruke, a Roman brow, a child's broad jowls . . .? (pp. 48-9)

The Golden Basket is something of an anomaly too, but a more harmonious one however much it appears to flout the canons of book design by inserting what amount to unframed paintings, deep compositions with strong chiaroscuro, in the two-dimensional text pages. Though not a picturebook in proportions, it is wholly pictorial in conception, the workings of an inn and the byways of Bruges as seen by two little English girls. Celeste and Melisande wake in a strange red room, rose to crimson to scarlet to tomato; it is still night, and the square outside is bathed in blue, the street lamps and the finials glisten. . . . The scene is one to dream upon and back to bed they go; at breakfast, more wonders: two English ladies, look-alikes, with matching fur pieces—but one of the red foxes is cross-eyed, "and that is how they were told apart." (pp. 49-50)

A more sophisticated affair than *Hansi*, *The Golden Basket* is otherwise notable for the debut of Madeline, exquisite Madeline, at the end of a staid double line of little girls. (p. 50)

Castle Number Nine is Bemelmans's best story, and also his most interestingly illustrated book, a kind of running picture-story with everything in place—uniforms and pumps and wigs, innkeeper and courtyard, guard at his post, boy and gate and mountains beyond. Let the action narrow, and the picture cuts in—the count's poodle chases Baptiste's cat, followed by Baptiste's foot; let it spread, let dog pursue cat from cellar to tower, and we get a cross-section of the castle. It is an illustrated manuscript with the fluidity of a film.

With *Madeline* Bemelmans settled down to charm all and sundry and succeeded. Does anyone who knows it not know the story, not remember the verses, not summon up the two as one? The words are the story / and phrase by phrase they are the images / that Bemelmans paints page by page: there is hardly another book quite so compact and close-knit and self-reinforcing. (pp. 50-1)

From The Golden Basket, *written and illustrated by Ludwig Bemelmans.*

One comes to think of **Madeline** in terms of color but actually there is full color at only four openings, where outdoor scenes occur, which should be a lesson of several sorts. Most of the illustrations are in black, or black and white, against a yellow ground, and they have the character of drawings as distinct from the Dufy-like paintings. . . . That the two don't conflict, that the abbreviated cartoon style of the former is for the most part not violated by overdevelopment in the latter, has much to do with making the book an artistic whole; when the reverse occurs in **Madeline's Rescue,** when the drawing becomes cruder and more cursory, the painting more dense and detailed, the illustration suffers as such and the total design falls apart.

In no respect do the later books have the integrity of **Madeline,** and one looks thereafter to his adult work for the best of Bemelmans. (p. 51)

> *Barbara Bader, "Foreign Backgrounds: Bemelmans," in her* American Picture Books from Noah's Ark to the Beast Within *(reprinted with permission of Macmillan Publishing Company; copyright © 1976 by Barbara Bader), Macmillan, 1976, pp. 47-51.*

HANSI (1934)

["**Hansi**"] is as fresh and zestful as the air up in those high [Austrian] valleys. It tells of Hansi, a small boy who goes from his village up into the higher mountains to visit his uncle and aunt and cousins at Christmas time. In the end-papers we get a view of Uncle Herman's house and the things in it that will absorb boys and girls who have a feeling for detail. Everything is there, from the ax and the wood-block to the rocking-horse! The story is an appealing one, so real that we confidently expect to see Hansi and Lieserl the next time we travel through the Tyrolean valleys. It is vivid and alive, full of the feeling of the winter season in high places, of crisp snow and cold, far peaks against a brilliant sky. The Christmas service at midnight in the white church holds the very heart of Christmas in the old world. . . .

There is humor in both story and pictures, but we find ourselves wondering why the drawings hover so near to the burlesque. Not all of them—the little white church is real. And so is Waldl, the dachshund, dashing down the snowy slopes on skis. Looking at this picture, children will wonder if Waldl got his skis, and what happened to him at the end of the exciting journey. In some of the pictures you feel the background, the atmosphere of the mountains and the quaint little village, but there is, too, a quality that is almost caricature. It is a pity, because to the children the story will seem entirely true—as well it might be.

> *Mary Gould Davis, in a review of "Hansi," in* New York Herald Tribune Books *(© I.H.T. Corporation; reprinted by permission), November 11, 1934, p. 8.*

From The Castle Number Nine, *written and illustrated by Ludwig Bemelmans.*

Here is a book which promptly takes us to another country, not as a mere tourist, but as one who has for guide a friend to whom that country is dear and familiar. Ever after we shall have the feeling that we have stayed in the Austrian Tyrol long enough to feel at home, and to be on friendly terms with its people. (p. 17)

The artist-author of **"Hansi"** has put down his own recollections in a way that will not only make the Christmas celebration and the Austrian Tyrol vivid to child readers, but will intensify their enjoyment of their own experiences and their own country. Mr. Bemelman has kept the ability to see with children's eyes and he remembers vividly what a small boy enjoys. The pictures are delightful; they give a real feeling of the country, and have a humor that children will find irresistible. The colors used are warm and pleasing. A good book for a Christmas gift for 7 to 9 year olds and even for grown-ups who love the Austrian Tyrol. (p. 24)

Anne T. Eaton, in a review of "Hansi," in The New York Times Book Review (© 1934 by The New York Times Company; reprinted by permission), November 11, 1934, pp. 17, 24.

["**Hansi**"] should come high in any list. Mr. Bemelmans has done both pictures and text, and both are original and delightful. . . . It is done with great freshness and simplicity and a sense of humor. I find myself wanting to quote many things, which is always a good sign. I wish I might also show the book's end-papers which depict the interior of Uncle Herman's house and are a delight for children. There is a curious underlying wisdom and nostalgia in this book, as if Mr. Bemelmans were remembering his own childhood. It is remarkable that anyone who had done sophisticated murals for a New York restaurant can be versatile enough to sustain a childlike mood so well.

Rosemary Carr Benét, in a review of "Hansi," in The Saturday Review of Literature (© 1934, copyright renewed © 1962, Saturday Review Magazine Co.; reprinted by permission), Vol. XI, No. 18, November 17, 1934, p. 296.

THE GOLDEN BASKET (1936)

Ludwig Bemelmans, in his pretty volume, **The Golden Basket** . . . , makes a strong appeal to the imagination of an adult. Taking the old Hôtel du Panier d'Or in Bruges for his setting, and two little girls and their English father as travelers, Mr. Bemelmans has put them in such intimate touch with the cook, Monsieur Meulen, and his son Jan, who embody the spirit of art and pride in the smallest service, that they come to love the whole city of Bruges and learn a lot about it. While the story is not so clearly drawn as that of **Hansi** . . . , it is a book containing the quintessence of the spirit of travel in any land; and, most important of all, it is concerned with the live interests of children rather than with those of the teacher or parent traveler. One has an enlarged conception of Bruges, of all Belgium, after reading and looking at the pictures Mr. Bemelmans has drawn for this book.

Anne Carroll Moore, in a review of "The Golden Basket," in The Atlantic Monthly (copyright © 1936, by The Atlantic Monthly Company, Boston, Mass.; reprinted with permission), Vol. 158, No. 4, October, 1936, p. 13.

Often stories for children about other lands inform but do not convince. The facts are there but not the spirit. Thus it is a heartening experience to discover such a book as **"The Golden Basket,"** which, like the magic traveling cloak of the fairy tales, carries the reader away to the very place and the very people described in the story. When Mr. Horatio Coggeshall, manufacturer of pianos, brings his two little daughters from London to visit Bruges, we are not told how they came and what they did—we arrive with them, hearing the horses' hoofs on the cobblestones; seeing the Golden Basket, the sign of the inn, lit up by a street lamp; waking up with the little girls in the room with the red rose wall paper and the big red furniture; making friends with Jan . . . and with Monsieur ter Meulen . . . ; enjoying an acquaintance with Monsieur Carnewal, the maitre d'hôtel. . . .

There are carillons and canals, there are bridges and squares and weathered gabled houses, there is greenness and coolness, light and shade, and life quietly lived against a background of tradition. In the midst of it all three very lively children contrive to amuse themselves enormously, and are described so naturally that the reader feels as though he were eavesdropping in the next room.

Text and drawings must be thought of together, for together they tell the story and together they make the reader feel the atmosphere of this grave and charming city. The pictures have the gayety and humor and satisfying detail that have made the illustrations in Mr. Bemelmans's **"Hansi"** so popular and, like **"Hansi," "The Golden Basket,"** because of its zest, its light-heartedness and its sincerity, is a book that will be cherished and enjoyed not only by 7 to 10 year olds, but by their elders.

Anne Eaton, in a review of "The Golden Basket," in The New York Times Book Review (© 1936 by The New York Times Company; reprinted by permission), October 4, 1936, p. 12.

From Hansi, *written and illustrated by Ludwig Bemelmans.*

[Arriving very late at the Golden Basket Inn, Celeste and Melisande slept in] a singularly engaging room, and with the enviable capacity of children for coming all at once awake all over, took in the details of its furnishings. It was all red, different shades, but all loud and cheerful. The plush curtains had pompons; the chair cushions were the color of a very ripe tomato. "It's very lovely," breathed the little girls, climbed out of the towering bed, looked out of the casement window and saw the beautiful town. Mr. Bemelmans shows it to you in many colors, as you would see it if you were very happy, quite young, and held your head over on one side. The result, as in all his pictures, is gay and exhilarating. . . .

The ingenuity of the little girls in not being bored with the rain is little less than dazzling. . . .

If any one reading [the passage where the girls ask Jan for something with which to steer their play submarine] has the least doubt that this author knows just how children talk and act when their minds are set on something really important, and even how they feel when in this state of mind, he does not know as much about this as Mr. Bemelmans does. Or as Jan does; he gets the coffee-mill without more ado, the meat-grinder being fastened to the table. It is obvious that the submarine will be made of chairs and need this steering-gear.

So it goes; nothing alarming, nothing that might not conceivably happen almost anywhere in the neighborhood of such ingenious and sociable little girls, but that here gets the co-operation of everybody in a cheerful foreign *pension* and indeed of most of the people the children meet in Bruges. But because the humor of its telling is so constant, unforced and what one might almost call *sotto voce*, all this makes entertainment on which one looks back with gratitude. One is sorry to see the last of the little girls in Bruges. . . .

The pictures of this jolly artist grow on one. These are not deliberately grotesque, like those Hansi, in an earlier story, is supposed himself to have made. They do, however, continue

to take the law into their own hands, watch the world askew, and set it down in riotous colors that express the emotional effect of nature quite as much as the outward appearance. The result is one of pure and contagious exuberance.

> *May Lamberton Becker, "Boys Sail Off: Girls Reach Bruges," in* New York Herald Tribune Books *(© I.H.T. Corporation; reprinted by permission), November 15, 1936, p. 12.**

[Hotel of the Golden Basket] is the background of Mr. Bemelmans' latest and successful book for children of third and fourth grades. . . . The author-artist has the gift of seeing as a child sees, so that in his text and in his illustrations he unerringly selects details significant to young readers. As a story, as a book of pictures, and as an introduction to the quaint charm of Bruges, *The Golden Basket* is a distinguished book. (pp. 929-30)

> *Marjorie F. Potter, in a review of "Golden Basket," in* Library Journal *(copyright © 1936 by Xerox Corporation), Vol. 62, No. 19, December 1, 1936, pp. 929-30.*

To present-day readers [Celeste, Melisande, and Jan] seem like paper dolls. Much of the information included would interest adults more than children. For example, the author gives a detailed history of one of the great church towers they visit. The illustrations, done in the same exuberant manner as those of the Madeline stories, are far more distinguished than the text. It would seem that it was the intention of the Newbery Committee to honor the illustrations. The Caldecott Award for outstanding picture books had not been established at the time this book was written.

> *Linda Kauffman Peterson and Marilyn Leathers Solt, "The Newbery Medal and Honor Books, 1922-1981: 'The Golden Basket'," in their* Newbery and Caldecott Medal and Honor Books: An Annotated Bibliography *(copyright 1982 by Marilyn Solt and Linda Peterson), G. K. Hall & Co., 1982, p. 63.*

THE CASTLE NUMBER NINE   (1937)

The amusing tale of Baptiste, the perfect butler, who had a uniform of a different color for each day of the week. When he came to Castle No. 9 in Austria, his master renamed many objects in his home and the resulting confusion was as great as in the folk tale "Master of all masters" and, this time, most tragic. Attractive illustrations. The story will appeal to third to fifth grade children and to some younger ones when read aloud.

> *A review of "The Castle Number Nine," in* The Booklist *(reprinted by permission of the American Library Association; copyright © 1937 by the American Library Association), Vol. 34, No. 5, November 1, 1937, p. 96.*

[*Castle Number Nine*] is an enchanting book, written and drawn for the pure enjoyment of every imaginable child. Count Hungerburg-Hungerburg's old Austrian castle with its lovely baroque furnishings is the setting. The old count in his ruffles, laces, and wig, and the conscientious Baptiste . . . are its dignified comedians. The pictures are irresistible.

> *Irene Smith, in a review of "Castle Number Nine," in* Library Journal *(copyright © 1937 by Xerox Cor-*

poration), Vol. 62, No. 19, November 1, 1937, p. 808.

This variant of the legend of Master of All Masters—not so well known to all children as it is to all folk-lorists—becomes something new under Mr. Bemelmans's familiar method of treatment. . . .

The pictures are high, wide and handsome, the rococo court costumes coming out especially well in colors. The poodle, too, is a sight to remember.

May Lamberton Becker, "Salt Water, High Water, Magic and an Island," in New York Herald Tribune Books *(© I.H.T. Corporation; reprinted by permission), November 14, 1937, p. 9.* *

What happened as a result [of renaming household items], and why the Count changed the names back again, makes a story which children find uproariously funny and one in which older readers, if they choose, may see a deeper meaning.

"The Castle No. 9" has the sturdy quality of a fine old fairy tale, it has also the atmosphere of a gracious country and a gentle age, the age of Mozart's music, of Baroque and Biedermeier. The pictures have a detail that delights children and an enchanting humor. At Baptiste's side we may, young and old, visit a story book castle which is at the same time strangely real, seeing it complete from cellar to topmost tower. May Mr. Bemelmans give us many more picture-story books with the beauty, freshness and fun of Castle No. 9.

Anne T. Eaton, "A Bemelmans Story," in The New York Times Book Review *(© 1937 by The New York Times Company; reprinted by permission), November 14, 1937, p. 14.*

QUITO EXPRESS (1938)

In **"Quito Express,"** Pedro's trip is more or less involuntary. He is so small his talk is limited to "Dadadada," and when he crawls up on the seat in the train and goes to sleep between two ladies, each thinks he belongs to the other till he is far from home. . . . When at last the train returns to Quito there is his little sister, who says "That's Pedro"—and everybody is blissful, including me, for the little book charmed me, it is so unexpected and lovable. The pictures are in brown chalk, at first somewhat baffling but soon capturing the affections, for the book is Bemelmans at his kindest.

May Lamberton Becker, in a review of "Quito Express," in New York Herald Tribune Books *(© I.H.T. Corporation), October 23, 1938, p. 8.*

Ludwig Bemelmans brings to every new experience a lively curiosity and a ready sympathy and thus children are delighted at finding in his books an enjoyment and zest that is like their own. . . .

[The astonished conductor], the sleepy passengers, the tourists, the conductor's brother who ran the motor boat Gloria, the conductor's patient efforts to return Pedro to his family and the aplomb of Pedro himself are drawn and described with a delicious humour.

"Quito Express" will be as much fun for the adult who reads it aloud as for the children who listen. The drawings are in Mr. Bemelmans's best vein and the pleasure he so plainly had in making them is contagious.

Anne T. Eaton, "Mr. Bemelmans Again," in The New York Times Book Review *(© 1938 by The New York Times Company; reprinted by permission), October 30, 1938, p. 12.*

What of Mr. Bemelmans and his lost Inca baby in Ecuador? To me it is the least appealing of all his amusing books, and the attempt to show a small child Ecuador is one not worth making in this way. The way he sprinkles things around on pages—a nightgown, a baby's bottle, the sun—is always engaging. But the usual child does not like the full page pictures, in my experience. For the open-minded parent it is a book to experiment with. There should be inspiration for the young artist in the ease and strength of these sophisticated sketches.

Louise Seaman Bechtel, in a review of "Quito Express," in The Saturday Review of Literature *(© 1938, copyright renewed © 1965, Saturday Review Magazine Co.; reprinted by permission), Vol. XIX, No. 4, November 19, 1938, p. 18.*

MADELINE (1939)

Ludwig Bemelmans's sense of fun, genuine enjoyment of the absurd and feeling for places are all thoroughly congenial to children.

"Madeline" is a slighter tale than his earlier ones, but there is a brisk and amusing quality in this account of twelve little Parisian school girls who "in an old house covered with vines," practically lived their lives "in two straight lines." For "in two straight lines they broke their bread, and brushed their teeth and went to bed." Rain or shine, they took their walks in the same formation, carrying on their daily occupations with the utmost regularity till Madeline broke the pattern by having appendicitis. Though the beginning of her illness was painful, recovery in the hospital with visits and flowers and kind attention from the nurses proved so pleasant that all the other little girls clamored for the same experience!

Gayety is the keynote of the book in text and pictures, nevertheless Mr. Bemelmans's drawings of the opera, of Notre Dame in the rain, of the sun shining on birds and children in the Luxembourg and Tuileries Gardens have put an authentic Paris within the covers of this book. The rhyme and strongly marked rhythm with which the tale is told make it one that children of pre-school age will enjoy repeating with the aid of the pictures as they turn the pages. For children 6 to 8, and for readers of any age who love Paris.

Anne T. Eaton, "Charm in Paris," in The New York Times Book Review *(© 1939 by The New York Times Company; reprinted by permission), September 24, 1939, p. 12.*

[Madeline] is certainly one of the people you will want to meet, not only for her sake, but because the pictures in the book include some beautiful reproductions of real scenes in Paris. The fact that the story is told in couplets will make it doubly popular, I believe. If children have a chance to see it, they will like it. So far, the adults seem to have been enjoying this story. . . . [It] should be seen to be appreciated; but, "For goodness' sake—read **Madeline**!"

Josephine Smith, in a review of "Madeline," in Junior Libraries, *an appendix to* Library Journal *(reprinted from the November, 1939 issue of* Junior Libraries, *published by R. R. Bowker Co./ A Xerox*

Corporation; copyright © 1939), Vol. 64, No. 19, November, 1939, p. 848.

A funnier book in its own demure and different way I have not seen this year, nor one more likely to please both little people and their elders without appealing to precocity in one or sophistication in the other. Madeline has appeared to great applause in a stylish magazine for grown-ups: on the other hand, there is a child in a New York school who owes a considerable popularity largely to being able to recite her story from one end to the other with appropriate action.

It would not take long. It is practically in the big color pictures. . . [You] should see Mr. Bemelmans's cockeyed Paris landscapes through which [the girls] walk in the rain or sun. . . .

I suppose there's a moral [in **Madeline**]; I didn't look for it. I was too busy laughing. This is fun that won't go out of style.

May Lamberton Becker, in a review of "Madeline," in New York Herald Tribune Books *(© I.H.T. Corporation), November 12, 1939, p. 14.*

Among the most treasured of pre-war memories is that of the lovely picture-books, imported from the U.S.A., by the Haders, the D'Aulaires, Artzybasheff, and many others. My own favourites among these were the joyous, colourful books—**The Castle Number Nine** stays most firmly in my memory—in which Ludwig Bemelmans exactly matched his stories with pictures of incomparable vigour and simplicity. . . . [And now we have **Madeline**], one of the best of these books. . . .

Not much of a story, and in doggerel at that, but drawn with a sweet simplicity which is quite irresistible. Mr. Bemelmans draws like a child of genius and he sees the world through a child's wondering eyes.

This is a picture book of the highest quality, original, true and beautiful. It will be an earnest of hope for the book world if it has a tremendous sale.

A review of "Madeline," in The Junior Bookshelf, *Vol. 17, No. 1, January, 1953, p. 12.*

Readers usually think of this as merely a delightful picture book, which it certainly is, without realizing that the accompanying verse has its own enchantment:

> In an old house in Paris that was covered with vines
> Lived twelve little girls in two straight lines.

How nicely this falls on the ear, and how clearly it appeals to the small child's sense of arrangement, delineation, and proportion. Marianne Moore has written: "We call climax a device, but is it not the natural result of strong feeling? It is, moreover, a pyramid that can rest either on its point or on its base, witty anticlimax being one of Ludwig Bemelmans' best enticements, as when he says:

> They smiled at the good
> and frowned at the bad
> and sometimes they were very sad."

Virginia Haviland and William Jay Smith, in a review of "Madeline," in their Children & Poetry: A Selective, Annotated Bibliography *(reprinted by permission of Virginia Haviland and William Jay Smith),* The Library of Congress, 1969, p. 3 [the excerpts of Ludwig Bemelmans's work used here were originally published in his Madeline (copyright 1939 by Ludwig Bemelmans; copyright © renewed 1967 by Madeleine Bemelmans and Barbara Bemelmans Marci-

ano; reprinted by permission of Viking Penguin Inc.), Simon and Schuster, 1939].

[**Madeline**] is one of the first early Award Books to introduce a digression from the sedate, low-keyed books that dominate the early years of the Caldecott Medal. This rhyming text . . . moves the story along with action, both in word and picture. The repetition in the illustrations and the long and narrow spatial feelings resulting from this repetition move the eyes up and down with the rhythmic verse of the text. . . .

[The story] nearly begs to be reread and perused.

The illustrations, full of motion and life, expertly expand the text and the artist's conception of such abstractions as good, bad, and sad. Eight full-color illustrations are interspersed among pages of yellow, black, and white watercolor, pen, and ink, adding variety and interest to the book's format. The full-color pages contain much more detail than the others, but the expressionism, present in all the illustrations, is an integral part of the book. As "Miss Clavel ran fast/and faster," the diagonal tilt of her body and of the hallway offers an abstract visualization of the motion present in the situation. It is just this ability to express the essence of an idea in the simplicity of a few lines, shapes, and words, that makes Bemelmans' work, text and illustrations, an integrated, cooperative unit that does not lose its flavor, reading after reading.

Linda Kauffman Peterson and Marilyn Leathers Solt, "The Caldecott Medal and Honor Books, 1938-1981: 'Madeline'," in their Newbery and Caldecott Medal and Honor Books: An Annotated Bibliography *(copyright 1982 by Marilyn Solt and Linda Peterson), G. K. Hall & Co., 1982, p. 244.*

ROSEBUD (1942)

That wily African great-great-granddaddy of Br'er Rabbit has popped up again. At least Mr. Bemelmans claims his story is based on an old African folktale and certainly his Rosebud is as tricky and ingenious as Uncle Remus's practical joker.

Rosebud, in some way accountable only by Mr. Bemelmans, has gotten hold of a book of natural history and is greatly disturbed by its invidious comparisons drawn between the lion, the whale, the elephant, and the rabbit, who it says "is scared, shy and hysterical." Looking like an irritated professor, Rosebud decides he must redeem the reputation of all rabbitdom and so forthwith he challenges the whale, a gorgeous violet creature basking amidst ultramarine waves, to a tug of war. Likewise the elephant. The contest is at night and in the dark it is a simple matter for one of Rosebud's wit to rope the unsuspecting mammoths together and let them tug it out to a violent finish, and equally simple to bluff each one into thinking that he, Rosebud, is a creature of superb muscle and sinew.

The fable certainly seems to bear the earmarks of a genuine folktale, even dressed up in brisk dialogue which carries its own latter-day punch. The pictures are Mr. Bemelmans at his most extravagant, which in this case isn't Bemelmans at his best. You couldn't indeed, without information or a good deal of imagination identify Rosebud as a rabbit offhand. But that perhaps is just doing arithmetic in the mouth of a merry little gifthorse, and certainly the colors, purple, blue and peppermint pink, are a delight to the eye.

Ellen Lewis Buell, "The Tricky Rabbit," in The New York Times Book Review *(© 1942 by The New York*

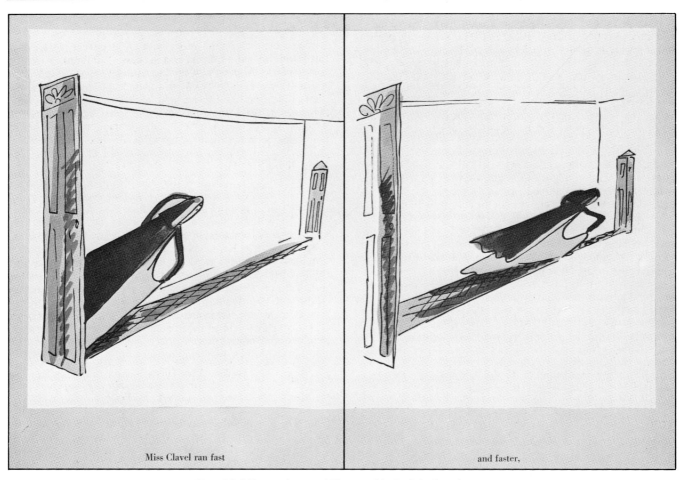

Miss Clavel ran fast   and faster,

From Madeline, *written and illustrated by Ludwig Bemelmans.*

Times Company; reprinted by permission), October 4, 1942, p. 35.

Rosebud was a rabbit the like of which you never saw save in dreams, of a color we now call shocking pink, to match his conduct. . . .

This fable, related in colored pictures of Bemelmans' mad design, makes up for technique by extraordinary vigor, such as you might expect from the dynamic Rosebud.

> *May Lamberton Becker, in a review of "Rosebud," in* New York Herald Tribune Books (© *I.H.T. Corporation), November 22, 1942, p. 12.*

Rosebud was a rabbit, though the pictures in varied colors do not make the fact too plain.

Pictures and text are absurd, but children will like this new funny book which has a certain folktale quality. . . .

> *Alice M. Jordan, in a review of "Rosebud," in* The Horn Book Magazine *(copyrighted, 1942, by The Horn Book, Inc., Boston), Vol. XVIII, No. 6, November-December, 1942, p. 417.*

SUNSHINE (1950)

Not entirely for the children is this latest by the fine-knifed master of satire. Although the "juvenile" Bemelmans of *Made-*

line has an imaginative, gentle whimsy, here the verse is often over-sophisticated and relies on experiences familiar only to adults—room renting, lawyers and leases. However, the situations are delightful. . . . The illustrations by the author, full color and black with one color, are delightful. The rain has never rained so hard over New York, nor the snow snowed in Central Park with such glittering brilliance. . . . Bemelmans' followers will gobble it up.

> *A review of "Sunshine," in* Virginia Kirkus' Bookshop Service, *Vol. XVIII, No. 9, May 1, 1950, p. 260.*

Awaited most eagerly, at last the new Bemelmans is here. Does it do for New York what the beloved **"Madeline"** did for Paris? Does it tell a clear, crisp little tale like that one, close to the hearts of all from four to eighty? No, it does not. But a lusty sense of contemporary city life is here, and some of the big, full-page paintings give back our New York with swift stabs of surprise and beauty. There are gorgeous end papers of Manhattan from the East River, in the snow. And, of course, the funny people are the same old master's inimitable characters—mean old man Sunshine, the daft music teacher, the lawyer, the policeman, the two U.N. delegates. There is no hero or heroine, little or grown-up, to clasp to the heart as we have Madeline, but there is lots of fun, on an older level.

The story is told in pretty informal verse, and it will amuse those young New Yorkers who are fairly sophisticated, of eight or nine, as well as all Bemelmans's adult fans. "Sunshine," evidently so-called in satire, at last found the seemingly perfect tenant for his apartment, a quiet old lady. But she was a music teacher, with dogs and cats and dozens of noisy pupils, who seem always to take lessons as an orchestra. Sunshine kept trying to get her out, and had to move out himself. She almost lost when she bought, by mistake, at an auction, not one umbrella, but all the 2,000 found in the subways. Never mind, the rain came, and she and the children went all over the city selling the umbrellas. . . .

At the end, Christmas is thrown in, with Sunshine coming back, repentant for no known reason, to live again in the same apartment house. It is an odd, inchoate sort of story, and it is a pity that the famous author has not the sort of rhyming ability possessed by, for instance, the author of "Albert the Camel." . . . But one must not complain of Mr. Bemelmans: he is a law unto himself, and if that is how he imagined the real music school on Gramercy Park, we take it as it comes. He gives us a fresh sense of the possibilities for fun in looking at our city, and as art his work is far above that in any other spring picturebook.

> *Louise S. Bechtel, "Prize Books," in* New York Herald Tribune Book Review *(© I.H.T. Corporation), May 7, 1950, p. 7.**

Even small children are aware of the housing shortage. Still, it is doubtful if they will enter whole-heartedly into Ludwig Bemelmans' story of a snide landlord. Mr. Bemelmans, who has written some wonderful nonsense stories for children, is certainly not at his best in his account of a feud between [Sunshine and Miss Moore]. . . . The story is more extravagant than funny and the verses are often heavy-footed. This is very sad because the pictures are so delightful. Both children and parents will enjoy the New York City scenes, the pictures of the orchestra in full swing and of the children in full cry, all done with Mr. Bemelmans' special brand of wacky fun and faultless sense of color.

> *Ellen Lewis Buell, "Curmudgeon's Rout," in* The New York Times Book Review *(© 1950 by The New York Times Company; reprinted by permission), May 14, 1950, p. 30.*

The few children who appreciate Bemelmans' art will enjoy these illustrations. This is, however, an adult book and it should be treated as such. Too much of the humor depends on an adult understanding and, when this is lacking, leaves the child with concepts that are not only un-funny but are actually wrong. Recommended for all *adult* departments in libraries.

> *A review of "Sunshine," in* Bulletin of the Children's Book Center *(reprinted by permission of The University of Chicago Press), Vol. 3, No. 7, June, 1950, p. 44.*

The individuality and flavor of Bemelmans' work are apparent in this picture book of New York, though the freshness, spontaneity, and originality of *Madeline* are missing. . . . [The tale is] told in labored rhyme. End papers and a few of the illustrations are most effective.

> *Alice McQuaid, in a review of "Sunshine," in* Library Journal *(copyright © 1950 by Xerox Corporation), Vol. 75, No. 14, August, 1950, p. 1305.*

THE HAPPY PLACE   (1952)

Bemelmans in an animal story with a bittersweet moral, narrated with his calm humor, is a success. Winthrop, a forlorn Easter bunny, is bought at the last minute[, soon ousted from his new family, and chased by a whippet]. . . . He befriends a frog, then hops to the zoo and befriends a lonely but sympathetic elephant who sends him back to the frog with a present of a glass frog—the elephant's only companion piece—which in turn gets eaten by and causes the death of a cormorant. Adults too will enjoy seeing the wonderful Bemelmans' pictures. (pp. 499-500)

> *A review of "The Happy Place," in* Virginia Kirkus' Bookshop Service, *Vol. XX, No. 16, August 15, 1952, pp. 499-500.*

[Winthrop's adventures] make up a light-hearted extravaganza. Like most of Mr. Bemelmans' nonsense tales it is put together with scant regard for logic but with abundant originality and humor. Much of this humor (as one also expects from the author) is of the adult variety, like the prose. Once launched in the story however, any normal youngster will undoubtedly be caught up in the suspense of Winthrop's hairbreadth escapes and relax happily when peace and good-will are finally established in the Happy Place.

> *Ellen Lewis Buell, "Adventures of Winthrop," in* The New York Times Book Review *(© 1952 by The New York Times Company; reprinted by permission), September 21, 1952, p. 32.*

The story has an adult humor and sophistication that will be meaningless to most children who will, however, enjoy Winthrop as an unusual rabbit. The story will be fun to read aloud, and children and adults alike will enjoy Bemelmans' drawings.

> *A review of "The Happy Place," in* Bulletin of the Children's Book Center *(reprinted by permission of The University of Chicago Press), Vol. 6, No. 2, October, 1952, p. 12.*

In ***The Happy Place,*** Ludwig Bemelmans serves up the recipe that he first concocted many years ago for adult consumption; it consists of some absurd character put down in a setting that is just around the block and dolloped with matter of fact nonsense. . . . Winthrop chums up with other park animals, and together they create a typical Bemelmans mixture in a world of magic which is entered, naturally and easily, "at 104th Street and Central Park West." (p. 106)

> *"The Children's Hour," in* Time *(copyright 1952 Time Inc.; all rights reserved; reprinted by permission from* Time), *Vol. LX, No. 23, December 8, 1952, pp. 106, 109.*

MADELINE'S RESCUE   (1953)

AUTHOR'S COMMENTARY

There is one life that is more difficult than that of the policeman's and that is the life of the artist.

I have repeatedly said two things that no one takes seriously, and they are that first of all I am not a writer but a painter, and secondly that I have no imagination. It is very curious that, with my lack of these important essentials, the character of Madeline came to be. It accounts perhaps for her strength; she insisted on being born. Before she came into the world, I painted. That is, I placed canvas or paper on an easel before me and made pictures. I found in this complete happiness and satisfaction.

The unfortunate thing about painting is that the artist must exhibit, and at exhibitions, along with his work, exhibit himself; that he has to see his work, which is as his children, sold; see it wrapped up and taken away. I felt sorry for many of my pictures and those of other painters. I wish that there were a way of acquiring dogs or paintings other than by walking into a store and paying for them. The art market, then, the faces of the people who come and look at pictures, the methods of arriving at success, which entail self-advertisement and the kissing of hands, were not my dish.

I looked for another way of painting, for privacy; for a fresh audience, vast and critical and remote, to whom I could address myself with complete freedom. I wanted to do what seemed self-evident—to avoid sweet pictures, the eternal still lifes, the pretty portraits that sell well, arty abstractions, pastoral fireplace pictures, calendar art, and surrealist nightmares.

I wanted to paint purely that which gave me pleasure, scenes that interested me; and one day I found that the audience for that kind of painting was a vast reservoir of impressionists who did very good work themselves, who were very clear-eyed and capable of enthusiasm. I addressed myself to children.

You will notice in **Madeline** that there is very little text and there is a lot of picture. The text allows me the most varied type of illustration: there is the use of flowers, of the night, of all of Paris, and such varied detail as the cemetery of *Père la Chaise* and the Restaurant of the *Deux Magots*. All this was there waiting to be used, but as yet Madeline herself hovered about as an unborn spirit.

Her beginnings can be traced to stories my mother told me of her life as a little girl in the convent of Altoetting in Bavaria. I visited this convent with her and saw the little beds in straight rows, and the long table with the washbasins at which the girls had brushed their teeth. I myself, as a small boy, had been sent to a boarding school in Rothenburg. We walked through that ancient town in two straight lines. I was the smallest one, but our arrangement was reversed. I walked ahead in the first row, not on the hand of Mademoiselle Clavel at the end of the column.

All this, as I said, for many years hung in the air and was at the back of my mind. Madeline finally began to take shape in France, where I had gone to paint. (pp. 270-71)

[While riding his bicycle on the Isle d'Yeu, Bemelmans collided with a car and was hospitalized]. Here were the stout sister that you see bringing the tray to Madeline, and the crank on the bed. In the room across the hall was a little girl who had had an appendix operation, and, standing up in bed, with great pride she showed her scar to me. Over my bed was the crack in the ceiling "That had the habit, of sometimes looking like a rabbit." It all began to arrange itself. And after I got back to Paris I started to paint the scenery for the book. I looked up telephone numbers to rhyme with appendix. One day I had a meeting with Léon Blum, and if you take a look at the book, you will see that the doctor who runs to Madeline's bed is the great patriot and humanitarian Léon Blum.

And so Madeline was born, or rather appeared by her own decision.

Now we come to the sequel. . . .

In this story Madeline shares the pages with a dog. This dog came about in a strange way. My wife's parents live in Larchmont, and in a house next door to them is a family of outwardly respectable folk—that is, no one in that solid community would suspect that this quiet and respectable suburban house was occupied by a poet. Her name is Phyllis McGinley and she writes for *The New Yorker*.

She has two little girls, and they said, "Why don't you write another **Madeline**?" So I offered them fifty cents apiece if they would give me an Idea, for I was paralyzed with lack of imagination. The children did not even go out of the room. They came with hands held out, and after I paid them they stated the plot:

"There's a dog, see—Madeline has a dog. And then the dog is taken away but it comes back again, maybe with puppies so all the girls can have dogs."

That was tight and clever dramatic construction, and now there remained the dog to find. I said, "What kind of a dog?"

"Oh, any kind of a dog."

I went back to Paris and started to look for any kind of a dog. And of that breed Genevieve is a member.

I had a studio at the time in a house on the Seine at number one *Git de Coeur,* and I walked down to the quay and promenaded along there. Under one of the bridges there lived an old man with his dog. He loved it very much and he combed its fur with the same comb he did his own hair, and they sat together watching the fishermen and the passing boats. I started to draw that dog, and observed it. It loved to swim.

I now had the dog and I sat along the Seine, and thought about the new book. But as yet there wasn't a plot I could use, and the little girls who might have done it for me were in America.

Then one day something happened. An object was floating down the Seine, and little boys ran along the quay, and as the object came near it turned out to be an artificial leg. (pp. 273-74)

At that same moment a long line of little girls passed over the bridge *des Arts,* followed by their teacher. They stopped and looked, holding onto the iron rails with their white-gloved hands. The leg was now very close, and the dog jumped into the Seine and retrieved it, struggling ashore and pulling it from the water by backing up the stones.

There suddenly was a great vision before me. The plot was perfect.

There are many problems ahead. Who are Madeline's parents? Who are the other girls, what are their names, what new disaster shall Mademoiselle Clavel rush to? The next **Madeline** on which I have been working for two years concerns a boy called Pepito, the son of the Spanish Ambassador who lives next door to the little girls and is a very bad hat.

I'm looking for him now. That is, I've been to Spain three times and searched for him and for his house. As yet, nothing has come up, but with patience it always does, for somewhere he is, lives and breathes. The portrait of life is the most important work of the artist and it is good only when you've seen it, when you've touched it, when you know it. Then you can breathe life onto canvas and paper. (p. 275)

Ludwig Bemelmans, "Caldecott Award Acceptance"
(originally a paper read at the meeting of the American Library Association on June 22, 1954), in The

Horn Book Magazine *(copyrighted, 1954, by The Horn Book, Inc., Boston), Vol. XXX, No. 4, August, 1954, pp. 270-75.*

In a fine big book
With nice large printing
And dozens of pictures,
Gleaming and glinting,
There's news this spring that's simply fine.
For guess who's back?
Madeline!
Does she still dwell
With Miss Clavel?
She does;
And a noble dog, as well,
Whom you must see to believe,
And whose name is Genevieve.
Perhaps the author would as lief
We all pronounced it "Genevief,"
But call her anything you choose,
Still she is delightful news.
Though Madeline's a total stranger,
G. rescues her from dreadful danger,
And then all sorts of things occur
To Madeline, the school, and her
Which I shan't say a word, indeed, about,
Because it's much more fun to read about.

The rhymes are rather
Off the cuff;
There's not much story,
But story enough
To please the hundred thousand fans
Of Mr. Ludwig Bemelmans.
And lightsome or thunderful,
The pictures are wonderful
That tell this tale of Madeline.
(I think I counted forty-nine,
Though if you add the jacket, you
Might count as high as fifty-two);
All full of witty sweets and spices
As Miss Clavel's is full of crises.

So what if it's been a rainy spring?
April news is a cheerful thing
Since Genevieve, that Gallic hound,
Has brought back Madeline,
Safe and sound.

> *Phyllis McGinley, "Madeline and Genevieve," in The New York Times Book Review (© 1953 by The New York Times Company; reprinted by permission), April 26, 1953, p. 30.*

[*Madeline's Rescue*] takes us all over Paris through pictures by someone who knows how to evoke the charm of the place, without any sentimentality and with a subtle humor which has occasional sharp edges no one can possibly mind because of the irresistible talent of the painter.

This is not only an amusing story, but a trip to Paris, for adults as well as children. And you will want to take it over and over again. What a break at that price!

> *A review of "Madeline's Rescue," in The Saturday Review, New York (© 1953 Saturday Review Mag-azine Co.; reprinted by permission), Vol. XXXVI, No. 20, May 16, 1953, p. 48.*

Come to Paris again with Madeline and Miss Clavel, a happy trip to make in spring. It is a journey long awaited, for no other Bemelmans picture book has matched the ageless appeal of "**Madeline.**" We left her proudly showing off her appendicitis scar. This time, she tumbles into the Seine and is rescued by a dog who comes back to school with the famous two-line walk of little girls. The story goes on to a search all over Paris for the poor dog Genevieve who returns of her own accord and solves the riotous problem of "whose bed tonight" by having the right number of puppies.

This sort of tale will amuse and delight children. For grown-ups, the joy will be in the Bemelmans views of Paris, eight elegant full-color plates, and enchanting end papers, a view of the Seine flowing around the Ile de la Cité. Young and old will laugh at the details of the big spread of the Tuileries Gardens. Or you may like best the bright clarity of the scene on Montmartre, or the eerie charm of the night scene looking toward the Eiffel Tower.

We are not disturbed any longer by this artist's often ghastly rhymes, nor are we upset that the line drawings here are not so good as in the first book. To have two books about Madeline in one lifetime is great good fortune.

> *Louise S. Bechtel, in a review of "Madeline's Rescue," in New York Herald Tribune Book Review (© I.H.T. Corporation), May 17, 1953, p. 10.*

Ludwig Bemelmans's newest picture-story book is far too good to be kicked round the house by a child of the age for which, at first glance, some might think it had been produced.

Everything Bemelmans has ever written has had a naïvely simple yet vivid quality of kindness. That is in this story: first a little heartbreak because, as every child knows, that is the way the world works; and then, because Bemelmans is fundamentally kind-hearted, a happy ending. In my own house, three-years-old and eight-years-old followed the gently rhymed and illustrated story with as great interest as I did myself. My annoyance at the man who first produced the cliché about a book being "for children of all ages" is increased by the belief that it cannot have been so true of his book as of this, about which I may not use his phrase because it is too hackneyed.

Above all, of course, the gaiety, clarity and richly right colours of Bemelmans' pictures make them live and joyous scenes, both for the child and the painter.

Posterity, in observing Bemelmans to have been as outstanding as a children's illustrator in his own time as Kate Greenaway was in hers, may also know that, while Kate Greenaway's work has become a period piece, Bemelmans' colouring, child-simplicity and compassion were universals, in time, as in place, so that they have endured datelessly.

> *J. A., "Madeline's Rescue," in The Spectator (© 1953 by The Spectator; reprinted by permission of The Spectator), No. 6545, December 4, 1953, p. 682.*

[*Madeline's Rescue*] combines the virtues suggested by the words "picture book" but seldom provided with real generosity in one package. It is big, colorful, humorous; has real story; is crammed with pictures, upon which hang the interest and suspense. Those who may not know the changeless popularity of the predecessor, *Madeline,* might judge at first glance that these pictures are too sophisticated for small children's choice. The truth is, however, that they could not please the audience better. They are joyously racy, yet simple at heart and easy to understand.

> *Irene Smith, "The Medal-Winning Books: 'Madeline's Rescue'," in her* A History of the Newbery and Caldecott Medals *(copyright © 1957 by Irene Smith; reprinted by permission of Viking Penguin Inc.),* The Viking Press, *1957, p. 94.*

THE HIGH WORLD (1954)

Laid in the mountains of the Austrian Tyrol, this is a poignant account, based on fact, of three years in the life of simple Tobias Amrainer, who with his wife and five children lives an uncomplicated existence until the arrival of the Oberminister-ialrat, Dr. Julius Stickle, with plans for a hydro-electric plant. In a reminiscent and nostalgic mood Bemelmans tells of the simple day-by-day occurrences, of the good-natured tricks played by the friendly gendarme on Tobias, of the training of the children in the lore of the wild, of Frau Amrainer's efforts to save her home from the din and clatter of the cable and bucket, reaching the climax in the avalanche and the timely rescue of the children and the mellowing of the unpopular high official. This latter is more or less a stock figure and a little hard to accept. The many pen-and-ink sketches and four full-page illustrations in color add to the charm. The story may have more appeal for adults, but could be read aloud to children of ten to twelve; all will receive a vivid impression of life in the high mountains and of the integrity and sincerity of the people who live there. A distinguished book of somewhat limited appeal.

> *Elizabeth A. Groves, in a review of "The High World," in* The Saturday Review, *New York (© 1954 Saturday Review Magazine Co.; reprinted by permission), Vol. XXXVII, No. 46, November 13, 1954, p. 76.*

The new Bemelmans brings us the master whose picture books of Madeline in Paris delight all ages, and whose adult books, especially the latest, **"Father, Dear Father,"** entertain many young people. His own "high world," the Austrian Tyrol of his boyhood, now is the background for a story and a mood rather different from those of any previous book. With its many dashing line drawings and six color pages, it will lure boys and girls over ten. Its style, its moral, its humorous yet biting study of contrasting German or Austrian types and of village psychology, will delight older readers of any age. . . .

It's a story you can't put down, with surprises in each brief chapter, and such humor, such rare village talk, such food and such an inn as only Ludwig "Le Pauvre Bemelmans" could give us.

> *Louise S. Bechtel, in a review of "The High World," in* New York Herald Tribune Book Review *(© I. H. T. Corporation), November 14, 1954, p. 2.*

In its essence, Mr. Bemelmans' narrative is a winning one. . . .

In locale and theme, this is all pretty snowy and delightful. Indeed, all would be well were it not for the strangely uneven manner in which Mr. Bemelmans has written it. The impression is of a smooth, swift, lively story (in that urbane deadpan style which carries Mr. Bemelmans' wit so well) crossed with tedious and lumpy dollops of information on Tyrolean ways (it is Mr. Bemelman's home ground). Happily, midway in **"The**

High World" Mr. Bemelmans uncrosses his skiis, and from there on in the story slaloms home with considerable verve.

There is nothing wrong with the illustrations. In black and white and in color, they are rakish, witty and authoritative, and Mr. Bemelmans is generous with them.

> *Alice S. Morris, "Tyrolean Ways," in* The New York Times Book Review *(© 1954 by The New York Times Company; reprinted by permission), November 14, 1954, p. 32.*

[Mr. Bemelmans tells his story with] a warmth which springs from his love of the Austrian Tyrol and his understanding of little children. . . . The pictures in color and in black and white are wonderful; one depicting a thrilling escape from an avalanche takes seven consecutive pages! A Christmas book that is not limited to this season.

> *Jennie D. Lindquist, in a review of "The High World," in* The Horn Book Magazine *(copyrighted, 1954, by The Horn Book, Inc., Boston), Vol. XXX, No. 6, December, 1954, p. 441.*

[Out] of his memories and his abundant zest for the rich wisdom and absurdity of life, [Mr. Bemelmans] has made this enchanting book about the high world of the mountains. . . . The impact of "progress" on this community makes for rich comedy and exciting drama.

This is a very funny book. It is much more; for if Mr. Bemelmans laughs at his peasants as well as his officials he does not disguise his delight in their way of life. *The High World* is, in its gay way, a study of the mountains and the simple wisdom of those who live there. The author's drawings enrich and interpret the story. In the fullest sense a "good" book.

> *A review of "The High World," in* The Junior Bookshelf, *Vol. 22, No. 4, October, 1958, p. 205.*

PARSLEY (1955)

A gnarled old pine tree and a canny stag with a firm belief in the health-giving properties of parsley share the honors in Mr. Bemelmans' new picture book. A whimsical combination, certainly, and a whimsical story this is. The beginning is a poetic account of the two growing up and growing old together. Abruptly the mood and the tempo change as a hunter invades this craggy Eden. Then it is the tree, barren, useless, who saves the stag and also presents him with the hunter's binoculars—a safeguard against future marauders.

Satisfying as this may be to a child's innate sympathy for the poor and the unwanted, this still seems a shaky vehicle for the pictures. These, however, are wonderful—dramatic, comic, touching—as the story demands—and all of them luminous with color.

> *Ellen Lewis Buell, "Stag at Bay," in* The New York Times Book Review *(© 1955 by The New York Times Company; reprinted by permission), September 25, 1955, p. 34.*

Measuring over a foot long, and ten inches high, this big book gives lovers of Bemelmans reproductions of his paintings bigger than any yet offered. But the greatest surprise is that it is about America. The charming text, very brief, tells of the tiny pine that grew on the edge of a windy abyss. So it was not cut down, taken to a sawmill, made into houses, toys and

From The High World, *written and illustrated by Ludwig Bemelmans.*

furniture for New Englanders, as we see happening in several of the best pictures. . . . [At the end] comes the one touch of the traditional humor of this artist—the stag using the hunter's binoculars to spy out more hunters.

On the text pages are a score of familiar Eastern wildflowers, painted with great charm. If you can't guess them, a list is given at the end. This picture-book reflection of our great northern forest life is most original, touching, and dramatic, and will appeal to all ages who like Bemelmans.

> *Louise S. Bechtel, in a review of "Parsley," in* New York Herald Tribune Book Review, *Part II (© I. H. T. Corporation; reprinted by permission), November 13, 1955, p. 2.*

In *Parsley,* as in all Ludwig Bemelmans' books for children, there is a wonderful wedding of words and pictures. The balance is perfect—short, witty text and succinct, humorous illustration, beautifully reproduced in full color. (p. 474)

[This] is a simple tale, simply told, but with undercurrents of meaning, some mysterious and cloaked, about the strength of the weak and the weakness of the strong, the joy and pain and humor of life.

There is a rich array of pictures: the gentle, idyllic ones of the forest animals, those showing lumbering and the making of

furniture from the trees that surrounded the crooked pine, and the boldly designed pages about the hunter and his fate.

In the quiet beginning of the book, the second picture shows life in the forest and the pine starting to grow. There are shy rabbits and deer peering through all sorts of blue flowers, with a large yellow-green snail in the foreground studying the little dark green pine. Around all this is a border of bright red ladybugs. The whole effect is one of delicacy and tenderness but with no trace of sentimentality. There is subtle humor in every line.

Particularly delightful are the pages depicting work in the forest, at the mill, a craftsman's workshop and a cozy home. The first of these . . . is painted in dense, almost sombre greens and browns, beautifully accented by the yellow ends of the newly felled trees, the pale yellow wood chips and the fragile wild flowers. These colors are further enriched by the powerful blues of the woodsman's shirt and the little girls' dresses. The blue in turn is made more intense by the vivid red galluses on the man and the red ribbons in the girls' yellow hair. The actual drawing is exceedingly expressive. There is sly humor in the serious-faced, bearded men and in the homely farm horses, one munching on a flower that is left standing between two fallen trees. In the left foreground the woodsman, a surprised look on his face, stops in mid-swing as the tremendous tree starts to fall. The solemn gestures of the other men lead one's eyes to the focal center: the charming little girls holding bouquets. This is a most satisfactory picture, fresh without affectation or contrived design. It is substantial, funny and beautiful. Who could ask for more?

The pictures dealing with the hunter are remarkable for their strong and daring composition. He is seen close up, looking menacingly through his huge binoculars. He climbs up over the edge of the abyss to begin his assault on Parsley. He is tripped in a wonderfully mysterious way by the old tree (this picture is superb in its power), and finally just his two feet are seen disappearing as he plunges "far below—to hunt no more." The drawing of these boots is very funny and telling, as is the text. "Good-by—my luck she is running out!"

An enchanting added attraction is the series of common wild flowers, one on each page of text and named at the back of the book. These delicate drawings, whimsical and touching, added a final joyous note to the delight and satisfaction I got from this wonderful picture book. (pp. 474-75)

> *Margaret Bloy Graham, in a review of "Parsley," in* The Horn Book Magazine *(copyrighted, 1955, by The Horn Book, Inc., Boston), Vol. XXXI, No. 6, December, 1955, pp. 474-75.*

The book has some of Bemelmans' loveliest art work, and for this reason could be of value for art collections. The story is adult rather than childlike, and the valuing of animal above human life makes it questionable even from an adult point of view.

> *A review of "Parsley," in* Bulletin of the Children's Book Center *(reprinted by permission of The University of Chicago Press), Vol. 9, No. 6, February, 1956, p. 66.*

MADELINE AND THE BAD HAT (1957)

More nonsense about Madeline . . . versifies her encounters with the Spanish Ambassador's son. . . . The Bemelmans col-

From Parsley, *written and illustrated by Ludwig Bemelmans.*

ored pictures present a panorama of Paris that is far more humorous and amusing than the awkwardly rhymed and ordinary story. Bemelmans is usually cleverer than he is here.

> *A review of "Madeline and the Bad Hat," in* Virginia Kirkus' Service, *Vol. XXV, No. 4, February 15, 1957, p. 138.*

In an old house in Paris
That was covered with vines
Lived twelve little girls
In two straight lines.

These are, probably, the best-known opening lines in contemporary American juvenile literature—the beginning of Ludwig Bemelmans' "**Madeline**." And, happily, they begin this third story about that impish little schoolgirl. As a matter of fact Madeline is a little restrained—for her. Now it is the next-door neighbor, the Spanish Ambassador's son, who provides most of the fun and a touch of the macabre. Pepito, the Bad Hat, is a Katzenjammer Kid with Chas. Addams inspirations—like building a guillotine for the cook's chickens. What he is really trying to do is to impress the young misses of Miss Clavel's school and, failing, takes out his frustration in staging the biggest cat-and-dog melee ever seen in the Bois de Boulogne. Naturally his fall is swift and painful, his disgrace complete, but his reformation is excessive. Even Miss Clavel said, "This is too much" when out of his new love for animals, he releases the inmates of the Paris zoo. In that crisis it's Madeline who, with feminine wisdom, brings him into line.

Blithe as ever, Mr. Bemelmans tells it all in the familiar rhythms and unexpected rhymes that children love. The pictures of Paris, the school, the little girls and Pepito are just as funny and handsome as you'd expect.

> *Ellen Lewis Buell, "Fall and Rise of Pepito," in* The New York Times Book Review (© *1957 by The New York Times Company; reprinted by permission), March 10, 1957, p. 36 [the excerpt of Ludwig Bemelmans's work used here was originally published in his* Madeline *(copyright 1939 by Ludwig Bemelmans; copyright © renewed 1967 by Madeleine Bemelmans and*

> *Barbara Bemelmans Marciano; reprinted by permission of Viking Penguin Inc.), Simon & Schuster, 1939].*

Irresistible Madeline is back again. . . . Although the story is contrived and overlong and the text awkwardly rhymed, the charming Paris scenes and the other amusing pictures are as much fun as those in the earlier books.

> *A review of "Madeline and the Bad Hat," in* The Booklist and Subscription Books Bulletin *(reprinted by permission of the American Library Association; copyright © 1957 by the American Library Association), Vol. 53, No. 15, April 1, 1957, p. 410.*

Magic pictures meticulous
Verse sublimely ridiculous
Madeline's always ubiquitous.

Said our Viking Junior log of the third Madeline book and we agree in all but the "meticulous." Ludwig Bemelmans is not "over careful about minute details." His charm is quite in the other direction, a humorous seizing of the spirit of a scene, a genius for selecting the gay oddity. As in "**Madeline's Rescue**" the pictures of Paris are bathed in a warm and sunny light not in the delicious misty grays of the first "**Madeline**." The scene at the flower market is the gayest, but there is also a delightful view of Notre Dame from the Quai, which alas, is only on the end papers. . . .

Fine topsy-turvy humor in a gay French setting with a very Spanish "bad hat" giving marvelous piquancy and contrast.

> *Margaret Sherwood Libby, "The Three 1957 Prize Books," in* New York Herald Tribune Book Review (© *I.H.T. Corporation; reprinted by permission), May 12, 1957, p. 6.**

MADELINE AND THE GYPSIES (1959)

[If] "**Madeline and the Gypsies**" isn't absolutely top-drawer Bemelmans—being a little haphazard in structure and not very polished as to rhythm—it provides the kind of escapade that children dream about. Madeline, that most famous of Parisian schoolgirls, and her friend Pepito, the reformed "Bad Hat," are marooned in the top of a Ferris wheel in a gypsy carnival. They are rescued by the gypsies and are introduced to an idyllic life. . . . Their adventures provide Mr. Bemelmans with the opportunity to show us carnival life and some of the choice scenes of France, such as Chartres, Mont Saint-Michel, the beach at Deauville, the Castle of Fountainblue (sic)—all as gay and handsome as you please.

> *Ellen Lewis Buell, "In Rhyme and Rhythm," in* The New York Times Book Review (© *1959 by The New York Times Company; reprinted by permission), September 13, 1959, p. 58.**

Another picture book about the intrepid Parisian orphan will be hailed with delight by Bemelmans fans. . . . The familiar enjoyable combination of mild text and improbable plot are enhanced by colorful scenes of Paris and of the circus. Like the other books about Madeline, this affords pleasure for reading aloud, although there are awkwardnesses in the writing style which are obtrusive.

> *Zena Sutherland, in a review of "Madeline and the Gypsies," in* Bulletin of the Center for Children's Books *(reprinted by permission of The University of*

Chicago Press), Vol. 13, No. 2, October, 1959, p. 26.

The halting verses grow more casual and the French scenes less recognizable with each succeeding book. Here Notre Dame, Mont St. Michel and Carcassone are barely suggested though the Monet-like Gare St. Lazare is pleasantly Gallic. However, the exuberance and the verve of the pictures remain, and the affection for Madeline, while her gypsy adventures are sure to please her innumerable young friends.

Margaret Sherwood Libby, "Laughter and Jollity in Picture Storybooks from Far and Near," in New York Herald Tribune Book Review *(© I.H.T. Corporation; reprinted by permission), November 1, 1959, p. 4.**

The combination of circus-like background with scenes of actual places, such as Chartres, Deauville, and Avignon, makes these typically Bemelmans pictures gayer, livelier, and more full of interest than ever, but the verse seems inexcusably limp.

Margaret Warren Brown, in a review of "Madeline and the Gypsies," in The Horn Book Magazine *(copyright, 1960, by The Horn Book, Inc., Boston), Vol. XXXVI, No. 2, April, 1960, p. 124.*

The fourth of the Madeline books has all the excellences of its predecessors. The scene is new . . . and there are enchanting glimpses of Fontainebleau, Chartres, Mont-saint-Michel, Carcassonne and the other places as well as a lovely end-paper of the Pont d'Avignon which should set the reader singing. The fairground too is admirable material for Bemelmans' exuberant art. The verse is as bad as ever—but who would wish for neatly turned couplets? There is no one like Bemelmans, and certainly no one else would get away with such a deliciously improper story.

A review of "Madeline and the Gypsies," in The Junior Bookshelf, *Vol. 25, No. 6, December, 1961, p. 336.*

WELCOME HOME! (1960)

Ludwig Bemelmans has done it again; he has taken what is a concept of mature wit and imagination and fashioned it into a story which will be the delight both of children and parents. . . . [Told] in the delightful verse of Ludwig Bemelmans and illustrated in his flavorful drawings, [this story] assumes the proportion of a comic and wistful fable, a wry metaphor of the life struggle.

A review of "Welcome Home!" in Virginia Kirkus' Service, *Vol. XXVIII, No. 18, September 15, 1960, p. 815.*

The story of a foxhunt . . . Although there is humor in the story, it requires knowledge of hunting to appreciate the distortion in this presentation. The illustrations are magnificent, some of the outdoor scenes meriting inclusion in an art collection.

Zena Sutherland, in a review of "Welcome Home!" in Bulletin of the Center for Children's Books *(reprinted by permission of The University of Chicago Press), Vol. 14, No. 1, November, 1960, p. 37.*

Fox and hounds and the thrill of the chase are celebrated in Ludwig Bemelmans' **"Welcome Home!"** . . . The sly fox

triumphs of course and "When he gets home / And bolts the latch / He heaves a sigh and says, 'No catch.'" The verse is smart and bouncy but it is Bemelmans' brush that carries the day with scenes of the woodland hunt, of the fox's comfortable lair, of the setting sun's rays on the dejected hunters, all superbly painted in glorious color. (p. 59)

George A. Woods, "A Child's Best Friend Can Be a Picture Book," in The New York Times Book Review, Part II *(© 1960 by The New York Times Company; reprinted by permission), November 13, 1960, pp. 58-9.**

Tally ho! The red-coated hunters and the Holiday Hounds are after Mr. Bemelmans' glorious red fox. . . . As the basis for his latest picture book, the author-artist has embellished a rollicking poem by Beverley Bogert. Although identical in size with **"Parsley,"** this lacks the truly distinguished format of the earlier book. Typical Bemelmans, with illustrations full of action, humor, and striking colors. Should be popular.

Nancy Festa Elsmo, in a review of "Welcome Home!" in Junior Libraries, *an appendix to* Library Journal *(reprinted from the November, 1960 issue of* Junior Libraries, *published by R. R. Bowker Co./ A Xerox Corporation; copyright © 1960), Vol. 85, No. 20, November, 1960, p. 4217.*

A short, simple but sly ballad of a fox outwitting the hunt is the framework for some of the funniest and, at the same time,

From Madeline in London, *written and illustrated by Ludwig Bemelmans.*

most beautiful pictures that Mr. Bemelmans has ever done. In radiant colors, horses, hounds, and foxes sweep across the large pages to make a true picture book which today's children will surely be reading to equally delighted grandchildren in fifty years or so.

> *Margaret Warren Brown, in a review of "Welcome Home!" in* The Horn Book Magazine *(copyright, 1960, by the Horn Book, Inc., Boston), Vol. XXXVI, No. 6, December, 1960, p. 506.*

MADELINE IN LONDON   (1961)

Would the reader like to go to London? He can—with Ludwig Bemelmans' Madeline and her school mates, for a birthday visit with Pepito. . . . ["**Madeline in London**"] is a full verse report of that trip, including what happens when a retired guard's horse answers the trumpets' summons with Pepito and Madeline aboard. Mr. Bemelmans offers a colorful tour . . . in a breathlessly gay adventure. (p. 54)

> *George A. Woods, "To Travel, to Travel, with Many a Wonderful Port-of-Call—For the Very Young, That Is," in* The New York Times Book Review, *Part II (© 1961 by The New York Times Company; reprinted by permission), November 12, 1961, pp. 54-5.**

Another improbable ploy by Madeline and her fellow orphans. . . . The text is bland in tone and nonsensical in message, a combination that is happily complemented by the lively and colorful illustrations. The rhyming is occasionally jarring, especially when the book is read aloud, but this is of minor import in a story rife with tongue-in-cheek exaggeration.

> *Zena Sutherland, in a review of "Madeline in London," in* Bulletin of the Center for Children's Books *(reprinted by permission of The University of Chicago Press; copyright 1961 by The University of Chicago), Vol. 15, No. 4, December, 1961, p. 54.*

Any Bemelmans book has charm, but this seems a little more slap-dash in invention and execution than it should be. It might be stronger if it ended with Pepito's birthday celebration after the horse presented by Miss Clavel's charges leads a wild chase through town. The sentiments and their versification are often strained, sometimes strange, the horses' legs are dreadful, the finale forced, and the background poor to excellent, but Bemelmans fans will want it.

> *Janice H. Dohm, in a review of "Madeline in London," in* School Library Journal, *an appendix to* Library Journal *(reprinted from the January, 1962 issue of* School Library Journal, *published by R. R. Bowker Co./ A Xerox Corporation; copyright © 1962), Vol. 8, No. 5, January, 1962, p. 72.*

Mr. Bemelmans' storytelling has inventions as jolly as ever and his paintings are just as lively as they provide new London backgrounds for the exploits of Madeline. . . . However, there is lacking now that easy swinging rhythm which made the first stories about Madeline such fun to read aloud.

> *Virginia Haviland, in a review of "Madeline in London," in* The Horn Book Magazine *(copyright, 1962, by The Horn Book, Inc., Boston), Vol. XXXVIII, No. 1, February, 1962, p. 41.*

Madeline goes out in a blaze of colour. This, presumably the last of the series, is the best since the first. It has some of the sparkle of the original. The doggerel is as bad as ever, but the author takes an audacious delight in it which is infectious, as with Pepito's horse; "Some poor old dobbins are made into glue, But not this one—Look, he's as good as new." The pictures of London scenes are charming, although Londoners will regret that Mr. Bemelmans is casual about topography. A nice jolly book.

> *A review of "Madeline in London," in* The Junior Bookshelf, *Vol. 27, No. 1, January, 1963, p. 23.*

Arna Bontemps

1902-1973

(Born Arnaud Wendell Bontemps) Black American author of fiction, nonfiction, poetry, short stories, plays, and essays, critic and editor.

Bontemps was one of the first black writers for children to replace stereotyping with an accurate portrayal of black life. He also pioneered the use of realistic black speech in children's books. Seeking to instill cultural esteem in young readers, he wrote biographies of notable black men and women, a critically praised black history, realistic fiction, and humorous tall tales. Whether writing for adults or children, Bontemps conveyed optimism and pride in his culture.

A distinguished figure in the history of black American literature, Bontemps published his first work during the Harlem Renaissance. His literary career spanned a fifty-year period, and his versatility is seen in his creation of books of several genres directed to all age levels. A noted educator and librarian, Bontemps progressed from high school teacher and principal to librarian at Fisk University, professor of English at the University of Illinois, and curator of the James Weldon Johnson collection at Yale University.

Bontemps combined erudition with a lucid writing style in his children's books. Critics generally see these works as expressing balanced restraint, sensitivity, and directness. Reviewers commend *The Story of the Negro* for its impartiality, objectivity, and detached views, but judge *Young Booker* as superficial and melodramatic. *Lonesome Boy*, the tale of Bubber and his trumpet, is praised for its poetic beauty, but considered too mystical for a child to comprehend. Despite this, Bontemps will be remembered for his popularizations of black history and for his positive impact on black American children. *The Story of the Negro* was a Newbery Honor Book in 1949 and received the Jane Addams Book Award in 1956.

(See also *Contemporary Literary Criticism*, Vols. 1, 18; *Something about the Author*, Vols. 2, 24 [obituary]; *Contemporary Authors New Revision Series*, Vol. 4; and *Contemporary Authors*, Vols. 1-4, rev. ed., Vols. 41-44, rev. ed. [obituary].)

AUTHOR'S COMMENTARY

In the eighteenth century, I have been told, there was a popular saying to the effect that nobody would ever have fallen in love if he had not first read about it in the poets. Whether or not this is true, there is certainly something to be said for the proposition that experience owes much—if not everything—to the writers, the storytellers, the moralists who make us aware of the heights and depths, the brilliance and shadow of many-splendored existence.

Perhaps memory is the common element or ingredient that works the miracle of merging poetry, writing, art with experience. If you have read Saint Augustine's essay on memory in his *Confessions,* you will know what I am thinking; but a more recent example can be found. My own experience as a reader of fiction is long enough to make me aware of changes that have occurred in my time in the outlook of writers. The attitude toward memory which their stories reflect is particularly noticeable.

Photograph by Roy Lewis

Fiction of the twenties—when I was a college student and immediately after—books like *My Antonia* by Willa Cather, *Three Black Pennys* by Joseph Hergesheimer, *The Grandmothers* and *Good-bye Wisconsin* by Glenway Westcott, even *Main Street* by Sinclair Lewis had at least one element in common: nostalgia, a quality which was warmly appreciated in those days, but which tended to come into disfavor with critics, if not readers, about the time of the Depression. Perhaps the change was inevitable, but as nostalgia was purged from fiction, something else was also lost. The abracadabra by which the writer got some of his own vision into the reader's experience stopped working so well. What happened, I suspect, was that the medium of transmission was impaired. It was a failure of memory.

Another instance of preoccupation with memory, which did not involve longing or nostalgia, is found in *The Hunted Man and the Ghost's Bargain* by Charles Dickens. The hero of this story, a chemist, wants to forget a life blighted by sorrow and wrong. His nemesis, having convinced him that his memories are his curse, makes a bargain with him to take away the disturbing memories on condition that the hero will pass along a similar oblivion to everyone he meets. The chemist tries to carry out the terms, but discovers to his horror (as our generation must learn, I fear) that the blotting out of remembrance of the past also blots out his life and the lives of those about him such qualities as gratitude, repentance, compassion, and forbearance. Only the intervention of a good angel, as it were, gets him out of this unfortunate compact.

The Greeks were bothered by unpleasant memories too. The waters of Lethe, the river of forgetfulness, appear to have had a strong attraction for them.

Another concern of storytellers at least as far back as Dickens— if not all the way to the Greeks—strikes me as related in a different way. It has to do with a kind of spiritual malnutrition resulting from a deficiency or poverty of memories. Here in the United States we might call it the theme of the boy from the country. In Europe, no doubt, it was the young man from the provinces, and it was represented by such novels as Dickens' *Great Expectations,* Dumas' *The Three Musketeers,* and a host of other fictional works. The standard situation involved an eager youth making his way to the city in the hope of acquiring experience, standing outside in his callowness and naïveté, seeking to enter and participate. His memories, if he came from some of the areas we used to hear about, Mississippi, for example, left as much to be desired as did the pot-liquor and sow-back diet on which his body had been nourished in childhood. But these recollections I have found almost too poignant, too disturbing, for children's books.

With me the lonesome-boy theme has persisted. Consciously or unconsciously, it too reflects influences. I used to avoid the first person singular in my writing; for some reason or other it embarrassed me. But despite my efforts—despite careful stratagems—I am afraid I did not always avoid autobiography. Born in Louisiana, carried by my parents to California at a very early age, I suspect that it is myself I see as I look back in each of the guises in which the lonesome boy has appeared since I introduced him in *God Sends Sunday,* my first book. (pp. 672-74)

[Here Augie, who loved horses, had a chance one spring morning. It was] more than just a chance to get away from the plantation, more than just a chance to ease his itching feet. It was a chance to somehow deal with loneliness itself. When Little Augie began hanging around the old fair grounds in New Orleans and got an opportunity to ride racing horses as a jockey, he thought he had surely found the way. . . .

When *God Sends Sunday* failed to sell well, despite favorable reviews, the publisher told me that perhaps it was because the year was 1931 and the publication of the book coincided too well with the great thud of depression that followed the crash of 1929. I told myself soon after, however, that if the adult world had become too miserable from other causes to remember or respond to loneliness, I was not sure the same was true for children.

So I wrote about Slumber the *Sad-Faced Boy* . . . , and the younger readers bore me out, I think. (p. 675)

[*Lonesome Boy*] came much later. In it, I think, the eagerness and the longing that troubled Little Augie and Slumber in a vague way they could not fully understand are made sufficiently explicit. But it brought no smiles immediately. Some people have found *Lonesome Boy* puzzling. (I get the impression that some adults who work with children have felt that with young people you should leave no uncertainty, no vagueness.) Some have wondered whether or not it is a folk tale. It is not, but it is told somewhat in the manner of a folk tale because I thought that style suited the material. Was Bubber dreaming when all the last part happened?

A difficult question. Coming back to autobiography, I can remember instances in my own childhood when I was not sure whether I had experienced or dreamed certain things. That is as much as I can say about the mystery of the story that gives me a title for these remarks. (pp. 675-76)

> *Arna Bontemps, ''The 'Lonesome Boy' Theme''*
> *(originally a lecture given at The New York Public*
> *Library on May 5, 1966), in* The Horn Book Mag-
> azine *(copyright © 1966, by The Horn Book, Inc.,*
> *Boston), Vol. XLII, No. 6, December, 1966, pp. 672-*
> *80.**

GENERAL COMMENTARY

Not everyone, of course, was really taken in [by the degrading depiction of the black child in American children's books of the 1930's]. Members of the black community certainly were not. Around the beginning of the 1930's, in an era of black literary and artistic production known today as the Harlem Renaissance, Langston Hughes and Arna Bontemps produced ***Popo and Fifina, Children of Haiti.*** . . . Hughes' poetic language and rich metaphors effectively complimented Bontemps' feeling for childhood playfulness and parental concerns. . . . Bontemps went on in the '30's without Hughes to produce more books about the black child, at the same time searching for a more realistic way to depict the black child's speech. From a total use of standard English in *Popo and Fifina,* he reverted to moderate representation of regional Alabama dialect through phonemic levels of speech in *You Can't Pet a Possum* . . . but later produced in *Sad Faced Boy* . . . a replication of syntactic levels of expression, foreshadowing the method such writers as John Steptoe, Lucille Clifton, and James Baldwin would use thirty years later to represent the black child's speech patterns. Bontemps' books are perhaps even more important, however, for providing the black child with the perspective of a black adult observing the segregated worlds of rural Alabama as well as urban Harlem. (p. 118)

> *Nina Mikkelsen, ''Censorship and the Black Child:*
> *Can the Real Story Ever Be Told?'' in* Proceedings
> of the Ninth Annual Conference of The Children's
> Literature Association: The Child and the Story, An
> Exploration of Narrative Forms, *edited by Priscilla*
> *A. Ord (copyright © 1983 by The Children's Liter-*
> *ature Association),* Children's Literature Associa-
> tion, *1983, pp. 117-27.**

POPO AND FIFINA, CHILDREN OF HAITI (with Langston Hughes, 1932)

Here is a travel book that is a model of its kind. Facts, indeed, the reader acquires, but unconsciously, for what he feels is the atmosphere of the island of Haiti, dusty little roads that wind along the hills, sun-drenched silences only broken by the droning of insects and the cry of tropical birds, silver sails on clear green water, sheets of warm white rain.

Little black Popo and Fifina and their father and mother . . . [create] in the reader's mind the feeling of reality. One follows their adventures, the simple everyday happenings, with interest. The book has some of the simple homelike atmosphere that has made ''The Dutch Twins'' such a favorite. Older readers will recognize that the beauty of the style has much to do in holding the reader's attention, and younger readers will unconsciously be held by the same quality. **''Popo and Fifina''** tempts us to wish that all our travel books for children might be written by poets. (pp. 13, 16)

> *Anne T. Eaton, in a review of "Popo and Fifina: Children of Haiti," in* The New York Times Book Review *(© 1932 by The New York Times Company; reprinted by permission), October 23, 1932, pp. 13, 16.*

Popo and Fifina, Papa Jean, Mamma Anna, and the baby . . . traveled from the hills to live on the seacoast so that Papa Jean might be a fisherman. What they saw and what they did will interest children of fourth and fifth grades. The story is told with sincerity and appreciation of the simple, colorful life of the native black people of Haiti.

> *A review of "Popo and Fifina, Children of Haiti," in* The Booklist *(reprinted by permission of the American Library Association; copyright © 1932 by the American Library Association), Vol. 29, No. 4, December, 1932, p. 118.*

YOU CAN'T PET A POSSUM (1934)

Shine Boy, the little Negro who lived with his Aunt Cindy in an Alabama cabin, had no one to play with until he found Butch, a homeless, yellow pup, and then the age-old partnership of boy and dog was quickly established. Together they had many adventures. . . .

This is a story of hot, sunny days in the Alabama countryside, of the amusing escapades of an 8-year-old boy. The dialect is particularly characteristic and well written, so that it can be easily understood by children.

> *A review of "You Can't Pet a Possum," in* The New York Times Book Review *(© 1934 by The New York Times Company; reprinted by permission), September 23, 1934, p. 9.*

Simplicity, clarity and a cool and luminous tenderness make this story . . . stand out not only among stories about Negro children but above many of the stories for children this year. **"Popo and Fifina"** . . . presented its children with the sort of touch by which one who understands them ushers a shy child safely into company; I saw them more clearly than any other foreign children the year that book came out. . . .

"At first Shine Boy had nobody to play with, no friend." Thus the story begins, in a sentence whose cadence catches the ear. Through scenes sometimes downright funny—for the 'possum of the title turns out to be a polecat—but more often with the gentle merriment that comes from honest enjoyment of small things, Shine Boy reaches his birthday anniversary and a dinner in the cabin and a white cake with nine pink candles and his good friends the triplets at the table and Butch under the table. There is a curious poignancy in the happiness of the day. The young Cratchits would have understood it. Children get these overtones, and should have stories like this that rouse them.

> *A review of "You Can't Pet a Possum," in* New York Herald Tribune Books *(© I.H.T. Corporation; reprinted by permission), January 20, 1935, p. 7.*

SAD-FACED BOY (1937)

No one writes for children with a style more limpid than Arna Bontemps, or in an English whose turns of phrase are more likely to give a child not only pleasure, but a taste for words used with distinction as against clichés or sloppy sentences. It would be a pity if his writing only about colored children should keep him from exerting this beneficent influence on white ones, especially as he has succeeded in rendering Negro speech simply by the use of appropriate rhythms, so that no child's budding English will be distorted by misspellings.

Any one living in New York or in any large city of the North is likely to have seen one of those impromptu musical outfits of little black boys who make melody and harmony on and out of almost anything, creating as they go. The Dozier brothers, three little chaps from Alabama, are stricken in the South with a deep sense that New York is the place to be, and float rather than beat their way, like migratory birds, to their Uncle Jasper, janitor of an apartment house away uptown. He sets them all to work about the place: Slumber, the sad-faced boy (whose face grows sadder the happier his thoughts become) mops to a rhythmic chant that comes naturally out of the motion and the thought in his mind, a true work-song. They all sing, play, and make their own music and when they need pocket money they make it by playing, first in Harlem backyards, then outside theaters downtown in the evening intermissions. They never think of shining on the stage, but they put on a good show. Then it is spring, and as instinctively as they once realized it was time to drift North, they now have the South in their bones and are gone in a moment, Alabama-bound. But their brief season lingers in the mind like music, a good thing to be said about a book for an eight-year-old.

> *"Stories of Now and Long Ago from Mathematics to Movies: 'Sad-Faced Boy'," in* New York Herald Tribune Books *(© I.H.T. Corporation; reprinted by permission), May 9, 1937, p. 10.*

Arna Bontemps has told the odyssey of . . . three small adventurers with real distinction and a crisp humor peculiar to our day. Its comedy, moreover, is enriched with a mellowness rooted in a real understanding of boyhood, and 9 and 10-year-olds will find convincing as well as diverting the trigger-quick impulses of the boys and their flavorsome speech, so truly recorded that one can fairly hear in it the rhythms of the South.

> *Ellen Lewis Buell, in a review of "Sad-Faced Boy," in* The New York Times Book Review *(© 1937 by The New York Times Company; reprinted by permission), May 9, 1937, p. 12.*

Although [the boys'] trip to New York is plausible, their confidence in exploring the city seems somewhat improbable. This was one of the first books, however, to show the poor conditions where the Negroes lived.

> *Charlotte S. Huck and Doris Young Kuhn, "Realistic Fiction: 'Sad-Faced Boy'," in their* Children's Literature in the Elementary School *(copyright © 1961, 1968 by Holt, Rinehart and Winston, Inc.; reprinted by permission of Holt, Rinehart and Winston, Publishers, CBS College Publishing), second edition, Holt, Rinehart and Winston, 1968, p. 229.*

THE FAST SOONER HOUND (with Jack Conroy, 1942)

Of all the funny picture books in this year's crop, none satisfied me more than *Fast Sooner Hound.* . . . Sooner, a long-legged, lop-eared hound, so named becase he'd "sooner run than eat," belonged to a boomer fireman. Not being allowed to ride in the cab with his beloved master, Sooner simply ran along beside the train, to the chagrin of the roadmaster, for Sooner made even the fastest train look slow, so easily could he out-distance it.

Ruth Hill, in a review of "The Fast Sooner Hound," in Library Journal *(copyright © 1942 by Xerox Corporation), Vol. 67, No. 18, October 15, 1942, p. 882.*

This "tall tale" from the early days of the railroad is a cheerful bit of American folklore very welcome in a wartime year. . . . What happened when the Sooner raced the Cannon Ball, the pride of the road, makes a hilarious climax to the tale. . . .

A fresh, original picture-story book. . . .

Anne T. Eaton, "Early Railroad Days," in The New York Times Book Review *(© 1942 by The New York Times Company; reprinted by permission), November 15, 1942, p. 8.*

Boy or man, this tall tale pleases. It began as one of those "industrial folk-stories" with which Americans in lumber camps, steamboat gangs or the like, test a newcomer's powers of belief and their own ability to keep a straight face. This is a railroading story, and because small boys like railroads as well as men do, it belongs to both alike—especially as the instinctive and trained gift for literary style possessed by Arna Bontemps has put Mr. Conroy's piece of Americana into a form that makes it a treasure for storytellers.

May Lamberton Becker, in a review of "The Fast Sooner Hound," in New York Herald Tribune Books *(© I.H.T. Corporation), January 17, 1943, p. 8.*

WE HAVE TOMORROW   (1945)

Twelve stories of Negroes who have "made good" against the all too obvious odds. In varied fields, commercial art, public nursing, symphonic conducting, hat designing, aeronautics, chemistry, night club entertainment, sociology, etc., including such famous names as Hazel Scott, Dean Dixon, Col. Benjamin Davis, Jr., head of the 332nd Fighter Group, E. Simms Campbell, James E. Luvalle. Almost all the stories are treated the same—the early years, the struggle against poverty or prejudice, the beginning of success. . . . I could only wish the book were better written, but that they exist at all is a note of hopefulness.

A review of "We Have Tomorrow," in Virginia Kirkus' Bookshop Service, *Vol. XIII, No. 14, July 15, 1945, p. 318.*

[These are] dignified story biographies. . . . And they treat with calm, dispassionate frankness the great issue of racial discrimination. Adults, as well as older boys and girls, will find this an arresting book.

Alice M. Jordan, in a review of "We Have Tomorrow," in The Horn Book Magazine *(copyrighted, 1945, by The Horn Book, Inc., Boston), Vol. XXI, No. 5, September, 1945, p. 354.*

The fact that these are young Negroes at the beginning of their careers rather than persons who have already won fame gives added meaning to the book. Useful both for promoting more democratic attitudes and for vocational guidance with Negro boys and girls.

A review of "We Have Tomorrow," in The Booklist *(reprinted by permission of the American Library Association; copyright © 1945 by the American Library Association), Vol. 42, No. 3, October 15, 1945, p. 60.*

SLAPPY HOOPER, THE WONDERFUL SIGN PAINTER   (with Jack Conroy, 1946)

When art critics coined the phrase "magic realism" a few years ago they didn't mention Slappy Hooper but the term fitted the work of the world's biggest, bestest and fastest sign painter to a T. We hadn't heard about him either so we are grateful for this introduction to an impressive American folk hero.

His story hasn't exactly the dash nor the completely satisfying climax which the authors brought to their tale of **"The Fast Sooner Hound,"** but 7 to 10 year olds with a taste for native extravaganza will enjoy the description of Slappy's painting of a loaf of bread on which hungry birds broke their bills. (Remember the grapes of Zeuxis?) They will chuckle over and sympathize with his troubles when he advertised the Jimdandy Hot Blast Heating Stove with such skill that the town bums hung around the sign in cold weather to heat their shaving water.

[The prose is] full of fun and spirit. . . .

Ellen Lewis Buell, in a review of "Slappy Hooper, the Wonderful Sign Painter," in The New York Times Book Review *(© 1946 by The New York Times Company; reprinted by permission), December 8, 1946, p. 22.*

STORY OF THE NEGRO   (1948)

This concise history of the Negro has the accuracy required for so hotly debated a subject, the sense of form that gives the gist of many facts without making them into a digest, and the balance that keeps emotions alive but under control. Arna Bontemps's style has distinction and a touch of deep, troubled beauty. . . .

Offered to the teens, it is for anyone old enough to think and young enough to keep on thinking.

May Lamberton Becker, in a review of "Story of the Negro," in New York Herald Tribune Weekly Book Review *(© I.H.T. Corporation), May 30, 1948, p. 6.*

[Mr. Bontemps] has given us the answer to a librarian's prayer. With an aroused consciousness of the contribution of Negro Americans to our national life, thoughtful teachers everywhere are sending their students to "read up" on this contribution. The shelves are pretty bare. There are comic dialect stories, stories in which the Negro figures as a devoted servitor, and of late some excellent books designed to inspire better understanding. But of factual history there is almost nothing. The present volume exactly meets that lack.

It begins with a clear description of the African peoples at home, pointing out that they differed from one another as sharply as do Americans from Mexicans and Canadians. . . . Most of the book is devoted to outstanding Negroes of the past and present century. High school readers will find their stories both thrilling and informative. Their elders too might read the book with profit.

Nina Brown Baker, in a review of "Story of the Negro," in The New York Times Book Review (© 1948 by The New York Times Company; reprinted by permission), June 20, 1948, p. 21.

[*The Story of the Negro*] I find the most absorbing presentation of Negro history that I have ever read. Here again is a book that has been warmed in the heart while it hews to the line in giving the history of the race as far back as it goes in terms that any boy or girl will thoroughly respect and will read with imagination alight. Mr. Bontemps has made notable contributions to children's books, and his name is a familiar one to American boys and girls.

Anne Carroll Moore, in a review of "The Story of the Negro," in The Horn Book Magazine (copyrighted, 1948, by The Horn Book, Inc., Boston), Vol. XXIV, No. 4, July, 1948, p. 267.

["**The Story of the Negro**"] is a short book which, in its simplicity and drama, would make excellent reading for children as well as adults. The theme is probably one of the most vivid in human development. . . .

Black men have been in America as long as white men, and Bontemps brings a simple and compelling understanding to their part in American history, their economic contribution as slaves, their struggles for freedom, their part in the Civil War and reconstruction, and their dogged climb into education and citizenship.

It is a painful and proud history, and Bontemps wastes no hyperboles but tells it as a matter of simple record.

Henrietta Buckmaster, "Proud History and Urgent Problem," in The Christian Science Monitor (reprinted by permission from The Christian Science Monitor; © 1948 The Christian Science Publishing Society; all rights reserved), July 1, 1948, p. 15.*

This is an unusual book, and one that all one-world-minded people should take under consideration. It is the story of the Negro race, from the liberation of the Egyptians in 1700 B.C. to an informed and unprejudiced word picture of the status of the American Negro today. It tells, dramatically but without bias, the ghastly story of the slave ships, the underground railway, the insurrection in Haiti, the years that preceded the American Civil War. . . . The freshness, the impact in the story is partly due to Mr. Bontemps's complete detachment. He establishes a continuity in time for the history of the Negro race. He gives it its place in the development of civilization in a way that keeps the atmosphere always free of prejudice and propaganda. It is a story that must have developed slowly in a scholarly and balanced mind. . . .

[This is] a book that in text and format presents a vitally important subject with conspicuous success.

Ruth Hill Viguers, "The Spice of Life: 'The Story of the Negro'," in The Saturday Review of Literature (© 1948, copyright renewed © 1976, Saturday Review Magazine Co.; reprinted by permission), Vol. XXXI, No. 33, August 14, 1948, p. 36.

The simplicity with which the author unfolds the story of the Negro people from earliest times, the objectivity with which he presents the problems of his race, and the wealth of material, much of it not available elsewhere, make this book a valuable contribution to children's literature. (pp. 4-5)

A review of "The Story of the Negro," in Notable Children's Books 1940-1959, edited by Rosemary E. Livsey & others (copyright © 1966 by the American Library Association), American Library Association, 1966, pp. 4-5.

SAM PATCH, THE HIGH, WIDE, AND HANDSOME JUMPER
(with Jack Conroy, 1951)

An unsuccessful attempt to capture the tall-tale flavor of the folk legend in this story of a Bunyanesque young man famous for jumping. . . . Too thin in folk background to compete with the stories of Irwin Shapiro (*Joe Magarac, Casey Jones*), the *Jack* tales of Richard Chase and these authors' *The Fast Sooner Hound,* and the jumping device wears rather thin until Sam is allowed to jump horizontally.

A review of "Sam Patch: The High, Wide and Handsome Jumper," in Virginia Kirkus' Bookshop Service, Vol. XIX, No. 2, January 15, 1951, p. 24.

Back in the early nineteenth century—even before Steve Brody—there was Sam Patch. He thrilled citizens of New Jersey and New York State by his daring leaps, until he jumped the Genesee Falls once too often. After that people began making up some remarkable tales about him.

Now Arna Bontemps and Jack Conroy, who gave us "**The Fast Sooner Hound**" and "**Slappy Hooper,**" present their own lively version of the Sam Patch legend. They tell of how young Sam met Hurricane Harry, the Kaskaskia Snapping Turtle, and joined the circus to outjump that braggart. The rivalry between them raged back and forth across the land, somewhat complicated by Hurricane Harry's bear, Chucklehead, until Sam triumphed in the most fabulous jump of all. The prose doesn't quite keep pace with the action, but the exaggeration and the dead-pan humor will tickle many a young funnybone.

Ellen Lewis Buell, "Jumping Sam," in The New York Times Book Review (©1951 by The New York Times Company; reprinted by permission), February 25, 1951, p. 30.

More folklore in the Bontemps-Conroy style. . . . The first part of the story moves rather slowly and lacks the folk-lore flavor that is usually found in the writing of these two authors. The climax, however, is thoroughly satisfying and overcomes the slow build-up.

A review of "Sam Patch, the High, Wide and Handsome Jumper," in Bulletin of the Children's Book Center (reprinted by permission of The University of Chicago Press), Vol. 4, No. 4, March, 1951, p. 26.

American tall tales, whether truly legendary or mostly invented, as one assumes this one to be, are fine material for picture books for "middle age" reading. Their rambunctious humor and lack of condescension to a child audience make them particularly good competitors for the comics. So, boys of nine to twelve, hurry to meet Sam Patch and his rival, Hurricane Harry. . . . It's a book you will want to read aloud to every one you meet, of any age. . . .

It is all very funny, and ever so well written, as Mr. Bontemps' name would guarantee. Sam's mother, with her good advice, ties the magic to earth and home; she is timeless, and might be any washerwoman you know, just as Sam and Harry might almost be seen at any country carnival today.

Louise S. Bechtel, in a review of "Sam Patch: The High Wide and Handsome Jumper," in New York Herald Tribune Book Review *(© I.H.T. Corporation), May 13, 1951, p. 7.*

CHARIOT IN THE SKY: A STORY OF THE JUBILEE SINGERS (1951)

The author of **The Story of the Negro** contributes to *The Land of the Free* series a fictional account of the plight of the Negro youth in the years during and just after the Civil War, in the South. . . . Although the characters seem somewhat sterile and the story stretched to include landmark events, the subject matter should inspire any young person interested in the practical results of the American promise of freedom for all people.

A review of "Chariot in the Sky," in Virginia Kirkus' Bookshop Service, *Vol. XIX, No. 5, March 1, 1951, p. 129.*

A worthy member of the "Land of the Free Series." In the story of Caleb Willows, sixteen year old slave, Arna Bontemps portrays realistically and without rancor or bitterness the life of the slave and freeman. He gives a well-rounded, accurate picture that reflects a great deal of research and yet the book is a very good story with adventure and even with a romantic interest. Fisk Jubilee Singers were world-renowned, and older boys and girls will find it exciting to know how they started and how they helped build Fisk University so that today it is one of the finest universities in the South. Teachers and librarians will find this an excellent book to use with other material on slavery, Civil War, and the Reconstruction Period. Arna Bontemps has done a superb job in telling a story and in presenting a historical slice of America.

Augusta Baker, in a review of "Chariot in the Sky: A Story of the Jubilee Singers," in Library Journal *(copyright © 1951 by Xerox Corporation), Vol. 76, No. 11, June 1, 1951, p. 970.*

In "Chariot in the Sky," a distinguished Negro scholar looks at the impact of liberation upon his people. With compassionate understanding and unobtrusive skill Arna Bontemps tells the whole story through the life of Caleb Willows. . . .

A thoughtful, enlightening book.

Nina Brown Baker, "Where Freedom Rings," in The New York Times Book Review *(© 1951 by The New York Times Company; reprinted by permission), June 17, 1951, p. 24.**

Chariot in the Sky is another of those inspiring stories based on one of the most phenomenal aspects of American culture—the rise of the Negro above the bonds of slavery. With a smooth, moving style—lively, genuine, and realistic—Dr. Bontemps has here presented to young people one of the most memorable and heart-stirring stories since Booker T. Washington's *Up from Slavery*.

In a highly effective manner, the book combines stirring qualities of fiction with the authenticity of historical research. (p. 717)

This story is truly a great one, and it inspires the reader with a new appreciation for an important aspect of the great American heritage—the culture of the Negro race. (p. 718)

Evelyn Perkins Burke, in a review of "Chariot in the Sky: A Story of the Jubilee Singers," in Notes: The Quarterly Journal of The Music Library Association *(copyright 1951 by the Music Library Association, Inc.), Vol. VIII, No. 4, September, 1951, pp. 717-18.*

A beautifully written story that presents the full impact of slavery and racial discrimination as few stories for young people have ever done. Particularly good is the way in which the author has managed to convey the full flavor of southern dialect without resorting to the exaggerated spellings that are so difficult to read.

A review of "Chariot in the Sky: A Story of the Jubilee Singers," in Good Books for Children: A Selection of Outstanding Children's Books Published, 1950-65, *edited by Mary K. Eakin (reprinted by permission of The University of Chicago Press; © 1959, 1962, and 1966 by The University of Chicago), third edition, University of Chicago Press, 1966, p. 39.*

Twenty years have passed since this whitewashed version of the Civil War period first appeared. . . . The book has several serious defects. For example, after an unsuccessful runaway attempt Caleb, formerly a field hand, is sent to work with a tailor in Charleston, where he is reunited with his parents. This was hardly the typical fate of runaway slaves! No attempt is made to present dialect. No black person is ever referred to as a "nigger"; characters are often described as "colored" but never as "black." This alone would make the book unacceptable in these times of increasing black awareness. Caleb is a one-dimensional character, and his attitude throughout the novel is one of accommodation. . . . Caleb never has a bad word to say about any of his white masters, and the only villains he battles are two black men. A much more realistic picture of the black man's struggles at this time can be found in Margaret Walker's *Jubilee*. . . . (pp. 142-43)

John F. Caviston, in a review of "Chariot in the Sky: A Story of the Jubilee Singers," in School Library Journal, *an appendix to* Library Journal *(reprinted from the April, 1972 issue of* School Library Journal, *published by R. R. Bowker Co./A Xerox Corporation; copyright © 1972), Vol. 18, No. 8, April, 1972, pp. 142-43.*

THE STORY OF GEORGE WASHINGTON CARVER (1954)

The humility of true greatness and his avid quest for knowledge about the world combine to make Carver an inspiration to all young readers. The simplicity of style of this well-rounded biography should prove valuable for upper grade remedial reading as well as for character building and developing and understanding of minority groups.

Harriet Morrison, in a review of "The Story of George Washington Carver," in Library Journal *(copyright © 1954 by Xerox Corporation), Vol. 79, No. 9, May 1, 1954, p. 864.*

Of these three narrative biographies [which include "The Story of General Custer" by Margaret Leighton and "The Story of Clara Barton" by Olive Price, all part of the Signature series], Arna Bontemps' life of Dr. Carver has the most enduring value. Addressed to a slightly younger age group than was Anne Terry White's recent study, this is simpler in approach. It is not quite incisive enough in its summary of Carver's achievements, but it is, none the less, a moving portrait, unsentimentalized, written with restraint and sensitivity.

Ellen Lewis Buell, "Three Americans," in The New York Times Book Review (© 1954 by The New York Times Company; reprinted by permission), June 20, 1954, p. 16.*

A superior biography for children of from eight to twelve, written with simplicity and deep feeling, and particularly felicitous in its depiction of the scientist's homeless youth and his struggle to acquire even a grade-school education.

Katharine T. Kinkead, in a review of "The Story of George Washington Carver," in The New Yorker (© 1954, 1982 by The New Yorker Magazine, Inc.), Vol. XXX, No. 41, November 27, 1954, p. 220.

LONESOME BOY (1955)

Mr. Bontemps has written books for children with varying degrees of success, and ranging all the way from a rather thin retelling of the legendary Negro *Sam Patch* . . . to the excellent *Story of the Negro.* . . . Now he tells another simple story that could happen to anyone. But as excitingly colored as it is with the atmosphere and music of the South, it has a mystic quality and meaning that makes us wonder whether more than a few children will appreciate it.

A review of "Lonesome Boy," in Virginia Kirkus' Service, Vol. XXIII, No. 5, March 1, 1955, p. 170.

This is an eerie little tale with something of the quality of legend. It might be read simply as a ghost story or as a fable of those who forget the world of people and lose themselves in their own private worlds. It's an off-beat, tantalizing story that leaves one still wondering a little and therefore remembering it.

Ellen Lewis Buell, "The Silver Trumpet," in The New York Times Book Review (© 1955 by The New York Times Company; reprinted by permission), May 1, 1955, p. 28.

The pulse of silver notes pouring out in a boy's passionate devotion to music fills each page of this haunting story. Bubber . . . , who loved his trumpet, was lonesome if he walked without it. His old Grandpa cautioned him . . . [that carrying a horn around could lead to devilment]. Bubber grew up and learned that lesson, because he couldn't help carrying that trumpet. But was it a dream, his learning? Was it a devil's ball where he played through the night and found himself sitting in a pecan tree? Perhaps it is all symbolic of the spell of jazz— such magic as creates a Louis Armstrong. Each reader, the unusual young person or, perhaps, the adult, will seek his own interpretation. . . . [This is an] extraordinary tale. . . . (pp. 194-95)

Virginia Haviland, in a review of "Lonesome Boy," in The Horn Book Magazine (copyrighted, 1955, by The Horn Book, Inc., Boston), Vol. XXXI, No. 3, June, 1955, pp. 194-95.

With the co-operation of a superb artist [Feliks Topolski], this beautifully written short story by Mr. Bontemps makes a slim but very distinguished little book. . . .

The fearsome finale of Bubber's playing at a "devil's ball," used so vividly, will be recognized as folk material by some adults. To many children, it will be new and very strange, as will be grandpa's advice: "A horn can't do nothing for lonesomeness but make it hurt worse." This was not the advice

followed, probably, by the great Louis Armstrong, or by even greater musicians, but it is worth thinking about.

Louise S. Bechtel, in a review of "Lonesome Boy," in New York Herald Tribune Book Review (© I.H.T. Corporation; reprinted by permission), August 7, 1955, p. 8.

There is a lyrical and human feeling in this book. Grandpa's advice to Bubber proves to be more insightful and helpful about contemporary issues than it was considered when the story was first published.

"Fiction: 'Lonesome Boy'," in Adventuring with Books: 2,400 Titles for Pre=K-Grade 8, edited by Shelton L. Root, Jr. & others (copyright © 1973 by the National Council of Teachers of English), second edition, Citation Press, 1973, p. 47.

FREDERICK DOUGLASS: SLAVE-FIGHTER-FREEMAN (1959)

Probably most young people today have never heard of this "slave-fighter-freeman," as the subtitle describes this Negro leader. For the 10-14's here is a biography of a boy born in a plantation cabin, made to feel he was from an inferior race, kept from learning in order that he might be content with slavery. It might be the story of any ambitious gifted little Negro boy in the pre-war South. How he taught himself to read, improved his opportunities, and escaped only to help others is vividly told.

Millicent Taylor, "Men and Women Never to Be Forgotten," in The Christian Science Monitor (reprinted by permission from The Christian Science Monitor; © 1959 The Christian Science Publishing Society; all rights reserved), May 14, 1959, p. 11.*

In this simply written, easy-moving biography, Arna Bontemps deals mainly with Douglass' youth, that part of his life which would make the most dramatic appeal to boys and girls. Here are the early plantation days in Maryland, the decisive interim in Baltimore, the return to the Eastern Shore and the shock of working under a hard rather than a kind master, the hideously brutal treatment by a "slave-breaker," and, finally his escape to the North. His subsequent career is briefly but clearly summarized, and although one wishes there had been a little more concerning his post-Civil War work, the whole is sufficient to indicate the quality of the man who refused to be broken by slavery.

Ellen Lewis Buell, "Escape to Freedom," in The New York Times Book Review (© 1959 by The New York Times Company; reprinted by permission), June 21, 1959, p. 22.

Mr. Bontemps has used great restraint in this account of the sufferings of [Douglass during his] early years, but even so this is an exciting story of struggle against almost insurmountable odds, and of the triumph of human greatness. Direct style, large type and good illustrations make this an appealing book for children as young as nine or ten, but there is no writing down and junior high school boys and girls should find this absorbing. (pp. 293-94)

Ruth Hill Viguers, in a review of "Frederick Douglass: Slave-Fighter-Freeman," in The Horn Book Magazine (copyright, 1959, by The Horn Book, Inc., Boston), Vol. XXXV, No. 4, August, 1959, pp. 293-94.

The possibility of presenting both social and personal history is particularly well developed in some of the year's better biographies. In Arna Bontemps's skilful **"Frederick Douglass"** . . . wise presentation of the hero's motives establishes the rather subtle point that the wrong of slavery is intrinsic and that physical maltreatment is not the crux of the matter.

> *Joan Winsor Blos, "Importance of the Cherry Tree,"* in Saturday Review *(© 1960 Saturday Review Magazine Co.; reprinted by permission), Vol. XLIII, No. 7, February 20, 1960, p. 40.**

FAMOUS NEGRO ATHLETES   (1964)

Joe Louis and Sugar Ray Robinson, Jackie Robinson and Willie Mays, Jessie Owens, Wilt Chamberlain, Jimmy Brown, and Althea Gibson are all introduced here. Coverage includes their early years, school days, and eventual triumph as stars. The struggles of each to succeed, as an athlete and as a person, are told frankly, without sentimentality. A strong collection of capsule biographies, certain to be popular with sports fans. Recommended.

> *Jeraline N. Nerney, in a review of "Famous Negro Athletes,"* in School Library Journal, *an appendix to* Library Journal *(reprinted from the October, 1964 issue of* School Library Journal, *published by R. R. Bowker Co./A Xerox Corporation; copyright © 1964), Vol. 11, No. 2, October, 1964, p. 210.*

Arna Bontemps, who has written so variously about his people, writes in **"Famous Negro Athletes"** . . . with passion and acceptable melodrama about the career of [several] champions. This is, of course, tendentious image-making, but the image is needed. (p. 54)

> *Donald Barr, "A Great Issue Confronts the Writer— and Haunts Us All,"* in The New York Times Book Review, Part II *(© 1964 by The New York Times Company; reprinted by permission), November 1, 1964, pp. 3, 54-5.**

A collection of biographical sketches of Negro athletes, with emphasis on their accomplishments in the sports world but with a balanced attention paid to their personal lives. . . . The material has great popular appeal; the book is weakened by florid writing: ". . . colored folk sitting tensely before radios suddenly fell off their chairs with warm, fond laughter" or "She played more like an exciting stranger from another continent than a truant tomboy from a nearby neighborhood." . . . [An] index is appended. (pp. 3-4)

> *Zena Sutherland, in a review of "Famous Negro Athletes,"* in Bulletin of the Center for Children's Books *(reprinted by permission of The University of Chicago Press; copyright 1965 by The University of Chicago), Vol. 19, No. 1, September, 1965, pp. 3-4 [the excerpts of Arna Bontemps's work used here were originally published in his* Famous Negro Athletes *(reprinted by permission of Dodd, Mead & Company, Inc.; copyright © 1964 by Arna Bontemps), Dodd, Mead, 1964].*

MR. KELSO'S LION   (1970)

Percy and his grandfather travel by bus to Sidonia, Alabama to visit great-aunt Clothilde. Next door a man is boarding the lion that belongs to Mr. Kelso, and they all agree that the lion is both dangerous and unsanitary. A complaint to the authorities does no good, since no zoning regulation covers the matter. The lion gets out, knocks down but does not seriously injure Grandfather, and is lured back into his cage. Grandfather stays on to rest and recuperate, while Percy prepares to return home and go back to school. The writing style is adequate and the story has potential; unfortunately, it is not realized. There is some action but no development, a situation but no focus. (pp. 102-03)

> *Zena Sutherland, in a review of "Mr. Kelso's Lion,"* in Bulletin of the Center for Children's Books *(reprinted by permission of The University of Chicago Press; © 1971 by The University of Chicago), Vol. 24, No. 7, March, 1971, pp. 102-03.*

The life of the people in the black neighborhood is made miserable by Mr. Kelso's pet lion which is boarded there because zoning ordinances prevent this kind of a nuisance in the other end of town. Percy and his grandfather confront the local government agencies without success. . . . Percy returns home, convinced by Grandpa to study hard in school and learn how to solve such problems of injustice. This inconclusive ending will be disappointing to children, but the warmth of the low-keyed story outweighs the plot deficiency.

> *Marguerite M. Murray, in a review of "Mr. Kelso's Lion,"* in School Library Journal, *an appendix to* Library Journal *(reprinted from the March, 1971 issue of* School Library Journal, *published by R. R. Bowker Co./A Xerox Corporation; copyright © 1971), Vol. 17, No. 7, March, 1971, p. 126.*

YOUNG BOOKER: BOOKER T. WASHINGTON'S EARLY DAYS (1972)

Based heavily on Washington's autobiography, "Up From Slavery," this should be rated an inspirational work primarily suited for young readers. Arna Bontemps' portrait of the turn-of-the-century black leader is simplified and glamorized to the point of superficiality. It is a quite readable work that ranges through Washington's early career, romanticizes his three marriages, and carries up to the year 1895 when he made his famous address at the Atlanta Exposition.

> *A review of "Young Booker: Booker T. Washington's Early Days,"* in Publishers Weekly *(reprinted from the September 18, 1972 issue of* Publishers Weekly, *published by R. R. Bowker Company, a Xerox company; copyright © 1972 by Xerox Corporation), Vol. 202, No. 12, September 18, 1972, p. 67.*

[Bontemps] here attempts to retell the story of the life and work of the father of Tuskegee Institute, whose name is today almost a synonym for Uncle Tom. Bontemps shows Washington inadvertently contributing to the rationale of segregation through his acceptance of a separate-but-equal status and through his emphasis on training a black labor force. He clearly traces his enthusiastic embrace of white standards and culture. Yet without far deeper historical analysis than is presented here, we gain little insight into the tragic choices facing a young black teacher in the South of the Reconstruction. Somehow Washington comes off as a bit ridiculous, as well as gullible and insensitive; his autobiography, *Up from Slavery,* should correct that impression.

> *Aurora W. Gardner (Aurora G. Simms), in a review of "Young Booker: The Story of Booker T. Wash-*

ington's Early Days," in School Library Journal, *an appendix to* Library Journal *(reprinted from the October, 1972 issue of* School Library Journal; *published by R. R. Bowker Co./ A Xerox Corporation; copyright © 1972),* Vol. 97, No. 18, October, 1972, p. 3306.

Arna Bontemps's **"Young Booker"** is a readable popular account of the life of Washington. . . . Bontemps, a dean of Afro-American writers, ignores questions concerning the nature or sources of Washington's power and the many sides of his complex personality while providing a sketch of his youth, adolescence and rise to prominence. His account is rather close to that offered by Washington himself in his autobiographical "The Story of My Life and Work" and in "Up From Slavery" . . . and doesn't tell us much that is not already known. The explanations of Washington's actions and decisions are overly dramatic, the entire narrative is episodic—and the ending is abrupt.

On balance, however, Bontemps vividly reports the hardships that Washington endured while educating himself, and later while founding and building Tuskegee into the nation's most prominent black educational institution. The tone . . . [indicates] that this is not a book intended for the professional scholar or serious laymen. It is another of Bontemps's fine efforts at enlivening the history of black Americans. . . . (pp. 34-5)

John H. Bracey, Jr., "A Master of Role Playing, Strategem, Power," in The New York Times Book Review *(© 1973 by The New York Times Company; reprinted by permission), March 4, 1973, pp. 34-7.**

Nan Chauncy

1900-1970

English-born Australian author of fiction and nonfiction and scriptwriter.

Chauncy is credited with changing the course of Australian children's literature from melodrama to realistic fiction. Using rich Tasmanian settings, wholesome family relationships, convincing characters, and absorbing adventures, she stressed the wisdom of living in harmony with nature; her Badge Lorenny trilogy—*Tiger in the Bush, Devil's Hill,* and *The "Roaring 40"*—successfully reflects these traits.

As a child, Chauncy moved with her family from England to Tasmania, where she grew to love the wilds. After traveling around the world and teaching English in Denmark, she returned to Tasmania. She and her husband lived in her childhood home, where they founded the wildlife sanctuary Chauncy Vale. Chauncy's deep compassion for the extinct Tasmanian aborigines is movingly expressed in *Tangara* and *Mathinna's People,* often considered her best books. Her work is sometimes called historical writing, since many of the events she details are based on fact and personal experience. However, critics feel that she brings warmth and imagination, as well as a gift for description and expressive dialogue, to the telling of her stories.

In addition, critics praise Chauncy's development of character, her quiet compassion, and her effective presentation of reality. They note, however, that her portrayals of wicked people are not as persuasive as her descriptions of good characters. They also believe that her use of local language hinders her non-Australian audience and necessitates the use of a glossary. Chauncy's books challenge readers to become acquainted with a small world whose people and problems are nevertheless universal in nature. Her awards include the Australian Book of the Year Award in 1958 for *Tiger in the Bush,* in 1959 for *Devil's Hill,* and in 1961 for *Tangara. Devil's Hill* also received the Boys' Club of America Junior Book Award in 1961.

(See also *Something about the Author,* Vol. 6; *Contemporary Authors New Revision Series,* Vol. 4; and *Contemporary Authors,* Vols. 1-4, rev. ed.)

GENERAL COMMENTARY

Being lost in a book is far from being lost in the bush, but it is a good way to know how it feels to be someone else, somewhere else. And [Nan Chauncy] can fill the imagination of her 9-12-year-old readers with new sights, sounds and smells and the lilt of an unfamiliar accent. Her two most successful books are probably "Tiger in the Bush" and "Devil's Hill."

> Pamela Marsh, "Widening Horizons," in The Christian Science Monitor *(reprinted by permission from* The Christian Science Monitor; © *1961 The Christian Science Publishing Society; all rights reserved), June 29, 1961, p. 7.*

[In *They Found a Cave,* four] English children are sent to Tasmania to stay with their mother's twin sister for the duration of the war. When their aunt goes to Melbourne for a serious operation they rebel at the abnormally unkind treatment of the

housekeeper and her husband and, with a Tasmanian boy, run away to a well-concealed cave in the hills. Published simultaneously in the United States . . . are two other books by Mrs. Chauncy: *World's End Was Home* and *A Fortune for the Brave.* All three give glimpses of a beautiful part of the world where seasons are reversed and Christmas falls in the summer vacation, yet where life is remarkably like that in certain parts of the United States (with the addition of some unusual animal life) and young people's pleasures are very similar. All the books incline to sensationalism and the latter two particularly are reminiscent of fiction of a generation or so ago in which the happy outcome depended on melodramatic revelations of identity or unknown fortune. *World's End Was Home* has an appealing heroine and fewer unbelievably unpleasant people than *Fortune for the Brave,* but *They Found a Cave* reveals more of the rugged beauty of the bush country. Of this author's books, however, *Tiger in the Bush* and *Devil's Hill* are to be preferred unless there is special need for more stories with Tasmanian background.

> Ruth Hill Viguers, in a review of "They Found a Cave," in The Horn Book Magazine *(copyright, 1961, by The Horn Book, Inc., Boston), Vol. XXXVII, No. 4, August, 1961, p. 342.*

Some not-very-perceptive critics were unkind to *Half a World Away.* Coming after an unquestionable masterpiece [*Tangara*] it may have seemed altogether too slight and formless a piece. A story so autobiographical and so clearly important to the writer must nevertheless receive the earnest attention of those who find in Mrs. Chauncy's work some of the most stimulating, vigorous and sensitive elements to be seen in children's literature today. In it Mrs. Chauncy underlines, with perhaps a little less than her usual subtlety, one of the basic themes of all her stories, the contrast between the futility of conventions and the practical wisdom of life lived close to the realities of nature. The young Lettengars, in their preposterous Kentish home, are sensitive, when their awful governess lets them, to the beauty of everyday life, of "new beech leaves unfolding like tender green butterflies," but it is the escape from a society which does not allow them to do anything practical or useful to a new land "the shape of a heart" where their survival depends on their efforts which opens their eyes and gives skill to their hands. There is a nice simple symbolism when Jaffy, who had once longed to spend her birthday at the White City, receives as her first birthday present in her new world a cow. Not Mrs. Chauncy's best book, certainly, but full of her characteristic warmth.

I have started, in classical manner, in the middle. When Mrs. Chauncy came to write **Half a World Away** she had already completed six books and had three "Best Australian Book" awards to her credit. Before these successes she had got through her 'prentice period in three books, all of them interesting and characteristic. **They Found a Cave** . . . has one of her basic themes, that of a secret refuge. It is of course one of the recurrent dreams of childhood. The Pinners, whose awfulness sends the children into the wilds, may be unconvincing—this author has never been at her best in portraying wicked people—but life in the cave is convincingly described. Two familiar themes appear: the grief-haunted recluse, and the tragedy—not less poignant for being long past—of the aborigines. Immaturities in writing can be found, notably a weakness for anticipation—of the "little did he know. . ." kind. The book has nevertheless been widely popular, and has been the subject of a film in Australia. It stands up better to re-reading than **World's End Was Home** . . . and **A Fortune for the Brave**. . . . The former has an "escape" theme and a memorable heroine in Dallie, but the plot leans overmuch on coincidence. **A Fortune for the Brave** stands outside the main body of Mrs. Chauncy's work. For the most part the scene is "civilised," in England and in one of the early Tasmanian settlements; and the appeal is to adolescent readers. The detestable Goguds, a family living on past glories and quite ruthless in pursuing selfish ends, are just too much to bear, although Mrs. Chauncy's reclamation of the youngest shows some of the sympathetic subtlety of her later studies in character. The book is at its best when the action moves to Green End Island, whither a treasure hunt takes the Goguds and their cousin Huon—the days which Huon and friend Jimmy spend there marooned are full of a realistic delight in the wild—and in the intense interest of the details of the craft of bee-keeping.

With **Tiger in the Bush** . . . Mrs. Chauncy found herself and her principal character, Badge. Badge's world, tucked between the mountains "like a drop of dew between cabbage leaves," must be something like her own home in the pioneering days, and Badge's shared delight in the farm and the bush has the intensity of a personal experience. In **Tiger in the Bush** and, more markedly, in **Devils' Hill** . . . , the author shows the close and complex relationship between people and their environment. The first book about Badge is mainly a story about the creatures of the bush. There is a lovely passage in which Badge

watches a platypus at work, ignoring the mosquitoes which sing "ping" in his ear "as a grace before their meat, which was himself" and the leaches which suck his blood, and realises the personal relationship and understanding which he has with wild animals. In **Devils' Hill** Badge learns to live not only with animals but with humans. This long story about the search for a lost cow is in fact an extended study of the way in which people grow through experience and contact with one another. Badge, the boy who is at home in the wild, is the touchstone of the story, but the interest lies in Sam, his cocky cousin from "Outside," Sheppie, the little girl who embraces each new experience joyfully, and Bron, the timid shadow of a child who has her moment of glory. The episode in which Bron finds the cow's track is worthy of Ransome. **Devils' Hill,** technically a simple, almost plotless book, shows Mrs. Chauncy in the first full height of her powers, in a story which is rich in understanding and wisdom, no less profound for being expressed in Badge's artless words. Badge, defending the rights of the Tasmanian devil—"We was devils to them, Bron. They was here first, see? Minding their own business they was, when we come along"—is surely speaking for the author too.

Devils' Hill shows the author in full maturity. In most authors, however, there lies hidden a book better than their best, if only some miracle can release it. For Mrs. Chauncy the miracle happened. **Tangara** . . . is not just her best book. It is a book on a different plane. It is written out of experience, understanding and—to use the word carefully—inspiration; it is written, too, as an atonement. The theme of the destruction of the Tasmanian aborigines reappears again and again in Mrs. Chauncy's books. As a sensitive person must, she is haunted by the horror of it and takes upon herself a share of the guilt. Is her work in the preservation of Tasmania's threatened rare animals prompted—perhaps unconsciously—by the same feeling? Certainly in **Tiger in the Bush** she saw that the threat to the Tasmanian tiger was precisely like that to the aborigines, that both were threatened with death not from bullets but from a broken heart.

Tangara shows great technical mastery. The slow opening chapters, with their skilfully handled dialogue, set the tone most successfully, showing an ordinary sheltered society against which the tragedy is to be displayed. Mrs. Chauncy has a gift for the portraiture of small children, but Lexie is her masterpiece. When she comes to meet her future companion, nurse and stepmother, armoured with a "breastplate of kitten," she goes straight into the reader's heart and stays there. **Tangara** shows a mastery of economical writing. In earlier books Mrs. Chauncy sometimes scatters her sensitive descriptions of nature with too liberal a hand. Here she uses description sparingly and with precise effort. How beautifully she prepares the reader for the first appearance of the aboriginal child Merrina by building up an atmosphere, not of unreality but of sharper awareness. Lexie looks at the leaves behind which the little ghost-child is hiding. "When she stared very hard there was movement, lots of movement . . . hundreds and hundreds of quick silvery things sliding down the leaves in a shimmer of brightness, their toes wrapped in their silver hair."

There is an inner restraint in **Tangara**. So delicate a thread of story could be destroyed by one rough touch. Mrs. Chauncy never falters, never blunders into explanations. Her book is deeply moving. Difficult and demanding, as the best books have a right to be, it can be for the right reader, child or adult, a major emotional experience.

In her latest books Mrs. Chauncy has moved to a different scene and to a slightly different manner. **The Roaring 40** . . .

and *High and Haunted Island* . . . are stories in which the sea plays an important part, a beautiful and terrible sea which destroys lives and swallows the strange ship *Circle*. For the first time since her earliest books Mrs. Chauncy has used strong and complex plots. The stories are exciting, even if they strain the reader's credulity. I wonder, however, if the author is following her inclinations in writing like this, or if she has been driven by too literal a reading of critical reviews into writing not as she feels but as she thinks she ought. *High and Haunted Island* has a startling theme, and it took courage to create the extraordinary society of the Circlists and to show both its oddity and its wisdom. I find the handling of the story, with its shift in time, not entirely happy. The scene-painting, both of wild Port Davey and of the storm-torn rocks of Reef Island, is magnificent. In *The Roaring 40* Mrs. Chauncy is nearer to her home ground. This is the third "Badge" book. The interest here lies more in action than in observation. It is a mystery story, in which the old mystery—dating back to *Tiger in the Bush*—of old Harry the "hatter" is matched with the new mystery of Ned Kelly, the boy living naked in a cave beside the raging seas of Davey. Some of the sadness of *Tangara* lingers in this book, in the loneliness of Ned, waiting for his boat, which Badge, who has the bushman's feeling for "loneliness and beauty," can understand and share. Another of Mrs. Chauncy's favourite themes reappears here, that of the right to privacy. When Badge sees the label which Ned carries and which holds the clue to his identity, he feels ashamed and guilty at spying into another's secret. Although *The Roaring 40* is a moving and sad story, it has its own gaiety, in the character of the huge prospector, Vik, and its sweet humanity, in the affinity between Sheppie and the wild boy. (pp. 135-40)

In Nan Chauncy we have a writer with a rare and exciting scene, a vision and a philosophy. With increasing power and mastery of her medium and its technique, she has drawn a picture of a satisfying and sane way of life, "shut in and secret" indeed, but nevertheless sharply relevant to those who are bound to the wheel of an urban society. (p. 140)

Marcus Crouch, "Half a World Away," in The Junior Bookshelf, *Vol. 29, No. 3, June, 1965, pp. 135-40.*

Firsthand experience is the basis for all [Mrs. Chauncy's] books, but only as a springboard for her imagination. Living in her childhood setting must help Nan Chauncy to re-create the child's world, to see things with a child's outlook, and to say things in authentic dialogue form. As a skilled adult, she shapes memory into creative stories. . . .

[She] recalls the wrench of leaving home—and of being left behind—in several of her books. But the vacations were thrilling. On one holiday, the children found a wind-eroded cave—she pointed up the canyon—that had once been the hideout of a bushranger. The setting worked on Nan's memory, and half a century later it became the background for *They Found a Cave*. The story is not an account of a mistreated convict-turned-bandit. Rather it concerns the adventures of five children in a Crusoe-like existence. The children are morally justified in defying adults, the rascals who have seized their aunt's farm.

The situation is highly satisfactory to young readers, who keep on demanding the book after more than twenty years. (p. 442)

A thorough knowledge of animals plays a part in the trilogy about the Lorenny family. *Tiger in the Bush* is a fascinating

story of the Lorenny children finding a Tasmanian marsupial tiger, while hunting for a lost heifer. . . .

Its sequel, *Devil's Hill*, seems to me to have more character development. . . . (p. 444)

In *Tangara*, a lonely modern child slips into the past to make friends with a mysterious Aboriginal girl and relives the old terrors. One librarian described the book as "genuinely tragic, so moving that it is not for the too young or too sensitive child. Girls of twelve and over shouldn't miss it, however." [It] is, to me, the most memorable of Nan Chauncy's books.

More recently, *Mathinna's People* documents the tragedy of the Tasmanian race. Although in places the writing is almost poetry, yet the wide time range, the combination of fact and fiction, and the sense of doom combine to produce a book that is less satisfying than *Tangara*. . . .

None of Nan Chauncy's books can be considered a "tract." She has no tendency to whip up national pride or make a conscious effort to interpret Australia to outsiders. Such by-products are all to the good, of course, but to Nan Chauncy, "the story's the thing." (p. 445)

Lyn Harrington, "World's End Is Home for Nan Chauncy," in The Horn Book Magazine *(copyright © 1969 by The Horn Book, Inc., Boston), Vol. XLV, No. 4, August, 1969, pp. 441-45.*

With many fine new stories appearing, it's easy to forget Nan Chauncy's tales from the sixties, yet when difficult messages are in question, she is certainly the writer to remember. Who else has written explicitly and for children about the destruction of the Tasmanian Aborigines? *Mathinna's people* makes that situation terribly clear. At the same time, she never forgets the beauty and challenge of the land, its potential for adventurous children, and *The lighthouse keeper's son* strikes me as the most delightful way of learning the geography of the Australian East Coast, from lighthouse to lighthouse, as a family has to move with the job. Following Captain Cook's route, passing the Great Barrier Reef, she surely catches the spirit of place. Again in *Tangara*, which has as its epigraph 'let us set off again', she seems to be making a plea for the children of the Aborigines, remembering the atrocities of *Mathinna*, but introducing a note of reconciliation in the white children who hear the story and can learn from it. The device of matching two pairs of children, one Aborigine girl of the past and her white friend, one Aborigine girl of the present and her friend, brought together by evocations of the past—this is an old storytelling mechanism but it works. That is perhaps because of the sad endings, which Nan Chauncy does not shirk. In *Tangara*, the Aborigine child, who has led her friend away from danger remains obsessively in the mind of that friend. She can see her beside a small red fire in a hidden place in the bush. 'There for ever squatted Merrina, her thin arms reaching up imploringly. Merrina alone—alone, and calling to her dead.'

A bonus with this writer is the fidelity of her parent-children, brother-sister, children's-group relationships. I enjoy the lighthouse as a setting in *Lizzie Lights* but also Lizzie's mother: 'the broad face with the ugly hairs on the chin (and too few in her eyebrows)—the wrinkles round the eyes, the brown dress a little too tight, fastened in front with a Woolworth jewelled brooch.' Just as truthful are the appalling little spoilt sister in *The lighthouse keeper's son* and the false friend in *Lizzie Lights*, who puts everybody into a bad humour by her dangerous disobedience—on a lighthouse, remember—and calculated malice. (pp. 13-14)

D. J. Atkinson, "Waltzing Matilda: Children's Stories from Australia," in The School Librarian, Vol. 29, No. 1, March, 1981, pp. 12-15.*

THEY FOUND A CAVE (1948)

Any author who dares to give such a title to her book must have confidence in her powers to put over the most hackneyed of themes for a children's adventure story. And to a great extent her optimism is justified, for the cave is not introduced as a bit of sure-fire stock-in-trade. It is in fact actually existent in the author's Tasmanian homeland and both the background of the story and the children who are lucky enough to share in the adventures are drawn with sincerity and conviction. Even truly unpleasant parents are not spared! An unusual and worthwhile addition to the school library.

A review of "They Found a Cave," in The School Librarian and School Library Review, Vol. 4, No. 5, July, 1949, p. 297.

There is something more in [They Found a Cave] than an adventure, entertaining and spiced with discomfort; there is something more than the entrancing details of housekeeping with a difference. There is a feeling for character, for the behaviour of the various members of a family when faced by a crisis. (p. 274)

Margery Fisher, " 'Little Birds in Their Nests Agree': Family Stories," in her Intent Upon Reading: A Critical Appraisal of Modern Fiction for Children (copyright © 1961 by Margery Fisher), Hodder & Stoughton Children's Books (formerly Brockhampton Press), 1961, pp. 270-96.*

WORLD'S END WAS HOME (1952)

This story of family life in Tasmania makes a robust appeal because of the freshness of the material, the delightfully unfamiliar scene and the completely different shape of everyday life there. Exuberance bursts through the author's pen and makes up for the inexperience which has not yet learned how to let good characters take charge of events. The weakness of the story lies in the tiresomely novelettish plot which is clamped on it and by which the stranger in their midst, mild Dallie, is pursued melodramatically and not at all convincingly by a wealthy, designing Aunt and lawyers, successfully foiled by poor, practical Gran. It should nevertheless generally go down well with boys and girls in the ten to thirteen stage of reading.

Eleanor Graham, in a review of "World's End Was Home," in The Junior Bookshelf, Vol. 16, No. 3, October, 1952, p. 171.

The style of this book is lively, and children will learn something of the attractions of the Tasmanian countryside and its animals. . . . Here we find that hard work, friendliness and loyalty are qualities which bring fun and happiness to a family. . . . Girls in particular will like the story, though it is meant for both boys and girls of between nine and thirteen. (p. 205)

M.E.E., in a review of "World's End Was Home," in The School Librarian and School Library Review, Vol. 6, No. 3, December, 1952, pp. 204-05.

The story of Dallie, an orphan of eleven, who disliked the rich aunt with whom she lived, and went off in secret to live with the Wilde family in a remote and unsettled region of Tasmania. Characterization is good, and the writing style has ease and pace. The weakness of the book is in the improbable turn of the plot: the friend of the family, Uncle Dan, turns out to be Dallie's uncle just at the moment when her snobbish aunt appears to claim the girl. A long-lost member of the family is Uncle Dan, and he has just come into a title and proposes to take Dallie off for a year in England. The great strength of the book is in the atmosphere of wild back country, described in loving and evocative detail.

Zena Sutherland, in a review of "World's End Was Home," in Bulletin of the Center for Children's Books (reprinted by permission of The University of Chicago Press; copyright 1961 by The University of Chicago), Vol. 15, No. 1, September, 1961, p. 4.

A FORTUNE FOR THE BRAVE (1954)

Tasmania makes a pleasant and welcome change of setting for any tale, but the tale is even more pleasant when it is itself original in outcome. Huon Trivett, plucked from the lazy pleasures of racing on the Thames to learn farming on a friend's farm in Tasmania, finds himself staying with cousins who are only interested in him because he may hold a clue to an island on which treasure may be found. They are not a nice family and go to some lengths to cheat him of a suspected inheritance. Fortunately Huon finds his own allies and, eventually, his own unexpected treasure. More important, he finds himself. Miss Chauncy has a feeling for country and situation and makes the most of both in a quiet, effective style. (pp. 140-41)

A review of "A Fortune for the Brave," in The Junior Bookshelf, Vol. 19, No. 3, July, 1955, pp. 140-41.

Good writing style and good characterization, but there is in this story an unpleasant and unjustifiable hostility among some of the characters that weakens the book. . . . [The] ending of the story is a happy change from the usual plot, with a logical explanation of [the cousins'] mistake and a protagonist satisfied with his lot.

Zena Sutherland, in a review of "A Fortune for the Brave," in Bulletin of the Center for Children's Books (reprinted by permission of The University of Chicago Press; copyright 1961 by The University of Chicago), Vol. 14, No. 10, June, 1961, p. 155.

TIGER IN THE BUSH (1957)

The strength of this book lies in the Tasmanian setting. It is beautifully and sensitively brought before the mind of the reader, not as a mere description, but in the people who live in the valley, whose lives are a part of it and whose personalities it governs.

The story centres round Badge, the eleven year-old youngest member of this family in the valley, who discovers a secret about the rare Tasmanian tiger and, in an unguarded moment, gives that secret away to two scientists, one of whom he greatly admires. His remorse on realisation, followed by his plans to remain true to the valley and its life yet still wishing to help his scientist, is excellently handled by the author. Badge is a down-to-earth honest thinking boy who comes out of trouble the better for it. The rest of his family—Liddle-Ma, Dad, brother Lance and sister Iggy—are all individuals and yet part of that valley team. Each character is fully rounded in portrayal, and the personal relationships truly interpreted.

The result is a worth while book, meat for any boy or girl with a liking for something different, it is also a book that can be read again and more extracted at every reading. It can open new pathways and open new realms of experience as enjoyment increases for the young reader.

> *A review of "Tiger in the Bush," in* The Junior Bookshelf, *Vol. 21, No. 3, July, 1957, p. 132.*

This has the same compelling interest [as *Devil's Hill*] in its intimate, detailed picturing of Badge's family. . . . The family relationships are important and are fully developed. . . . Colloquial speech has wisely been reduced to make this story much less formidable on the page than was *Devil's Hill.*

> *Virginia Haviland, in a review of "Tiger in the Bush," in* The Horn Book Magazine *(copyright, 1961, by The Horn Book, Inc., Boston), Vol. XXXVII, No. 3, June, 1961, p. 265.*

Interest centers on Badge, . . . who resents the close relationship between his older brother and sister; during the course of the story Badge gains self-confidence and independence. Good relationships, marvelous background of Tasmanian wild life; the weaknesses of the book are in the heavy use of local terminology and idiom, and the rather slow pace of development that results from the detailed narration of events.

> *Zena Sutherland, in a review of "Tiger in the Bush," in* Bulletin of the Center for Children's Books *(reprinted by permission of The University of Chicago Press; copyright 1962 by The University of Chicago), Vol. 15, No. 2, October, 1962, p. 25.*

Children for whom nature is a way of life will be able to identify with Badge even though it is wombat and platypus he watches and not rabbit and hedgehog in the fields or birds at a city bird-table. They may envy him the freedom and variety of his days, but they may notice that he suffers like any other youngest child from the casual teasing and neglect of his elders and that like any other boy he has to learn through trial and error. Nan Chauncy understands the difficulties of a solitary child suddenly challenged by new relationships or (as with *Lizzie Lights*) a new environment. In all her books, too, a racy, amusing and expressive dialogue gives the right clues—and never too many—to the basis and changes of individual personality. All this in a setting that will have the attractions of the unfamiliar for English readers, described with economy and always in the interest of the story. . . . (pp. 1756-57)

> *Margery Fisher, "An Old Favourite," in her* Growing Point, *Vol. 10, No. 2, July, 1971, pp. 1756-57.*

DEVIL'S HILL **(1958)**

There is something about Badge, the Tasmanian boy living in what might euphemistically be described as the back of beyond, which compels admiration and a certain unsentimental wonder. To the son of a white man and wife engaged literally in wresting a living from a reluctant land, the thought of school in a distant township after this freedom looms as an impossible restraint, especially as it will entail sharing life on intimate terms with cousin Sam who has always seemed to despise his isolated kinsman and his parents' way of life. An accidental epidemic

and a family crisis puts an end to the immediate prospect of school, and the death of Badge's family cow causes an emergency in which Sam and his two sisters are involved. The fascination of Miss Chauncy's addition to the Badge saga is the steady development of *all* the characters involved in her story, a story which has none of the artificial elements of plot-making, and the impact of the natural background which is always apparent. The fact is, Miss Chauncy is what used to be confidently called an artist and one still cannot give higher praise than that.

> *A review of "Devil's Hill," in* The Junior Bookshelf, *Vol. 22, No. 5, November, 1958, p. 276.*

The children and the adults, their relations one with another, and the carefully observed unfolding of the children—all this is beautifully done.

Miss Chauncy is not afraid of squalor, does not see it as squalor any more than she sees it as romantic poverty. When her family sits down to tea, the table is "festive . . . " [with newspapers for a cloth and candles stuck in bottles and a huge fire for lighting]. This is life, and there is no more self-consciousness about this than there is about the children staring at the glory of the sunset streaming over the hills. . . . This is a lovely book, full of warmth, vitality and reality. . . .

> *"Unhappy Far-Off Things," in* The Times Literary Supplement *(© Times Newspapers Ltd. (London) 1958; reproduced from* The Times Literary Supplement *by permission), No. 2960, November 21, 1958, p. xxi.**

An interesting picture of life in the Tasmanian Bush. . . . With its abundance of dialect and unfamiliar words, however, it is not for the slow, reluctant reader. The curious child who reads eagerly and well will find it a rewarding account of a difficult way of life very different from ours.

> *A review of "Devil's Hill," in* Publishers Weekly *(reprinted from the June 13, 1960 issue of* Publishers Weekly, *published by R. R. Bowker Company; copyright © 1960 by R. R. Bowker Company), Vol. 177, No. 24, June 13, 1960, p. 98.*

[The plot] comes vividly to life through the author's intimate knowledge of her setting. It is the realistic portrayal of this setting and of the characters who move within it which imparts to this book its particular appeal.

> *Patricia D. Beard, in a review of "Devil's Hill," in* Junior Libraries, *an appendix to* Library Journal *(reprinted from the October 15, 1960 issue of* Junior Libraries, *published by R. R. Bowker Co./A Xerox Corporation; copyright © 1960), Vol. 85, No. 18, October 15, 1960, p. 3859.*

"Devil's Hill" has a powerful setting; the reader comprehends the loneliness and danger of man against the wild. Sharply contrasted, to good effect, is the basic simplicity of the story, and the forthrightness of the characters. The style is terse; the vocabulary requires attention but—with the aid of a brief glossary—is fully understandable. The best of intermediate readers should be offered this book, and encouraged to persevere in it.

> *Mary Louise Hector, "What Badge Learned," in* The New York Times Book Review, Part II *(© 1960 by The New York Times Company; reprinted by permission), November 13, 1960, p. 42.*

TANGARA: "LET US SET OFF AGAIN" (1960; U.S. edition as The Secret Friends)

[*Tiger in the Bush* and *Devil's Hill*] seemed to add a third dimension to the author's always interesting projection of the Tasmanian countryside and its people, and now she adds the fourth dimension and gives the original Tasmanians their place in the picture. In a deceptively simple, approachable manner she introduces the people surrounding motherless eight year-old Lexie, all very pleasant, following their own pursuits, undoubtedly living. Yet no one seems so full of life as the little naked native girl, Merrina, whom Lexie meets daily for a brief period. Merrina is a delightful piece of creation, and Lexie's entry into her world is most vividly described; her traumatic vision of its brutal destruction comes as a personal shock, and with it the realisation of the essential wrongness of the natives' fate.

The whole experience is driven too deep for conscious memory, but after years filled with normal happy activities, at school, with Guides, on family holidays, another crisis brings Merrina back for a moment, and for the first time it is established that she has come a very long way indeed, for her tribe was destroyed before the eyes of Lexie's great-great aunt. But it is Lexie's zipper which is displayed to the elders, and Lexie's brother who is saved by Merrina's agency, so there is much to ponder over when the end is reached. If it can be called an end, for Mrs. Chauncy is very good at conveying a sense of life going on: Lexie is still growing up with much before her, the affectionately described old dog, Uncle Podger, dies, as is natural and right. So there is nothing morbid or mystical about this tale of the supernatural, but a deep appreciation of life, especially of life in Tasmania. . . . [*This*] story will stand. . . . (pp. 143-44)

> *A review of "Tangara," in* The Junior Bookshelf, *Vol. 24, No. 3, July, 1960, pp. 143-44.*

An unusual setting for a time-displacement fantasy. . . . The ending is anticlimactic and over-extended, but the portion of the book that describes the culture of the aborigines and the friendship of Lexie and Merinna is absorbing. The writing style is highly fragmented and rather difficult, in places, to follow. It is unfortunate that—for the greater part of the story—Lexie is only eight, since the difficulties of style and vocabulary demand older readers.

> *Zena Sutherland, in a review of "The Secret Friends," in* Bulletin of the Center for Children's Books *(reprinted by permission of The University of Chicago Press; copyright 1962 by The University of Chicago), Vol. 15, No. 10, June, 1962, p. 156.*

The unusual setting of this story, the convincing characterization, and the smooth stepping back and forth in time make this an outstanding fantasy.

> *Charlotte S. Huck and Doris Young Kuhn, "Modern Fantasy and Humor: 'Tangara: "Let Us Set Off Again"'," in their* Children's Literature in the Elementary School *(copyright © 1961, 1968 by Holt, Rinehart and Winston, Inc.; reprinted by permission of Holt, Rinehart and Winston, Publishers, CBS College Publishing), second edition, Holt, Rinehart and Winston, 1968, p. 364.*

Nan Chauncy used the character of Lexie as a medium for her own feeling about the now extinct Tasmanian aboriginals and their fate at the hands of the white settlers of the last century. It is a subject she explored again later in the historical story *Mathinna's People. Tangara* is emotionally closer to the subject because the theme is explored through the feelings of a child who mysteriously enters into the experience of another like herself in the past. The two little girls are delightfully real as they dance together, but Lexie is just as believable as a schoolgirl. She is not in any sense a disturbed child but one whose solitary, imaginative temperament responds uniquely to the influence of the necklace [given by Merrina to Lexie's great-great aunt Rita] and of the gully round which hung the shadows of old gaiety and old unhappiness.

> *Margery Fisher, "Who's Who in Children's Books: Lexie," in her* Who's Who in Children's Books: A Treasury of the Familiar Characters of Childhood *(copyright © 1975 by Margery Fisher; reprinted by permission), Holt, Rinehart and Winston, 1975, Weidenfeld and Nicolson, 1975, p. 173.*

Australian critics agree that [Chauncy's] outstanding book is *Tangara.* . . . Ultimately, the loving sympathy between the black and the white girls cancels out some of the hideous cruelty inflicted on one race by another. This is a book that could appeal to a much wider audience than its Australian readers. (p. 23)

> *Vida Horn, "Children's Books in the Commonwealth of Australia," in* Printed for Children: World Children's Book Exhibition *(© 1978 by K. G. Saur Verlag KG, München), Saur, 1978, pp. 19-28.**

HALF A WORLD AWAY (1962)

[Nan Chauncy] has written a kind of historical novel, capturing with uncanny precision the atmosphere of 1911. *Half A World Away* is a little bit of her own story. . . . One hopes that her childhood was not as distressing as the one described here, for in the days of their father's affluence the Lettengars are left to the care of a remarkably foolish governess and nurse. It is only when father's money is embezzled that parents and children get together and discover a common objective.

Nevertheless it is this book's particular quality that it conveys the idea of the family as a self-contained unit made up of interdependent parts. The sum of Ben, Jaffy, Wolfe and Roddy is greater than the individual parts. Lest this should sound boringly portentous it should be added that the story is told with pace and a homely style. The new book has not the passionate quality of *Tangara;* it is a sweet, joyous, honest book which rings true in every page. (pp. 258-59)

> *A review of "Half a World Away," in* The Junior Bookshelf, *Vol. 26, No. 5, November, 1962, pp. 258-59.*

From a 19th-century world of cooks, gardeners and governesses, the Lettengar children rather suddenly find themselves aboard a ship headed for Tasmania and a pioneer life filled with the freedom and responsibilities they've yearned for. The very English beginning may prove thick going for young readers, but once under way to Tasmania they will enjoy this story.

> *A review of "Half a World Away," in* Publishers Weekly *(reprinted from the January 28, 1963 issue of* Publishers Weekly, *published by R. R. Bowker Company; copyright © 1963 by R. R. Bowker Company), Vol. 183, No. 4, January 28, 1963, p. 260.*

There is interesting contrast between the two settings and in the adjustment of a well-to-do family to wilderness life, but there is an oddly outdated quality to the writing. . . . The end of the story is a bit sugar-frosted. . . .

> *Zena Sutherland, in a review of "Half a World Away,"* in Bulletin of the Center for Children's Books *(reprinted by permission of The University of Chicago Press; copyright 1963 by The University of Chicago), Vol. 16, No. 8, April, 1963, p. 124.*

[Family stresses produced by a move from England to Tasmania], and the personal and material problems involved, is the theme of Nan Chauncy's autobiographical novel *Half a World Away*. . . . This is not in the first flight of Mrs Chauncy's books, but it meant much to her for personal reasons. . . . The former section of *Half a World Away* is a Nesbitish social comedy, the latter a story of pioneering adventure. The division does not help artistic unity, but this is a book to judge not on structural grounds but as a personal document. It is flooded with nostalgia, but this for once produces not a sentimental cloud, but a deeper authenticity. (p. 180)

> *Marcus Crouch, "School—Home—Family," in his* The Nesbit Tradition: The Children's Novel in England 1945-1970 *(© Marcus Crouch 1972; reprinted by permission of the author), Ernest Benn, 1972, pp. 161-84.**

THE "ROARING 40" (1963)

Badge, whom we have met in previous books, is growing up and Iggy, his sister, is talking of her "career." But the family is still a united one and "Liddle-ma" is the warm centre of it.

Badge accompanies his father and Vik Viking to Port Davey to find the hiding place of a lost lump of gold. They find no gold but they do discover a lost boy. He is all alone on this uninhabited coast and the mystery of his identity and his connection with Old Harry's wrecked boat, makes a stange and moving tale.

This story has not the haunting beauty of *Tangara*, but nevertheless it has positive and admirable qualities. The background of the wild uninhabited country and the great lonely beaches where the surf thunders unheard, is conveyed vividly. . . . As usual Mrs. Chauncy . . . has given us a story of distinction, originality and warmth. (pp. 209-10)

> *A review of "The 'Roaring 40'," in* The Junior Bookshelf, *Vol. 27, No. 4, October, 1963, pp. 209-10.*

[The lost boy's] story is wildly impossible yet, as the author tells it, completely believable. She shows how Badge, whose heart is as soft as his behaviour is practical, comes to realise the cruelty men are capable of, to realise and in the end to accept it as part of a life that holds also trust and affection. Past touches present, in a moving story . . . that will make a strong impression on any thoughtful child. (p. 263)

> *Margery Fisher, in a review of "The 'Roaring 40'," in her* Growing Point, *Vol. 2, No. 7, January, 1964, pp. 262-63.*

HIGH AND HAUNTED ISLAND (1964)

Nan Chauncy's books are already popular with young people in this country and this story of shipwreck and survival on the wild coast of Tasmania will add to her already high reputation.

The plot takes some time to develop, but once one meets the two schoolgirls, wrecked during the First World War, it is full of suspense and vivid story telling. They are rescued by some very odd Scandinavians, who belong to a religious cult called the Circle. The girls are taken, rather unwillingly, with them to found a settlement on an inaccessible part of the coast called the Reef. Many years later they are discovered by the brother of one of them, who has been searching for them, but they do not want to return to the outside world.

Some of the descriptive passages make one long to visit the coastline. Older boys and girls will read this novel with pleasure and will learn a great deal from it. The development of the girls' characters, under great stress, is skilfully and realistically drawn and will prove especially interesting to them. (pp. 230-31)

> *A review of "High and Haunted Island," in* The Junior Bookshelf, *Vol. 28, No. 4, October, 1964, pp. 230-31.*

Part of the attraction of this book is its deep familiarity with the country and people, customs and ways of speech. Nan Chauncy writes of a world she knows and there is nothing superficial about it.

> *"Sporting the Field," in* The Times Literary Supplement *(© Times Newspapers Ltd. (London) 1964; reproduced from* The Times Literary Supplement *by permission), No. 3274, November 26, 1964, p. 1076.**

The book begins with an account of the [rescuers] and their background and is very slow to get into the story of Tess and Vicky; the writing style is rather clogged and heavy.

> *Zena Sutherland, in a review of "High and Haunted Island," in* Bulletin of the Center for Children's Books *(reprinted by permission of The University of Chicago Press; copyright 1965 by The University of Chicago), Vol. 19, No. 4, December, 1965, p. 59.*

An enchanting novel on two time planes. . . . Skillful plotting and characterizations and a perfect conclusion make this a memorable story.

> *Jeanette Hotchkiss, "Australasia and Oceania: 'High and Haunted Island'," in her* African-Asian Reading Guide for Children and Young Adults *(copyright © 1976 by Jeanette Hotchkiss), The Scarecrow Press, Inc., 1976, p. 201.*

MATHINNA'S PEOPLE (1967; U.S. edition as *Hunted in Their Own Land*)

We have seen some notable revolutions in writing for children these past few decades, many of them marking a corresponding evolution of thought in the adult world. Slowly and painfully people are learning to question much that was taken for granted in the past and occasionally someone is able to crystallise the resulting self-discovery of the race so that even a child can comprehend matters which were hidden from their ancestors. That is what happens in this story, where the white man's rape of Tasmania is made clear without any undue weighting or underlining, but by a simple and dignified reconstruction of the life of two neighbouring tribes, with special emphasis on Wyrum, who becomes leader of his little group. They are not noble savages, but human beings who have worked out an astonishingly successful way of life, one of the most innocent and elementary "civilisations" ever achieved, but totally unprepared for any intrusion of the outside world. When the outside world does intrude and goes on intruding until the aborigines are almost totally extinguished it comes as a real blow to the reader, particularly to the white reader who sees what his own kind has perpetrated in wanton ignorance and greed. The horrible cheat of putting the remaining tribesmen on a worthless island and forcing them to copy meaningless aspects of western life is made especially vivid to the reader who has learned to admire these people in their proper setting. Nothing is said of the White Man's Burden in the Kiplingese sense, nor of the new burden of shame for what our race has wrought, but real feeling is evoked for the peaceful people who were once natives of Tasmania. We might not want to share their lives, but it is salutory to share their humanity and to respect it. Books like this should help foster our own development, for the material is good, the writing excellent and the last chapters are unforgettably moving. (pp. 178-79)

A review of "Mathinna's People," in The Junior Bookshelf, *Vol. 31, No. 3, June, 1967, pp. 178-79.*

[A] fictionalized but conscientious reconstruction of the last days of the Toogee of Tasmania. . . . From Wyrum's first sighting of a "whale with wings" to another able young chief's gradual destruction years later and the postscripted story of his daughter's subsequent sad fate, the Toogee people are recalled with a fidelity and restraint that make the chronicle all the more moving.

A review of "Hunted in Their Own Land," in Kirkus Reviews *(copyright © 1973 The Kirkus Service, Inc.), Vol. XLI, No. 5, March 1, 1973, p. 259.*

The poignant and relevant theme is that of the white man's conquest of the west coast of Tasmania and the indignities he inflicted on the aboriginal Toogee people. . . . The reading is difficult as the prose incorporates both fragments of an ancient tribal language and a primitive logic. Because of the sophisticated approach and style, the book will appeal more to a guilt-ridden population than to children.

Barbara K. Rodes, in a review of "Hunted in Their Own Land," in Children's Book Review Service *(copyright © 1973 Children's Book Review Service Inc.), Vol. 1, No. 8, April, 1973, p. 48.*

The story of the coming of the first white men to Tasmania gives a colorful picture of the tribal cultures and the richness of their traditions, but it moves slowly, the details that are interesting as a study of Aborigine patterns too intricate for literary smoothness.

Zena Sutherland, in a review of "Hunted in Their Own Land," in Bulletin of the Center for Children's Books *(reprinted by permission of The University of Chicago Press; © 1973 by The University of Chicago), Vol. 26, No. 9, May, 1973, p. 135.*

The tragic history of Tasmanian aborigines comes to life in a reconstruction of fact and legend which speaks movingly of one more Eden destroyed, and of man's cheating injustice to its displaced people. Teachers will find much potential in the

book. The scenery is fresh and vivid, and the all-too-believable characters will spark imaginations as they haunt consciences.

Lois Belfield Watt, in a review of "Hunted in Their Own Land," in Childhood Education *(reprinted by permission of the Association for Childhood Education International, 3615 Wisconsin Ave., N.W., Washington, DC 20016; copyright © 1973 by the Association), Vol. 49, No. 8 (May, 1973), p. 421.*

Haunting, somber fiction. . . . In this book, the author's writing is at her best as she tells of the ritual celebrations based on aboriginal mythology of Moon, Sun, and Sea, and tells of the mounting terror brought by "Meester Robeenson's" men and their "firesticks." Behind the narrative is the splendidly detailed picture of the environment. . . . The book may be a challenge to the young reader, who will be confronted with words from aboriginal dialect (not all listed in the Glossary), but the highly provocative presentation will be rewarding. (pp. 275-76)

Virginia Haviland, in a review of "Hunted in Their Own Land," in The Horn Book Magazine *(copyright © 1973 by The Horn Book, Inc., Boston), Vol. XLIX, No. 3, June, 1973, pp. 275-76.*

LIZZIE LIGHTS (1968)

[*Lizzie Lights* has an] uncommon setting—a lighthouse on a lonely island off Tasmania. The descriptions of Shag Island, with its windswept houses and enormous cliffs, of ships and rocks, and birds, and above all the changing sky and sea, are much the best part of the book. The people by contrast seem less real and their problems less urgent, until the climax of the story when we realize what it has all been leading up to— Lizzie's feelings about her Mum when she discovers that she is an adopted child, and the conflict between her desire to help after her Mum's accident and her fear of flying. Lizzie herself is an appealing character, and Mum stands out as real and solid as the lighthouse itself.

"People Who Live in the Country," in The Times Literary Supplement *(© Times Newspapers Ltd. (London) 1968; reproduced from The Times Literary Supplement by permission), No. 3446, March 14, 1968, p. 259.**

Mrs. Chauncy, like some other fine writers, needs to relax and recoup after a supreme effort. So, after that devastatingly moving book *Mathinna's People*—a book surely written in the author's heart's blood—comes *Lizzie Lights,* which is indeed light. Here however is a writer who, at her slightest, is still always herself, a person of integrity. The weakness of *Lizzie Lights* is largely structural. It is a book insufficiently designed. The picture of life on a lighthouse rock, and of the girl who sheltered there from the realities of life is drawn with tenderness, and with a deep understanding both of people and of landscape. Mrs. Chauncy is less successful with the dreadful Myra Jaffy who plays serpent in this Eden; she is not the first fine writer who fails to portray the unpleasant. If *Lizzie Lights* is not a distinguished book, it is an honest and an amusing one, and should appeal strongly to growing-up girls, including those who, like Lizzie, find difficulty in adjusting to adult life.

A review of "Lizzie Lights," in The Junior Bookshelf, *Vol. 32, No. 3, June, 1968, p. 174.*

THE LIGHTHOUSE KEEPER'S SON (1969)

Nan Chauncy's new book, *The Lighthouse Keeper's Son,* is even more of a disappointment after *Lizzie Lights.* It is meant for rather younger children. Chessy is nearly ten; Lizzie was thirteen. He is also a loner, but he is a cardboard character compared with Lizzie, and his family—the unfailingly annoying small sister, the mother who understands so little that she thinks a rare shell can be replaced by something bought—are by Mrs. Chauncy's own high standards cardboard people too. There is none of the warmth of the Lorenny books, none of the intensity and involvement of a book like *Tangara.* In the new book, Mrs. Chauncy never focuses entirely on a place or a situation. Nothing much happens except that the family moves from lighthouse to fruit market, to another lighthouse and another. It is only at the end that the low-pressure narrative gathers pace and finally resolves itself into a neat little last paragraph:

> So that was all right; the cyclone had passed,
> Chessy had his dog, his shell was safe—and
> he had made a new friend.

(p. 1203)

> *"Half a World Away," in* The Times Literary Supplement *(© Times Newspapers Ltd. (London) 1969; reproduced from* The Times Literary Supplement *by permission), No. 3529, October 16, 1969, pp. 1202-03.**

This is a kind of by-product of *Lizzie Lights.* The earlier book was dictated at least as much by the interest of the main char-

acter as by the author's fascination with lighthouses. Now that fascination has taken charge.

Chessy is torn protesting from a light on the Tasmanian coast to go and grow—in fact to sell—fruit in Queensland. That enterprise fails and the family return to lights, this time off the Great Barrier Reef. That is about all the story. Apart from the extraordinary interest of the enclosed society of the lighthouse men, the story is sustained by some minor conflicts of character, in which Chessy's horrid little sister—Mrs. Chauncy never could manage really nasty characters—plays a part.

Here in fact is a minor Chauncy. Her lesser achievements are better than a great many people's best, but one misses the penetration, the compassion which are this fine writer's hallmarks. In compensation, however, there are some magnificent land- and sea-scapes.

> *A review of "The Lighthouse Keeper's Son," in* The Junior Bookshelf, *Vol. 33, No. 6, December, 1969, p. 382.*

This is a rambling story. . . . There's a dog, a little sister who's a nuisance, some excitement in storms and a cyclone, and lots of interesting information to be picked up on the way. Chessy has a passionate interest in shells, and a proper curiosity about history and geography, but the book makes no demands on the imagination.

> *Alex McLeod, in a review of "The Lighthouse Keeper's Son," in* The School Librarian, *Vol. 18, No. 2, June, 1970, p. 242.*

Vera Cleaver

1919-

Bill Cleaver

1920-1981

American authors of fiction.

The Cleavers are major writers for today's pre-adolescent and young adult audience. They are known for the vivid settings, authentic dialogue, and grim realism of their novels, which present perceptive, honest portrayals of human nature. Their protagonists, usually female, experience inner conflicts connected with growing up while confronting such contemporary social and moral issues as divorce, suicide, poverty, illegitimacy, and mental retardation. The Cleavers present these topics in a way that is thought-provoking rather than didactic. Exhibiting traditional values of independence, endurance, family responsibility, and respect for education, Cleaver heroines and heroes fight against great odds and mature in the process. Their stories mirror the good and bad in life, and incorporate humor and levity to temper seriousness of plot.

Raised during the Depression, the Cleavers experienced many of the struggles depicted in their works. Unable to complete their formal education, they taught themselves in public libraries. Early in their marriage, the Cleavers composed over 275 stories for pulp magazines. Wishing to stretch their creativity and produce writings of more lasting value, they then began to write for children. Bill usually generated the ideas which were developed in collaboration. He then performed the technical research which Vera later incorporated into the writing of the story.

Critical reception of the Cleavers's books has generally been very favorable. Reviewers especially applaud *Where the Lilies Bloom* for its realistic Appalachian dialogue, its accurate descriptions of the mountain terrain and wildcrafting (a gathering of herbs and plants for medicinal purposes), and its notable portrayal of Mary Call Luther. Mary Call is fiercely determined to overcome the odds of her father's death, her family's poverty, and their possible disunity. In *Ellen Grae* and *Lady Ellen Grae*, the heroine is the independent daughter of divorced parents. She deals with a lying problem and matures from tomboy to young lady. While these books are praised for their faithful depiction of human nature and their graphic Florida setting, some critics feel that Ellen's thoughts are occasionally too adult. Reviewers praise *Me Too* for its honest treatment of mental retardation: Lydia fails to educate her afflicted twin sister but grows in her understanding of the emotions of the retarded; critics see the twins as sensitively and realistically drawn. In contrast to their strong, young main characters, Cleaver adults often appear fallible and prone to emotional disaster: they desert their children, commit suicide, become criminals, and are generally ineffectual.

The Cleavers do not moralize on the universal issues they treat; instead, they present differing views on these topics and allow readers to form their own conclusions. However, the Cleavers

Courtesy of Lothrop, Lee & Shepard Company

do not dwell on the problems themselves. Rather, they incorporate humor into the stories and stress the indomitability of the human spirit to transcend situations despite setback or defeat. It is these aspects, critics say, that save their books from being depressing. Several of their books have been designated as ALA Notable Children's Books and have appeared on the New York Times Annual List of Best Juveniles. Four of their books have been finalists for the National Book Award: *Where the Lilies Bloom* in 1970, *Grover* in 1971, *The Whys and Wherefores of Littabelle Lee* in 1974, and *Queen of Hearts* in 1979. *Dust of the Earth* won the Lewis Carroll Shelf Award and the Western Writers of America Spur Award in 1975.

(See also *Contemporary Authors*, Vols. 73-76 and *Something about the Author*, Vols. 22, 27 [obituary].)

AUTHORS' COMMENTARY

Ideally the writer of fiction comes to the task of doing so with an understanding of what fiction is. For me it is not so much the said but the unsaid. It is that which holds incident and character together, the questing voices that whisper, 'What is it? Why is it? Where are we going? What's on the other side?'

The question of why I write is put to me often but in all my years at this art or craft or madness or whatever it is I have not yet been able to translate the why of it into a distinct description. I can suppose that it is an inherent energy that pushes me toward some kind of self-validation. I say 'inherent' because I believe that only the mechanics of creative writing may be taught. As a very young child I knew that I was going to be a writer. Also, in that way children know things without being told or shown, I knew that I was going to have to be my own teacher. I have been my own teacher. I am a graduate of the public libraries of the United States of America.

I like the peace of my daily performance of brooding and poring and study and I revel in the attempts to set to page that which goes beyond the presentation of mere human behaviour. All of this digging and pushing and grinding and examination is not a bid for immortality. It is to put to work that which was given me to use for a while.

I have written of the Ozark mountaineer, of the South Dakotan, the Floridian, the rural Appalachian dweller, and so again and yet again there comes this:

Question: Do you write for any deliberately chosen audience?

Answer: No. I write of what I know. My audience is volunteer.

Question: Do you feel the need to explain the elements of your settings?

Answer: No. The explanations flow, or they should, from the philosophies in the work, from its intellectual meaning, from invested detail. If explanations are needed then, in my opinion, the work is either weak or has failed.

Question: Is the backdrop scenery in your work incidental?

Answer: Of course not. Months before I start a work I begin to gather my research material. It is requisite absolute that I know the speech of my fictional companions, know their lore. I must see their geography.

Question: Readers readily identify with stereotypes. Why do you avoid using them?

Answer: I have never seen a stereotyped situation or person. For me there resides, even in the most common, the unusual, and I want to know what it is and then through the selection of word and event tackle a demonstration.

Question: As a team how do you work together?

Answer: Well, let me tell you a little story. We have a close friend with whom we lunch several times a month. He tells us that he has trouble recognizing us when we are not together. He is serious. We have been married that long. We are joint and so all of our endeavours and opinions are joint. This is not a hedge, you understand. That is simply the way it is. (pp. 39-40)

> *Vera Cleaver and Bill Cleaver, in an extract from "Vera and Bill Cleaver," in* A Sounding of Storytellers: New and Revised Essays on Contemporary Writers for Children *by John Rowe Townsend (copyright © 1971, 1979 by John Rowe Townsend; reprinted by permission of Harper & Row, Publishers, Inc.; in Canada by Penguin Books Ltd), J. B. Lippincott, 1979, pp. 39-40.*

GENERAL COMMENTARY

[*Ellen Grae* and *Lady Ellen Grae* do] a good deal of entertaining in the process of portraying the dilemma of eleven-year-old Ellen—bright and talkative almost to the point of precociousness. In her situation—the child of divorced parents, who lives with neither of them—this precociousness and most of her actions give an effect of psychological disturbance. It may be that children will find the elements of entertainment in one or other of these two books outweigh the problem situations, but I wonder? The presentation of such problems, adult created, highly emotional and in the main not such as can be satisfactorily resolved, do seem to represent a slightly morbid trend in children's books. (p. 367)

> *Doreen Norman, in a review of "Ellen Grae and Lady Ellen Grae," in* The School Librarian, *Vol. 21, No. 4, December, 1973, pp. 366-67.*

There is an unusual freshness and spontaneity about Vera and Bill Cleaver's characters which awaken and surprise the reader, compelling him to be attentive to every fresh move. There is eccentricity in many of the characters which they create but their stories are no fanciful dreams. They are firmly rooted in the reality of everyday life, showing its variety of people and the effect which they have upon each other. (pp. 39-40)

The two authors have gained a considerable reputation which is well deserved. Their attitude to young people—and to adults—is sensitive and revealing, and the picture of life which they create is very true but seen from a differently orientated aspect, and is the more arresting because of that. They arouse varied thoughts about characters and give us an extra perception of a community and its richness. (p. 40)

> *A review of "Delpha Green and Company," in* The Junior Bookshelf, *Vol. 40, No. 1, February, 1976, pp. 39-40.*

The Cleavers know human nature and they portray many facets of it in a truly believable and arousing manner. Their stories highlight the humor as well as the pathos characteristic of the human experience. They know how people react to the trials and adversities brought on by poverty, the loss of a loved one through death, divorce, or incapacitating illness. They know how stultifying it can be to be living in a decaying fieflike town, a geographically isolate area, or among bigoted, ignorant, or insensitive people. All of their stories are connected with life—life as they see it. And one need only read their books to realize how well Vera and Bill Cleaver know human nature! They firmly believe that children are capable of all human responses. Thus their literature depicts the gamut of human experience—just like Henry James, long ago, said it should. They believe that children can cope when given the opportunity.

> Parents, teachers and other people concerned with children should consider the potential in treating them with maturity. Most children enjoy being treated that way, in fact some even demand it so why not oblige them and at the same time give them some forewarning knowledge? The fact is that children are not allowed to be strong.

The human experiences they portray are done with an honesty, a sensitivity, and a realism that are unique in children's literature today. They include many aspects of reality in their novels—the tragedies and the sufferings and the violence as well as the beautiful, the humorous, and the pleasantries one might find somewhere in the real world. . . . When the writer's version of the truth appears grotesque and not typical to some, "well, that is regrettable," say the Cleavers. They believe the writer must consider his truth to human nature. He must exert a fidelity to the situations portrayed in the fiction in his own terms rather than in terms that are designed to please a segment of his audience. (pp. 338-40)

The Cleavers stated that they hoped to offer their readers food for thought, stories that contained enough complexity in them to create the habit of critical reading. In correspondence with me they said:

> The phenomenon of language is an instrument for thinking. The nature of words affects the nature of thought, and if, in his selection of words, the writer of fiction is able to provoke thought, whether favorable or unfavorable to his own views and philosophies, then he can rest for a moment for he has met at least one of his functions. . . . There seems to be a notion that children are not so perceptive as adults and therefore the slipshod books which present no outlook on life or philosophy, slight stories which rush from motion to motion, which present no imagery, which do not ask the reader to pause and reflect, are perfectly acceptable.

The readers of *Ellen Grae* are led to do some serious thinking about Ellen Grae Derryberry's decision to tell the sheriff that her story about Ira was just another one of her fabrications when actually it was one of the few times she told a story that was not the product of her very active imagination. The repeated emphasis that "dependence is a perpetual call upon humanity" and the habit of impoverished and neglected Luke Wilder to take advantage of the more privileged Ussy Mock will no doubt stir up some thinking and raise some questions in the minds of the readers of *The Mock Revolt*. The statement that Betty Repkin made to Grover, "Suicide is a coward's way," will shock some young readers, but it is one that will lead them to do a bit of philosophizing, too. In most of their novels, Vera and Bill Cleaver exemplify the desirability of uniqueness of personality and the importance of "doing your own thing." A thoughtful reader will notice that the authors dramatize the advantages as well as the disadvantages of implementing these values. This is especially so in *Ellen Grae, I Would Rather Be a Turnip,* and *Dust of the Earth.* (pp. 340-41)

One could go on and on with the many questions about social and moral values that are raised and commented upon in the stories created by Vera and Bill Cleaver. Without doubt, their books alert the readers to the pluralistic values and diverse value concepts held today by the popular culture and the elitist culture. The readers are not presented pat answers. They are told how the book characters think and what action they decide to take, but, in the main, the Cleavers let their readers know that they have to arrive at their own judgments about the behavior of, and the values held by, the book characters. One of the major objectives of this talented writing team is to get children to think, and it is an objective that has been realized. Of course, one can read the novels by Vera and Bill Cleaver for the pleasures they will bring to one. Also, their books are an excellent medium to use to inform oneself more thoroughly about diverse life-styles and human needs, about some of the social, cultural, and economic wants of contemporary society.

One can use their literature as the medium to inform oneself more thoroughly about which opinions, attitudes, and positions one believes to be correct, and which are wrong. One can use their literature to identify some newly emerging problems in our society, areas in which one's opinions, attitudes, and positions are not yet defined.

The Cleavers have chosen to involve their characters in timeless and universal problems and conditions endemic to all humanity: poverty, death, incapacitating and/or terminal illness, mental retardation, divorce, and alienation (or at least lack of communication between parents and child). They are presented seriously and forthrightly, but they are interspersed, oftentimes, with humor and levity. In at least three books (*Ellen Grae, Lady Ellen Grae,* and *Delpha Green and Company*) they make use of very sophisticated and surrealistic conversations that positively fracture the reader with their humor on the one hand and jar him or her with their insight into the human condition on the other hand. Within the context of these human conditions, the authors offer themes and messages that highlight, but not didactically, such values as independence and self-sufficiency, determination and persistence, responsibility for the welfare of others, a respect and a value for education, and individuality. So, as the reader gets a glimpse of the various aspects of life, he or she also learns about some of the values that are persistently treasured in a democratic society. (pp. 341-42)

The protagonists in at least three very moving and well-written novels by the Cleavers are characterized by two qualities—a headstrong determination to accomplish one's goals, and spunk. These traits are established as worthy of emulation and yet their disadvantages are also clearly identified in *Dust of the Earth, The Whys and Wherefores of Littabelle Lee, Where the Lilies Bloom,* and *The Mimosa Tree.*

People like Littabelle Lee, Mary Call Luther, Marvella Proffitt, and Fern Drawn do not give up easily when their world seems to crumble and fall apart. These protagonists, like their creators themselves, bounce back and keep on trying—*to spite* their adversaries, it seems, rather than *in spite* of them. They exemplify many of the qualities the modern-day feminists are advocating. (p. 342)

Littabelle's experiences, rough and challenging as they are, lead her and the readers to gain an understanding and even an acceptance of the needs and drives and frailties of human nature. Her desire to go to the place where teachers are taught how to be teachers and learn to be a "real one" creates a positive image of educators who are worthy of emulation and respect—an image not too many authors of children's literature choose for educators these days. (pp. 342-43)

A tenacious spirit is . . . seen in fourteen-year-old Mary Call Luther, heroine of *Where the Lilies Bloom,* as she struggles to keep her brother and sisters alive and together after their father dies. Her brother, Romey, bitterly comments during a snowstorm, "The Lord has forgotten us. This land is forgotten. We're forgotten. We're forgotten people." Mary Call thinks, and finally decides that " . . . By the Grace of the Lord we're here and what we make of it is our own affair. It's everybody's affair of what they make of being here. . . ." She insists that one cannot just stand there and let people beat on one. She recognizes that her weapons to combat hardships are inadequate, and they certainly are. She is convinced, also, that she can correct her ignorance, and proceeds to do something about her plight.

Again, in *The Mimosa Tree,* if it were not for Marvella's staunchness, the Proffitt family, consisting of a blind father, an unstable and unreliable stepmother, and four children, would not have survived the depressing and unhappy experiences they had when they moved from their unproductive farm in North Carolina to the slums of Chicago. When the stepmother deserts the family, Marvella becomes "head of the family." (p. 343)

It is interesting to compare the life-styles of the Proffitt family, Littabelle Lee's family, and the Luther family, all of whom were mountaineers, with the life-styles of the mountaineers recorded by the psychiatrist Robert Coles in *Children of Crises.* He validates so much of what the Cleavers have portrayed in their stories about the mountaineers past and present: their sense of family and sense of allegiance to parents and grandparents; their attitude about doing things together with the home or land; their intimacy with the soil and land and the elements; their need for resources that capital investment provides, for their minds are quite able to handle resources; the fact that the offer of charity may well offend their sense of self-sufficiency; and the fact that the school unites them in a personal way and tends to dramatize that they are all members of one community, bringing together all those whose fate is similar. The Cleavers are astute students of people, especially the impoverished and struggling mountaineers.

The determination put forth by Lydia Birdsong to raise the mental capacities of Lornie, her retarded twin sister, is passionately and sensitively portrayed in *Me Too.* . . . Though Lydia fails in her efforts to accomplish her avowed goal, she is not disillusioned. Nor are the readers, for that matter. Lydia's persistence does pay off. It leads her to new understanding and knowledge about love and how people—"normal" and "exceptional" people—find happiness. This story about a family's handling of mental retardation is portrayed in a beautifully intimate manner. The tragedy and the realities of this element of life are honestly portrayed and are so skillfully heightened that one's response to them makes for an intensely emotional experience.

Mental retardation is dealt with in some of the Cleavers' other novels, namely *Ellen Grae* and *Where the Lilies Bloom.* In these books, and in *Me Too* as well, the authors demonstrate that these people are worthy of, and in need of, love and acceptance. It is in *Me Too* that the authors demonstrate so competently the terrific challenge of raising and educating a retarded child, and they present a point of view that is personal, humane, factual, and sensitive. There is food for some mighty solid thinking offered and some sincere, compassionate feelings aroused in *Me Too.* (pp. 343-44)

Until very recently, the theme of death was taboo in juvenile literature, but this theme is quite prevalent in the contemporary literature for children. The way it is treated varies from author to author. In several of their novels, Vera and Bill Cleaver have shown their young readers ways people may react to the death of a loved one or to their own death. (pp. 344-45)

The focus is on people's reaction to the act of dying, rather than on the details of a death, in *Grover* and *Where the Lilies Bloom.* In both books the topic is treated with considerable sensitivity. The reaction that Grover and his father have to the mother's malignant cancer and her subsequent suicide is dealt with honestly. The survivors are shown to struggle with their loss, and each, in his own way, eventually succeeds in making an adjustment. Like Grover, the young readers will " . . . wish I could figure out what being dead is and I wish I could

get it settled in my mind where people go when they die." . . . The readers of this story will understand Grover's thoughts as he witnesses his father's self-isolation and grief. Grover decides that eventually one has to stop grieving; one cannot expect people to continue to sympathize with one about one's tragic loss. Eventually, says Grover, "you have to depend on your own gumption and common sense." (p. 345)

Children reading *Grover* will have to decide for themselves whether suicide is wrong or right; the authors neither condemn nor condone this form of dying. They do, through the utterances of some of the characters, state the various positions people espouse on this issue. The authors do help the readers appreciate the valuable lesson there is to be learned from Grover's strength and ability to cope with and adjust to his mother's suffering and death.

Expression and repression of emotion occur in *Where the Lilies Bloom,* as they did in *Grover;* but when Roy Luther died, his children were not allowed the luxury of introspection, as was Grover when his mother died. The Luther children needed to use all their strengths and wits for mere survival. They simply had to accept Roy Luther's death. There wasn't even time for an adjustment period; their extreme poverty precluded that. This does not mean that the children are portrayed as being unaffected by their father's death. They were grieved, but Mary Call promised her father that neither she nor the others in the family would "carry on" about his death. So, each of the four children must express his grief alone and get on with the business of living and surviving without the presence and help of their father.

Death and violence is presented in *The Mimosa Tree,* a moving story in which one views the effects that poverty in a large metropolitan area such as Chicago has on people. The Cleavers have depicted death as an everyday experience in this novel. . . . *The Mimosa Tree* constitutes quite an indictment about poverty in the big cities today and the inhumanity to man that occurs there. Important, too, although it does not condone such things, is the fact that it does dramatize to the young readers why some people become so hardened and cynical, why they are sometimes forced to live dehumanizing, violent, and lawless lives.

Some of the novels by the Cleavers depict what happens to children when a family structure is fragmented because of divorce, alienation, or illegitimacy. The parents of Ellen Grae, who is the heroine of *Ellen Grae* and *Lady Ellen Grae,* are divorced, but they are on amiable terms. Ellen Grae is comfortable with them; she obviously respects them and loves them. They, in turn, demonstrate that they are concerned about her, despite the fact that the everyday family interaction is missing. They come to her aid when she is in need of their moral support and help. Nonetheless, because her parents are divorced and living in another city, Ellen Grae boards with Mrs. Mc-Gruder. . . . Ellen Grae must go it alone much of the time; she must rely on her own resources to solve her problems. Some adults might see that her constant chatter and vivid imagination in telling surrealistic macabre stories are evidence of some degree of insecurity; they serve as a defense mechanism to compensate for feelings of rejection and self-inadequacy. But her tales are marvelously humorous, and one wonders if these whoppers are not merely signs of a very intelligent and imaginative child who is anxious for some excitement and eager to entertain those she thinks need entertainment. (pp. 345-47)

The parents and children in *The Mimosa Tree, I Would Rather Be a Turnip, Grover, The Mock Revolt, Delpha Green and Com-*

pany, and *Dust of the Earth* fail to communicate with one another. The father of the children in *The Mimosa Tree* is blind and withdrawing into his own thoughts; as he becomes psychologically helpless, he isolates himself from the world and his family. . . . In *I Would Rather Be a Turnip,* the father is no more than a respected presence. . . . The heroine of *Delpha Green and Company* takes it upon herself to contact the residents of the decaying town of Chinquapin Cove about the Church of the Blessed Hope which her father (an ex-con and self-proclaimed preacher) has started. Seldom, if ever, does she talk with her parents about the family's economic struggles and living conditions, her father's conversion to an unknown religious sect (and thus his family's affiliation with that religious sect!), or her convictions and enthusiastic proselytizing of astrology. (pp. 347-48)

A rapidly disappearing part of our American culture is authentically portrayed in the Cleavers' novels about mountaineers, *The Whys and Wherefores of Littabelle Lee* and *Where the Lilies Bloom.* From these books the reader can learn about such aspects of our American inheritance as mountain crafts and wild-plant food, home remedies and herbal medicine. One gets a personal look at midwifing, burial customs, and ghost stories. An examination of such informative volumes as Eliot Wigginton's *Foxfire* books will demonstrate how authentically the Cleavers have portrayed the way the mountaineers have dealt with these particular problems of survival. (p. 348)

A writer is successful when he includes in his writing something he knows well and feels strongly about. One reason the Cleavers' stories are so successful is that they do exactly that. The settings for their stories are in places they have lived and know well. They know the climate, the terrain, the vegetation, and the animal life of the areas. They know the life-styles of many of the people that live in these places. They know thoroughly the cultural and sociological characteristics of the people that populate these areas. Important, too, they are astute students of human nature. They know people's frailties, strengths, needs, and desires.

As with all good writers, the characters and events which appear in the Cleavers' novels originated from their own experiences. Vera's sister had one blue eye and one green, and Bill's mother, who lives in Seattle, is named Delpha: thus, the character Delpha Green. Vera's sister was mentally retarded, and so is Lydia Birdsong's sister, Lornie. The settings for their novels include Washington state, North Carolina, Florida—all of which reflect areas of the country where the authors once lived. Their stories pertain to such circumstances as poverty, divorce, illness—all of which the Cleavers experienced and/or observed in their growing up. Their biographical background obviously influenced their writing.

Vera and Bill Cleaver are good writers; they have the talent to include all their marvelous knowledge and sensitivity about the human condition in stories and still give young readers pleasurable and thoughtful reading fare. They view their job as writers as being to provide educators something with which to work and which can be appreciated. To be "appreciated," according to the Cleavers, is to be "relished, respected, recognized as being something of quality. And after that it is the job of the educator to provide guidance to the student through books." (pp. 349-50)

Patricia J. Cianciolo, "Vera and Bill Cleaver Know Their Whys and Wherefores," in Top of the News (reprinted by permission of the American Library Association), Vol. 32, No. 4, June, 1976, pp. 338-50.

Rereading the Cleavers' books for children—a dozen of them up to the time of writing—one is struck most obviously and forcibly by their gallery of fierce, determined heroines like Mary Call and Littabelle; by their vividly drawn settings in Allegheny or Ozark mountain country, in Florida small town or Dakota badland; and by the ordeals their young people have to face. Like the Australian writer Ivan Southall, with whom they have little else in common, the Cleavers tend to put their central characters into situations which are at or beyond the limits of what they can cope with. In their first book, *Ellen Grae* . . . , Ellen has to carry an insupportable burden of knowledge about the deaths of her friend Ira's parents. Grover, in the book named after him, has a mother who is dying of cancer and who kills herself to shorten the agony. In *Where the Lilies Bloom,* Mary Call Luther struggles to keep together a parentless family of four, including 'cloudy-headed' older sister Devola, while they scratch a precarious living by gathering wild plants among the mountains. Annie Jelks in *I Would Rather Be a Turnip* . . . is oppressed by small-town censoriousness over the illegitimate child in her family. Intelligent Lydia, in *Me Too* . . . , has not merely to live with her mentally-handicapped, unresponsive twin Lornie after their father has had enough and decamped; she feels she must try to improve Lornie's behaviour and to teach her when the special school has failed. Littabelle looks after her aged grandparents in desperate circumstances when their house has burned down, winter is coming, and their children refuse to support them. Other characters face difficulties hardly less daunting.

The Cleaver novels are rooted in an unyielding realism. No wind is tempered to the shorn lamb; no rich uncle or equivalent turns up with infusions of love and money; no dying parent recovers or absconding one returns repentant. Real life probably contains more happy accidents, more unexpected bonuses, more merciful softening of harsh situations than the Cleavers ever permit themselves. The circumstances of each story assert themselves ruthlessly and dictate the solution. While some of the protagonists win through, others are defeated. Lydia can do little or nothing for sister Lornie; the Proffitts in *The Mimosa Tree* . . . can find no way to survive in a Chicago slum; Ussy Mock in *The Mock Revolt* . . . cannot escape from his small-town ambience and his own sense of responsibility.

Yet the overall impression left by individual books and by the Cleavers' work as a whole is not a depressing one. The fight must be fought, but if the end is defeat, very well then, the end is defeat and there is no disgrace in it. It is better to have fought and lost than not to have fought. Lydia realizes at the end of *Me Too* that 'in failure there is certainty and in certainty there is release'. And though there is self-sacrifice in the Cleaver novels, sometimes on a heroic scale, there is also the recognition that even the most self-sacrificing people have a duty to themselves. Lydia must save herself from being dragged down by Lornie, just as she must save herself from the sinkhole that opens up beneath her in the scrub. Littabelle in *The Whys and Wherefores* and Mary Call at the end of *Trial Valley* (. . . the sequel to *Where the Lilies Bloom*) are determined to overcome their ignorance, get some education and make something of their own lives; and having seen them in action we know that nothing can stop them.

This sense of the indomitability of the human spirit is undoubtedly the major reason why in the end the Cleaver books are more likely to lift up than cast down the reader, to offer an astringent yet stimulating experience. There is also a strong minor reason, in that wry humour, salty dialogue and intriguing surface incident are counterpointed against the grave underlying themes. Ellen Grae is a teller of tall tales which are often extremely funny, as are her conversations with friend Grover and room-mate Rosemary. In *Grover* . . . , the adventures of Grover and Ellen Grae while delivering telegrams, and the comedy of their being outwitted by small boy Farrell, occupy the foreground during the time in which Grover is coming to realize that his mother will die. Light incidents such as these do nothing to diminish the seriousness of the book, but they save it from being constantly harrowing, and they give all the more force to moments such as the one when, after a day on the river, Grover lies awake at night and says aloud to himself that his mother is going to die; 'testing the words for the truth that was in them and hearing it there'.

The Cleaver heroines, though bearing a family likeness to each other, are clearly distinguishable (with the possible exceptions of Mary Call and Littabelle, who chime very closely together). Ellen Grae is a bright imaginative eccentric, Mary Call and Littabelle are dourly practical, Delpha in *Delpha Green and Company* . . . is a lively extrovert who changes the lives of those around her. Annie Jelks, in *I Would Rather Be a Turnip*, oppressed by small-town censoriousness, is a particularly memorable character. Annie is bad-tempered and unlikeable, and bitter in her resentment of the harmless illegitimate child who provokes this censoriousness; but she is a true Cleaver heroine all the same, and by the end, when she has crossly saved Calvin's life and rudely rejected his thanks, one finds oneself liking and even admiring this graceless character; one knows that her loyalty to Calvin, her family, or anyone she accepted as a friend would be grudging but unbounded.

One would infer from the Cleaver novels that women are the stronger sex: a correct inference, in my view, and for the same reason in the books as in life. Women are stronger because coping makes them so. 'Men, God pity them, are such poor sticks,' says Mary Call, and there are some feeble men in these books. Roy Luther, Mary Call's father, cannot help it that he is dying, but even in health he doesn't seem to have done much to win a decent life for his family. Grover's father goes to pieces when his wife dies, and it is the black housekeeper Rose who keeps things going. There are other portraits of weak and unsatisfactory men, though it would be wrong to suggest that the Cleavers are anti-male sexists. Grover himself comes through his ordeal: he is solid, strong, reliable, he aims to be a veterinarian when he grows up, and one knows that he will be a good one. Lydia, in *Me Too*, suffers from attempts at ostracism by people who think her sister's mental deficiency may run in her family, but her friend Billy Frank is firmly loyal to her: 'We're friends,' he says, 'and can't nobody stop us.'

Apart from Grover, Ussy Mock in *The Mock Revolt* is the Cleavers' only male central character so far. One can hardly call him a hero, he isn't even particularly impressive; but he wins respect and—a very Cleaverlike touch—his own self-respect. Ussy, trying to save up money to get away from the 'deadlies' in his small town, finds himself supporting the deadweight of Luke Wilder and his hopeless family. The demands of the Wilders consume Ussy's hard-earned vacation pay; the escape dream fades. It is borne in on Ussy that, in the words of the novelist W. M. Thackeray, 'dependence is a perpetual call on humanity'. He doesn't even *like* Luke, but Luke is there; and roaring off on a motorbike to New Orleans and San Francisco is not an option that is open to Ussy. For all his

wish to be different, he knows that one day he will be a little baggy old man like those he sees in the town, trotting around his garden with a watering-can.

Of villainy in the traditional sense there is none in the Cleaver novels, but there is some brute ignorance, and there is the mental cruelty of those who will make young people suffer for an illegitimate or backward sibling or a parent who shot herself. And there is the cold selfishness of Hutchens, Ora and Estie in *Littabelle Lee*, who leave their aged parents to sink or swim. (It is a fine, all too realistic touch that when Littabelle brings an action on the old people's behalf and wins support for them from their defaulting children, they are totally ungrateful and consider it a disgrace.)

I have heard it suggested that there are passages in these books that are too gruesome to be suitable for children: the description, for instance, of Littabelle's help to a woman who is giving birth without medical or nursing care, or her operation on the windpipe of a choking child, carried out with a penknife. Gratuitous horrors are, I think, always bad art, and in a children's book are morally objectionable; but there is of course an opposite error of falsely smoothing the rough edges of life, and to me it seems that when the Cleavers shock they do so almost invariably for good reasons and within current tolerances. There is much in the account of mentally-handicapped Lornie's behaviour in *Me Too* which makes painful reading, but which surely is required for the honest treatment of the theme. This book has a fearful and unforgettable moment at the end when Lornie, returned at last to her special school, re-encounters her fellow-pupil Jane. . . . In all the twelve books, the one passage that troubles me is the description in graphic detail of how Grover, taking bloody revenge on a woman who tormented him over his mother's death, kills her turkey by chopping off its head. I am not convinced of the artistic necessity or psychological accuracy of this; and, if it is unnecessary, it is pointless and repellent violence.

Settings are of great importance in the Cleaver novels. Trial Valley, in the Appalachian mountain country, is 'fair land, the fairest of them all'; and through all the tribulations of the Luther family, this landscape in which and on which they live is never lost sight of. Ellen Grae deeply loves the small Florida town of Thicket—'day after sunny day and night after starlit night Thicket is as neat and as beautiful as a rose garden'—and an unsuccessful attempt to take her away from it is the principal material of *Lady Ellen Grae*. . . . The South Dakota badlands, in *Dust of the Earth* . . . , bring to Fern Drawn's mind 'a picture of an old, lost royal city I have never seen'. . . . In *Littabelle Lee*, the old unspoiled hills, the hollows and watered valleys of the Ozark mountain country are just as much a vital part of the book.

In these landscapes a sense of the presence of God is strong, and indeed the rural communities in which the Cleavers' novels are set are communities reared on God's word. But religion is in the air, in the common culture, a felt religion rather than a thought one; and attitudes can be permeated by a down-to-earth cynicism that is not the same as doubt. . . . Mary Call Luther's trust in God is accompanied, typically, by a shrewd scepticism about what God will actually do for her; it is not the kind of trust that excuses one from keeping one's powder dry. Grover, after his mother's death, has some pertinent questions to put to the Reverend Vance, and the answers do not satisfy him—though of course the shortcoming may be that of the Reverend Vance rather than of the Christian religion. The novels are not concerned with religious inquiry or speculation, and offer no conclusions on the subject; religion, however, is there in people's backgrounds and cannot be ignored. It is intriguing that in the very first sentence of the first book Ellen Grae proclaims herself a Pantheist, but this is pure Ellen; a Pantheist is just what she *would* be. A curious sidelight is cast in *Delpha Green and Company*. Delpha's ex-convict father is now the Reverend Green, minister of his own one-man Church of Blessed Hope; Delpha herself has taken up astrology and thinks it helps her to help people solve their problems. Father's church and Delpha's astrology may well be phoney, but nevertheless Father and Delpha between them bring the people of a half-dead small town to life. It could be that what is phoney and what is genuine is to be judged by results.

A systematic appraisal of the twelve books would obviously take far more space than is available here. To me it seems that the Cleavers have not yet written a better one than *Where the Lilies Bloom,* a singularly beautiful and moving novel. Their first book for children, *Ellen Grae*—serious, funny, perceptive, splendidly crafted and holding a great deal within its few pages— is just as remarkable in its different way, but does not give quite the same sense of dealing with universal emotional experience. *Grover, Me Too* and *The Whys and Wherefores of Littabelle Lee* show the Cleavers in their most challenging vein; they are rewarding, and even in the end enjoyable, but the enjoyment is bought at a cost of some pain. They are not light reading, and it is possible to feel that *Littabelle Lee* in particular piles on the agony too heavily. The remaining books I find slighter or less successful, though I would be sorry not to have met Ussy Mock in *The Mock Revolt* or Annie Jelks and her bright mild illegitimate nephew Calvin in *I Would Rather Be a Turnip.*

By and large it is a poor, rural and curiously innocent America that emerges from the novels of Vera and Bill Cleaver. Life is hard, and must be faced with determination and without illusion. Subsistence has to be worked for. Values are traditional, good people are upright and self-respecting and inclined to be stern. The Bible is known, religion is not an embarrassment or a discarded superstition, people are conscious of God, though whether He is in their hearts or in the landscape or 'out there' somewhere is not determined, and does not need to be. Though the action takes place in the present, the past is all around it, and sometimes one feels oneself to be reading about a surviving pocket of the past. 'Endurance' is a key word. Such strenuous—indeed, pioneering—virtues are surely still to be admired and still relevant; not least in the early stages of life, which, whatever technology may do for us, remains and must always remain a long uncertain journey to the West. (pp. 31-8)

> *John Rowe Townsend, "Vera and Bill Cleaver," in his* A Sounding of Storytellers: New and Revised Essays on Contemporary Writers for Children *(copyright © 1971, 1979 by John Rowe Townsend; reprinted by permission of Harper & Row, Publishers, Inc.; in Canada by Penguin Books Ltd), J. B. Lippincott, 1979, pp. 30-40.*

Although there had been other books about children of divorce before *Ellen Grae* . . . was published, none had so firmly stated by implication the fact that a parent's love and responsibility are not changed by divorce. Ellen Grae tells her own story, and it becomes instantly apparent that she is an accomplished and artistic teller of tall tales and that she is a child with great sensitivity and loyalty. Despite the seriousness of the problem that faces Ellen Grae and despite its less than satisfactory res-

olution, the story is permeated with humor. Its sequel, *Lady Ellen Grae,* has less impact but is written with vivacity and sharp characterization. The hero of *Grover* . . . is Ellen Grae's friend, and his adjustment to his mother's suicide (she has cancer) and to his father's grief is described in a story that shows the sensitivity of the young.

The heroine of *Where the Lilies Bloom* . . . is one of the strongest characters in children's fiction. Fourteen-year-old Mary Call Luther buries her father herself, and valiantly tries to hold together the family . . . so that the four children will not be sent to a county charity home. This is an excellent example of the need for security as well as of the need to achieve. In the sequel, *Trial Valley* . . . , Mary Call is just as responsible in coping with suitors as she is with family problems. Another strong character, Fern Drawn in *Dust of the Earth* . . . , works at the difficult job of sheepherding to help her family survive, and has the joy of seeing a disparate group of children and parents become a united family.

In *I Would Rather Be a Turnip* . . . twelve-year-old Annie Jelks faces a problem that is seldom presented in children's books, the acceptance of an illegitimate child. . . . The Cleavers deal perceptively with the intricacies of serious problems yet lighten the stories with humor. These books are prime examples of the changes that have occurred in what has been considered appropriate in children's books. (pp. 326-27)

> *Zena Sutherland, Dianne L. Monson, and May Hill Arbuthnot, "Modern Fiction," in their* Children and Books *(copyright © 1981, 1977, 1972, 1964, 1957, 1947 by Scott, Foresman and Company; reprinted by permission), sixth edition, Scott, Foresman, 1981, pp. 308-32.**

ELLEN GRAE (1967)

"Ellen Grae" might have been a great book. Its authors give you a girl, and she is a very real as well as unique girl. They give her a difficult moral problem to solve and she solves it. (The reader's approval or disapproval of the way she solves it has no bearing on the quality of the book.) They catch the reader with their first sentence and don't release him until their last. So? What's the flaw in the diamond? The flaw is this: told in the first person, when Ellen Grae talks she talks like the highly intelligent, highly aware eleven-year-old that she is. When she thinks, the authors make her think like Kathleen Norris, in phrases like: "His dark eyes [that] have a very old man's sadness in them"; and "A strange kind of soft sweet excitement crept into his eyes." It's impossible to reconcile the two—a girl who talks like a tart lemonade and thinks like a chocolate mousse. But don't miss "Ellen Grae." It's an unusual story. And don't forget its authors' names; they're worth watching. (pp. 80-1)

> *A review of "Ellen Grae," in* Publishers Weekly *(reprinted from the April 10, 1967 issue of* Publishers Weekly, *published by R. R. Bowker Company; copyright © 1967 by R. R. Bowker Company), Vol. 191, No. 15, April 10, 1967, pp. 80-1.*

Ever since "Harriet the Spy" crashed into the juvenile book world, an odd disease has been afflicting its authors. They are beginning to tell the truth. Children are behaving like children, and parents are being revealed as the vulnerable souls they are. I rejoice in this and in "Ellen Grae": a serio-comic work which deals with a matter of conscience. . . .

Suffice it to say that this is an unusual book, rich in characterization, and keenly observant of childhood.

> *Barbara Wersba, in a review of "Ellen Grae," in* The New York Times Book Review *(© 1967 by The New York Times Company; reprinted by permission), May 7, 1967, p. 39.*

Although the story has poignant moments, it is funny most of the time and perceptive all of the time. The seldom-explored situation of divorce is nicely handled, with Ellen Grae's parents on friendly footing and no less responsible and loving toward their child because they don't live under the same roof. (p. 36)

> *Zena Sutherland, in a review of "Ellen Grae," in* Saturday Review *(© 1967 Saturday Review Magazine Co.; reprinted by permission), Vol. L, No. 24, July 17, 1967, pp. 35-6.*

Like *Harriet the Spy*, this book has the potential to frazzle book selectors while dazzling juvenile readers. . . . The writing is excellent and its combination of comedy, near-tragedy, and suspense are rare in juvenile fiction. The ending is tantalizing, and ambiguous adult values are penetrated as the unforgettable Ellen prys the lid off the platitude about honesty being the best policy. That question, the book, and its heroine are worth talking about. (pp. 116-17)

> *Lillian N. Gerhardt, in a review of "Ellen Grae," in* School Library Journal, *an appendix to* Library Journal *(reprinted from the September, 1967 issue of* School Library Journal, *published by R. R. Bowker Co./ A Xerox Corporation; copyright © 1967), Vol. 14, No. 1, September, 1967, pp. 116-17.*

A daring and honest treatment of a girl's experience with an unexpected problem, the sympathetically told story reveals the irony and the tragedy that often face a child on the road to maturity. But although the narrative is serious, it is not solemn. (p. 65)

> *Paul Heins, in a review of "Ellen Grae," in* The Horn Book Magazine *(copyright © 1968 by The Horn Book, Inc., Boston), Vol. XLIV, No. 1, February, 1968, pp. 64-5.*

LADY ELLEN GRAE (1968)

It's a wonder no movie company hasn't snapped up the Cleavers: they write some of the best dialog around these days—some of the truest, straightest dialog. And some of the wackiest. Because Ellen Grae, their heroine, is a wacky 12-year-old who must read the dictionary as avidly as other girls read the latest Nancy Drew. When the Cleavers record what Ellen Grae is thinking and feeling, their hearing is not so perfect—the thinking and feeling become too adult for the likes of Ellen Grae. But don't let that scare you off—from this hilarious account of Ellen Grae's trip from Thicket, Florida, to Seattle, Oregon, and back again.

> *A review of "Lady Ellen Grae," in* Publishers Weekly *(reprinted from the August 12, 1968 issue of* Publishers Weekly, *published by R. R. Bowker Company, a Xerox company; copyright © 1968 by Xerox Corporation), Vol. 194, No. 7, August 12, 1968, p. 55.*

"Then there surged in me an increase in reason and understanding and my obligations to what I had been fell away and

were replaced with a new indebtedness to what I was." Alas, this is not Henry James speaking, but an 11-year-old girl named Ellen Grae. Ellen first appeared on the literary scene in 1967, delighting readers with her rambunctiousness. . . . In this sequel, she seems to have aged 40 years while still remaining 11. Faced with the problem of being sent to live with relatives who will teach her to be a "lady," Ellen uses childish strategies to defeat the plan—yet her attitude is so philosophic that she reminds one of a dowager. This is neither her fault nor the authors', but that of the sequel itself: a form that often fails because its energy has been exhausted by the original creation. But if the once-sparkling Ellen now seems old, it doesn't matter. Readers like myself will remember her happily in that first book, **"Ellen Grae."**

> *Barbara Wersba, in a review of "Lady Ellen Grae," in* The New York Times Book Review *(© 1968 by The New York Times Company; reprinted by permission), September 8, 1968, p. 38.*

[**Lady Ellen Grae** contains a] superbly ironic ending. With her linguistic virtuosity, tireless imagination, independence, and precocious wisdom ("Sometimes it's best to agree with people even when you don't. It stops them from pressing and gives you time to think"), Ellen Grae is thoroughly refreshing and enormously real. (p. 560)

> *Ethel L. Heins, in a review of "Lady Ellen Grae," in* The Horn Book Magazine *(copyright © 1968 by The Horn Book, Inc., Boston), Vol. XLIV, No. 5, October, 1968, pp. 559-60.*

The Cleavers have squandered their considerable writing talents on a sequel that subverts the essence of the excellent **Ellen Grae.** In fact, in **Lady Ellen Grae,** their 11-year-old heroine becomes the only extant juvenile variation on the adult novel's bitch-heroines—the ones like *Rebecca*, who gambled with death (suicide made to look like murder) to achieve their own ends. The juvenile difference is that Ellen Grae not only survives but gets away with getting her own way; she purposely sits still so that a sailboat boom handled by another child concusses her and so is allowed to return to her Florida small town from Seattle. Her divorced parents had sent her to live with a widowed aunt and an ultra-feminine cousin in the hope that she would become neater and more socially aware. That transformation had begun before the determined girl got back to the town she early on announces she'll never leave until she dies. But she's also transformed from the first book—in which she was sensitive enough to become feverish over an ethical dilemma in honesty and responsibility to others—into a child who gambles and wins with a possible suicide that would leave someone else gathering guilt. This time, she doesn't notice that honesty and responsibility to others are central here, too. The Cleavers write well—but they either didn't realize what they created the first time or don't see how they've devalued Ellen Grae in attempting to trot her out again. (pp. 152-53)

> *Lillian N. Gerhardt, in a review of "Lady Ellen Grae," in* School Library Journal, *an appendix to* Library Journal *(reprinted from the October, 1968 issue of* School Library Journal, *published by R. R. Bowker Co./ A Xerox Corporation; copyright © 1968), Vol. 15, No. 2, October, 1968, pp. 152-53.*

[With **Ellen Grae** and **Lady Ellen Grae,** Vera and Bill Cleaver] have succeeded in restoring to their rightful places a good portion of harmless, necessary horror and fine, purple prose. . . . I enjoyed [**Lady Ellen Grae**] and found it too short. The authors left me wishing to know more about the neighbors and the admiral, and hungering for more adventures in Seattle: Ellen's contretemps with a garter belt, the saga of the home permanent, and the false eyelashes at $6.00 a set. Girls and people who have been girls, and males as well, will probably enjoy this book. It is a nightshade sundae, but the helping is too small.

> *Martha Bacon, "The Children's Trip to the Gallows," in* The Atlantic Monthly *(copyright © 1968, by The Atlantic Monthly Company, Boston, Mass.; reprinted with permission), Vol. 222, No. 6, December, 1968, p. 148.*

WHERE THE LILIES BLOOM (1969)

I have just read Vera and Bill Cleaver's **"Where the Lilies Bloom."** Most appealing in the story is the sense of earnestness and determination in the central character and narrator, Mary Call Luther. . . .

Only 14, Mary Call is determined to keep the family together and to make do—that's the thing the girl is after. The appeal of her effort is profound, because this impulse is the heroic impulse of all achievement, adventure, art and the making of character.

The soul asks, "What do we have?" And when it knows, it calculates usage in terms of time and life. This concern, this awareness of hard limits and cautious usages of stocks, is good to observe in action. Life has purpose and the purpose is good, because in it is intelligence and pride. Having so much responsibility and awareness of the hazards ahead makes the beautiful little girl seem ugly and mean, especially to the kid brother Romey, who works with her to keep the noses of outsiders away from the Luther story, which is nobody's business but their own. These two will protect the beautiful Devola. And in doing so they will fight and hate one another, only to discover that they have learned new truth and acquired new humor. The whole book is immersed in a sense of the deep kinship between human beings, animals and plants, recognized, accepted and rejected or cherished with humor.

This is a story of good people, with real natures, living under conditions of hardship, in poverty, in the midst of bereavement, maintaining their independence, wit and dignity. Everybody in the family—including 5-year-old Ima Dean Luther—has a common sense that is very attractive. Even "villain" suitor and landlord, Kiser Pease, is not really villainous. (Oh, this has got to be a children's book.) . . .

Only now and then does the natural simplicity of the narrator become noticeably literary. Most of the time she speaks as effortlessly as Huck Finn, another orphan. . . .

These four Luther kids don't want help from anyone, and of course that kind of thinking just won't do in our society. In fact, it may even be un-American. This is a grand book, but only if you don't happen to be an adult.

Reading the book has been like eating a good meal of bread, cheese, onion and cold water. I tend to have this feeling of hunger satisfied when I read very good writing.

> *William Saroyan, in a review of "Where the Lilies Bloom," in* The New York Times Book Review *(© 1969 by The New York Times Company; reprinted by permission), September 28, 1969, p. 34.*

Authors Vera and Bill Cleaver had everything going for them in this story of Mary Call's struggle to keep her promise. There is, first, the child's eccentric, obstinate character; there are the strange ways of the hill people, who treat pneumonia with applications of hot onion slices; finally there is the unusual occupation of wildcrafters, the harvesters of medicinal herbs and plants in the Great Smokies. But the Cleavers blow the lot by failing to leave their own sophistication outside when they enter Mary Call's primitive world.

The chic cleverness and strained metaphors pile up, and at last they bury the appeal of Mary Call's heroic, resourceful and often amusing efforts to hold her little family together.

> *Robert Ostermann, "In Tackling Youthful Emotions, 'Sounder' Is Best of Four Tales," in* The National Observer *(reprinted by permission of* The National Observer; *© Dow Jones & Company, Inc. 1969; all rights reserved), December 29, 1969, p. 17.*

This is a humorous, tough story. . . .

Seasons and landscape are imaginatively described as important elements in the family's life; adults seen with the coolness and limited sympathy of children. The Luthers' loyalty and occasional disruptive bitterness are well-observed, using only Mary's insight. Indeed, the story is skilfully told since, apart from the hospital scene, the authors succeed in keeping sophisticated vocabulary and opinions outside the narrative, while allowing the reader to notice more than Mary Call does.

Mary is likeable and sensitive as well as shrewish and hard when desperation drives her. Romey, her chief support, is sharply portrayed as a mischievous boy made adult too soon.

The story reaches a satisfying and credible conclusion. Strongly recommended as a warm and honest story for readers of eleven up.

> *Judith Aldridge, in a review of "Where the Lilies Bloom," in* Children's Book Review *(© 1971 by Five Owls Press Ltd.; all rights reserved), Vol. 1, No. 1, February, 1971, p. 19.*

I would like to think that this book . . . is one of those rarities which has ready appeal as well as being an excellent piece of writing, though it is a pity that the title is somewhat off-putting. . . .

[Mary Call] tells her story with confident toughness, humour and unsentimental honesty. Battles with environment have always made popular reading from Robinson Crusoe onwards, and the tale of Mary Call's resourcefulness should be no exception.

A 'must' for the library shelf. . . .

> *P. Robertson, in a review of "Where the Lilies Bloom," in* The School Librarian, *Vol. 19, No. 1, March, 1971, p. 62.*

[There is an] astonishing chapter in Vera and Bill Cleaver's classic **"Where the Lilies Bloom,"** in which the authors begin with something unbearable, the death of the only remaining parent in the family, and go on to double, triple and take the square of the unbearableness. Two of the children drag the father's body up the mountain and bury it in secret so that the county people will not know he is dead. . . .

The gravity of the setting, the grim urgency of the occasion and the stubborn bravery of the children transmogrify our horror into awe and delight.

Jane Langton, "Five Lives," in The New York Times Book Review (© 1974 by The New York Times Company; reprinted by permission), May 5, 1974, p. 16.*

[**Where the Lilies Bloom**] has important implications about leadership in troubled families. In this book, there are no parents. The heroine is delegated as parent by her dying father and takes on the mantle with a vehemence. The siblings become a family that is defined, organized, and united by its peril in the world. It is in some ways a secret and conspiratorial unit operating under a state of siege. If the siblings cannot succeed as a family, they will be broken up—each one sent a separate way. Mary Call, the child-delegated parent, struggles with her role. To assume it and to be the guiding light who can concoct all sorts of plans for survival, she must repudiate dependency. She must be self-sufficient, or perhaps family-sufficient. The preservation of the family unit has a primacy over and above individual need and particularly individual hopelessness, depression, and longings for comfort. To maintain her role, Mary Call must deny all feelings of sorrow. This is most poignant in a scene in which she and her brother, Romey, bury their father. . . . This is all handled gingerly with amusement and tenderness. The story is somewhat fantastic and delightfully so.

But here . . . in this story we see the dilemma of autocratic leadership. Mary Call repeatedly criticizes the father's past leadership for its passivity—for the fact that it kept the family economically disenfranchised and degraded. Mary Call becomes, understandably, controlling, and sees everything outside the family as suspect. This suspiciousness causes her to deny the needs of her siblings to form outside attachments. In the course of her struggle as leader, she learns to acknowledge both her sister's wish to marry and her own need for help from without. There are some fine interior monologues in which we can see the various forces conflicting—her fear and conquest of fear, her longing and overcoming of longing. And in the end, we see the autocratic role give way—not to its passive opposite, but to a kind of independence that is not wholly self-sufficient.

The transformation of character forms the moral center of this story. Particularly important in this change is the function of work—of the family sustaining itself through wildcrafting (the collection of wild medicinal herbs). Although the book does have its aphoristic moments, these are lightened by humor and so seem less heavy-handed and obtrusive. . . . (pp. 92-4)

Kate Fincke, "The Breakdown of the Family: Fictional Case Studies in Contemporary Novels for Young People," in The Lion and the Unicorn (copyright © 1980 The Lion and the Unicorn), Vol. 3, No. 2, Winter, 1979-80, pp. 81-95.*

GROVER (1970)

That children's books are richer by the Cleavers there is no doubt. Their characters are whole grain, their imagery absorbing, with such as "rain-colored eyes" and "soup-warm water." Still "**Grover**" comes as something of a disappointment after "**Where the Lilies Bloom**" (and where and when one wants to ask will that book be *properly* lauded?) for it lacks the same poignancy.

The place is Thicket again, of "**Ellen Grae**" and "**Lady Ellen Grae**" but this time it's Grover's story—a strong, sensible boy of 11 now, he must come to grips not only with the death of one parent but also with the resulting emotional instability of the other. And Grover has a strange, fine perceptiveness about the people around him—"He is a good man, my father . . . but were anybody to ask me if I wanted to be like him I would have to say no. . . . He doesn't look at things or listen. It strains him to talk to people."

A series of isolated incidents tinged with humor and pathos and subordinate to the main narrative—what happens when Grover's mother dies—creates the story. One stands out: a gruesome act of retribution toward the bitter woman who tells him "You're the kid whose mother blew her brains out." It's no easy road and Grover must go it alone but with time some of his questions have answers and some of his hills are plains again.

Ingeborg Boudreau, in a review of "Grover," in The New York Times Book Review (© 1970 by The New York Times Company; reprinted by permission), March 15, 1970, p. 49.

Again the authors have presented a difficult subject with sensitive honesty, keeping within the bounds of a child's understanding. The act of suicide is neither condemned nor condoned. Grover has to arrive at his own understanding and acceptance of what has happened. The adults he trusts have no answers for his questions. He comes to realize that his father also must meet the tragedy in his own way and on his own terms. The reader is made aware of the alternatives but left to make his own judgment. A sad, but not a somber story, in which there is humor to counterbalance sorrow, and action as well as introspection. The language is strong and rich in imagery; the narrative is absorbing. A profoundly wise and real tale. (pp. 158-59)

Diane Farrell, in a review of "Grover," in The Horn Book Magazine (copyright © 1970 by The Horn Book, Inc., Boston), Vol. XLVI, No. 2, April, 1970, pp. 158-59.

Grover is another successful story by the authors of **Where the Lilies Bloom**. Some of the same qualities appear, in particular the sympathetic, realistic and unsentimental portrayal of children's concerns and conversations, their bafflement and occasional cool contempt of adult's behaviour. There is the same deft mingling of humour, seriousness and sadness and the ability to convey more to the reader than Grover, from whose viewpoint the story is told, is aware of. All the characters, whether central or peripheral, are made credible and alive; and the setting, a small town drowsing in the heat of a Florida summer, almost tangible. . . .

Delicately, often indirectly, Grover's grief and bewilderment are depicted, through, for example, his internal debates about his father's uncommunicative grief, through the account of this normally gentle boy's cruel slaughter of a turkey. Supported by his friends, Grover reaches some understanding of his new emotions and of his father.

Highly recommended for everyone over eleven.

Judith Aldridge, in a review of "Grover," in Children's Book Review (© 1971 by Five Owls Press Ltd.; all rights reserved), Vol. I, No. 2, April, 1971, p. 51.

The novel is an art form and not a photograph-cum-gramophone-record of selected individuals behaving. It is not the writer's business either to protect us from real life or to depict it literally but, rather, to rouse us into awareness of his own telescoped view of a corner of it. In this, dialogue can be an ally for him or a way of evading his responsibilities. The authors of *Grover* convince me that . . . (by exploiting that habit of "talking in sentences" that belongs naturally to certain temperaments and ages) . . . Grover and Ellen Grae and the gregarious Farrell might chatter as they do while bathing, fishing and tracking through the environs of the little town of Thicket in Florida. The flickering humour of the book is not the result of adults smiling indulgently at the cuteness of the young; the dialogue is selected and shaped to demonstrate the way human beings come to terms with grief. And yet not human beings but individuals, for the characters in the story (Rose the warm-hearted daily, self-centred father, wise little Ellen and the rest) are cut out of whole cloth. No, we don't all talk like this, but Grover and his friends do, and what they say has a sharp meaning in terms of life as well as of literature. (pp. 1743-44)

> *Margery Fisher, in a review of "Grover," in her* Growing Point, *Vol. 10, No. 1, May, 1971, pp. 1743-44.*

This is an elegant book. Its concern is with life, death and life after death. These are pretty big problems and one is forced to wonder if the average nine to eleven-year-old who will provide the bulk of its readers will really appreciate Grover's problem. . . . The fact that he comes to terms with the problem and how he does so are the main themes of the book, but it does seem rather too adult in its approach for more than say five per cent of its potential readership. The style is beautiful, one gets the feeling of heat and of being stifled by both the environment and the atmosphere. I think what I am trying to say is that this is a Faulkner type book, where the authors have spent their talents on the creation of the hero and the background, but have failed in their minor characters and plot. I hope young readers will be encouraged to read it for in parts it is of very high quality. The descriptive passages could well be read aloud to inspire children to write similar ones of their own surroundings.

> *A review of "Grover," in* The Junior Bookshelf, *Vol. 35, No. 4, August, 1971, p. 240.*

Grover, Ellen Grae, whose parents were divorced and who baited her own fish hooks, Farrell, a 'hick' town in the Mid West, all this would seem to add up to the usual American kid's novel: how tempting it is to make snap judgment after twenty pages. But *Grover* is different. . . . Against a background of heat and dust and hopelessness the authors have created a very real world, a picture of America that perhaps readers of ten-to-fourteen do not often find. There is nothing glamorous here, it is a raw book, but one which is much nearer to everyman's, or every child's, experience than we care to think.

> *Joan Murphy, in a review of "Grover," in* The School Librarian, *Vol. 19, No. 4, December, 1971, p. 370.*

THE MIMOSA TREE (1970)

The story deals with socioeconomic problems and runs the risk of being labeled a case study. It has a strong ring of truth; the living conditions have been noted as by the scrutinizing eye of a social worker. Five children with their blind father and unstable stepmother leave their bit of mountainside in Goose Elk, North Carolina, in despair because they claim neighbors have poisoned their hogs. They go off to Chicago in their old car, to a most unsavory and discouraging new set of circumstances. Their stepmother soon deserts them; a relief worker demands that fourteen-year-old Marvella cease working in a pawnshop (for the needed ten dollars a week); the promised government money never comes; and Marvella joins her younger brother in purse-snatching on the Loop. At last, with new stolen tires on the old car, they drive back to their shack in the hills where their erstwhile hog-poisoning neighbors receive them with warmth and generous hospitality. The penetrating characterizations, scenes, and incidents brilliantly define social ills resulting from the impersonality of the city; and the children's justification of theft becomes all too understandable. A disturbing book.

> *Virginia Haviland, in a review of "The Mimosa Tree," in* The Horn Book Magazine *(copyright © 1970 by The Horn Book, Inc., Boston), Vol. XLVI, No. 5, October, 1970, p. 477.*

The upgrading of rural poverty is a transparent evasion: the idea that being poor in the country is dignified and humane (while only urban poverty degrades) is stuff and nonsense.

> *Dorothy Broderick, "The Young Teen Scene," in* The New York Times Book Review *(© 1980 by The New York Times Company; reprinted by permission), November 8, 1980, p. 10.**

[The Profitt's] hand-to-mouth existence and experiments at thievery, their attempts to obtain welfare, and their relationships with fellow slum-dwellers are fairly interesting and believable, but the too-easy solution to their problems leaves readers unconvinced. . . . [They] find that the Critchers, mortal enemies who originally drove them from their home, have undergone a miraculous transformation and are now loving, generous friends who welcome them back with gifts and the happy news that they have found a cure for the blight that ruined the farm. It's a bit too much.

> *Ruth M. Pegau, in a review of "The Mimosa Tree," in* School Library Journal, *an appendix to* Library Journal *(reprinted from the January, 1971 issue of* School Library Journal, *published by R. R. Bowker Co./ A Xerox Corporation; copyright © 1971), Vol. 17, No. 5, January, 1971, p. 58.*

Realism . . . is the theme of Vera and Bill Cleaver's **The Mimosa Tree**. The setting is Chicago and this time life is very, very grim. . . . The mood of oppression, man's inhumanity to man, is almost completely unrelieved.

Poverty . . . presents the children with a choice—to steal or to starve. Here you can't live by the "Golden Rule". "Sometimes things got between you and it. It was fine if everything was at least tolerably equal. But when you had little brothers and a blind father at home hungry and there wasn't even rent money coming because your job was against the law, well, then you had to forget about doing to others as you would have them to do unto you." Grim stuff, eh? For good measure we also get treated to vivid details of mugging, epilepsy, drugs and more than a hint of matricide.

It is certainly one of the bleakest children's books I have come across and the moderately happy ending does little to mitigate the despair. Nevertheless, if you can stomach the depression, it's an excellent book, and you'll never find it boring. As for the mimosa tree of the title, which the daughter pictures outside the slum dwelling—that doesn't exist. Everybody knows that. Even her old blind father.

Peter Fanning, "Illusion and Reality," in The Times Educational Supplement *(© Times Newspapers Ltd. (London) 1978; reproduced from* The Times Educational Supplement *by permission), No. 3265, January 6, 1978, p. 17.*

Once more the Cleavers present a teenage girl coping single-handed with overwhelming problems: it is romance, but modern style. . . . The vivid evocation of country and city, the understanding of the pressures on the really poor, and the impact of the city on country innocents who suffer from conscience make this a moving, very readable story. (pp. 35-6)

A review of "The Mimosa Tree," in The Junior Bookshelf, *Vol. 42, No. 1, February, 1978, pp. 35-6.*

I WOULD RATHER BE A TURNIP   (1971)

The story of Annie Jelks, aged twelve, depends more upon situation than on plot; and yet, by the time all has been told, the girl has lived through a crucial summer. The daughter of the local druggist in a small Southern town near the Gulf of Mexico, she felt that her local reputation "was being periled" when Calvin, the illegitimate son of her sister Norma in California, came to live with them. Ostracized by her friends, harassed by the uncertainties of life and of her own physical and mental development, she scorned and resisted the possibilities of her little, blond, bespectacled, precocious nephew. . . . The events are vividly told, often hilariously and sometimes a bit melodramatically. And if one cannot believe that Annie really shot a bull dead, one will at least laugh at her experiences during her piano recital and at her misfortunes on a horse. Father, daughter, grandson-nephew, and Ruth—their black housekeeper—emerge as distinct individuals in the story of an Ellen Graelike character, whose conflicts are fought out as much with herself as with her environment. (pp. 171-72)

Paul Heins, in a review of "I Would Rather Be a Turnip," in The Horn Book Magazine *(copyright © 1971 by The Horn Book, Inc., Boston), Vol. XLVII, No. 2, April, 1971, pp. 171-72.*

The Cleavers have enriched children's literature through the creation of three memorable characters: Ellen Grae, Grover, and the incomparable Mary Call of *Where the Lilies Bloom*. . . . They are each revealed to us as they struggle to surmount problems which are not of their own making but rather have their genesis in an adult world the children cannot control. Here, 12-year-old Annie Jelks is upset when her father agrees to provide a home for her sister's illegitimate son. . . . Certainly the authors have succeeded in some measure in their exploration of the painful responses to illegitimacy that develop within and outside the Jelks' household. Readers will yearn for Annie to return Calvin's proffered affection without losing sympathy for her outraged sense of betrayal, the depth of which is revealed in a moving confrontation with her father. But only Annie's problem will lodge in their minds, not Annie herself. Real-life situations yield to such devices as a mad-bull episode which rings false from inception to its shotgun-blast conclusion. If the final chapter suggests a rapprochement between Annie and Calvin, it is too late and too faint; believable resolution and closure signaling the end of a tale have eluded the

authors, as has the kind of pulsing life they breathed into Mary Call. (pp. 102, 104)

Janet French, in a review of "I Would Rather Be a Turnip," in School Library Journal, *an appendix to* Library Journal *(reprinted from the April, 1971 issue of* School Library Journal, *published by R. R. Bowker Co./ A Xerox Corporation; copyright © 1971), Vol. 17, No. 8, April, 1971, pp. 102, 104.*

One of the hazards facing prolific writers is a tendency on the part of the reading public to greet a new book less on its own terms and more in relation to its predecessors. This is unfair; but, when the writing follows a formula, comparison becomes inevitable.

In the case of Vera and Bill Cleaver, the formula is that of an irascible young girl besieged by what is known as a social problem: divorced parents, feebleminded friends, dire poverty, urban displacement—the list can get as long as your arm.

"I Would Rather Be a Turnip" will be touted as a courageous book about illegitimacy, but it is no such thing. Annie Jelks is placed in what might have been a challenging predicament. . . .

Unlike Mary Call (in **"Where the Lilies Bloom"**), whose family was literally dying of poverty, or Marvella Profitt (**"The Mimosa Tree"**), who suffered a plunge into a Chicago slum, Annie Jelks is furnished with a loving and intelligent father, a black mother figure who apparently has not heard of the Revolution, and a secure middle-class home. She suffers no deficiency of brains or opportunity. With all this equipment at her disposal, one wonders why Calvin should be such a cross. If his illegitimacy is her problem, the authors haven't let her explore it.

The idea of illegitimacy is abstract, absurd, adult and, in a sense, evil. How can one human being be legitimate and another not? But Annie Jelks never thinks past the whispered innuendos of her peers, let alone tests the concept against her own reality. She never wonders how Calvin regards his supposed stigma nor even if he is aware of suffering social disability. No one snubs him. Instead, the authors trot Annie through a brief truancy, a performance at a piano recital, the shooting of a mad bull and an extended tour of the local library. Each of these experiences enhances her self-esteem but in no way deals with the issue.

One must wonder why writers of the Cleavers' stature rushed this underdone book into print. In **"Where the Lilies Bloom,"** they painted a compelling portrait of a girl whose fortitude matched the starkness of her circumstance. The very narrowness of Mary Call's view of the possible enabled her to survive disaster. Mary Call evoked the reader's respect and compassion because she was involved in a life-and-death struggle. Annie Jelks isn't fit to polish her boots.

"I'd Rather Be a Turnip" comes perilously close to being an inversion of the series book. The current marketability of "problems" does not justify such a misuse of the Cleavers' talents.

Feenie Ziner, in a review of "I Would Rather Be a Turnip," in The New York Times Book Review *(© 1971 by The New York Times Company; reprinted by permission), May 2, 1971, p. 4.*

Annie Jelks, the heroine, inhabits the same enclosed, hot-summered, small-town world in the American South as Frankie

Addams in *Member of the Wedding*. She too, like Frankie, is twelve, motherless and cared for by a forthright, homely black housekeeper. But there the similarity ends, for this is a children's book, not an adult novel. . . . Her confusion, conflicting emotions and gradual, stumbling awareness of herself are portrayed with humour and sensitivity. This is an excellent book to offer young adolescents.

> *Vivienne Furlong, in a review of "I Would Rather Be a Turnip," in* The School Librarian, *Vol. 20, No. 3, September, 1972, p. 252.*

Only as she sees the corrosive effect of the prejudiced behavior of others does Annie gain perspective. She's a wonderfully belligerent character, and the gentle, amiable Calvin a striking contrast. Their relationship is perceptively developed, and the loving, no-nonsense black housekeeper's relationship with both children is warm and sensitive. It is surprising that the term "bastard" is several times referred to tangentially as the "name" that some girls have called Calvin, but neither the housekeeper nor the father uses it when Annie remarks on it. A very small flaw in a well-constructed book that is written with verve, humor, and compassion.

> *Zena Sutherland, "Review of Books: 'I Would Rather Be a Turnip'," in her* The Best in Children's Books: The University of Chicago Guide to Children's Literature, 1966-1972, *edited by Zena Sutherland (reprinted by permission of The University of Chicago Press; © 1973 by The University of Chicago), University of Chicago Press, 1973, p. 77.*

THE MOCK REVOLT (1971)

"I want to go out and battle the world. . . . I just got to do it before I get so old I won't want to." During 1939, the Great Depression was still an economic factor in the United States, but thirteen-year-old Ussy Mock's concerns—distaste for a comfortably mundane existence, determination to be different from the respectable Medina "deadlies" (including his father)—will not be particularly startling to the decade which defined the "generation gap." The references are topical—Adolf Hitler, radio soap operas—but the tone is 1971 as Ussy painfully discovers that being different is more than exterior change. Thus, the defiant "scalped" haircut and secret tattoo acquired in early summer become less important at summer's end than securing a fair trial for the father of a luckless migrant family. "'I'm going to tell the judge what William Makepeace Thackeray said about dependence being a perpetual call upon humanity,'" he informs Mr. Suffrin, the teacher who first introduced Thackeray's ideas to him. "'*That'll* give him something to think about.'" Essentially an introspective study of a boy's maturation, the plot is developed episodically, concentrating on details revealing character rather than on story line. Although the pace seems slower than that of *Ellen Grae* or *Where the Lilies Bloom,* the Cleavers' flair for unusual character vignettes—a technique which often stops just short of caricature—is evidenced in the descriptions of the eccentric teacher who "encouraged his students to have and express their own opinions" and in the brief sketches of "Directly" and Turner Ensley, a pair of social iconoclasts in the Huck Finn tradition.

> *Mary Burns, in a review of "The Mock Revolt," in* The Horn Book Magazine *(copyright © 1971 by The Horn Book, Inc., Boston), Vol. XLVII, No. 5, October, 1971, p. 488.*

The Cleavers have added another excellent title to their backlist of distinguished novels. . . . [Ussy Mock's] revolt, which seems to be a gradual exchange of youthful discontent for informed compassion, is described with understanding and insight, and the story effectively recreates the Depression era.

> *Brooke Anson, in a review of "The Mock Revolt," in* School Library Journal, *an appendix to* Library Journal *(reprinted from the October, 1971 issue of* School Library Journal, *published by R. R. Bowker Co./ A Xerox Corporation; copyright © 1971), Vol. 18, No. 2, October, 1971, p. 118.*

What the Cleavers are saying about our responsibility to our fellow men, about migrant workers and about an egocentric kid who is more harshly judgmental than the deadlies he despises, escapes me.

> *Dorothy M. Broderick, in a review of "The Mock Revolt," in* The New York Times Book Review *(© 1972 by The New York Times Company; reprinted by permission), January 16, 1972, p. 8.*

Vera and Bill Cleaver have established a territory for themselves in books about the young coming to terms with that other America—of small town narrowness, and sometimes desperate poverty. Their subjects are grim, even horrifying, but the treatment is tender, funny and humane. This book lacks the sublime macabre tenderness that informed *Where the Lilies Bloom* but is good and interesting nevertheless. . . . This book is good fiction and without cheaty preaching didacticism, puts the case for human decency, without turning it into a case for the establishment. Wholesome food for thought for young rebels—and a good read too.

> *Jill Paton Walsh, in a review of "The Mock Revolt," in* Children's Book Review *(© 1972 by Five Owls Press Ltd.; all rights reserved), Vol. II, No. 5, October, 1972, p. 148.*

This is a *very* American book. Ghosts from *Catcher in the Rye, The Grapes of Wrath* and from Mark Twain stalk its pages. The very specific period of its setting (summer 1939) means the fag-ends of the depression and isolationism. Migrant workers cross the South and the middle classes call them trash. Only a few hear the disturbing rumbles from across the water.

However, this book is no mere plagiaristic historical mishmash. The child here may have to make an effort to adjust to it: the effort will be well worth while. . . . Often very funny, always observant, the book yet wears its conscience on its sleeve rather obviously; some characters—one thinks of Mr Suffrin, the wise oddball of a history teacher, to whom Ussy turns in moments of crisis—are a little hard to take. But there are some minor triumphs as well; Ussy's younger brother Pody is in children's fiction's great tradition of memorable younger brothers—inscrutably wilful, he stands as a creation with James in *The Warden's Niece* and Paul in *Bedknobs and Broomsticks*. It is a pity he does not appear more often.

This book is recommended for children in the 11-15 age-group—they will get a lot out of it. (pp. 343-44)

> *Dennis Hamley, in a review of "The Mock Revolt," in* The School Librarian, *Vol. 20, No. 4, December, 1972, pp. 343-44.*

DELPHA GREEN AND COMPANY (1972)

[Factory owner Mr.] Choate's proximity to caricature hardly matters, though the resemblance of Mr. Green's gospel to Con III conventional wisdom is more disappointing in light of his messianic role here. Even Delpha's sunny charm gets pretty thick, but just when we've had enough of the Ellen Grae-Mary Call Luther grit, Delpha disarmingly admits her excesses and determines to stop "looking for rainbows"—proving once more that there's no foretelling what the Cleavers' are up to. Here as previously, though, their most auspicious configurations are reserved for the outlandish minor characters and their sharply surreal conversations—such as when the disposition of several futures evolves quite rationally into a discussion of whether to be in love with a mule is "credible." Then there are those tantalizing chapter headings, and if it all adds up to an elaborately ingenious system that overshadows the mundane machinery beneath, that is just what Delpha Green and company are into.

A review of "Delpha Green and Company," in Kirkus Reviews *(copyright © 1972 The Kirkus Service, Inc.), Vol. XL, No. 6, March 15, 1972, p. 98.*

This rambling, virtually plotless family tale of a ne'er-do-well father—at the moment he's the minister of an offbeat church of his own creation—and his brood compares poorly with the authors' previous successes. Supposedly written by the astrology-smitten oldest daughter, Delpha, the story employs an amateurish stream-of-consciousness style and is overfilled with characters who come and go, talking interminably all the while. Even the family members are sketchily drawn—one's only distinguishing characteristic is that he says "sholey" instead of "surely"; another seems confined to the phrase "'Oh, my conscience.'" Delpha contends that, "'You could find out what I am saying is the truest thing you ever heard if you wanted to . . . ,'" but most readers would be left too confused and too bored to try.

Ruth Pegau, in a review of "Delpha Green and Company," in School Library Journal, *an appendix to* Library Journal *(reprinted from the May, 1972 issue of* School Library Journal, *published by R. R. Bowker Co./A Xerox Corporation; copyright © 1972), Vol. 18, No. 9, May, 1972, p. 75.*

It's hard to say how Cleaver fans are going to take this new book, seeing that the Cleavers, long known for lighting single candles in oceanic darks, are now presenting a comedy. . . .

Loosely hung on Delpha's enthusiasm for astrology—she shows people their true, benevolent selves by exposing them to the meaning of their signs—the plot cavorts to a happy conclusion never for a moment in doubt. The Cleavers obviously mean the whole thing to be taken lightly in spite of foster homes, penitentiaries, and so on. The characters, with names like Hershel, Tillie, and Honey Bunch, are to a man rakish, eccentric and purely one-dimensional. The reader is never burdened by any particular belief in them or sympathy for their problems, he simply enjoys them.

This brings us to a flaw: Delpha, for no apparent reason, drops her optimism in the end, at the very moment when you might expect her to feel it was most justified, and announces: "I have changed in the last day or two. . . . From now on I am going to show everything I feel. I am not going to pretend like I see a rainbow when I don't." In a story constructed of rainbows, this seems unnecessary.

Perhaps the Cleavers felt that one nail was needed to keep it all from floating away; but they would have done better to leave things as they were. Writers needn't apologize for fluff if it is good fluff, well-written, consistent, and truly funny. There *are* moments in "Delpha Green" when the rakishness gets a little too broad; but there are many more moments of genuine comedy with a decidedly Wodehousian cast.

Natalie Babbitt, in a review of "Delpha Green and Company," in The New York Times Book Review *(© 1972 by The New York Times Company; reprinted by permission), May 28, 1972, p. 8.*

The Cleavers have always relied on the bizarre and unusual to bring their characters to life, drawing people a little larger than life in communities strange by reason of their remoteness. In some of their books—notably, *Where the lilies bloom*—the method has worked supremely well. In *Delpha Green and Company* the oddity seems to have gone a little sour. One of the troubles is that the book is episodic, with some of the chapters reading almost like perfunctory gap-fillers in the narrative. . . . [Delpha's] crude interference in people's lives and the self-conscious oddity of her idiom give an uneasy and unreal tone to this loosely-planned book. Oddity is not enough in itself to make a good story, and this one seems to lack the inner motivation it needs. (pp. 2739-40)

Margery Fisher, in a review of "Delpha Green and Company," in her Growing Point, *Vol. 14, No. 5, November, 1975, pp. 2739-40.*

THE WHYS AND WHEREFORES OF LITTABELLE LEE (1973)

In the tradition of Mary Call Luther (**Where the Lilies Bloom**), Littabelle Lee at sixteen faces up to the whys and wherefores of inherited responsibility with gutsy resolution. . . . We appreciate the absence of **Delpha Green's** astrological trappings here, and Littabelle Lee demonstrates once more that there is plenty of mileage left in the Cleavers' archetypal gritty heroine . . . but we're beginning to get the feeling that only the names have been changed. (pp. 122-23)

A review of "The Whys and Wherefores of Littabelle Lee," in Kirkus Reviews *(copyright © 1973 The Kirkus Service, Inc.), Vol. XLI, No. 3, February 1, 1973, pp. 122-23.*

Books pour from the writing factory known as Vera and Bill Cleaver in a succession so rapid as to be frightening, and like all writers of prolific production they have their low moments along with their high. "The Whys and Wherefores of Littabelle Lee" is, happily, one of the latter. . . . [It] is a tight, controlled, touching and unsentimental piece of work—a novel that is charming but not cloying.

That is a fault the Cleavers have not always been able to avoid. Their books are usually set in the "folksy" surroundings of the Appalachian South, and they have a tendency to let their rusticity become mannered—as in their last book, "**Delpha Green & Company**"—and to churn out flowery back-to-nature descriptive passages that smack heavily of the literary arts-and-crafts class, passages that mar their otherwise fine "**Where the Lilies Bloom**."

But in "**Littabelle Lee**" the mountains and their people are wholly believable; the prose is graceful; the story is both engaging and thematically purposeful. It is of the caliber of William Armstrong's "Sounder" and Laura Ingalls Wilder's "The

Little House in the Big Woods''—and coming from one who grew up on and loved the Wilder books, that is high praise indeed. . . .

"**Littabelle Lee**" is very much a "Cleaver book," which is to say it is about a teen-aged girl placed in circumstances that test her resourcefulness and her loyalty to family. The typical "Cleaver girl" is, or thinks of herself as, homely and faintly tomboyish. She entertains few thoughts of boys, and those she does are largely scornful; marriage is the last thing on her mind, although one usually senses (Women's Lib notwithstanding) that she will get there eventually. She is ambitious: "I want to be better than I was," Littabelle says. "And smarter." She is tough and competent and ingenious. She has her rough moments, but her native wit and industry pull her through, and in the end she has learned some important lessons about life and herself. . . . (p. 6)

The story is direct and modest, and the Cleavers offer its morals without belaboring them. But they are there, and they are sound. "**Littabelle Lee**" is about the dignity of poor people who struggle to live on a demanding mountain land that they love. . . . It is about children who are faithful to family, and children who are not. It is about a law in which there is mercy and true justice. Most of all, it is about growing up, about meeting the responsibilities that are one's "whys and where-fores." (pp. 6-7)

[This is a] thoughtful and affecting book. "**Littabelle Lee**" is genuinely mature, written with no condescension toward its youthful readers. . . . The Cleavers, in this book, grant their readers the respect they deserve, using language that is forth-right and honest, telling a story that touches on life's truths. "**The Whys and Wherefores of Littabelle Lee**" is a book that children ought to read, precisely because it does not treat them as "children." (p. 7)

> *Jonathan Yardley, in a review of "The Whys and Wherefores of Littabelle Lee," in* The New York Times Book Review *(© 1973 by The New York Times Company; reprinted by permission), March 4, 1973, pp. 6-7.*

The Cleavers are off on another folksy nostalgia trip, this time to the Ozarks. This book is written with more care and style than their **Delpha Green & Company** . . . , but it will not appeal to the intended age group. . . . The story is predictable, talky, and dull, and just stops—it doesn't conclude, it quits and gives up.

> *Ruth Pegau, in a review of "The Whys and Where-fores of Littabelle Lee," in* Library Journal *(reprinted from Library Journal, June 15, 1973; published by R. R. Bowker Co. (a Xerox company); copyright © 1973 by Xerox Corporation), Vol. 98, No. 12, June 15, 1973, p. 2000.*

Those who have read **Where the Lilies Bloom** may find the opening pages of this book a bit too familiar. . . .

To read this book, full of truth and the natural life of the country, is a rewarding experience. It contains much eventful incident, and much simple, wise reflection. Our modern age introduces great tension into the attempt to live the self-reliant existence of the countryman and the characters are all firmly set in their ambivalent society. Less exuberant than the author's other books, this one is no less genuinely alive.

> *M. H. Miller, in a review of "The Whys and Where-fores of Littabelle Lee," in* Children's Book Review

Vol. IV, No. 2, Summer, 1974, p. 64.

Few readers are likely to find themselves in the situation of the sixteen-year-old heroine of **The Whys and Wherefores of Littabelle Lee:** few will put down the book without the feeling that they have been enlarged and enlightened by reading it. . . . Something in the sardonic hill-billy idiom of Littabelle as she tells this story, something of the taut, economical plan of the book, makes perfect sense of an outlandish plot.

> *Margery Fisher, in a review of "The Whys and Wherefores of Littabelle Lee," in her* Growing Point, *Vol. 13, No. 4, October, 1974, p. 2479.*

ME TOO (1973)

"**Me Too**" is the sort of warm, rich book one has come to expect from Vera and Bill Cleaver, and yet it lays bare one of the most difficult things the family of an exceptional child must face: their own complicated feelings toward the child.

The story concerns two girls, twins, 12 years old. Lydia is bright and intelligent; Lorna is an exceptional child with a mental age of about 5. During the summer in which the father deserts the family, Lydia takes on the care and education of Lornie. Her dream is that she will make Lornie so much like herself that no one will be able to tell the difference. . . .

Her efforts—the failures, the bursts of frustration, the unex-pected success followed by more failure—all have the ring of truth, and the dialogue between the two girls is fine. Although Lydia's plan is obviously doomed from the start, this is not a depressing book. The build-up to the climax is sure and ex-citing, and in the end Lydia finds that although she has failed, there is in the certainty of failure a kind of release. This is so skillfully done that the reader feels released too.

> *Betsy Byars, "Twins and an Anthem," in* The New York Times Book Review *(© 1973 by The New York Times Company; reprinted by permission), October 21, 1973, p. 8.**

The contrast between the twins is dramatic, the interplay fas-cinating, and Lydia's efforts and self-searching moving. But her failure is neither pathetic nor sad; for she has grown during her trials and frustrations, has learned to accept the reality of her father's desertion, and has come to an understanding of the "exceptional" status of her sister. This vital, self-reliant, and unusually perceptive child takes her place beside other strong and highly individual characters created by the authors.

> *Beryl Robinson, in a review of "Me Too," in* The Horn Book Magazine *(copyright © 1973 by The Horn Book, Inc., Boston), Vol. XLIX, No. 6, December, 1973, p. 590.*

This is a single-problem novel with a vengeance that never looks up from the contrived relationship of a pair of 12-year-old twins. . . .

There are some telling moments in the story, and there is need to probe the problems of the retarded. But **Me Too** is distorted by a pat situation and facile adult characterizations. (p. 236)

> *Richard Peck, "Young Adult Books: Teenagers' Tastes," in* American Libraries *(reprinted by per-mission of the American Library Association; © 1974 by the American Library Association), Vol. 5, No. 5, May, 1974, pp. 235-36.**

The country community, the mountain, pond and railway tracks, the neighbours whose reactions to the Birdsongs are a challenge to Lydia—these elements are fused through dialogue, description and comment into a fluent narrative with the sisters as its focal points. They are, if you like, two sides of human nature—extrovert and introvert, quiescent and striving, dominant and passive, open and secret. Through a story about individuals the Cleavers have shown, in their uniquely quirky, shrewd, almost shockingly actual way, certain truths about family relationships and their complexity. (pp. 2642-43)

> *Margery Fisher, in a review of "Me Too," in her* Growing Point, *Vol. 14, No. 1, May, 1975, pp. 2642-43.*

This is a challenging and deeply moving book. . . .

Vera and Bill Cleaver seem to be able to see into a child and to create its world with incredible accuracy. But it is a very narrow world and it is, if I remember correctly, usually that of a girl. Ellen Grae bears a remarkable resemblance to Lydia. However, *Me Too* should appeal to the thoughtful twelve- to fifteen-year-old and lead to wide-ranging discussions within a group.

> *Joan Murphy, in a review of "Me Too," in* The School Librarian, *Vol. 23, No. 4, December, 1975, p. 338.*

The chronicles of Lorna's behavior, especially her erratic speech patterns, upon examination are somewhat off-target descriptions of reality. And while Lydia is a perceptive child, the contention that she could know that the composer whose music she heard was going through an ordeal when he wrote it is highly unlikely: "Deaf and still able to write music like that. How was it she knew beforehand the music hadn't come from any normal person?" However, the Cleavers are in top form in terms of pacing and style and the deceptively simple novel makes some sophisticated demands on its readers, asking them to consider the philosophical aspects of love, its limitations, and its contradictions. Some existential and religious questions are raised and some shocking insights into people's responses to stress are effectively presented. (pp. 148-49)

> *Barbara H. Baskin and Karen H. Harris, "An Annotated Guide to Juvenile Fiction Portraying the Handicapped, 1940-1975: 'Me Too',"* in their *Notes from a Different Drummer: A Guide to Juvenile Fiction Portraying the Handicapped (reprinted with permission of the R. R. Bowker Company; copyright © 1977 by Barbara H. Baskin and Karen H. Harris), Bowker, 1977, pp. 148-49.*

DUST OF THE EARTH (1975)

This book reminds me somehow of a very odd patchwork quilt, one in which delicate floral patterns and sophisticated abstracts are stitched side-by-side with sturdy muslin and rough homespun. Its method is that mixed, even indecisive, and the result is half-enchanting, half-annoying. . . . (p. 10)

Fourteen-year-old Fern Drawn tells the story of how her family, "poor as potato scrapings" and scant on love, inherits a run-down farm near the South Dakota Badlands and, while making a go of it, discover themselves and each other, becoming a family for the first time. (pp. 10, 12)

[Through] episode after episode of matter-of-fact survival, each of the Drawns both copes and blossoms, confronting terrors,

discovering unsuspected strengths, and, perhaps most important, learning to see and value each other in the light of a common challenge. . . .

[Through] Fern swirl currents of discovery, the multitude of minute separate awakenings which compose the new sense of oneself, of others, of one's aloneness at 14. It's a good age to write a story through, and the Cleavers capture excellently the half-formed, inarticulate but compelling way things come to one "in a bewildered flow of feeling." In counterpoint to these delicate and moving intuitions is the solidly practical stuff of making do on the farm—lots of satisfying information on sheep raising and frontier history—and it bursts with the exhilaration of mastering touch tasks.

The problem is that the authors can't quite decide whether they're writing in a 14-year-old's voice or a reminiscing grown-up's, in folk speech or artistic language. Fern's "voice," an often unsettlingly beautiful blend of folk rhythms and knowing poetry, tends to slip left and right into "aw-shucks" corn and sophisticated authors' prose respectively—itself quite beautiful, but not out of the head of any young frontier girl. This inconsistency of voice is matched by a wobbliness of narrative structure, an uncertainty of form. Are the Cleavers writing a dramatic narrative, a letter, or a prose poem? Bits of all three, it would seem. The narrative texture has the spontaneity of a letter, a confidence or a reminiscence (awkward at times, as when Fern turns to the reader in an abrupt aside: "Imagine our worry . . ."), but this mode is too fancy-free and haphazard to support a dramatic structure. So, as a story with an emotional shape, the book is full of slips and flaws. The big blizzard, hinted at early as a climactic event, comes and goes in a few anticlimactic paragraphs, and important moments of dawning awareness between family members are described in brief lyrical generalizations rather than written out as dramatic scenes. The reader's emotions, when tempted to take hold, are often unseated by a sudden shift of mode. An odd patchwork, then—earthy events and poetic emotions, but no firm dramatic ground on which the twain may meet. (p. 12)

> *Annie Gottlieb, in a review of "Dust of the Earth," in* The New York Times Book Review *(© 1975 by The New York Times Company; reprinted by permission), October 19, 1975, pp. 10, 12.*

[*Dust of the Earth* is] penned by Fern in a slightly formal but brilliantly individualistic style. . . . *Earth* is rich with humor and human feeling and facts about farming, but it is richest in the personality of Fern herself. Like Ellen Grae Derryberry in *Ellen Grae* . . . or Mary Call Luther in *Where the Lilies Bloom* . . . , Fern has spirit and intelligence and is an extremely nice person to know. (pp. 87-8)

> *Shirley M. Wilton, in a review of "Dust of the Earth," in* School Library Journal *(reprinted from the November, 1975 issue of* School Library Journal, *published by R. R. Bowker Co./ A Xerox Corporation; copyright © 1975), Vol. 22, No. 3, November, 1975, pp. 87-8.*

The strength and charm of this novel lie in the characterization of Fern Drawn, who is a courageous, strong, resourceful young girl, with leadership qualities and a mind of her own.

This is a beautifully written book which young readers will enjoy. (p. 178)

> *"The Analyses: 'Dust of the Earth',"* in Human—and Anti-Human—Values in Children's Books: A

Content Rating Instrument for Educators and Concerned Parents *(copyright © 1976 by the Council on
Interracial Books for Children, Inc.), CIBC Racism
and Sexism Resource Center for Educators, 1976,
pp. 177-78.*

Many of [the Cleaver's] books have resourceful and embattled
young heroines, coping with extraordinary difficulties, but they
differ from the usual run of "problem" novels for young readers in their emotional intensity and their literary, often self-
conscious, flavour. Cleaver heroines can be cloying—they are
apt to say things like "nobody ever said love was easy", but
they are seldom dull.

Dust of the Earth doesn't really advance the Cleaver's work
very much. . . . Fern's first person narrative, with its biblical
overtones, is often more irritating than moving and the plot is
slight. There's no mistaking the sincerity behind the writing,
though, and the Cleavers are strong on the behaviour of both
older brothers and of sheep.

> *Rosamond Faith, "Treacherous Earth," in* The Times
> Literary Supplement *(© Times Newspapers Ltd.
> (London) 1977; reproduced from The Times Literary
> Supplement by permission), No. 3931, July 15, 1977,
> p. 865.**

Another most unusual but moving novel featuring the plight
of an adolescent girl who feels she must carry the entire weight
of the responsibility for her down-and-out family. This is a
familiar theme for this unusual writing team. Their books will
not appeal widely but they have a special power of evoking a
particular desolate landscape (in this case the Badlands of South
Dakota) and because the theme is survival—physical and emotional survival—against great odds they have a special place
in children's literature.

> *A review of "Dust of the Earth," in* Books for Your
> Children *(© Books for Your Children 1977), Vol.
> 12, No. 4, Autumn, 1977, p. 11.*

TRIAL VALLEY (1977)

Mary Call Luther has grown some since we met her in ***Where
the Lilies Bloom,*** but she's as level-headed and hard working
as ever. Now sixteen, she continues to support herself and her
brother and sister by wildcrafting; the details of their daily
tasks give a rich flavor. To complicate her life further, Mary
Call has two very different suitors, as well as the care and
feeding of little Jack Parsons, whom she finds locked in a cage.
The inevitable Cleaver bizarreness is in evidence. Ima Dean
and Romey's grumbling and feistiness make a nice balance to
Mary Call's earnestness. This is a successful sequel that contains all the elements Cleaver fans expect.

> *Nelda Mohr, in a review of "Trial Valley," in* Chil-
> dren's Book Review Service *(copyright © 1977 Chil-
> dren's Book Review Service Inc.), Vol. 5, No. 9,
> April, 1977, p. 89.*

Vera and Bill Cleaver's latest book, **"Trial Valley"**, the sequel
to **"Where the Lilies Bloom"** is equally captivating . . .

On one level, this book deals with what will become of the
child and which suitor Mary Call will accept. But on another
level, it is a beautiful depiction of a young girl growing up
and finding her direction in life. The characters are finely
drawn, the mood is poetic at times. A sensitive book for a
thoughtful reader.

*Wendy Moorhead, "From Appalachia to China-
town—Adventures in Americana," in* The Christian
Science Monitor *(reprinted by permission from* The
Christian Science Monitor; *© 1977 The Christian
Science Publishing Society; all rights reserved), May
4, 1977, p. 132.**

Vera and Bill Cleaver have written a coming-of-age book with
wit, grace and humor. By using language that is rich and varied
rather than literal and slangy, they have reminded us that dignity is not just a province of the affluent. Mary Call Luther is
a young woman in touch with herself. Young readers coming
away from **"Trial Valley"** will feel in touch with themselves,
too.

> *Bryna J. Fireside, in a review of "Trial Valley," in*
> The New York Times Book Review *(© 1977 by The
> New York Times Company; reprinted by permission),
> June 12, 1977, p. 31.*

[***Trial Valley***] is a follow up story to ***Where the Lilies Bloom,***
but it seems to lack the same richness and strength. Nevertheless, Mary Call, the sixteen-year-old heroine, continues to display her sense of mountain tradition and self-reliance. With
less minor character development and more emphasis on Mary
Call, the reader will be satisfied to discover that she retains
her independence and her sense of protection and responsibility
for those she loves. The Cleavers have again written in a lively
and authentic style.

> *A review of "Trial Valley," in* The Babbling Book-
> worm *(copyright 1977 The Babbling Bookworm
> Newsletter), Vol. 5, No. 7, August, 1977, p. 4.*

The writing in this book is of the same high quality [as in
Where the Lilies Bloom]. Mary Call . . . is the character through
whose eyes the reader experiences the action. She is strong-
willed and disillusioned in the best sense in that her expectations of human beings and especially of the children for whose
upbringing she is responsible (both her parents are dead) are
realistic, without being embittered. Her wry realism on the
other hand demands the understanding of a mature reader, e.g.
where she says of her younger brother and sister, "I love these
two but can hardly stand them." The arrival in their lives of
an abandoned child, Jack Parsons, brings in a personality almost as strong as Mary's, an added responsibility in a life
where there has already been too much. Kiser, her brother-in-
law, is concerned that her great strength in the end does not
lead to a terrible hardness with which she seems threatened.
In the background is the country of Indian legend where the
children "wildcraft" for a living, gathering roots and herbs.
It is beautiful and contributes something to the strength and
individuality of all the characters. It is a book that shows the
reader "the steeples" just as the book borrowed from Mary's
much loved teacher showed to Mary. This is a book to "pull
you out of yourself".

> *Norah Napiontek, in a review of "Trial Valley," in*
> Book Window *(© 1978 S.C.B.A. and contributors),
> Vol. 5, No. 3, Summer, 1978, p. 26.*

QUEEN OF HEARTS (1978)

I continue to be astonished that the Cleavers have not received
the Newbery Medal. It is a gross oversight; perhaps it will be
remedied, soon. ***Queen of Hearts*** is not an easy read. But
learning to live with the complex rhythms of intimacy is not
easy, either. It's even harder when the two people thrown

together are an alert, cantankerous, spirited seventy-nine-year-old and a stubborn, detached, day-dreaming adolescent. When Granny Lincoln suffers a small stroke and then refuses to budge from her own home, Wilma discovers the deeper layers, the special joys and pains that accompany aging. At a time when so many elderly are being "put away," this novel shines forth with another, far wiser and more loving vision. The writing sings. (pp. 75-6)

Leigh Dean, in a review of "Queen of Hearts," in Children's Book Review Service *(copyright © 1978 Children's Book Review Service Inc.), Vol. 6, No. 8, March, 1978, pp. 75-6.*

Now meet Granny Lincoln, the feisty creation of Vera and Bill Cleaver in **"Queen of Hearts."** You won't catch her taking her life to make things easier for her folks; she would not lift a little finger for them. Her grandchildren give her the "nervous snits," and, as everyone knows, crossing her is more "dangerous than gargling with household bleach." Still, it is only after her fall that she becomes a problem. The doctor says she can't live alone. One after another, three women are hired, but none lasts more than a few days. Finally Granny allows she might put up with Wilma, her 12-year-old granddaughter, and Wilma moves in.

At the outset of this story Wilma's emotions have "never been called upon to make any big responses," but that soon changes. By turn Wilma is humiliated ("Your hair is your only redeeming feature," Granny tells her), angry ("You think because you're old . . . you can treat people any old way?" Wilma asks), repulsed ("God must hate people," Wilma thinks, "to make them go through this awful business"). Nevertheless Wilma learns to stand up to the cantankerous old soul, to follow her into her past, and she even finds a way to make her grandmother feel useful. Not that this improves Granny's disposition. When other people are found to take over the job, Wilma is, of course, fervently grateful. But "oh dearest God," she prays, "please take care of my Granny, for she is old and some of her wires are twisted."

As usual, the Cleavers face tough situations with spunk and deliver language so lively that it crackles. And, as usual, they hit the mark, so it is no surprise that Granny makes short work of the new people and Wilma returns. It is quite clear, however, that Granny is not just getting her way again. Wilma is going because she has decided to go. Why? Perhaps because she has come to grips with the sorry fact that, however ornery, Granny, like all old people, is the real loser.

Jean Fritz, in a review of "Queen of Hearts," in The New York Times Book Review *(© 1978 by The New York Times Company; reprinted by permission), April 30, 1978, p. 51.*

In the present time of proliferating isms the authors characteristically transcend a fashionable theme and produce a fine novel. . . . The incongruity of [Wilma and Granny's] relationship is seen in a devastatingly honest tragicomedy. In the sometimes fierce struggles that ensued, Wilma fought back, toughened, and matured; she perceived the old woman's deterioration, her isolation, her outrageous loss of dignity, and above all, her terrible fear—"of living, of dying, of herself, of having now to depend on others to tell her what to do." And she determined to provide Granny with a source of purpose and pride. A brave, humane book, wholly individual in conception and in style.

Ethel Heins, in a review of "Queen of Hearts," in The Horn Book Magazine *(copyright © 1978 by The Horn Book, Inc., Boston), Vol. LIV, No. 3, June, 1978, p. 275.*

There's no false sweetness-and-light ending to the story, which has good characterization and dialogue but is weakened by an ending that simply trails away and by the frequent evidences of overwriting: ". . . a man with . . . large, greedy ears . . ." or, "The power in her was a hard and steady beat. Drawing on its flattering worth and its mysterious ambition . . ." (pp. 172-73)

Zena Sutherland, in a review of "Queen of Hearts," in Bulletin of the Center for Children's Books *(reprinted by permission of The University of Chicago Press; © 1978 by The University of Chicago), Vol. 31, No. 11, July-August, 1978, pp. 172-73.*

Though the authors are writing about the problems of old age and how youth copes with this, natural feelings of warmth and compassion seem awkwardly expressed. . . . [There] is a dryness and lack of easy humor in comparison to previous Cleaver books.

A review of "Queen of Hearts," in The Babbling Bookworm *(copyright 1979 The Babbling Bookworm Newsletter), Vol. 6, No. 12, January 1979, p. 3.*

Queen of Hearts . . . is a painful—at times brutal, never sweet or sentimental—look at aging. . . .

The story is poignant and bitter-sweet, a book for adolescents that should also be read by adults, particularly adults who are involved in decisions about the care of aging parents. The Cleavers' treatment of the relationship between Granny and her son (Wilma's father) as she fights to retain the parent-child dominance and he fights to reverse it, is particularly relevant to adults.

For all of its strengths, the book also has some weaknesses. Claybrook, Wilma's six-year-old brother, is sometimes portrayed as both more mature and thoughtful than his twelve-year-old sister. More seriously, racial stereotypes are thrown—almost dragged—into the story. For instance, Wilma envisions an Eskimo in one of her imaginary scenarios: "He was fat and his greasy grin exposed teeth shaped like blocks." In addition, the book's resolution is based on fraud, with Wilma lying to Granny "for her own good" and thus causing Granny to lose control of her own life.

Powerful, painful and poignant, ***Queen of Hearts*** is definitely not light reading, but it is a thought-provoking book that should be read and discussed. The specific instances in the book that are sexist, racist and ageist should be discussed with young readers, however.

Patricia Campbell, in a review of "Queen of Hearts," in Interracial Books for Children Bulletin *(reprinted by permission of Interracial Books for Children Bulletin, 1841 Broadway, New York, N.Y. 10023), Vol. 10, No. 8, 1979, p. 18.*

A LITTLE DESTINY (1979)

"It has to be old, this instinct to let evil be its own slave," the Cleavers conclude in the epilogue, but more stirring than the gem of a sermon, more sweeping than the riptide plot, and more touching than the wry dialogue is the love story here—

the quietly thunderous spectacle of six closely bound people who face personal loss with fear and grief, find security "a slippery commodity," and manage to save one another with flying colors.

> *Laura Geringer, in a review of "A Little Destiny," in* School Library Journal *(reprinted from the September, 1979 issue of* School Library Journal, *published by R. R. Bowker Co./ A Xerox Corporation; copyright © 1979), Vol. 26, No. 1, September, 1979, p. 154.*

The plot verges on turgidity and, although there are passages of facile writing, the book is marred by other passages that are ornate and by phrases that are redolent of an earlier time (". . . he felt bleary of a sudden . . ." or, "The woman . . . wore an ankle-length dress of linsey-woolsey . . .") although the setting, undated, includes references to an automobile.

> *Zena Sutherland, in a review of "A Little Destiny," in* Bulletin of the Center for Children's Books *(reprinted by permission of The University of Chicago Press; © 1979 by The University of Chicago), Vol. 33, No. 3, November, 1979, p. 44.*

A story of evil and peril and the question of revenge, set in rural Georgia early in the century. . . . Along with moral questioning of unusual depth and the tensions brought about by the kidnapping of Lyman and Lucy by Cleggs's men, there are occasional flashes of humor and a feeling for the immense courage and fortitude of Lyman and Lucy. (pp. 667-68)

> *Virginia Haviland, in a review of "A Little Destiny," in* The Horn Book Magazine *(copyright © 1979 by The Horn Book, Inc., Boston), Vol. LV, No. 6, December, 1979, pp. 667-68.*

A decade ago, few writers were better known for their spunky country heroines than Vera and Bill Cleaver. . . . The scene of the Cleavers' latest book, **"A Little Destiny"** . . . , is postbellum Georgia, and protagonist Lucy Commander is a gently-bred, home-tutored girl who joins forces with a no-account drifter to get revenge on the local big shot whose scheming has contributed to her father's death and the loss of her inheritance.

Lucy's terse yet round-about speaking style adds some piquancy to the action scenes and to her relationship with her devoted side-kick, who turns out to be only 26 (we at first picture him as an old codger) and eager to change his ways to win her approval. But Lucy has neither the repertory of mountain lore nor the poor-folks' savvy that have made other Cleaver heroines so arresting. The outwitting of Tom Clegg's henchmen is good fun. You will not be surprised to learn, however, that Lucy finally changes her mind about shooting Clegg. Faced with a subtle and devious enemy, there's not really much satisfaction in blowing his brains out with a pistol. It's just disappointing that a girl with all that home tutoring behind her is never able to come up with a superior plan.

> *Joyce Milton, in a review of "A Little Destiny," in* The New York Times Book Review *(© 1980 by The New York Times Company; reprinted by permission), January 13, 1980, p. 26.*

THE KISSIMMEE KID (1981)

Twelve-year-old Evelyn and her younger brother Buell come to the Kissimmee Prairie region of Florida to visit a married sister, Reba, and her husband Camfield; they find that Reba's working in a nearby town and Cam sees her only on weekends. Both children adore Cam, who works for Major Peacock as a cowboy. The crusty Major finds Evelyn's tart independence appealing, christens her "The Kissimmee Kid," and tries to win her affection; this minor thread in the story should be (but is not quite) overshadowed by the major plot line: Evelyn's discovery that gentle, affectionate Cam is helping rustlers steal the Major's cows. The book presents convincingly the strong conflict for Evelyn between her love and feelings of loyalty for Cam, and her ethical sense. With pain, she reports her knowledge of his culpability. The conflict and decision are perceptively handled; less convincing is the catalyst for Evelyn's action, a bird's song. The characterization is strong, but the book is marred by pretentious writing: "Fond was she too of her dreams and inward visions and her ability to take a dull fact and make such a remarkable thing of it that her listener or listeners would gasp. She liked her gloomy tales best, for she was a tall, strong child of abrasive personality." (pp. 147-48)

> *Zena Sutherland, in a review of "The Kissimmee Kid," in* Bulletin of the Center for Children's Books *(reprinted by permission of The University of Chicago Press; © 1981 by The University of Chicago), Vol. 34, No. 8, April, 1981, pp. 147-48.*

The story has the familiar Cleaver imprint in its vinegary heroine and cadenced style, but here both these elements are heavily managed. Also, key secondary figures such as Cam or the miserly Major Peacock need more definition. The tension coming from Evelyn's knowledge of Cam's dealings helps focus things, however, and the pain of her final decision will make its mark with Cleaver readers.

> *Denise M. Wilms, in a review of "The Kissimmee Kid," in* Booklist *(reprinted by permission of the American Library Association; copyright © 1981 by the American Library Association), Vol. 77, No. 17, May 1, 1981, p. 1194.*

Evelyn Chestnut is twelve years old, a sort of graceless, lumpish girl with few friends and a feeling that she has few talents. But she possesses a gritty, uncompromising honesty and a strong affection for her family, especially for Camfield. . . . The reader cannot help sympathizing with Evelyn and even with Cam; Evelyn is admirable for that central core of determination which impels her to cling to her values in the face of destroying someone she loves. The transcendent symbol of that determination—a bird whose song seems to Evelyn to promise all that is good—seems somewhat thin and contrived. But the book's exposition is masterly; the language, with its light touch of Southern dialect, is just right; and the characters fairly spring forth from the page.

> *Ann A. Flowers, in a review of "The Kissimmee Kid," in* The Horn Book Magazine *(copyright © 1981 by The Horn Book, Inc., Boston), Vol. LVII, No. 3, June, 1981, p. 301.*

In **The Kissimmee Kid** Vera and Bill Cleaver have achieved that quality which separates the best novels for young readers from the merely good ones. They have dealt with the thorniest of life's moral dilemmas without ever once being moralistic. The issue here is honesty, specifically telling the truth when lying might protect someone you love very much. By the novel's conclusion truth has triumphed, yet so have loyalty and love. . . .

The Cleavers handle their material with sensitivity and skill, carefully laying down each segment of the path Evvie takes from innocence to understanding. They portray her, from the beginning, as perceptive, strong, and individualistic, so that the outcome she chooses in her moral dilemma is convincing when it comes.

> *Alice Digilio, in a review of "The Kissimmee Kid,"* in Book World—The Washington Post *(© 1981 The Washington Post), June 14, 1981, p. 11.*

Although Vera and Bill Cleaver always seem to draw on the same ingredients for their heroines—grit, humor, clear-sighted practicality, they are somehow able to come up with a distinctly individual character each time. . . .

But why would Cam stoop so low? We are told that it is because his spirit has been broken. Once an art teacher, he has given up art because a group of vicious, small-minded boys who had no use for art ran him out of his job. I don't doubt that this could happen. But not to the Cam whom the Cleavers have given us. Indeed, the Cam we know would not even have let Buell lie for him.

Then there's the matter of the bird that suddenly makes Evelyn feel the beauty of the prairie. Fine. But the bird keeps coming back. To persuade Evelyn to tell the truth. To comfort her when she thinks Cam may go to jail. Well, it's hard for me to take much stock in that redbird. A Cleaver plot shouldn't need such an easy symbol to get it over the humps.

This is not to say that I did not enjoy the book. The fresh, witty dialogue is reason enough to enjoy it.

> *Jean Fritz, in a review of "The Kissimmee Kid," in* The New York Times Book Review *(© 1981 by The New York Times Company; reprinted by permission), June 21, 1981, p. 37.*

HAZEL RYE (1983)

This is the last of the novels by the Cleavers, finished by Vera after Bill's death, and the best, in many ways, of the couple's award winners. Touching and funny, the story also has a serious core that readers won't forget.

> *A review of "Hazel Rye," in* Publishers Weekly *(reprinted from the January 28, 1983 issue of* Publishers Weekly, *published by R. R. Bowker Company, a Xerox company; copyright © 1983 by Xerox Corporation), Vol. 223, No. 4, January 28, 1983, p. 86.*

[Hazel Rye] is one of those indelible Cleaver heroines, feisty and determined. . . . The Cleavers project Hazel's awakening, her father's pathetic treachery, the struggles within and between them, and her changing views of [her brother] Donnie and his wife, the Pooles, and the world in general in uncomplicated scenes of direct, emphatic action and punchy conversations that ring with that special colloquial power. (pp. 306-07)

> *A review of "Hazel Rye," in* Kirkus Reviews *(copyright © 1983 The Kirkus Service, Inc.), Vol. LI, No. 6, March 15, 1983, pp. 306-07.*

A smashing book! The characters are alive with personality and the telling has the twang of the Southern hills. The parent-child relationship is well explored. This should be a popular title as well as a Newbery candidate.

> *A review of "Hazel Rye," in* Children's Book Review Service *(copyright © 1983 Children's Book Review Service Inc.), Vol. 11, No. 9, April, 1983, p. 92.*

Although Hazel, eleven, and her father squabble about everything, they're really good friends. . . . [Hazel is] tough, inventive, loquacious, and self-satisfied. And then the Pooles move in next door, and Hazel—who owns their house—relishes the idea of ordering Felder Poole around. She can't understand why all the Pooles love and talk about books, since she scorns reading; she can't understand why Felder gets so excited about plants. Then Hazel becomes smitten with a new love for plants, and soon Felder is the dominant figure in the relationship; unfortunately, this makes her father jealous and his irritation mounts when Hazel and Felder, with the help of an elderly friend, start a successful money-raising project to buy fertilizer. He evicts the Pooles, but Hazel has been changed forever by knowing them: she has learned that reading is not to be despised, and she has learned to love the land. Like other resilient Cleaver protagonists, this is, even if she's not likeable, a girl with grit. She's just a bit too pert, her father just a bit too callow, and Felder just a bit too patient and knowledgeable to be true; save for the evidence of this in dialogue, the writing style is competent. (pp. 163-64)

> *Zena Sutherland, in a review of "Hazel Rye," in* Bulletin of the Center for Children's Books *(reprinted by permission of The University of Chicago Press; © 1983 by The University of Chicago), Vol. 36, No. 9, May, 1983, pp. 163-64.*

The Cleavers' heroines are unmistakable, but while all share certain common characteristics—independence and ingenuity, for instance—each character is a unique creation, enigmatic but also endearing; and . . . Hazel Rye is no exception. . . . The conflict [between Hazel and her father] is serious but handled with humor and with compassion for the pain underlying Millard Rye's pronouncement: "'It's natural and a good thing for a young one to want to . . . be his own boss, but he shouldn't ever . . . quit his daddy or say he's smarter.'" Through skillful balancing of description and dialogue, the characters develop believably. And while the Florida Ridge setting seems particularly suited to their temperaments and attitudes, the theme is universal. Hazel Rye, like Ellen Grae and Mary Call Luther, is a character to be reckoned with—and not easily forgotten.

> *Mary M. Burns, in a review of "Hazel Rye," in* The Horn Book Magazine *(copyright © 1983 by The Horn Book, Inc., Boston), Vol. LIX, No. 3, June, 1983, p. 301.*

Nikki Giovanni

1943-

(Born Yolande Cornelia Giovanni, Jr.) Black American author of poetry, fiction, and essays and editor.

Giovanni adapts the voices, feelings, and traditions of her childhood into words and images in her poetry for children. A strong identification with her black heritage is also a focal point in her works. Of her three books for younger readers, *Spin a Soft Black Song* and *Vacation Time* explore the everyday experiences of children while *Ego-Tripping* focuses on black life and contains some poems of a serious, militant nature.

Critics believe Giovanni to be at her best when writing light verse which reflects her happy, loving family life and her early black awareness. The poetry which results from her involvement in civil rights and black movement groups functions well within her adult works; when included in her children's books, however, the poems are often thought to be inappropriate for their intended audience. Critics also complain of occasional forced rhyme schemes and uninspired verses. Despite this, reviewers generally agree that Giovanni portrays children accurately and that she successfully combines sadness, fear, happiness, and humor in her work.

(See also *Contemporary Literary Criticism*, Vols. 2, 4, 19; *Something about the Author*, Vol. 24; *Contemporary Authors*, Vols. 29-32, rev. ed.; *Dictionary of Literary Biography*, Vol. 5; and *Authors in the News*, Vol. 1.)

AUTHOR'S COMMENTARY

When I write poetry, . . . I write out of my own experiences—which also happen to be the experiences of my people. But if I had to choose between my people's experiences and mine, I'd choose mine because that's what I know best. That way I don't have to trap the people into some kind of *dreams* that I have about what they should be into. An artist's job is to show what he sees. I can do "**Nikki-Rosa**" . . . because that's the way I look at my early years. I had a really groovy childhood and I'm really pleased with my family. Of course I can say my father drank a lot and we had conflicts here and there, but essentially everything was groovy. A person with an unhappy childhood can't dig the poem. For him it is useless. To reach him I would have to do one of those 'I can't stand those m.f.'s who birthed me' kind of poems 'cause for him *that's* the truth. (p. 49)

> *Nikki Giovanni, in an extract from "Nikki Giovanni: 'I Am Black, Female, Polite . . .'" in* Ebony *(reprinted by permission of the author), Vol. XXVII, No. 4, February, 1972, pp. 49-56.*

SPIN A SOFT BLACK SONG: POEMS FOR CHILDREN (1971)

Though some of these prose-poems seem more likely to be appreciated by an adult sensibility, others, like "**Daddies**" (they "teach you how to walk and wear a hat and pee"), hit the mark. The verses draw on the everyday world of sneakers and Sesame Street in the context of the experience of black children, and the diction is comfortably colloquial. [Giovanni and illustrator Charles Bible] . . . have tried to recapture lost

innocence . . . , and their effort to produce positive, black poetry for kids is admirable despite occasional signs of strain. . . . Some of the poems may be too self-conscious to reach their intended audience, but, on the whole, they're worth a try.

> *A review of "Spin a Soft Black Song: Poems for Children," in* Kirkus Reviews *(copyright © 1971 The Kirkus Service, Inc.), Vol. XXXIX, No. 20, October 15, 1971, p. 1126.*

Nikki Giovanni's poems for children, like her adult works, exhibit a combination of casual energy and sudden wit. No cheek-pinching auntie, she explores the contours of childhood with honest affection, sidestepping both nostalgia and condescension. Her poems focus on the experiences of children—naps and baths and getting bigger, dreams and fears and growing up.

The poem "**two friends**" is an example of simplicity and quiet grace:

> lydia and shirley have
> two pierced ears and
> two bare ones
> five pigtails

two pair of sneakers
two berets
two smiles
one necklace
one bracelet
lots of stripes and
one good friendship

The words are natural, the images sunny and clear.

Mamas and their elusive logic figure in several poems: punishing wet pants despite an ingenious explanation, fussing about school, keeping a child away from the street and summer games "because she loves me." . . .

Many of the poems feature individual children, touching on an experience or gesture with lingering warmth. For the Debbies and Rodneys who find their names, there will be sure satisfaction; for others there is the pleasure of recognition because the people have familiar identities. . . .

Besides homey concerns like sneakers and collard greens, there are larger issues dealt with by the poems—being big and badddd. These fantasies include the usual power dream ("one day I'll be seven feet tall . . .") and a good-natured list of strengths ending

i can rap so hard Rap
Brown hates to be
in the same town with me
and i'm only ten
this year coming

In the poem **"sleep,"** however, a boy uses everyday imaginings to cope with the very real and ugly horror of a rat in his bed. . . .

[This] book is not for black children alone. The poems that represent the black experience are open to any reader, and the others, like **"springtime"** . . . , record the changeless traditions of all childhoods. . . .

> *Nancy Klein, in a review of "Americana, City-Style and Country Style: 'Spin a Soft Black Song: Poems for Children',"* in The New York Times Book Review *(© 1971 by The New York Times Company; reprinted by permission), November 28, 1971, p. 8.*

[A collection of] short, evocative poems. . . . Some of the poems deal with universal childhood feelings and concerns while others are unique to the black experience, but all are honest and nonsentimental in concept and expression. Disparate but generally interesting.

> *A review of "Spin a Soft Black Song: Poems for Children,"* in The Booklist *(reprinted by permission of the American Library Association; copyright © 1972 by the American Library Association), Vol. 68, No. 17, May 1, 1972, p. 770.*

Nikki Giovanni and Charles Bible "decided to write a book with poems and pictures for and about children 'cause when we were growing up there were precious few of them. Especially for us." This self-consciously cute approach to children and the attempt to emulate childish language is painfully evident throughout the introduction and the 35 poems. Most of the 35 are unsuccessful in capturing or conveying feelings of childhood—e.g., "'come on sugar dumpling mommy has to go / to the store' / I'd better not be too easy / 'Abxyn qpotx?' / let her coax me / 'come on apple cake put your coat on' /

maybe I'll push her a little / 'Qpy Skt?'"—or in providing black children with points of identification. . . . There are many other books which can be especially enjoyed by black children, as well as children of other races, among them Adoff's *I Am the Darker Brother* (Macmillan, 1970), Langston Hughes' *Don't You Turn Back* (Knopf, 1969), Larrick's *On City Streets* (Evans, dist. by Lippincott, 1968), and Lewis' *Miracles* (S. & S., 1966). All of these should be selected before this one.

> *Alice Miller Bregman, in a review of "Spin a Soft Black Song,"* in School Library Journal, *an appendix to* Library Journal *(reprinted from the June, 1972 issue of* School Library Journal, *published by R. R. Bowker Co./A Xerox Corporation; copyright © 1972), Vol. 97, No. 12, June, 1972, p. 2230.*

[*Spin A Soft Black Song*] aiming at poetry, not verse, contains . . . complex images and ideas. . . . Describing Black children's lives from infancy to ten years, the poems use the experiences, the vocabulary, and the speech patterns of children in the inner city. According to Giovanni, to say things the way children say them when they are very young is, in adult language, "the profundity of the noble savage" ("Introduction"). Many of the poems offer a child's perspective on the tiresome rules grownups devise for children, but the child's original, ingenious and ingenuous verbal response reduces them to humor—even the ridiculous (**"trips," "one of the problems of play,"** and **"parents never understand"**); others affirm the possibility of growing up strong and wise, despite oppression (**"10 years old," "the drum"**). Some contain complex ideas, perhaps totally comprehensible only by adult readers. In **"stars,"** a child speaker has just learned that "stars are a mass of gases that burned / out a long time ago only we don't know / that because we still see the glow." Innocently the child asks a big brother who has said that he "burned out a long time ago," if he's "a star." The confusion of meanings for star may be entertaining to children who have made similar mistakes, but adults will see the waste of human life implicit in the parallel. Usually best when her tone is lighter, Giovanni's serious poems are sometimes too insistent on message. **"If,"** her parallel to Kipling's poem, is heavyhanded and finally as unrealistic in its application to reality as his.

> *Alice Fannin, "Black Poetry: Three for the Children,"* in Children's Literature Association Quarterly, *Vol. 6, No. 2, Summer, 1981, p. 35.**

EGO-TRIPPING, AND OTHER POEMS FOR YOUNG PEOPLE (1973)

Nikki Giovanni is a poet who often seems impatient with words, but when she grabs hold (as happens here on page one with "if i were a poet i'd kid / nap you") it's a rare kid, certainly a rare black kid, who could resist being picked right up. The poems selected here for younger people . . . are also her best known celebrations of black soul, black music and personal dreams, "revolutionary" and otherwise. While much of *Spin a Soft Black Song,* a collection written especially for children often seemed forced, older children will probably be the ideal audience for the sly, queenly procession of **"Ego-Tripping"** . . . , the rhythmic **"Revolutionary Music"** which amplifies the message of Sly, Aretha and James Brown, or the quiet itchy frustration of "i was / lonely alone / now i'm lonely / with you / something is wrong / there are flies / everywhere i go." Upbeat, proud, and confident.

A review of "Ego-Tripping and Other Poems for Young People," in Kirkus Reviews (copyright © 1974 The Kirkus Service, Inc.), Vol. XLII, No. 1, January 1, 1974, p. 11.

Most of the poems assembled here are pulled from Giovanni's other published works. Her readers will easily recall the reflections in **"Nikki-Rosa"** or **"Revolutionary dreams."** . . . And if the stuff of **"Revolutionary dreams"** carries a strident militancy, the opening **"Kidnap poem"** is a suitable contrast with its melodic study of gentleness. A nice, all-around introduction to the poet.

A review of "Ego-Tripping and Other Poems for Young People," in The Booklist (reprinted by permission of the American Library Association; copyright © 1974 by the American Library Association), Vol. 70, No. 15, April 1, 1974, p. 873.

Both the poet and the artist in **"Ego-tripping"** are Black, and this book is very conscious of its Blackness.

[George Ford's illustrations] are kinder and happier than some of the verses which reflect the anger, even hatred, of the civil rights struggle in the '60's. But other poems are sheer poetry, and they all crackle with feeling, originality, zest.

Neil Millar, "Dancing Poetry, Chantable Verse," in The Christian Science Monitor (reprinted by permission from The Christian Science Monitor; © 1974 The Christian Science Publishing Society; all rights reserved), May 1, 1974, p. F5.*

[In] **"Spin a Soft Black Song,"** Miss Giovanni used warm, unaffected language to describe being young and black. In **"Ego-Tripping"** . . . , the poems are directed at older readers able to handle heavier subjects and more ambitious poetry. . . . They are sly and seductive, freewheeling and winsome, tough, sure and proud. Miss Giovanni pursues both personal and cultural matters: loneliness, private dreams, love and survival, all with a boundless enthusiasm for the essences of black life. In the best poems, language and spirit rebound and join forces. The title poem is a celebration of African heritage and modern dignity. . . .

She can chide herself for "radical dreams," joke about more common ones. . . . Throughout the book Miss Giovanni shares her razor-sharp perceptions with energy and passion.

Nancy Rosenberg, "A Tree Grows in Print," in The New York Times Book Review (© 1974 by The New York Times Company; reprinted by permission), May 5, 1974, p. 38.*

What the child experiences [in juvenile poetry] is awe of fabled archetype, unaware of the fiction's complex origins.

[In *Ego-Tripping*], the archetype is a monster. . . . Nikki Giovanni's monster is Life envisioned by a black in a white world. . . .

Nikki Giovanni doesn't convert her monster into symbol. *Ego-Tripping* . . . is a proud, exuberant confrontation with monster as reality. Giovanni corrects the white man's misconception of the black man's world:

> Black love is Black wealth and they'll
> probably talk about my hard childhood
> and never understand that
> all the while I was quite happy

On both autobiographical and cultural level, she evokes a black, Whitmanesque "Song of Myself." And like Whitman, she catalogues the elemental details of her world: "I always like summer / best / you can eat fresh corn / from daddy's garden / and okra / and greens / and cabbage." . . . Such stylistic simplicity reveals the joy of the child or the primitive poet in just naming things. Each word seems a tiny, triumphant stone hurled at that white monster, Life. The cumulative effect is that of a mysticism which celebrates spontaneity and fearlessness.

Norma Procopiow, "A Melee of Monsters," in Book World—The Washington Post (© 1974, The Washington Post), May 19, 1974, p. 4.*

While books of ethnic poetry are often marred by the inclusion of pedestrian and poorly constructed material, they also contain some of the most expressive poems we have for children. In *Ego-Tripping*, Nikki Giovanni, one of the best of today's writers of the Black experience, has put together twenty-two poems . . . which she felt young readers would like. Although the poems vary in quality, this collection appeals to the intellect as well as to the emotions. . . . Sometimes she jokes, sometimes she is serious, at other times she is angry or sad. (pp. 196-97)

Alethea K. Helbig, "Trends in Poetry for Children," in Children's Literature: Annual of The Modern Language Association Seminar on Children's Literature and The Children's Literature Association, Vol. 6, edited by Francelia Butler (© 1977 by Francelia Butler; reprinted by permission of Francelia Butler), Temple University Press, 1977, pp. 195-201.*

VACATION TIME: POEMS FOR CHILDREN (1980)

The well-known poet presents a little book with a collection of her original, economic and richly meaningful works. It is an anthology with new and previously published poems, designed for parents to share with children, and one that perceptive boys and girls can read on their own. In her singing lines, Giovanni shows she hasn't forgotten childhood adventures in family living, in play and in exploring the world with a small person's sense of discovery. Some, like **"Tommy's Mommy,"** also slyly express a parent's viewpoint.

A review of "Vacation Time: Poems for Children," in Publishers Weekly (reprinted from the May 23, 1980 issue of Publishers Weekly, published by R. R. Bowker Company, a Xerox company; copyright © 1980 by Xerox Corporation), Vol. 217, No. 20, May 23, 1980, p. 77.

Twenty-two uninspired rhymes, ranging from the wan wistfulness of **"Rainbows"** to a feeble pun on watching the soaps. There are a couple of so-so attempts at light humor (as in **"Jonathan Sitting in the Mud"**), a passable crack at nonsense (**"Prickled Pickles Don't Smile"**), one apt, rueful comment on studying joy, and several trite images of sweet childhood, with the words spaced out in a modern manner to disguise the staleness of the ideas. Without a sign of spoofing, Giovanni stoops to such artificial and outmoded constructions as "Vacation time is nigh" and "The moonbeams call me so." And despite a "hooray for women's lib," there are several hints that the endorsement is only skin deep.

A review of "Vacation Time: Poems for Children," in Kirkus Reviews (copyright © 1980 The Kirkus

Service, Inc.), Vol. XLVIII, No. 17, September 1, 1980, p. 1165.

Many of the selections included here are available in anthologies; all of them are brief and many are humorous, some are lyric, some narrative. The number of poems that have vision or depth is minimal, most of them being slight or even superficial if merry. The subjects are appropriately chosen, but there's an occasional contrivance to achieve scansion (". . . In her rocker she does stay / Neat and prim throughout the day . . .") or an occasional rhyme that seems forced ("flowers for houses / Remain inert / But when the bees pass / They flutter and flirt / The bees come down / To steal a kiss / Then off they fly / To some other miss.")

Zena Sutherland, in a review of "Vacation Time: Poems for Children," in Bulletin of the Center for Children's Books *(reprinted by permission of The University of Chicago Press; © 1980 by The University of Chicago), Vol. 34, No. 2, October, 1980, p. 31.*

Nikki Giovanni, [a] radical antiformalist, in her latest collection for children, strikes a contemporary note in jingling stanza form:

> Yolande the panda
> sat with Amanda
> eating a bar-be-cue rib
>
> They drank a beer
> and gave a big cheer
> "Hooray! for women's lib"

This has the engaging brashness of skip rope rhymes, and Giovanni's collection, *Vacation Time,* contains a few other pieces that children will easily beat time to. Unfortunately, like many another poet for children who isn't at home in traditional verse, Giovanni too often writes in a careless, condescending way. In formal verse, a writer's incompetence and self-indulgence are hard to conceal. These appear in rhymes coupled by violence, lines crammed with extra words in order to fill up a metrical pattern, things said not for the sake of meaning anything but to pay lip-service to symmetry. And so Giovanni lets herself describe a grandparent: "In her rocker she *does* stay / Neat and prim throughout the day" (italics ours, to indicate only one word of unnatural stuffing). A boat is "locked up in a moat," the only visible need for the word *moat* being that it supplies a rhyme. (pp. 75-6)

X. J. Kennedy and Dorothy M. Kennedy, "Tradition and Revolt: Recent Poetry for Children," in The Lion and the Unicorn *(copyright © 1981 The Lion and the Unicorn), Vol. 4, No. 2, Winter, 1980-81, pp. 75-82 [the poem by Nikki Giovanni used here was originally published in her* Vacation Time: Poems for Children, *(copyright © 1980 by Nikki Giovanni; by permission of William Morrow & Company), Morrow, 1980].**

[Nikki Giovanni] writes first-rate stuff for her peers, second-rate for children. Is she self-conscious with them, or smug about her position among them even though she has an 8-year-old son? Has she abandoned her childhood ear, or is it just different from mine? I was often irritated to see that lines didn't parse or scan or sing, that rhymes were haphazard or "wrongly" placed.

Take this, from **"The Sun"**:

> Sunsets are so pretty
> the clouds and colors leap
> Across her deep red belly
> as she flutters off to sleep

Does "her" refer to sunsets? Do sunsets flutter? What a lame rhythm the poem has.

Or take **"Masks"**: "Sis wears a mask / when she makes a scene / Dad wears a mask / when he is mean / I wear my mask / when it's Halloween / But Mom wears her mask / for beauty purposes." Is this satire? It's cute, arch. Eight-year-old humor that I wouldn't let my 8-year-old get away with on paper.

But Giovanni is a good poet (that's why I demand so much) and many of the thoughts, images and stanzas in *Vacation Time* ring appealingly true. A child watching bubbles in the bathtub or telling us why he likes chocolate and scary movies is familiar to us. Little girls tiptoeing through a strawberry patch call up nostalgia. We echo the lament of the little boy who cannot climb the sky: "And others steer the rainbow past / While I just hang around."

Nikki Giovanni is at her best describing real experiences in a simple "unpoetic" way, not striving for fantasy or conventional rhythm and rhyme. (pp. 10-11)

Rose Styron, "A Pocketful of Rhyme," in Book World—The Washington Post *(© 1981, The Washington Post), March 8, 1981, pp. 10-11.**

Kate Greenaway

1846-1901

English author/illustrator of poetry and nonfiction and illustrator.

Greenaway was among the first authors to look at childhood from the child's viewpoint. She is best known for her illustrations of children in unique old-fashioned dress, and her solemn-faced characters reflect the serious essence of childhood. With the help of Edmund Evans, an entrepreneur and printer who also promoted the illustrations of Walter Crane and Randolph Caldecott, Greenaway created picture books that were vibrant and rich in color. Crane, Caldecott, and Greenaway are considered the great triumvirate of English picture book illustrators. Unlike the others, however, Greenaway coupled her artistic talent with original poetry intended to please and entertain children. Her artistic vision, her personal view of childhood, and her naive poetry brought a freshness to nineteenth-century literature for the young.

There were many influences which contributed to Greenaway's career choice and her illustration style. Her mother was an enterprising children's seamstress in London and her father a wood engraver for the *Illustrated London News*. Greenaway began drawing at a young age and was instructed by her father until she entered art school at the age of twelve. She learned to appreciate children's clothing during her youth; she admired delicate styles and remembered the details and exact colors of her favorites. When Greenaway turned to illustrating, her models wore self-designed empress gowns and large mob caps. She illustrated children's books and greeting cards until she decided that, despite her lack of writing experience, she would be more satisfied illustrating her own words.

It has been said that Greenaway was a true picture book author, integrating her texts and illustrations into a balanced whole. During her career, she wrote and illustrated six books and chose to illustrate works by Jane and Ann Taylor, John Ruskin, Robert Browning, and Bret Harte. She also created yearly almanacs and *The Illustrated Language of Flowers*, which is noted for its detailed, early Renaissance style reminiscent of Botticelli. Her first book, *Under the Window*, was an instant success and brought her international acclaim. It was popular among book buyers and received praise from reviewers for its beauty, simplicity, and timeless fashions. In France, her influence was so strong that a style of dress modeled after her picture books became a trend known as "Greenawaisme." Greenaway's poetry, however, was occasionally deemed insignificant, and even today critics comment that if she had been only a poet her work would probably be unnoticed. Others feel that her verses complement her illustrations and focus on universal themes. As an artist, Greenaway had difficulty with limb and feet proportions and with depth perception in her outdoor scenes. While many critics acknowledge these technical defects, the errors are usually considered insignificant enough not to detract from the high quality of her work.

Greenaway's most important influence was undoubtedly art critic John Ruskin. He considered Greenaway a major artist and appreciated her early Renaissance style, her ability to capture the innocence of children, and her exclusion of in-

dustrial settings. He was also a stern critic of her picture books and frequently became infuriated when he saw they lacked artistry. Ruskin felt Greenaway was wasting her talent on children's books and advised her to concentrate on painting. Although she applied some of his suggestions, Greenaway knew that her livelihood and happiness came through children and picture books, which is where she directed most of her professional energy. Later, however, she became frustrated by the changing popular opinion of her works and began to see herself as a passing fashion. In a sense, this was true: critics began to use such terms as "typical Greenaway style" and did not notice her work's technical improvements. The eulogies after her death, however, lavishly commend the characteristic beauty of her style and her quaint poems. Greenaway once told a friend, "People laugh at me, I am so delighted and pleased with things, and say I see with rose-colored spectacles. What do you think—is it not a beautiful world? Sometimes have I got a defective art faculty that few things are ugly to me?" Nineteenth- and twentieth-century critics praise Greenaway's "defective art faculty," which brought originality, a preservation of preindustrial England, and a new respectability to the picture book. In 1955 the Library Association of Great Britain established the Kate Greenaway Medal, which is now the highest honor given to an English illustrator.

(See also *Yesterday's Authors of Books for Children*, Vol. 2.)

AUTHOR'S COMMENTARY

[*English essayist and reformer John Ruskin was perhaps the most important art critic of the nineteenth century. He influenced Kate Greenaway's artistic development through steady correspondence with her. Below are extracts from her letters to Ruskin from November 11, 1895 to December 5, 1899, taken from M. H. Spielman and G. S. Layard's biography,* Kate Greenaway.]

I am still in a state of great perplexity as to what work to do and as to what to agree to about books. (p. 197)

Some beautiful picture or drawing will make me long to do something. The worst of it is, I ought always to do everything the moment it suggests itself, or very likely by the time I go to do it the spirit of it has vanished.

I do the technical part of painting so badly, and every one else seems to do it so well. I have no settled way of working—I am always trying this or that. That is why I get on better when I am doing a cottage because I naturally do just what I see and do not think of the way to do it at all. (pp. 197-98)

. . . . .

I am still doing all sorts of drawing—pencil ones with colour—I think them rather pretty. I wish you would like a new sort—a little—I seem to want to put in shade so much more than I used to. I have got to love the making out of form by shade—the softness of it. I love things soft and beautiful—not angular and hard as it is the fashion to like them now. To be an impressionist opens a good wide space for leaving a good deal that is difficult to do *undone*—at least so it seems to me. It is so easy to begin, so difficult to finish. (pp. 198-99)

. . . . .

A great many people are now what they call modern. When I state *my* likes and dislikes they tell me I am *not* modern, so I suppose I'm not—advanced. That is why, I suppose, I see some of the new pictures as looking so very funny. . . . Oh dear! I believe I shall ever think a face should look like a face, and a beautiful arm like a beautiful arm—not that I can do it—the great pity I can't. Why, if I could, they should have *visions*. . . . Isn't it hard sometimes when you have felt the beauty of something in a certain way and have done it so and *no one* you show it to seems to see it at all. But I suppose if it is really a good thing you have done that, after years, some one does feel it, while if it is not worth finding out it goes into oblivion—so Time sifts it all out. Such is not my fate, for I unfortunately can only think of all the beautiful things and have not the skill to do them. (p. 205)

. . . . .

I can never define what art really is—in painting, I mean. It isn't realism, it isn't all imagination, it's a queer giving something to nature that is possible for nature to have, but always has not—at least that's my idea. It's what Burne-Jones does when he twists those roses all about his people in the Briar Rose. They don't often grow like that, but they could, and it's a great comfort to like such things, at least I find it so. (p. 209)

. . . . .

Isn't it a funny thing I can't copy? All the morning I have been blundering over a baby's face from a little study. I can't do it a bit; it is odd. I can't get it a bit like the original. I put it in and take it out, and so it goes on getting worse and worse. And I wish I could do it so much but I never have been able, and it don't matter what it is—it is everything—the most trifling thing. I never do it well except direct from the object or my own mind, but I can't copy a flat thing—it really is curious. (p. 216)

. . . . .

I often think, just for the pleasure of thinking, that a little door leads out of the garden wall into a real old flowering garden, full of deep shades and deep colours. Did you always plan out delightful places just close and unexpected, when you were very young? I did. My bedroom window used to look out over red roofs and chimney-pots, and I made steps up to a lovely garden up there with nasturtiums growing and brilliant flowers so near to the sky. There were some old houses joined ours at the side, and I made a secret door into long lines of old rooms, all so delightful, leading into an old garden. I imagined it so often that I knew its look so well; it got to be very real. And now I'd like somehow to express all this in painting, especially my love of old gardens with that richness of colour and depth of shade. (p. 218)

. . . . .

I feel I *do* such weak things and think strong ones, and it is dreadfully tiresome. I do want to do something nice—beautiful—like I feel—like I see in my mind, and there I am trammelled by technical shortcomings. I will never begin a lot of things together again because then you can't do new ideas or try different ways of work, and I always could only do one thing at once. I live in the one thing and think about it, and it's like a real thing or place for the time. Even now, the moment I'm doing a new drawing the morning rushes by—I'm so happy, so interested, I only feel the tiredness when I can't go on because it is too late or too dark. (p. 229)

. . . . .

I wish I did not have to make any money. I would like to work very hard but in a different way so that I was more free to do what I liked, and it is so difficult now I am no longer at all the fashion. I say fashion, for that is the right word, that is all it is to a great many people. (p. 232)

. . . . .

Isn't it curious how one can like good things so much and not do them? I do love one figure or a number put into a little space with just room for what they are doing. I don't think figures ever look well with large spaces of background. . . . For one thing, my mind runs to ornament or decoration in a way, though it has to be natural forms, like foxgloves or vine-leaves. I can't like a flower or leaf I invent, though I often love those I see done. (p. 232)

. . . . .

I told you, didn't I, that I was going to try if I could do portraits of children? I don't at all like it. I don't feel near strong enough for the strain of it. I know what the children are like—quite unaccustomed to sitting still, and then to have to get a real likeness! I prefer the little girls and boys that live in that nice land, that come as you call them, fair or dark, in green ribbons or blue. I like making cowslip fields grow and apple-trees bloom at a moment's notice. This is what it is, you see, to have gone through life with an enchanted land ever beside you—yet how much it has been! (pp. 239-40)

. . . . .

There are not any very good children's books about just now that I have seen. The rage for copying mine seems over, so I suppose some one will soon step to the front with something new. Children often don't care a bit about the books people think they will, and I think they often like grown-up books—at any rate I did. (p. 245)

. . . . .

There is going to be an exhibition for children at the Fine Art—the Private View is on Saturday—but I think it is very likely the children won't appreciate it. I often notice that they don't at all care for what grown-up people think they will. For one thing, they like something that excites their imagination—a very real thing mixed up with a great unreality like Blue Beard. How I used to be thrilled by 'Sister Ann, Sister Ann,' done by the servants in the agonised voice of Blue Beard's wife, and I could hardly breathe when the stains would not come off the key.—Those wonderful little books they used to sell in coloured covers, a penny and a halfpenny each—they were condensed and dramatic. They are spoilt now by their profuseness.

I never cared so much for *Jack the Giant-Killer*, or *Jack and the Beanstalk*, or *Tom Thumb*, as I did for *The Sleeping Beauty in the Wood*, *Cinderella*, and *Beauty and the Beast*. I did not like *Puss in Boots* as well either. Of course they were all deeply fascinating, but the three pretty ones I liked best. It would be curious to do a book of them from one's remembrance of them in one's early thoughts. I know my Blue Beard people were not dressed as Turks then. (pp. 246-47)

> *Kate Greenaway, in extracts from twelve of her letters to John Ruskin from November 11, 1895 to December 5, 1899 in* Kate Greenaway *by M. H. Spielmann and G. S. Layard, G. P. Putnam's Sons, 1905, pp. 197-247.*

GENERAL COMMENTARY

The great softening of the English mind, so manifest already in John Leech, shows itself in a decisive manner by the enthusiasm with which the public have lately received the designs of Mr Walter Crane, Mr Caldecott, and Miss Kate Greenaway. . . . [In] the works of all these three artists, landscape plays an important part—familiar landscape, very English, interpreted with a 'bonhomie savante' (no translating that), spiritual, decorative in the rarest taste, strange and precious adaptation of Etruscan art, Flemish and Japanese, reaching, together with the perfect interpretation of nature, to incomparable chords of colour harmony. These powers are found in the work of the three, but Miss Greenaway, with a profound sentiment of love for children, puts the child alone on the scene, companions him in his own solicitudes, and shows the infantine nature in all its naiveté, its gaucherie, its touching grace, its shy alarm, its discoveries, ravishments, embarrassments, and victories; the stumblings of it in wintry ways, the enchanted smiles of its spring time, and all the history of its fond heart and guiltless egoism.

From the honest but fierce laugh of the coarse Saxon, William Hogarth, to the delicious smile of Kate Greenaway, there has passed a century and a half. Is it the same people which applauds to-day the sweet genius and tender malices of the one, and which applauded the bitter genius and slaughterous satire of the other? After all, that is possible—the hatred of vice is only another manifestation of the love of innocence. (p. 243)

> *Ernest Chesneau, in his extract from "Fairy Land: Mrs. Allingham and Kate Greenaway," translated*

by John Ruskin (originally published in La peinture anglaise, *A. Quantin, 1882), in* The Art of England: Lectures Given in Oxford *by John Ruskin, George Allen, 1883 and reprinted in* A Peculiar Gift: Nineteenth Century Writings on Books for Children, *edited by Lance Salway, Kestrel Books, 1976, p. 243).*

Monsieur Chesneau doubts if the charm of Miss Greenaway's work can be carried farther [see excerpt above]. I answer with security—yes, very much farther, and that in two directions: first, in her own method of design; and secondly, the manner of its representation in printing.

First, her own design has been greatly restricted by being too ornamental, or, in your modern phrase, decorative; contracted into any corner of a Christmas card, or stretched like an elastic band round the edges of an almanack. Now, her art is much too good to be used merely for illumination; it is essentially and perfectly that of true colour-picture, and that the most naïve and delightful manner of picture, because, on the simplest terms, it comes nearest reality. No end of mischief has been done to modern art by the habit of running semi-pictorial illustration round the margins of ornamental volumes, and Miss Greenaway has been wasting her strength too sorrowfully in making the edges of her little birthday books, and the like, glitter with unregarded gold, whereas her power should be concentrated in the direct illustration of connected story, and her pictures should be made complete on the page, and far more realistic than decorative. There is no charm so enduring as that of the real representation of any given scene; her present designs are like living flowers flattened to go into an herbarium, and sometimes too pretty to be believed. We must ask her for more descriptive reality, for more convincing simplicity, and we must get her to organize a school of colourists by hand, who can absolutely facsimile her own first drawing. (pp. 244-45)

[The style of Greenaway's work agrees] in one thing—minuteness and delicacy of touch carried to its utmost limit, visible in its perfectness to the eyes of youth, but neither executed with a magnifying glass, nor, except to aged eyes, needing one. Even I, at sixty-four, can see the essential qualities of the work without spectacles. . . .

And now please note this, for an entirely general law, again and again reiterated by me for many a year. *All great art is delicate*, and fine to the uttermost. Wherever there is blotting, or daubing, or dashing, there is weakness at least; probably affectation; certainly bluntness of feeling. But all delicacy which is rightly pleasing to the human mind is addressed to the *unaided human sight*, not to microscopic help or mediation. (p. 246)

There are two other points I must try to enforce in closing, very clearly. 'Landscape,' says M. Chesneau, 'takes great part in these lovely designs.' He does not say of what kind; may I ask you to look for yourselves, and think?

There are no railroads in it to carry the children away with, are there? No tunnel or pit mouths to swallow them up, no league-long viaducts, no blinkered iron bridges? There are only winding brooks, wooden foot-bridges, and grassy hills without any holes cut into them!

Again—there are no parks, no gentlemen's seats with attached stables and offices! No rows of model lodging houses! No charitable institutions! It seems as if none of these things which the English mind now rages after possess any attraction whatever for this impressionable person. She is a graceful Gallio—Gallia gratia plena—and cares for none of these things.

And more wonderful still, there are no gasworks! No water-works, no mowing machines, no sewing machines, no telegraph poles, no vestige, in fact, of science, civilization, economical arrangements, or commercial enterprise!

Would you wish me, with professorial authority, to advise her that her conceptions belong to the dark ages, and must be reared on a new foundation? Or is it, on the other hand, recommendably conceivable by *you* that perhaps the world we truly live in may not be quite so changeable as you thought it; that all the gold and silver you can dig out of the earth are not worth the kingcups and the daisies she gave you of her grace; and that all the fury, and the flutter, and the wonder, and the wistfulness of your lives will never discover for you any other than the ancient blessing: 'He maketh me to lie down in green pastures, He leadeth me beside the still waters, He restoreth my soul'?

Yet one word more. Observe that what this unimpressionable person *does* draw, she draws as like it as she can. It is true that the combination or composition of things is not what you can see every day. You can't every day, for instance, see a baby thrown into a basket of roses; but when she has once pleasantly invented that arrangement for you, baby is as like baby, and rose as like rose, as she can possibly draw them. And the beauty of them is in *being* like. They are blissful, just in the degree that they are natural; and the fairy land she creates for you is not beyond the sky nor beneath the sea, but nigh you, even at your doors. She does but show you how to see it, and how to cherish. . . . (pp. 246-47)

John Ruskin, "Fairy Land: Mrs. Allingham and Kate Greenaway," in his The Art of England: Lectures Given in Oxford . . . *During His Second Tenure of the Slade Professorship, George Allen, 1883 (and reprinted in* A Peculiar Gift: Nineteenth Century Writings on Books for Children, *edited by Lance Salway, Kestrel Books, 1976, pp. 233-47).**

In color Miss Greenaway is almost a purist. If you could see her paint-box it is doubtful if you would find that it contained many colors outside the primaries and their attributes. Look at any one of her studies; red, blue, yellow, and black would be colors enough to paint almost any one of them. This simplicity runs through all her work. Her composition is equally simple; it is in fact Anglo-Saxon art at its best; pure, simple, matter-of-fact subject-matter, with refinement enough in it to lift it out of the commonplace, pure sentiment enough to save it from hollow dilettantism, and yet so near to nature that although our little folks are not as they are depicted, yet they are prototypes of what we would have them be. In her studies Miss Greenaway uses almost pure colors, or, as the artists put it, she rarely mixes flake or Chinese white with her paints. The outline is firmly drawn either with the pen or pencil, the shadows are then struck in, mostly in gray, and over all wash after wash of color is put; of course there are numerous retouchings and 'heightenings,' till the right tone required is obtained, but Miss Greenaway's method is that simple one, 'wash,' as handled by all the greater of the greatest painters in water-colors. (p. 58)

"Three Christmas Fairies: Miss Kate Greenaway," in The Critic, *New York, Vol. 6, January 31, 1885, pp. 57-8.*

The little paragraph in the papers a week ago stating simply that Kate Greenaway was dead must have come as a shock to thousands of people. One had never thought of death in con-

nection with this delicate and joyous artist. Her name had called up for so long only pleasant, sunny associations; memories of green meadows with grave little girls and boys a-maying; quiet, restful rooms, with tiny fireplaces, daffodils in blue vases on the high mantelpieces, and grave little girls and boys a-playing; and trim village streets where everything was well-kept and well-swept, and all the roofs were red and all the garden gates and fences green, and more grave little girls carried dolls, and more grave little boys rolled hoops, and very young mothers with high waists gossiped together over their grave little babies' infinitesimal heads. Some such scenes as these have for twenty years been rising before one whenever Kate Greenaway's name was heard, bringing with them a gentle breath of ancient repose and simplicity and a faint scent of potpourri. And now the hand that devised this innocent communism of quaintness and felicity, this juvenile Arcadia, is still forever!

For some years Miss Greenaway has not been the power that once she was. Her greatest triumphs were in the early eighties, when she illustrated Jane and Ann Taylor's "Original Poems," and wrote and illustrated verses of her own writing, and put forth every Christmas a little almanac, with scenes fitting to every month, and delicate and dainty borders of the old-world flowers she loved best. It might almost be said that she invented the daffodil. That was the time when flowers were being newly discovered, and while the aesthetes were worshipping the sunflower and the lily Miss Greenaway was bidding the cheeriest little daisies spring from the grass and the chubbiest little roses burst from the bushes, and teaching thousands of uninitiated eyes how beautiful the daffodil is. . . . Kate Greenaway came like a fresh southern breeze after a fog. The aesthetes were useful, but they were artificial; they never attained to her open-air radiances. (p. 724)

Her genius bent rather to repose than action; or, at least, to any action more complex than skipping or dancing, picking flowers, crying or taking tea. (No one in the whole history of art has drawn more attractive tea-tables.) Drama was beyond her capacity, and her want of sympathy with anything unhappy or forceful also unfitted her. Her pictures prove her the soul of gentleness. Had she set out to draw a tiger, it would have purred like the friendliest tabby; nothing could induce her pencil to abandon its natural bent for soft contours and grave kindlinesses. Hence her crones were merely good-natured young women doing their best—and doing it very badly—to look old; her witches were benevolent grandmothers. To illustrate was not her *métier*. But to create—that she did to perfection. She literally made a new world where sorrow never entered—nothing but the momentary sadness of a little child—where the sun always shone, where ugliness had no place, and life was always young. No poet has done more than this. It seems to me that among the sweet influences of the nineteenth century Kate Greenaway stands very high. The debt we owe to her is beyond payment. . . . (p. 725)

E. V. Lucas, "Kate Greenaway" (reprinted by permission of the Literary Estate of E. V. Lucas), in The Living Age, *Vol. XIII, No. 2997, December 14, 1901, pp. 724-25.*

Kate Greenaway is dead. To how bright a star would the Greeks have assigned her pure intelligence! With what thronging escort of child angels would the mediaeval Italians have accomplished her entry into the heavenly mansions! To us plain folk of the twentieth century no such imaginative consolations are possible, and those of us who would fain hang up some slight wreath to her memory must do so by means more prosaic.

Surely (to adapt to our purpose words applied to another artist) all British people, even the most confirmed bachelors and invincible old maids, must have had a friendly feeling for Miss Greenaway—her children are so happy, so healthy, and so gay. What a wonderful family that is that peeps out at us from a score of delightful volumes! What a series of studies of young life in all its stages, from the baby with its "pretty little infant wiles" to the young girl-wife with the mystery of her motherhood still brooding over her.

"Which is the way to Somewhere Town?" sings the little girl in **"Under the Window,"** as pulling on her lace mittens she steps bravely across the red-tiled roof of her home towards the broad yellow disc of the sun. Who at one time or another in life has not wished to make just such a determined start for that strange undiscovered country that lies somewhere far, far away in those hidden spaces of the visible world which Mr. Sully tells us are the locality of our childish day-dreams? . . . Curious how universal is this longing for the vague unknown. In the town-bred child the natural desire is to escape from the confinement of the streets to the freedom of the open country. Such a one is the little London girl in **'Marigold Garden,'** who, seated under her green umbrella recounts the charms of rural life. With country children, on the other hand, it is often roused by the thought of the great city, still untried, sometimes, as in the case of Margery Brown (a charming little person in blue) not without a foreboding of possible misfortune. . . . Connected with these feelings of the child are those other and subtler manifestations of his dawning recognition of the mysteries of time and space, and it is often the irrevocable lapse of the former, or the passing away of familiar things, that casts the first shadow over the young mind. An admirable illustration of this represents two children in quaint mob-caps and aprons, gazing after a disappearing ship which only the "white birds" can follow. . . . Miss Greenaway's children are, however, by no means always sad or sentimental. On the contrary, they romp and rolic by scores, up and down, across, and all around her pages:—

> "Pipe the high, and pipe the low,
> Let the little feet go faster;
> Blow your penny trumpet,—blow!
> Well done, little master!"

Well done, indeed! The quaint urchin seated on the stile "blows out his brains" not "upon the flute" but on a penny trumpet, with all the vigour of his little lungs, while his companions foot it with the gravity peculiar to their tender years. Another charming page, full of life and movement, is that devoted to the Dancing Family in 'Marigold Garden'. . . . (pp. 16-18)

It would be difficult to convey in words the fresh and elegant charm of the seven little figures that almost encircle the text, each in a different but equally natural pose, and each a careful study in itself. There are many similar studies in these books; we can only instance the chain of five baby-girls on the last page of **'Under the Window'**. . . . Just at this point we are tempted to digress for a moment. Long ago Ruskin observed of Miss Greenaway's babies that they were as like babies as babies could be [see excerpt above]—an obvious criticism, perhaps, but deeper than it seems. For of how many artists (in book-illustration especially) before her time can as much be said? Not of the mighty George Cruikshank certainly; . . . nor of John Leech . . . ; nor yet of Richard Doyle. . . . But to return to our artist. What sympathy she shows with those other moods of the child when, tired of more boisterous play, he sets himself to act the everyday drama of life around him. On

a trim old-fashioned lawn the tea-things are set: "Do you take sugar? and do you take milk?" asks the little hostess of **'Marigold Garden'**—"she'd got a new gown on, a smart one of silk"—of her four young friends, who make such a pretty picture in their simple frocks and sashes. In the background is one of those diminutive but cosy houses, red brick with diamond-paned windows, the architecture of which was Miss Greenaway's secret. . . . Then there is the pleasant little *ménage* of our old friends Mr. Jack Spratt and his wife (to the expressive drawing of the latter's pretty back we would direct particular attention) in **'Mother Goose,'** and many more.

Sometimes the childish imitation goes a step further, and more solemn rights are introduced, as in the picture of the funeral of the favourite bird, where the naturally-expressed grief of the mourning children is not more happily rendered than the resolutely cheerful air of the little master of the ceremonies. . . . And here we may remark that when the artist handles her pen, she does so in that simple, natural, and straightforward manner eminently suited to her purpose. Her "rhymes" as she modestly calls them, in spite of occasional irregularities, have often true poetical feeling. (pp. 18-19)

But what of all those tiny figures, instinct with the very spirit of youth, scattered like stars singly or in constellations throughout her books—must they pass unnoticed? Each reader will have his special favourites; we can only mention a few of our own for the pleasure of looking at them once more. First then comes the little girl in an inimitable hat, who, rope in hand, skips towards us out of the page with such energetic and frank abandon; then that mite in green seated on the top of a gate with his hands under his chin thinking those "long, long thoughts" of a boy, and that other who clasps his together so joyously as he leaps away, and yet another who drives his hoop with such fine vigour on his half-inch of white paper; next come two little women in their grandmothers' bonnets curtseying to each other with all the formality of aldermen's ladies, and those other two, no longer children, whose exquisitely designed costumes (studies in pink and blue?), set off their budding beauty to such perfection; lastly, the New Year (1883), scattering roses, a figure recalling in its refined and elegant *bizarrerie* the charm of Botticelli or some early Italian painter. Here we must pause—as children revelling in some flowery meadow, not from satiety or lack of unplucked blossoms, but because our hands are full. . . . (pp. 19-20)

It would be interesting if it were possible to trace the influences which have wrought in so individual an artist as Miss Greenaway. That she had all her countrywomen's love of fresh air and exercise, **"On the Wall Top"** and many another breezy little scene will show. Nor must we omit to mention her delight in flowers, which she introduces into all her books with such excellent taste, and which next perhaps to her charmingly invented costumes proclaim her purely decorative talents with the greatest effect. Among the wider influences of the time there have been two movements, roughly speaking synchronous with her life, in both of which it seems to us she has consciously or unconsciously taken part. The one is that movement—at present nameless—which has for its focus the child and all that concerns its welfare. Miss Greenaway could never have been what is popularly called a "faddist," yet she undoubtedly represented this movement on its artistic side. The other, of a widely differing character, was the movement which, beginning about the middle of the last century in a renewed interest in every-day forms of beauty, culminated towards its close in that aesthetic revival which may fittingly be called our English renaissance. In this movement, not the least striking or significant of those which distinguished the Victorian era, she certainly shared. In the nursery of the House Beautiful Kate Greenaway reigns supreme. (pp. 20-1)

[She] was essentially original, and had, too, that fine perception which enabled her always to draw the line between pathos and bathos—a slender one at times in her subject. Her drawing may not be invariably correct, but her sentiment is never false. Nor are the influences of the older world of art, rejuvenated by their passage through a mind always fresh and young, to be forgotten, tinged as they often are with that curious Gothic (or should we say Celtic?) mysticism so characteristic of the highest imaginative efforts of the time. (p. 21)

> *Francis Ernest Williams, "Kate Greenaway: An Appreciation," in* Temple Bar, *Vol. 125, No. 494, January, 1902, pp. 16-21.*

It is true that what Kate Greenaway mainly did was to draw Christmas cards, illustrate a score or two of toy-books, and produce a number of dainty water-colour drawings; and that is the sum of her work. Why, then, is her name a household word in Great and Greater Britain, and even abroad where the mention of some of the greatest artists of England of to-day scarcely calls forth so much as an intelligent glance of recognition? It is because of the universal appeal she made, almost unconsciously, to the universal heart.

All who love childhood, even though they may not be blessed with the full measure of her insight and sympathy, all who love the fields and flowers and the brightness of healthy and sunny natures, must feel that Kate Greenaway had a claim on her country's regard and upon the love of a whole generation. She was the Baby's Friend, the Children's Champion, who stood absolutely alone in her relations to the public. Randolph Caldecott laboured to amuse the little ones; Mr. Walter Crane, to entertain them. They aimed at interesting children in their drawings; but Kate Greenaway interested us in the children themselves. She taught us more of the charm of their ways than we had seen before; she showed us their graces, their little foibles, their thousand little prettinesses, the sweet little characteristics and psychology of their tender age, as no one else had done it before. What are Edouard Frère's little children to hers? What are Fröhlich's, what are Richter's? She felt, with Douglas Jerrold, that 'babes are earthly angels to keep us from the stars,' and has peopled for us a fairy-world which we recognise nevertheless for our own. She had a hundred imitators (from whom she suffered enough), but which of them is a rival on her own ground?. . . And not babies and school-girls only, but maidens who are past the ignorance though not the innocence of childhood; not roses only, but all the flowers of the garden; not the fields only, but the fair landscape of the English country-side,—all these things Kate Greenaway has shown us, with winning and delightful quaintness, and has made us all the happier for her own happiness in them; and, showing us all these things, she has made us love them and her drawings the more for the teaching and the loveliness in them, and herself as well for having made them. (pp. 2-3)

She has flown away for ever now; but the gift she left behind is more than the gift of a book or of a row of books. She left a pure love of childhood in many hearts that never felt it before, and the lesson of a greater kindness to be done, and a delight in simple and tender joys. And to children her gift was not only this; but she put before them pictures more beautiful in their way and quaint than had ever been seen, and she taught

them, too, to look more kindly on their playmates, more wisely on their own little lives, and with better understanding on the beauties of garden and meadow and sky with which Heaven has embellished the world. It was a great deal to do, and she did it well—so well that there is no sadness in her friends' memory of her; and their gratitude is tinged with pride that her name will be remembered with honour in her country for generations to come.

What Kate Greenaway did with her modest pencil was by her example to revolutionise one form of book-illustration. (pp. 3-4)

Indeed, Kate Greenaway is known on the Continent of Europe along with the very few English artists whose names are familiar to the foreign public—with those of Millais, Leighton, Burne-Jones, Watts, and Walter Crane—being recognised as the great domestic artist who, though her subjects were infantile, her treatment often elementary, and her little faults clear to the first glance, merited respect for originality of invention and for rare creative quality. It was realised that she was a *tête d'ècole*, the head and founder of a school—even though that school was but a Kindergarten—the inventor of a new way of seeing and doing, quite apart from the exquisite qualities of what she did and what she expressed. (p. 4)

The touchstone of all art in which there is an element of greatness is the appeal which it makes to the foreigner, to the high and the low alike. Kate Greenaway's appeal was unerring. (p. 5)

In speaking of Kate Greenaway as a 'great' artist, we do not, of course, mean that she was technically accomplished in the sense or degree that a great picture-painter or a sculptor may be. Her figure-drawing was by no means always impeccable; and the fact of the design and composition being generally 'right' arose, we imagine, as much from intuition as from the result of scholarly training. And that is the chief thing. As he grows older, even the artist who is primarily technician and purist is apt to ask, 'What does technical excellence matter so long as the gist of the thing is there? Is not that a finer thing which convinces us from the instinct of the painter than that which satisfies us from his knowledge of it?' Yet Kate could draw an eye or the outline of a face with unsurpassable skill: firmness and a sense of beauty were among her leading virtues. The painter with whom she had most affinity was perhaps Mr. G. D. Leslie, for her period and treatment are not unlike. Her sense of humour is allied to that of Stacy Marks; and her sentiment to that of Fred Walker. Yet she was wholly personal . . . , and full of independence, courage, and fixity of purpose. And just as G. F. Watts in his portraits of men and women invariably sought out the finest and most noble quality in his constant search for beauty in the sitter, not only in features but in character, so did Kate Greenaway in her quiet little drawings show us all that was sweet and pleasant and charming in children's lives of days gone by in country-side and village, and left out all that was ugly, wrong, or bad. (pp. 6-7)

In order to judge of Kate Greenaway as an artist, and appraise her true place and position in British art, we must bear in mind not only what she did, but what she was. It must be remembered that she was a pioneer, an inventor, an innovator; and that, although she painted no great pictures and challenged no comparison with those who labour in the more elevated planes of artistry, is sufficient to place her high upon the roll. Just as Blake is most highly valued for his illustration and Cruikshank and Goya for their etched plates, rather than for their pictures, so Kate Greenaway must be judged, not by the dignity of her materials, or by the area of her canvas, but by the originality of her genius, and by the strength and depth of the impression she has stamped on the mind and sentiment of the world. As Mr. Holman Hunt, Millais, and their associates invigorated the art of England by their foundation of the Pre-Raphaelite Brotherhood, so Kate Greenaway introduced a Pre-Raphaelite spirit into the art of the nursery. That is what Dr. Max Nordau, with curious perversion of judgment and lack of appreciation, denounced as 'degeneracy'!—accusing her of creating 'a false and degenerate race of children in art,' while at the worst she was but giving us a Midsummer Day's Dream in Modern England. For him Kate Greenaway, the healthy, sincere, laughter-loving artist, is a 'decadent' such as vexes the soul of a Tolstoi. It is the result, of course, of misapprehension—of a misunderstanding which has revolted few besides him.

The outstanding merit of Kate Greenaway's work is its obvious freedom from affectation, its true and unadulterated English character. What Dr. Nordau mistook for affectation is simply humour—a quaintness which is not less sincere and honest for being sometimes sufficiently self-conscious to make and enjoy and sustain the fun. Such grace of action, such invariable delicacy and perfect taste of her little pictures, belong only to a mind of the sweetest order—the spontaneity and style, only to an artist of the rarest instinct. Animated by a love of the world's beauty that was almost painful in its intensity, she was not satisfied to render merely what she saw; she was compelled to colour it with fancy and imagination. . . . The truth is, her poetic emotion and the imagination which so stirred the admiration of Ruskin and the rest, inspired her to express a somewhat fanciful vision of the flowers, and children, and life which she saw around her. She gave us not what she saw, but what she felt, even as she looked. Her subtle and tender observation, one writer has declared, was corrected and modified by her own sense of love and beauty. Her instinctive feeling is, therefore, nobler than her sense of record; it is big in 'conception' and style, and is immeasurably more delightful than bare appreciation of fact. (pp. 265-66)

[She] drew children with the grace of Stothard and the naturalness of Reynolds, investing them with all the purity and brightness that we find in her drawing and her colour. Although her cantata was simple, it was ever notable for its exquisite harmony and perfect instrumentation.

Faults, no doubt, of a technical sort Kate Greenaway shows in many of her drawings, and . . . mannerisms at times betrayed her. She would exaggerate in her faces the pointed chin that was a charm of her model Gertie's face. She would draw eyes too far apart, as Ford Madox Brown came to do; yet how exquisitely those eyes were drawn, and how admirably placed within their sockets! perfect in accuracy of touch, and delightful in their beauty. The knees of her girls are sometimes too low down; the draperies are often too little studied and lack grace of line; her babies' feet are at times too large, and are carelessly drawn, or at least are rendered without sufficient appreciation of their form. A score of drawings substantiate every one of these charges—but what of that? The greatest artists have had their failings, cardinal in academic eyes, for the faults are all of technique. . . . In Kate Greenaway's case her faults are forgotten, or at least forgiven, in presence of her refined line and fairy tinting, her profiles and full faces of tender loveliness, and her figures of daintiest grace. (pp. 266-67)

Original as she was in her view of art and in the execution of her ideas, Kate Greenaway was very impressionable and frequently suffered herself to be influenced by other artists. But that she was unconscious of the fact seems unquestionable, and that her own strong individuality saved her from anything that could be called imitation must be admitted. The nearest semblance to that plagiarism which she so heartily abhorred is to be found in the likeness borne by some of her landscapes to those of Mrs. Allingham. . . . The artist herself has clearly felt the defect, and obviated it on other occasions. The love of red Surrey cottages, green fields, and groups of little children was common to both artists, and Kate's imitation is more apparent than real; her renderings of them are honest and tender, full of sentiment, and of accurate, vigorous observation. She does not seem to have studied landscape for its breadth, or sought to read and transcribe the mighty message of poetry it holds for every whole-hearted worshipper. Rather did she seek for the passages of beauty and the pretty scenes which appealed to her, delighting in the sonnet, as it were, rather than in the epic. (p. 269)

There are those who sneer at nationality in art. You can no more speak of English art, laughed Whistler, than you can speak of English mathematics. The analogy is entirely a false one. You can say with truth 'English art' as you can say 'German music'; for although art in its language is universal, in its expression it is national, or at least racial; and it is the merit of a nation to express itself frankly in its art in its own natural way, and to despise the affectation of self-presentation in the terms and in the guise of foreign practice not native to itself. It is a matter of sincerity and, moreover, of good sense; for little respect is deserved or received by a man who affects to speak his language with a foreign accent. Kate Greenaway was intensely and unfeignedly English: for that she is beloved in her own country, and for that she is appreciated and respected abroad. Like Hogarth, Reynolds, and Millais, she was the unadulterated product of England, and like them she gave us of her 'English art.' (pp. 270-71)

When all Miss Greenaway's work is carefully judged, it will, we think, be seen that it is with the point rather than with the brush that she touches her highest level, whether her manner be precise as in her book-plates, or free as in her sketches. (p. 276)

In the *Language of Flowers* and *Marigold Garden* Kate Greenaway rose to her highest point in decision and firmness allied to the perfect drawing of flowers and fruit, although it must be allowed that those who have not seen the original designs can form no accurate judgment from the printed work. The annual *Almanacks,* too, . . . showed her endless resource and inexhaustible faculty of design; yet it is perhaps to be regretted that so much conscientious effort and executive ability should have been wasted in the almost microscopic rendering of the innumerable illustrations which embellish these tiny books. . . . She returned to her more formal manner in *A Apple Pie* . . . , as it was more suitable to the large page she had to decorate; and she gives us a greater measure of combined humour and invention than had previously been shown, for the subject fitted her mood of fun and fancy exactly. . . . (p. 282)

The survey of her work in the aggregate shows convincingly that even had her technique been on a lower level Kate Greenaway would still have succeeded as the interpreter-in-chief of childhood. Follower though she was in point of time of Mr. Walter Crane and Randolph Caldecott, inspired in some respects no doubt by their example, she nevertheless stands alone in her own sphere. From Lucca della Robbia to Ludwig Richter and Schwind, to Bewick and Thackeray, Cruikshank and Boutet de Monvel, no one has demonstrated more completely the artist's knowledge of and sympathy with infant life, or communicated that knowledge and that sympathy to us. Her pictures delight the little ones for their own sake, and delight us for the sake of the little ones; and it may be taken as certain that Kate Greenaway's position in the Art of England is assured, so long as her drawings speak to us out of their broad and tender humanity, and carry their message to every little heart. (pp. 283-84)

M. H. Spielmann and G. S. Layard, in their Kate Greenaway, *Adam & Charles Black, 1905, 300 p.*

Greenawayland is not Fairyland. . . . Hers is, rather, a country of red cottages and green fields, of formal gardens edged with box, of an eighteenth century England, idealized and illuminated by a romantic imagination. There may be fairies in it, but it is not a fairy world.

The children who roam through the pages, who run lightly along the paths in twos and threes, skip rope, play gracefully in ring-a-rounds, or walk sedately with their elders, are simplicity itself. Their fresh little faces, their touching innocence, their naiveté and seriousness reflect the winning and gentle spirit of the artist.

You may look in vain, in her pictures, for children who are not well-mannered, prim little folks with pointed chins and confiding eyes. When these children climb apple trees they do it tidily, with gloves on their arms and frocks unruffled. Even the two little boys fighting in *A Apple Pie,* despite doubled fists and lifted arms, are not really very angry.

Not to please the moralist, or stickler for right behaviour, did Kate Greenaway draw only good children, but because she thought of childhood with affection and tenderness and wished to surround it with happy thoughts. She set it in the midst of gardens and flowers, clad it in flowing garments in summer, protected it warmly in winter. She liked the skies to be blue and white, the fields and hedgerows to be green and well kept, with blossoms everywhere. Her sensitive spirit could not bear anything harsh or cruel. (p. 10)

Flowers were always among her greatest joys, and her delicate delineation of them, in clear, charming colour, is one of her leading characteristics, suggesting the springtime of life. In *Marigold Garden,* where her drawing of flowers and fruit is counted perfect, her lines firm and decided, the pages are fragrant with nosegays of roses and tulips, daffodils and lilies, or garlanded with apples and pears and primrose chains. . . .

[Kate Greenaway's books] are loved for their happy-heartedness, the sweet pure beauty of their flowers and, especially, for the single-minded purpose in which they are designed to please children.

If the dainty frocks and frills, the sashes, capes and hats, once so popular on both sides of the Atlantic, now seem a little fussy and elaborate for present day children, they suit Greenawayland, with its old-fashioned houses and demure inhabitants. Kate Greenaway may be counted long secure of an honoured place on the children's book shelves. The grandmothers will see to that and her own sincerity will win the hearts of the children. (p. 11)

Alice M. Jordan, "Kate Greenaway and Randolph Caldecott," in The Junior Bookshelf, *Vol. 10, No. 1, March, 1946, pp. 9-14.**

From Marigold Garden, *written and illustrated by Kate Greenaway.*

Kate Greenaway brought [children's books] sheer beauty and picturesque charm. . . .

The enthusiastic reception of all Kate Greenaway's books from ["**Under the Window**"] on is an old familiar story; of how her quaint costumes influenced the clothes and manners of the children of three continents, of how her fame rivaled that of the foremost artists of the day (as well it might).

This wonderful skill in the use of costumes was no free gift from the gods, not just "a flair for costume." Like Kate Greenaway's skill in drawing it was the result of years and years of loving study, of meticulous labor and attention to detail. All her life, from childhood on, she *worked* with costumes, material and designs, cutting and stitching, herself, most of the lovely dresses which appeared in her drawings.

The name "Kate Greenaway" has become a household word. . . . But it is well to remember those ten years of art school boning, those ten long years of hack work, the lifetime of studying and working with costumes and the children who wore them. . . .

[Here] for the first time, children's books were given a true dignity and importance. Here, for the first time, children were regarded as real, intelligent human beings, worthy of the very best of draughtsmanship, imagination and publishing integrity.

Robert Lawson, "The Art of Caldecott and Greenaway," in The New York Times Book Review *(©1946 by The New York Times Company; reprinted by permission), March 17, 1946, p. 7.**

If you have not opened your copies of *Under the Window* and *Marigold Garden* for years, open them now. Do they not look more beautiful than ever in these days, their grace and charm freshly blooming like flowers, and creating delight and hope? What have the years to do with these books except to bear witness to their life?

> Bertha E. Mahony, "Kate Greenaway and Randolph Caldecott," in The Horn Book Magazine (copyright © 1946 by The Horn Book, Inc., Boston), Vol. XXII, No. 2, March-April, 1946, p. 95.*

It was a very human world in which real children dance and play and sing in sunlit streets and gardens or beside the sea that Kate Greenaway recorded for the nineteenth century in "Under the Window" and "Marigold Garden".

Clear memory of the wonder of her own happy childhood in country and city was behind these essentially English scenes. It is said that "K. G.", as she was familiarly known in her own time, never forgot the colour or form of anything she had looked upon in childhood. She seems to have been born with the rare sense of colour and design which has distinguished her work as the pioneer among picture books of a new order. (p. 5)

Of the many ABC books published in recent years "A Apple Pie" is by far the most popular with the children of the libraries. "Kate Greenaway's Mother Goose" has not been superseded by any of the moderns in the eyes of those who are looking for a little one of perfect design.

"Under the Window", "Marigold Garden" and "The Pied Piper" are still without rivals and are better known and loved to-day than they were twenty-five years ago. (p. 13)

> Anne Carroll Moore, in her A Century of Kate Greenaway (copyright Frederick Warne & Co. Ltd. London 1946), Warne, 1946, 15 p.

Kate Greenaway's pictures for *Under the Window, Marigold Garden, A Child's Day* and all her other picture books are filled with natural, happy children. . . . Her picture children are shown against delicate spring-like landscapes of old cottages with formal gardens or farmhouses set in fields of bloom. Part of the charm of her pictures is their effortless, unstudied look as well as the gay yet delicate color. The verses which accompany the pictures are her own, and without pictures would have little to commend them to succeeding generations. Without the inversions they would be little more than a running comment in prose, and in their verse form they often lack both rhythm and good rhyme. Although her pictures have little forceful activity, sensitive children are drawn to Kate Greenaway's books by the strength of her affectionate and understanding portrayal of what Austin Dobson called "the coy reticences, the simplicities and the small solemnities of little people" and by the fresh beauty of her flowers and gardens. (p. 120)

> Lillian H. Smith, "Picture Books: Kate Greenaway," in her The Unreluctant Years: A Critical Approach to Children's Literature (reprinted by permission; copyright © 1953, 1981 by the American Library Association), American Library Association, 1953, pp. 119-20.

Kate Greenaway, in a sense, was not an illustrator at all. She was an artist whose pictures comprised the soul of the book in which they appeared: the soul, that is, as she saw it. . . . She even invented and made the public believe in the costumes the children wore. . . . Her light and gentle fancy made her text and her fidelity to it of secondary importance. The book she illustrated, whatever it was, was Kate Greenaway's: not more so, but only more happily so, if she had no author to follow, as in her own *Under the Window* . . . and could live in her enchanting and enchanted private nursery world, sharing it with children in frocks she made for it, but loved wholeheartedly by children in the less beautiful actual patterns of 1873 to 1900. (p. 286)

> F. J. Harvey Darton, "The 'Sixties: 'Alice' and After," in his Children's Books in England: Five Centuries of Social Life, second edition, Cambridge at the University Press, 1958, pp. 259-98.*

Kate Greenaway is the most beloved, if not the greatest, of the trio of picture-book artists of the 'seventies. . . . She created with her pen and brush a realm of her own for children's delight, an Arcadia where tidy little boys in long pantaloons and prettily-dressed little girls in frilly gowns and sunbonnets played games, gathered flowers or took tea in cottage gardens. Kate Greenaway's engaging infants are always spotless and neat, even when they climb apple-trees or go fishing. Flowers were her joy, and her pages are much decorated with them. Occasionally something more fearful appears, such as the witch and the queer old man who runs away with Billy in *Under the Window*, but such darker aspects are rare.

Criticism has been made of Kate Greenaway for her technical faults, but her charming, original style more than outweighs any such deficiencies. (p. 203)

Kate Greenaway was both author and illustrator of what is perhaps her most attractive book, *Marigold Garden* . . . , as she was for her first success, *Under the Window*. Although there is nothing remarkable about her verses, they are so happily interpreted in line and colour, that the whole book is a triumph of artistic invention. (pp. 203-04)

Today some of Kate Greenaway's picture-books still please the young, although they may not possess the fascination they once had for their great-grandmothers. Her work has been imitated, but never equalled in the style she created. She gave to boys and girls not merely some picture-books of real charm and artistic quality, but her own vision of innocence and happy childhood. (p. 204)

> M. F. Thwaite, "Picture-Books and Books for Young Children," in her From Primer to Pleasure: An Introduction to the History of Children's Books in England, from the Invention of Printing to 1900 (© M. F. Thwaite 1963), The Library Association, 1963, pp. 194-206.*

In the practice of art, as in every human activity, each generation learns from the generations that have gone before. The lesser artists will imitate. The greater ones will turn to their forerunners not to find models but to start reverberations in their own imaginations. Among these a few may become the originals of their generation. Kate Greenaway was one of these. (p. 13)

In Kate Greenaway's garden the sun is always shining. We look at her pictures much as we look at a blossoming garden, seeing only the light on the flowers, forgetting the rain or the toil that went into the creation of that beauty. Her drawings show color, humor, grace, but no hint of the effort and drudgery inevitable in the giving of form to vision.

That Kate Greenaway deserved the fame she attained can be seen by the reproductions of her paintings, drawings, and sketches . . . ; her fame actually rested on her illustrations for relatively few books. A bibliography of those she illustrated that children of later generations have loved and that future generations will be most likely to enjoy would be short. . . .

Yet every book containing her pictures is enhanced—even one of mincing verse or spurious prose—by the purity of her vision of childhood. She stands with Walter Crane and Randolph Caldecott. (p. 14)

She stands also by herself. Kate Greenaway was an innovator who brought to her pictures of flowers and flowerlike children a freshness that none of her many imitators could capture.

Her childhood stayed with her always. . . .

> I suppose my imaginary life made me one long continuous joy—filled everything with a strange wonder and beauty. Living in that childish wonder is a most beautiful feeling—I can so well remember it. There was always something more—behind and beyond everything—to me; the golden spectacles were very big.

It is that "behind and beyond" that one feels in her pictures which gives them their depth and an indefinable essence. (pp. 14-15)

The most blessed of the artists and poets can give to children experiences that start imaginations growing. Kate Greenaway is one of these. She is unique in that the most beautiful impressions of her childhood not only became part of the woman but remained in her memory so clearly as to be essential in the expression of the artist. This expression, endowing childhood and the actions, moods, and games of childhood with the beauty she felt, is a rightful inheritance of each new generation. (p. 15)

Quaint though her children are—charmingly dressed in a costume of many years before her own birth—they are truly children, alive, moving, their faces solemn with the natural intentness of young children at play. What could be more real than the concentration of the little boy blowing his penny trumpet for the children dancing on the curve of the hill in *Under the Window?* Or more characteristic than the picture in the same book of girls at tea, playing most seriously at being grown-up ladies?

When a critic called the expression on her children's faces woebegone, Kate Greenaway agreed that it was absurd for children to be playing a game and for their faces to be "plunged in the deepest despair and sadness," and she said that she hoped to do better. Few have been troubled by mournfulness in the children of her pictures, however. . . . In her *Book of Games* and in her other books, if the faces appear solemn, they are also pleasant and unself-conscious. Kate Greenaway children have the rapt faces natural to those children who are uninterrupted in their absorption with a world of wonders they are only beginning to discover or experience. (p. 17)

Although her pictured children, with their quaint dress and flowerlike faces, may appear like figures in an exquisite dream, each new generation sees them as real children. They have none of the coyness, the self-conscious parody of childhood of which many lesser artists are guilty. (p. 18)

[Kate Greenaway's] verses for children are in complete harmony with her drawings. They are unpretentious, amusing, sometimes touched with surprise or mystery, and true to the feelings of childhood. They give evidence that although she lacked the power of great poetic expression, she had, in Austin Dobson's words, "the root of the matter in her." (p. 22)

> *Ruth Hill Viguers, in an introduction to* The Kate Greenaway Treasury: An Anthology of the Illustrations and Writings of Kate Greenaway, *edited by Edward Ernest with Patricia Tracy Lowe (copyright © 1967 by The World Publishing Company), World Publishing Co., 1967, pp. 13-23.*

[Kate Greenaway was] an artist of great charm and sensibility, very narrow range, and limited technical ability. She never really learned to draw, but she had a fine feeling for colour and a strong sense of design. At her best, in *Marigold Garden* for example, she was not just drawing charming pictures but producing a complete and calculated work of art—minor art, certainly, but very precious.

> *A review of "The Kate Greenaway Treasury," in* The Junior Bookshelf, *Vol. 32, No. 6, December, 1968, p. 350.*

Kate Greenaway is a unique figure in the history of books for children. At first thought it seems absurd to couple her name with William Blake, yet the two had something in common for, unlike as their work was, both artists discovered and understood the spirit of innocent childhood and transferred it to their pages. (p. 233)

Kate Greenaway would never have called herself a poet, but her simple verses are a perfect accompaniment to her drawings. They appeal to children as do the pictures themselves, for so true to real childhood are Miss Greenaway's children that modern boys and girls recognize them as children like themselves, in spite of the quaint costumes of an earlier day in which the artist dressed them, and which are one of the charms of her books. "I like making cowslip fields grow and apple trees bloom at a moment's notice," she wrote in a letter to Ruskin, "that is what it is, you see, to have gone through life with an enchanted land ever beside you." This enchantment and child-like wonder she kept alive in her own heart and filled her pictures with them for others. (p. 234)

> *Anne Thaxter Eaton, "Illustrators Who Were More Than Illustrators: The Quaint and Beautiful Art of Kate Greenaway," in* A Critical History of Children's Literature *by Cornelia Meigs, Anne Thaxter Eaton, Elizabeth Nesbitt, and Ruth Hill Viguers, edited by Cornelia Meigs (copyright ©1953, 1969 by Macmillan Publishing Co., Inc.), revised edition, Macmillan, 1969, pp. 233-35.*

With all due deference to the charm and felicity of [Kate Greenaway's] inimitable powers of decoration, her range is limited and even her 'pretty maids all in a row' are not to be compared with Caldecott's. (p. 170)

She was not, let it be admitted, a great artist. Her target was a modest one; but she created a small world of her own, a dream-world, a never-never-land, above all a world at least as remote from the one in which she lived as from our own. Yet it was a world familiar to her audience, the world of nursery-rhyme and make-believe. What did she do with it? She peopled it with beings, idealised maybe, but dressed in the clothes of everyday folk—even if always their best clothes—and behaving as they might behave—even if it was always their best behaviour.

Her prim children, starry-eyed and innocent, betray little sign of life. They play their decorative and ornamental games with unnatural decorum, their nimble fingers weaving natty posies and garlands with an assuredness and neatness equalled only by the grace and regularity with which their feet weave the patterns of simple country dance measures. Quite literally they never put a foot wrong. Their elders are grave and beautiful even in extreme old age: never a minx nor a larrikin defaces her immaculate pages. All is maypoles and smock frocks, beauty and tranquillity, simplicity and charm. (pp. 170-71)

It will not do to say, with certain critics, that she has survived because her work enshrines the Victorian age. It is not true. Her dimity-clad damsels and demure little boys are not representative of an age which, although it had its points, was essentially an age of dirt and ugliness. . . . On the other hand, if it were true, it would mean that her work dates, and, despite the fact that her pictures represent things of the past, they definitely do not date. They are as fresh and beguiling to us as ever they were to her contemporaries; and that begins to point to immortality. . . .

The quality of Kate Greenaway as an artist for children lies in her ability to provide pictures which are really illustrations. They help to tell the story, and they helped the young readers to project themselves into the company of the children she depicted.

One relevant criticism of nearly all early books for children is that the authors and artists saw a child as a small adult. The tendency persists in some modern illustrations intended for children, which are all too fanciful and modernistic. Kate created no single outstanding character, but she knew that children wanted something they could recognise. 'I often notice that children don't at all care for what grown-up people think they will', she wrote on one occasion, and again: 'I think they often like grown-up books—at any rate I did'. Perhaps to solve the difficulty she designed books to please both children and adults. Thus she drew a nursery-rhyme land, raised to the *n*th degree of sublimation if you like, a mortality that had taken on immortality, a corruption clothed in incorruptibility, and her pictures fitted the words like a glove.

Why does she still enchant us? If we are children, because we find her children still real enough to convince us, yet fanciful enough to be true denizens of fairyland, who obviously have wonderful opportunities of dressing-up. If we are adults the appeal is more subtly explained. First there is what might be called a second childhood, if there were no offensive connotation with that term—let us call it a perpetuation of youth. They appeal to us in direct proportion to our ability to look at them with the eyes of a child. (p. 171)

Percy Muir, "The Advent of Colour: Kate Greenaway," in his Victorian Illustrated Books *(© Percy Muir 1971), B. T. Batsford Ltd, 1971, pp. 170-74.*

Kate Greenaway wrote undistinguished verse for children, but she did write with artless gaiety, and her illustrations have all the lyric grace the verses lack. Her balanced pages. . . . possess a freshness and charm, and a kind of rhythmic grace that seem to lift the accompanying quatrains into the realm of genuine poetry. Without the pictures, the rhymes probably would not have survived, but the two in combination constitute a unique contribution to children's books. (p. 338)

In the Greenaway books, we see and read about children racing and skipping, dancing to the piper's tune, flying kites, rolling hoops, chasing each other, going primly to tea, or quietly enjoying their own little red house—in short, real children. For this is Kate Greenaway's contribution to children's poetry: verses that are simple in language and idea, but with a spark of humor that brings a smile, because her children are truly childlike. (p. 339)

May Hill Arbuthnot and Zena Sutherland, "Poets and Children's Poetry: Kate Greenaway, 1846-1901," in their Children and Books *(copyright © 1972, 1964, 1957, 1947 by Scott, Foresman and Company; reprinted by permission), fourth edition, Scott, Foresman, 1972, pp. 338-39.*

Nostalgia for the past—for one's own childhood or even for the fleeting moment—and a generalized sentimentality toward childhood and children are two quite separate phenomena. From the first have come some of the English language's richest books for the young. . . . From the latter come many of those books clucked over by doting great-aunts and assorted well-meaning adults who have, alas, long ago mislaid their own childhoods. (p. 31)

The work of the nineteenth-century illustrator and author Kate Greenaway and the contemporary artist and writer Joan Walsh Anglund provides superior examples of these opposite states of mind from which children's books may spring. (pp. 31-2)

In each instance, the children of their books are presented as being out of some not quite specified past era. In Miss Greenaway's case, they wear a country costume half remembered from the small, rural town of Rolleston where she spent considerable time as a child and half created out of her admiration for late-eighteenth-century costume. . . .

As important to Miss Greenaway as costume, however, are the particulars of the English countryside which she first discovered as a visiting London child and cherished ever after. Fields and flowers, orchards and hedges, houses and gently rolling vistas are all set down with lyric fidelity and made eternal somehow by the quaint timelessness of the beautifully clothed children and adults who trod lightly through them. The freshness of springtime, the clarity of country air, the lightness of the human spirit in such a setting—these are Miss Greenaway's subject matter. (p. 32)

While both authors are consummate craftsmen whose work bears the indelible imprint of their personal styles, Mrs. Anglund's intelligence is applied to the manipulation of her readers' latent sentimentality concerning childhood and children, Miss Greenaway's to conveying a vision of life.

Neither speaks primarily *to* children. They write *of* childhood: Mrs. Anglund in a way that uses children as a means of escape from adult realities which may not be so pleasing—the pain of growing old, the sameness of daily routine—and Miss Greenaway in a way that enlarges our appreciation of all green and growing things in nature—children among them.

This said, a child once introduced to Kate Greenaway via her *Mother Goose* or her own verse in *Under the Window* is likely to be hooked. . . . [The] magic of her richly costumed children (a dress as unfamiliar and literary to late-nineteenth-century England as it is to us today) appeals immediately to most children's love of drama and make-believe. What child's self-esteem or sense of importance is not greatly enhanced by seeing Miss Greenaway's solemn, grandly turned-out infants engaged in such wholly mundane and familiar activities as skipping rope, playing tag and holding tea parties?

The real difference in Miss Greenaway's and Mrs. Anglund's work lies in the opposing life views which inspire them. Behind Miss Greenaway's cheerful, idyllic English scenes there lies the artist's essentially tragic view of life. (pp. 33-4)

To Kate Greenaway, childhood was a metaphor for life at its richest and most bountiful. As an adult, she often recalled her early years with a nostalgia that bordered on pain. . . .

That shady lane with high hedges and wide grassy places—Miss Greenaway's Eden—recurs like an obsession in her illustrations. It is the locale of her world. (p. 35)

Her work is fraught with poignancy not because she strains or in any way reaches for it, but because this awareness of life's evanescence permeates her whole life view. . . .

Something alive and breathing is at the heart of Miss Greenaway's world. When her "Little Maid" walks down the lane in **Mother Goose,** there is no question that she has a real destination in a real landscape and that we are merely privy to a passing moment. Children do not care "about children in an abstract way. That belongs to older people," Miss Greenaway once noted. Entirely devoid either of abstraction or condescension, Miss Greenaway's work appeals both to grownups and to children by virtue of its matter-of-fact naturalness. In her landscapes, children and adults alike are merely part of the architecture of her vision of English life. They have neither more nor less importance than roses or a blossoming apple tree. Take them or leave them, you can never doubt the reality of Kate Greenaway's scenes. Even at their most absurd (a state they occasionally reach), her costumes are so distinctive and convincingly realized that we suppress a smile in admiration of her unique vision. (p. 36)

The real world informs her every pen stroke and gives backbone to her work. "There is no charm so enduring as that of the real representation of any given scene," Ruskin remarked of her work as a whole, and Miss Greenaway's vision neither fades nor dates. England may one day be transformed into an industrial wasteland like the flatlands of New Jersey, but we can always return to her loving little landscapes for an authentic flavor of the rural English past. (p. 37)

Miss Greenaway's airy landscapes, being closely observed from the English countryside she knew and loved rather than fabricated as backdrops for adult-inspired games of pretend, have the bracing flavor of ginger. (p. 39)

[Her] nostalgic costuming and improvised child's play always serve to enhance her particular vision of nature and the poignancy of life as she observed it through passing seasons and years in the English countryside. . . . Like her pictures, her own verse, at its best, was honestly observed and from life. . . . (p. 40)

One readily sees how Stevenson found inspiration in such work for his later *Child's Garden of Verses.* Miss Greenaway's children look forward. They do not exist merely as vehicles to corroborate a grownup's sentimental looking backward. (p. 41)

[Childhood] never ends in the best of people or in the best of writing for children. George MacDonald noted this in *The Princess and Curdie:*

> There is this difference between the growth of some human beings and that of others; in the one case it is a continuous dying, in the other a continuous resurrection . . . the child is not meant to die, but to be forever freshborn.

This Kate Greenaway instinctively understood, and it is the constant resurrection—the springtime of childhood—that her work timelessly celebrates. (pp. 42-3)

Selma G. Lanes, "Greenaway Went Thataway," in her Down the Rabbit Hole: Adventures and Misadventures in the Realm of Children's Literature *(copyright © 1971 by Selma G. Lanes; reprinted with the permission of Atheneum Publishers, New York), Atheneum, 1972, pp. 31-43.*

Kate Greenaway's verses are innocuous, ordinary, and of no significance away from the pictures; but the pictures are an endless delight—clear, fresh, innocent, individual. Anyone can recognize Kate Greenaway children. They are always cool, neat and self-possessed, and one is convinced that they will never get dirty or come to any harm. On one page of **Under the Window** three tiny children are rowing in a flooded field in what look like bathtubs. They are calm and happy, and obviously in no danger whatever; it is a sweet dream of childhood. The Greenaway costumes belong, with modifications, to the earlier part of the century. Miss Greenaway did not follow contemporary fashion in children's dress; it followed her. Her young ladies, in **The Language of Flowers** . . . and elsewhere, are as lovely and innocent as her children. They obviously never need to blow their noses or perform any of the grosser physical functions. They are the immortals of the broad, smooth lawns and the rich flower-beds; it is unendingly late May, the trees are in bloom, the clear girlish laughter ripples out to eternity, and there is honey for tea forever.

Kate Greenaway often put quite large numbers of children into a picture; she had a fondness for arranging them in lines or clusters or in the patterns of play, and perhaps she had also a shrewd understanding that children love detail and enjoy illustrations that can be pored over rather than taken in at a glance. (pp. 152-53)

John Rowe Townsend, "Pictures That Tell a Story: Kate Greenaway," in his Written for Children: An Outline of English-Language Children's Literature *(copyright © 1965, 1974 by John Rowe Townsend; reprinted by permission of Harper & Row Publishers, Inc.; in Canada by Penguin Books Ltd), revised edition, Lippincott, 1974, pp. 152-53.*

[Kate Greenaway] reflected the grim attitude toward age that was presumably more prevalent at the turn of the century. In **Marigold Garden** . . . we find the only appearance of an older character in **"When we went out with grandmamma."** Grandma makes the children walk stiffly, chides them and generally makes life uncomfortable for them. One can argue that such were the modes of the day, i.e., grandma was instilling traditional values ("conformity" in our matrix). Greenaway's **Under the Window** . . . also features only one rhyme about an older person, **"Some geese went out a-walking."** In this case, the older person is definitely not engaged in instilling tradition. She is simply unpleasant. (p. 7)

Edward F. Ansello, "The Rocking Chair Syndrome in Action," in Interracial Books for Children Bulletin *(reprinted by permission of* Interracial Books for Children Bulletin, *1841 Broadway, New York, NY 10023), Vol. 7, No. 6, 1976, pp. 7-10.**

Kate Greenaway has few peers when it comes to conveying the beauty of children and the world in rose-colored images. (p. 60)

YES, it is sad of them—
Shocking to me ;
Bad—yes, it's bad of them—
Bad of all three.

Warnings they've had from me.
Still I repeat them—
Cold is the water—the
Fishes will eat them.

Yet they will row about,
Tho' I say "Fie !" to them ;
Fathers may scold at it,
Mothers may cry to them.

From Under the Window, *written and illustrated by Kate Greenaway.*

Characterized by elegance, delicacy, and grace, children from Greenaway's brush reflect her vision of childhood as a time of happy innocence. . . . During the years of Britain's industrial revolution, Kate hewed to the Pre-Raphaelite injunction to venerate the simple and poetic in nature.

For the unique impression of childhood her illustrations have left on the minds and hearts of readers, Kate Greenaway's name has a place in children's literature not easily matched. (p. 61)

> *Bernice E. Cullinan with Mary K. Karrer and Arlene M. Pillar, "A Historical View of Children and Books: Profile, Kate Greenaway," in their* Literature and the Child *(copyright © 1981 by Harcourt Brace Jovanovich, Inc.; reprinted by permission of the publisher), Harcourt Brace Jovanovich, 1981, pp. 60-1.*

Surfeited now with images as we are, it may be less captivating to fall under the spell of those Kate Greenaway figures, placed in a landscape so redolent of the past—at least the magical past as arranged in Queen Anne style—but their very air of charming contrivance, of being nowhere, their very unreality, in fact, preserves them from inevitable decay. . . . Pensive, grave, their expressions allow for new elaborations and interpretations; they are not the fixed forms of a specific time, typical but limiting; instead they have something of the availability of timeless images. (p. 409)

> *Sonya Rudikoff, "A Past Recaptured," in* The American Scholar *(copyright © 1983 by Sonya Rudikoff;*

reprinted by permission of the publishers, the United Chapters of Phi Beta Kappa), Vol. 52, No. 3, Summer, 1983, pp. 406, 408-11.

UNDER THE WINDOW: PICTURES AND RHYMES FOR CHILDREN (1878)

[*Before she became an author/illustrator, Greenaway received encouragement from H. Stacy Marks, whose paintings of birds are often considered brilliant. Marks suggested that Greenaway dress her figures in quaint costumes similar to those she knew as a child. He continued to offer Greenaway artistic advice throughout her career.*]

Dear Miss Greenaway—Very many thanks for your very pretty and charming book, which has afforded me and my household much pleasure. Where so many designs are delightful, it seems hard to select any special one, but I think, as a happy method of filling up a page, the girls with the shuttlecocks bears the palm; and how useful is the verse between! [p. 33].

I like page 41 for its naïve defiance of all rules of composition, and pages 23 and 47 are very sweet.

I am not going to be 'severe,' but I *must* ask you not to repeat those funny little black shadows under the feet of your figures—looking in some places like spurs, in others like tadpoles, in others like short stilts. . . . Why you have done this (much to the detriment of the drawings) in special instances and not in others I can't see. I will only find another fault—the drawing of the *feet* on page 31—the tallest girl's are very funny, but all are queer. A cast of any foot placed a little below the level of the eye would teach you how to foreshorten feet better.

There, I have done! But I know you well enough to feel assured that you would not be content with unqualified praise, and that you are grateful for a little honest criticism.

Don't bother about painting too much. You have a *lay* of your own, and do your best to cultivate it.

Think of the large number of people you charm and delight by these designs compared with those who can afford to buy paintings. You have a special gift and it is your duty in every sense to make the most of it.

By the way, did you write the verses also? If so, there is another feather for your cap, for I know how difficult it is to write verses for children.

I hope I have not sermonised too much, and thanking you once more for your pleasant, happy book, to which I shall turn again and again. . . . (pp. 80-1)

> *H. S. Marks, in a letter to Kate Greenaway on October 22, 1879, in* Kate Greenaway *by M. H. Spielmann and G. S. Layard, G. P. Putnam's Sons, 1905, pp. 80-1.*

This is a lovely little book—all through—the New and Old Years are chiefly delightful to me. But I wish some of the children had bare feet—and that the shoes of the others weren't *quite* so like mussel-shells.

> *J. Ruskin, in a letter to Kate Greenaway on December 27, 1882, in* Kate Greenaway *by M. H. Spielmann and G. S. Layard, G. P. Putnam's Sons, 1905, p. 110.*

[Of **Under the Window**], it is no exaggeration to say that it was epoch-making; its popularity was such that Kate tasted the bitter-sweet experience . . . of finding her work coolly appropriated by others. (p. 60)

Alone [her verses] would probably not have attracted much serious attention, and doubtless would have met with criticism. For there are in them faults of scansion, rhythm, and rhyme which it is easy enough to reprobate. But their sincerity, gaiety, and feeling appealed to such unimpeachable judges as Frederick Locker and Mr. Austin Dobson. . . .

Other verses were obviously cleverer and daintier than hers, but her own simple thoughts were more in harmony with her delightful little pictures.

It was not only the critics but the public who acclaimed her, for she had got at the secret of the beauty and charm of childhood, and the appeal was universal. (p. 62)

> *M. H. Spielmann and G. S. Layard, in their* Kate
> Greenaway, *Adam & Charles Black, 1905, 300 p.*

Everything about **"Under the Window"** was fresh and different from any picture book that had been seen before—the lovely cover design, the pictorial title-page, the unique table of contents, reproducing in miniature and in colour the figures from each complete drawing in the book.

No one who had known the book in childhood seems to have forgotten its form or any of its pictures. And what a variety of activities and sheer nonsense appear ranging from the Five Little Sisters standing in a row in their big hats with their muffs, the supercilious Prince Finikin sipping tea with his mamma in the garden of his castle, the children just let out of school, the Proud Girl that struts about to the sheer loveliness of the Maying Party with their baskets of wildflowers and flowering branches. (pp. 10-11)

> *Anne Carroll Moore, in her* A Century of Kate
> Greenaway *(copyright Frederick Warne & Co. Ltd.
> London 1946), Warne, 1946, 15 p.*

Kate Greenaway loved a nice white blank. She followed Crane in designing the book as a whole, letting no department escape her attention: the contents pages of her first book *Under the Window* . . . are among the prettiest, each title being represented by a miniature edition of the picture in the text. Her pages are full of light, grace and variety. The pretty borders of coloured lines are never quite the same; sometimes she decorates the four corners of a page, sometimes makes a circular design round a centre of text. Those with a little block of text, a great expanse of white, and a delicate flowery border look as inviting as a box of chocolates wrapped up in smooth white paper and pretty ribbons. (p. 34)

> *Janet Adam Smith, "The Classic Picture-Books:
> 'Under the Window'," in her* Children's Illustrated
> Books *(reprinted by permission of the author), Collins, 1948, pp. 34-5.*

MOTHER GOOSE; OR, THE OLD NURSERY RHYMES (1881)

[The following is an extract from a letter by H. Stacy Marks to Kate Greenaway.]

In many respects you have improved, and the *drawing* is firmer and better. But let me have my fault-finding first, for 'I am nothing if not critical.' You have got rid of the spur-like shadows, but where, even in England, do you see such cabbagy

From Under the Window, *written and illustrated by Kate Greenaway.*

trees as on pages 5, 7, 29? You might find a better pattern even in the elm, which *is* cabbagy.

The action of the figure on page 40 is impossible coming downhill—how about the centre of gravity, madam? You know I am not conventional, but I am troubled to know why you don't make the hero of your story more conspicuous. Thus on page 47 Tom the Piper's son is the least prominent figure in the composition, and where are the boys?

Again—the Beggars coming to town are in the far distance, and there's only one dog! What I mean is, that these two don't tell their story, but I suppose you have some good reason for your treatment.

As instances of fearlessness, I admire the pluck which can place a face directly against a window with each pane made out as on page 12, and the arrangement of the stick in Jack Horner which coincides with his *head* and *both hands*, and as it (the stick) is not continued to the ground we can only suppose it to be resting on the boy's knees.

And now I have done being disagreeable. Despite its little faults, it is a charming book. Your backgrounds of old houses are delightful. The two most pictorial drawings are 'Polly, put the kettle on' and 'Cross-patch.' The latter is especially good and might be painted—the right fore-arm only should be a bit more foreshortened.

A last look gives me a last fault to find—the chins, especially in some of the boys, are still very pointed. (p. 104)

Stacy Marks, in a letter to Kate Greenaway on October 11, 1881, in Kate Greenaway *by M. H. Spielmann and G. S. Layard, G. P. Putnam's Sons, 1905, pp. 104-05.*

[*The folllowing is an extract from a letter by John Ruskin to Kate Greenaway.*]

You are fast becoming—I believe you are already, except only Edward B. Jones—the helpfullest in showing me that there are yet living souls on earth who can see beauty and peace and Goodwill among men—and rejoice in them.

You have sent me a little choir of such angels as are ready to sing, if we will listen, for Christ's being born—every day.

I trust you may long be spared to do such lovely things, and be an element of the best happiness in every English household that still has an English heart, as you are already in the simpler homes of Germany.

J. Ruskin, in a letter to Kate Greenaway on December 25, 1881, in Kate Greenaway *by M. H. Spielmann and G. S. Layard, G. P. Putnam's Sons, 1905, p. 105.*

[In] **Mother Goose** we meet a collection of children depicted so free from constraint (except in the matter of their Kate Greenaway clothes) that we may reflect that 'the children's century' has already begun. As so often happens, the sensitivity of the artist is preparing the way for the educationists.

Bettina Hürlimann, "Picture-Books in the Twentieth Century: 'Mother Goose'," in her Three Centuries of Children's Books in Europe, *edited and translated by Brian W. Alderson (© Oxford University Press 1967; reprinted by permission; originally published as* Europäische Kinderbücher in drei Jahrhunderten, *Atlantis Verlag, 1959), Oxford University Press, Oxford, 1967, p. 203.*

The benign brush of Kate Greenaway has recorded an idealised English countryside, but if all her hedges are neatly clipped and all her children clean (whether they are little cowherds or little gentlemen) it is still childhood that she sees. Tom steals his pig with youthful glee and Jack Sprat and his wife are obviously a brother and sister playing Mothers and Fathers. Choosing the shorter nursery rhymes, and those that give scope for her prettily visualised gardens and cottages, Kate Greenaway has given a period and yet an ageless look to them. This little book, with its neat and elegant format, would be a fine gift for any child.

Margery Fisher, "Two Old Favourites," in her Growing Point, *Vol. 2, No. 5, November, 1963, p. 228.* *

[Kate Greenaway's] **Mother Goose or Old Nursery Rhymes** is, after Caldecott, an awful letdown. It is the great ancestor of the sentimental Mother Goose books, and it is hard not to blame Kate Greenaway for founding the line. For all its delicacy of design and exquisite color, for all its refinement of taste, there is little of the real Mother Goose in this lovely but antiseptic affair. The rhymes have been flounced out in a wardrobe of quaint Greenaway frocks, and they look stiff and inanimate; Greenaway's surface charm does not mitigate the atmosphere of chilly Victorianism at the heart of her prim interpretation. See, for example, the two disdainful young ladies who seem to rush off in shocked distaste at the amusing verse they sup-

posedly illustrate. All they lack are scented hankies to disguise the bad odor of Goosey, Goosey, Gander.

If Greenaway fails, perhaps it is due most of all to her error in tangling with Mother Goose, a doomed relationship that glaringly exposed her shortcomings. When Greenaway illustrates Greenaway, as in her perfect, tiny almanacks, she ranks with the best. (p. 38)

Maurice Sendak, "Mother Goose's Garnishings," in Book Week—New York Herald Tribune *(© 1965, The Washington Post), October 31, 1965, pp. 5, 38-40.* *

[**Mother Goose: or, The Old Nursery Rhymes**] is a tiny book to fit small hands and pockets and to fill small hearts with delight. It contains forty-four of the brief rhymes, each with its own picture in the quaint Kate Greenaway style. The print is exceedingly small, but for nonreaders this does not matter. The illustrations are gently gay, the colors are soft, and the people exquisitely decorative.

Zena Sutherland, Dianne L. Monson, and May Hill Arbuthnot, "Books for the Very Young: 'Mother Goose: or, The Old Nursery Rhymes'," in their Children and Books *(copyright © 1981, 1977, 1972, 1964, 1957, 1947 by Scott, Foresman and Company; reprinted by permission), sixth edition, Scott, Foresman, 1981, p. 82.*

KATE GREENAWAY'S LANGUAGE OF FLOWERS (1884)

AUTHOR'S COMMENTARY

Mr. Ruskin thinks [**Language of Flowers** is] very bad. He says he's ashamed to show it to any one—I hope it won't affect you so fearfully. I am very disgusted myself—*only* I *don't* feel I *am* so much to blame as the printers, who have literally blotted every picture out.

Kate Greenaway, in a letter to Mrs. Arthur Severn on November 9, 1884, in Kate Greenaway *by M. H. Spielmann and G. S. Layard, G. P. Putnam's Sons, 1905, p. 128.*

The fact is that [**Language of Flowers**] was printed on unsuitable paper and much effect was thereby lost; still the illustrations, although not always very apposite, include some of the daintiest and most exquisitely drawn figures and flowers she ever produced. (p. 128)

M. H. Spielmann and G. S. Layard, in their Kate Greenaway, *Adam & Charles Black, 1905, 300 p.*

The Language of Flowers appeared first in 1884 when Kate Greenaway was at the height of her powers. . . . Nostalgic oldies, and some of the teenagers who, inexplicably, support the current vogue, will respond to these delicately faded charms and the equally faded sentiments. I doubt whether today's children will care much either for the careful matching of flower and quality or for the exquisitely static drawing of flowers and prettily draped maidens.

Marcus Crouch, in a review of "The Language of Flowers," in The Junior Bookshelf, *Vol. 41, No. 5, October, 1977, p. 277.*

From A Apple Pie, *written and illustrated by Kate Greenaway.*

A APPLE PIE   (1886)

[*The following are extracts from John Ruskin's letters to Greenaway from the biography by Spielmann and Layard.*]

I am considerably vexed about Apple Pie. I really think you ought seriously to consult me before determining on the lettering of thing so important—

The titles are simply bill-sticking of the vulgarest sort, over the drawings—nor is there one of those that has the least melodious charm as a colour design—while the feet—from merely shapeless are becoming literal paddles and flappers—and in the pretty—though ungrammatical—'Eat it' are real deformities.

All your faults are gaining on you every hour that you don't fight them. (p. 156)

. . . . .

I have no idea what state of mind you are in when you draw stockings down at the heel, and shoes with the right foot in the left and the left in the right—and legs lumpy at the shins—and shaky at the knees. And when, ever did you put red letters like the bills of a pantomime in any of *my* drawings? and why do it to the public? (p. 160)

> *John Ruskin, in extracts from two of his letters to Kate Greenaway on November 9, 1886 and Novem-*

ber 14, 1886, in Kate Greenaway *by M. H. Spielmann and G. S. Layard, G. P. Putnam's Sons, 1905, pp. 156, 160.*

[*A, Apple Pie*] is full of beautiful colour and all the charms of childish manners, joy, and gentleness as they are revealed to the artist. It takes the form of an alphabet of designs illustrating a world of youthful beauty and grace, from *A*, dancing round a monumental tart, to *Z*, where the white-clad maidens trudge off to bed, each bearing her portion of the repast. The grace, vivacity, homeliness, and Englishness of the pretty little figures in the whole series of designs more than justify the reputation of the artist.

> *A review of "A, Apple Pie," in* The Athenaeum, *No. 3085, December 11, 1886, p. 788.*

No list [of alphabet books] could leave out this exquisite posy of children, with its neatly evasive ending ('U V W X Y Z All had a large slice and went off to bed') and its procession of scenes, lovely, touching and cleverly chosen.

> *Margery Fisher, in a review of "A Apple Pie," in her* Growing Point, *Vol. 1, No. 4, October, 1962, p. 64.*

The prints have a curiously washed-out appearance compared with the bold colours we are used to today. Nonetheless, they

From Kate Greenaway's Book of Games, *written and illustrated by Kate Greenaway.*

give an indication of the debt that children's book illustration owes to Kate Greenaway. Although looking old-fashioned to our eyes, these are real children who fight, run, jump and mourn for a piece of pie.

> *Pat Garrett, in a review of "A Apple Pie," in* Children's Book Review *(© 1971 by Five Owls Press Ltd.; all rights reserved), Vol. 1, No. 2, April, 1971, p. vi.*

KATE GREENAWAY'S BOOK OF GAMES (1889)

Besides brief descriptions of sports for little children, boys as well as girls, **Kate Greenaway's Book of Games** . . . contains many charming designs by the renowned artist, most of which, in addition to the excellence of their colouring, as reproduced by the skilful hands and rare taste of Mr. E. Evans, are equal to the lady's best, while nearly all of them are as true, graceful, and fresh as Stothard's. Than this we could not say more. '**Puss in the Corner**' is very pretty and exquisitely naïve. It would be hard to over-praise similar qualities which are discoverable in the dainty figures of two little girls playing at '**Ball,**' or to admire too much the infantile joyfulness of '**Frog in the Middle**' and similar compositions, such as '**Mulberry Bush**' and '**Hunt the Slipper.**' Very pretty is '**See-Saw.**' (p. 748)

> *"Art for the Nursery," in* The Athenaeum, *No. 3240, November 30, 1889, pp. 748-49.**

This is a charming book, with its delicate colours . . . and scenes of little masters and misses in country houses and gardens. Each page is decorated, in addition, with flowers and boughs of fruit. The games, even where recognisable, have interesting variants from ours in procedure and name: 'I Spy', for instance, was 'Schoolmistress' to the Victorians. It is noticeable that games are not played for prizes, no-one "wins". They merely "change places" or "take turns". There is the same quaint appeal of more spacious days as in some Beatrix Potter books, well worth reproducing for a new generation of children, though sadly, nowadays, they no longer possess the verbal dexterity or skill in drawing required by many of the games.

> *Mary Hobbs, in a review of "Book of Games," in* The Junior Bookshelf, *Vol. 41, No. 1, February, 1977, p. 34.*

THE KATE GREENAWAY TREASURY: AN ANTHOLOGY OF THE ILLUSTRATIONS AND WRITINGS OF KATE GREENAWAY (1967)

The Kate Greenaway Treasury brings to everyone interested in children's book illustration a valuable insight into the life and work of a truly creative artist whose vision of childhood was translated into gay and tender picture books, enormously popular in her day and still represented in library collections. . . .

The Kate Greenaway Treasury is not an art book in the sense of *The Art of Beatrix Potter* (Warne) which uses direct reproduction of original drawings and publisher's plates printed on glossy paper, but it is well named a treasury and should be in the collections of many libraries, library schools, and private individuals along with *The Art of Beatrix Potter.*

> *Aileen O'Brien Murphy, "Greenaway Collection," in* School Library Journal, *an appendix to* Library Journal *(reprinted from the February, 1968 issue of* School Library Journal, *published by R. R. Bowker Co./ A Xerox Corporation; copyright © 1968), Vol. 14, No. 6, February, 1968, p. 57.*

In the last quarter of the Nineteenth Century, the English artist Kate Greenaway broke with tradition that insisted children's literature must moralize and instruct. She thought it should be diverting, whimsical, and happy, qualities that infused her rhymes, alphabet books, and songs. **The Kate Greenaway Treasury** has a lot of Kate Greenaway in it. . . . It is a treasure.

> *Robert Ostermann, "Tales of Jonah and Joan of Arc Survive Time's Test Quite Well," in* The National Observer *(reprinted by permission of* The National Observer; *© Dow Jones & Company, Inc. 1968; all rights reserved), March 18, 1968, p. 23.**

This definitive work of an original nineteenth-century artist who helped change the course of juvenile book illustration manages to encompass the spirit and freshness of her art, life, and philosophy. Black/white photographs, pen-and-ink drawings, and Greenaway's much-imitated watercolors decorate, illustrate, and enliven a rich collection.

> *Ruth M. Stein, in a review of "The Kate Greenaway Treasury," (copyright © 1979 by the National Council of Teachers of English; reprinted by permission of the publisher and the author), in* Language Arts, *Vol. 56, No. 6, September, 1979, p. 687.*

Hergé

1907-1983

(Pseudonym of Georges Rémi) Belgian author/illustrator of fiction and cartoonist.

Tintin, the perennially adolescent hero of over twenty comic books, is one of Europe's most recognized cartoon characters. Created in 1929 for a Belgian newspaper, the escapades of Tintin and his dog Milou (Snowy) were immediately successful, taking them from the ocean floor to the moon, from Egypt to America. As each adventure unfolds, Tintin meets with characters such as Captain Haddock, a bleary-eyed seaman; Dupon and Dupont (Thomson and Thompson), an identical pair of bumbling detectives; and Professor Tournesol (Calculus), an absent-minded scientist who is nearly deaf. Together they battle the various forces of evil which turn up in every situation in which the group finds itself. It is, however, Tintin's mental agility and Snowy's helpfulness that right the wrongs and bring the group to safety.

Critics comment that Tintin seems to represent both independence and innocence. His involvement in outlandish episodes of travel and intrigue without benefit of parental supervision complements his childish appearance—round face, plume of red hair, plus-fours, and oxfords. He is the medium between his adult companions and his loving and dependent pet. Several of the books are seen as representations of Hergé's moral and political convictions. He presents intolerance and prejudice negatively, and underscores his books with the theme of universal justice. No country visited by the band of travelers goes completely unscathed by Hergé's satire. Reviewers regard the dialog and plot of the *Tintin* adventures as exceptional. They also note that his use of color and authenticity of detail place the books far above the traditional comic in concept and design. Because Hergé believed that no item was too trivial to be overlooked, he and his school of cartoonists devoted themselves to careful research and study to guarantee the precise depiction of period automobiles and airplanes, landscapes, and modes of dress.

Tintin appeals to all ages: he is the hero of every child's dream, while Hergé's subtle wry humor and development of plot and secondary characters keep older readers intrigued with the series. Although Hergé wrote additional works for children, the *Tintin* books remain his most popular creations. Having been translated into over thirty languages as well as adapted to stage and screen, the *Tintin* series is indeed universal.

(See also *Something about the Author*, Vols. 13, 32 [obituary] and *Contemporary Authors*, Vols. 69-72.)

GENERAL COMMENTARY

A few months ago the French Government forced down the aircraft in which five Algerian nationalist leaders had taken seats. The serious daily *Le Monde* said that this move was rather like a *Tintin et Milou* operation. In one of the most sophisticated Parisian literary reviews, André Breton was recently described as the Professor Tournesol of Surrealism.

Suppose that in two or three hundred years people do research on French colonial problems or on modern verse and they come across such allusions, the Bibliothèque Nationale having mean-

while been destroyed. These students might conclude that Tintin, Milou, and Tournesol were important figures in a mythology produced by the French-speaking civilisation of the early twentieth century. They would not be far wrong. . . .

[The influence of the *Tintin et Milou* saga] is so widespread and unquestioned in all strata of the population that one interested in France should know what they are about: not only because children's books, good ones and bad ones, are an important part of culture, but because when grown-ups become passionately interested in them some kind of nostalgia is involved.

The spirit of this kind of publication changes considerably from one generation to another. Fifty years ago children were brought up on the positivism of Jules Verne and on the sadistic moralism of Madame de Ségur. Before the last war, the Pieds-Nickelés were favourites. . . . In the 'thirties and 'forties we were also interested in Bibi Fricotin, a young detective who was virtuous enough but rather remote, perhaps too much at ease with ordinary adults.

Tintin is different in many ways, and his companions are more friendly. Of course he is endowed, like the majority of these heroes, with reassuring metaphysical qualities. Like substance, he does not change. He is ageless; time does not exist as far as he is concerned. . . . [Like] all true gods he is eternal. . . .

He never worries about hunger, fatigue, or money matters. His physical endurance is formidable, rather like that which allows children to go on playing and running about long after their parents are exhausted. He will never need tranquillisers: that is partly why we need *him*. (p. 512)

Tintin does not have to eat or wash or go to bed at regular hours. Identification is therefore attractively easy. He is very good at disguising himself with any handy rug or towel. Yet he remains recognisable, except by those he is trying to deceive in the plot. There seems to be a tacit agreement with the younger readers that he is not to overdo his disguising. Those who can follow happenings only through the perfectly explicit pictures are not left out by his impersonations. Tintin and Hergé know that children enjoy being frightened and deceived all the more if they have asked for it as part of the 'let's pretend' ritual. As detective stories go, the Tintin albums are strings of suspicious pursuits. As in Guignol, the French Punch and Judy shows, the spectators are always given more than a fair share of omniscience.

To my mind Tintin himself is often perfectly dull and dully perfect, though he is not meant to be. He is as righteous as Corneille's characters but he is not faced with their dilemmas. A professional free-lance journalist, he is excellent at unravelling riddles. A piece of paper, a cigarette stub, a toy gun in a shop window get him ratiocinating in no time, and that brings him dangerously close to Holmes' most tiresome inductive and deductive brainstorms, only just redeemed by his good-natured naivety. . . . He does not have to aim at universality: he is universal. Natives address him in their own pidgin versions of French.

Fortunately, like a good existentialist subject, his real being proceeds from others. His ever-present associates provide him with a personality he would not have on his own, which indeed he did not have in the earlier albums when he was almost alone. He owes a great deal to his dog Milou, a white fox-terrier with a sense of humour, who is not taken in by his master and conducts his own asides without pomposity. A series of stage conventions relate Milou to Tintin and to us. Milou understands when he is spoken to. He talks freely. But although the readers know that he is speaking, the other human characters in the tale do not. Milou has problems. He is, say, forced to decide whether he is going to carry the long-sought-for sceptre of the King of Syldavia or a particularly succulent bone. He goes through a variety of emotions before doing his duty. That definitely makes him more human than his master. Milou is also a necessary link with the animal world. After being with him for a while, it seems perfectly natural to hear an elephant talking.

The most picturesque character, however, is beloved Captain Haddock. A retired black-bearded, whisky-loving sailor, he swears in 145 different ways, all original and proper. Almost on the same level is Professor Tournesol, a gentle, deaf, and very vague scientist who spends most of his time being kidnapped and burning the plans of his inventions when they could be used for evil purposes. Then come, in step, the two bowler-hatted twin policemen, Dupont and Dupond. They symbolise bureaucratic inefficiency and stupidity but not the cruelty with which the police are generally credited in Latin countries. They are the best and probably the only example of Bergson's theory of laughter produced by mechanical repetition and break-down.

Around Tintin, Milou, Captain Haddock, Professor Tournesol, and Dupont and Dupond swarm hundreds of richly described,

perfectly differentiated secondary humours, from the South American general turned music-hall artist, through Nestor the butler, to the singer Bianca Castafiore. Even purely episodical characters, a fireman, a passing motorist, a talkative salesman, have strong unforgettable individualities. General types always emerge from particular traits.

More remarkable still, although there are plenty of conventional villains, it is always assumed that they can change for the better. They have no fixed essence, like Tintin. During a trip to the moon, Wolff, Tournesol's traitor assistant, repents and sacrifices himself by jumping into space to provide more oxygen for the other passengers of the expedition. Heroism in *Tintin et Milou* is useful, not absurd or whimsical. This systematic effort at understanding human beings diffuses a light, refreshing optimism. Hergé is, in fact, a moralist who manages to put his convictions over without preaching tediously. His stories are worked out in such a way that solidarity, justice, tolerance, and democratic liberties, are shown to be positive features in the world; international power-politics, racial prejudice, and totalitarianism negative ones. His contribution to literature is one of the best antidotes against all the crude comics that are sold by the million in France every week to children and adults.

Hergé obviously tries to be fair, even if he does not always succeed when he sets his tales in a complex contemporary political setting. By now he has given almost everybody reason for displeasure with his satires: the Japanese when he sends Tintin to China during the war; the Russians and the Germans with his imaginary semi-nazi, semi-stalinist state of Borduria; the French with his comments on colonialism; the Americans with his parodies of gangsterism, the British with his descriptions of Middle-East affairs. Hergé panders to no one. In his own quiet way he is equally far from Jdanovism and McCarthyism—perhaps the correct place of a European humanist. On religious questions his sympathies seem to be with Catholicism, but all creeds are respected, up to superstition—surely an excellent lesson for children and adults who have a tendency to think that anything which is different is automatically absurd. (pp. 512-13)

The albums are packed with factual information. Within the ordinary framework of classical adventure they make the universe an exciting, happy hunting-ground, always understandable by reason. Nothing is ever impossible. It is well known that Hergé and his team aim at accuracy, precision, and more generally truth, in their drawings. Their poetical realism sometimes recalls if not the art at least the spirit of Flemish painters. They imply considerable regard for young readers and are opposed to the irrationalism of ordinary comics. No detail is considered trivial. Everything, from the uniform of a Swiss *gendarme* to a primitive statuette, is faithfully reproduced. Difficult new words and expressions are introduced intelligently. I have been able to watch my six-year-old son enriching his vocabulary through these books.

The narrative technique used in the presentation of the pictures—every album contains more than 600 of them—is truly cinematographic. Gags, close-ups, climaxes, suspense are liberally intertwined, and one does not drop a Tintin any more than one walks out in the middle of a good film. Hergé's craft can be assessed by comparing the early, uninteresting black-and-white vignettes with the latest coloured pictures, or by examining closely the expressions of his characters' eyes, and their hands so full of life and feeling.

A few years ago a group of Americans intended to bury a good many feet underground specimens of contemporary civilisation, in case most of us were wiped out and no trace left on the surface of the earth. If these well-meaning people are interested in some of the best aspects of European humanism, measure, equilibrium, a taste for justice, humour, generosity, and an un-maudlin liking for human beings, I feel they ought to put a couple of *Tintin et Milou* albums with the other vestiges. Whoever digs them up would find them enlightening: and useful, if we have to go through another Stone Age. (p. 513)

Olivier Todd, *"Tintin, Milou, and European Humanism"* (© British Broadcasting Corp. 1957; reprinted by permission of Olivier Todd), in The Listener, *Vol. LVIII, No. 1488, October 3, 1957, pp. 512-13.*

There are no other strip-cartoons in this class. Tintin enjoys the benefit of meticulous drawing, excellent colour-printing, tireless invention, enormous humour, a gallery of memorable characters . . . the catalogue might be extended indefinitely.

The Tintin stories are essentially French in style and point-of-view. Inevitably they lose a great deal in translation. The swift dialogue slows down. The verbal mannerisms of those absurd detectives Dupont and Dupond (now Thompson and Thomson) seem a little artificial. Above all Captain Haddock's language loses some of its splendour. (One can't translate "Mille de mille sabords de tonnerre de Brest"!) For all that, it is very good to have the stories in English. They are the perfect answer to the American comic, for, using the traditional comic technique, they offer something incomparably better in background, conception and performance. They have as much excitement as anyone could demand, but the fantastically improbable stories are matched with such personable characters and have so clearly realised a setting that the reader must accept their inner truth. Moreover, almost alone among "comics" they are comic. They are full of good jokes, simple and subtle, and the laughter is singularly free of malice. Good clean fun! [*The Crab with the Golden Claw* and *King Ottokar's Sceptre*] are two richly rewarding books. I hope that teachers and librarians will not be discouraged at a superficial glance, but will give them the support they so thoroughly deserve. (pp. 206-07)

A review of "The Crab with the Golden Claws" and "King Ottokar's Sceptre," in The Junior Bookshelf, *Vol. 22, No. 4, October, 1958, pp. 206-07.*

Unique in its kind, [the *Tintin* saga] is a really first-rate comic strip. . . .

Among all [the characters] it is only the disagreeable characters who are unconvincing. Those supposed masters of villainy, Müller, Dawson and Rastapopoulos, are quite the least interesting figures in the series; a strange infringement of the conventions normally governing comic strips, if not modern literature as a whole.

There have been strips with the same wealth of characterization before, notably the excellent Popeye. . . . What distinguishes the Tintin books at once from all others is the high quality of the drawing and printing, and the richness of the colour.

This was already so in the earlier volumes, and the parodies of medieval manuscripts in *King Ottokar's Sceptre* (last of the pre-Haddock era) are a real *tour de force.* Since the 1940s, however, there has been a steady improvement, both in subtlety of colour—so that one may now find four shades of green and

three shades of blue in a single small picture—and in detailed observation. The two highly topical volumes about a trip to the moon, for instance, and, perhaps even more, *L'Affaire Tournesol* that followed them, strike a brilliant balance between lively caricature and accurate, informative drawing. The characters remain as vivid and absurd as ever, but they now move among apparently convincing scientific apparatus; they travel in recognizable types of car or aeroplane, with correct markings; they miss a train at a real Swiss railway station, and are rescued after an explosion by a real Swiss fire brigade. (p. 697)

The basic layout is of four equal strips per page, with three or four pictures to a strip and liberal use of balloons, coloured stars and other standard strip conventions. But within this general pattern the medium is handled in a most resourceful and intelligent way. Size and proportion of the pictures will change: suddenly there may be a full-page drawing, or perhaps a sequence of tiny pictures tracing out some secondary incident. Often, by skilful cross-cutting, two threads of the story are kept going at once; thus in *Le Temple du Soleil* while Tintin and Haddock are waiting to be sacrificed by the Incas we are repeatedly taken back to the follies of the Dupondts the other side of the globe. Nor is the story told by the pictures alone: apparently documentary material such as photographs and Press cuttings is logically introduced, while the writing of documents and dialogue alike demands to be carefully read. . . . Even in

THE BATTLE OF ZILEHEROUM
After a XVth century miniature

From King Ottokar's Sceptre, *written and illustrated by Hergé. Art © by Casterman, Tournai. Text © by Methuen, London/Little, Brown, Boston.*

Haddock's vast repertoire of insults alone there is much to enrich the vocabulary. . . .

"Un point de départ très simple. Une affabulation très linéaire. Là-dessus, le plus possible de 'gags' et de 'suspenses'." Such is Hergé's recipe. Often this point of departure is purely and simply travel . . . though the actual story will be of smuggling (arms or dope), kidnapping, hidden treasure, espionage or the thwarting of some Master Criminal.

In all circumstances the suspense is unfailing, rising nearly always to a minor crisis or uncertainty at the foot of each left-hand page, then a point of real tension at that of the right. Most of the stories start with a bang on the very first page. . . . And there are several inspired sequences which would not disgrace one of the great film comedians: Haddock's description in *Le Secret de la Licorne,* for instance, of his ancestor's struggle with Red Rackham the pirate, where Haddock's gestures as he tells the story exactly match and are cross-cut with those of the Chevalier de la Hadoque slashing away at the ruffians boarding his ship; or the passage in its sequel *Le Trésor de Rackham le Rouge* where the uninhabited island at first seems to be full of mysterious voices hurling Haddock's favourite epithets—descendants of those parrots who picked them up from the Chevalier two hundred years before.

In the handling of his themes Hergé combines topicality with a markedly liberal point of view. Before the 1939 War, for instance, Borduria was aggressively trying to overthrow King Muskar XII of Syldavia by means of the Iron Guard leader Müsstler, while *Le Lotus Bleu* was bitterly anti-Japanese. Today Borduria is ruled by the melancholy looking Plekszy-Gladz . . . and has acquired a Soviet style of architecture and other less pleasant features of People's Democracy. Syldavia, on the other hand, having found valuable uranium deposits in the Zmylpathian mountains, has recruited an international team who, in conditions of the strictest and most American security, are developing the use of atomic energy for exclusively peaceful ends, starting by sending a missile full of instruments round the moon.

The slightly vague mistrust of Big Business in the pre-war volumes, where the Bohlwinkel Bank and General American Oil and Sir Basil Bazaroff of Vicking Arms were all blackly villainous, gives way to the much more convincing scandals of the Emirate of Wadesdah by the head of the Red Sea, where Abdallah's indulgent but unscrupulous father has to deal first with a conspiracy against the British-owned oil company *(Tintin au Pays de l'Or Noir),* then (in *Coke en Stock*) with a secretly armed pretender who reintroduces slave-dealing and is supported by the air line Arabair. Lynch law and Prohibition and the beastly members of the Occidental Private Club in Shanghai are succeeded as satirical targets by the astronomer in the alarming *L'Étoile Mystérieuse,* who observes "une ÉNORRRME boule de feu" in the sky and is truly disappointed when his estimate of the end of the world is proved wrong, or by those Bordurian military experts who watch the televised destruction by a secret weapon of "une gigantesque cité d'outre-Atlantique qu'il est inutile de nommer," and are then told that it was only a model. "Oui, je vois une vive déception se peindre sur vos visages . . . ", says the demonstrator, but, "Confiance, Messieurs!"—the real thing will come. With that we cut to the Szohôd Opera, where they are, of course, performing *Faust.*

This outlook has its limits. Tintin may treat Zorrino, the little Indian, and Tchang, the Chinese orphan, as friends and equals, but he seems to see the Negroes as something of a White Man's Burden, and all through *Tintin au Congo* they are presented as comic figures. This very early volume also involves the whole-sale slaughter of wild animals, mainly for fun: a pastime that is luckily given up later (apart from a brief massacre of alligators in *Le Temple du Soleil*) but is recalled by the slightly repulsive amusement sometimes got out of injuries to Milou's tail. Even Captain Haddock's drinking may perhaps be over-done for some tastes, though the consequences of his occasional bouts are always impressively disastrous.

But generally speaking the atmosphere of the whole saga is delightful, and any principles which a child picks up from these books are likely to be good. For Tintin is the nearest equivalent we have to that pillar of modern Soviet criticism, the "positive hero." He is brave, resourceful, kind, clever and invariably polite, always taking an adult's pretensions at their face value, however absurd. He is strong and serious, a born leader of men like Haddock, though Tournesol is too self-contained and the pair of policemen too idiotic for him to control. He has no girl friends and no parents. Like the positive hero he has no doubts or hesitations, or complicating emotions, or anything else that would make him interesting as a person. He is the antithesis of complex undesirables like Dr. Zhivago: a model pattern of behaviour, into which the reader can only project himself.

We cannot ignore this aspect of the stories, because the revoltingly low quality of most "comics" has led parents here to watch over their children's reading in very much the same way as the Soviet Communist party watches over that of its adults. Such an attitude does, however, conflict rather queerly with our exaggerated suspicion of moral content in adult fiction, or almost any other sphere of art, and both need to be reconciled in a more balanced point of view. The real strength of Tintin is not so much that he exemplifies a sensible moral outlook as that the books are works of high quality and even beauty, put together with obvious enjoyment and brimming over with intelligence and life. They share with many great works of art a tremendous generosity, throwing in all sorts of allusions, jokes and details which are quite gratuitous but gave pleasure to their creators and now lend even the simplest episode a wide range of reference which the reader can explore.

Even considered just as illustration this is among the most interesting work being done to-day, for at a time when the expensive illustrated book has become something of a farce Hergé and Casterman his printer are using a precise offset technique and clear colours to produce not perhaps Goyas and Hokusais but worthy successors to the *Images d'Épinal* or the *Münchner Bilderbogen* of Wilhelm Busch. Nothing could be a greater contrast to those well-intentioned but usually shoddy drawings which set out to retell the classics, or the lives of the saints, or other improving stories, in comic strip form. For the high standards of the Tintin series apply not only to their ethics but—and a long aesthetic argument could be based on this coincidence—to their visual and intellectual sides. Their merits are all-round.

In thus redeeming the comic strip Hergé has justified an interesting and immensely popular medium, made it vastly more entertaining and turned it into an art. In a sense this is what Cervantes did for the novel; except that the media which appeal to our visually conscious age call for organizing ability as well as individual talent, so that the pioneer of to-day has to combine both. It is not yet easy for us to grasp such developments, for the present industrial revolution in the arts goes dead against the individualist faith and specialist outlook of many critics, who often ignore the well-organized wood in favour of the isolated tree. But we can usually recognize technical mastery and brilliant teamwork even if we fail to analyse them, and it is good to see the collective skill normally thrown away on advertising now at last being devoted to a more creative end. Nothing could be more upsetting to those cultural historians who claim that our lack of any overriding Cause must necessarily drive the artist into a private corner and prevent any collective or semi-anonymous work. This does not mean that Hergé's team have as yet built a Gothic cathedral or compiled an Homeric epic; but they have to exploit a new and complex medium, and they have used it with a happy blend of inspiration and care. It is a cheerful omen for the future of the popular arts, for it shows that good planning can stimulate a touch of genius, first-rate work out-sell trash, and true originality give life to the most unpromising form. (p. 698)

> *"The Epic Strip: Tintin Crosses the Channel," in* The Times Literary Supplement *(© Times Newspapers Ltd. (London) 1958; reproduced from* The Times Literary Supplement *by permission), No. 2962, December 5, 1958, pp. 697-98.*

[*The Secret of the Unicorn* and *Red Rackham's Treasure*] in fact record one single story, of the quest for the treasure which Captain Haddock's ancestor, Sir Francis Haddock, stole from the pirate Red Rackham. It is a long story to follow in strip-cartoon style, and this suggests both the strength and the weakness of Hergé's method. He is a consistent artist who picks up and develops hints made originally a hundred or more drawings back. Excellent if his readers have a good enough memory to follow him.

Tintin is not merely the aristocrat among strip-cartoons; it is a strip-cartoon for egg-heads. It is unlikely to do much for the reluctant reader, but to the connoisseur of fun, nonsense and good narrative it will give a great deal of pleasure. There is much good stuff in these two volumes: Aristides Silk, a charming old gentleman who collects other people's wallets, the first appearance of the memorable Professor Calculus, some lovely underwater scenes, a treasure island inhabited by swearing parrots . . . , and many others. It is all very exciting and funny, often very well drawn and with excellent colour. I hope the publishers will not be discouraged that the public (as opposed to the critical) response is slow. *Tintin* is an acquired taste.

> *A review of "The Secret of the Unicorn" and "Red Rackham's Treasure," in* The Junior Bookshelf, Vol. 23, No. 3, July, 1959, p. 134.

Tintin, Haddock and Calculus in Peru, Incas and their mysterious rites, treasure, mountain passes and recurring danger. These two linked adventures [*The Seven Crystal Balls* and *Prisoners of the Sun*] will please all Hergé's admirers. I think many children will get most fun from Haddock's feud with a llama (who has the last word) and Snowy's involvements with a Siamese cat and a suit of armour—the humorous detail is superb.

> *Margery Fisher, in a review of "The Seven Crystal Balls" and "Prisoners of the Sun," in her* Growing Point, Vol. 2, No. 7, January, 1964, p. 269.

In 1938 the American strips were banned from Italy. By a phenomenon that was to be repeated in France, far from encouraging home production this event caused it to degenerate, and mediocre imitations of the major American series burgeoned everywhere.

From The Seven Crystal Balls, *written and illustrated by Hergé. Art © by Casterman, Tournai. Text © by Methuen, London/Little, Brown, Boston.*

This period witnessed the birth, in Belgium, of what was to become the star performer of the European comic strip: **"Tintin,"** . . . the success of which was to surpass that of "Zig et Puce," but not until after the war. . . . While the characters were, and always will be, caricatures (in the beginning Tintin bore a particularly strong resemblance to Bécassine), the settings presented an increasingly detailed realism, and the balloons—the weak point of Saint-Ogan, who inserted them anywhere—are clear and rectangular. The general appearance of the strip is carefully finished, orderly, and less whimsical and unrestrained than the style of Saint-Ogan. Whereas the latter was satisfied with combinations of black-white-red or red-brown-blue, Hergé played skillfully with colors, sometimes using cool colors for beautiful night effects, sometimes warm colors in which a scale of browns and beiges predominates. (p. 79)

[It] was Hergé who dominated this era and that of the fifties. Skillfulness of narrative, integrity of execution—in drawing, background information, and finesse of color—and an impeccable and unobtrusive technique, all assured **"Tintin"** of international success. . . . (p. 101)

[A] self-confident **"Tintin"** has been pursuing its career on a steady level of solid craftsmanship. A trip to the moon, a book of exegesis, and a film adaptation mark the high points of its career. That it has been less talked of in recent years is due solely to a certain moderation in self-promotion, for which we may be grateful to Hergé. . . .

Some people may find it cause for regret that Hergé has not concentrated on being a storyteller for adults, in the manner of the American masters. His chief talent, however, is that he has been able to create an *oeuvre* in which every age group can delight. (p. 127)

> *Pierre Couperie, Maurice C. Horn & others, in their* A History of the Comic Strip, *translated by Eileen B. Hennesy (copyright © 1968, by Crown Publishers, Inc.; used by permission of Crown Publishers, Inc.; originally published as* Bande Dessinee et Figuration Narrative, *S.E.R.G., 1967), Crown, 1967, 256 p.**

It is quite possible that [the comics], which may be regarded as a smaller and apparently less flamboyant brother of the cinema, will penetrate the Continent of Europe as it has done America. It behoves us, therefore, in my opinion, to be on our guard. In this context it is perhaps worth mentioning the use to which Hergé has put comic-strip techniques in his interminable **Tintin** stories. . . . So far as they deploy ideas and situations which are original and which truly catch-up the reader's attention they are worth careful investigation, but their impact fails all to rapidly from the sheer quantity of the production. (pp. 170-71)

> *Bettina Hürlimann, "Wham! Sok! Thinks!" in her* Three Centuries of Children's Books in Europe, *edited and translated by Brian W. Alderson (© Oxford University Press 1967; reprinted by permission; originally published as* Europäische Kinderbücher in drei Jahrhunderten, *Atlantis Verlag, 1959), Oxford University Press, Oxford, 1967, pp. 160-72.**

Tintin is fast becoming an "in" figure: one of the clan of children's heroes cerebralized by students and eggheads into high-flown figures of intellectual poppery. . . . [Three] generations of children have appreciated the one important thing about Tintin: he is entertaining. . . .

As early as 1929 Tintin was dumped on his first mission—to Soviet Russia. In 1968, the "Sunday Times" hymned, "He's right up there with the Cohn-Bendits, on trial with the ineffable Haddock"—a remark I take exception to, on Tintin's behalf. He is more amusing, more alive, more intelligent than that rampaging student of the temporary revolt. And, far from being the revolutionary the "Sunday Times" libelled him, Tintin is an upholder of all things traditional, established, and legal. Imposters he can't abide, while Haddock has names for them quite as uninhibited as any that get past watchful children's editors.

Like Biggles and Bond, Tintin has a taste for foreign places; he shares too their penchant for exotic, eccentric opponents, weapons, and a belief in his own righteousness. He acts first and philosophizes (if at all) afterwards. Fair-dealing, a quick brain, faithfulness to his happy band of pals are the limits of Tintin's preoccupations. The rest is action. Where he outstrips, even transcends, the Bond-Biggles syndrome is in the humour that underlies all the stories, that bursts out in every incident through slapstick pictures, verbal gags, and best of all, the great big sent-up situations.

[**"The Adventures of Tintin: Flight 714"**] continues the adventures in the formula as before. Who cares? As comic strip, it knocks holes in its rivals: the draughtsmanship is high in standard, simple in conception, never over-stated. The colouring is accurately set, muted, tasteful, and each scene has its predominant basic colour that suggests time, place and at-

mosphere, while relieving the eye from the monotony that so mars other comic strips. In few others is the language in the balloons so essential to the story. The language has the merit, too, of being consistent for each character. Professor Calculus could never be mistaken for Haddock, nor Haddock for Tintin, and none of them for the Thomson twins.

In the classroom and library **"Tintin"** is invaluable. Immediately attractive to children (one of the few books truly attractive to "008-0015"), it has enormous educational advantages. Teachers get almost mindlessly furious about comics. Here is one they can like, and use—not too dogmatically, please—to compare with the usual product, and do so from the strength of personal enthusiasm and genuine enjoyment. The very fact that each story is 64 pages long requires a modicum of sustained reading and encourages it. Too, the words in the balloons are as vital as the pictures to an appreciation of the story, the basis of which is always humour rather than escapist violence or "adventure". And making the French and English versions available together does more for the teaching of French than most language-teaching gimmicks.

This being said, let's not kill Tintin stone dead by making him a classroom tool. Let's leave him around where children are, to be what he is meant to be: an entertainer. We're short of them in children's books, those that can do the job with compelling plots, clear-cut characters and—this above all—*fun*. Vive le Tintin!

> *Aidan Chambers, in a review of "The Adventures of Tintin: Flight 714," in* Children's Book News *(copyright © 1969 by Baker Book Services Ltd.), Vol. 4, No. 1, January-February, 1969, p. 9.*

[**Tintin** books] have an irresistible fascination for all children, immigrants included. It is very tempting to use them as a sedative which instantly silences an unruly class of any nationality. But they do not, in my experience, lead on to any other reading. They become an addiction and once having allowed a class to have them there is trouble if they are not given out next week and every week. (p. 42)

> *Cecilia Gordon, "The Immigrant Child in the School Library," in* Children's Book Review *(© 1971 by Five Owls Press Ltd.; all rights reserved), Vol. 1, No. 2, April, 1971, pp. 40-2.**

One of the continuing questions in a democracy is whether or not high artistic quality can ever be combined with genuine mass popularity. Tocqueville's answer more than a century ago was negative; and, "Pop Culture" notwithstanding, there seems little reason to question the fundamental soundness of his judgement now, when the vastly accelerated commercialization of American culture seems in fact to have made him more right than ever. If the outlook for a truly popular yet truly humanizing art in America is therefore rather gloomy in general, the outlook from the point of view of those who are interested in children's literature may be gloomier still in particular. Trapped in an imposed passivity our children constitute the largest and most uniform single audience in the country. It has become vitally important therefore, to try to find some model for children's literature that would hold out the possibility of surmounting the dilemma of art in a democracy. There may be such a model for us in Belgium.

Three years ago the world sales of a series of children's books published in nine languages passed beyond the twenty-five million mark. The author of this series, an anglophile Belgian artist in his sixties, has been called a genius; his work has . . . ample testimony to its impact within the English-speaking world. And yet this series is virtually unknown and virtually unobtainable in the United States. (p. 93)

The fact that Tintin's adventures are narrated through strip cartoons in color is probably why they have had no success in the United States. The American parents who buy books for their children are likely to be the same parents who find the very idea of "color comic books" appalling, though they probably allow their children to watch the morally dubious and aesthetically vulgar animations on American television until their eyes pop out. The Golden Press, which tried unsuccessfully to introduce the Tintin series several years ago, apparently has no further plans for a second try. Certainly the failure of the series in the U.S. is a pity. As an anonymous front-page reviewer for *The Times Literary Supplement* remarked, "The real strength of Tintin is not so much that he exemplifies a sensible moral outlook as that the books are works of high quality and even beauty, put together with obvious enjoyment and brimming over with intelligence and life." [see excerpt above] They are clearly worthy of serious critical consideration not merely as an international phenomenon but also as works of art.

The creator of Tintin has described the plot line of his adventures as "linear," episodic, adorned with as many *gags* (in, of course, the French sense) and as much suspense as possible. To take one example: *The Red Sea Sharks*, like all of Tintin's adventures, runs to precisely sixty-four pages including the title page. This length, one fascicle, is dictated by the economics of publishing but has the effect of imposing an almost Joycean "closed field," restricting the scope of each adventure to roughly predetermined limits. Each page is slightly larger than a sheet of typing paper, though considerably heavier, and usually holds four strips of three color frames. The last frame on each page provides either a gag or a point of suspension to the onward movement of the story, while the first frame on each page provides what we might call relief. A succession of pages thus creates a kind of emotional oscillation, rather as if one were riding an aesthetic roller coaster. And one suspects that it is in large part this roller-coaster effect that endears the adventures to children. The plot line meanwhile serves merely to provide opportunities for this effect and to spread it over the largest possible background of land- and seascape, in Europe, Africa, Asia, or the Americas.

The Red Sea Sharks begins with Tintin and Captain Haddock encountering an old acquaintance, who reappears thereafter in only one frame. This encounter leads them on, however, into investigating the machinations of an international armaments combine apparently controlled by a mysterious American named Dawson. From Europe their investigation takes them next to a fictitious country in the Middle East, where another old acquaintance has just been overthrown as ruler with weapons supplied by the combine. They are nearly killed several times, but eventually find themselves on a raft in the middle of the Red Sea, having in the meantime picked up an airplane pilot who has deserted from the criminals. By chance they meet a pleasure-cruising yacht, which turns out to be owned by one Rastapopoulos, the real master mind behind the combine. Rastapopoulos rescues and entertains them, then hands them over unsuspecting to the crew of the *Ramona*, another ship in the combine's fleet who plan to kill Tintin, Captain Haddock, and the pilot but instead simply abandon them when the *Ramona* catches fire. Finally, now in control of the burning ship, the

castaways put out the fire, release a cargo of intended slaves, and are attacked by one of the combine's submarines, only to be rescued at the last moment by the U.S. Navy. Meanwhile the ingenious Rastapopoulos escapes again to fight another day.

A plot like this one finds its best analogy in the plot of a good opera, the function of which is to provide what Gian-Carlo Menotti has called meditative moments, occasions for the effective singing of arias. And like the plot of a good many operas, it has minor moral significance. The real moral vision of the Tintin series resides instead almost wholly in the self-respecting character of Tintin himself and in the moral judgments the reader is invited to make, from Tintin's point of view, upon each of the characters he meets. We encounter, not only the bad and the good among these characters but also the bumbling, the stupid, the greedy, the naive, the misled, the silly, the innocent—a wide variety of human types.

The striking visual beauty of the Tintin books can be exemplified by a page from another adventure, *The Crab with the Golden Claws*. On page twelve Tintin and Captain Haddock, in trouble at sea again, float on an overturned life boat, while a small airplane makes strafing runs at them. Suddenly the next page is devoted to a single picture, rather than to the usual four strips of small frames: from a vantage point deliberately placed level with the rolling surface of the sea, as if to make one share the sensation of a castaway, the reader sees the plane about to sweep almost directly over his own head, while in the background Tintin and Captain Haddock sit on their overturned boat, looking dismayed. The sky is pastel blue, the sea is green with white flecks and crests, the plane is ochre against the sky where the sun strikes its edges, shadowy beneath, and its engine housing is actually rounded (incredibly enough in an age of publishing short-cuts) by subtle gradations of color from pearl to dark gray. The dramatic composition of this picture is faultlessly effective and the extra-ordinary care devoted to printing the color values is worthy of an art book. One suspects, in fact, that though the picture works very well to enhance the drama of the story, it represents really an act of creative gusto on the part of the author and his staff.

Such meticulousness and gusto constitute the endearing aesthetic overplus of the Tintin books, an overplus that admirers of Tintin delight to discover exemplified in small features: the wonderful imitations of medieval manuscripts and the clever use of the Cyrillic alphabet in *The Scepter of King Ottokar;* the attempt to spell out "Tintin" and "Haddock" in Arabic on a poster in the background of one frame in *The Red Sea Sharks;* the brilliant green cloth and the decorative nails in the background of another full-page picture in *The Crab with the Golden Claws;* the subtle distinctions in drawing made between the shapes of the Andes and the Himalayas; the absolutely authentic motor cars that roar and put-put through all the adventures; the mere arrangement of frames by size and colors upon a page.

One always returns, however, to the character of Tintin as the greatest source of the books' appeal. To a child Tintin (who cannot be more than fourteen) must naturally stand for what he himself would like to be. One notices for example that Tintin is absolutely and almost mysteriously autonomous. He lives alone in his own simple flat. There is no hint of anything parental in his relationship with Captain Haddock, who in fact seems much more childish than Tintin. Furthermore there is only one woman of any importance in all the Tintin adventures, Bianca Castafiore, an aging opera-singer who, though plenteously bosomed, offers not the remotest suggestion of a mother surrogate. In a couple of instances Tintin establishes friendly

From The Crab with the Golden Claws, *written and illustrated by Hergé. Art © by Casterman, Tournai. Text © by Methuen, London/Little, Brown, Boston.*

relations with other boys, a Peruvian and a Chinese, but one notices that they are in many ways essentially reflections of Tintin himself. Tintin seems to realize, in other words, the wish for total and perfect self-sufficiency.

Tintin is always treated by adults as an adult, whether they wish to do him harm or good. He is taken seriously and without any condescension by everyone he meets. Though he is often threatened and sometimes feels ridiculous, he is never humiliated and never reduced in his independence. Though the world he lives in is an adult world, he understands and navigates within it much better than any of his elders. Identifying himself with Tintin, the young reader must therefore feel the unusual satisfaction of finding that here the situations that prevail within his prolonged babyhood are not merely altered but reversed, though it should also be pointed out that Tintin is never in the position of becoming anything like a quasiparental tyrant. The independence of others is respected just as much as his own, even though Tintin stands over all, made superior to them not merely by his greater resourcefulness and energy for good but also by his knowledge and intelligence. He is after all, we are continually reminded, just a boy, smaller and weaker physically than any of his foes, and therefore he must depend on brains instead of brawn.

One would guess, in fact, that it is specifically the disparity of Tintin's physical smallness and mental largeness in relation to the adult world that accounts in considerable part for his appeal to children: he satisfies them as a simultaneous reflection of both childhood reality and childhood dream, which the author keeps always securely balanced against each other, allowing neither reflected element to predominate. Balance is the secret of Tintin's morality, a balance that can be seen as resting upon [his creative intelligence]. . . . (pp. 94-6)

The world of Tintin offers satisfactions to the most sophisticated adult. A world utterly without the imposed, philosophically naive design of absolute cause and effect, it is subjected to no general thematic conceptualization and therefore remains very real as well as morally humanistic. The headlong series of loosely related incidents that I have summarized from *The Red Sea Sharks,* for example, is adorned not only with *gags* (again, in the French sense) but with accidents and reminiscences, (as, I take it, is life itself), which the linear narrative and oscillating aesthetic effects make no attempt to define for us as a "lesson for a child." The world of Tintin thus reaches out of the epistemological innocence of children to touch something highly adult and highly sophisticated in the best sense of those words. In contrast with this world, the worlds offered to us by the novels that grown-ups customarily read have continued to be made up for a hundred years out of essentially nineteenth-century ideal solipsistic structures masquerading as reality. Only in the last two or three decades has the novel been able consciously to break out of its nineteenth-century epistemological molds and get back to something like the episodic vigor and the artistic freshness of, say, a Henry Fielding. It has done so, sometimes at the expense, unfortunately, of its own traditional humanism, by returning deliberately to the great literary tradition that Fielding saw his work as belonging to, and to which the Tintin books quite equally belong. This is the tradition not of the "story" but of the "tale." It includes the *Odyssey,* the *Satyricon,* the *Golden Ass, A Thousand and One Nights, Tom Jones, Moby Dick,* the *Arthur Gordon Pym of Poe,* as well as the tales of Isak Dinesen. It would be pleasant to think that American children could be as easily introduced as their European cousins are to this humanizing tradition, as well as to a little realism, a little "sensible morality," and a great deal of visual beauty. (pp. 96-7)

> *John Rodenbeck, "The Tin-Tin Series: Children's Literature and Popular Appeal," in* Children's Literature: Annual of The Modern Language Association Seminar on Children's Literature and The Children's Literature Association, *Vol. 1, edited by Francelia Butler (© 1972 by Francelia Butler; reprinted by permission of Francelia Butler), Temple University Press, 1972, pp. 93-7.*

Tin Tin's are swift, inventive adventure tales [told] . . . with a concise, economical cartoon style and a sprightly, careful use of color. . . .

The humorous tone, plus the caricature drawing style, should help reassure parents of what every youthful reader knows, but grownups tend to forget—that adventure tales (be they in literature, on film, in comics or on TV) are fine hokum, usually frivolous as expressions of the outer "real" world, but are very important as probing expressions of what goes on deep inside the psyche.

The action, the violence, the gunplay, are to be taken symbolically, as is the violence in all myth.

Of course, there is violence and crime in *Tin Tin:* Indeed, **"The Crab with the Golden Claws"** is about opium smuggling. Imagine an American kids' comic on that subject . . . !

But, for that matter, imagine an American comic given good quality paper, press and color work.

And yet, the comic strip is an American invention—if you will, an American art form. And Tin Tin also owes obvious specific debts to Roy Crane's "Wash Tubbs," Frank King's Skeezix, and to Harold Grey's "Little Orphan Annie."

> *Martin Williams, "Continental Comics," in* Book World—The Washington Post *(© 1974, The Washington Post), May 19, 1974, p. 4.*

To me, the most striking thing about the Tintin books is their art work, reproduced in meticulous offset reminiscent of the original Babar books. People and animals are drawn very simply, flatly, little more than a firm outline. (The camels in **"The Crab With the Golden Claws"** are gloriously camelly; I wonder what many readers will make of the caricatures of the Arabs in the same adventure.) Machines—especially airplanes and ships—are done with the precise detail and loving care of the German Duden Pictorial Encyclopedia. Suddenly, there will be a set piece—a full-page pastiche of a Persian miniature, a 17th-century sea battle, a parrot-filled jungle, a Transylvanian town, an aerial panorama, an under-seascape. The shifts are dramatically and esthetically effective, and, I think, unique.

I can't be as enthusiastic about the plots or the humor. They're both pretty simple-minded. The humor is largely based on a supporting cast of regulars. . . . The plots run to stolen crown jewels, smuggled opium and pirate treasure. Violence, happily, is minimal: A presumably dying pirate makes a comic face, and an informer shot on Tintin's doorstep recovers in the hospital.

Hergé (whose real name is Georges Remi; reverse the initials and give them a Gallic pronunciation) originated the strip as a weekly supplement for a Catholic party newspaper in Brussels, and it appears to have been solidly right-wing at first. By now, it's completely apolitical. Which is O.K. But with its growing success, Hergé has expanded into an assembly-line approach—hardly Disney-size, but with a dozen or so assistants back in the studio, and spin-offs like TV shows and merchandising tie-ins, and the cannibalizing of old episodes. Hergé insists that he still writes everything himself and does all the basic character drawings, but there's an air of blandness about the whole thing. Fine for a child who's going to read comics anyhow: harmless at worst, tasteful at best. For the under-25's-at-heart: of interest as an exercise in something better than camp. For me, not a patch on "Krazy Kat" or "Barnaby" or "Pogo" or "B.C."

> *Sherwin D. Smith, in a review of "The Adventures of Tintin," in* The New York Times Book Review *(© 1974 by The New York Times Company; reprinted by permission), August 11, 1974, p. 8.*

Although the [texts of **The Crab with the Golden Claws, King Ottokar's Sceptre, Red Rackham's Treasure,** and **The Secret of the Unicorn** are] dotted with Britishisms that may stump young readers, the humor is on the Three Stooges level with pratfalls, inebriated follies, doggish pranks, and good-humored derring-do. The lively cartoon strip stories are well drawn in crisp colors and will appeal to the same crowd who enjoys the adventures of Dr. Dolittle.

> *Estelle Jussim, in a review of "The Crab with the Golden Claws," "King Ottokar's Sceptre," "Red Rackham's Treasure," and "The Secret of the Unicorn," in* School Library Journal, *an appendix to*

Library Journal *(reprinted from the September, 1974 issue of* School Library Journal, *published by R. R. Bowker Co./A Xerox Corporation; copyright © 1974), Vol. 21, No. 1, September, 1974, p. 83.*

Tintin is to French popular culture what Little Orphan Annie is to that of the U.S. . . . With the appearance of four volumes—the texts are British rather than American English translations—Tintin should rapidly develop a following in this country. In **King Ottokar's sceptre,** a colorful volume, Tintin with his loyal dog, Snowy, and his bumbling detective friends, Thomson and Thompson, all become entwined in a secret plot to steal the vital royal sceptre of the Balkan kingdom of Syldavia. . . . It is a delightful and suspenseful story; the color and artwork are engaging; and the blend of humor and drama is impressive. Like the other books in the series, this volume contains about 700 pictures and about 8,000 words of intelligent text. **The crab with the golden claws** is another exciting tale. Dressed in a trench coat and knickers, Tintin here uncovers a complex opium-smuggling operation which takes him from his European home to the Moroccan desert. With him in this adventure, along with Snowy and Thomson and Thompson, is his friend Captain Haddock. . . . The story of this group's hardships in bringing the smugglers to justice is excitingly related through the colorful art, humor, and plot line. Pirates and treasure and exciting chases and narrow escapes are the principal ingredients of **The secret of the unicorn.** . . . It is an exciting story with many unexpected twists. As usual, the art is engaging and elaborate in detail, and the text is urbane and literate. . . . [In **Red Rackham's treasure**], Tintin and his friends—including a new character, the hard-of-hearing inventor Professor Cuthbert Calculus—are off to an uncharted island to find . . . [buried booty]. After several adventures the treasure is finally discovered in a most unexpected place. Of these four Tintin volumes this is the only disappointment. There are several extraneous diversions in the story, and the treasure-hunt exploits are predictable. Nevertheless, the art is again impressive, and the personalities of the familiar characters are entertaining. The sophistication of its text and story makes **"The adventures of Tintin"** series most suitable for older children and adults who seek diverting entertainment. These stories might also be suitable for public, high school, and college libraries eager to possess examples of French, indeed European, popular culture.

> *A review of "The Crab with the Golden Claws," "King Ottokar's Sceptre," "Red Rackham's Treasure," and "The Secret of the Unicorn," in* Choice *(copyright © 1974 by American Library Association), Vol. 11, No. 8, October, 1974, p. 118.**

The comic strip in Belgium, just as in any other country, is an image of daily life. Anyone trying to understand daily life in Belgium would do well to bear in mind that it is a small, bilingual country, and that the two languages have radically different origins. Flemish is a Germanic language, French is Romance. The differences are not only linguistic, but also ethnic: one type is strong and sanguine, while the other has a smaller body frame but greater dignity. Brussels is where the twain meet in the most confused manner, and the large influx of foreign immigrants since the end of World War Two currently gives rise to situations like the one in the food store with a Greek owner; a Flemish customer with broken French fails to communicate with the Greek whose own vocabulary is limited, so an African woman has to step in and muster up a dozen words of Flemish to help patch things up. Against this background the Belgian comic strip artist is particularly fond of intricate linguistic performances and elaborate situation plots. Imagery plays a major role in Belgian jokes, as my example showed. There, we had a candid Babel where funny faces and mimicry compensated for the imperfection of it all. Too perfect diction is often resented, if you speak too well, then you should look somewhat feeble, or naive, or incompetent, so that no-one will take offence.

Drawn by Hergé, the Belgian comic strip hero Tintin is the best known outside his own country. He has a bosom friend, Captain Haddock, the insult specialist, who whenever he loses his temper, lets fly a volley of oaths made up of snatches of phrases in which oriental market exoticism mingles with history and caboose vocabulary. The resulting effect is that of an endless verbal bric-a-brac. The two police detectives Dupond and Dupont are past masters at the art of spoonerism and redundancy. Repeating each other's words, which they echo back at their speaker like parrots, they use orotund and empty sentences, conveying the clear impression that any attempt at decorous diction is automatically branded as parrot-like. For Belgians readily acknowledge their crossbred culture and look down upon any gravitation toward linguistic accomplishment. Another personage of Hergé's cast is Tournesol, the absent-minded, stone-deaf but highly sociable professor; every conversation with him is one long misunderstanding. Castafiore also may be ranked among the major characters: she is a monstrous prima-donna who sings so loudly that she scares her listeners away with her ear-shattering voice. (p. 144)

Belgian heroes are small. Take Tintin: he wears his hair in a topknot like a baby, has no beard, is clad in plus-fours like a kid in the 1930s. He is the size of an adolescent, but all his mental attitudes are those of a very gifted boy of twelve. In fact, he has none of the problems of adolescence: he neither drinks nor smokes, and has no thoughts for women. There is no room for women in his adventures, apart from Castafiore, the whirlwind prima donna, who has very little sex appeal. Psychologists consider that the adult age of childhood is twelve. That is about as far as Tintin has gone: he is a good, intelligent lad, capable of courage, and endowed with a deductive mind. Victory awaits him at the end of every adventure, with practically no help from anyone. His more colourful allies, hovering around him, are rather in his way and only provide a picturesque setting. In fact, Tintin's most helpful friend is his dog, Milou. . . . The comic strip hero's chief preoccupations are how to get out of a fix, how to defend himself against gangs, how to evade the rules of society or simply to escape from the drudgery of seriousness. Tintin is a case in point; he fights without hatred or violence. He aims to put things straight and at the same time land on his feet. His only weak point, if he has one, is to underestimate others. Hergé's primitive people are consistently presented as very dumb and very childish. Put in two lines, Hergé's equation would go something like this: everybody is childlike, except Tintin, who alone looks it. (pp. 144-45)

Micheline van Lier, "David and Goliath," in Studio International, *Vol. 188, No. 970, October, 1974, pp. 144-45.*

[Tintin, Captain Haddock, and Snowy] grow on the reader, who is soon lost in comic-strip chronicles marked by great wit, suspense and true humor rising both from character and from a remarkably sophisticated view of the world. . . . [Hergé] . . . fills his small frames with marvelous detail. If he draws a 1955 Peugeot 403 or the old Geneva Airport, everything is

exactly right. Occasionally he breaks out into a full-page picture recreating such things as a complete Persian miniature version of a 15th century battle with the Turks, or the havoc wreaked by an Alfa Romeo slaloming through a European square on market day.

Much is lost in translation. Even so, these books amply prove that 50 million Frenchmen can't be wrong. (pp. 72-3)

A review of "The Adventures of Tintin," "The Secret of the Unicorn," "Red Rackham's Treasure," "The Crab with the Golden Claws," and "King Ottokar's Sceptre," in Time *(copyright 1974 Time Inc.; all rights reserved; reprinted by permission from* Time), *Vol. 104, No. 26, December 23, 1974, pp. 72-3.*

Alas! These new adventures of Tintin [**The Black Island, Cigars of the Pharaoh, Flight 714,** and **Tintin in Tibet**] are seriously disappointing. While earlier stories—**The Crab with the Golden Claws, King Ottokar's Sceptre, The Secret of the Unicorn, Red Rackham's Treasure** . . .—retained a sense of spluttering fun, these are heavy-handed and close to television fare. Tintin is no longer a boy reporter but a miniature Mannix, Cannon, and FBI agent. Women hardly ever enter the pages of these "boy adventures," but there's lots of heroin smuggling, spying, machine guns, and endless violence perpetrated in the name of the "good guys." **Tintin in Tibet,** originally published in England in 1962, is the only one which has the old Hergé vitality.

A review of "The Black Island," "Cigars of the Pharaoh," "Flight 714," and "Tintin in Tibet," in School Library Journal *(reprinted from the September, 1975 issue of* School Library Journal, *published by R. R. Bowker Co. / A Xerox Corporation; copyright © 1975), Vol. 22, No. 1, September, 1975, p. 104.*

There is one comic series . . . that stands out markedly from the general mediocrity of the genre. It is called **The Adventures of Tin-Tin**. . . . While no claims can (or should) be made for the series as serious literature, **The Adventures of Tin-Tin** uniquely demonstrates that comic book comedy need not be incompatible with the tastes of those who take literature seriously. (p. 54)

What probably appeals most to adult readers is the quality of the drawings, which, by comic book standards, are exquisite. Herge's ambition in his youth was to become a fine artist. . . . His artistic skill . . . is evident in nearly every frame of the books. Each scene is rendered in almost photographic detail— individual plant species can be identified, for example, in jungle settings—which is augmented by an exceptionally subtle handling of color. (p. 55)

Apropos comedy, our concern here, **Tin-Tin** is likewise remarkable but for different reasons. Surprisingly (or so it seems), Tintin himself is neither the subject nor the object of much laughter in the books. In fact, he is rather bland. Both visually and literarily, he is the most underdrawn of the characters. . . . His personality is likewise tepid ("Crumbs!" is his most powerful epithet) and, except for some noteworthy departures, his dialogue is as laconic as the generic schoolboy's outfit he wears (light sweater, dark knickers). Tintin is an exactly life-size character, neither very shrewd nor very gullible, neither heroically outsized nor cutely miniaturized. And yet, these same "characterless" qualities are what make him the key to the entire series, the vital center and focal point for the action.

To explain this seeming paradox, we must note the important fact that Tintin never appears alone in the stories. He is perpetually flanked by his two boon companions, Captain Haddock and Snowy. Taken together, this triad of personalities constitutes a subtle and extremely well-handled literary device: the hero as a composite character.

The contrasting natures of Haddock and Snowy offer a clue to their literary meaning. Haddock is large, swarthy (he wears dark seaman's clothing and a black beard) and menacing. Snowy is small, pure white, and generally timid. Haddock is apparently in his thirties or forties, Snowy barely out of the puppy stage. The man is heavy and slow-witted, the dog lively and clever. In short, the two are totally antithetical.

The same is true of their personalities. While Haddock is unfailingly deferential to Tintin, to others he is violent, erratic and unpredictable, a rough-talking, swaggering old lush. Snowy, significantly, is soft, sweet, and accommodating.

On a psychological level, the two represent a displacement of certain aspects of Tintin himself. Haddock is the aggressive, potentially destructive male principle, whose literary antecedents include such figures as Long John Silver and the brutish father of Huckleberry Finn. He is what Jung called the "Terrible Father," but one tamed in the *Adventures* by an unswerving loyalty to the boy. Indirectly, he adds depth and texture to the character of Tintin, since he is unconsciously perceived as an extension of him. And (as will be discussed shortly) he also provides a potential for comedy that Tintin lacks.

Snowy, on the other hand, represents the female side of the hero, expressing his fears and vulnerability. The dog also has a streak of inventiveness in her (or him). Frequently she will stray off on some adventure of her own, often with fateful consequences to the story. If Haddock is an agent of destruction, Snowy is no less one of creativity.

Literarily, the pair embody the qualities of Innocence (Snowy) and Experience (Haddock), the child and the adult. They provide an appropriate milieu within which Tintin can exist, partaking positively of both, without the extremes of either. His position, like theirs, is imaged pictorially: he is of middling size, and his clothing is equally light and dark; his features are boyish/girlish, with a peachlike bloom; his hair is neither black nor white, but sandy. Unlike Haddock, he has no discernible past life. And thus he completes the triangulation of characters, being a perpetual youth living in an eternal present, forever poised between the ages of innocence and experience. It is no surprise, then, that this composite "hero" offers as much appeal for adults as for children.

More to the point, it is the cohesion of this tripartite arrangement that enables Herge to surround them with comic devices of an extraordinary range and diversity. For Herge is a most eclectic humorist. On any given page, he may give us sparkling wit, low farce, ingenious situation comedy, or whatever other curiosities he wishes to pull from his ragbag of humor.

At one end of the spectrum, for example, are such characters as a nitwit pair of twin brothers named Thomson and Thompson, one of whom is an echo to the other. The two are introduced as detectives, but they are extraneous to the plot. They exist instead for such comic bits as this: trying to learn tobacco-chewing in order to mingle with a ship's crew, they are startled when the horn sounds and both, in tandem, swallow their quids. The same is true of an absent-minded professor (stock characters abound) named Calculus, a male Mrs. Malaprop whose irrelevancies soon become very predictable. This is bargain-basement comedy, played strictly for "laffs."

At the other extreme, however, are moments of comedy that fairly crackle with wit, sophistication, even erudition. In "**Flight 714,**" for example, a tycoon is seen talking by phone with his financial consultant in New York. In one panel he says,

> Hello? . . . Yes . . . Of course: the Parke-Bennet sale . . . Well? . . . Three Picassos, two Braques and a Renoir . . . Junk! . . . Anyway, I haven't an inch of space to hang them.

In the next panel:

> What's that? . . . Onassis after them? . . . Then buy! . . . Get them all! What? . . . I don't care how much, buy!

Here, as in the Thomson and Thompson business, a certain delicacy must be used so as not to lose readers of too great or too little sophistication. Wisely, Herge employs a hit-and-run approach and keeps the story moving swiftly along.

Visual humor is handled with the same adroitness and often to the same end, i.e., to add leavening to stories that are basically serious. One memorable sight-gag occurs while a sinister character named Rastapopoulos is waiting in ambush for Our Hero. Suddenly, out of a jungle thicket dashes a proboscis monkey (the species is named), its long nose dangling prominently as it scurries through the clearing and disappears. One of Rastapopoulos' henchmen begins to giggle: "My, what a sight! . . . What a conk! . . . Did ever you see such a conk? Reminds me of someone . . . Now, who can it . . ." So saying, he turns to his pendulous-nosed boss, who is decidedly not amused. Such comic bits are not only funny in themselves, but deflate the forces of evil to a level consistent with that of Tintin and his companions.

As mentioned above, Captain Haddock contains much greater comic possibilities than does Tintin, and Herge uses them all. Most are fairly conventional, as in Haddock's drunken-sailor escapades (e.g., forgetting his diving helmet), and he even hits such low notes as the ancient "flypaper bit" of vaudeville days, i.e., transferring a sticky piece of paper from one part of the anatomy to another. But even with Haddock, Herge will occasionally indulge his penchant for whimsical erudition. The old tar's primary comic expressions take the form of streams of alliterated imprecations, such as "Thundering typhoons!" and "Billions of blistering blue barnacles!" But when he and Tintin are captured by Peruvian sun-worshipers, we see this not-untypical variation of the form:

> Stand back, anachronisms! . . . Keep off, you imitation Incas, you! . . . Tramps! . . . Zapotecs! . . . Pockmarks! . . . Pithecanthropuses! . . . Bashi-bazouks! . . . Let me go, you savages!

Could the rough-hewn Haddock know how appropriately he was using the words "anachronisms" and "pithecanthropuses"? Or even what they mean? To judge from the context, probably not. But no matter, the rhythms and juxtapositions of the words are really the point.

As for Tintin himself, his comedy poses an intriguing puzzle. For the most part, he operates intellectually at about the level of a precocious 14-year-old. But at certain, very infrequent moments he will suddenly step out of character and deliver some preposterously esoteric piece of knowledge. A striking example occurs in "**Red Rackham's Treasure,**" when Tintin solves a mystery by spotting and identifying a statue of St.

John the Evangelist, and then recalling the vital fact that John was known as the "Eagle of Patmos" after the island on which he wrote his Revelation! Did Herge intend this bizarre passage as comedy or as a convenience of plot (something Herge is definitely not above)? Whatever the intention, if comedy has at its core surprise and sense of the incongruous, then Tintin must be credited with some of the books' best lines.

Taken as a whole, Herge's sense of humor may be likened to that of a very charming and learned host at a dinner party, who is determined not to let the conversation get serious but who also can't resist a bit of wry drollery for the few who might get it. Thanks to the effectiveness of his hero (meaning the three) and his innate sense of tact and judgment, Herge is able to carry off this feat with great finesse. The man has class, and so do his books. (pp. 55-60)

> *Nicholas Pease, "The Seriocomicstrip World of Tin-Tin," in* The Lion and the Unicorn *(copyright © 1977 The Lion and the Unicorn), Vol. 1, No. 1, 1977, pp. 54-61.*

[Hergé] is a man of many skills which meet together in his cartoon stories. He is strong on plot and sub-plot—each Tintin adventure could be written as a children's novel of the Kästner *Emil and the Detective* genre. He understands, and uses to the full, the conventions of the detective story—which brings him dedicated adult readers too. His characters may be stereotypes but they have quirks and weaknesses that make them lovable

From Red Rackham's Treasure, *written and illustrated by Hergé. Art © by Casterman, Tournai. Text © by Methuen, London/Little, Brown, Boston.*

and interesting. He is an artist of exceptional quality whose clean, clear, detailed 'frames' are combined ingeniously with one another to give the reader solid plot here, a humorous little breathing space there. Hergé's strips contain more dialogue—an integral part of the design of each frame—than any other. Through the pictures and dialogue, without recourse to the narrative sequences that lesser artists (see Schick's *Frankenstein* and Kahlstrom's *Biggles*) resort to all the time, Hergé tells his intricate stories. (pp. 36-7)

> *Elaine Moss, in a review of "The Adventures of Tintin: The Calculus Affair," in her* Picture Books for Young People: 9-13 *(copyright © 1981 Elaine Moss), The Thimble Press, 1981, pp. 36-7.*

TINTIN EN AMÉRIQUE [*TINTIN IN AMERICA*]   (1932)

Tintin admirers will be glad to have a reprint of this book, . . . for although Captain Haddock and the Thompson-Thomsons do not appear, there is a profusion of cliff-hanging episodes and a fresh, headlong variety of verbal fun which contrasts a little with the sometimes jaded style of more recent books. In contrast to the allusive wit of the Asterix books, Hergé's satire is direct and explicit, directed mainly at events and institutions and contained more in the choice of scenes and episodes (that is, in the artwork) than in words. Determined to clean up gangster-ridden Chicago, Tintin and his faithful dog Snowy . . . race enthusiastically through city and desert. Indian village and factory, escaping death by torture, drowning, lynching, express train (a beautiful look back at silent film disasters); they fall over a precipice, are shut in a tunnel, are shot at or bashed by innumerable weapons, and depart for Europe in a liner after a Wall Street ticker-tape farewell. The balloon-text is on the whole low-keyed and neutral in tone, though there are some nice upper-case moments and a neat parody of the Holmes deductive method. . . .

Hergé's meticulous research is shown everywhere in his pictures, in the exact details of terrain, costume, architecture which underpin caricatured faces and visual parody. His admirers will point to other aspects of his art, like the subtle deploying of colour or the sharp felicity of his line. For me, a fresh look at Tintin after (I confess) some years of boredom has renewed my admiration for the brilliant pacing and composition by which the adventure is diversified and activated and the masterly integration of words and pictures in this doubly readable tale.

> *Margery Fisher, in a review of "Tintin in America," in her* Growing Point, *Vol. 18, No. 1, May, 1979, p. 3504.*

Every new Tintin release is an event and . . . *in America* . . . is no exception. As always Hergé's precise, imaginative cartoon line and wide range of vivid and subtle colors are unsurpassed this side of the Atlantic. Too bad the art work here props up a story without many surprises or memorable characters as the quinquagenarian boy reporter and his faithful dog Snowy, called to Chicago to clean up the Capone mob, battle a number of lightweight baddies. This disappointing entry is testimony to the fact that a champion can't always be a winner. (pp. 70-1)

> *Pamela D. Pollack, in a review of "Tintin in America," in* School Library Journal *(reprinted from the January, 1980 issue of* School Library Journal, *published by R. R. Bowker Co. / A Xerox Corporation; copyright © 1980), Vol. 26, No. 5, January, 1980, pp. 70-1.*

LES CIGARES DU PHARAON [THE CIGARS OF THE PHARAOH] (1934)

Beside the unrestrained high spirits of Asterix Tintin seems pale. . . . Tintin in English lacks the crispness and sparkle of the French text. *Cigars of the Pharaoh* is nevertheless highly entertaining. The action is complicated and fantastically improbable, but the little journalist goes through each terrifying episode with quiff unruffled.

The latest adventures . . . concern a charming Egyptologist, Sophocles Sarcophagus, whose scientific work is hindered by extreme eccentricity. He shakes hands with Tintin's dog instead of Tintin, apologizes to a ship's ventilator. Even before he becomes technically insane and thinks he is Rameses II travelling incognito, Sophocles is distinctly odd. Still in the front rank of comic strips, Tintin seems now just a little démodé.

> *"Striptease," in* The Times Literary Supplement *(© Times Newspapers Ltd. (London) 1971; reproduced from* The Times Literary Supplement *by permission), No. 3634, October 22, 1971, p. 1332.**

L'ISLE NOIRE [THE BLACK ISLAND] (1938)

[*The Black Island*] is Tintin's one adventure to date on British—mainly Scottish—soil. He pursues a mysterious gang who fly about in unregistered aircraft, drive fast cars, and are eventually run to ground in the ruined castle of Craig Dhu, where they keep a gorilla named Ranko to frighten away intruders. The story features the detectives Thompson and Thomson, but not Haddock or Calculus, who had not yet joined the cast. . . . Tintin spends most of the second half in a kilt.

The book has been redrawn since that first appearance, though structure and dialogue remain the same. It is interesting to note the changes. Partly they stem from Hergé's increased resources in draughtsmanship; the pictures are more detailed, the details more accurate. Partly they pay tribute to eighteen years' advances in technology; for instance, the criminals now have strip lighting and air-conditioning in their workshop; electric locomotives have replaced steam (so Tintin gets much less black in the tunnel incident). . . .

There are visual amendments of many sorts. The Scottish quayside pub is no longer half-timbered or named Ye Dolphin, though the Sussex pub is as rustic as can be, complete with new horse-brasses and fox's mask; Dr. Müller's mansion has also become opulently baronial. Abstract paintings hang on the criminals' office walls. With this increased sophistication goes a greater awareness of the splendours and miseries of publicity; the advertisements for Haig and Guinness have vanished from the bars, while Snowy may no longer get drunk on Johnny Walker but has to make do with something called Loch Lomond Scotch Whisky instead. It is all in its way a reflection of our changing society, just like the stepping-up in denomination of the forged banknotes from fifty francs to 100 and from £1 to £5.

Even the one element that should be unchanged—the eternally fixed personalities of Tintin and the two asinine detectives—seems to have been subtly affected. It is not just that Tintin has given up wearing a tie and thrown away the belt to his mackintosh. He also looks in some mysterious way more grown-up; his hair less orange; his face longer and less blank; his amazing resourcefulness somehow less incongruous than in the old days. Indeed, one can envisage the 1965 model Tintin

winning the Duke of Edinburgh's Award. Whether this flight from improbability is exactly an advantage is debatable; however, the book's gain in beauty of colour and flexibility of layout makes it well worth while.

> *"Tintin in Tartan," in* The Times Literary Supplement *(© Times Newspapers Ltd. (London) 1966; reproduced from* The Times Literary Supplement *by permission), No. 3351, May 19, 1966, p. 428.*

TINTIN AU PAYS DE L'OR NOIR [THE LAND OF BLACK GOLD] (1951)

Why have English Tintin fans had to wait so long for *Land of Black Gold*? Two ten-year-old mysteries, caused by translations appearing out of sequence, are at last cleared up. The first arose in *Explorers on the Moon* . . . , when Thomson and Thompson, as usual up to their necks in ineptitude, started sprouting yards of green hair. Tintin remarked "Oh dear, it's what I feared: another attack . . . the trouble they developed after eating those strange pills in the Arabian desert!" Now they are seen in the desert at last, driving round and round in circles, unable to tell a waterhole from a mirage. Better still, fiendish little Prince Abdullah, son of Mohammed Ben Kalish Ezab (already shown tormenting Captain Haddock in *The Red Sea Sharks* . . . , is properly introduced in *Land of Black Gold*—a dreadfully credible royal delinquent. The back of the title page lists the many countries where Tintin's adventures are published—including Egypt and Israel: nice to think that young Arabs and Israelis can laugh at the same jokes.

> *"Strips for Action," in* The Times Literary Supplement *(© Times Newspaper Ltd. (London) 1972; reproduced from* The Times Literary Supplement *by permission), No. 3692, December 8, 1972, p. 1490.**

ON A MARCHE SUR LA LUNE [EXPLORERS ON THE MOON] (1954)

As Tintin and Captain Haddock explore caves on the moon, Snowy, the dog in a specially designed space suit, moon-hops ahead—into great danger: ice. This new exciting strip-cartoon story with its well designed pictures, and balloon talk that has to be read because it is necessary to the plot, keeps the series well in the lead as a motivator for older non-readers.

> *Elaine Moss, "Paperback Editions: 'Explorers on the Moon'," in* Children's Books of the Year: 1974, *edited by Elaine Moss (© Elaine Moss), Hamish Hamilton, 1975, p. 119.*

TINTIN AU TIBET [TINTIN IN TIBET] (1960)

Tintin is as engaging as ever, and I can justify calling this a picture/story book, for seldom have human faces and gestures, in and out of caricature, expressed so much. Captain Haddock is as full of original pejorative adjectives as ever, and Tintin as resourceful, as they scour the Himalayas for their friend Chang, meeting as they go with deep snow, hospitable llamas and an Abominable Snowman with a heart of gold. Wonderful fun for all ages.

> *Margery Fisher, in a review of "Tintin in Tibet," in her* Growing Point, *Vol. 1, No. 6, December, 1962, p. 93.*

From Tintin in Tibet, *written and illustrated by Hergé. Art © by Casterman, Tournai. Text © by Methuen, London/Little, Brown, Boston.*

POPOL ET VIRGINIE AU PAYS DES LAPINOS [POPOL OUT WEST] (1968)

Readers of the French (i.e. Belgian) edition of Tintin may have noticed among Hergé's lesser works listed on the back covers something called **Popol et Virginie au pays des Lapinos.** Now republished after some thirty years and issued in an English translation, it proves to be a kind of simplified animal version of Tintin, performed by rabbits (the Red Indian tribe of *Lapinos* or Bunnokees), dogs (firemen) and two bears as hero and heroine. They, Popol and Virginia, are itinerant hatters, trying to develop the trade in the Wild West, and travelling with a villainous but inexhaustible sky-blue horse called Bluebell. For a time the Bunnokees have a craze for the new-fangled bowlers and toppers, till their feather-loving chief rouses them against the strangers, who are driven out after showing great resourcefulness and courage in war. Then they fall foul of a characteristic, if canine, Western baddie called Bully Bull, and the ensuing cliff-hanging episodes fill the second half of the book.

Colour and drawing are good, though less sophisticated than Tintin. Popol is an interesting personality, being a reincarnation of Tintin himself in bear form, with many of Tintin's early facial expressions. But the real treat is Virginia, who sings blithely, hardly says a word, knits Popol's socks and remains cool and demure, with cast-down eyes, in all but the most

urgent crises. To think what Tintin missed through his early commitment to the celibate life of a boy scout. . . .

A review of "Popol Out West," in The Times Literary Supplement *(© Times Newspapers Ltd. (London) 1969; reproduced from* The Times Literary Supplement *by permission), No. 3536, December 4, 1969, p. 1394.*

VOL 714 POUR SYDNEY [FLIGHT 714] (1968)

Flight 714 is a Qantas flight from London to Sydney, carrying Tintin—still his usual plus-foured self—and friends to an astronautical congress in that city. The story is not about the flight at all, but about what happens when the party leave it and are given a private lift by the millionaire Laszlo Carreidas in his supersonic three-jet executive aircraft. The plane is hijacked and Carreidas kidnapped by Rastapopoulos, who uses a truth drug to try to extract the number of his secret account in a Zurich bank, which he means to drain. Tintin, Haddock, Milou/Snowy and Tournesol/Calculus (a bit of a passenger in this volume of the saga), reinforced by the Esthonian pilot Skut, do their best against the bandits, and finally get their disagreeable host away. Then about two-thirds of the way through everything goes magic on us. The party is guided to a mysterious cave, full of prototypical science fiction sculptures, where they meet their *deus ex machina,* a slightly questionable interplanetary quisling who has them rescued by flying saucer and hypnotized to forget everything they have seen.

The plot, in other words, is broken-backed; the same weakness as beset its two predecessors: **Tintin in Tibet** and **The Castafiore Emerald.** But Carreidas himself, from his first appearance as a lonely, decrepit old man tipped five dollars by the charitable Haddock, is an admirable new recruit to the series, while his treasonable ginger-moustached English yes-man also deserves to fight another day. There is a good scene where both Carreidas and Rastapopoulos (who seems fatter than before, and now dresses in Texan style) are under the influence of the truth drug, competing to see which can produce the more disgraceful confessions. In the dialogue too there are some new flashes: "Breathalyser!" (insult by Haddock), "Mdjrk" (expletive by Rastapopoulos), "an ill-gotten camel gathers no gain" (Turkish proverb); also Haddock's revealingly non-committal expression of sympathy on Milou's supposed death: "I . . . er . . . well . . . yes . . . him . . . er." The relationship between Tintin's friend and Tintin's dog might well be worth deeper exploration.

"The Tintin Saga," in The Times Literary Supplement *(© Times Newspapers Ltd. (London) 1968; reproduced from* The Times Literary Supplement *by permission), No. 3475, October 3, 1968, p. 1115.*

Randall Jarrell

1914-1965

American author of fiction, poetry, and essays, critic, journalist, editor, and translator.

Jarrell is considered one of the most gifted contemporary poets of his generation. It was not surprising that he turned to the writing of children's fantasy late in his career, since childhood and fairy tale images figure prominently in his poems. Even such mature themes as personal growth, family love, and loneliness find gentle expression in Jarrell's four books for children: *The Gingerbread Rabbit*, *The Bat-Poet*, *The Animal Family*, and *Fly by Night*. Combinations of prose and poetry, these works are often concerned with the search for self-expression and inner peace. They are seen as sensitively and lyrically written, characterized by tenderness and emotional honesty. Underscoring the books are Jarrell's concerns about his life and art, and several of his characters—especially the bat-poet—are symbols of himself.

Jarrell loved the sounds of words and is often praised for his use of language. In addition to producing his own works, he taught poetry and read avidly, often turning to Grimm's fairy tales and *The Wind in the Willows* for inspiration. As a writer for a young audience, Jarrell received much critical acclaim, though reviewers debated whether his poetry and prose flowed well together. Most critics regard *The Bat-Poet*, which relates the difficulties of being a poet, as insightful, quietly lyrical, and accurate in its animal characterizations, while some feel that not much happens and that Jarrell is too didactic. *The Animal Family*, his longest work for children, has been compared to *The Little Prince* for its restrained beauty. The need for love and family are explored in a delicate text which combines wit and warmth. Critics find *Fly by Night* to be poetic and peaceful in tone, yet feel the story might be too sophisticated for children. Jarrell produced relatively few works for children, but his fantasies, three of which are enriched by Maurice Sendak's illustrations, are considered distinguished contributions to children's literature. *The Animal Family* was a Newbery Honor Book in 1966 and received the Lewis Carroll Shelf Award in 1970.

(See also *Contemporary Literary Criticism*, Vols. 1, 2, 6, 9, 13; *Something about the Author*, Vol. 7; *Contemporary Authors New Revision Series*, Vol. 6; and *Contemporary Authors*, Vols. 5-8, rev. ed., Vols. 25-28, rev. ed. [obituary].)

AUTHOR'S COMMENTARY

[The following excerpt is by Randall Jarrell's wife, Mary von S. Jarrell. It introduces the transcript of an interview with Jarrell by Aaron Kramer.]

My husband said *The Bat-Poet* was a story "half for children and half for grown-ups" and that makes for a book as peculiar among books as bats are among animals, and poets are among people. The children and grown-ups who enjoy *The Bat-Poet* do so because somewhere inside themselves they are—or want to be —Different. This book speaks to them about the personal world one finds, and how one is treated by the conventional world, when one *is* different. . . .

About a year before his death, my husband had a conversation with Aaron Kramer about his last book of poetry *The Lost World* and, by chance, *The Bat-Poet*. This was taped for WBAI and when Kramer asked Randall how he came to add children's literature to his career . . . Randall told their listeners of a time when he'd not been able to write poems at all for some months. He said that his friend, Michael di Capua, happened to ask him, "What about writing for children? Have you ever thought of that?" And Randall went on to say, "So, that spring I often lay in our hammock outdoors and wrote everyday on a little story about a rabbit. And I'd read what I'd written to my wife who was gardening there. I enjoyed it, but it wasn't a *real* book. But it was fun. And I finished it. Later, four or five months later, I started another book half for children and half for grown-ups called *The Bat-Poet* and that felt just like a regular book to me. (Pause) And . . . and . . . you know how it is . . . you work on it all the time. You stay awake at night . . . you wake up in the middle of the night . . . and . . . and I did it just like a grown-up book. By good luck, we had some bats on our porch and so I imagined a bat who would not *write* poems, but anyway make them up. And so, *I had to make up poems* for him. . . . Oh, but in fact, I *wanted* to make up poems for him. And, anyway I did. And a couple of the poems were pretty much like grown-up poems. Anyway, the *New Yorker* printed them . . . I didn't tell them they were children's poems. (Laugh) It was probably a great shock to them to find that out later.''

Kramer: "Did these bats hang upside down in a clump inside your porch?''

Jarrell: "Exactly. We have a kind of Moravian star there with an electric light in the middle and the bats cling to a rafter about a foot away. I think they like the insects that come to the light. And then . . . uh . . . uh . . . they *do* have . . . uh . . . 'little ones.' These were small brown bats—very small— and their babies were about the size of a quarter. (Laugh) And with no fur. (Laugh) They're not beautiful—except to a bat. And anyway, there really was one bat that was a different color from the rest. He was a kind of cafe-au-lait brown and I made him the Bat-Poet. (Pause) Queerly enough, he was the one who stayed with us the longest.''

Kramer: "And isn't there a mockingbird in the book? And isn't he a poet, too?''

Jarrell: "Oh, *yeah!* I've known a lot of artists and poets . . . and . . . I write poetry myself—or anyway, I write verse my-self—and anyway, several times when I've talked to writer friends about this book I'm amused to see how they immedi-ately identify with the mockingbird. (Laugh) But the hero of the book is the bat who is really quite nice. And there's a charming chipmunk. And, well, the mockingbird is pretty bad. But he's a *real* artist. (Pause) Some of the time, as Keats says, 'when a poet looks at sparrows playing in the gravel he *is* those sparrows' but the funny thing is . . . the rest of the time . . . most of the time, if he's a *normal* poet, he's just as vain as he can be and he's obsessed with *himself.* And mockingbirds are! Mockingbirds are the best birds in the world at imitating other birds. And everything else. They can imitate cars, distant trains, chipmunks. . . . But at the same time they imitate 'em, *perfectly,* get their real essence—*echte* chipmunk, and so on— they can't stand 'em. They drive 'em away. (Pause) Uh . . . uh . . . territoriality at its strongest is in mockingbirds. I've really seen a mockingbird try to drive away seventy or eighty birds off our porch during a snowstorm. You know . . . when they were all eating seeds from the porch? He worked so hard for a day and a half trying to drive them away, he couldn't fly anymore. He couldn't eat. Or anything! (Pause) So, it seemed to me that . . . uh . . . mockingbirds are not only more like artists than other birds, they're more like people, too.''

Kramer: "Well, you're certainly not that kind of poet, Jar-rell.''

Jarrell: "Oh . . . but . . . but if I'm not . . . I'm not a poet, I'm afraid. I mean . . . I mean . . . (Laugh)''

Kramer: "The critics who have been praising *The Bat-Poet* have acknowledged that it is not only a great children's classic, but a classic for grown-ups as well.''

Jarrell: "I've been awfully happy about what readers have said to me and what I've read in the reviews. But . . . but . . . Oh, you know . . . sometimes you feel you have good *luck* with a book, you know? Things *come* to you. And I feel that way about it. That . . . that *The Bat-Poet,* for what it is, *is* done right.'' . . .

[*The Bat-Poet*] is mainly prose, but there are three "portrait" poems. In the onomatopoetic one about the owl the many l's and w's and legato vowels are directed more to a listener than a reader to help him hear, as it were, the way air stirs when a large object made of aerated feathers swoops downward thru the air to its prey. By the same token, the chipmunk's poem is made of short, quick words and deft, staccato phrases to remind one of the speed the chipmunk relies upon for his very life. The mockingbird poem is altogether different. It is de-scribing the artist at his art: imitating life—that is, creating song from Life and the world around him, and then rejecting the world he imitated. With this poem the bat, too, had good luck. Things, came to him, all right, in a philosophical and even Yeats-ian vein! Perhaps the best luck he had (as far as *he* was concerned) was with his final poem, the one his own dear brother and sister bats would listen to and comprehend and say about it, "This is *so!*" In it the bat-poet used all the bizarre but authentic biological and biographical facts that seemed incredible to the chipmunk (and perhaps will to us) but that to bats are sound and true, and comfortable to think about. That poem is called just **"Bats"** and when he completes it to memory he rejoins the others "high up under the roof in the farthest corner of the barn, where the bats were hanging upside down, wrapped in their brown wings." Then, "the bat said to himself sleepily: "I wish I'd said we sleep all winter. That would have been a good thing to have in." He yawned and thought, "as soon as they wake up I'll say them the poem. The chipmunk said they'd love it . . ."" the story ends, "His eyes were closed; he yawned, and screwed his face up, and snuggled closer to the others.''

> *Mary von S. Jarrell, "Notes" (reprinted by permis-sion of the author), taken from the phonograph re-cord album cover for* Randall Jarrell: The Bat-Poet, *Caedmon Records, 1972.*

GENERAL COMMENTARY

The Bat-Poet is a gentle, satiric commentary on poets and their audiences, but the author's conscious effort to write for children is evident. The book does show, however, his tenderness and graceful style that make *The Animal Family* . . . one of his most poetic achievements.

The Animal Family has been compared with *The Little Prince* because it too has the beauty and impact of poetry in the art form of the fairy tale, and because each reader finds an indi-vidual import in a story that is universal in emotion, yet per-sonal in meaning. It tells of the hunter who lived alone in his log house near the sea. (p. 453)

In time the mermaid came to live with him, and then a bear cub, a lynx kitten, finally a little boy whom the sea had cast ashore, and the family was complete. It is a story warm with the need of earth's creatures for each other; disparities and adjustments are only hinted at; in the concept of wholeness they are of little importance. But very clear is the mosaic of realities—clumsy, clever, humorous, tender—that make a home where each member, often startlingly different from the others, finds completeness, as though life without the others would not be life at all. (p. 454)

> *Ruth Hill Viguers, "Worlds without Boundaries: Lit-erary Fairy Tales and Fantasy," in* A Critical His-tory of Children's Literature *by Cornelia Meigs, Anne Thaxter Eaton, Elizabeth Nesbitt, and Ruth Hill Vi-guers, edited by Cornelia Meigs (reprinted with per-mission of Macmillan Publishing Company; copy-right © 1953, 1969 by Macmillan Publishing Company), revised edition, Macmillan, 1969, pp. 446-83.**

The hero of **"Fly by Night"** is a boy named David, who lives alone, with none save animals for friends, and who at night evidently lifts up out of his bed and skims through the moonlit air in the nude. The nudity is unspecified in the text but looms specific in Sendak's illustrations. (p. 25)

Flying of course is a euphemism in more than one language for sexual activity, and a man can recall those disorienting intimations of potency that visited him in bed at about the age David seems to be. The sensations of the blankets' weight, the illusions of changing direction and inert voyage, prepare the onanistic mystery; launched, the child glides with criminal stealth into his parent's room. His father is a substantial lump in the bed, with his head out; his mother, however, has placed her head beneath a pillow. Mother, as she was for Oedipus, is unrecognizable. David invades their dreams, and sees himself in process of replacing his father: "his father, looking very small, is running back and forth with David on his back, only David is as big as ever. His father is panting." His mother's dreams, like her head are eclipsed by feathers. These feathers, outdoors, become the face of a mother owl, "with its big round brown eyes: each of them has a feathery white ring around it, and then a brown one, and then a white one, and then a brown one, till the rings come together and make big brown and white rings around its whole head." This concentric vaginal apparition holds in its claws a "big silvery fish." David thinks to himself, "I didn't know owls could catch *fish*."

Himself a fish in air, he swims after the owl, and watches her feed her young, and listens as she recites to her owlets a long bedtime poem, about a lost owl making its way back to the nest. Floating back into his bed, David gropes after who the owl's gaze reminds him of, wakes to his own mother's gaze, and after a moment of confusion perceives by sunlight that "his mother looks at him like his mother." Finis. The story-teller should be commended for the tact of his language and the depth at which his imagery seeks to touch, amid its feathery circles gripping big silvery somethings, the forbidden actual. All of Jarrell's children's tales have a sinister stir about them, the breath of true forlornness felt by children. But the stir tends to remain unsettled, unresolved by the clarifying power adult-hood promises. All successful children's literature has a con-spiratorial element; but the conspiracy is not among equals, one side is pretending. With Jarrell there is little pretense; he shares with his young readers as one child shares with others a guilty secret, and imparts his own unease.

The poems he includes in **"The Bat-Poet"** and **"Fly by Night"** are not as good as they should be. They aspire to a tender sharpness achieved elsewhere, by his contemporary Theodore Roethke, whose animal poems catch Nature's flip cruelty in a line (in "The Heron": "He jerks a frog across his bony lip") or brood with the grief of a helpless god:

Where has he gone, my meadow mouse,
My thumb of a child that nuzzled in my palm?
To run under the hawk's wing,
Under the eye of the great owl watching from the elm-
    tree,
To live by courtesy of the shrike, the snake, the tom-
    cat.

By comparison Jarrell's own owls are symbolic menaces: "The ear that listens to the owl believes /In death." If he was no Roethke, he was no A. A. Milne either; his poems do not address themselves to children, exclusively and positively, but are included, with disturbing *double-entendre*, in his collec-tions of "serious" poetry as well. As they appear in the chil-dren's books, they seem stuck-on, and a bit stuck-up. What is most poetic about the bat-poet is the author's prose description

of him, "the color of coffee with cream in it," as he sleeps among his fellow-bats, the wriggling of one forcing a wriggling of all, so that "it looked as if a fur wave went over them."

Jarrell saw a strangeness in the daylight, and loved inhuman nature. The longest and best of his children's books, **"The Animal Family,"** holds no formal poetry, but most intensely presents his habitual themes of individual lostness, of estrange-ment within a family, of the magic of language, of the wild beauty beyond our habitations. . . . [The union of the hunter and mermaid is a] disquieting match, as if Jarrell had taken literally Roethke's lovely erotic line, "She'd more sides than a seal." As in **"Fly by Night,"** the mother's role is flooded with strangeness, and a male child's egotism is grotesquely served. . . . With the acquiescence of his four-footed siblings, the human child takes over the prime place in the animal family, and is told by his adopted mother, in her liquid accent, that he has been with them always. With this lie, the book ends. To Jarrell's vision of bliss adoption by members of another species seems intrinsic. His first book for children, **"The Gin-gerbread Rabbit,"** deviated from its gingerbread-man model in the cookie's adoption by a childless pair of real rabbits, while the human mother who had concocted the hero of pastry fabricated a substitute of cloth and thread, bringing yet another texture into the patchwork of fur, skin and dough.

The writing in **"The Animal Family"** is exquisite, and all of Jarrell's little juveniles are a cut above the run in intelligence and unfaked feeling. The feeling, however, remains somewhat locked behind the combinative oddness, the mix of pluralism and isolation and warping transposition; these tales of boys active at night and bats active in day bend, as it were, around an unseen center. They are surreal as not even **"Alice"** is surreal, for the anfractuosities of Carroll's nightmare wind back to the sunny riverbank, while Jarrell's leave us in mist, in an owl's twilight, without that sense of *emergence*, of winning through and clearing up, intrinsic to children's classics from **"Cinderella"** to **"Charlotte's Web."** (pp. 25, 36)

John Updike, "Randall Jarrell Writing Stories for Children," in The New York Times Book Review *(© 1976 by The New York Times Company; reprinted by permission), November 14, 1976, pp. 25, 36 [the excerpts of Randall Jarrell's work used here were originally published in his* Fly by Night *(reprinted by permission of Farrar, Straus and Giroux, Inc.; copyright © 1969, 1976 by Randall Jarrell), Farrar, Straus and Giroux, 1976].*

[In his adult poetry, Jarrell] wrote of war and death and aging, but he often wrote about them in terms of a child's failed expectations, as if amazed that life could grow so complex and so vicious. His poems are poems of disillusionment; "heart-breaking," Robert Lowell called them.

His children's books are possessed of this quality in a way that the children themselves rarely notice. And I suspect this is especially true of *Fly By Night*. . . . It evokes feelings in an adult that do not—I think could not—touch my six-year-old. . . .

It's a frustrating tale with the same fascination but also the same horrible impotence that dreams often convey. David tells himself time and again as he drifts through the night that he ought to remember flying, because if he could he could fly in the day. But of course he can't. And the things he sees as he drifts through the night—the mice, the sheep—he longs to pet, but he is powerless to move his arms, incapable of touching them.

Jarrell once wrote that children ask of a story "what they ask of a dream: that it satisfy their wishes." But David's wishes are beyond his grasp, finally lost even to his memory.

"Do you like the story?" I asked my little boy while reading him *Fly By Night.* "Oh . . . sure."

When I had read him other books by Jarrell they set him laughing and giggling and begging me to go on. *The Bat Poet,* which I thought a mildly witty allegory of the literary world, was for him a simple, delightful bedtime story. *The Animal Family,* a more ambitious tale on every level, struck me as a gentle masterpiece, unforgettable, delicate and full of surprises. My son was also enthralled. . . .

In his poem "**Children Selecting Books in a Library**" Jarrell wrote that "children's cries / Are to men the cries of crickets, dense with warmth / —But dip a finger into Fafnir, taste it / And all their words are plain as chance and pain," and he went on to argue that the experience of escape, of change, which children seek from their literature is little different from what the adult seeks from his.

But there is a difference, and it becomes clear in some of the last pieces Jarrell wrote: in his poem "**The Lost World,**" in *The Animal Family,* and in *Fly By Night.*

In them we meet a child worried by the stories he's been told. In *Fly By Night* David is disturbed by his helplessness to remember or act; in the poem the little boy has read about a mad scientist bent on destroying the universe; in *The Animal Family,* the hunter and the mermaid have told the boy that once he had another mother, before they found him in a boat washed up onto shore. But when the children seem disturbed, the adults reassure them. David's mother "looks at him like his mother." There is someone to say, "No, that's just play, just make believe." "Oh we just told you that. . . . We've had you always."

This is the voice we want to hear, no matter how old we are— even more, in fact, as we grow older: the voice spoken by someone who knows all about us, saying that everything will be all right, this life, these worries, this helplessness is all a dream from which we will wake. It is the voice adults lie awake all night waiting to hear, but it only comes to children.

Christopher Dickey, "Voices of Childhood," in Book World—The Washington Post *(© 1977, The Washington Post), January 9, 1977, p. K4.*

In a flickering of prose and poetry that is curiously weightless, Randall Jarrell catches the movement in and out of daily life and dreaming [in *Fly By Night*]. Firmly located in his house by the woods, David flies by night. . . . In making a beautiful fable [*The Bat-Poet*] Jarrell presents (with a deep gravity) the poet's way of looking. The chipmunk, on hearing the bat's poem about the owl, asks, "Why do I like it if it makes me shiver?"

The lyric directness of the poems themselves, entwined in story and pictures, produces a metaphor of art for the young so memorable that all that is required of readers, who have moved through the story pattern in a kind of clear trance, is to say at the end: that is how that is. Seen and heard at once, both books have a powerful coherence. *The Bat-Poet* is more clearly detached from the mundane; its avowed intention is to make the reader see things from the bat's viewpoint. David's flying, located firmly in the present, affirms the imaginative skill of the reader.

Margaret Meek, "Reaching below the Surface," in The Times Literary Supplement *(© Times Newspapers Ltd. (London) 1977; reproduced from* The Times Literary Supplement *by permission), No. 3949, December 2, 1977, p. 1413.**

It is not surprising that Randall Jarrell would be a writer of children's stories. Throughout his poems, we find again and again the subject matter of childhood. There are the poems derived from well-known fairy tales and other works for children: for example, "**The Sleeping Beauty,**" "**Cinderella,**" and "**The Marchen.**" Then there are the poems which tell of the daily lives of children: "**A Girl in a Library,**" "**A Sick Child,**" "**The Girl Dreams That She Is Giselle.**" The most important literary figures of his time—his friends and admirers—recognized Jarrell as *the* poet of childhood. Robert Lowell said that the subject of childhood was for Jarrell, "what it was for his two favorite poets, Rilke and Wordsworth, a governing and transcendent vision." He was, "Monstrously knowing and monstrously innocent—one does not know just where to find him . . . a Wordsworth with the obsessions of Lewis Carroll." Reflecting on the "literary commonplace that American literature is essentially a child literature," Karl Shapiro observed that, "Our poetry studies behavior and leads us back to the child. With Jarrell, too, the child becomes the critic and center of value." He was, "the poet of the *Kinder* and the earliest games of the mind and heart. All those wounded soldiers and shot-down men turn back again into children, for a wounded man is again a child." Shapiro is specifically thinking of Jarrell's war-poems here, but he rightfully suggests that all his poetry shows an overriding concern not only with the experiences of childhood but with a general theme of childhood as a human experience continuing well into maturity. As James Dickey notes:

> The poems are one long look . . . into a child's face, as the Things of modern life happen around it, happen to it, so that you see the expressions change, and even feel the breath change over you, and you come to be aware that you are staring back in perfect centered blindness, in which everything to pity is clear as death, and none of the reasons for any of it.

While helping us note the central place a childlike experience of the world has in Jarrell's poetry, it must be admitted that Dickey's reading makes us a little leery about what we might expect to find in his children's stories. There seems little reason to want to show a child that aspect of the world which is amorally brutal and dumb, and which renders even us adults impotently childlike ourselves. Yet the stories, [*The Bat-Poet, The Animal Family,* and *Fly By Night*], are wonderful, filled with life and hope. Perhaps coming at the end of his poetic career and life, they reflect the culmination of the long struggle for selfhood going on in the poems. Perhaps they are merely an escape. Nonetheless, the vision is generally hopeful; for the heroes of the children's stories, life is a negotiable condition. (pp. 73-4)

[A survey of the poems helps us see] the rich meanings and values which the stories are meant to have, despite their matter-of-fact evocations of reality and seemingly limited sense of what defines the heroic and triumphant. The victories of the stories' heroes may seem small, but they are clearly an advance over the plight of the poems' protagonists, who are, in the main, passive victims, oppressed by outside forces, at best naive makers of their fate. (p. 74)

In some ways [the stories] may be seen as a gradual turning away from a real world and an entry into a private, phantasmagoric realm. In *The Bat Poet* the hero confronts the everyday problems of making friends while simultaneously discovering what it means to make poems and find an audience. *The Animal Family* seems more escapist. It is a fairy tale world in which a hunter catches a mermaid, takes her as a mate and adopts animal children. In *Fly By Night,* the familiar daylight world dissolves completely. The rudiments of plot are replaced by a midnight ride of pure happenings—a ride of sights, sounds, feelings which are purely for their own sake.

But all in all, the course of the main characters is upward. The bat-poet is abandoned by his brothers and sisters, but he does brave the strange and somewhat unyielding world of daylight, and, despite a sinister suggestion about it, makes it back into the barn for a winter's hibernation with his natural family. If we are told that the hunter-hero of *The Animal Family* still nostalgically yearns for his long-dead parents, he does manage to make a mate of the mermaid, and with her becomes a loving and responsible parent of a bear, a lynx, and a real-life boy. And while the hero of *Fly By Night* is a lonely child, in his dreams he is able to lift off for a wondrous flight with a powerful mother-substitute, a great Owl, who leads him through the otherwise unfathomable night, assuring him of its beauty and safety. . . . In the boy's dream, at least, the problem of the negligent parent has been resolved.

The path through the poems and into the stories is an existential one. Left behind more and more is the image of man fatally anchored to his role in society; what emerges is an explorer, a seeker. The heroes of the children's stories want least to hide themselves from pain, want most to discover what the great outside consists of. When we read the stories, we experience as much uncertainty and doubt as we feel a coming through. But the uncertainty and doubt and the coming through are necessarily and intricately linked. We learn through trial and error, and Jarrell does not spare us the details. Matter-of-factly we are introduced to circumstances that are often disturbing and threatening. But, with his heroes, we survive and even profit from them. And when the story is over we accept life.

The Bat-Poet opens with a quietly revealed but essentially traumatic abandonment.

> Towards the end of summer all the bats except
> the little brown one began sleeping in the barn.
> He missed them, and tried to get them to come
> back and sleep on the porch with him.

But they of course don't change their minds. Unlike the strangely nonconformist little bat, they must do what comes naturally and move to more protective quarters for a winter's sleep. Jarrell is non-committal in communicating this; the little bat hardly seems to mind. This silence on the part of the bat and his author is an example of what James Dickey has commented on above. The events which shape our destinies are often absurdly circumstantial, undeniably unfair. There is nothing we can do: we can only accept and go on. Yet it is this that makes a difference. Bereft of the comfort and company of his brothers and sisters, the bat begins to "hang there and think" and contemplates the difficult but dazzling world of daylight. It fascinates him, and, despite a poor response from his brethren—"the sun *hurts*," . . . they complain—follows the lead of the mockingbird and begins to translate it into poetry.

The bat's experience with the mockingbird and a family of cardinals restates the underlying assertion that growing up means getting used to living with mixed blessings and partial victories,

as well as inevitable defeats here and there. The mockingbird whom he so admires and emulates is a disappointment. Beyond his natural gift for imitating life, he pays notice neither to the world which gives him his material, nor the bat who appreciates his talents. . . . And when the little bat tries out his own poetry—strongly felt, an original and striking evocation of the owl's menacing power—the mockingbird is pedantic, restrained, impersonal. "'Why, I like it,' said the mockingbird. 'Technically it's quite accomplished. The way you change the rhyme-scheme's particularly effective.'" After this kind of response, the bat can only feel a mixed satisfaction; "Partly he felt very good—the mockingbird had liked his poem—and partly he felt just terrible. He thought: 'Why, I might as well have said it to the bats. . . . The owl nearly kills me and he says he likes the rhyme-scheme!'" . . . (pp. 77-81)

The bat's efforts to describe a cardinal and his family represent another problematic step into the world; again the world resists, denies satisfaction. Although the baby cardinals are "old enough to feed themselves" their father still has to "fly down and stuff . . . the seed." . . . In truth, it seemed wrong for him to be a father at all.

> The father was such a beautiful clear bright red,
> with his tall crest the wind rippled like fur, that
> it didn't seem right for him to be so harried
> and useful and hardworking: it was like seeing
> a general in a red uniform washing hundreds
> and hundreds of dishes. The babies followed
> him everywhere, and kept sticking their open
> mouths up by his mouth—they shook all over,
> they begged so hard—and he never got a bite
> for himself. . . .

Before this the bat-poet is rendered impotent. "I watch him and he's just beautiful, he'd make a beautiful poem; but I can't think of anything". . . . Perhaps the bat suffers this strange case of writer's block because he cannot separate the beautiful bird from the trying circumstances in which he is found, and he isn't capable just yet of completing a total portrait of all that is before him. Perhaps the subject matter is too painful. It is difficult even for us the readers to identify what is going on among the cardinals. We may be disturbed because we are seeing a painful moment in a weaning process that will turn out well in the long run. Or we may indeed be viewing an unfit parent struggling to fulfill an impossible assignment. Whatever is the truth, the bat is facing a world which can only be partially rendered and imperfectly understood.

In its entirety, *The Bat-Poet* depicts the kind of simple learning we all have to do from day to day. The young bat wins some, loses some, and gets enough of what he needs out there to return home for a long winter's rest. Yet there is something heroic in the journey, an experience of life that is mysterious and deep. In his very first poem, **"The Owl,"** the bat tells us about a life-experience which is real but in no way commonplace. A poem of three stanzas, it opens suddenly with an image of sinister power.

> A shadow is floating through the moonlight
> Its wings don't make a sound. . . .

The shadow in the second stanza becomes a frightening bird of prey whose presence, once recognized, brings knowledge of death.

> The ear that listens to the owl believes
> In death. . . .

The owl symbolizes what is really to be feared in life, a more certain danger than the darkness, the unknown.

> The owl goes back and forth inside the night,
> And the night holds its breath. . . .

The poem thus brings together fact and symbol—the owl as predator and truly dangerous to the bat; the owl as the natural representative of the deadly nature of biological existence—to provide an existential ground for the whole story. It is within the very real limits of a hazardous existence that the bat will grow. The night can be overcome, but death—as an everyday possibility, as an ultimate fact—cannot. Such knowledge must simply be taken in.

The last poem, **"The Bat,"** affirms that the bat has come to a new awareness of self. He recognizes that he is limited and dependent by nature:

> A bat is born
> Naked and blind and pale
> His mother makes a pocket of her tail
> And catches him. . . .

However, the bat later recognizes that the poem is not a complete portrait of a bat. Returning to the barn to begin his own period of hibernation, the bat is troubled by the omission. It is hard to keep out of mind Frost's "Stopping by the Woods on a Snowy Evening" as the drowsy bat tries to pick up the poem and include what he has left out.

> He went back to the beginning. He said,

> A bat is born
> Naked and blind—

but before he could get any further he thought: "I wish I'd said we sleep all winter." . . .

There is something disturbing about the bat's need to certify that the very sleep he is now on the verge of entering is clearly defined and included as part of a bat's life. Perhaps he is not certain just yet that the normal processes of renewal do not lead to death.

The Animal Family introduces another alienated figure, a lonely hunter, who culls a family and happiness from the forest world around him. From a nostalgic yearning for his dead parents, well into his maturity, it is they he thinks about before sleep. He "would lie in his bed, warm under the bearskin and listen to the great soft sound the waves made over and over. It seemed to him that it was like his mother singing." One day the sound of the waves is replaced by a real voice, that of a mermaid who cannot speak or understand human speech. He brings her home with him and so begins a difficult dialogue of love and understanding in which each becomes more fully conscious of the other and their needs and value.

What the presence of the mermaid brings to the hunter, admittedly, is a far more striking experience of life, an existential one. He no longer dreams of his long-dead parents, but finds out instead about a more basic emptiness—in life itself. As he teaches the mermaid to speak, he as well as she learns that a house as well as a log is "hollow," and that his human water is more hollow than her sea-water. Thus a new perspective is added, one that stresses what is not there, as a definition of things—negativity. We can know ourselves according to what we don't have, according to what we are not. And it is language which permits such new and difficult knowledge. For a few marvelous paragraphs in **The Animal Family** the narrative becomes a meditation on thought and language as problematic essentials of being human. It is words and their boundary-making—the saying of what is light and dark, edge and impasse—which *invents* the hollow and dry spaces. Only with words can there be the experience of nothing, of negative space. Yet it is only with words that such experience can be transcended and the somethings found which can adequately fill the void. For the hunter the possibility of nothing is found to replace the self-defeating and sentimental longings for others, e.g. his parents, that he is burdened by. For the mermaid the "other"—a feeling, a care and concern for—is found to fill the void she had been taught to create when loss was imminent.

> When it storms for the people, no matter how terribly it storms, the storm isn't real—swim down a few strokes and it's calm there, down there it's always calm. And death is no different, if it's someone else who dies. We say: "Swim away from it"; we swim away from everything. . . .

She is by definition a cold creature; the closeness and warmth that are natural for humans are unnatural for her. She slept by the hunter "every night, but on top of the bearskin, not underneath it—she was used to the cold sea". . . . Her limits are not completely unfamiliar to us, nor unhuman. When she brings the hunter a necklace which he affirms as "the best gift he ever had" her reply emphasizes her prowess, a chauvinism about her race, rather than a pleasure in his pleasure. "You can find anything down in the sea. The ships sail over us for a while but at last they sink—in the end everything comes to us". . . . True or not, it is a chilling statement to human ears; a show of absolute power, not of love.

In **The Bat-Poet** growth comes as the bat enters more and more into the forest world outside the family nexus. In a sense, the process is reversed in **The Animal Family**. The hunter, who knows the forest-world well, grows through entering into family life. The development of his relationship with the mermaid is solidified through their finding and caring for the bear, the lynx, and finally, an orphaned boy. Caring for these foundlings enlists the couple in common cause, and gives them less reason for dwelling on the differences between them. In this regard, the boy provides a resolution to the issue of the mermaid's natural discomfort with the hunter and his world. She is charmed by the boy's beauty. But most important she sees at last the hunter, once a boy too, from a new perspective: "I never knew what it was like when you lived here with your mother and father, I never had seen a little one. He's half like a little man and half—oh, *different!*". . . . (pp. 81-5)

Whatever the boy's charms and meaning for the hunter and mermaid, the best of Jarrell can be found in the long and leisurely middle section of the story; the antics of the floppy-clumsy and every place bear and the gorgeous and sinewy lynx call to mind Marianne Moore's observation that, "In Randall Jarrell, we have an author who somehow unshackled himself from *self* and could have a good time." (p. 85)

Bringing these two up involves more than indulging occasional minor accidents such as that with the bees. The hunter and the mermaid do have to provide room and space, have to accommodate. But by and large the bear and the lynx grow quickly, learn by themselves, are soon self-sufficient. The bear hibernates all winter, and the lynx makes his own way to the bureau-drawer set aside for him. The boy, the human element, demands much more.

The lynx finds the boy in a shipwrecked boat, huddled next to his dead mother. Suddenly bereft of love and security, he naturally turns to the hunter and the mermaid, and they do not fail him. This way of responding to their foundling son's questions about his origins is a demonstration of the subtlety and humor we must call on in bringing up the human child, and, as at the end of *The Bat-Poet*, brings the reader face to face with some of life's imponderable issues. The hunter does not wait for his son to ask about where he came from, but instead challenges the boy directly:

> One day the hunter smiled back and said, "You must think you've lived with us always." The boy didn't know whether to say yes or no, and gave a laugh of confused joy, so that the mermaid smiled and said, "Yes, you think you've lived with us always."
>
> The boy's heart beat faster, but he said, "No, the lynx found me." And this got to be a game of theirs. Because he knew it wasn't so, the boy enjoyed saying the lynx had found him; and the hunter and mermaid enjoyed saying that the boy had lived with them always, because of—because of many things. . . .

The "game" is, of course, not thoroughly enjoyable. The subject-matter is discomforting. The ultimate answers, for the adopted or natural child, must carry the disturbing news of man's essentially lonely place in the cosmos. For even if the boy is really his parents', he must gradually recognize that he and they are not and never can be absolutely secure, safe from adversity and death, the human condition. The most we can do is to bridge the gap gracefully between the time when the questions are posed and that time when the total discovery about our place in things can become known. The boy in this story is all children who need to know the truth, but only when they are ready; until then they want it withheld out of love. The boy's "joy" is his pleasure in knowing he can risk the truth without it having to become too soon a part of his life. *The Animal Family* closes with the boy stepping more fully out into the realm of truth, and his parents, cautiously using "the game," holding him close still with love. When he and his father spy the lynx down on the beach, it is the boy who bravely picks up the game and playfully alludes to his beginning.

> The boy looked and saw [the lynx] and said laughing, "That's where he found *me!*"
>
> "Oh, we just told you that," said the hunter, starting their old game. "The very first day your mother and I came to the house, there you were in the corner, fast asleep.
>
> "That's right, fast asleep with *him,*" said the boy, giving the bear a push.
>
> "Oh no," said the mermaid, "that was years before the bear came. We've had you always."

With such a sense of security, a boy might dare to dream, to seek new adventure, new worlds. *Fly By Night* provides a boy, David, with such an opportunity.

It would be wrong to speak of *Fly By Night* without at least mentioning Maurice Sendak's contribution. Sendak also did the "Pictures" for *The Bat-Poet* and the "Decorations" for *The Animal Family,* but only in the last work's "Pictures" do we have to recognize the demands of a collaboration, an integrity of words and music. The narrative *needs* the marvelously substantial and provocative drawings. The full publica-

tion of David's pubescence, his delicately formed yet full-bodied nakedness, helps keep the work from being too narrowly a tone poem, a meditation. For this is Jarrell's most poetic story, not dream-like but literally a dream of a young boy and a poem for one fifth of its content.

Yet, beginning it, one might think quite otherwise. More than the previous stories, the opening is mundanely realistic, deceptively like a popular novel, or even a formula Hollywood movie of the forties.

> If you turn right at the last stoplight on New Garden Road and go north for a mile and a half, you come to a lake on a farm. Beyond, at the edge of the forest, there is a house . . .

The theme of loneliness is more immediately felt here than in the previous works. For David, the hero, "there aren't any children . . . to play with." And animals, pets, do not provide relief. When he takes it into the tree with him, "the cat never stays long." Each morning David waits, "so that the mailman can hand the mail to him instead of putting it in the box". . . . When we consider David's predicament, we can perhaps adjust to Jarrell's recourse for him:

> At night David can fly. . . .

David *can* fly because he must. He needs a perspective, a way of understanding his loneliness; he needs to try out a new way of being, and he needs to be where he has the chance to create the things and creatures which can help him "work it out." It becomes so much easier for us to do it with him because of the brilliance—the sheer perfection, the simple clarity and balance—of the writing. This is the way we have always lifted up from our beds and into the stratosphere:

> He looks out into the moonlight. Then he stretches his legs out as far as they will go, with the feet together. He can feel the sheet and the blanket and the counterpane pushing down against his toes. He presses his hands against the sides of his legs, with the fingers together, and stretches his head back as far as it will go. Then he takes a deep slow breath, and shuts his eyes and holds his breath; and after a minute he feels himself float up from the bed. He is flying. . . .

Soon the world of David is magical. He floats over his parents, merging briefly with a Bergmanesque dream of his father. . . . Then he is a master of the sky, admired by appreciative forest animals. . . . He sees the dreams of sheep, he sees ponies who dart away from him. By sight he owns the world.

The climax of the story, and perhaps of all Jarrell's work, occurs when he encounters a powerful owl, who is really the same awesome creature of *The Bat-Poet,* but more accessible and supportive—a mother-owl in real fact. . . . He hears a poem telling of its having flown the night to catch fish "for my nestlings' sake" . . . and feels how it protects him by gliding "around and around him". . . . This portrait answers the doubt raised by the cardinal-father of *The Bat-Poet.* David notes that although the baby owls have a "sad absurd look" . . . , and are ugly little things, he cannot deny that their mother's "eyes look loving". . . .

"The Owl's Bedtime Story" . . . seems to be an optimistic version of "Out of the Cradle Endlessly Rocking." A young owl is sent out into the world by its mother, finds an orphaned female owl, and brings her home with him where they are both taken in by the mother-owl. "She opened her wings, they nestled to her breast". . . . But as such it seems precious and forced, and not really as true to the nature of the owl as the portrait in *The Bat-Poet*. While there is something truly lovely about this last view of the owl, the happy ending is unconvincing. Friends and mates are not so easy to find, nor mothers so receptive to additional burdens.

Perhaps it is for this reason that the by now predictably uncertain quality of Jarrell's conclusion to *Fly By Night* seems so satisfying. On the one hand, the owl in this story does represent the resolution of a loss-of-mother theme we recognize in the poems and stories. When David returns to his own world, he is full of an awesome experience with a soaring, majestic, yet nurturing presence. Home in the kitchen, his real mother offers him breakfast, and David almost discovers in her the wondrous substitute he had been with. His mother, he considers

> looks at him like—
>
> "Like—" thinks David, "like—"
>
> The owl? No, not quite.
>
> . . . his mother looks at him like his mother. . . .

Like Dorothy in *The Wizard of Oz* David has flown so high only to come down to earth and discover that his dreams are not unlike his own real world. But it would take powerfully wishful thinking to say that it is as good as the one just visited.

Here, as in the two previous stories, Jarrell cannot deny the difficulty and disappointments of "reality." All these stories fulfill his commitment to a particular personal perspective. He is a modern; the world is existentially flat. In responding to it, we must resist the desire to color what we cannot change, to embellish or invent new worlds which deny the real. If life thus experienced is sometimes a little empty—in the nights and even the days of the bat, in the days of the hunter and David—such an emptiness is part of a complex human reality. Beginning to know it as early as we can will insure that we make good use of it sooner, and be less tempted to evade what is our only life. (pp. 91-2)

> *Leo Zanderer, "Randall Jarrell: About and for Children," in* The Lion and the Unicorn *(copyright © 1978 The Lion and the Unicorn), Vol. 2, No. 1, Spring, 1978, pp. 73-93 [the excerpts of Jarrell's work used here were originally published in his* The Bat-Poet *(reprinted with permission of Macmillan Publishing Company; copyright © Macmillan Publishing Co., Inc. 1963, 1964), Macmillan/Collier, 1964; also in his* The Animal Family *(© copyright, 1965, by Random House; reprinted by permission of Pantheon Books, a Division of Random House, Inc.), Pantheon Books, 1965; and also in his* Fly by Night *(reprinted by permission of Farrar, Straus and Giroux, Inc.; copyright © 1969, 1976 by Randall Jarrell), Farrar, Straus and Giroux, 1976].*

THE GINGERBREAD RABBIT (1964)

In Randall Jarrell's tale the gingerbread rabbit comes to life just prior to getting baked, then flees the giant, who turns out to be, as a matter of fact, a very pretty mother who had wished to surprise her daughter. This "impossible" rabbit experiences a number of adventures during his flight from humanity, the most delightful of which is an encounter with a fox who insists he is a rabbit and whose blasé attitude is a mixture of Sartre and Noel Coward at his best. All relations are ultimately re-

stored to order so that the young reader experiences the tumultuous magic and yet escapes the pain of chaos.

Randall Jarrell is one of our foremost poets and critics. As always, his prose here is straightforward, the tone is right, the learning informs subtly, the sensibility is in control. In short, the tale is in perfect taste. He needs only to explain to the adult why the gingerbread rabbit doesn't know what a rabbit is and why, on seeing a squirrel, knows what *it* is at first sight. But, then, I suppose, children need no explanation for such inequities because they are at home in the realm of non-Euclidean logic.

> *Harvey Breit, in a review of "The Gingerbread Rabbit," in* The New York Times Book Review *(© 1964 by The New York Times Company; reprinted by permission), March 29, 1964, p. 20.*

Mr. Jarrell has mixed almost everything into this story, the main elements of which are the gingerbread man and the crafty fox. I realize that the book is supposed to be a spoof of folk tales and people's reaction to them, but why is the gingerbread rabbit saved from the cruel (?) fate of being cooked and eaten— unless this is poking fun at those who always want a happy ending? Some children will enjoy the story; there are a few amusing moments in it. . . .

> *A review of "The Gingerbread Rabbit," in* Saturday Review *(© 1964 Saturday Review Magazine Co.; reprinted by permission), Vol. XLVII, No. 17, April 25, 1964, p. 41.*

The story itself has some nice touches—the reaction of the frightened gingerbread rabbit when told he might be eaten by the woman who baked him as a surprise for her little girl, and the scene with the wily fox who manages to persuade him that despite the pointed nose, sharp teeth and long bushy tail, he too is a rabbit. We think 5- to 8-year-olds will enjoy the story, especially the ending.

> *Margaret Sherwood Libby, "Adjustment Problems," in* Book Week—The Sunday Herald Tribune *(© 1964, The Washington Post), May 10, 1964, p. 25.*

The Gingerbread Rabbit has much more of a shape to its story [than Myra Berry Brown's *Pip Camps Out*], and has borrowed to good effect from the standard folk tale of the bun, johnny-cake, gingerbread boy, who escapes directly his baking is done. . . . Agreeably told . . . , this tale shows an affectionate interest and understanding in what the child wants to hear. (p. 1136)

> *"Consumer Goods or Durables?" in* The Times Literary Supplement *(© Times Newspapers Ltd. (London) 1967; reproduced from* The Times Literary Supplement *by permission), No. 3431, November 30, 1967, pp. 1136-37.**

THE BAT-POET (1964)

This is a shining jewel of a book. Poet Randall Jarrell says us his own song in a luminous, flawless prose that dances from the tongue and in bat-poems of piercing lyric sweetness. . . . The totality charms by turns the eye, the ear, and the imagination and, as true poetry must, it satisfies the heart. This book cries to be read aloud at story hours, in classrooms, and at bedtime. Do not relegate it to the "special" shelf, for it speaks to every child, not just the dreamy ones.

Ellen Rudin, in a review of "The Bat-Poet," in School Library Journal, an appendix to Library Journal (reprinted from the May, 1964 issue of School Library Journal, published by R. R. Bowker Co./ A Xerox Corporation; copyright © 1964), Vol. 10, No. 9, May, 1964, p. 84.

[The Bat-Poet] has been hailed as a masterpiece, and if it is not quite that, it is well worth attention. . . . The Bat-Poet is in essence about imitation—about poetry; it has some fine imaginative detail and the mood is warm and welcoming. . . . Yet for all its delicate precision, the book lacks the dramatic element that great children's books always possess. Nothing really happens in The Bat-Poet and no character emerges distinctly as a character. There is nothing very batty about the bat and the style of the bat's poems has little of the airiness of a flickering, fluttering creature. Still, Jarrell's book contains a mystery and magic rarely met with today. . . . (p. 634)

William Jay Smith, "The Bobbsey Twins at an Orgy," in The Nation (copyright 1964 The Nation magazine, The Nation Associates, Inc.), Vol. 198, No. 26, June 22, 1964, pp. 633-35.*

A curious book. A symptomatic book, I think. Certainly a book of a type more and more conspicuous in recent years. That is, a book by a very gifted writer who for a long time has ridden the crest of a literary wave, and who attempts, as the wave crashes into its trough, a louder, less sophisticated call, perhaps in the hope that some ordinary landpeople will come to his rescue. Significantly, most such books fail. Significantly also, many of them are written for children.

Jarrell's The Bat-Poet does not carry the customary age-group recommendation that publishers of juvenile books put on their products, and I presume this is at his own insistence; he wishes his book to seek its audience unaided. Judging from the style, however, one can see the sort of children he is looking for: bright, reasonably advanced, but still receptive, free from the conformities of adolescence. (p. 194)

[The bat's] songs turn out to be poems, rather Jarrellish poems. When he says his poems to the other bats, he is rejected as a bizarre and possibly dangerous fellow; when he says them to the mockingbird, he is snubbed. In the end his only friend is a rather simpleminded but impressible chipmunk. Choosing names only from the past, you could call the bat Keats, the mockingbird Southey, the chipmunk (stretching the point) Leigh Hunt. The writing is colloquial, vigorous, and precise, and the observations of animal life are acute, just the things that children see but that most adults, urban and suburban, have lost sight of. And Jarrell has taken extraordinary pains to insinuate the allegorical connections in such a way that they will not intrude.

Nevertheless, they do intrude, as they must. Isn't the idea of subliminal allegory a peculiarly modern contradiction in terms? An allegory, like any double entendre, needs to be openly acknowledged if it is to succeed; but here it is hidden, disguised, the author is trying to put something over on the reader. Very likely he must do this, since what he is attempting to infuse in the minds of his readers—a certain rationalization of culture—had few points of prior reference in their lives. But art is not a substitute for experience, and in any event the kids will see through it. After all, one of the points of the story is that writing, any writing, should be enjoyable, yet here is Jarrell himself, preaching. The kids won't like it and I don't blame them. I doubt I shall give the book to any children of my acquaintance, who have more interesting things to think about. Besides, can any author as calculating as Jarrell—which is to say, as calculating as a self-conscious artist must be—produce a book that kids will really enjoy? Granted, they like animal stories, but I think they want either the straight facts or something completely whacky. In my own case I remember taking equal delight in books by Seton and in Dr. Dolittle; but I loathed Uncle Remus. In spite of its sophisticated gloss, The Bat-Poet is only Remus again: sugar-coated esthetics instead of sugar-coated morality. What a bloody bore!

On the other hand, now that Stephen Dedalus has finally turned into a bat, maybe we can get rid of him and go on to the more important things that all of us—children, reviewers, and poets—have to consider. (pp. 194-95)

Hayden Carruth, "Daylight," in Poetry (© 1964 by The Modern Poetry Association; reprinted by permission of the Editor of Poetry), Vol. CV, No. 3, December, 1964, pp. 194-95.

It is a most unusual theme which is dealt with here and one treated with great sensitivity. Not the least of the reader's fine surprise comes from the portrait of the bat, a creature more often associated with night and witchcraft. . . . Mr. Jarrell's "Bat-poet" sees his world clearly, and it is one where "small is beautiful". It seems to make a gentle and perceptive book sound dull to state that motifs of vanity and happiness are handled with tenderness and humour, especially when the bat-poet appears in the role of despised prophet in his own country. . . . [This story] never strikes a false note of sentimentality. . . . The characters of chipmunk (hesitant and wholesome), the mocking-bird (somewhat severe, sceptical, and excessively vain) are nicely differentiated. As a critic of weight, the mocking-bird's comments on the bat's verse add a comfortable feeling of cleverness to the unconscious artistry of his poetry. No concessions are made to the sparse and mechanical school of debased poetry thought in some circles still to be appropriate to the taste of children. The rhymes and rhythms are subtle and true. This is a book which will continue to delight not only the child but the sophisticated adult also. It will stand the test of time. (pp. 11-12)

Margaret Walker, in a review of "The Bat-Poet," in Book Window (© 1977 S.C.B.A. and contributors), Vol. 5, No. 1, Winter, 1977, pp. 11-12.

[The Bat-Poet] is a small tale of gentle lyricism in which are distilled certain truths about the poet, the reader, and the child, Its story is simple, a linear skeletal plot such as one would find in a lyric of Blake or of Wordsworth. (p. 453)

The Bat-Poet swings easily from prose to verse, emerging as a seamless whole that can be a fine introduction to the idea and practice of poetry. The poet is seen as one who is apart but not cut off from ordinary experience. The bat's poems spring from a keen observation of the lives of his subjects. He struggles with the raw material of words but not in conscious analytical terms. It is for the didactic mockingbird to talk about " 'iambic trimeter.' " In his search for an audience the bat works on a subject he assigns himself, a chipmunk poem for a chipmunk (offered in exchange for six crickets), but he cannot write on demand for the cardinal. He finds that the truths his poems embody are not always welcome to the recipient. And he finds that his own memory and experience are the richest poetic source of all. Thus the many ideas of a poet's role— observer, participant, artisan, counterfeiter, dreamer, and truth-teller—are introduced and contemplated.

But *The Bat-Poet* is as much about the audience as about the poet. An audience for his poems is essential to the bat, and he is discouraged by the analytical coldness of the mockingbird. The chipmunk's response is at the other extreme, a visceral participation in the poem in which the subject and the words are seen as identical:

> "Shall I start on the poem about you?" asked the bat.
>
> "All right," said the chipmunk. "But could you put in lots of holes? The first thing in the morning I'm going to dig myself another."

The bat's own response to poetry—although it eventually leads to questioning, imitation, and analysis—is initially one of sheer joy. Jarrell is not telling us how to read poetry; he is telling us what poems can be if we let them.

A story which is essentially about poets and poetry could easily be remote, inward-looking, or closed. Jarrell escapes these pitfalls with a quality of deep innocence, of childlikeness, in his writing. He makes the connections to shared childhood experience. The circumstances that first lead the bat to poetry are described, for example, in terms accessible to all:

> Sometimes he would open his eyes a little and look out into the sunlight. It gave him a queer feeling for it to be daytime and for him to be hanging there looking; he felt the way you would feel if you woke up and went to the window and stayed there for hours, looking out into the moonlight.

This combination of quietness and restlessness, the familiar world seen with one dimension changed; here begins poetry.

Likewise, the central image of flight connects to an archetypal child dream. In his essay **"Poets, Critics and Readers"** Jarrell quotes an image of Freud's to give advice on how truly to listen. " 'Free-floating' " or " 'evenly-hovering' " are seen as positions from which one can guess, intuit, and fully understand. Children need no such analogy or theory. They know, with the bat-poet and with David of *Fly By Night* . . . , that flying gives one the freedom truly to see.

A master stroke in *The Bat-Poet*, not made explicit until the final poem, is that, of course, the bat "sees" to a large extent with sound. (pp. 454-55)

The Bat-Poet is a book to be read aloud. Only orally do the transitions from prose to verse achieve their total smoothness. Perhaps only the preschooler or the child just beginning to read is close enough to poetry to connect fully with Jarrell. . . .

Echoing Yeats's line "How can we know the dancer from the dance," the bat-poet asks in the mockingbird poem:

> A mockingbird can sound like anything.
> He imitates the world he drove away
> So well that for a minute, in the moonlight,
> Which one's the mockingbird? which one's the world?

This is the integrated vision of the poet and the child. And the two will meet on common ground in this small book. (p. 455)

Sarah Ellis, "A Second Look: 'The Bat-Poet'," in The Horn Book Magazine (copyright © 1981 by The Horn Book, Inc., Boston), Vol. LVII, No. 4, August, 1981, pp. 453-55 [the three excerpts of Randall Jarrell's work used here were originally published in his The Bat-Poet (reprinted with permission of Macmillan Publishing Company; copyright © Macmillan

Publishing Co., Inc. 1963, 1964), Macmillan/Collier, 1964; in addition, the third excerpt first appeared as "The Mockingbird;" in The New Yorker, Vol. XXXIX, No. 37, November 2, 1963].

In a book he called "half for children and half for grownups," Randall Jarrell explores the dilemma of the artist in maintaining his individuality in his work, or finding his voice, and yet approaching an audience. *The Bat-Poet* records a character's attempt to find the correct voice in a world that holds both danger and security. Through the development of and responses to three full-length poems (and another poem that the bat is allowed only to begin), the novice bat-poet learns important lessons about his craft and his audience and about his relation to both. As Karl Shapiro has noted about the main concern of the book: "Whether to be a bat or a poet: that is the question." From this central question, the bat-poet's state of individual and artistic awareness rests. (p. 71)

Through his separation [from the other bats], the bat becomes aware of a new world, both physical and creative, that he has never known before or ever will be separate from again. He becomes, first, an observer of the world of day with its bright colors, light, incessant activities, and sounds, especially those of the mockingbird and his songs. He tries to make a poem to tell the other bats about the world they are missing and to share with them this new world of experience. . . . Even before the bat can finish his first poem, the other bats rebuke him with the displeasure they receive from its images—strange, unbelievable, and even frightening images of a world they unyieldingly refuse to try to imagine or stay awake to see for themselves. They express further displeasure with that which the little bat finds most pleasing, the mockingbird's songs; the sounds are too different from their own to like. With this harsh rebuttal, the bat goes his own way, aware that if he wants to continue to enjoy the world by day, he must abandon the familiar.

The bat willingly suffers this rejection in order to listen to the mockingbird's songs. He decides, after listening to these songs for a while, to "make up a song like the mockingbird's." . . . Although he fails to imitate the mockingbird's sounds, he is able to put together some words that to him sound beautiful, and he decides that "'If you get the words right you don't need a tune.'" (pp. 71-2)

Jarrell presents this same philosophy in suggesting that works of art be treated as a form of nakedness, "a means by which the reader, writer, and subject are able for once to accept their own nakedness . . . not merely of the 'naked truth,' but also of the naked wishes that come before and after the truth." Jarrell wants to divorce the writer, reader, and subject from all confines of the past: the way of thinking, writing, and reading. From the same freedom and from the "wishes that come before and after the truth," the bat becomes a bat-poet, a dual identity that prompts him to search his own potentials and resources to become a maker of songs, a poet.

The more poems the bat makes, throws away, and forgets, the more he feels the need for someone to hear a poem. After escaping an owl, the bat makes a poem about his frightening closeness to death and decides to tell the poem to the mockingbird, whose look is "peremptory, authoritative . . . as if he were more alive than anything else and wanted everything else to know it," and who on the "good days" does not regard the world as much "but just song" and on the "bad days" makes it his business to chase everything away. . . . The mockingbird is the symbol of the poet in the world about whom

Jarrell speaks specifically as the "real artist" who "some of the time, as Keats says, 'when a poet looks at sparrows playing in the gravel he is those sparrows' but the funny thing is . . . the rest of the time . . . most of the time if he's a real poet, he's just as vain as he can be and he's obsessed with *himself*." Jarrell continues, "Mockingbirds are not only more like artists than other birds, they're more like people, too."

To the bat-poet's owl poem, the mockingbird responds as master-poet, technician, craftsman. He instructs the bat on such matters as line, meter, and rhyme. Certainly unaware at this point of such matters of craft, the bat-poet is dumbfounded by the mockingbird's emphasis on the poem's technicalities and his virtual ambivalence to the poem's content: "What do I care how many feet it has? The owl nearly kills me, and he says he likes the rhyme-scheme!" The mockingbird's response to technique drowns the bat's voice. The mockingbird's concern is with how the piece of art is put together; and the bat's concern is with putting his experience together in a poem.

Although the bat does get the mockingbird's attention, his totally technical response to the poem and lack of sensitivity to the depth of the experience intimated in the poem angers the new poet. Likewise, the bat's poem receives disconcerting remarks from the other bats who find the poem incomprehensible through their inability to transfer their experiences into his poem and through their lack of willingness to suspend their disbelief long enough to imagine the world the poem describes. With these frustrating experiences, the bat-poet realizes a crucial problem of the poet: "'The trouble isn't making poems, the trouble's finding somebody that will listen to them.'" (pp. 72-3)

The absence of what the bat-poet considers appropriate listening, much less response, compels him to reexamine his own verse. He finds the poem credible in its representation of his experience with the owl and knows that the "owl would like it," but because of his fear of the owl, the bat cannot tell him his poem. . . . The bat is not yet ready to meet certain realities of the world; the owl represents a greater danger to him. As a result, the bat continues to yearn and search for an audience that will find pleasure in hearing a poet who has a true sense of what he knows and experiences rather than a sense of rules and rhetoric. He finds that audience in the chipmunk.

After reciting his owl poem to the chipmunk, the bat-poet is happy with the chipmunk's responses: "'He didn't say any of that two-feet-short stuff,' the bat thought triumphantly; 'He was scared!'" . . . Even if the chipmunk's response is a literal and pragmatic one, the bat-poet feels as if, perhaps, now, he has found an ear for the meaning of the poem and, correspondingly, for the meaning of his experience.

In a poem that the bat makes for the chipmunk, he records as much of the realities of the chipmunk's life as of the ever-near and yet unseen presence of death in the owl's poem. The world of warmth, security, and community that the bat had known with the other bats now becomes integrated with this other world of uncertainty and even death. In yet another poem that he tries to write about a father cardinal, the neophyte experiences his first disappointment as a writer, his first failure of creativity.

The bat cannot write about the cardinal. His problem with making a "portrait" of the cardinal represents another step of the new poet's initiation into an art that requires understanding, even if the understanding is subliminal. The experience of the father cardinal in feeding his young is outside the bat's realm of knowledge, and he is relieved when he is not made re-

sponsible for a poem about aspects of life that he does not understand: the nature of sacrifice, the demands of love, the frustrations of potential. . . . (p. 73)

The bat-poet consoles himself in his inability to "make portraits of the animals after all" by admitting to the chipmunk, "'It was just so I'd have somebody to say them to. Now that I've got you I'm all right—when I get a good idea about it and say it to you.'" . . . In a sense, the bat-poet has acquiesced to his lack of range of experience; in another sense, he has opened himself for the need for that experience. Regardless, the bat-poet has found a new community in the chipmunk, or at least, he thinks he has.

The bat's poem about the mockingbird is a crucial point in his creative development. In this poem, he describes the artist imitating life and then rejecting the life he has imitated; he describes the artist accepting the imitation for the real. . . . The bat-poet responds to the world as he sees it, and such response angers the mockingbird who sees in the poem an accusation about the nature of his imitation. The mockingbird even fails to notice the craftsmanship of the poem; the subject, this time, is too close.

The poem speaks of the dangers of imitation, and in this new world, the bat-poet is learning that there exist fine lines between the real and the imaginary, between listening and hearing, between seeing and understanding. As he develops knowledge about the ways of this world, he also develops a greater sense of self-awareness; he wishes originally to imitate the mockingbird but realizes that he is not the mockingbird. . . . In realizing what he is not, the bat remembers what he is and desires to make a poem about bats. The bat leaves the inspiration of the mockingbird and the security of the chipmunk and finds his own voice and seeks his true audience.

The bat, not the poet, remembers his old world—the warmth and protection of the other bats, the "first things" about a bat and its mother—and yearns to return to this time, and if not to the time, then to the feelings intrinsic to his own physical world. While he readies himself for the change in weather, still unaware completely of the change in himself, he creates a poem about bats that pictures this new self-awareness of limitation and dependencies—and yet it is still not a complete portrait. . . . The bat-poet discovers that writing this poem is "easier than the other poems, somehow: all he had to do was remember what it had been like and every once in a while put it in a rhyme." . . . What is essential to the bat becomes the subject of his most important and accomplished poem; the voices of the bat and of the poet integrate fully to catch the essence of life as a bat, any bat. The bat-poet returns to his fellows because his poetry is intended to tell them about themselves.

Like the bat in the poem, the bat-poet still depends upon his community. His separation from the familiar is only temporary: as he has ventured out into the world, so must he return to his home. He has spoken to a world that has only heard the voice that it wishes to hear; the bats who live by hearing will learn by hearing. The bat-poet senses, however, that something is missing from the poem; something must be added to his poem to make it complete, just one more experience, and yet he returns to sleep with his community before he can remember what that experience should be.

The bat-poet is on the brink of mature experience—whether critical or existential, it does not matter. He is changed, certainly, from the self in the book's beginning. He is wise, he is different, and he is aware of a world that he can no longer ignore like the rest of the bats because he has not only become a part of it physically but creatively as well.

Yet at the closing of the book with the bat-poet on the brink of sleep, he has failed to recite his poem to the others. What is missing from the poem is the bat-poet's telling it, sharing it, voicing it to the others. Whether or not he remembers the poem and recites it after they all awaken is a question left unanswered at the close of the book; the bat has still to decide whether to remain a bat or to become a bat-poet. It is all a matter of voice. The bat-poet's voice is stilled; it is not silent. (pp. 73-6)

> Pamela R. Howell, *"Voice Is Voice Whether a Bat or a Poet"* (1982), in Proceedings of the Ninth Annual Conference of The Children's Literature Association: The Child and the Story, An Exploration of Narrative Poems, *edited by Priscilla A. Ord (copyright © 1983 by The Children's Literature Association), Children's Literature Association, 1983, pp. 71-6 [the excerpts of Randall Jarrell's work used here were originally published in his* The Bat-Poet *(reprinted with permission of Macmillan Publishing Company; copyright © Macmillan Publishing Co., Inc. 1963, 1964), Macmillan/Collier, 1964].*

THE ANIMAL FAMILY (1965)

Occasionally, very rarely—like the spirit of delight—comes a book that is not so much a book as a kind of visitation. I had not known that I was waiting for **"The Animal Family"** but when it came it was as though I had long been expecting it. . . .

Nothing could be simpler than this story, if indeed one can call it a story. A lonely hunter finds a mermaid, takes her to live in his hut and with her adopts successively a bear-cub, a lynx kitten and a boy from a drifting lifeboat. That is all—and yet, reading it, one is convinced that this all is everything, each happening inevitable, essential, right. The secret lies, of course less in the plot than in the telling. The author lingers over the facts with the absorption, the inner delight of the true storyteller, letting them play and range as they will; he listens to what they say, he notes down every informing detail, above all he takes his time.

Taking time takes one into timelessness. And thus the story, like the traditional fairy tale, seems to be without beginning and without end in the sense that one is aware of it existing long before the flyleaf and long after the back page. Was, is now and ever shall be is the meaning both of Once Upon a Time and Happy Ever After; and this is the world the book inhabits.

All good stories have this feeling of continuity, of going on and never ending. Moreover, the good story never explains. The courtship of the hunter and the mermaid is taken as a matter of course much as it is in the old Scottish ballads where, after all, mermaids who wive with humans are two-a-penny. There is nothing here of Hans Andersen's mawkish portentousness and nostalgia, no longing for an immortal soul, no craving for a pair of legs. *Our* mermaid accepts herself as she is, a sea-creature in love with the land, eager to understand its language, willing to submit to its limitations. She toils happily, if awkwardly, over the meadows, propelling herself by her own tail, lives on a diet of raw fish and when she takes up her abode in the hut proves to be an indifferent housewife. But there is more to homekeeping than sweeping floors or stirring the stew; it is relationship that matters. And here every domestic

detail of their mutual life throws light upon the characters of the hunter and the mermaid and the affinity between them. . . .

The book, indeed, is a paean to family life and its long unending thread. The reciting of its small, factual, intimate daily round constitutes, as it were, an epic in reverse. The reader is made party to all its lights and shadows, its souvenirs, heirlooms, problems; one grieves with the hunter when he dreams of his dead parents, is concerned for him in his moments of masculine uncertainty in front of the mermaid's feminine sureness, rejoices with them both when with the advent of the first child—the bear-cub—two and one make three. The animal children are beautifully drawn and juxtaposed; the clumsy, slow-witted bumbling bear and the quick lithe lynx—each becomes more truly himself when placed beside the other. After two such fully realized characters the author could artistically go no further in the world of beasts. The third child *had* to be a boy and with him the family is complete—at peace, with the charm wound up.

The story is a medley of lyrical factuality. Never once does its sentiment decline into sentimentality—"the bear's table manners were bad, but so were the mermaid's"—nor our belief into skepticism. There is the truth of fact and the truth of truth, as D. H. Lawrence said, and any child reading this book would know to which category **"The Animal Family"** belonged.

Is it a book for children? I would say Yes because for me *all* books are books for children. There is no such thing as a children's book. There are simply books of many kinds and some of them children read. I would deny, however, that it was written *for* children. But is any book that these creatures love really invented for them? "I write to please myself," said Beatrix Potter, all her natural modesty and arrogance gathered into the noble phrase. Indeed, whom else, one could rightly ask. And this book bears the same hallmark. Someone, in love with an idea, has lovingly elaborated it simply to please himself—no ax to grind, making no requirements, just putting a pinch of salt on its tail—as one would with a poem—and setting it down in words. How, therefore, could a child—and children come in all ages, remember—fail to read and enjoy it?

> P. L. Travers, *"A Kind of Visitation,"* in The New York Times Book Review *(© 1965 by The New York Times Company; reprinted by permission), November 21, 1965, p. 56.*

If the values to be found in juvenile literature were, in the future, to be measured against the wealth in this golden fable . . . , I suggest that we would witness a renaissance which would be applauded by the Brothers Grimm, Hans Andersen, and Lewis Carroll. If I sound strident it is because I'm afraid that adults upon discovering the virtues in this book will appropriate it for themselves. No! Let the kids of all ages get at this, for this tale of a lonely hunter and how he acquires a family consisting of a mermaid, a bear, a lynx, and finally a boy, is the stuff from which a lifetime of dreams and epiphanies are made, a veritable boot camp for the imagination! Everything is here: the fascination, delight, and accommodation with reality as it is—and yet, the attraction to and desire for a new reality, that could and should be. If this all sounds dully philosophical, let me assure you that all these elements are evoked through a poetic mood, a harmony of images that favorably compares with Saint Exupéry's *Little Prince.*

> James D'Anna, in a review of *"The Animal Family,"* in School Library Journal, *an appendix to* Library Journal *(reprinted from the December, 1965 issue of* School Library Journal, *published by R. R. Bowker*

Co./A Xerox Corporation; copyright © 1965), Vol. 12, No. 4, December, 1965, p. 78.

A most unusual book, handsome in format and in the quiet illustrations; the pictures complement the subtle simplicity of the fanciful story. This is an idyll, a Utopia book. . . . The author has miraculously avoided whimsy and sugar-coating; the writing style is gentle and delicate, with the nuance of latent content and a trace of pointed humor. Simple enough to read aloud to children too young to read the book by themselves, the story is probably best suited to the sensitive reader who can appreciate the perceptive writing.

Zena Sutherland, in a review of "The Animal Family," in Bulletin of the Center for Children's Books *(reprinted by permission of The University of Chicago Press; copyright 1966 by The University of Chicago), Vol. 19, No. 6, February, 1966, p. 100.*

Many of Randall Jarrell's poems were inspired by fairytales. The strange appropriateness of the *Märchen* to an exploration of family relations and sexuality is a central factor in some of his best work: these myths were in his blood. It seems odd, then, to encounter a children's story by Jarrell which has in it very little of Grimm. . . . There is no suspense, no riddles or spells, no horror. There is no real fable.

And yet the story is a perfect example of Jarrell's delicate blend of humour and pathos. Love is evoked through strangeness and the way in which alien habits are described and understood by the poet and his characters. Ordinary things are seen afresh, and the games and rituals of family life exalted by a splendid accuracy of description and the overriding tenderness that Jarrell's admirers will of course expect. The mermaid holding her breath ("She would do it to amuse him, occasionally pointing to her closed mouth and narrowed nostrils") or the stung bear licking himself ("As the fire got his wet fur warmer and warmer, a little cloud of steam rose from him; he smelled like four or five wet dogs and a beehive") are small examples of such invention and observation. The role of the mermaid, half-wife, half-daughter, is particularly fine and the affection between her and the hunter beautifully understated. . . .

[*The Animal Family*] establishes the child's role as newcomer, having to learn the differences between parent and parent or between pet and child, with care and love. The masterly tone of the book is matched by Maurice Sendak's illustrations. . . . Slight though it is, *The Animal Family* has a rare sort of magic and will not be easily forgotten.

John Fuller, "Perfect Bliss," in The Times Literary Supplement *(© Times Newspapers Ltd. (London) 1976; reproduced from The Times Literary Supplement by permission), No. 3864, April 2, 1976, p. 392 [the excerpts of Randall Jarrell's work used here were originally published in his* The Animal Family *(© copyright 1965, by Random House, Inc.; reprinted by permission of Pantheon Books, a Division of Random House, Inc.), Pantheon Books, 1965].*

This may be one of those books . . . which win the warmest critical acclaim yet pass the child by. I hope I am wrong. There are things here which will undoubtedly appeal to a child—the closely observed descriptions of animal behaviour; even the sheer improbability of the story—but its finely tooled craftsmanship has a calculated quality in it which may alienate some readers.

It is certainly a beautiful book. The story . . . is told with an exquisite sense of style, atmosphere and timing. The book is

neither myth nor allegory but there seem to be universal undercurrents of truth beneath the elegant fantasy. Sendak's decorations . . . [convey] the quiet charm of the atmosphere, more than the sentiment or the humour. The succes d'estime of *The Animal Family* seems as assured here as in the States, and it should become a collector's piece if not a nursery favourite.

Marcus Crouch, in a review of "The Animal Family," in The Junior Bookshelf, Vol. 40, No. 4, August, 1976, p. 232.*

The Animal Family begins with a full realistic description of a hunter living in a cabin on a meadow next to an ocean, very much aware that he is alone. One day he hears a voice singing in the water, and, after returning to hear the voice day after day, finally identifies the singer as a mermaid. He learns her song, sings it, she sings back, and what seems like the beginning of a courtship ensues:

> The hunter had lived so long with animals that he himself was patient as an animal. He waited a long time, and then went home; he was not disappointed that she had gone, only certain that she would be back. He kept remembering how the laugh and the last notes of the song had sounded. When he was so nearly asleep that he could hardly tell whether he was remembering them or hearing them, he was still certain that she would be back—after he was fast alseep, neither thinking nor dreaming, he still smiled.

If this were a strictly realistic story, "she" would be a woman and the tale a romance, but it isn't, quite, because "she" lives in the sea. She sings, she responds to his attempt to sing her song, she goes away, and he is "only certain that she would be back." If a robin sings in my yard day after day, I can justifiably expect it to return on subsequent days, but that is not quite the hunter's situation. He is certain "she" will come back to him, and because of him, which is why this feels so much like a romance. Jarrell alerts us, thus, to two possibilities: "she" is human, somehow, and will become the hunter's mate; "she" is "animal" nonetheless and will become his guide, his pet, something not a mate. The word "mermaid" covers both possibilities without stressing one to the exclusion of the other.

The mermaid and the hunter learn to talk by her learning his language, but the major distinction Jarrell keeps making between them cuts across the two possibilities mentioned above, still without denying either: he is male, she is female; he is human, she is not. These distinctions, though, are then superseded by another: she is sea, and he is land. . . . [Gradually] she comes ashore, finds out about fire, and cooked food, and fresh water, and the occasional boredom of the hunter.

In these pages Jarrell faces his biggest hurdles, and we can be aware of them even reading the book for the first time. The first concerns the part of the mermaid that is a fish and her ability to adapt to land. Jarrell solves part of the problem by making her breathe through her human mouth to gain oxygen, so while in the water she must occasionally surface, like a whale or a dolphin. He tries to solve the more difficult question of her perambulation by just ignoring it until late in the book, after she has been on land for years, and even then he explains nothing. A book so much concerned with physical detail and animal behavior is marred, thus, because its most interesting figure is a mermaid moving about on land. The second problem is perhaps more serious, and concerns the relation of *The Animal Family* to Andersen's ''The Little Mermaid.'' It seems for long stretches as though Jarrell's book is best seen as a critique of Andersen's values. In ''The Little Mermaid,'' . . . life in the sea is inferior to life on land, as much so as life on earth is inferior to life in heaven; only human beings have immortal souls, and the best and brightest of mermaids is willing to suffer agonies in order to gain the love of a mortal prince and thereby to gain an immortal soul as well. Perhaps Jarrell's story can read perfectly well for a reader who has never read Andersen, but unquestionably it is in the awkward position of being tilted so it can be set against Andersen's tale. Jarrell's land is not superior to the sea, only different, and Jarrell delights in working back and forth between showing us the mermaid as animal—thus, given over to gathering food, sleeping, and unreflectiveness—and the mermaid as human—thus, able to talk, be interested in new things, eager to adapt to conditions for which she was not physically designed. Everything around her keeps strictly realistic bearings, but her presence, her questions and puzzlements about the ways of people and the land force Jarrell and the hunter into fresh examinations of the land, and of the difference that being human does and does not make. Jarrell insists we cannot grant Andersen's assumptions about the superiority of the human unless we can demonstrate it. But the hurdle of this book's relation to ''The Little Mermaid'' remains, for me, not so much jumped as walked around; little as I am fond of Andersen's tale, little do I enjoy what seems *The Animal Family*'s parasitic relation to it.

What Jarrell wants, we soon see, is a romance, but one whose bearings are very different from Andersen's. I am going to break off the following quotation in mid-sentence for the purpose of asking what our expectations are about the way the sentence will end:

> She loved the look of the fire, but she hated anything cooked over it—she ate nothing but raw fish she herself had swum after and caught. (When one was particularly appetizing she couldn't resist offering the hunter a bit. ''It's so good when you don't burn it in the fire,'' she would say.) She helped the hunter with the cooking as—

It is a comparison that is set up by that ''as.'' If our expectations are derived from at least parts of our own world, or from Andersen's, the sentence might read ''as a bride who had never learned to cook.'' Jarrell's text actually continues as follows:

> She helped the hunter with the cooking as a husband helps his wife: when he had gone out to hunt and had left something to stew, she would take the pot off the fire. But she never knew when to take it off; sometimes the meat was hard, and sometimes it was cooked to pieces, and she never got it right except by accident.

This is perhaps realistic, but not what we would expect nonetheless. Jarrell's realism wants, first, to alert us to the problems of mermaids and to the possibility that cooking is not the ''natural'' event we usually take it to be; and he wants, second, to reverse or negate our sense of the ''natural'' roles for the hunter and the mermaid. She is not the hunter's ''husband,'' to be sure, and she is not his mate or his bride, but an outsider trying to be helpful.

We are now on the thirty-seventh page of a book of one hundred and eighty pages; where is it going to go? Not into an Andersen romance, not back into the sea, and not, unless it alters its engrossed tone, into a satire against mankind. The best we can say is that Jarrell thus far has employed his one nonrealistic element, the mermaid, to ask about and point our attention toward the land, so it should be that that Jarrell is interested in. And so it is. What follows is a myth of the family that is clearly designed to replace Andersen's myth of the romantic lovers. The hunter shoots a bear one day in order to escape from it, and he then captures her cub, brings it home, and feeds it, so the bear is soon part of the family. The hunter steals a lynx cub, claiming its mother will not miss it for long, and soon it too is part of the family. The lynx finds a boy in a boat that has washed up on the beach, and the boy is brought home and soon no one remembers a time before he came. The bear, being well fed, remains peaceful and sleeps most of the time. The lynx enjoys its loving family and yet remains independent in a feline way. The boy grows more slowly than the other two and knows instinctively not to put his hands in the fire. Jarrell makes it as close to realism as he can, and gains this kind of effect:

> That night they put deerskins and sealskins on the bed and let the cub sleep on the bearskin, in the corner. Sometimes he would wake and cry for a while, and then huddle in the corner with his face pushed into the bearskin, and go back to sleep. And in two days he was sitting on the floor by the table when they ate, eating with them; in a week it was as if he had lived with them always.

The hunter and the mermaid thus become parents to the bear cub; the young thing instinctively acknowledges its need of protection and food, and they, apparently just as instinctively, offer it to him. None of the three sees anything remarkable in what has happened, but Jarrell himself does, and expects us to.

Then comes the lynx. . . . These aren't ''magic'' animals, not even talking animals, but the aim of Jarrell's realistic rendering of them is not so much realism as myth, and, as we begin to see this, we can also see why Jarrell wanted to begin with the mermaid, for all the awkwardness he gets into with her. The mermaid wants to live with the hunter, not as his mate, but because she is curious about life on land; he sleeps underneath the skins and she on top. The mermaid, however, being herself ''magical,'' sets us up to expect the magical, so Jarrell then offers, as something magical but tantalizingly possible, his mythical version of the real. Having started with a mermaid, rather than a woman, our questions about the romantic and sexual possibilities between the mermaid and the hunter are transformed into assurances about their grand worth as parents, since the cubs and the boy want warmth, food, and protection, and, receiving it, they grow into themselves, fully and peacefully. Start with the mermaid, and use her as the one magical ingredient in a myth of the real and the natural.

Hovering over the entire story is a question: why couldn't life be like this? Why do we live in isolation and division when harmony seems possible? When we first ask it, the answer is obvious: because this is a story with a mermaid, and mermaids don't exist. As the story unfolds, however, that answer comes to seem shallow and inadequate, and another, though never offered explicitly by Jarrell, seems more to the point: because we don't separate family life from sexual and procreative life. The hunter and the mermaid are of different species, so they don't mate, and, since they are not the natural parents of the bear, the lynx, and the boy, there is never any fuss about father-roles or mother-roles, any more than there is about husband-roles and wife-roles, and male-roles and female-roles. They nurture instinctively, not because they love to—though they do—but because they must. Jarrell cannot, to be sure, solve our sexual and procreative problems by avoiding them, but he can show us the animal family we could make were we able to solve, or ignore, those problems.

How wonderful, or so it all seems to the alien, the mermaid, who tells the hunter near the end of the book, as they are lying on the beach one day:

> "And then I knew how you feel when it rains and there's nothing for you to do. I knew, but none of them knew. They don't know how to be bored or miserable. One day is one wave, and the next day the next, for the sea people—and whether they're glad or whether they're sorry, the sea washes it away. When my sister died, the next day I'd forgotten and was happy. But if you died, if he died, my heart would break."

The point, she insists, is not that she is female and he is male, not that she is "animal" and that he and the boy are "human," for these are subsidiary points. The crucial difference is still that she is sea and they are land, and she has come to live with them:

> "But on land it's different. The storm's real here, and the red leaves, and the branches when they're bare all winter. It all changes and never stops changing, and I'm here with nowhere to swim to, no way ever to leave it or forget it. No, the land's better! The land's better!"

The lynx is moving away down the beach, and presumably at some point it will not come back. The bear, at the end, is sound asleep, because bears sleep. The boy, at the end, is talking to his parents, because boys talk and ask questions because they are curious. The family doesn't change the nature of any of its members, and it must be strong enough to protect against the pain of those who feel pain for longer than a moment or two. The family is the land's great creation, made possible by the magical mermaid, and the longing that lies behind the resultant myth wants it to be true that such a family does not need a mermaid in order to be made real.

The crucial use of the talking mermaid for Randall Jarrell is to help make a myth, and in this making we are not strongly aware of story beyond the opening sequences. Our task as we read is to see what we know to be prefitted parts being fitted into their prefitted places. In such a book, nothing is a mere thing, a mere dialogue, a mere animal or person, and such books always run the risk of seeming too pat and too preachy, and perhaps concerning that little more need be said here than that Jarrell runs these risks better than most such books. In such a book, also, we don't, I think, become actively aware of an "A is B, animal is like person" metaphor, at least not past the opening scenes, because we are being asked to say, in effect, A (animal) and B (person) belong to class C (family), and the real metaphor is between C and the "real world." (pp. 84-90)

> *Roger Sale, "Animals," in his* Fairy Tales and After: From Snow White to E. B. White *(copyright © 1978 by the President and Fellows of Harvard College; excerpted by permission), Cambridge, Mass.: Harvard University Press, 1978, pp. 77-100 [the excerpts of Randall Jarrell's work used here were orig-*

> *inally published in his* The Animal Family *(© copyright 1965, by Random House, Inc.; reprinted by permission of Pantheon Books, a Division of Random House, Inc.), Pantheon Books, 1965].**

FLY BY NIGHT (1976)

A warm, wispy, enfolding dream of owls in their nest and of David, who can fly at night, with a bed to return to. . . . Hardly a story, and the **"Bedtime Story"** is slack as a poem compared to the animal portraits in *The Bat Poet*. . . . Despite their thematic relationship the two parts don't synergize. (Who knows what Jarrell had in mind?) Still, more than the poem, the framing prose has a hypnotic pull. . . .

> *A review of "Fly by Night," in* Kirkus Reviews *(copyright © 1976 The Kirkus Service, Inc.), Vol. XLIV, No. 20, October 15, 1976, p. 1137.*

[Finished before Jarrell's death, this story] makes us realize again how special his contributions to children's literature are and deepens our sense of loss. . . . The writing is lyrical prose, interspersed with rhymes and a long poem. . . . This book is a rarity, sure to find a warm welcome everywhere.

> *A review of "Fly by Night," in* Publishers Weekly *(reprinted from the October 25, 1976 issue of* Publishers Weekly, *published by R. R. Bowker Company, a Xerox company; copyright © 1976 by Xerox Corporation), Vol. 210, No. 17, October 25, 1976, p. 74.*

A deeply resonant mood piece, *Fly By Night* is as hard to catch hold of as a dot of mercury or a half-remembered dream. This is, in fact, one long, extended image of dreaming. . . . Jarrell writes with simple force and grace about the essential loneliness of life (during his dream voyage David is unable to touch or communicate with the animals he encounters) but above all he is writing about love—family love, especially, which is shown to be strong and constant. . . . Although this will probably fly over the heads of most readers, a special audience will find a powerful voice and vision here. (pp. 59-60)

> *Jane Abramson, in a review of "Fly by Night," in* School Library Journal *(reprinted from the November, 1976 issue of* School Library Journal, *published by R. R. Bowker Co./ A Xerox Corporation; copyright © 1976), Vol. 23, No. 3, November, 1976, pp. 59-60.*

There is a great distance between the callow clutter of books-for-kids and the high haunted aeries of American fantasies as told by Randall Jarrell. . . .

Jarrell was a master of the pleasant seemings of American juvenile literature that hide grim truths. *The Animal Family* . . . is a seemingly peaceful pastoral about a hunter who seeks and finds companions. It is an idyllic tale so tranquil that we are apt to overlook the fact that the hunter befriends each of his "sons" over a cashiered mother. That fact, and that the only female of the book is a mermaid in whom the hunter sees his dead mother, hints that something is amiss in Eden.

Fly By Night is likewise an embodiment of the wish for companions. . . .

David is as powerless as Huckleberry Finn, another floater, when in his tree perch he cannot save his friend Buck; as powerless as the aerial Peter Pan trying to persuade Wendy. David cannot help the mice, cannot ask a fleeing rabbit to wait, and his hovering presence makes the ponies shy. Though he exercises Superman's power of flight, all his potential companions are the retiring Clark Kents of the animal world who take flight at his appearance.

And so he turns away from them and looks above, to a winged superior, to a night bird awake like himself. A striped owl with a small fish in its claws befriends him. The owl speaks to David in poetry and invites him to her nest where two owlets rest. To hardnosed David the unfeathered owlets make a sorry picture but he sees in the loving eyes of the mother owl that she "doesn't know how they look."

The owl tells her three nestlings a bedtime story, one that they can fall to sleep by before daybreak, and one that is the keystone to *Fly By Night*. It is the story of an owlet who is all alone and wishes for company. A great owl comes and tells him this will only come to pass if he leaves his mother's nest and flies in the daylight. The owlet departs, struggles in the tumult of "unfriendly day," clumsily finds footing on a branch, and finally meets and makes a sisterly companion of another owlet in a tree at whose base a dead owl lies. The two of them wend their way back through the harsh sunlight and the crows to the original nest where they welcome the arrival of night, the moon, and the owl they call "Mother" against whose breast they nestle making brooding sounds.

Once the owl has told the bedtime story she accompanies David home where he wakes to sunlight and forgets. Twice David struggles to remember, to link night and day in a simile: "the owl looks at me like . . . like . . .—" but before he can remember sunlight streams into the kitchen and "his mother looks at him like his mother." (p. 30)

David lives in the same superstitious and myth-filled world where angels are made. It is a world where "like" carries no force and invisible passions or emotions must be wholly made over into visible and physical shapes: gods, and angels, wise owls. And it is a world of strict separations of night from day, child from companions, mother from child that become other separations: "dancing mice" and frightened mice, unfeathered owlets and lovable offspring, hardnosed literality and what is figured in dreams.

Fly By Night will be read by dreamy youths like David, those same youths who in their tree houses have read of others that were ordinary too but, like Tarzan or Superman or Peter Pan, were gifted with aerial mobility. It is a gift of . . . the author of *The Bat-Poet* to youths in love with night and the creatures that, like Batman or Dracula or Zorro, are vivid then but grow anemic at daybreak.

And it is a book that speaks to their parents, to those youths' fathers nestled in their easy chairs with books that transport them to the knightly world of detectives. It speaks to their mothers, knees under their chins, reading of the possessions that were Salem's lot, who have gone with the wind and wish to go again to moonlight trysts on mansion savannahs. *Fly By Night* is for us, Davids, hardnosed and slow to "like," for whom fantasy provides what we cannot find at daybreak: a way to be in dreams awake. (p. 31)

Jerry Griswold, in a review of "Fly by Night," in The New Republic *(reprinted by permission of* The New Republic; © *1977 The New Republic, Inc.),* Vol. 176, Nos. 1 & 2, January 1 & 8, 1977, pp. 30-1.

Randall Jarrell's evocation both of David's daytime and his dream world is vivid and recognisable, in particular the feeling of being invisible to others and unable to make them hear, and floating so easily, yet being powerless to move each separate limb. . . . Unfortunately, we also have **'The Owl's Bedtime Story'** which he overhears, five pages of what must be the most embarrassingly lame iambic pentameters outside William McGonagall.

Mary Hobbs, in a review of "Fly by Night," in The Junior Bookshelf, *Vol. 42, No. 1, February, 1978, p. 27.*

Genuine fantasy, such as Randall Jarrell's *Fly by Night* . . . , is by its very nature an imaginative journey away from something: constraint, laws, normality. Like other fantasies, it contains the element of opposition: the quality imagined, wished for, fantasized is opposed and animated by what it rejects. As the naturalistic waking world at the beginning of the story opposes the night flight of fantasy, so Sendak's realistic illustrations . . . oppose the dreamlike quality of the text. In this way they present perfectly the quality of hallucination, which is only hallucination when we think it is real.

Fly by Night is a performance encouraging the participation of the audience. Jarrell and Sendak give the child-reader a narrative through which to pursue possible combinations of haunted fantasy and mature self-conscious adult perceptions. The narrative moves with the perspective of the main character, David, through three different levels of imagination and sleep, from David's conscious, naturalistic reality through his night flight of dream or hallucination to his most subtle power to create a fictionalized parable from his most painful deprivations. At all three levels the narrative voice is coeval with David's imagination, but the voice cannot be David's because he cannot yet use a language which would integrate dream and reality.

The line that announces that *Fly by Night* is fantasy is "At night David can fly." Up to that point the perspective is matter-of-fact, the completely naturalistic description of David's home following a strictly ordinary set of directions. . . . With the statement "At night David can fly," the fantastical non sequitur, we have the abrupt jump to the extraordinary or disordinary perspective. Most children blithely accept the non sequitur—the shift from one point of view to its opposite—by shifting their perspective. They have not yet been educated about the potential chaos of simply accepting a fantastical narrative as though it were "real." The non sequitur initiates their new, but still naturalistic, point of view. Adults, suspicious, trained to bifurcate fantastic and real, are confused and likely to remain so by the directness of the statement: Is it ingenuous? Is it meant ironically? Is it actually saying "At night David *dreams* that he can fly"? Narrative directions are harder for adults to follow because adults hear directions with more predispositions. The line indicates, basically, that participation in the story, involving suspension of the reader's sense of natural law, is welcomed. In fact, children, remembering their own vividly experienced fantasies, and adults who can still summon up good faith in fantastic narrative, will yield readily to the authority of the sentence. David himself is not really surprised by his ability to fly, nor by anything else in the story except his discovery that owls catch fish.

Following the announcement of David's fantastical nighttime ability, David goes one whole step further than *the good dream*, often found in children's literature, for example, in Sendak's *Where the Wild Things Are* and *In the Night Kitchen*. Floating through the house—a kind of omniscient sleep-wanderer—David can see the good dreams of his father, mother, and dog. All are presented as stereotypes but with some element of childlike charm. The dreams are contained in glowing nimbuses and present David's wishful version of reality: his miniaturized father is giving full-size David a piggyback ride; his mother is preparing a stack of pancakes; Reddy (the dog) is chasing something furry. (Later, outside, he sees that the sheep are dreaming of eating or sleeping.) In contrast to the self-contained, stereotyped dreams, David's physical motion is expansive. Even though he has little control (he can use his feet like a rudder), he floats over the dreams, out of the house, into a mysterious black-and-white-striped world: part of David's bed was shadow, part was "white with moonlight"; outside, the garden is black-and-white-striped, as is one of the ponies; there are white limbs and black shadows, white and dark ducks, and crows "all black against the snow." All of the oppositions of dark and light culminate in the marvelous description of the owl. . . . (pp. 125-28)

In this night world, itself a series of oppositions of light and dark, many other sorts of reversals seem plausible, as natural laws are dominated by the laws of imaginative perspective. The cat, the mice, and the rabbit (and later the owl) talk to David. The animals' manner of speaking is animated by some fundamental quality of "opposition." The cat, for example, in the style of incantation, says,

> Wake by night and fly by night,
> The wood is black, the wood is white,
> The mice are dancing in the moonlight. . . .

As David's shadow touches the mice, one says, "What's that great big black thing in the sky?". . . . The rabbit, which is the only animal without companions, seems to play at sharing with David. And as the rabbit speaks, the visual patterns of opposition seem to influence the rhythm:

> A squash for me, a beet for you,
> A beet for me, a squash for you. . . .

The animals talk to David, but to a great degree David is enclosed in himself. He is an observer, a passive wanderer in the tradition of Huck Finn. Huck can be involved with people on shore and then reject them and return to the raft, but David has small effect on the world of "nature" which surrounds his flow of motion. His shadow interrupts the mice at play, but they still hide from the cat; and when David tries to talk to the cat and rabbit, he cannot. (pp. 128-29)

There is, in fact, an element of sadness in **Fly by Night.** Frequently there is the suggestion that our deprivations—our lack of ease, our isolation, if not our fear and pain—are closely related to the movement of our imaginations. Our daydreams, our nightdreams, our nightmares, also our works of fiction are often our haunted responses to our memories and desires. Waking preoccupations occupy, intrude upon, our dreams. Immediately following the description of the desolate field, David is adopted—to be an owl till morning—by a mother owl, who speaks with the sound and rhythm of Blake's *Songs of Innocence.* . . . At this point, on the verge of yet another fantasy world, David discovers that, in contrast to the animals, he is able to give shape to his perceptions by creating analogies, or, the equivalent at the level of language, similes and metaphors. Early in his night flight, his parents' images—as seen by David—are naive, pictorial, cartoonish. But as he flies further, deeper into the fantasy world of his subconscious, he develops much more subtle ways of shaping reality in terms of imagery. He learns that human beings can express feeling and idea as *image*. David begins to experience reality in terms of analogy before he explicitly and self-consciously realizes his power. He sees

the sheep as "six woolly gray mounds the size of the mound his mother makes in the bed" . . . , and at the end of the description of the owl the narrative voice says, "the fish in its claws shines in the moonlight like a spoon". . . . David's epiphany follows an extended description of the owlets, in which the similes subserve a general feeling of buoyancy and exuberance:

> They look as if somebody had poured handfuls of white woodshavings over them, or as if they had stayed outside all winter and had got covered with patches of wet snow. And when they have gobbled up the fish and sit by each other again, instead of looking beautiful, like puppies or kittens, they have a sad absurd look, as if they were sitting there waiting for their real feathers to come. *But when the big owl turns its head toward them its eyes look loving— David thinks, "It doesn't know the way they look."* [. . . critic's italics]

David perceives and figuratively *names* the way they look, and he realizes that the pure look of love of the mother owl indicates that the animal can immediately experience the elemental love between herself and the owlets, but she cannot mediately describe that love. For the mother it doesn't *matter* how they look.

The owl's bedtime story is the third narrative level within the book; it takes the form of a narrative-within-a-narrative. The mother owl is the ideal storyteller; she is ideal because it is David's own imagination which gives her shape, substance, style. She is David's projection, his character. When we are told "the owl floats along by David, and says to him in such a low deep voice it is almost like hearing it inside his head . . . ," we realize that even if we aren't all our own mothers, at least we are all the mothers of our own dreams. At this deepest level of fantasy and sleep, David both creates the story and listens to it with total absorption. He translates his serious waking problem of loneliness into articulate narrative terms: character, action, language, plot, and so forth. David is unaware that the narrative elements express—in a sort of pure metaphor—the truths of life. As David "listens" to the story, the more naive reader simply enters a different narrative world; his selfconsciousness is dominated by the authority of the voice presenting its own point of view. The more mature reader begins to recognize the deeper metaphorical parallels expressed through the story.

First, the owl narrator demonstrates sympathy for her audience. Even though the ostensible purpose of the narrative is a bedtime story for her children, she seems to tell the story directly to David, and lets the owlets listen in. The pain of the isolation of the owlet she describes in her story is perfectly congruent with David's loneliness and longing for a playmate in his waking world. The story begins with the utterly mundane fairy tale opening, and from then on sounds a good deal like a version of the opening of *Fly by Night* itself.

> There was once upon a time a little owl.
> He lived with his mother in a hollow tree.
> On winter nights he'd hear the foxes howl,
> He'd hear his mother call, and he would see
> The moonlight glittering upon the snow.
> How many times he wished for company
> As he sat there alone! . . .

We remember the first picture of David sitting alone in his tree (he already has an owl's perch; the sparrows are used to him) and the isolation he faces in the naturalistic opening of the book. As the narrative continues, the owl addresses the needs of the listener—David himself and the child reading the book—in an imaginative manner, so that the listener can participate in the experience of fulfillment. First there is the challenge, the test of owl-hood or boyhood/manhood. The leap into the untried element must be made. . . . The leap of faith and courage of the owlet into the naked air is a harsh revision of the naked David's flow through the gently mysterious air of his night. But soon comes the reassurance and the confidence which will provide the core for the rest of the adventure:

> How good it felt to him,
> That solid branch. . . .

Having found the second owlet, discovered that she can be his sister-friend, evaded dogs, boys, crows, and played and eaten, the two owlets nestle to the mother's breast. At this point, as "the white of the moonlight and the black of the shadows are beginning to be gray," the fantasy experience of David's night, including as it does his fictionalization of his own feelings, must end. He has learned (albeit unconsciously) about his loneliness and discovered his urge to return home, to awaken to the loving reality of his mother.

The central premise of *Fly by Night*, that which gives it the feeling of a parable that can in its simplicity explain a good deal of our imaginative life, is this:

> "Why do I always forget? I always forget. If
> I remembered in the daytime I could fly in the
> daytime. All I have to do is remember." . . .

David cannot translate the experience, perceptions, or point of view of his fantasy worlds into his naturalistic world. Jarrell, of course, encompassing all perspectives in the world of his book, could have his narrator make the translation, but he refuses to do so. Perhaps the reason is that he wants to place the child-reader in what I might call a position of potential awareness. In this position the child is exposed to the variety of perspectives, and it is up to him—a function of his mental sophistication—to make or not make the connections implicit in Jarrell's act of shaping the whole book. The child can remain totally naive or reach Jarrell's level of mature selfconsciousness. A good deal of the appeal of the book is that the character David is more naive than most of the child-readers of the book, while expressing as much imaginative potential as any of them. The vividness of his fantasy—the non sequitur is not at all a non sequitur for him—is largely caused by his *inability* to remember or articulate the deepest level of his fantasy when he returns to the waking naturalistic world. When it comes time for him to reenter that world, in other words, to wake up, David can't finish his images:

> When they come to the house the owl sails up
> to David and tilts its wings so that it stops still

in the air; then it looks at David with its shining eyes, almost the way it had looked at the owlets, and flies away. David thinks, "The owl looks at me like—"

But he can't think. . . .

His imagination continues to stutter: "I slept so late because I—because I—"

Finally, his mother looks at him like—

"Like—" thinks David, "like—"

He can remember, he can almost remember; but the sunlight streams in through the windows, he holds his hand out for the orange juice, and his mother looks at him like his mother. (pp. 128-33)

The naturalistic world—orange juice, pancakes, sunlight, a loving mother—overwhelms the pain and the benefit of the night fantasy. Jarrell's presentation of David's naiveté—David's ability to create and enter opposing perspectives on reality, but only one at a time—gives the reader the chance to translate, if he can, one world into the other. Thus the child hearing the last page of the book is likely to shout, with all the enthusiasm of making the important connection,

> "The owl looks at me like *my mother;*
> his mother looks at him like *the owl.*"

If David could remember, he could join his two worlds; he could be the mature author of his own life or, more modestly, he could write *Fly by Night* rather than be a character in it. As it is, his waking reality can intrude on his fantasy; his fantasy can actualize his preoccupations and longings; his waking reality will eventually be haunted by the imitations of the night world as he travels down the path of his fantasy toward maturity. It is in this sense that David's flying and consequent night-time world are both the consequence and source of imagination. Imagination is the combination of memory and desire expressed as metaphor. It is the power of metaphor, of one's personal ability to shape feeling into image, which provides the firmest confidence—"The branch will not break." (p. 134)

Thomas H. Getz, "Memory and Desire in 'Fly by Night'," in Children's Literature: Annual of the Modern Language Association Group on Children's Literature and the Children's Literature Association, *Vol. 11, edited by Francelia Butler (copyright © by Children's Literature An International Journal, Inc.), Yale University Press, 1983, pp. 125-34 [the excerpts of Randall Jarrell's work used here were originally published in his* Fly by Night *(reprinted by permission of Farrar, Straus and Giroux, Inc.; copyright © 1969, 1976 by Randall Jarrell), Farrar, Straus and Giroux, 1976].*

Steven Kellogg

1941-

American author/illustrator of picture books, fiction, and non-fiction and illustrator.

Kellogg is admired for his ability to combine artistic skill with a knowledge of children's interests to create a variety of books which delight and entertain them. His highly detailed illustrations include playfully innocent oversized animals, chubby unangelic children, and practical parents. His themes focus on the concerns of childhood and frequently have clever, unexpected conclusions which appeal to the young reader's sense of humor. Among Kellogg's works are realistic easy-to-read mysteries, family and pet stories, animal fantasies, fairy tales, and adaptations of classic folk songs. Critics praise Kellogg's works for their creative blend of fantasy and reality and for the comic details which complement and add depth to his texts.

Kellogg is consistently praised for illustrating fantasies from the imaginations of characters involved in real activities, a technique he uses in his picture books and mysteries. These mystery stories are well-received for their depiction of normal children, spare use of line and color, perceptive themes, and original endings. Kellogg's picture book illustrations, however, are filled with unusual color combinations, lots of lines, and clever additions to the central action. This style receives mixed reviews from critics. Some say that Kellogg clutters his pages, thus making his books inappropriate for large groups of children, while others applaud the humorous and expressive qualities of the works, which they say make great entertainment reading after reading.

Some of Kellogg's works, such as *Can I Keep Him?*, have elicited controversy. Based on a child's longing for a house pet, it depicts his mother cleaning the toilet, putting away the groceries, and imagining what her home would be like with such pets as a python, bear, or deer while her husband ignores the situation. Critics occasionally disapprove of the roles Kellogg assigns each parent. Sexist stereotyping is also a reaction to two later books, *The Island of the Skog*, which is notable for its strong female leader, and *Steven Kellogg's Yankee Doodle*, in which a line is changed to avoid sexism.

Perhaps Kellogg's most popular works are his "Pinkerton" stories, based on the antics of his own Great Dane. Critics see Pinkerton as a lovable, laughable character, and Kellogg's illustrations are praised for their use of both action and subtlety. Kellogg has said that he recognizes individuality in the tastes of children and the need for a variety of styles in illustration and text. The popularity of his works reflects Kellogg's satisfaction of these needs. *Can I Keep Him?* was included in the American Institute of Graphic Arts Children's Book Show selection of best books in 1971-72 and was a New York Times Choice as Best Illustrated Children's Book of the Year in 1973. American Institute of Graphic Arts selections were also given to *The Orchard Cat* for 1971-72 and to *Pinkerton, Behave!* in 1980. *The Mystery of the Missing Red Mitten* was a Children's Book Showcase selection in 1975, *Steven Kellogg's Yankee Doodle* was an ALA Notable Book selection in 1976, and *The Mysterious Tadpole* won the Irma Simonton Black Award in 1978.

Photograph by Tom Crider

(See also *Something about the Author*, Vol. 8; *Contemporary Authors New Revision Series*, Vol. 1; and *Contemporary Authors*, Vols. 49-52.)

GENERAL COMMENTARY

Steven Kellogg has illustrated a number of delightful and original picture books in recent years. . . . His simple caricatures of people and animals combine ingenuity and wit with a feeling for the ridiculous that appeals to the imagination of many young children. . . . [*The Mystery of the Missing Red Mitten* and *The Mystery of the Magic Green Ball*] are two delightful mystery stories aimed at children just learning to read. The books are slighter than most of his earlier ones but still retain the same sense of fun and appeal to young children. The stories are simple with short sentences leaving much of the detail and humour to the clear black and white illustrations. . . .

In both books, Steven Kellogg skilfully blends text and illustrations to make a very pleasing and humorous whole.

> *Judith Elkin, "Simply Enticing," in* The Times Literary Supplement *(© Times Newspapers Ltd. (London) 1980; reproduced from* The Times Literary Supplement *by permission), No. 4034, July 18, 1980, p. 809.*

CAN I KEEP HIM? (1971)

You don't need to read the jacket blurb on this rollicking story to discover its author-illustrator has a houseful of children: it is apparent on each laugh-provoking page. It's easy to visualize all Steven Kellogg's six children looking over his shoulder as he drew the pictures, suggesting and criticizing. It's even easier to believe that their father listened to them as he wrote and illustrated his story of small Arnold, an avid animal lover and liberator, who wants to give all the animals he meets a home in his home.

> *A review of "Can I Keep Him?" in* Publishers Weekly *(reprinted from the March 1, 1971 issue of* Publishers Weekly, *published by R. R. Bowker Company, a Xerox company; copyright © 1971 by Xerox Corporation), Vol. 199, No. 9, March 1, 1971, p. 58.*

Thoroughly childlike, with humorous details, this picture book gets better with each reading and viewing. After bringing home a large, shaggy dog and a very small kitten, neither of which his mother will let him keep . . . , Arnold begins to imagine other animals he might have as pets, but there is an objection to each. . . . The text consists of the conversation between Arnold and his mother. The boy's arguments for each new pet take into account all his mother's objections to previous ones and make for a very nice cumulative effect. Much of the story's meaning, however, is carried in the well-placed illustrations: the homey, realistic scenes (e.g., showing Arnold's mother cleaning the toilet and replenishing a closet full of cans of yams) are done in pen and ink with black sketchy lines and some grey washes; the scenes of Arnold's fantasies have added touches of blue, yellow and green.

> *Janet Strothman, in a review of "Can I Keep Him?" in* School Library Journal, *an appendix to* Library Journal *(reprinted from the May, 1971 issue of* School Library Journal, *published by R. R. Bowker Co./ A Xerox Corporation; copyright © 1971), Vol. 17, No. 9, May, 1971, p. 59.*

The book becomes a merry romp as large, droll pictures on each page bring entirely different dimensions to the mother's logical replies. When Arnold brings such imaginary pets as a bear, a tiger and a python, the situation approaches hilarity. (p. 33)

> *Christina Carr Young, in a review of "Can I Keep Him?" in* Childhood Education *(reprinted by permission of the Association for Childhood Education International, 3615 Wisconsin Ave., N.W., Washington, DC 20016; copyright © 1971 by the Association), Vol. 48, No. 1 (October, 1971), pp. 32-3.*

Ralph [the boy Arnold brings home], with a finger in his mouth, saves Mum from a nervous breakdown and produces Mr. Kellogg—who clearly relishes every kind of animal, but especially small boys—with a happy ending to a very happy book. (He also relishes comic detail and has supplied pictures wan in colour but full of entertainment.)

> *Brian W. Alderson, in a review of "Can I Keep Him?" in* Children's Book Review *(© 1973 Five Owls Press Ltd.; all rights reserved), Vol. III, No. 6, December, 1973, p. 171.*

Amusing illustrations capture the light humor of a story that successfully blends realism and a child's fanciful imaginings. . . . A merry story, and one that has every possibility of raising dissension among proponents of feminine liberation

From Can I Keep Him? *written and illustrated by Steven Kellogg.*

because the illustrations show mother (with a ruffled apron, too) engaged in menial household tasks while the one picture of father shows him reading.

> *A review of "Can I Keep Him?" in* The Best in Children's Books: The University of Chicago Guide to Children's Literature: 1966-1972, *edited by Zena Sutherland (reprinted by permission of The University of Chicago Press; © 1973 by The University of Chicago),* University of Chicago Press, *1973, p. 224.*

A delicately drawn, delicately coloured, rather pathetic story of deprivation. In Arnold's mother, material values reign supreme: she lives in accordance with what people will think, and the illustrations slyly show her wrong-headedness.

> *Mary Hobbs, in a review of "Can I Keep Him?" in* The Junior Bookshelf, *Vol. 38, No. 1, February, 1974, p. 14.*

THE MYSTERY BEAST OF OSTERGEEST (1971)

The six blind men and the elephant in a European village, via a lightweight spoof that plays down the allegory and plays up the slapstick possibilities for more than they're worth. . . . This has none of the fond drollery of *Can I Keep Him?* . . . , and in fact the populace of Ostergeest is a singularly revolting crew. Children might be diverted by the minute and innumerable comic-strip details (silly signs and sideshows on every page), but even sighted wise men won't agree on whether this is the Indian fable, costume low comedy, or Smokey Stover.

> *A review of "The Mystery Beast of Ostergeest," in* Kirkus Reviews *(copyright © 1971 The Kirkus Service, Inc.), Vol. XXXIX, No. 20, October 15, 1971, p. 1114.*

Steven Kellogg is a rising talent in the children's book world, his greatest asset being a fresh and varied style. This tongue-in-cheek adaptation of a classic tale is one of the funniest books we've seen in a long time. It tells of a clown who brings a mystery beast to the town of Ostergeest where six blind scholars are asked by the king to identify it. Their conclusions will delight young children, as will the detailed comic illustrations.

A review of "The Mystery Beast of Ostergeest," in Publishers Weekly *(reprinted from the October 25, 1971 issue of* Publishers Weekly, *published by R. R. Bowker Company, a Xerox company; copyright © 1971 by Xerox Corporation), Vol. 200, No. 17, October 25, 1971, p. 50.*

A mod, tongue-in-cheek treatment of the traditional Indian fable, *The Blind Men and the Elephant.* . . . Much of the book's sophisticated humor lies in the amusingly detailed color illustrations and in the clever dialogue which floats across the pages in cartoon-style balloons. Even younger children who might miss the satire will chuckle over the depiction of the circus. (pp. 56-7)

Barbara S. Miller, in a review of "The Mystery Beast of Ostergeest," in School Library Journal, *an appendix to* Library Journal *(reprinted from the February, 1972 issue of* School Library Journal, *published by R. R. Bowker Co./ A Xerox Corporation; copyright © 1972), Vol. 18, No. 6, February, 1972, pp. 56-7.*

Both [*The Mystery Beast of Ostergeest* and *Mumps!*] rely on fantastic exaggeration of recognisable people and situations, with an immense amount of irrelevant and delightful detail in the illustrations, but Steven Kellogg's has a success the Ostrovsky's book misses, not only by a surer sense of how far he can go, but by a story-line sufficiently remote from reality for a willing suspension of disbelief. At the same time, his setting, a seaside town (you can almost smell the salt air) with steep streets, vulgar shops, entertainments and holidaygoers, not to mention loud Queen Lulu yacking away on the phone, the ineffectual King, convinced that the unidentified beast brought ashore by a cheerful clown (who plans a circus round it) will constitute a "threat to the entire nation", the thuggish royal entourage, the sacrosanct (and empty) royal areas, all draw from daily experience, if only of television. Mr. Kellogg follows the style of nineteenth-century caricaturists like Leech and Cruikshank, even in his choice of colours, which suggest hand-tinting. He shows the increasingly ridiculous attempts to guess the creature's identity, until blind University scholars, judging only by what they can touch, pronounce with certainty such solutions as a spear, a tree or a fan. It takes a child to find the elephant in an alphabet book (neat little moral!).

Mary Hobbs, in a review of "The Mystery Beast of Ostergeest," in The Junior Bookshelf, *Vol. 41, No. 5, October, 1977, p. 280.*

THE ORCHARD CAT (1972)

The flap copy calls this a "whimsical morality tale," but unfortunately it's more moral than whimsy and falls short of Kellogg's earlier works (e.g., *Can I Keep Him?* . . .). An old alley cat prods her son to win the fame and power she never achieved. Armed with a chart showing terrain to be conquered and fired by Mama's motto—"'You gets what you takes and you takes what you gets.'"—Cat proceeds to the orchard, where he threatens and bullies Mouse, Owl, Mole, etc., while proclaiming himself king. But his intended subjects repulse him, and it is a lonely Cat who moves on to the next destination—the people's house. There, frolicking children almost bring on an identity crisis, but the sight of a layer cake strength-

ens literal-minded Cat's ambition (Mama had said, "'You'll be rolling in cake.'"). So he romps in and chomps at the cake, gets sick, and is rescued by one of the children who then plays with him and makes him feel ". . . like a new cat. The old ways were gone." Returning to the orchard, Cat throws a party for his former victims. Kellogg's gray-washed pen-and-ink drawings are typically detailed and amusing, and the format is attractive with well-arranged pictures offset by red type. But there's nothing particularly catlike about Cat, the verse is neither clever nor catchy, and the all-join-hands ending is predictable and anti-climactic. Moreover, Mama's motto and Cat's braggadocio are jarring and in the end pointless.

Diane Gersoni-Edelman, in a review of "The Orchard Cat," in School Library Journal, *an appendix to* Library Journal *(reprinted from the May, 1972 issue of* School Library Journal, *published by R. R. Bowker Co./ A Xerox Corporation; copyright © 1972), Vol. 18, No. 9, May, 1972, p. 67.*

In rhymed red words and slyly affectionate black and white line and wash pictures, a cat who sets out to be king learns that friends are better than subjects. . . . An open house ending that might in other hands be cloying is here, as the jacket puts it, "gloriously overstuffed." . . . Kellogg's offhand visual embellishments, like the grinning buzzards that carry off the dead mother, add new twists of wit to the old story.

A review of "The Orchard Cat," in Kirkus Reviews *(copyright © 1972 The Kirkus Service, Inc.), Vol. XL, No. 10, May 15, 1972, p. 575.*

WON'T SOMEBODY PLAY WITH ME? (1972)

The author-illustrator tracks the heroine from dawn's early light through a morning so full of grievous disappointments they occasion several fantasized revenges on three seemingly no-good friends. Though Kellogg has a disconcerting tendency to render the human figure boneless, he has an unerring sense of what will invest fantasy scenes—an orgy consisting entirely of desserts, a solitary romp through the perfect toy shop—with the felt-reality of childhood.

Selma Lanes, in a review of "Won't Somebody Play with Me?" in The New York Times Book Review *(© 1972 by The New York Times Company; reprinted by permission), November 5, 1972, p. 44.*

This is a comically illustrated picture book detailing a day spent by a child anxiously awaiting 5:30 P.M. (when her father comes home and she may open her birthday presents) . . . but there is so much more! She realizes at 8:30 A.M. that time can be unbearably long when you're waiting for something so she decides to find someone to play with. Humorous imagined play scenes follow with illustrations so complex that they will provide an exercise in reading skills for the child tenacious enough to look in detail. Surprise ending too! Well done!

A review of "Won't Someone Play with Me?" in Children's Book Review Service *(copyright © 1972 Children's Book Review Service Inc.), Vol. 1, No. 4, December, 1972, p. 22.*

An acceptable story marred by below-average illustrations. . . . Kellogg's unappealing, pastel illustrations rely heavily on gimmickry, and are filled with superfluous jokes and dialogue which are not aimed at the picture-book audience. The overcrowded, jumbled pictures burdened with excessive detail make this unsuitable for story hours.

> *Corinne Liva, in a review of "Won't Somebody Play with Me?" in* School Library Journal, *an appendix to* Library Journal *(reprinted from the January, 1973 issue of* School Library Journal, *published by R. R. Bowker Co./ A Xerox Corporation; copyright © 1973), Vol. 19, No. 5, January, 1973, p. 62.*

Won't Somebody Play With Me? has little story but a great deal of perception. Kim must wait for her father before opening her birthday presents. To make the time pass, she tries to get one friend after another to play with her. On her way, she imagines their fantastic makebelieve games together, on which Steven Kellogg really goes to town. . . . The exaggerated abandon of expression and movement is a joy. (p. 18)

> *Mary Hobbs, in a review of "Won't Somebody Play with Me?" in* The Junior Bookshelf, *Vol. 42, No. 1, February, 1978, pp. 17-18.*

THE ISLAND OF THE SKOG   (1973)

This is Kellogg at his finest. The pictures are intricately drawn and full of all kinds of action and information that add to and embellish the text. The mice are real with an individualism that is carried throughout the book. For Kellogg monster fans— yes, there is one. Children are sure to ponder over this book time and time again regardless of age.

> *Ann L. Kalkhoff, in a review of "The Island of the Skog," in* Children's Book Review Service *(copyright © 1974 Children's Book Review Service Inc.), Vol. 2, No. 5, January, 1974, p. 34.*

This acceptable adventure tale of mice and a mysterious skog is highlighted by the illustrations which are superior to both the plot and writing style. A band of hardy mice embark on a sea voyage seeking a land of safety and freedom. A perilous journey leads them to a suitable island, but their delight is soon clouded by the discovery of a fearsome skog. How they bravely face up to the monster, only to find that he's a scared little creature even weaker than they, provides the action. The mood is effectively set through the minutely detailed, humorous pen-and-ink drawings with full-color wash which depict mice cavorting through the pages. Good for sharing with a small group, but have them sit up close!

> *Patricia McCue Marwell, in a review of "The Island of the Skog," in* School Library Journal, *an appendix to* Library Journal *(reprinted from the February, 1974 issue of* School Library Journal, *published by R. R. Bowker Co./ A Xerox Corporation; copyright © 1974), Vol. 20, No. 6, February, 1974, p. 54.*

Although the story and dialog are choppy, the animal characters emerge nicely as individuals. Kellogg's painstakingly detailed illustrations, richly shaded in full color, are at their best in the two-page spreads where they are not marred by the busy juxtaposition of different scenes.

> *A review of "The Island of the Skog," in* The Booklist *(reprinted by permission of the American Library Association; copyright © 1974 by the American Library Association), Vol. 70, No. 14, March 15, 1974, p. 821.*

This should be a good choice for feminists, as Jenny's calm ideas always prove more practical than those of hot-headed Bouncer, self-proclaimed leader of the group. The lavish illustrations, in pastels, are filled with humorous details, such as notes sent off in bottles by the sea-bound mice. Kellogg's book should prove especially successful with one or two children who can spend time enjoying the pictures, rather than with a larger number.

> *Barbara Dill, in a review of "The Island of the Skog," in* Wilson Library Bulletin *(copyright © 1974 by the H. W. Wilson Company), Vol. 48, No. 8, April, 1974, p. 633.*

Kellogg is at his best at this kind of blithe nonsense: appealing animal characters, an unsubstantial but busy plot, a happy ending, and a light, humorous style; the frosting on his cakes are always the illustrations, full of charming details that are not overstressed, but left for the child to find for himself or perhaps pore over after they've been pointed out: the chart hung upside down, the telephone on an island that's deserted, the impossibly long pennant on the mast.

> *Zena Sutherland, in a review of "The Island of the Skog," in* Bulletin of the Center for Children's Books *(reprinted by permission of The University of Chicago Press; © 1974 by The University of Chicago), Vol. 27, No. 9, May, 1974, p. 146.*

THE MYSTERY OF THE MISSING RED MITTEN   (1974)

Kellogg never seems to run out of ideas for endearing themes and people. This book ought to be a big hit with the smallest set; it offers a mystery in miniature, a tiny book that will fit comfortably into little hands.

> *A review of "The Mystery of the Missing Red Mitten," in* Publishers Weekly *(reprinted from the March 18, 1974 issue of* Publishers Weekly, *published by R. R. Bowker Company, a Xerox company; copyright*

From The Island of the Skog, *written and illustrated by Steven Kellogg.*

© 1974 by Xerox Corporation), Vol. 205, No. 11, March 18, 1974, p. 52.

The familiar Kellogg child-face crops up again but this time in a fresh story right out of the mouth of a little girl with a universal child-problem. To her dog she confides, "Oscar, I lost my other mitten. That makes five mittens this winter. I'm in big trouble." The two search everywhere, stumbling along a snowy trail strewn with articles their friends have left behind and dallying with imaginative games and conversations along the way. . . . The mitten's appearance is a real surprise; and in contrast to some of the artist's more cluttered work, these pictures make effective use of spare, delicate lines and white space, lit up by an occasional spot of red. (pp. 875-76)

A review of "The Mystery of the Missing Red Mitten," in The Booklist *(reprinted by permission of the American Library Association; copyright © 1974 by the American Library Association), Vol. 70, No. 15, April 1, 1974, pp. 875-76.*

Annie's remaining red mitten and the one in her pictured day-dreams about what might have become of the other make up the only bits of color in these nicely contained line drawings. . . . Kellogg's visual aides are fewer and subtler here than usual, his ebullient imagination trimmed to a perfect fit for the undersized pages and small scale pursuit.

A review of "The Mystery of the Missing Red Mitten," in Kirkus Reviews *(copyright © 1974 The Kirkus Service, Inc.), Vol. XLII, No. 8, April 15, 1974, p. 419.*

Humorous black-and-white line drawings—highlighted by red mittens—illustrate Annie's adventures and fantasies; however, they are too small and colorless to be used successfully with a group. This pleasant winter story is best suited to sharing with individual children.

Patricia Berglund, in a review of "The Mystery of the Missing Red Mitten," in School Library Journal, *an appendix to* Library Journal *(reprinted from the May, 1974 issue of* School Library Journal, *published by R. R. Bowker Co./ A Xerox Corporation; copyright © 1974), Vol. 20, No. 9, May, 1974, p. 48.*

Annie is a typical little girl who does everyday things like losing her mitten; but the sequence of events encompassed by the author in the hunt for it will capture the imagination of all young readers. How many adults, I wonder, would envisage a mitten as the heart of a snowman, or as a hat for a baby hawk? Read this enchanting short story to any young child and you may be convinced.

Richard H. Jones, in a review of "The Mystery of the Missing Red Mitten," in The School Librarian, *Vol. 28, No. 3, September, 1980, p. 255.*

THERE WAS AN OLD WOMAN (1974)

In a departure from his usual style, Kellogg offers cartoon pictures here to embellish his adaptation of the old folktale. Many children will find the verses (and added dialogue by Kellogg) familiar, since Burl Ives and others have recorded a song also based on the story. "There was an old woman who swallowed a fly; I wonder why, she swallowed a fly." She goes on to swallow a spider and increasingly larger creatures until she swallows a horse and dies "of course." As the woman,

A snowman with a heart!

From The Mystery of the Missing Red Mitten, *written and illustrated by Steven Kellogg.*

Rosebud, keeps on eating sundry animals and things (including a barn), she becomes enormous, almost as huge as the steed who does her in. The whole treatment is, frankly, too much and a little sick-making in tone and pictures. It's an indication that this silly tale is more effective as a song.

A review of "There Was an Old Woman," in Publishers Weekly *(reprinted from the April 8, 1974 issue of* Publishers Weekly, *published by R. R. Bowker Company, a Xerox company; copyright © 1974 by Xerox Corporation), Vol. 205, No. 14, April 8, 1974, p. 83.*

Steven Kellogg goes right over grownups' heads with his unabashedly vulgar line and watercolor pictures for *There Was An Old Woman*. . . . [While Rosebud] grows monstrous enough from her voracious rampage to become a pampered circus fat lady, Kellogg's slovenly pages become crammed with debris, crass billboards, sideshow freaks and cartoon speech balloons. Kellogg is sure to gross out impressionable parents, but it's the sort of spread that kids can swallow without a qualm.

Sada Fretz, "Once Upon a Picture," in Book World— The Washington Post *(© 1974, The Washington Post), May 19, 1974, p. 4.**

This [is a] jazzed-up cartoon version of the favorite old song. . . . Kellogg's frenetic pastel ink-and-watercolor illustrations are full of slapstick gags and raucous sound effects, but because of the heavy dose of sick humor, librarians may prefer to stick with Mills and Bonne's traditional version, *I Know an Old Lady* (Rand McNally, 1961). (pp. 63-4)

Phyllis Yuill, in a review of "There Was an Old Woman," in School Library Journal, *an appendix to*

Library Journal (*reprinted from the September, 1974 issue of* School Library Journal, *published by R. R. Bowker Co./ A Xerox Corporation; copyright © 1974), Vol. 21, No. 1, September, 1974, pp. 63-4.*

The words are familiar . . . but the interpretation quite new. Steven Kellogg has hit on the agreeable notion of making the progression of consumables an entirely logical one. Rosebud is a gun-toting farmer's wife who "jest hates flies", and has an irritating parrot. The sequence of pictures showing the cat looking ever more apprehensive as the bird is consumed is horribly funny, as is the determination with which Rosebud decides on her sixth course (worried looking cow: "Moo?" "You!"). . . . Drawn in a wicked Caldecott style using the familiar format and earthy palette, this gruesome story with its rhyming ballooned interpolations will delight everyone but the obese or squeamish.

Sarah Hayes, "The Power of Pictures," in The Times Literary Supplement *(© Times Newspapers Ltd. (London) 1978; reproduced from* The Times Literary Supplement *by permission), No. 3979, July 7, 1978, p. 763.**

STEVEN KELLOGG'S YANKEE DOODLE (1976)

Kellogg has created an irresistible picture of a young boy sticking a feather in his cap, crawling up behind his father, and with his small fuzzy dog alongside, setting off for camp along with Captain Good'in. . . . The excitement, patriotism, and spirit of the day Washington took command of the American army is captured completely and matches the lilting, sprightly familiar melody. Full-color illustrations rich with lush greens and warm yellows, accented by the reds and blues of the armies' jackets, are set off in soft parchment-toned borders printed with a green-and-red pattern. In contrast to the more explanatory historic presentation by Quackenbush, . . . the artist includes his usual humor and detail, from an oppossum hanging upside-down by his tail to the Redcoat caught with his boots off. Definitely a feather in Steven Kellogg's cap. (pp. 851-52)

Barbara Elleman, in a review of "Steven Kellogg's Yankee Doodle," in The Booklist *(reprinted by permission of the American Library Association; copyright © 1976 by the American Library Association), Vol. 72, No. 12, February 15, 1976, pp. 851-52.*

The color illustrations are zesty and action filled. . . . But Kellogg's rewording of some of the well-known verses are downright silly. In an attempt to please feminists, for instance, he has changed, "Mind the music and the step, and with the girls be handy" (which meant something) to "with the folks be handy" (which means nothing).

A review of "Steven Kellogg's Yankee Doodle," in Publishers Weekly *(reprinted from the March 15, 1976 issue of* Publishers Weekly, *published by R. R. Bowker Company, a Xerox company; copyright © 1976 by Xerox Corporation), Vol. 209, No. 11, March 15, 1976, p. 58.*

Steven Kellogg's **"Yankee Doodle"** transforms the well-known ditty into a slender tale of a boy ingenuously entangled in a Revolutionary battle. While the illustrations properly capture the flavor of colonial dress and landscape, their overall tone is disconcertingly inappropriate. Kellogg's pictures, largely because of their cartoonish derivation and emphasis, have turned the song into a slapstick farce; his British soldiers in particular

radiate a vaudevillian aura. There's no denying that Yankee Doodle is a jaunty song, funny and frivolous by turns, but buffoonery it isn't.

Of further interest is Kellogg's tinkering with Yankee Doodle's famous chorus. According to a press release, Kellogg was convinced by the editors at Parents' that the familiar chorus was "sexist." So, instead of the traditional "Mind the music and the step/And with the girls be handy," the last line now reads "And with the folks be handy." Kellogg explains in the book's prefatory note that the chorus has been changed in the past "to suit the realities" of other times, and that "this Bicentennial edition alters that very chorus to suit the realities of our own." Considering the respective "realities" involved, this is specious logic of the highest order. Besides, not only is the change of dubious historical propriety, but such misguided sensitivity is solely a triumph for the sort of people who want to integrate "penpersonship" and "personkind" into the English language.

Stephen Krensky, in a review of "Yankee Doodle," in The New York Times Book Review *(© 1976 by The New York Times Company; reprinted by permission), May 2, 1976, p. 27.*

The artist's lively, meticulously detailed pictures in warm colors suggest Peter Spier's illustrations. Processions, battlefield action, and a little boy spectator, wearing a feather in his cap and usually waving a flag, fill the pages of a visually satisfying book.

Virginia Haviland, in a review of "Steven Kellogg's Yankee Doodle," in The Horn Book Magazine *(copyright © 1976 by The Horn Book, Inc., Boston), Vol. LII, No. 3, June, 1976, p. 296.*

MUCH BIGGER THAN MARTIN (1976)

All the frustrations of being younger and smaller than an older sibling come pouring out in this humorous treatment of a very real problem. Henry doesn't like being Martin's little brother when he's victim in games, gets the smallest piece of cake, or finds the basketball loop too high for his shots. Stretching and watering himself doesn't help, while eating a lot of apples only makes him sick; there seems to be no remedy. However, the Kellogg who surprised his readers with giraffes in his illustrations for Mahy's *The Boy Who Was Followed Home* . . . once more adds an ingenious twist to his ending—Henry makes stilts! The imagination scenes, where Henry perceives himself as a giant towering over Martin, are where Kellogg's touches of subtle humor and whimsical detail are most effective.

Barbara Elleman, in a review of "Much Bigger than Martin," in Booklist *(reprinted by permission of the American Library Association; copyright © 1976 by the American Library Association), Vol. 73, No. 1, September 1, 1976, p. 39.*

The ambivalence a younger brother feels toward an older one is humorously conveyed through a minimal but precise text combined with color-washed line drawings. . . . [**Much Bigger Than Martin** is] a thoroughly childlike story about a familiar situation.

Mary M. Burns, in a review of "Much Bigger than Martin," in The Horn Book Magazine *(copyright © 1976 by The Horn Book, Inc., Boston), Vol. LII, No. 5, October, 1976, p. 492.*

Any child with a sibling problem will empathize with Henry's wish to grow **Much Bigger Than** . . . older brother Martin. . . . The illustrations, done in Kellogg's usual style with sturdy impish-looking boys, add a lot of humor to this enjoyable look at a common problem.

> *Jane E. Gardner, in a review of "Much Bigger than Martin," in* School Library Journal *(reprinted from the November, 1976 issue of* School Library Journal, *published by R. R. Bowker Co./ A Xerox Corporation; copyright © 1976), Vol. 23, No. 3, November, 1976, p. 48.*

[This] book fails, I think, because in both text and illustration it swings uncomfortably between realism and fantasy. It would have been better had Mr Kellogg maintained the tone of his opening pages with their sympathetic and intelligent realisation of a common sentiment, resentment of being the 'littlest'.

> *Gabrielle Maunder, in a review of "Much Bigger than Martin," in* The School Librarian, *Vol. 26, No. 2, June, 1978, p. 128.*

THE MYSTERIOUS TADPOLE (1977)

Uncle McAllister's birthday gift for Louis seems to be an innocent looking, soon-to-be-frog tadpole. However, when Alphonse outgrows a jar, the sink, and the bathtub, it quickly becomes apparent that Louis' cheeseburger-eating friend is no ordinary creature. . . . Humor, emphasized by an understated text, vibrates through Kellogg's expressively detailed black line drawings awash in mellow colors. The cohesively integrated text and illustrations will lead to a thoroughly enjoyable picture book experience.

> *Barbara Elleman, in a review of "The Mysterious Tadpole," in* Booklist *(reprinted by permission of the American Library Association; copyright © 1977 by the American Library Association), Vol. 74, No. 7, December 1, 1977, p. 613.*

Picking up where he left off in **Can I Keep Him?** . . . , Kellogg eliminates any parental opposition to exotic pets by having Louis' nice old Scottish uncle send him a tadpole for a birthday present. . . . Illustrations in the author's typical style show Alphonse to be a sort of bulbous, polka-dotted salamander. Moderately amusing, he may satisfy readers who like their monsters tame.

> *Janet French, in a review of "The Mysterious Tadpole," in* School Library Journal *(reprinted from the January, 1978 issue of* School Library Journal, *published by R. R. Bowker Co./ A Xerox Corporation; copyright © 1978), Vol. 24, No. 5, January, 1978, p. 78.*

The extravagant, sunlit pictures could almost carry the story alone, but the matter-of-fact text heightens the humor. Action and detail in the illustrations are balanced by quiet scenes, so the eye is not overwhelmed by the busyness that occasionally threatens the artist's work.

> *Charlotte W. Draper, in a review of "The Mysterious Tadpole," in* The Horn Book Magazine *(copyright © 1978 by The Horn Book, Inc., Boston), Vol. LIV, No. 1, February, 1978, p. 36.*

Lightly caricatured, the animal cavorts on pages crowded with detail, stippled paint and line used on pages like instalments

of a fantastic film; the final page, showing Uncle producing a curious egg as next year's present, might encourage young readers (say, eight or so) to write their own sequel before the artist comes up with one.

> *Margery Fisher, in a review of "The Mysterious Tadpole," in her* Growing Point, *Vol. 18, No. 4, November, 1979, p. 3610.*

The scene of **The Mysterious Tadpole** is city America, which makes the dilemma even more acute.

Mr. Kellogg draws with a neat, explicit line, meeting all the technical problems presented by his delightful and original story, and making it all acceptable through his soft colours and gentle humour. The balance between text and picture is beautifully maintained. I do not know who will like this one most, the youngest in the family or Grandpa, but it is a sure guarantee of delight and domestic harmony, for everyone will come under Alphonse's spell. (p. 117)

> *Marcus Crouch, in a review of "The Mysterious Tadpole," in* The Junior Bookshelf, *Vol. 44, No. 3, June, 1980, pp. 116-17.*

THE MYSTERY OF THE MAGIC GREEN BALL (1978)

Timmy and his friends are the author-illustrator's specialty, full of life and appeal and, as usual, Kellogg has an engrossing story to tell. Timmy gets a present from his brother Alfred, a big green ball with a "T" imprinted on it, making it the boy's very own. But he shares it with Albert and all their friends, except Sara Bianco. She won't let anyone play with her magic set. One day, the ball goes flying into the woods and nobody can find it. The disconsolate children keep looking as the year passes and spring rolls around. Then Sara Bianco puts on a magic show and offers to tell fortunes with her magic ball which turns out to be Timmy's missing gift. She refuses to admit that the ball isn't her property, a contretemps which induces Timmy and his smart pals to outdo the mean magician

From The Mysterious Tadpole, *written and illustrated by Steven Kellogg.*

in trickery. This opus will rival Kellogg's **"Mystery of the Missing Red Mitten"** in popularity.

> *A review of "The Mystery of the Magic Green Ball," in* Publishers Weekly *(reprinted from the August 7, 1978 issue of* Publishers Weekly, *published by R. R. Bowker Company, a Xerox company; copyright © 1978 by Xerox Corporation), Vol. 214, No. 6, August 7, 1978, p. 82.*

A slight, slightly unbenevolent, if narrowly satisfying little tale about Timmy's green ball. . . . Timmy and friend Peggy fool Sara with their own gypsy switch, arranging a distraction and then substituting a green-painted grapefruit for the disputed toy. Fair enough, but a little short on charity . . . and substance.

> *A review of "The Mystery of the Magic Green Ball," in* Kirkus Reviews *(copyright © 1978 The Kirkus Service, Inc.), Vol. XLVI, No. 18, September 15, 1978, p. 1015.*

PINKERTON, BEHAVE! (1979)

Humor abounds in this exuberant tale of a Great Dane's confrontation with obedience school. Reluctant to learn to "come," "fetch," or "get the burglar," Pinkerton is enrolled in a class, where he not only continues to counter behavior commands but also has all the dogs following his lead. After making chaos of the schoolroom, Pinkerton is sent home in disgrace. That night when a burglar intrudes, the young protagonist quickly and deliberately mixes the commands; hearing "fetch," Pinkerton promptly "gets the burglar," making himself a hero after all. Kellogg wittily captures expressions and movements of animal and human, wisely allowing the focal humor to emanate through the faces and action and forgoing the background detail usually found in his work. In addition, bright, lively colors and spare use of narrative blend to help make this a splendid comedic success. Kellogg at his best.

> *Barbara Elleman, in a review of "Pinkerton, Behave!" in* Booklist *(reprinted by permission of the American Library Association; copyright © 1979 by the American Library Association), Vol. 76, No. 6, November 15, 1979, p. 506.*

What comes through always in Kellogg's picture books is his essential kindliness. With his gentle wit and talent for blending reality into antic illustrations and stories, he describes here the "training course" of an enormous Great Dane.

> *A review of "Pinkerton, Behave!" in* Publishers Weekly *(reprinted from the November 26, 1979 issue of* Publishers Weekly, *published by R. R. Bowker Company, a Xerox company; copyright © 1979 by Xerox Corporation), Vol. 216, No. 22, November 26, 1979, p. 52.*

Based on Kellogg's experiences with his own harlequin Great Dane, this picture book will be loved by children of all ages. . . . The humor of the illustrations will make children very happy. This picture book should be included in all picture-book collections.

> *Virginia Gremillion, in a review of "Pinkerton, Behave!" in* Children's Book Review Service *(copyright © 1980 Children's Book Review Service Inc.), Vol. 8, No. 5, January, 1980, p. 42.*

From Pinkerton, Behave!, *written and illustrated by Steven Kellogg.*

Any kid who's tried to train a dog, a few more who have or want a dog, and (sneakier yet) any kid inclined to botch commands can be counted among Pinkerton's likely audience. . . . [Pinkerton's capture of the burglar is a] well-staged last laugh for dog and child, with much visual rambunction throughout.

> *A review of "Pinkerton, Behave!" in* Kirkus Reviews *(copyright © 1980 The Kirkus Service, Inc.), Vol. XLVIII, No. 4, February 15, 1980, p. 211.*

A cinematic effect is lent to **Pinkerton, Behave!** by the grouping of three or four framed pictures to a page, joined in a brisk narrative with a strong illusion of movement; besides, in keeping with the light-hearted, racy treatment, the artist has slightly Disneyfied his canine hero, exploiting that air that big, clumsy dogs . . . so often have of enjoying a joke against themselves. . . . There is humour in every fine line delineating facial expressions or boisterous action, in an inspired rearrangement of a situation familiar to dog-owners everywhere.

> *Margery Fisher, in a review of "Pinkerton, Behave!" in her* Growing Point, *Vol. 20, No. 4, November, 1981, p. 3962.*

We already know Steven Kellogg as one of the really funny makers of picture books. He maintains his reputation with **Pinkerton, Behave!** No fantasy this time, just a gentle exaggeration of an all too real situation. . . . This highly satisfactory tale is told in 'comic' style with lots of pictures full of shrewd and humorous detail.

> *Marcus Crouch, in a review of "Pinkerton, Behave!" in* The Junior Bookshelf, *Vol. 45, No. 6, December, 1981, p. 244.*

THE MYSTERY OF THE FLYING ORANGE PUMPKIN (1980)

Kellogg colors the seed, flower and fruit of a special pumpkin a brave orange in his jubilant new book. The one color appears in drawings of likable heroes, heroines and a villain. Mr. Bramble invites Brian, Ellis and Joan to plant their pumpkin seed in his garden and, with kind Mrs. Wilkins, helps the children care for the prize. . . . But Mr. Bramble moves away. Nasty Mr. Klug moves into his house and refuses to give the children their jack-o-lantern. Mrs. Wilkins, however, again proves a help, giving the boys and girls an idea that solves their problem hilariously and pleases almost everyone.

> *A review of "The Mystery of the Flying Orange Pumpkin," in* Publishers Weekly *(reprinted from the July 11, 1980 issue of* Publishers Weekly, *published by R. R. Bowker Company, a Xerox company; copyright © 1980 by Xerox Corporation), Vol. 218, No. 2, July 11, 1980, p. 91.*

Kellogg's slightly round, rumpled figures are appealing and his scenes are drawn with telling detail (the curmudgeonly neighbor reads "The Daily Complaint" with a sour look on his face). This warm and clever story would make even a goblin smile.

> *Alice Digilio, "The Pumpkin Papers," in* Book World—The Washington Post *(© 1980, The Washington Post), October 12, 1980, p. 8.**

The story is nothing but a good joke on Mr. Klug, but Kellogg's pictures pull you into the conspiracy. And he saves a good stroke for the end, when Mr. Klug scowls out from his devil suit to the general merriment of the pranksters.

> *A review of "The Mystery of the Flying Orange Pumpkin," in* Kirkus Reviews *(copyright © 1980 The Kirkus Service, Inc.), Vol. XLVIII, No. 20, October 15, 1980, p. 1352.*

A ROSE FOR PINKERTON (1981)

Kellogg, whose **Pinkerton, Behave!** gave Great Danes their own special place in picture books, brings the dog back in a zesty tale that is delivered with splendid flourish. Mellow shadings of color, unusual use of light, and effective crowd placement provide background for a funny and well-paced story that complements and is complemented by the dexterous illustrations.

> *Barbara Elleman, in a review of "A Rose for Pinkerton," in* Booklist *(reprinted by permission of the American Library Association; copyright © 1981 by the American Library Association), Vol. 78, No. 8, December 15, 1981, p. 548.*

The lure of Kellogg's latest is similar to that of Richard Scarry's and Wallace Tripp's books—the skilled, highly detailed illustrations, most with dozens of characters and tiny, amusing texts on billboards and in odd corners of the pictures. . . . The spare text, artless but inoffensive, occasionally becomes confusing because one can't always tell who is speaking. Still, this is a jolly, happy picture story, good for talking over with a child. (pp. 66-7)

> *Peter Neumeyer, in a review of "A Rose for Pinkerton," in* School Library Journal *(reprinted from the January, 1982 issue of* School Library Journal, *published by R. R. Bowker Co./ A Xerox Corpora-*

tion; copyright © 1982), Vol. 28, No. 5, January, 1982, pp. 66-7.

Pinkerton, the ungainly Great Dane puppy immortalized in **Pinkerton, Behave!** . . . is nearly upstaged by a feline interloper. . . . In a comic reversal of the expected, the kitten takes over the household, commandeering Pinkerton's sunny spot, eating his dinner, and chewing his bone. Pinkerton, in turn, begins to act like a kitten, drinking milk and sitting on laps. The illustrations, in glowing, sun-yellow colors, fully exploit the absurdity of the situation, juxtaposing each animal's actions with smaller drawings showing Pinkerton transformed into a kitten or Rose as a tiger-striped dog. And the artist gives full reign to his imagination when Rose and Pinkerton return to the pet show and disrupt the "Grand March of the Poodles." Cats, dogs, and outraged pet-owners burst the framed boundaries of the pictures in a chaotic end to a rollicking tale.

> *Kate M. Flanagan, in a review of "A Rose for Pinkerton," in* The Horn Book Magazine *(copyright © 1982 by The Horn Book, Inc., Boston), Vol. LVIII, No. 1, February, 1982, p. 34.*

Kellogg uses light, bright colors to sustain the mood of the story, puts imagined events into comic-strip style balloons, and offers visual contrast by providing both cozy scenes at home and larger canvases, filled with slightly caricatured pets and people, at the pet show.

> *Zena Sutherland, in a review of "A Rose for Pinkerton," in* Bulletin of the Center for Children's Books *(reprinted by permission of The University of Chi-*

From A Rose for Pinkerton, *written and illustrated by Steven Kellogg.*

cago Press; © 1982 by The University of Chicago), Vol. 35, No. 7, March, 1982, p. 132.

Zany, wholesome fun is offered readers 4-9 years of age by Steven Kellogg in *A Rose for Pinkerton*. . . . The chaotic events that occur . . . will have children doubled up with laughter. The predictable ending is bound to please. Cleverly detailed, cartoon-styled illustrations, which are black line drawings with full-color wash, are readily recognizable as Steven Kellogg's; they literally demand that one examine them carefully many times over.

> *A review of "A Rose for Pinkerton" (copyright 1982 by the International Reading Association, Inc.; reprinted with permission of the International Reading Association and), in* The Reading Teacher, *Vol. 35, No. 6, March, 1982, p. 751.*

Steven Kellogg, in *A Rose for Pinkerton,* satirizes the social scene with two basic devices: excesses in visual style and exaggerated plot complications. The story line lends itself to preposterous depictions of an overpopulated world of pets. (p. 610)

The illustrations are designed to convey both action and characterization, and the sparse text directs attention to certain aspects of the pandemonium. It also enhances a sense of immediacy and drama with its exclamations and present tense: "Pinkerton are you lonely? . . . Look! It's Rose! . . . Does she still think she's a poodle? . . . She's purring!"

Kellogg uses the same style he used in *Pinkerton, Behave!* to characterize the Great Dane, kitten, and other pampered pets. His technique includes odd combinations of yellow, pink, and blue, and thousands of minute lines scattered over the forms. This line work agitates surfaces until the images become disquieting. Added to the ironically opulent color and the scores of objects in each scene, the lines build up an aura of extravagance that is slapstick but also satirically suggestive. (p. 611)

> *Donnarae MacCann and Olga Richard, in a review of "A Rose for Pinkerton," in* Wilson Library Bulletin *(copyright ©1982 by the H. W. Wilson Company), Vol. 56, No. 8, April, 1982, pp. 610-11.*

THE MYSTERY OF THE STOLEN BLUE PAINT (1982)

The latest in Steven Kellogg's color mysteries . . . is as winning as its predecessors. Kellogg's children have an authentic look, with their droopy drawers and droopier socks, mismatched clothes, and flyaway hair. No spiffy preppies here.

The ensemble here includes Belinda Baldini, her implacable Basset hound Homer, and three ragtag pre-schoolers who bug Belinda while she paints in the park in hopes that she'll read to them. After a windstorm drives the small fry away, Belinda finds her blue paint is missing. Who has taken it? The mystery is solved by Homer the dog and the solution is illustrated by Kellogg in the cleverest way.

> *Alice Digilio, in a review of "The Mystery of the Stolen Blue Paint," in* Book World—The Washington Post *(© 1982, The Washington Post), April 11, 1982, p. 11.*

One reason for the popularity Kellogg enjoys is that children sense he's laughing with them when they explore his tenderly comic, always surprising stories and pictures. Splashed with blue, the drawings in the author-illustrator's new book will be

a special treat to fans of his previous jaunty puzzlers. . . . Here Kellogg introduces one of his jolly twists, linked to the two nuns who have been sitting near the artist. They are the only persons Belinda doesn't suspect. But she does accuse a third innocent, a mistake that she pays for conscientiously if not gladly.

> *A review of "The Mystery of the Stolen Blue Paint," in* Publishers Weekly *(reprinted from the April 16, 1982 issue of* Publishers Weekly, *published by R. R. Bowker Company, a Xerox company; copyright © 1982 by Xerox Corporation), Vol. 221, No. 16, April 16, 1982, p. 71.*

Brisk and almost ingenuous, a slight plot is lifted by the amicable tone of the story, and by the humor and action of the black and white drawings relieved by the blue of the stolen paint. . . . Belinda suspects the younger children, but the culprit proves to have been her dog, who (unlikely event) ate the paint. Ashamed of having accused the children, Belinda promises to read as many books as they want. Last picture: children returning with stacks and stacks of books. Not much mystery here, but plenty of action, a cheerful milieu, and rather a nice relationship among the children of varying ages.

> *Zena Sutherland, in a review of "The Mystery of the Stolen Blue Paint," in* Bulletin of the Center for Children's Books *(reprinted by permission of The University of Chicago Press; © 1982 by The University of Chicago), Vol. 35, No. 10, June, 1982, p. 190.*

Kellogg's multicolored mystery series takes on blue, as a dog, a gang of kids, and a can of paint romp through this funny, lighthearted tale. . . . Kellogg's black line drawings accented with blue are deftly and enthusiastically drawn with childlike expressions that are right on target, and background details add funny scenes that readers will enjoy following. Sure to be as popular with primary-graders as the red mitten, magic green ball, and flying orange pumpkin tales.

> *Barbara Elleman, in a review of "The Mystery of the Stolen Blue Paint," in* Booklist *(reprinted by permission of the American Library Association; copyright © 1982 by the American Library Association), Vol. 78, No. 21, July, 1982, p. 1445.*

Steven Kellogg knows just how a small child feels and thinks. . . . Kellogg's writing is good and often humorous. . . . Cartoon-like pictures in black ink with spots of blue wash are too tiny to show to a group of children. For a parent or teacher reading aloud or for a young reader this title would be well liked, making it a popular addition to a library.

> *Paula Gazess, in a review of "The Mystery of the Stolen Blue Paint," in* School Library Journal *(reprinted from the January, 1983 issue of* School Library Journal, *published by R. R. Bowker Co./ A Xerox Corporation; copyright © 1983), Vol. 29, No. 5, January, 1983, p. 61.*

TALLYHO, PINKERTON! (1982)

Kellogg's Great Dane conquered hearts in **"Pinkerton, Behave!"** and **"A Rose for Pinkerton."** Now the good-hearted, galumphing dog and his best friend Rose, the kitten, return in a third adventure, endearingly illustrated by the author-illustrator in action-filled, colorful pictures, as funny as the tale. The little girl and her mother who have adopted the dog and cat as pets take them along into the woods on a picnic, an outing combining pleasure with the child's homework assignment: to identify and report on wild birds and mammals. The report includes wilder types, Dr. Aleasha Kibble and members of her foxhunting academy, a hoity-toity group demoralized by affable Pinkerton who lands on their fox-spotting balloon and convinces them that he's a dangerous alien from outer space. That's only one of the episodes that Kellogg regales readers with in his new book, destined to be another favorite bedtime story.

> *A review of "Tallyho, Pinkerton!" in* Publishers Weekly *(reprinted from the November 26, 1982 issue of* Publishers Weekly, *published by R. R. Bowker Company, a Xerox company; copyright © 1982 by Xerox Corporation), Vol. 222, No. 22, November 26, 1982, p. 59.*

A day's outing in the woods turns into Kellogg's usual mayhem when Pinkerton the Great Dane and Rose the cat accompany their young owner on a search for ten birds and mammals. They encounter a group of fox-hunting academy students, with predictably funny results. To everyone's sorrow, the group tracks down the rare "striped fox". The skunk's retaliation is illustrated in such a bilious green that one would swear the page stank. This is a very funny romp.

> *Nelda Mohr, in a review of "Tallyho, Pinkerton!" in* Children's Book Review Service *(copyright © 1983 Children's Book Review Service Inc.), Vol. 11, No. 5, January, 1983, p. 42.*

Slapstick humour coupled with sly satire sharpens a story laid out in strip-form. . . . A short, swift text gives an illusion of brisk, surprising action as surely as the vigorous coloured scenes do.

> *Margery Fisher, in a review of "Tallyho, Pinkerton!" in her* Growing Point, *Vol. 22, No. 1, May, 1983, p. 4081.*

William Kotzwinkle

1938-

American author of fiction.

Kotzwinkle's works are ventures into the realms of science fiction, the imaginations of children, and the everyday activities of young boys. Critics consider *The Firemen, The Ship That Came Down the Gutter, The Day the Gang Got Rich*, and *Up the Alley with Jack and Joe* simple, accurate, and enjoyable reminiscences of various stages of childhood. In other books, Kotzwinkle takes the elements so prevalent in his adult works—the meshing of reality and the dream world, outrageous fantasies—and develops them for children. *The Oldest Man and Other Timeless Stories, The Nap Master, The Supreme, Superb, Exalted, and Delightful, One and Only Magic Building*, and especially *Dream of Dark Harbor* are based around plots in which the main character is constantly involved in a flight back and forth between the fantasy of dreams and the realism of the waking world. Most of Kotzwinkle's works are illustrated by Joe Servello. They have been greeted with mixed reviews: critics cite brilliant passages and images but do not give the books the same acclaim as a whole.

Probably Kotzwinkle's most popular book is *E.T., the Extra-Terrestrial and His Adventures on Earth*. Based on the screenplay by Melissa Mathison and not on Steven Spielberg's film, Kotzwinkle's *E.T.* is praised for its thoroughness and Kotzwinkle's ability to delve beneath the exteriors of the characters. Critics note the success of his emphasis on the adult characters and their motivations and his avoidance of the overt (but not necessarily detrimental) cuteness of the movie. Kotzwinkle is usually viewed as a children's author who creates original concepts and invests them with a romantic philosophy and a sense of humor.

(See also *Contemporary Literary Criticism*, Vols. 5, 14; *Something about the Author*, Vol. 24; *Contemporary Authors New Revision Series*, Vol. 3; and *Contemporary Authors*, Vols. 45-48.)

© *Joe Servello*

THE FIREMEN (1969)

[This] picture book, using a very realistic story, reminds the reader how strange and magical to the small child is his everyday world of household objects and backyard landscape. When a little boy receives a toy fire engine big enough to ride in, he and his little dog and his teddy bear travel through the house in search of fires, and then ride out into the yard and down the alley. . . . The illustrations are as simple and evocative as the text; . . . one feels that to read the book is to enter the realm of childhood.

> *Sidney D. Long, in a review of "The Firemen," in* The Horn Book Magazine *(copyright © 1969 by The Horn Book, Inc., Boston), Vol. XLV, No. 4, August, 1969, p. 397.*

A slight story. . . . In short sentences and simple language intended to be characteristic of the boy's thinking, the author describes the boy's trip through his house. . . . The simple ideas straightforwardly presented, the simple drawings, and the clean appearance of the book due to large amounts of white space surrounding text and drawings, make this a fair, if unexciting, choice for very young preschoolers. (pp. 111-12)

> *Eleanor Glaser, in a review of "The Firemen," in* School Library Journal, *an appendix to* Library Journal *(reprinted from the November, 1969 issue of* School Library Journal, *published by R. R. Bowker Co./ A Xerox Corporation; copyright © 1969), Vol. 16, No. 3, November, 1969, pp. 111-12.*

ELEPHANT BOY: A STORY OF THE STONE AGE (1970)

When you think about the Stone Age, if you think about it at all, you see the world then as a dark, threatening place with survival dependent on the most primitive skills. That's the way the author and illustrator [Joe Servello] describe and picture it as they tell the story of a small boy's struggles for survival in the Stone Age; they also see it as an age when the sun never shines. An effective look at the world way, way, way back.

> *A review of "Elephant Boy: A Story of the Stone Age," in* Publishers Weekly *(reprinted from the April 6, 1970 issue of* Publishers Weekly, *published by R. R. Bowker Company, a Xerox company; copyright © 1970 by Xerox Corporation), Vol. 197, No. 14, April 6, 1970, p. 61.*

Stone age boy and his father wander episodically thru fishing, hunting and various survival experiences, including simple family and religious life. Boy earns his name when he witnesses wooly mammoths thundering down the valley. Unfortunately, these ancient beasts with their furry coats and long curving tusks are referred to as elephants rather than by the more specific, accurate name of mammoth; accordingly, the boy is given the misnomer, Elephant Boy. In general, the text is bland and lacks the vigor, excitement and drama of the pictures. . . . The book is worth having just because of the art; also, there seems to be nothing available on the subject for this age level.

> *Margaret Riddell, in a review of "Elephant Boy: A Story of the Stone Age," in* School Library Journal, *an appendix to* Library Journal *(reprinted from the May, 1970 issue of* School Library Journal, *published by R. R. Bowker Co./ A Xerox Corporation; copyright © 1970), Vol. 16, No. 9, May, 1970, p. 60.*

The world of primordial man is presented in [*Elephant Boy: A Story of the Stone Age*] which reaches back through centuries of time to show man as he once was: primitive, vulnerable, but completely a part of his environment. . . . Though the text is simple, it should be even more spare; it is too wordy and conventional for the drama that the pictures reveal.

> *Sidney D. Long, in a review of "Elephant Boy: A Story of the Stone Age," in* The Horn Book Magazine *(copyright © 1970 by The Horn Book, Inc., Boston), Vol. XLVI, No. 3, June, 1970, p. 286.*

THE DAY THE GANG GOT RICH (1970)

Five dollars is a fortune when you're young, as this exuberant story proves. And to follow the neighborhood gang as they spend it, is to spend a glorious day with a gang of small boys as they fulfill their small boys' dreams. A happy book.

> *A review of "The Day the Gang Got Rich," in* Publishers Weekly *(reprinted from the August 3, 1970 issue of* Publishers Weekly, *published by R. R. Bowker Company, a Xerox company; copyright © 1970 by Xerox Corporation), Vol. 198, No. 5, August 3, 1970, p. 60.*

It doesn't figure—that the gang, flourishing George Dugan's five dollars, can get seven ice cream sodas for seventy cents or pretzels for a penny apiece—until a trolley heaves into sight and the nostalgic air takes on an old-time shape. The big splurge—banana splits and comic books and a free-for-all through the town—is potshot, unplotted fun ("They lost Willie Botchka" . . . and found him quite casually in a flower shop): like [the] very different *Elephant Boy*, something new is made of something stale. But then it doesn't exactly figure that kids who didn't have a baseball bat would have a tennis racket, or that they would use it instead of a stick, or that given five dollars when the racket's broken, they wouldn't buy a bat. Or that Mr. Grimble, running over the racket through no fault of his own, would hand over five dollars. Nor does one see how the racket got from the last batter to the apron of Mr. Grimble's garage. Loose, which is to the good; slack, which isn't.

> *A review of "The Day the Gang Got Rich," in* Kirkus Reviews *(copyright © 1970 The Kirkus Service, Inc.), Vol. XXXVIII, No. 16, August 15, 1970, p. 868.*

THE SHIP THAT CAME DOWN THE GUTTER (1970)

A partially successful, meager story about what a child might imagine in a gutter after a rain. Jack watches various articles flow down the gutter when along comes a galleon. Though no bigger than a walnut shell, it is manned by a full crew with a captain shouting orders. Jack runs alongside of it and by blowing into the sails saves it from going down the main sewer. He diverts it into an alley where it sails on out of sight. . . . The author, in his desire to make his little galleon real, is so convincing that one can't tell where reality slips off and imagination begins. Third graders should be able to read the relatively easy vocabulary, while younger children will listen and accept the story at face value.

> *Miriam C. Patton, in a review of "The Ship That Came Down the Gutter," in* School Library Journal, *an appendix to* Library Journal *(reprinted from the May, 1971 issue of* School Library Journal, *published by R. R. Bowker Co./ A Xerox Corporation; copyright © 1971), Vol. 17, No. 9, May, 1971, p. 59.*

Here is a striking and original idea. . . . The brief excitement is exactly child-sized, and the younger reader will not ask—as his parent may—how much was reality and how much imagination.

> *Marcus Crouch, in a review of "The Ship That Came Down the Gutter," in* The Junior Bookshelf, *Vol. 40, No. 3, June, 1976, p. 146.*

THE OLDEST MAN, AND OTHER TIMELESS STORIES (1971)

In an afterword, Kotzwinkle waives responsibility for these four antiqued tales—when he sits down at the typewriter a Little Old Man storms his head. . . . The Little Man's judgment doesn't seem as good as the author's own if that's the case; but the basic ideas, mostly old ones dealing with the margins between art and life, dream and reality, aren't bad. . . . [The last tale is] an original curiosity, the two laziest men on earth live forever. This one is oblique enough to engage reading-aloud adults but may puzzle the children; the others try to maintain both levels of interest but, with the exception of **"The Fairy King,"** dilute the impact of their ancient sources. . . . [There] is plenty of visual interest in the embroidered telling. (pp. 1013-14)

> *A review of "The Oldest Man," in* Kirkus Reviews *(copyright © 1971 The Kirkus Service, Inc.), Vol. XXXIX, No. 18, September 15, 1971, pp. 1013-14.*

Four gentle fantasies poetically told with flashes of realism and humor by the author of the simple, effective *Elephant Boy*. . . . Each is original in treatment or concept and each has a distinctive tone. All involve some meeting of the real and dream worlds. In the first tale, a butterfly-collector tires of a chase, lies down to sleep his usual dreamless sleep wrapped in darkness. . . . In another tale, two black stallions in a portrait come alive each night and go to visit the artist who painted them. . . . Children may find the changes which occur in the other tales more detached from their experiences and less affecting for what they portray than for the mood they create and for the lovely style of the telling.

> *Ruth M. McConnell, in a review of "The Oldest Man and Other Timeless Stories," in* School Library Journal, *an appendix to* Library Journal *(reprinted from the May, 1972 issue of* School Library Journal, *published by R. R. Bowker Co./ A Xerox Corporation;*

copyright © 1972), Vol. 18, No. 9, May, 1972, p. 78.

Four fanciful short stories are told in an elaborate style, each tale beginning with a realistic setting and moving into the mystical area in which the human being changes form—or perhaps dreams that he does. . . . The stories have imaginative touches but they also seem derivative, and the mysticism and writing style may limit the audience.

> *Zena Sutherland, in a review of "The Oldest Man and Other Timeless Stories," in* Bulletin of the Center for Children's Books *(reprinted by permission of The University of Chicago Press; © 1972 by The University of Chicago), Vol. 26, No. 2, October, 1972, p. 27.*

THE SUPREME, SUPERB, EXALTED AND DELIGHTFUL, ONE AND ONLY MAGIC BUILDING   (1973)

Among the many workers engaged in building the Emperor's Supreme, Superb, Exalted and Delightful Magic Building is Old Ridgepole, whose painstaking perfection is not appreciated until after the building is completed and then—on the night of its opening celebration—destroyed by an angry storm. Ruined also are the huts that the workers have built for themselves—all but that of Old Ridgepole, who made his so sturdy and so beautiful that it now stands alone, encircled by a glowing halo in which the gods dance and chant. The old worker is transformed too, "glowing with a mysterious inner light" so that even the Emperor now recognizes him as the Universal Monarch and his little hut as the true Magic Building. . . . Kotzwinkle's accomplished "original parable" has the ring of tradition—so much so that Old Ridgepole is treated with all the automatic piety (at the end the reader feels that he's expected to fall on his knees) accorded to the deity or prophet of a real religion. For those who revere graven images. (pp. 452-53)

> *A review of "The Supreme, Superb, Exalted and Delightful, One and Only Magic Building," in* Kirkus Reviews *(copyright © 1973 The Kirkus Service, Inc.), Vol. XLI, No. 8, April 15, 1973, pp. 452-53.*

From the Proclamation of the Emperor that a Magic Building is to be constructed, through the actual construction, destruction and finalization of the Magic Building, children are held spellbound. Children as young as seven can understand the full meaning of this book. It is truly a book for all ages!

> *Barbara R. McCoy, in a review of "The Supreme, Superb, Exalted and Delightful, One and Only Magic Building," in* Children's Book Review Service *(copyright © 1973 Children's Book Review Service Inc.), Vol. 1, No. 12, August, 1973, p. 76.*

An elusive parable concerning a proud Oriental Emperor and a humble carpenter called Old Ridgepole. "Smoothly did their blades go, and never bend, buckle or stick." Such tortuous locutions indicate the Eastern locale. It has escaped Mr. Kotzwinkle's attention that the Grimms's tales read in English do not "sound" German, nor Perrault's "sound" French. And is creating and describing mystery as simple as writing that Old Ridgepole is "glowing with a mysterious inner light"? . . . [The] author has failed to notice that imitating the East can sometimes be a royal road to the ridiculous.

> *Barbara Silverberg, in a review of "The Supreme, Superb, Exalted and Delightful, One and Only Magic*

Building," in The New York Times Book Review *(© 1974 by The New York Times Company; reprinted by permission), January 13, 1974, p. 10.*

UP THE ALLEY WITH JACK AND JOE   (1974)

Though Kotzwinkle concocts no story line to keep beginners turning the pages, his alley is both closer to home and more richly textured than the usual easy reader setting. . . . Sam and Jack and Joe jump, run, climb and explore their ramshackle but tranquil small town world while Kotzwinkle tells of their Saturday adventures. . . . Back home when Sam's mother asks him how he got the rip . . . in his pants, he answers only "Up the alley with Jack and Joe." A sympathetic inside view of "'Where did you go?' 'Out.'"

> *A review of "Up the Alley with Jack and Joe," in* Kirkus Reviews *(copyright © 1974 The Kirkus Service, Inc.), Vol. XLII, No. 15, August 1, 1974, p. 801.*

The boys' pastimes are often dangerous—e.g., swinging from the beams of a house under construction and accidentally taking a ride on the hook of a crane—but they are related in a matter-of-fact manner that takes this kind of boyhood bravado for granted.

> *Alice Ehlert, in a review of "Up the Alley with Jack and Joe," in* School Library Journal, *an appendix to* Library Journal *(reprinted from the December, 1974 issue of* School Library Journal, *published by R. R. Bowker Co./ A Xerox Corporation; copyright © 1974), Vol. 21, No. 4, December, 1974, p. 49.*

There's no story line, the only appeals being in the vicarious pleasure a reader may have in the idea of a day of freedom and companionship, and in the fact that the book is easy to read.

> *Zena Sutherland, in a review of "Up the Alley with Jack and Joe," in* Bulletin of the Center for Children's Books *(reprinted by permission of The University of Chicago Press; © 1975 by The University of Chicago), Vol. 28, No. 5, January, 1975, p. 80.*

THE LEOPARD'S TOOTH   (1976)

It's initially disappointing when the manic imagination of **The Fan Man** and **Dr. Rat** turns to juvenile fiction (there have been picture books) and produces this campy, Boy's Life dream of Darkest Africa. . . . Fortunately Kotzwinkle has something more in mind than nostalgia; his Africa is floridly trippy ("Charles felt as though he were in the garden of a mad giant") and the spells are truly magical—there's a spirit python with scales that sparkle like diamonds, and [when Sir Henry Turnbull is turned into a leopard by an angry witch doctor, the transformation] occurs, breathtakingly, before our eyes. Kotzwinkle performs with éclat, though like all feats of prestidigitation this requires collusion on the part of the audience.

> *A review of "The Leopard's Tooth," in* Kirkus Reviews *(copyright © 1976 The Kirkus Service, Inc.), Vol. XLIV, No. 7, April 1, 1976, p. 390.*

The setting and the element of danger may have some appeal to readers, but the story is neither well written nor convincing, and the characters are stereotypes.

Zena Sutherland, in a review of "The Leopard's Tooth," in Bulletin of the Center for Children's Books *(reprinted by permission of The University of Chicago Press; © 1976 by The University of Chicago), Vol. 30, No. 1, September, 1976, p. 12.*

Omens and oracles, hallucinations and dreams mingle to produce a vivid, fast-moving adventure yarn with supernatural overtones. The denouement is intriguingly inconclusive, and Charles experiences some of the pleasures of growing from childhood to adulthood. . . . [Short] chapters enhance the appeal of this book for slower or more reluctant readers.

Mike P. Healy, in a review of "The Leopard's Tooth," in Kliatt Young Adult Paperback Book Guide *(copyright © by Kliatt Paperback Book Guide), Vol. XVII, No. 3, April, 1983, p. 16.*

THE ANTS WHO TOOK AWAY TIME   (1978)

A far-out but filled-out sci-fi fantasy, about how some giant ants bring time to a stop but a slippery kid named Ducky helps start it up again. . . . Kotzwinkle clips along at a whirlwind pace, without stopping to introduce us properly to Ducky or to play with the implications of the time disturbances—for example, time runs backwards now and then but it's treated here merely as an annoying roadblock that momentarily delays the rushing heroes. . . . Much ado of little moment.

A review of "The Ants Who Took Away Time," in Kirkus Reviews *(copyright © 1978 The Kirkus Service, Inc.), Vol. XLVI, No. 22, November 15, 1978, p. 1248.*

Mr. Feldhammer—keeper of the Great Gold Watch that keeps Time marching on—decides to go on vacation outside of Time. Giant ants . . . take advantage of his absence to throw the world (and this book) into turmoil as they schlep the pieces of the watch off for their own devious ends. The world stops at 3:00. With some help from the Creator of the World (a woman who masquerades, sometimes, as a porcupine), Feldhammer's assistant, and a kid named Ducky Doodle (!), the plot is foiled. There are so many ridiculous side-line adventures and so many un-funny jokes that the story seems endless as indeed it is: almost 60 pages of the stuff. . . . Slipping in and out are flashes of unconnected cleverness. . . . But there's not enough of anything good to save this witless fantasy. (pp. 43-4)

Marjorie Lewis, in a review of "The Ants Who Took Away Time," in School Library Journal *(reprinted from the January, 1979 issue of* School Library Journal, *published by R. R. Bowker Co./ A Xerox Corporation; copyright © 1979), Vol. 25, No. 5, January, 1979, pp. 43-4.*

I suspect this picture-and-big-print book will be liked by those children barely old enough to read its words, but to anyone older than eight I think it will be dumb, childish, and corny . . . because kids of eight & up will have watched the more disciplined and "mature" sf on TV. . . .

Note: the characters are all males of various ages.

Richard E. Geis, in a review of "The Ants Who Took Away Time," in Science Fiction Review *(copyright © 1979 by Richard Geis; reprinted by permission of Richard Geis), Vol. 8, No. 2, March-April, 1979, p. 31.*

The story is too complex with too many incidents for the young readers who will be attracted to the format of this juvenile science fiction. . . . The statement on the quality and characteristics of Time disappears in the adventures which befall the Keeper of Time and his assistants. Some amusing segments do not make up for an incoherent whole.

Ruth M. Stein, in a review of "The Ants Who Took Away Time" (copyright © 1979 by the National Council of Teachers of English; reprinted by permission of the publisher and the author), in Language Arts, *Vol. 56, No. 4, April, 1979, p. 441.*

THE NAP MASTER   (1979)

"Wanted: Someone who can make our little boy, Herman Corderinkle, take his nap." Clutching the newspaper with the ad, a tiny man with a long white beard arrives at an apartment in Manhattan and tells vexed Mrs. Corderinkle: "I am the Nap Master." Rambunctious Herman will have nothing to do with the man. The boy runs into the hall where the elevator man, maintenance man and everyone is asleep but "Naps are for saps!" shouts Herman. With nothing to do, he flops into a cozy chair and into dream adventures beyond his imaginings, with the Nap Master. Kotzwinkle, master storyteller, clearly enjoyed writing this dandy fantasy as much as his readers surely will enjoy reading it. (pp. 126-27)

A review of "The Nap Master," in Publishers Weekly *(reprinted from the February 12, 1979 issue of* Publishers Weekly, *published by R. R. Bowker Company, a Xerox company; copyright © 1979 by Xerox Corporation), Vol. 215, No. 7, February 12, 1979, pp. 126-27.*

[The Nap Master takes Herman] on a typical Kotzwinkle fantasy trip where the . . . doorman, janitor, etc., join him underwater and he gets a taste for naps and dreams. "Enjoy yourself and don't be afraid [of dreams]," is the Nap Master's message, but the way he whooshes Herman from one wonder to another doesn't give anyone a chance to get involved.

A review of "The Nap Master," in Kirkus Reviews *(copyright © 1979 The Kirkus Service, Inc.), Vol. XLVII, No. 6, March 15, 1979, p. 323.*

DREAM OF DARK HARBOR   (1979)

The dreamlike vision of a wanderer's launching—in which readers, too, must set forth without a compass. Kotzwinkle begins in midflight, with one Jack "crouching low through the field," following his shadow which calls him to "learn the dark things," ducking and sliding and following the stream that calls him on to the sea. . . . Only those prepared to dive right in will embark on this at all, and they might reasonably turn back at the calling stream and dancing spirits. The second half benefits from the rushing urgency, the smashing waves, and the captain's watery strangeness.

A review of "Dream of Dark Harbor," in Kirkus Reviews *(copyright © 1979 The Kirkus Service, Inc.), Vol. XLVII, No. 4, February 15, 1979, p. 197.*

A boy of indeterminate age, conversing with the spirits of dead men and with anthropomorphized nature, moves across land, along a river, and (briefly) onto the sea, moved by—what? That's the mystery here, and we don't see enough of the boy's character to resolve it. Motivation is supplied by a muddle of some Jung ("*Follow me,* said the shadow, *and learn the dark things.*"), sentiment toward a nature at once solicitous and indifferent, and pretention ("*Of all the things I did in life,* said the ghost, *this* [jamming a stone into a tree fork] *was the only true one.*"). Allegorical aspirations weigh down the descriptions of nature and the runaway boy; the boundless romanticism doesn't compensate for the implausibilities. (During part of a dark, howling night the boy, a landlubber, builds a raft from an old shack, sews a sail, learns knot-tying and navigation from some dead sailors, and rides out a gale.) Purple patches sit uneasily alongside colloquialisms. The title is misleading: the "dream" dimension of the story is undefined, it's not chillingly "ghostly," and hardly qualifies as a "sea story." . . . [There is a] murky obscurity of mood and plot.

> *Patricia Dooley, in a review of "Dream of Dark Harbor," in* School Library Journal *(reprinted from the April, 1979 issue of* School Library Journal, *published by R. R. Bowker Co./ A Xerox Corporation; copyright © 1979), Vol. 25, No. 8, April, 1979, p. 58.*

[Kotzwinkle] seeks too often and obviously to impose significance upon his material, instead of letting it stand on its own merits as a ghost story/sea yarn. . . . Although the book manifests overall workmanship . . . , there is really nothing special about this book that makes essential its purchase.

> *Francis J. Molson, in a review of "Dream of Dark Harbor," in* Science Fiction & Fantasy Book Review *(copyright © 1979 by The Borgo Press), Vol. 1, No. 6, July, 1979, p. 84.*

Jack follows a stream and a river to the ocean, camps in a deserted shack, wakes to find he is marooned by the storm waves, is rescued by ghostly mariners, and decides to sail on in his improvised boat. The plot is ill-suited to either a ghost or an adventure story; the book has elements of both but succeeds in neither. The writing is determinedly poetic. . . .

> *Zena Sutherland, in a review of "Dream of Dark Harbor," in* Bulletin of the Center for Children's Books *(reprinted by permission of The University of Chicago Press; © 1979 by The University of Chicago), Vol. 32, No. 11, July-August, 1979, p. 194.*

E.T.: THE EXTRA-TERRESTRIAL (1982)

A ten million year old alien botanist is accidentally marooned on Earth. He is befriended by three children and in particular by Elliott, whose bedroom closet becomes his hideout. With their help he learns something of our planet's bewildering ways, puts together a beacon to call for rescue and thrives on a diet of M&Ms, Oreos and, even more important, the children's love. Of course, the government suspects his presence and is hunting him, but after he is captured Elliott helps him escape in time to rendezvous with his ship. It's a simple story, but Kotzwinkle tells it with great humor and zest. He makes the kids believable and successfully walks the fine line between genuine charm and exessive cuteness or bathos. If the movie does all that as well, the book should certainly be popular, but quite apart from the film, the novel's a delight in itself. This is not to be compared with the usual "novelization."

> *A review of "E.T.: The Extra-Terrestrial," in* Publishers Weekly *(reprinted from the June 18, 1982 issue of* Publishers Weekly, *published by R. R. Bowker Company, a Xerox company; copyright © 1982 by Xerox Corporation), Vol. 221, No. 25, June 18, 1982, p. 65.*

It may be unique that a writer as reputable as William Kotzwinkle has written a novel based on the screenplay of a film that is currently showing. But whether it is unique or not, one turns to the book version of "E.T." with a pleasant glow of anticipation.

That is partly because one looks forward to reading another book by [this] author. . . . It is partly because, having seen the Steven Spielberg film, one wants to experience again, though in different form, the thoroughly charming story. . . .

But it's also partly because one wants to clear up some of the fuzziness of the movie. Not that the film absolutely demands clarification. On the whole it works marvelously, despite its confusing passages. . . .

[One] turns to Mr. Kotzwinkle's novelization of Melissa Mathison's screenplay of "E.T." in the hope of understanding, say, the actual mechanics of the transmitting contraption that the space creature devises to "phone home"; or the nature of the powers that enable him to levitate objects or cause dying flowers to burst into bloom, or what really causes him to turn ashen gray as earth's alien environment works its malign effect on him.

And just as one suspected, the experience of reading "E.T." is extremely satisfying in its way. Not only does it answer many questions like the foregoing ones . . . , but it also solves certain problems of the film one was only subliminally aware of while watching it.

For example, I realize in retrospect that I was a little troubled by the apparent remoteness and indifference of the children's mother during the early scenes of the film. This remoteness is consistent with the fact that the whole story depends on our being in a children's world. Yet it still bothered me that the mother seemed so neglectful. In the book, this problem is cleared up by our seeing part of the story from the mother's point of view without her knowing what is really going on inside the children's heads. Writing can do this where film cannot, because film can't easily distinguish between thought and action, whereas writing can.

Similarly, the scientists who are tracking down E.T. do not seem so unnecessarily threatening in the book as they do in the film. Once again, Mr. Kotzwinkle can get inside the character's heads without giving their actions away to the children, where the film could not. Another significant difference is that in the book the leader of the scientific team is affectionately known as "Keys" because the large bunch dangling from his belt gives him access to so many "compartments" of the project. In the film, the same character is reduced to the ominous visual image of a bunch of keys hanging from an anonymous belt, which suggests unnecessarily that the owner of the keys is some sort of slave master or prison warden.

In these and similar ways, Mr. Kotzwinkle seems to improve upon and enrich Miss Mathison's screenplay and Mr. Spielberg's film. Most dramatically of all, he succeeds in making E.T.'s sickness a threat not only to Elliott, his devoted friend, but also to the entire planet Earth. And the only major drawback of putting the story into print is that Mr. Kotzwinkle seems to have the damnedest time figuring out how to refer to E.T. He calls him every awkward thing from "the old monster" to "the elderly voyager" to "the old genius" to "the ancient pilgrim from the stars."

Does this mean that "E.T." the book is really better than "E.T." the movie? For a while I thought so. But then I stopped and realized what it meant was that I was seeing the book against the background of the film: the best things about the story—from the flights of bicycles to the irresistible figure of the space creature himself—belong to the visual experience of the film. Even the story's underlying myths—our childlike wish for superior intelligence to exist in the universe, the possibility of death and resurrection—seem more effectively worked out in the film.

So let's concede that the book is very satisfying in its way, but most of all because it is an eloquent footnote to the film. Maybe it will seem the other way around to someone who reads the book before seeing the film. But I happen to have seen the movie first.

> *Christopher Lehmann-Haupt, in a review of "E.T.: The Extra-Terrestrial," in* The New York Times, *Section C (© 1982 by The New York Times Company; reprinted by permission), July 2, 1982, p. C20.*

The character of E.T., eating M&Ms, heart glowing, stranded three million light-years from home, and of 10-year-old Elliott who harbors and helps him, are well drawn. Kotzwinkle's narrative is polished, lush, humorous and Bradburyesque in an exuberance befitting a fantasy-adventure tale of boys, aliens, dogs, Halloween. But . . . he sometimes succumbs to the pitfall of novelizing: unnecessary, repetitive descriptions. And the never-ending parade of epithets for E.T. . . . can drive you crazy. Still, it's boy-summer-fun reading—maybe just the ticket while waiting on those long movie ticket lines.

> *Lisa Mitchell, in a review of "E.T.: The Extra-Terrestrial," in* Los Angeles Times *(reprinted by permission of the author), July 18, 1982, p. 12.*

William Kotzwinkle's **"E.T.: The Extra-Terrestrial"** is a novelization of Melissa Mathison's screenplay for the fabulously successful movie of the same name. The story in both forms is virtually the same. . . .

The characters too are virtually the same: the foul-mouthed but good-hearted kids, the distracted mom, the dog. And there is the same reassuring message: You not only *can* go home again, you can have a good laugh and a good cry and still be back in time for dinner.

Having reported all the parallels, I must also report that the book is much less appealing in every way than the movie. The reason, I think, is time lag. Modern science-fiction films seem to be recapitulating the history of modern science-fiction stories some 25 years late. In the 50's most movie aliens were inexplicably malign monsters who preferred to eat first and talk later. After this apparently endless parade of Blobs and Its and Things, friendly aliens seem innovative—on the screen. But in print this limited fairy tale (no real villains, no freshly "alien" point of view) is sadly out-of-date. In trying to disguise the unfortunate truth, the otherwise literate Mr. Kotzwinkle is reduced to sentences like: "She sensed that there was something at its core, unnameable, horrible, gathering everything to it."

I can hardly wait for the television series. (p. 11)

> *Gerald Jonas, "Imaginary People," in* The New York Times Book Review *(© 1982 by The New York Times Company; reprinted by permission), August 29, 1982, pp. 10-11.**

Movie tie-ins usually attempt only to evoke memories of the movie. Kotzwinkle has interpreted and expanded on the imagery of this film. He exposes the thoughts and motives of the characters, especially E.T., where the film showed only words and results leaving much to the process of audience identification. This is, in fact, a very subjective film and, by making the subjective concrete, Kotzwinkle has produced a story some moviegoers will barely recognize. The sequence of events is altered. E.T. is portrayed as "an ancient botanist" given to mid-life ruminations and unrequited passion for Elliott's mother. The emotional power of the movie is replaced by self-indulgent amusement wavering between sarcastic and pathetic. Kotzwinkle's style appears to be based on a thesaurus, particularly when he refers to E.T. by an annoying collection of synonyms. . . . If the relationship to the movie is ignored, the reader is left with a domestic comedy about misfits that is not science fiction. The real popularity of the book will be with the movie's fans who will find the contents disappointing.

> *Carolyn Caywood, in a review of "E.T.: The Extra-Terrestrial," in* Voice of Youth Advocates *(copyrighted 1982 by Voice of Youth Advocates), Vol. 5, No. 5, December, 1982, p. 38.*

E.T.: THE EXTRA-TERRESTRIAL STORYBOOK (1982)

While this claims to be based on Melissa Mathison's screenplay, a lot of liberties were taken with the plot. The film is much tighter—and after enjoying Mathison's gift for natural childlike dialogue, one can't help but wonder what this book might have been like if written by her. Many of the magical film scenes—Elliott liberating the frogs in biology class, E.T.'s learning speech from television's Sesame Street, the blooming revived geranium signaling E.T.'s recovery—are missing here. A new subplot involving Elliott's bratty enemy Lance (who reveals E.T.'s escape plans to the authorities) is very lame.

> *Marilyn Payne Phillips, in a review of "E.T.: The Extra-Terrestrial Storybook," in* School Library Journal *(reprinted from the October, 1982 issue of* School Library Journal, *published by R. R. Bowker Co./ A Xerox Corporation; copyright © 1982), Vol. 29, No. 2, October, 1982, p. 142.*

Illustrated by stills from the film from which this was adapted, the oversize format has a continuous text broken by a bar of color at points at which the scene shifts, which it often does with a jarring effect that is not in evidence in the visual medium. The story has appeal, and will probably have the greatest appeal for readers who have seen the film, but it doesn't have a smooth narrative flow. Kotzwinkle handles dialogue well, but the translation of action seen in film to action described in print is often awkward, and the adaptor's expository style often seems florid.

> *Zena Sutherland, in a review of "E.T.: The Extra-Terrestrial Storybook," in* Bulletin of the Center for Children's Books *(reprinted by permission of The University of Chicago Press; © 1982 by The University of Chicago), Vol. 36, No. 5, January, 1983, p. 92.*

Eda J(oan) LeShan

1922-

American author of nonfiction and editor.

LeShan is a noted psychologist whose works give young readers advice and insightful explanations about childhood emotions and problems. While there are many authors of works on child psychology, LeShan is one of the few who write to help children understand themselves and others. Critics approve of LeShan's forthright and sympathetic handling of difficult subjects and her use of examples to show children that their feelings are universal.

LeShan's first book for children, *What Makes Me Feel This Way? Growing Up with Human Emotions*, covers such topics as sex, empathy, and death. Critics praise LeShan for her approach, which assures the child that such emotions as jealousy and anger are normal. However, some critics find LeShan's discussions too complex and recommend that an adult read this book along with the child. *Learning to Say Good-by: When a Parent Dies*, perhaps her most popular book, resulted from LeShan's discovery that much of her mother's unhappiness as an adult was caused by society's ignorance about the capacity of children to deal with death. LeShan's grandmother died when her mother was a child, a fact kept from her for more than two years until she heard a neighbor discussing the tragedy. The trauma of her mother's disappearance and the confusion of not being able to face the pain, sorrow, and anger of death had lifelong effects. LeShan wrote *Learning to Say Good-by* so that other children would be able to understand and express their feelings. This book is considered a most reliable source for helping children cope with death.

LeShan is also the co-author of *The Incredible Television Machine* with Lee Polk. Although critics call the narrative condescending, they commend it for providing a practical assessment of the values and problems of television as they relate to children. LeShan has been the commentator for the television programs "How Do Your Children Grow" and "In Tune" and served as the consultant for "Dear Alex and Annie"—a section of "Kids Are People Too"—which answers children's letters on their everyday problems. As well as books for adults and children, she has written *You and Your Feelings* and *Roots of Crime* for young adults. LeShan applies her experiences, both personal and professional, to books which show respect and consideration for the emotional growth of children.

(See also *Contemporary Authors*, Vols. 13-16, rev. ed. and *Something about the Author*, Vol. 21.)

AUTHOR'S COMMENTARY

One day, just before I began writing this book [*In Search of Myself—And Other Children*], I was having lunch with a young father and we were discussing what I planned to write about. At one point he said, quite casually, "Well, you know, of course, Eda, that today children are an impediment." I couldn't understand why the walls of that quiet, elegant restaurant didn't begin to shake and tremble. I must have looked faint, because my companion looked very surprised. When he asked me what was the matter, I told him, "What you have said so casually is an idea that is almost entirely new to the history of human

Courtesy of Eda LeShan

civilization, and yet in the past few years it has become so ordinary that you say it without even expecting to be struck by lightning!" (p. 161)

For the last ten years or so, I have become increasingly frightened by what has seemed to me a turning against childhood and children. My second book, published in 1967, *The Conspiracy Against Childhood*, represented a growing feeling that in spite of appearing to be a child-centered nation, we were making childhood a more and more dangerous, difficult, and unhappy experience by pushing children too hard, creating an unhealthy environment for them to grow in, and by losing touch with our own humanity—largely determined by memories of our own childhood.

Now, looking back, that book seems ridiculously naïve; what has happened since has been far worse than I could have imagined.

Although I thought I'd done with writing about children, I found it was still a subject nagging at me; there *must* be something more I could do or say, for it seemed to me we were—are—on a suicidal course. And yet I had already written *so much* about childhood—was there anything more?

My hope is that there *must* be a way of turning the tide. When we turn away from childhood, we cut ourselves off from our own deepest needs and feelings, and we give up all hope for the future. (pp. 162-63)

I believe that concern for childhood is our only chance for survival. The child in us, the children yet unborn—the human and tender hope. I persist because the alternative—to give up— is unendurable.

The greatest gift any of us ever has is this tiny life we're given, and no matter what the odds of making that life count, it seems to me that one has to keep on trying; that that is what life is all about—the search, the struggle, the faith that goes beyond rational belief, that says, "No matter how things look, it's still possible. . . ." (p. 163)

What comforts me the most is the part of me that stays open and vulnerable, that stays curious and alive—that *hurts* so much. It is the part that doesn't ever get old and tired and tough, the part that remains a child full of wonder and sensitivity and lovingness. When I cannot bear to read another headline, or listen to another insane government official talk the gibberish of the theater of the absurd, I turn away from being a grown-up, middle-aged woman and try to get in contact with the innocence and courage of the child in me. It is not an escape from reality, it is an affirmation of my humanhood; and when I am refreshed, I go on working for life, no matter how discouraging the situation seems.

Ultimately, personally, as adults, the meaning of childhood is that each of us has a child companion who can be with us always—to love us, amuse us, help us continue to look at the world around us in wide-eyed wonder. It is this child part of ourselves that can keep us in closest touch with what we were most truly meant to be—what makes us unique, special, beautiful beyond measure; the child is the miracle of our humanness, and the more we allow that tender part of ourselves to be a companion, the more each of our lives will truly become an extraordinary and fulfilling adventure.

Recently my husband and I visited some friends on Fire Island, at a town in which the population is largely homosexual. Shortly after our arrival we went for a walk along the beach. It came as quite a shock to discover that I began to feel uneasy, uncomfortable—even anxious. This was quite out of character for me. Could it be that in spite of my professed indifference to the technical preferences through which human beings express love for each other, there lurked a prejudice after all? Larry and I had been fighting for the rights and dignity of the homosexual community for a lot longer than most people— way before it became fashionable. . . . Why then this disquiet, this apprehension?

It took me only a few minutes to figure it out. Here was a glorious beach, miles of sand, ahead and behind us, *and not a single child, anywhere*. It felt like the end of the world— some awful, unnatural, hopeless, and inhuman place. I tried to imagine what it would be like if this beach were the whole country—the whole world—and I realized in a new and deeper way than I ever had before why my life has been so preoccupied with childhood. *It is the essence of being human.*

Every time a child is born, we have another chance. The greatest miracle of all has happened; here is this mysterious and miraculous new person, with limitless possibilities for wonder and delight, tenderness and compassion, insights and gifts. Will we murder its humanity quickly, or slowly and torturously? Will we make this child glad to be alive, eager to love and be loved, or will we cripple it into a creature of self-hate and a

need to destroy? Partly this will depend on whether or not this child is deeply and truly *wanted*. That is absolutely essential; parents-to-be must choose deliberately to have a child, with all careful and responsible awareness of the personal and social commitment not to continue to haphazardly overpopulate the world. The newborn child is the only real hope we have for human survival; could a time come when we could truly nurture that miracle of life in order to save all life?

But there is even more to childhood than that. What was so painful and frightening for me, on that beach, was that if there were no children, ever, anywhere, then I would lose the child in *me*. Life is a continuum, a stream, and all that we have ever been is part of what we are now, and will be. Seeing children, loving their presence in my world, watching child nature express itself, is a constant reminder of the child within, which is my humanity, my possibilities for further growing. When I am happiest, most fulfilled, most loving, there is a child being nourished in a secret garden inside of me, a child I have not forgotten to love and to cherish, until death.

That is what all species of babies are about—the miracle of miracles, the rebirth of life. And nothing in our world can help us rekindle hope as much as a human child. A baby is the ultimate antidote to human terror and despair; it is our only hope, each new baby representing the possibility of tomorrow and of something good to come.

If we want to find our way out of the crippling that has come with the overkill of technology, the exhaustion of too much rationalism, the dehumanizing of the scientific age, the way back is through childhood—our own and that of our new children. We need to recognize that a child is not an *impediment* to life but the *source* of life, and that to parent a child is to parent one's own life as well as that of one's child.

What are children for? Not to help us survive economically, not to populate the world, not to hold a family together, not to give us a sense of immortality. Children are for loving— loving what they remind us of about ourselves, loving their being most human, loving the possibilities they bring, loving the miracle of life.

If we could begin to truly garden our children; if we could give them the nourishment they need to flower most fully and beautifully; if we could help them learn to care for their own lives and thereby to care for the lives of others; if we could let go and stop trying to teach and improve, but *garden*, maybe . . . maybe . . . yes, it *is* possible. Look at the faces of the babies in a hospital nursery; watch a baby nurse; look at your own sleeping child; watch the children building a sand castle at the shore; listen to a child singing to himself in the bathtub. What do you hear? I hear a new beginning; I hear something gentle and open and alive. I hear something that is most profoundly the opposite of "made by machine." I hear something unpredictable by any tests, something mysterious. I see what is most tender in being human. I see our only hope. (pp. 163-67)

Eda J. LeShan, in her In Search of Myself—And Other Children *(copyright © 1976 by Eda J. LeShan; reprinted by permission of the publisher, M. Evans and Company, Inc., New York, NY 10017), Evans, 1976, 167 p.*

WHAT MAKES ME FEEL THIS WAY? GROWING UP WITH HUMAN EMOTIONS (1972)

If an audience for self-applied psychology exists in the primary grades, this is the ideal manual—sane, undogmatic and reassuring. The author . . . counsels children to know and accept their own feelings, and the method is as much Socratic as Freudian (the introduction of theoretical concepts being limited to the recognition that emotions can be "unconscious" or "ambivalent"). Brief, easily recognizable examples demonstrate the different ways people have of expressing their feelings . . . ; the lesson is not to feel guilty about feelings because "Thinking thoughts cannot make bad things happen" and learning to find non-hurting ways of handling emotions is part of growing up—millions of shy people lead happy lives and the world needs worriers who express their concerns constructively. For children, the value will lie not so much in advice given, as in the soothing knowledge that their fears—about school, their appearance, sex roles, death—are universal human concerns.

> *A review of "What Makes Me Feel This Way? Growing Up with Human Emotions," in* Kirkus Reviews *(copyright © 1972 The Kirkus Service, Inc.), Vol. XL, No. 3, February 1, 1972, p. 139.*

The title promises to unveil explanations for "feeling . . . this way," but, fortunately, the text generally avoids discussions of antecedent conditions and focuses upon descriptions of children's emotional experiences through the use of brief, but sensitively written, examples. The examples, which only occasionally appear contrived, are drawn from a broad range of situations. . . . The principal thesis is to convince the young reader that the described feelings are universal and "natural." Such a tactic presumably leads to greater understanding and appreciation of one's self. Occasional analytic treatments are inadequately done, so that, for example, explanations of strict parental behavior (". . . it is only because someone, a long time ago, was very critical of them") may mislead the young reader. Complex dynamics associated with remarkable insights into behavioral phenomena (". . . when I hear the thunder . . . it's Daddy in disguise") are equally confusing. Reading and thinking about this book may be useful to some contemplative children and young adults. It is likely, however, that most children will need to discuss the book with an enlightened adult.

> *A review of "What Makes Me Feel This Way? Growing Up with Human Emotions," in* Science Books *(copyright 1972 by the American Association for the Advancement of Science), Vol. VIII, No. 2, September, 1972, p. 104.*

A straightforward, thorough presentation of emotions which covers a wide range of feelings and attitudes and how to handle them. The treatment is far more comprehensive than in such books as Alexander's *Hidden You: Psychology in Your Life* (Prentice-Hall, 1962) and includes feelings about sex and death. Rather than an exclusive focus on self, the discussion of feelings of parents, teachers, and children in the past broadens reader understanding. The experimental and clinical aspects of psychology are omitted. Children will surely identify with some of the hundreds of examples, and the examination of accepting feelings and learning to cope effectively is very readable.

> *Jeanette Daane, in a review of "What Makes Me Feel This Way? Growing Up with Human Emotions," in* School Library Journal, *an appendix to* Library Journal *(reprinted from the December, 1972 issue of* School Library Journal, *published by R. R. Bowker Co./ A Xerox Corporation; copyright © 1972), Vol. 97, No. 22, December, 1972, p. 61.*

A most needed book on human emotions, this book should be reassuring to children who may harbor feelings of guilt when very normal feelings of hate, jealousy, envy fill their beings. . . . Specific examples of emotion describing upset Carla, moody Ernie, angry Mother help to explain emotions and their importance in human beings. A sensible beginning psychology text for the young!

> *Virginia A. Tashijian, in a review of "What Makes Me Feel This Way?" in* Appraisal: Science Books for Young People *(copyright © 1973 by the Children's Science Book Review Committee), Vol. 6, No. 1, Winter, 1973, p. 21.*

This book is an excellent treatment of a rarely taught subject for elementary-age children. It may help some young people who read to understand that certain feelings are shared by others. . . . In addition to dealing with positive and negative (more emphasized, unfortunately) feelings, the book handles the "Future Shock" issues of present-day society: sexual feelings, death, prejudice, roles. Suggestions for handling feelings are given in this most useful book.

> *Anne E. Matthews, in a review of "What Makes Me Feel This Way?" in* Appraisal: Science Books for Young People *(copyright © 1973 by the Children's Science Book Review Committee), Vol. 6, No. 1, Winter, 1973, p. 22.*

Eda LeShan describes in simple and straightforward manner the role that various emotions play in our lives. . . . Encouraging children to "express themselves," of course, is a clinical cliché. Such advice often goes no further, and the problems behind their feelings are not dealt with. Mrs. LeShan does not make this error; she advises specific action.

I found particularly impressive her discussion-techniques to help the child appreciate the naturalness of ambivalence, the inevitability of parental imperfection, and the unavoidability of disappointment and struggle. I wonder, however, if all of Mrs. LeShan's message will be grasped by her child readers, if the wisdom here is sometimes too concentrated for young minds to absorb. More repetition, vignettes and anecdotal material would have helped. These qualifications aside, I strongly recommend the book. Every child (and certainly every parent) deserves the opportunity to read it. (p. 8)

> *Richard A. Gardner, "How the Head Works," in* The New York Times Book Review *(© 1973 by The New York Times Company; reprinted by permission), February 25, 1973, pp. 8, 10.**

LEARNING TO SAY GOOD-BY: WHEN A PARENT DIES (1976)

Children know death exists far sooner than we would like. They see death depicted on television as an act of violence or cruelty. Fairy tales and folk stories we read to them often contain characters who die or are killed. But when there is a death in the family, children are told the loved one has "gone to sleep" or "gone away," which can only arouse anxiety and doubt. Why aren't they told the truth?

Eda LeShan believes that denying feelings and painful truths is unfair to children of any age, and to help remedy this situation she has written a primer on grieving (which should not be limited by its subtitle). . . .

One of the best chapters in this fine book is **"Death Teaches Us About Life"** which focuses on earlier times when death was part of life and people died at home surrounded by their family. Now the rite has been removed to the impersonal atmosphere of hospitals and nursing homes. When a parent or loved one dies, a child must be allowed to express hurt, anger, guilt and face the heartache. There are no easy answers for, as LeShan counsels, wounds heal but the scar remains.

> *Vivian J. Scheinmann, "Questions of Life and Death," in* Book World—The Washington Post *(© 1976, The Washington Post), November 7, 1976, p. G 8.* *

Here is the outspoken and unequivocal book that has been needed for what seems like forever. It will and should get on everyone's best seller list, for it delivers just what it says it will in the title. LeShan . . . shows she knows what she's talking about from the first sentence in this book: "Just about the most terrible thing that can happen to a child is the death of a parent." In her introduction, she also states that some people might find her message shocking; they feel children should be protected from the agony of loss. But she stresses that children must not be shut out. They must grieve and mourn just as adults do when death strikes. The sharing of sorrow is a needed part of the healing process for everyone. This book . . . is immeasurably valuable.

> *A review of "Learning to Say Good-By: When a Parent Dies," in* Publishers Weekly *(reprinted from the November 15, 1976 issue of* Publishers Weekly, *published by R. R. Bowker Company, a Xerox company; copyright © 1976 by Xerox Corporation), Vol. 210, No. 20, November 15, 1976, p. 75.*

With great understanding, LeShan puts the bereaved children in touch with their grief. She then proceeds to explain the universality and validity of these feelings and how to cope with them healthfully. Actual examples illustrate many of her points. Although the style is choppy, jumping as it does from the universal to the particular, . . . this is valuable for recognizing and responding to the feelings of a sorrowing child, a subject on which very little is available for young readers. (pp. 55-6)

> *Celine O'Brien, in a review of "Learning to Say Good-By: When a Parent Dies," in* School Library Journal *(reprinted from the December, 1976 issue of* School Library Journal, *published by R. R. Bowker Co./ A Xerox Corporation; copyright © 1976), Vol. 3, No. 4, December, 1976, pp. 55-6.*

In a clear, simple, psychologically sound fashion, LeShan describes the multiplicity of feelings, behaviors and fantasies that usually occur when anyone (not only a child) experiences a serious loss. This book is a statement of the now accepted idea that denial and avoidance are unhealthy ways of dealing with problems and that they may enhance anxiety rather than reduce it. . . . Through the use of appropriate vignettes, personal experiences and dynamic descriptions of feelings, LeShan provides a clear exposition of grief and the grieving process. She utilizes a touching, human, insightful manner and includes a good explanation of professional help and at what point it should be sought. . . . While the subject of this book is sad, the book is not depressing at all; rather it is an affirmation of self and life. **Learning To Say Good-by** should be read by chil-

dren and families experiencing a loss and by anyone wishing to give help during others' bereavement period.

> *Maxine L. Penn, in a review of "Learning to Say Good-By: When a Parent Dies," in* Science Books & Films *(copyright 1977 by the American Association for the Advancement of Science), Vol. XIII, No. 1, May, 1977, p. 38.*

Although written for children, this is essentially a family book, with import for parents as well. . . .

Readers will be helped to understand their own feelings and the sometimes cryptic actions of the surviving parent. . . .

The author makes no attempt to talk down to the child or gloss over any difficult areas. Vocabulary is adult, but not beyond reach; subject matter is approached forthrightly and with simplicity.

Parents reading LeShan's book may well come to a deeper understanding of their own feelings and actions and of appropriate relationship with their child. A good bibliography is also provided.

> *Suzanne Krogh, in a review of "Learning to Say Good-By: When a Parent Dies," in* Childhood Education *(reprinted by permission of the Association for Childhood Education International, 3615 Wisconsin Ave., N.W., Washington, DC 20016; copyright © 1977 by the Association), Vol. 54, No. 2 (November-December, 1977), p. 96.*

Eda LeShan presents an approach that is very badly needed. She combines sensitivity, an understanding of the child's and adult's world with a humanistic perspective. Her book has become a widely used and respected resource in the field of thanatology. (p. 80)

[The] concern here is how a death is perceived by a child and how a child reacts to death. In her introduction, LeShan demonstrates her understanding of children's needs to accept their own feelings. She covers feelings of numbness, anger, loneliness, loss, grief and relief. Throughout **Learning to Say Goodby** there is the underlying theme, stated in the final few pages, that there are lessons for life in death for both children and adults. This is of great importance for the child whose parent has committed suicide or has died unexpectedly. Children must learn to cope with change and the feelings, 'good or bad', that go along with such change. There is no doubt that Eda LeShan has had experience with children and death, and can effectively communicate her feelings. I recommend **Learning to Say Goodby** to anyone who is concerned about death in childhood. (p. 81)

> *Richard Lonetto, "Death in the World of the Child," in* Canadian Children's Literature: A Journal of Criticism and Review *(Box 335, Guelph, Ontario, Canada N1H6K5), No. 20, 1980, pp. 80-1.* *

THE INCREDIBLE TELEVISION MACHINE (with Lee Polk, 1977)

In a condescending tone uncharacteristic of LeShan but reflecting perhaps Polk's background in children's TV, the authors begin by defending the medium against the common charges (too much violence, time-wasting), and their section on commercials repeatedly points out that the shoddy practices they cite are no longer allowed. . . . [The] medium's history is sneaked in via Polk's reminiscences about his own career; the "heavy stuff"—FCC, ratings, pressure groups—is discussed in an interview between the two authors (LeShan: "Don't tell me too much—I get confused by too many scientific facts")—and even then they seem nervous that their audience might switch channels before they get back to the entertainment with a skit in which detective Celery Keen sniffs out the MIP (most important person) in television. The answer? You, the audience. But you, the reader, deserve more respect. (pp. 729-30)

> *A review of "The Incredible Television Machine,"* in Kirkus Reviews *(copyright © 1977 The Kirkus Service, Inc.), Vol. XLV, No. 14, July 15, 1977, pp. 729-30.*

The authors introduce each other in separate introductions which have little to do with their text. These pages are paeans of mutual praise, and the sort of thing we could do without. The following chapters, however, get right down to the nitty-gritty. . . . On the positive side, young people are told exactly how to make themselves heard, whether they are protesting the cancellation of favorite shows or demanding better programming. Adults could profit from the book. It is concise, informative and well written.

> *A review of "The Incredible Television Machine,"* in Publishers Weekly *(reprinted from the September 26, 1977 issue of* Publishers Weekly, *published by R. R. Bowker Company, a Xerox company; copyright © 1977 by Xerox Corporation), Vol. 212, No. 13, September 26, 1977, p. 137.*

With comments slanted pro-industry, the authors answer the current criticisms of violence, commercialism, confusion of fantasy with reality, and child-watching addiction, then continue in a rather hodgepodge way to describe how shows and commercials are put together. . . . Despite its superficial coverage of important areas like the Nielsen ratings and a too-cutesy approach, the text provides up-to-date information and insights not found elsewhere for children. (pp. 482-83)

> *Barbara Elleman, in a review of "The Incredible Television Machine,"* in Booklist *(reprinted by permission of the American Library Association; copyright © 1977 by the American Library Association), Vol. 74, No. 5, November 1, 1977, pp. 482-83.*

An important first step in [examining television in children's literature] has been taken by the authors of **The Incredible Television Machine.** While much of the book is concerned with the history and workings of the television industry, and the actual mechanics of program production, and while the authors . . . are painfully careful not to alienate their television-loving young readers with any obvious agit-prop against television, many of the basic problems that television brings into a child's life are at least introduced, problems a child may never have thought about before: that television may be affecting his or her own development in certain adverse ways; that viewing may be robbing him of his powers of imagination, may be preventing her from discovering the pleasures of reading, may be distorting the sense of reality.

The authors hasten to say that not everybody agrees with these criticisms, and they present the industry's counterarguments with excessive fairness. I say excessive because the child reader is ill-equipped to judge the relative merits of each side of the argument—to take T.V. Guide's argument, for instance, quoted by the authors ("Television is actually helping some children to read!") and see it as a self-serving distortion of television's

profoundly negative influence on literacy and reading in America. (p. E4)

> *Marie Winn, "Caught in the Networks," in* Book World—The Washington Post *(© 1977, The Washington Post), November 13, 1977, pp. E1, E4.*

WHAT'S GOING TO HAPPEN TO ME? WHEN PARENTS SEPARATE OR DIVORCE (1978)

This is a book written for children whose parents are going through a divorce. It used to be that no one talked to the children and they guarded their fears and angers in silence. But now, when it's get in touch with your feelings or bust, family counselor and educator Eda LeShan has done for children in this book what Gail Sheehy did for their parents in *Passages.*

Basically, LeShan offers a positive approach to divorce, carefully including many anecdotes intended to prevent young readers from feeling singularly alone or afraid. She makes the point that keeping a bad marriage together "for the sake of the children" is not good for anyone involved, especially the children who will bring to their own marriages and future relationships the unhappy blueprint of their parents' experience. She also stresses that divorce is never, never, never the fault of the children.

Well, then, *how* did it happen? The issue LeShan doesn't raise is whether or not divorce is always necessary. Could the parents have worked out their problems and rebuilt the marriage?

Like their parents, children go through predictable stages and LeShan walks them through each one. First is surprise. Then comes panic. . . . This stage of uncertainty is the worse. Children also feel guilt and a sense of failure. It's a time when they become afraid of the dark again, do poorly at school, get stomach aches, shy away from friends.

At the same time, LeShan warns against seeing all of life's troubles through the prism of divorce. . . .

The author is careful not to make value judgments—almost too careful. The pain of some of the stories is brutal. Mothers run off to the big city "to find themselves" or stay in bed all day "sick in their feelings"; Daddies drink too much and gamble or they go away and never come back. One problem is that sometimes the style is too zippy to support the devastating vignettes. After a while, life gets started again. There are trips, new friends, and eventually new family groupings. It becomes clear that the theme of the book is that divorcing is a prelude to remarriage. There are anecdotes about how to greet Daddy's new girlfriend and advice about what to call the man who wants to come and live with Mommy. In contrast to the horror stories which lead to divorce, these anecdotes are almost too positive, raising children's expectations that divorce may be a first step on a yellow brick road to happiness. What happens when life seems to get worse?

Nevertheless this is a very good book for children when they are caught in the divorce dilemma. One of its main values is that children can use it to talk to their parents and bring those dark feelings out of the silence of childhood.

> *Abigail Trafford, "Children and Divorce," in* Book World—The Washington Post *(© 1978, The Washington Post), October 8, 1978, p. E 8.*

With the same straightforward approach that characterized **Learning to Say Good-bye: When a Parent Dies** . . . , LeShan goes through the "stages" of a divorce. . . . She addresses the child reader directly and personally, using frequent example situations. . . . There is a responsible balance between recognizing the pain involved and realizing divorce may be a necessary transition to better lives for those involved, with an underlying belief that "for most people marriage is a good arrangement—the best we have ever found for both parents and children." Thorough, realistic, and helpful.

> *Betsy Hearne, in a review of "What's Going to Happen to Me? When Parents Separate or Divorce," in* Booklist *(reprinted by permission of the American Library Association; copyright ©1978 by the American Library Association), Vol. 75, No. 4, October 15, 1978, p. 383.*

Adults and young people have benefited from LeShan's fluent, sympathetic writing in books addressed to those in trouble. Here, she gives practical advice to boys and girls ping-ponging between parents who split up. "You feel angry and scared," declares the understanding author, and she adds that unjustifiable guilts may deepen children's pains. From the introduction through the conclusions, the text contains discussions of various situations that can arise after a father and mother decide to break up a home. These instances are followed by comforting, sensible suggestions of ways for children of divorce to handle their problems and cope with their feelings. . . . LeShan's book is fail-safe for those who need it.

> *A review of "What's Going to Happen to Me? When Parents Separate or Divorce," in* Publishers Weekly *(reprinted from the October 30, 1978 issue of* Publishers Weekly, *published by R. R. Bowker Company, a Xerox company; copyright © 1978 by Xerox Corporation), Vol. 214, No. 18, October 30, 1978, p. 51.*

LeShan gives the same sort of sensible advice that Gardner does in *The Boys and Girls Book About Divorce,* but her tone is more gentle. . . . Inevitably, the writing is repetitive, but it is clear and candid.

> *Zena Sutherland, in a review of "What's Going to Happen to Me? When Parents Separate or Divorce," in* Bulletin of the Center for Children's Books *(reprinted by permission of The University of Chicago Press; © 1978 by The University of Chicago), Vol. 32, No. 4, December, 1978, p. 66.*

A lucid, objective presentation of a crucial problem facing many children. . . . Appropriate for use in a classroom setting, LeShan's examples may be used as a base for discussing different aspects of separation and divorce: before, during, and after. A useful awareness tool enabling readers to reflect upon their personal situations and gain insights.

> *Donald S. Leeds, in a review of "What's Going to Happen to Me? When Parents Separate or Divorce," in* School Library Journal *(reprinted from the January, 1979 issue of* School Library Journal, *published by R. R. Bowker Co./ A Xerox Corporation; copyright © 1979), Vol. 25, No. 5, January, 1979, p. 55.*

In direct, honest language, and with no less warmth and understanding, the author . . . answers many of the questions that assail children about divorce. . . . This book could be read as an accompaniment to counseling, could be read by parents and children together, and could prove valuable to friends of children whose parents are divorcing.

> *Sharon Spredemann Dreyer, in a review of "What's Going to Happen to Me? When Parents Separate or Divorce," in her* The Bookfinder: A Guide to Children's Literature about the Needs and Problems of Youth Aged 2-15: Annotations of Books Published 1975 through 1978, Vol. 2 *(© 1981 American Guidance Service, Inc.),* American Guidance Service, Inc., *1981, No. 402.*

Lois Lowry

1937-

American author of fiction and nonfiction and journalist.

Lowry's realistic fiction, which ranges from the serious to the humorous, incorporates compact plots, memorable characters, and witty dialogue. Her first books treated death (*A Summer to Die*) and adoption (*Find a Stranger, Say Goodbye*); her more recent works, such as the *Anastasia* series, are in a lighter vein. Prior to creating her children's books, Lowry engaged in photography, composed travel articles, and wrote two textbooks—one dealing with black American literature and the other with literature of the American Revolution. Her expertise as a photographer is evident by the sharp detail and discerning characterizations she brings to her works, while experience in writing travel articles honed her talent for portraying vivid settings.

Though they sometimes comment on Lowry's use of idealistic characters and pat solutions, critics commend her ability to enter into her protagonists' minds and to depict realistic relationships. They consider Anastasia Krupnik an exceptionally well-realized heroine. The personalities of her progressive parents and precocious brother are considered equally engaging. The elderly appear in all of Lowry's books, helping the central character to understand more about life and death. In *A Summer to Die*, Will's love for life encourages Meg to face her sister's death and her own future. Lowry has said of her writing that she wishes to help young people find their own answers to life, identity, and human relationships and to alleviate their sense of aloneness. Reaction to her works proves she has done this to a remarkable degree. *A Summer to Die* was awarded the International Reading Association Children's Book Award in 1978 and the Young Reader Medal in 1981. *Autumn Street* was placed on the l982 IBBY Honour List.

(See also *Something about the Author*, Vol. 23 and *Contemporary Authors*, Vols. 69-72.)

1977 issue of School Library Journal, *published by R. R. Bowker Co./ A Xerox Corporation; copyright © 1977), Vol. 23, No. 9, May, 1977, pp. 62-3.*

Photograph by Robert Jones; courtesy of Lois Lowry

A SUMMER TO DIE (1977)

Themes of birth and death are juxtaposed in this moving and perceptive story. Thirteen-year-old Meg, her pretty 15-year-old sister Molly, and their parents move to the country so that their father can write a book. Lonely at first and slightly jealous of popular, vivacious Molly, Meg befriends an elderly neighbor and a young couple living nearby; she also begins to recognize and develop her own talents. The sense of family security and the tranquility of surroundings, however, is shattered when Molly becomes terminally ill. As she weakens, her overwhelming interest becomes the baby expected by the young neighbors, and it is through the drama of their baby's birth at home, with Meg sharing in the experience, that the poignant link between birth and death is made. Lowry is skillful both in evoking a sense of place and in depicting realistic and sympathetic characters. Her story captures the mysteries of living and dying without manipulating the readers' emotions, providing understanding and a comforting sense of completion. (pp. 62-3)

*Linda R. Silver, in a review of "A Summer to Die,"
in* School Library Journal *(reprinted from the May,*

As Meg poignantly relates the story of her 15-year-old sister's death from leukemia, a warm picture emerges of a family bound together by caring and closeness that carries them through their immense loss. . . . Lowry is particularly apt at defining a sense of place, obviously developed through her photographer's eye. Death is woven into a story of life as the author delicately contrasts the seeming unfairness of Molly's death with the birth of the baby and the natural cyclic flow of the seasons. Meg's sorrow as well as her joy comes pouring out in this perceptive tale. . . .

*Barbara Elleman, in a review of "A Summer to Die,"
in* Booklist *(reprinted by permission of the American Library Association; copyright © 1977 by the American Library Association), Vol. 73, No. 17, May 1, 1977, p. 1354.*

This is Lowry's debut as a novelist, an auspicious one. She is sensitive; she infuses her story with feelings arising from personal experiences. . . . [The] author makes tragically clear what [Molly's] suffering and death mean. It's a marvelous book and a help in understanding loss.

A review of "A Summer to Die," in Publishers Weekly (reprinted from the June 20, 1977 issue of Publishers Weekly, published by R. R. Bowker Company, a Xerox company; copyright © 1977 by Xerox Corporation), Vol. 211, No. 25, June 20, 1977, p. 72.

[Meg's chronicle of Molly's death] is a sensitive exploration of the complex emotions underlying the adolescent's first confrontation with human mortality; the author suggests nuances of contemporary conversation and situations without sacrificing the finesse with which she limns her characters. Not simply another story on a subject currently in vogue, the book is memorable as a well-crafted reaffirmation of universal values. A remarkable first novel.

Mary M. Burns, in a review of "A Summer to Die," in The Horn Book Magazine (copyright © 1977 by The Horn Book, Inc., Boston), Vol. LIII, No. 4, August, 1977, p. 451.

This remarkable American first novel presents most sensitively and convincingly an intelligent 13-year-old's reactions to and gradual awareness and acceptance of the fact that her more beautiful, more popular older sister will die of leukemia at the end of their summer in the country. The family relationships are closely, often humorously, observed. . . . Meg learns important lessons about the inevitability of death, the stranglehold of convention, and honest values. The writing is beautifully unobtrusive, yet bracing and compelling. (pp. 224-25)

Mary Hobbs, in a review of "A Summer to Die," in The Junior Bookshelf, Vol. 43, No. 4, August, 1979, pp. 224-25.

This is an engrossing story. . . . The relationship between Meg and her neighbor is especially good, and her parents are supportive of Meg's feelings during Molly's illness and death. Unfortunately, the story is marred by several portrayals that are caricatures and by stereotyping of female and male sex roles.

Jeanne Bracken and Sharon Wigutoff with Ilene Baker, in a review of "A Summer to Die," in their Books for Today's Young Readers: An Annotated Bibliography of Recommended Fiction for Ages 10-14 (copyright © 1981 by The Feminist Press), Feminist Press, 1981, p. 7.

FIND A STRANGER, SAY GOODBYE (1978)

The one false note in Lowry's affecting A Summer to Die . . . was her treatment of the "hippie" couple and the town's far-fetched intolerance. But compared to the characters and relationships here—right down to such bit-players as Natalie's very undemanding boyfriend and a modern-type librarian who helps in her search [for her natural parents]—the entire previous novel was a model of precision and subtle modulation. This one is readable, but grating.

A review of "Find a Stranger, Say Goodbye," in Kirkus Reviews (copyright © 1978 The Kirkus Service, Inc.), Vol. XLVI, No. 5, March 1, 1978, p. 248.

Lucky Natalie. She's got an understanding mother and father, a loving grandmother, an adoring younger sister, dear friends, a handsome boyfriend, good marks, a college acceptance, all the middle class perks and beauty besides—only she's adopted and can't rest until she finds her "real" mother. For graduation, her adoptive family give her money, time, and a car to go on her search (also all the papers to make it easier). There are surprises—but very few; there are difficulties—but even fewer. There is thoughtfulness and just plain niceness wherever she goes. This novel, with an awkward title, has an old-fashioned naiveté about it. Everyone "smiles" or "grins"—there's not a louse or an argument or a dead end on the horizon. It strains hard to be modern—Natalie's boyfriend spits one or two obscenities like toads from a prince's mouth—but he never lays a hand on her; Mom and Grandma are a bit madcap, but endearingly so; even her newfound mother turns out to be a famous model now happily married and understanding about the whole thing. Its melodrama and sweetness will appeal to young teens who yearn for a comfortable amalgam of the romanticism of the 40s and 50s and the "new realism" of the 70s. (pp. 77-8)

Marjorie Lewis, in a review of "Find a Stranger, Say Goodbye," in School Library Journal (reprinted from the May, 1978 issue of School Library Journal, published by R. R. Bowker Co./ A Xerox Corporation; copyright © 1978), Vol. 24, No. 9, May, 1978, pp. 77-8.

[The author], a capable writer, is totally at ease with the topical novel; once again she is thoroughly au courant. . . . No sharp edges snag the fluent storytelling; everything has been neatly rounded off, and there is even one wonderfully funny episode. But the very attractiveness of the characters and the tidiness of the plot constitute the weakness of the book; for it is the kind of novel that reminds the reader that realism can often be less of an honest revelation of life than fantasy.

Ethel L. Heins, in a review of "Find a Stranger, Say Goodbye," in The Horn Book Magazine (copyright © 1978 by The Horn Book, Inc., Boston), Vol. LIV, No. 3, June, 1978, p. 258.

Lois Lowry proves that the Americans have not all forgotten that it is still possible to write in the third person, but, apart from that, there is not a great deal to be said for Find a Stranger, Say Goodbye. The title sounds rather like a women's magazine serial, and the book turns out to be weak and sentimental. It has an interesting theme, however. . . . [Much] of the narrative is concerned with the details of [Natalie's] search. This part of the story has an authentic ring to it and is well put together. But, in one way, it all sounds too easy: everyone Natalie meets is tremendously kind and helpful, and there at the end of the journey is her real mother, a glamorous fashion model. The characterization is paper thin, and the message of the book seems to be that if we all laugh and smile and are nice to each other the world's problems will simply disappear.

[The] femininity of Find a Stranger, Say Goodbye is false, almost as much as the masculinity of [S. E. Hinton's] Tex is phony. But the Lois Lowry is, marginally, a better read.

David Rees, "Starting Young," in The Times Literary Supplement (© Times Newspapers Ltd. (London) 1980; reproduced from The Times Literary Supplement by permission), No. 4018, March 28, 1980, p. 356.*

[Find a Stranger, Say Goodbye] has a plot which, by rights, should have made me groan with disbelief. . . . But, as one reads Lowry's perceptive book, one soon realizes that these apparently overly-romantic elements are essential to her purpose. Her 'message' is that filial love has nothing to do with biology, that one loves one's parents because they love you and want you and care for you, and not because they created you. Because Natalie is secure and happy at home, her search cannot be interpreted as an escape, and she is able to reject her natural mother's glamorous life because she doesn't need it and doesn't want it. *Find a Stranger, Say Goodbye* is a good, satisfying read, far more so than Lois Lowry's gloomy first book. I enjoyed it enormously. (p. 121)

> *Lance Salway, in a letter to Nancy Chambers in May, 1980, in* Signal *(copyright © 1980 The Thimble Press; reprinted by permission of The Thimble Press, Lockwood Station Road, South Woodchester, Glos. GL55EQ, England), No. 32, May, 1980, pp. 119-22.**

A Summer to Die showed [Lois Lowry's] deep understanding of human beings. This happier story is every bit as good and well-written. . . . The reader finds the people as real as Natalie herself finds those she meets in her travels. The book deals as much with unwanted schoolgirl pregnancy (sensitively depicted from her mother's diary) as with adoption, which is admittedly shown here rather more rosily than may transpire in real life. . . . Though an idealised world, however, it is still one to learn from over letting go of the past and preparing for adult life.

> *Mary Hobbs, in a review of "Find a Stranger, Say Goodbye," in* The Junior Bookshelf, *Vol. 44, No. 4, August, 1980, p. 194.*

ANASTASIA KRUPNIK (1979)

[Anastasia] seems always to have a hand on her emotional pulse. Not only does she get stomachaches and headaches when she's upset, but even worries that she will. Granted that she is given some heavy events to absorb—birth, death, ridicule (by a boy she likes) and, especially, jealousy. Still, the focus is relentlessly on Anastasia's reactions, and, to make matters worse, the author would have us believe that a child can do her important learning through conversation with adults. Nevertheless, there are some wonderful moments which include Anastasia's complaints about her name, which is so long that if it were stenciled on a tee shirt "the letters would go right into my armpits!" and the brief, unforgettable description of the irresistably flamboyant sixth grade boy she admires.

> *Mary B. Nickerson, in a review of "Anastasia Krupnik," in* School Library Journal *(reprinted from the October, 1979 issue of* School Library Journal, *published by R. R. Bowker Co./ A Xerox Corporation; copyright © 1979), Vol. 26, No. 2, October, 1979, p. 152.*

[Lowry] masterfully captures the heart and mind of a perceptive fourth grader. Anastasia, age 10, keeps track, in a green notebook, of the important things that happen to her, including a vacillating list entitled "Things I Hate/Things I Love." In a style typical of that age, items move back and forth paralleling her whims, and as Anastasia experiences rejection of a long labored-over poem, fights acceptance of the coming arrival of a baby sibling, deliberates about becoming Catholic (in order to change her name), has a crush on Washburn Cummings who constantly dribbles an imaginary basketball, and learns to understand her senile grandmother's inward eye, she grows and matures. Humor filters through the dialogue as superbly developed characters react to the vicissitudes of life; and through them Lowry creates situations that can give a reader insight.

The well-turned phrase amuses, and the unexpected turn of event surprises in a plot that is tightly strung.

> *Barbara Elleman, in a review of "Anastasia Krupnik," in* Booklist *(reprinted by permission of the American Library Association; copyright © 1979 by the American Library Association), Vol. 76, No. 4, October 15, 1979, p. 354.*

[Anastasia] is a girl of basic good sense and considerable insight; she responds to her problems with only a few outrageous actions. . . . The author maintains a balance between life and death: Anastasia is given the privilege of naming the new baby and vengefully considers naming him One-Ball Reilly, and her senile grandmother, whom Anastasia both loves and pities, dies of old age. Although the episodic story is somewhat slight, Anastasia's father and mother—an English professor and an artist—are among the most humorous, sensible, and understanding parents to be found in recent children's fiction, and Anastasia herself is an amusing and engaging heroine.

> *Ann A. Flowers, in a review of "Anastasia Krupnik," in* The Horn Book Magazine *(copyright © 1979 by The Horn Book, Inc., Boston), Vol. LV, No. 6, December, 1979, p. 663.*

As in other kids' stories with sympathetic college-teacher fathers, this dad seems stuffier and less bright than he's meant to be—and Anastasia's poem seems less genuine than intended. And with Anastasia's vindictive secret choice for the baby's name, Lowry seems to be playing to an adult audience. . . . Of course, she backs out and chooses her grandfather's name—more in memory of her grandmother, who dies just before the baby's birth. This way of remembering Grandmother is just one example of Lowry's linking of different threads and episodes, which she does well throughout the book. It is neatly crafted and stout for its genre, but entirely without the emotional conviction of *A Summer to Die.*

> *A review of "Anastasia Krupnik," in* Kirkus Reviews *(copyright © 1979 The Kirkus Service, Inc.), Vol. XLVII, No. 24, December 15, 1979, p. 1430.*

There are poignant moments like a holiday visit from a senile grandmother who can't remember Anastasia's name or recognize her, hilarious ones like a visit to her father's poetry class or a vigorous argument with her mother about changing her name. . . . The writing is lively, funny, and above all, intelligent. The relationship between Anastasia and her parents is superbly drawn, and the dialogue is a delight. In fact, the whole book is a delight.

> *Zena Sutherland, in a review of "Anastasia Krupnik," in* Bulletin of the Center for Children's Books *(reprinted by permission of The University of Chicago Press; © 1980 by The University of Chicago), Vol. 33, No. 5, January, 1980, p. 99.*

Anastasia's feelings and discoveries should be familiar to anyone who has ever been 10, and author Lois Lowry has a sensitive way of taking problems seriously without ever being shallow or leaning too far over into despair.

Lowry's writing never falters. Awaiting her turn to read a painstakingly written poem in front of her class, "Anastasia had begun to feel a little funny, as if she had ginger ale inside her knees." Each short chapter of this quick-moving book reads like a small story in itself, wonderfully clear and self-contained. There is a satirical scene of a college English class, taught by

Anastasia's father, with humor that isn't lost on an adult reader or, I suspect, a younger one.

This is a brightly written, entertaining book that does a convincing job of telling what it's like to be 10, or to be alive, for that matter.

> Brad Owens, "10 Years Old and Growing," in The Christian Science Monitor (reprinted by permission from The Christian Science Monitor; © 1980 The Christian Science Publishing Society; all rights reserved), January 14, 1980, p. B6.

AUTUMN STREET (1980)

In this bittersweet reminiscence, the narrator takes readers to a still sensitive spot in her past—the year she was six and had to move to her grandfather's home while her father was away fighting in World War II. There in the midst of ritual and refinement, the irrepressible Elizabeth holds her own. She becomes best friends with Charles, the six-year-old grandson of the Black cook. Considering that he is not allowed to appear in the front part of the house, inside or out, it seems strange that Liz's family doesn't object to the children becoming so tight. The family is pretty tolerant of Liz in general, which makes them likable, forgivable characters—even the cold and prissy grandmother. And Liz gives as well as takes a lot of love. . . . The book's painful ending, foreshadowed throughout, comes in a surprising form. It is Charles, not Liz's soldier father, who is killed—his throat slashed by the demented town bum. Liz almost dies herself from pneumonia but recovers to turn seven and see her father again. Obviously, this is a book for mature readers. Some teenagers will be put off by the young age of the main character. Those who aren't will be rewarded by a reading experience that touches the heart. (pp. 125-26)

> Marilyn R. Singer, in a review of "Autumn Street," in School Library Journal (reprinted from the April, 1980 issue of School Library Journal, published by R. R. Bowker Co./ A Xerox Corporation; copyright © 1980), Vol. 26, No. 8, April, 1980, pp. 125-26.

Lowry's new novel surpasses her finest stories in sensitivity and impact. . . . All the characters are wonderfully humanized and memorable but the author has devoted the most loving care to Tatie and Charles.

> A review of "Autumn Street," in Publishers Weekly (reprinted from the April 11, 1980 issue of Publishers Weekly, published by R. R. Bowker Company, a Xerox company; copyright © 1980 by Xerox Corporation), Vol. 217, No. 14, April 11, 1980, p. 78.

The myriad changes brought about "because of the war" are unsettling to six-year-old Elizabeth, and she responds with a candor, inquisitiveness, joy, and confusion that ring with honest truth. The story of the child is narrated by Elizabeth the adult, and the perspective of remembrance enriches the action. In the same way as the past surfaces in one's mind, a flurry of characters flickers in and out of an eventful plot that shifts smoothly to accommodate them. . . . With sharper skills than in *Anastasia Krupnik* . . . Lowry hones her writing to a high polish through which vivid settings and textured characters gleam in high relief. Though the trappings of the 1940s may go unrecognized and the young age of the protagonist may deter some, special readers who pursue this engrossing story, even from a distance of five to seven years, will find this

emotionally charged reverie understandable and unforgettable. Adults, too, will gain deeper-scored perceptions.

> Barbara Elleman, in a review of "Autumn Street," in Booklist (reprinted by permission of the American Library Association; copyright © 1980 by the American Library Association), Vol. 76, No. 16, April 15, 1980, p. 1206.

Noah's death earlier (and his perverse behavior), the loving, ample-bosomed black maid, the close but unequal black-white relationships, and the inevitable tragedy that Noah's death foreshadows—all give the story a touch of the ambience we associate with Southern fiction. Just once or twice, Lowry gives Elizabeth an egalitarian thought that would seem to be beyond her years. More often, she gives her a child's open sensitivity, a child's way of processing occurrences—her grandfather falls in the hall as the clock strikes: she is told next day that he had a stroke, and so she associates his illness with the clock, which she is sure is waiting to strike again—and a moving ability to recall an experience in its totality.

> A review of "Autumn Street," in Kirkus Reviews (copyright © 1980 The Kirkus Service, Inc.), Vol. XLVIII, No. 12, June 15, 1980, p. 779.

Many of the simple childlike reactions cover hidden ironies, as in the understated episodes suggesting the demeaning social position of Elizabeth's Black friends; but the casual, only half-understood experiences of the girl are presented in a somewhat overwrought style and concluded with a number of almost melodramatic scenes.

> Paul Heins, in a review of "Autumn Street," in The Horn Book Magazine (copyright © 1980 by The Horn Book, Inc., Boston), Vol. LVI, No. 4, August, 1980, p. 409.

Lowry has most adroitly woven . . . familial relationships into a story that has nuance, depth, poignancy, and insight; through Elizabeth's memories, she gives a child's candid, painful view of fear and love. A memorable book. (p. 58)

> Zena Sutherland, in a review of "Autumn Street," in Bulletin of the Center for Children's Books (reprinted by permission of The University of Chicago Press; © 1980 by The University of Chicago), Vol. 34, No. 3, November, 1980, pp. 57-8.

ANASTASIA AGAIN! (1981)

Anastasia Krupnik is one of the most intriguing female protagonists to appear in children's books since the advent of Harriet the spy nearly two decades ago. No less intrepid in the second chronicle of her adventures, Anastasia learns to cope with one of life's great puzzles: " 'The Mystery of Why Some People Make Decisions without Consulting Their Twelve-Year-Old Children.' " Faced with the prospect of moving to the suburbs, she complains in hyperbolic phrases such as " 'Ladies in the suburbs only wear cute cotton dresses from Lord and Taylor's. . . . And have affairs with the neighbors' husbands.' " . . . The author has perfected an anecdotal style, connecting incidents by incorporating Anastasia's attempts at writing a mystery novel. Although the book may be considered a sequel to *Anastasia Krupnik* . . . , it can be read independently, for the author skillfully integrates necessary references to earlier events. Genuinely funny, the story is a marvelously human portrait of an articulate adolescent. (pp. 535-36)

Mary M. Burns, in a review of "Anastasia Again!" in The Horn Book Magazine (copyright © 1981 by The Horn Book, Inc., Boston), Vol. LVII, No. 5, October, 1981, pp. 535-36.

A new home, a cute boy down the street and an intriguing elderly neighbor all provide the stimulus for Anastasia's remarkable perceptions and reactions. Precocious yet prone to the exaggerations and behavior typical of early adolescence, Anastasia faces new experiences with an outrageous blend of gusto, reluctance, determination and anxiety. Lowry's prose, timing and on-target humor combine to give this protagonist credibility, and she's no less precise with secondary characters. Lowry has the ability to describe common experiences and situations in an uncommon and exuberant manner, while at the same time providing easy access for readers who will undoubtedly find that many of Anastasia's notions bear a close relation to their own.

Marilyn Kaye, in a review of "Anastasia Again!" in School Library Journal (reprinted from the October, 1981 issue of School Library Journal, published by R. R. Bowker Co./ A Xerox Corporation; copyright © 1981), Vol. 28, No. 2, October, 1981, p. 144.

Undoubtedly this will be greeted with joy by those who became instant Anastasia fans with the publication of *Anastasia Krupnik* . . . and who appreciated the wit and warmth of her creative academic family. This time Anastasia's immoderate zest, pro or con, presages the turbulence of the teen years ahead. . . . Added to this story of adaptability and adjustment are a running theme of the protagonist's diary entries and the recurrent material about a precocious—but not cloying—baby brother. Lowry is adept at turning such characters to humorous use without in the least making fun of them, and she does it in part by particularly deft dialogue.

Zena Sutherland, in a review of "Anastasia Again!" in Bulletin of the Center for Children's Books (reprinted by permission of The University of Chicago Press; © 1982 by The University of Chicago), Vol. 35, No. 5, January, 1982, p. 90.

["Anastasia Again!"] is something of a disappointment. . . . The book does have its beguiling moments, but this time the author has let the Krupniks slip into sounding clever without always having something to say. Maybe that's because Anastasia doesn't deal with anything weightier than organizing a party or meeting the new boy down the street. . . .

As in most Lowry books, the elderly also have a role. Anastasia's eccentric neighbor, Gertrude Stein (Gertrustein to Sam), is likable enough, but she is never as fully realized as the senile grandmother in **"Anastasia Krupnik."** Nor is she as affecting as Will in Miss Lowry's **"A Summer to Die"** or the grandparents in **"Autumn Street."**

Lois Lowry is a talented writer. Perhaps in future Anastasia sequels she will do better by the Krupniks than to play them as just another briefly entertaining, warm and flippant TV sitcom family.

Judith St. George, in a review of "Anastasia Again!" in The New York Times Book Review (© 1982 by The New York Times Company; reprinted by permission), February 28, 1982, p. 31.

Anastasia Krupnik is a typical child of today! She has her own ideas about what things are or as she thinks they should be

. . . nor is she likely to change her views easily. This, though, is what gives her such an appealing personality. . . . Loaded within the pages are bits of dialogue, situation and character certain to bring chuckles, smiles and perhaps even a bit of insight into the personal lives of girls grades 3-6. Lowry is deserving of most high praise for this creation—it certainly will continue to reflect "how it was today!" Highly recommended.

Joseph B. Browne, in a review of "Anastasia Again!" in Catholic Library World, Vol. 53, No. 8, March, 1982, p. 356.

ANASTASIA AT YOUR SERVICE (1982)

For the third time straight, Lowry's right on target in capturing the thoughts and emotions of a 12-year-old girl and, on a broader scale, in proving herself as one of the consistently top children's writers in both appeal and quality. Punctuating her story with witty dialogue, she casts Anastasia in a more integrated story than before, which has her applying for a job as companion to a "really rich old lady." Upon reporting to work, however, Anastasia finds herself, to her horror, serving as maid at a birthday party for Mrs. Bellingham's granddaughter Daphne, a girl who will be Anastasia's classmate in the fall. Though Daphne's character and situation are not as completely realized as most of Lowry's characters, she proves to be a good foil for Anastasia. Despite differences, the girls become friends; and with the help of Anastasia's precocious brother Sam, they generate a plot that is rich, inviting, and very funny.

Barbara Elleman, in a review of "Anastasia at Your Service," in Booklist (reprinted by permission of the American Library Association; copyright © 1982 by the American Library Association), Vol. 79, No. 1, September 1, 1982, p. 46.

Fans of Anastasia will be delighted with this newest, if highly unlikely, adventure. . . . How [Anastasia's predicaments are] resolved is slapstick, an extended joke mitigated somewhat by an almost tragic accident that happens to Anastasia's little brother and teaches Anastasia what true love really is. Kids (including reluctant junior-high readers) who like their humor broad will probably get a kick out of this and its young heroine—themselves writ larger than life. (pp. 87-8)

Marjorie Lewis, in a review of "Anastasia at Your Service," in School Library Journal (reprinted from the November, 1982 issue of School Library Journal, published by R. R. Bowker Co./ A Xerox Corporation; copyright © 1982), Vol. 29, No. 3, November, 1982, pp. 87-8.

Anastasia addicts will welcome this third discerning romp about the enterprising daughter of a faculty family that is warm, supportive, and very funny. Anastasia always has problems (she's twelve) and this summer it's a combination of boredom, depression (the only friend she's made since they moved to town has gone to camp) and penury. . . . This is just as amusing as the earlier books, it's written with the same wit and polish; it isn't quite as substantial structurally.

Zena Sutherland, in a review of "Anastasia at Your Service," in Bulletin of the Center for Children's Books (reprinted by permission of The University of Chicago Press; © 1982 by The University of Chicago), Vol. 36, No. 4, December, 1982, p. 72.

Anastasia's good sense and kind heart bring everything to a satisfactory conclusion and, in addition, inspire Daphne to behave more reasonably. More important than the story, however, is the author's lively picture of a happy, devoted family. Anastasia is the fortunate possessor of two of the most sensible, sympathetic, cheerful, and amusing parents in children's literature, and her little brother Sam is a delight.

> *Ann A. Flowers, in a review of "Anastasia at Your Service," in* The Horn Book Magazine *(copyright © 1982 by The Horn Book, Inc., Boston), Vol. LVIII, No. 6, December, 1982, p. 650.*

Precise character delineations, dialogue that's right on the nose, and the element of authentic craziness raise Anastasia to Harriet and Ramona's level. The lesson learned at the charity ball—not to judge people by appearances—will have you laughing long after you've finished the story. My favorite in the series, and one of the best on the pains of growing up as seen by an adolescent.

> *Ruth M. Stein, in a review of "Anastasia at Your Service," (copyright © 1983 by the National Council of Teachers of English; reprinted by permission of the publisher and the author), in* Language Arts, *Vol. 60, No. 3, March, 1983, p. 360.*

TAKING CARE OF TERRIFIC   (1983)

Fourteen-year-old Enid is bright, sophisticated, and articulate, a typical Lowry child; she's lacking in self-esteem and bored by the prospect of a Boston summer. That's before she begins taking care of a precocious and lovable four-year-old, Joshua Warwick Cameron IV, who prefers to be called Tom Terrific, before she meets the friendly black musician in the Public Garden, or the bag ladies, before she discovers that that pest of a classmate, Seth, is really a very nice boy. And it all comes together in a story that is touching, inventive, believable, and hilarious, as all of the characters conspire to take a stealthy midnight ride on the Public Garden swan boats and are caught by the police. Great fun, with a solid base of sharp characterization and some pithy commentary on our society.

> *Zena Sutherland, in a review of "Taking Care of Terrific," in* Bulletin of the Center for Children's Books *(reprinted by permission of The University of Chicago Press; © 1983 by The University of Chicago), Vol. 36, No. 7, March, 1983, p. 129.*

A bright but most unlikely caper. . . . Lowry writes with verve and awareness, and she makes it clear that this is not to be taken for realism: "There was something about the whole enterprise that was like a fantasy, and that made the fake names seem okay." The trouble is that the fantasy comes off as a silly, sentimental-liberal pipedream that trivializes the realities she wants to transcend.

> *A review of "Taking Care of Terrific," in* Kirkus Reviews *(copyright © 1983 The Kirkus Service, Inc.), Vol. LI, No. 6, March 15, 1983, p. 310.*

Although the plot seems incredible, the book as a whole is somehow satisfying. The Boston setting is vividly evoked, and the diverse cast of characters adds variety and flavor to the narrative. But the strength lies, as it does in the **Anastasia** books . . . , in the author's ability to create a strong heroine whose determination and humorous outlook override her confusion and difficulties.

> *Karen Jameyson, in a review of "Taking Care of Terrific," in* The Horn Book Magazine *(copyright © 1983 by The Horn Book, Inc., Boston), Vol. LIX, No. 3, June, 1983, p. 304.*

Evaline Ness

1911-

American author/illustrator of fiction, illustrator, and editor.

Ness is considered one of the highly skilled author/illustrators in children's literature. Diversity of plot and technique contributes to the success of her works. Along with collages, woodcuts, and ink drawings, Ness uses washes of color that are bold and startling or soft and subtle. She purposefully utilizes colors which fit the plot and locale of each book. *Josefina February*, *A Gift for Sula Sula*, and *Do You Have the Time, Lydia?* are set in tropical areas, which Ness reflects in the warm tones of her illustrations. The muted colors of her Caldecott-winning *Sam, Bangs & Moonshine* effectively complement the coastal fishing village setting.

Ness left a career in advertising art to accept an offer to illustrate children's books. After successfully illustrating for other authors, it was suggested that she write a story around a series of woodcuts on Haiti that she had just completed. This story became her first book, *Josefina February*. Ness's writing style has received as much praise as her artwork. Critics admire her ability to incorporate the familiar details of childhood into poignant, witty stories. *Josefina February*, *Exactly Alike*, *Sam, Bangs & Moonshine*, and *Do You Have the Time, Lydia?* revolve around the particular habits or problems of children, such as lying, dealing with siblings, and making promises which prove difficult to keep. While some reviewers have found them simplistic and superficial, an overwhelming majority praise the expressiveness of her illustrations and the warmth and tenderness of her stories. Ness has also designed books which allow the reader to cut out and put together small cardboard replicas of historical houses, a palace, and four rooms from the Metropolitan Museum. Ness was awarded the Caldecott Medal in 1967 for *Sam, Bangs & Moonshine*. She received the *New York Herald Tribune* Spring Book Festival honor for picture books in 1963 for *Josefina February*, which was designated an ALA Notable Book in the same year. *Exactly Alike* and *A Double Discovery* were named *New York Times* Choice of Best Illustrated Children's Books of the Year in 1964 and 1965, respectively. Ness's illustrations for other authors have been included in Honor Book lists for the Caldecott Medal.

(See also *Something about the Author*, Vols. 1 and 26; *Contemporary Authors New Revision Series*, Vol. 5; and *Contemporary Authors*, Vols. 5-8, rev. ed.)

AUTHOR'S COMMENTARY

When Augusta Baker called me last January from New Orleans to tell me that I had been awarded the Caldecott Medal, I said, "Wow!" That comment indicates my ready talent as a writer. But since I think of myself as an artist who happens to write, I will get on with the art part. (p. 434)

About nine years ago Mary Silva Cosgrave, who was then children's book editor at Houghton Mifflin Company, asked me if I would illustrate a children's book. I was interested until I heard that the dole was only five hundred dollars with royalties. Royalties! What were they? Certainly not *real* money.

And who promised that the book would sell? A risky business. I said no.

But Mary persisted . . . and came up with a beautiful story that I wanted to illustrate regardless of those mythical royalties—*The Bridge* by Charlton Ogburn, Jr. During the months of work on the book, I realized the same kind of peace and enjoyment that comes when I paint for myself. There were no changes, no picking at details, no hot breath on my neck because of a deadline, which in advertising is always yesterday. . . . It was heaven and I did not want to leave. I was hooked.

After that I accepted almost every manuscript sent to me by publishers. Each one was a new exciting experience. The limitation of color separation, called overlay, fascinated me. . . . The name of that game is how to maintain freedom within a limitation. Because printer's ink is flat, my main concern was how to get texture into that flatness.

Some of the methods I have used are woodcut, serigraphy, rubber-roller technique (too complicated to explain here), scratching through black paint on acetate, ink splattering, and sometimes just spitting. Anything goes. (pp. 434-35)

[And this brings me] to *Sam, Bangs & Moonshine*. One day when I was looking through a portfolio in which I keep drawings I make for no reason at all, I found one of a ragged, displaced-person little girl who was quietly ecstatic over a starfish. In the same portfolio were drawings of fishing boats.

Before I did another thing I telephoned [children's book editor, Ann Durell]. . . . We talked about things, both nice and naughty, that we remembered as children.

I remembered me as a liar and a profitable one. My lies had a way of coming true. Three of them got me a piano, a telephone, and ballet lessons.

If I was a liar then, I am a thief today. I steal anything that will help me to resolve a piece of art: sunlight falling across a half-finished drawing, a dirty fingerprint, knots in wood, accidents like spilled ink, broken pens, ripped paper. Even the muddy water I rinse my brushes in can be the answer to a color problem.

Anyway, the shabby misplaced child of my drawing became Sam, who told lies. And what else could she be except a fisherman's daughter, with all those drawings of boats handy? I added the cat because I have a live one to draw from, and I decided to put Thomas under a racy bicyclist's cap I had seen in a photograph. The baby kangaroo got into the story because of a newspaper article. A child had written home from camp saying, "We got gerbils." (The parents were certain that the camp had been stricken by a new and horrible contagious disease.)

I really cannot tell you *how* I wrote the story. All I know is that I sat at the typewriter for four days and nothing happened. On the fifth day it struck. (pp. 435-36)

I had a story. But the worst was yet to come: illustrating it!

For some reason or other illustrating my own stories is torture. For days before I start, I generally mutter thoughts such as, "Why in heaven's name did I accept *this* book to do?" and "If the editor thinks it's so important for a story to stand on its own, why not let it stand?" All this, while I do what I call maid's work. I put my bureau drawers in order. I decide to redecorate my apartment. I read minutely the travel section of the newspaper. I get out my sewing machine and make a new suit which I don't need.

Then the art director closes my escape valves. She sends me galleys (text set in type) and the dummy (paper folded into the size and amount of pages the final book will be). Actual creative art work can still be put off until I have cut up the galleys and pasted them into the dummy, leaving blank spaces for the illustrations. When this is finished I always think it would be a good idea to publish the book as it is and let the children do their own illustrating. No one agrees with me.

The day that I actually produce my first illustration is the day that I stop muttering and start humming. I am involved. The book will be finished.

Months go by before the first bound book arrives. I have almost forgotten it. So much else has been in the works since then. I open it with a cold and critical eye. I look at all the unsuccessful parts first. This may sound like a negative action, but to me it is positive. I am not interested in what succeeded because that is a *fait accompli*. Things undone and unresolved are my loving antagonists, my agents who keep open paths that lead me to new experiments and experiences—forever expanding and always infinite. (pp. 436-37)

> *Evaline Ness, "Caldecott Acceptance Speech" (originally a speech given at the meeting of the American*
> *Library Association on June 27, 1967), in* The Horn Book Magazine *(copyright © 1967, by The Horn Book, Inc., Boston), Vol. XLIII, No. 4, August, 1967, pp. 434-48.*

GENERAL COMMENTARY

Evaline Ness is an artist of parts, who brings great vitality as well as craftmanship to each project she undertakes. . . .

But her prime satisfaction and interest lies in children's books, a fact reflected in the skill and freshness displayed in each of the many books she has illustrated. She says she is always experimenting with new techniques because "it's so boring to do the same thing over and over," and she therefore has become expert in many types of reproduction from woodcuts to her own inventive methods of achieving a particular effect. She recently bought a hand printing press "because I love type, and I want to try some experiments with type and woodcuts."

Each book, she feels, presents a new challenge which she welcomes. (p. 98)

Much as Evaline Ness loves new undertakings, she says she has a terrible resistance to taking the plunge into each new project. . . . But once she starts to draw, she works with absorption and enjoyment, "although there's always a terrible letdown when I finally finish and think, 'did I really achieve what I tried to?'" Although her own vision of perfection is never entirely satisfied, it would seem that she more than satisfies that vision in others! (p. 99)

> *Ann Durell, "Evaline Ness," in* School Library Journal, *an appendix to* Library Journal *(reprinted from the March, 1964 issue of* School Library Journal, *published by R. R. Bowker Co./ A Xerox Corporation; copyright © 1964), Vol. 10, No. 7, March, 1964, pp. 98-9.*

Sometimes the picture treatment reveals more about a book's characters than the text. . . . Sam [in *Sam, Bangs & Moonshine*] is presented in the text as something of a liar, and one of her lies is a dangerous one; but the line drawings with watercolor wash give a deeper view of Samantha—that of a splendidly dreaming child preoccupied with the textures, sights, and smells all about her. The first picture of her friend Thomas tells all that you need to know about him: that he is intent, gentle, and gullible! (No wonder imitations of Thomas are found in illustrations by lesser picture book artists.) (pp. 129-31)

Evaline Ness's woodcuts for *Josefina February* . . . have a solid rhythm with flowing orange, ochre, and lavender. The simple story of a little girl in Haiti searching for the owner of a burro she finds in a grove provides an attention-holding device for exploring the setting. *Do You Have the Time, Lydia?* . . . , set [on a tropical island] has a theme in keeping with the culture and setting. More than most illustrators, Ness imparts a feeling for locale combined with themes and plot ideas. (p. 271)

> *Sam Leaton Sebesta and William J. Iverson, "Picture Books and Folk Literature: Evaline Ness" and "Realistic Fiction: Evaline Ness," in* Literature for Thursday's Child *(© 1975, Science Research Associates, Inc.; reprinted by permission of the publisher), Science Research Associates, 1975, pp. 129-131, 271.*

Problems of relationships which give an accurate reflection of the society we live in, are . . . found at picture-book level. Evaline Ness, in **Sam, Bangs and Moonshine** and **Do You Have the Time, Lydia?** has written unusual and imaginative stories and illustrated them beautifully. In each case, as main character, there's a very believable, motherless, young girl who grows in maturity as the stories go on. Motherlessness in these stories, it might be noted, is not a cue for suffering but a cause for growth. (p. 40)

> *Bob Dixon, "Sexism: Birds in Gilded Cages," in his* Catching Them Young 1: Sex, Race and Class in Children's Fiction *(copyright © Pluto Press 1977), Pluto Press, 1977, pp. 1-41.*

Evaline Ness uses a variety of techniques ranging from hand-worked tapestry to woodcuts printed on tissue-thin paper, with separate blocks used for each color. Her constant experimentation brings freshness to her handsomely composed illustrations.

> *Zena Sutherland, Dianne L. Monson, and May Hill Arbuthnot, "Artists and Children's Books: Evaline Ness," in their* Children and Books *(copyright © 1981, 1977, 1972, 1964, 1957, 1947 by Scott, Foresman and Company; reprinted by permission), sixth edition, Scott, Foresman, 1981, p. 139.*

JOSEFINA FEBRUARY (1963)

Evaline Ness is responsible for some of the boldest and most original children's book illustrations. Now in startling olive green, tangerine, and mauve woodcuts she shows the 4-8's Haiti, and at the same time tells them the endearing story of a little girl called Josefina who found [a little burro]. . . . She knew she must search for his owner. That Josefina does all the right things with the right results goes to show that stories about good little girls need not be dull, nor sweet stories sentimental.

> *Pamela Marsh, "Girls in Whirls—Minor Royalty—Boys on Bikes and in the Apple Tree: 'Josefina February'," in* The Christian Science Monitor *(reprinted by permission from* The Christian Science Monitor; *© 1963 The Christian Science Publishing Society; all rights reserved), May 9, 1963, p. 3B.*

The most satisfying picture book we have seen in some time is written and illustrated by an artist whose work we have long admired. . . . This tender tale of little Josefina February has some of Miss Ness' finest work, beautifully reproduced with the same loving and expert care that made Marcia Brown's books . . . such a delight. The color harmonies from orange through dull greenish tan to black against bands of pale lavender are unusual and beautiful and the patterns of the wood cuts such that you come back to admire them again and again—the burro standing among the leaves of the coffee bush, the busy market place, Josefina braiding her hair ribbon into the mane of her pet.

For the sake of the children we are especially happy that a distinguished picture book has what is exceedingly difficult to find, a story they can delight in. It is a simple tale about a little Haitian girl whose whole heart goes out to a baby burro she finds in an orchard where she is gathering fruit to sell in the market in order to buy her grandfather a pair of real leather shoes for a birthday present. . . . Then came Mr. Hippolyte who offered to trade the burro for the pair of real leather shoes

that she had been too late to get, so wrapped up had she been in her exciting new acquisition, and Josefina was torn unbearably between two deep desires. We love her for her choice and even more we love the surprise ending. Surely children will cherish this book and want to hear the story again and again.

> *Margaret Sherwood Libby, "This Year's Top Winners . . . And Twelve Who Took Honors," in* Books *(© I.H.T. Corporation; reprinted by permission), May 12, 1963, p. 3.*

The words of Evaline Ness's first picture book story, and especially the warmly colored woodblock prints, are wonderfully evocative of tropical life and tempo. The story itself does have tender, poignant moments but never strays off the set path where an unselfish act earns a material reward. Children should sometimes travel the route where the signs point to generosity having its own, intangible reward.

> *George A. Woods, in a review of "Josefina February," in* The New York Times Book Review *(© 1963 by The New York Times Company; reprinted by permission), June 16, 1963, p. 28.*

[The outcome of the story] is happy and little children will be relieved and satisfied. The beautiful woodcuts in strong, warm colors—brown, purple, orange, and black—are very appropriate to the Haitian setting and make a stunning book; but they so overwhelm the gentle story that it is almost lost. (p. 379)

> *Ruth Hill Viguers, in a review of "Josefina February," in* The Horn Book Magazine *(copyright © 1963, by The Horn Book, Inc., Boston), Vol. XXXIX, No. 4, August, 1963, pp. 378-79.*

The text and the author's elegant woodcuts give substance and reality to a setting that must be unfamiliar to most young English readers. The illustrations amplify the text (for example, when a house is described as "like a kite on a string", the picture points up the force of the simile) in a way that demonstrates the value of a single hand controlling words and pictures. (pp. 386-87)

> *"Life-Patterns for the Under-Fives," in* The Times Literary Supplement *(© Times Newspapers Ltd. (London) 1971; reproduced from* The Times Literary Supplement *by permission), No. 3605, April 2, 1971, pp. 386-87.*

Evaline Ness used woodcut prints for the illustrations that appear in . . . [**Double Discovery**] and **Josefina February**. By and large, her woodcuts are fairly sophisticated in design. She evidences remarkable skill with the tools and is able to produce graceful and delicate lines with this art medium. The woodcuts that were made to illustrate **Josefina February** are especially effective. The pictures of the charming, skinny little Josefina with very unruly hair accentuate this compassionate story of a little Haitian girl. . . . The style of Ms. Ness' woodcuts and her use of color reflect the spirit of Haiti, its richness and its poverty, its beauty and its wretchedness. (p. 74)

> *Patricia Cianciolo, "The Artist's Media and Techniques," in her* Illustrations in Children's Books *(copyright © 1970, 1976 by Wm. C. Brown Company Publishers), second edition, Brown, 1976, pp. 58-93.*

From Josefina February, *written and illustrated by Evaline Ness.*

A GIFT FOR SULA SULA   (1963)

Evaline Ness, who captured the bold and vivid colors of Haiti in "**Josefina February,**" has moved her storybook location to the Aegean Sea. Her style here is softer, using pink, orange and chartreuse. . . . It is a well-written story, gentle and solid: the moral, plainly stated, will have a message for children. Yet it does not quite come to life—perhaps because it is *told,* rather than unfolding through action and emotion.

> *Alice Low, in a review of "A Gift for Sula Sula,"
> in* The New York Times Book Review, *Part II (©
> 1963 by The New York Times Company; reprinted
> by permission), November 10, 1963, p. 50.*

[Evaline Ness's books] are some of the happiest things that can happen to a reviewer. Her woodcuts make an instant impact in this season's "**A Gift for Sula Sula.**" . . . She has an exciting way with color combinations, yellow-greens, oranges, shocking pinks. Her design is superb. She contrasts narrow, decorative lines with bold strokes, textured surfaces with long curves, a dreamy fairy-tale quality with a Brueghel-like humor. The touching story . . . is made to match. It is about Miki, the pelican, . . . and the exotic, tangerine-colored bird that comes to his island. The lesson it teaches about pride and service never leaps out of the story to rebuke 4-8-year-old readers, but is there to satisfy them with a sense of justice and of the rightness of things.

> *Pamela Marsh, "To Unlock the Castle of Wonder,"
> in* The Christian Science Monitor *(reprinted by per-
> mission from* The Christian Science Monitor; © 1963
> The Christian Science Publishing Society; all rights
> reserved), November 14, 1963, p. 1B.**

The illustrations feature gold and orange against a pink wash. Miki points a moral for younger children than the audience for her recent *Josefina February* . . . which has a stronger story and more dramatic illustrations.

> *May H. Edmonds, in a review of "A Gift for Sula
> Sula," in* School Library Journal, *an appendix to*
> Library Journal *(reprinted from the December, 1963
> issue of* School Library Journal, *published by R. R.
> Bowker Co./ A Xerox Corporation; copyright © 1963),
> Vol. 10, No. 4, December, 1963, p. 42.*

EXACTLY ALIKE   (1964)

Elizabeth had four freckled-faced brothers, exactly alike. . . . The boys teased Elizabeth and she couldn't tell who was Benny or Bertie or Biff or Buzzie. She crawled under the bed and watched her brothers until she observed such small differences as a freckle out of place, a blue eye, etc. But she still didn't know which brother was which until. . . . This tale of a half century ago is pictured in gay shades of red and blue. Faces show the sadness of misunderstanding. Boys bellow until you hold your ears. To the loveliness of all her earlier books Miss Ness has added new spark and liveliness.

> *Eloise Rue, in a review of "Exactly Alike," in* School Library Journal, *an appendix to* Library Journal *(reprinted from the May, 1964 issue of* School Library Journal, *published by R. R. Bowker Co./ A Xerox Corporation; copyright © 1964), Vol. 10, No. 9, May, 1964, p. 86.*

The refreshing thing about this book is that the author doesn't preach. She allows her characters to find their own way out of their difficulties and gives her 5-8 readers a chance to think for themselves.

> *Patience M. Daltry, "The Coconut Caper," in* The Christian Science Monitor *(reprinted by permission from* The Christian Science Monitor; © 1964 The Christian Science Publishing Society; all rights reserved), May 7, 1964, p. 3B.*

While this book has charming and gay color, it has a truly extraordinary story—one that has all the setting of a realistic tale although we must accept it as an imaginary one, with perhaps some foundation in fact. . . . One wonders why Elizabeth could not at least place the brother who had one blue eye and one black, but the story ends happily with Elizabeth hugging all four brothers at once. It is one of the more artistic picture books of the spring, and children may accept it wholeheartedly.

> *Alice Dalgliesh, in a review of "Exactly Alike," in* Saturday Review *(© 1964 Saturday Review Magazine Co.; reprinted by permission), Vol. XLVII, No. 20, May 16, 1964, p. 55.*

Fortunately, the lesson [of "give and take"] slips plausibly into this spritely, delightful tale and the author's bold, slightly stylized drawings perfectly reflect the militant impudentness of the freckle-faced quads.

> *Polly Burroughs, in a review of "Exactly Alike," in* The New York Times Book Review *(© 1964 by The New York Times Company; reprinted by permission), August 30, 1964, p. 22.*

The story of Elizabeth and her four tormenting little brothers will bring cries of sympathy from girls who suffer similarly. . . . The solution [is] subtly conveyed. . . . The theme of human relationships and the problems of getting on together is handled in a way unusual in picture books, in an intelligent, well-written story. The illustrations, mainly in muted red and turquoise, exactly match the spirit of the story. Each opening has been planned as a whole, with a careful balance between pictures and text.

> *J. A. Cunliffe, in a review of "Exactly Alike," in* Children's Book News *(copyright © 1969 by Baker Book Services Ltd.), Vol. 4, No. 1, January-February, 1969, p. 17.*

PAVO AND THE PRINCESS (1964)

[*Pavo and the Princess*] is a variation of an old and somewhat faded fairy tale: a beautiful little princess who could not or would not cry. So her father, the king, gives her his splendid

From Exactly Alike, *written and illustrated by Evaline Ness.*

white peacock pet, Pavo, as a birthday gift. Why would that make her cry? We shall see in the end—when she loses him through her own nastiness. Evaline Ness has distinguished herself as an artist-author before—best in the earlier books illustrated with woodcuts. This time it is confectionery, mostly pink and turquoise candy. Best part of the characterization is the bratty face of Princess Phoebe, not beautiful at all as the text claims, but more appealing than all the rest. (p. 24)

> Fritz Eichenberg, "Familiar Themes and Variations," in Book Week—The Sunday Herald Tribune (© 1964, The Washington Post), November 1, 1964, pp. 24, 26.*

The plot here seems cold and is far less entertaining than the folk-tale situation, but children have enjoyed this invented princess story. Distinctively illustrated in brilliant overlays of deep pink, turquoise, and green.

> Virginia Haviland, in a review of "Pavo and the Princess," in The Horn Book Magazine (copyright © 1965, by The Horn Book, Inc., Boston), Vol. XLI, No. 1, February, 1965, p. 43.

A DOUBLE DISCOVERY (1965)

[This story] has the power to divert and amuse but not move. The pictures of Norio too often are monkey-like caricatures. The story is devoid of real Japanese feeling, and the woodcuts, while marvelously decorative, beautifully composed, and dramatically colored in aquas, grayed greens, and black, accented by vermillion, are only externally Japanese, lacking the delicacy of line characteristic of that country's art. As a whole, this is a disappointment from a distinguished illustrator.

> Elva Harmon, in a review of "A Double Discovery," in School Library Journal, an appendix to Library Journal (reprinted from the October, 1965 issue of School Library Journal, published by R. R. Bowker Co./ A Xerox Corporation; copyright © 1965), Vol. 12, No. 2, October, 1965, p. 220.

Saru was a monkey. Hoki was a wild pony. Norio was a farmer's son. Saru and Norio had two things in common. Both loved the pony and both suffered from double vision. Norio's condition was corrected with glasses, but poor Saru often leapt for branches that weren't there and landed on her face. The storyteller brings them all together cleverly and, as good friends should, they begin to share the essentials. In this instance, a monkey in glasses, seeing straight for the first time in years adds that extra dose of nonsense to a fantasy that will nudge the youngest listeners to laughter. Mrs. Ness, whose control of her technique does not vary, has achieved an oriental quality in her woodcuts this time that is color perfect.

> A review of "A Double Discovery," in Virginia Kirkus' Service (copyright © 1965 Virginia Kirkus' Service, Inc.), Vol. XXXIII, No. 19, October 1, 1965, p. 1035.

[In "A Double Discovery", Evaline Ness] comes out very well indeed, maintaining an exemplary professionalism in text, illustration and book design. The story [is told] in moving and economical prose. . . . The superb woodcuts, mutely colored, exquisitely spaced, are so telling that children listening with only one ear can still see exactly what is happening.

> Barbara Novak O'Doherty, in a review of "A Double Discovery," in The New York Times Book Review

(© 1965 by The New York Times Company; reprinted by permission), November 7, 1965, p. 62.

SAM, BANGS AND MOONSHINE (1966)

I knew it! Two minutes after I was foolhardy enough to list the new books I thought were going to have prominent places in the Christmas parade, . . . along came one so distinguished that it demands a place up front with the leaders. Evaline Ness may not agree, but to me all her other distinguished books were arrows pointing to "Sam, Bangs & Moonshine," her original, her perfect picture story. Up front, Miss Ness!

> A review of "Sam, Bangs & Moonshine," in Publishers Weekly (reprinted from the September 12, 1966 issue of Publishers Weekly, published by R. R. Bowker Company; copyright © 1966 by R. R. Bowker Company), Vol. 190, No. 11, September 12, 1966, p. 89.

Evaline Ness has written and illustrated a beautiful book about a lonely fisherman's daughter who invents fantasies which brighten her dreary life. Motherless Samantha, or Sam, has difficulty distinguishing between things which are "moonshine" and things which are real. Her father cautions her that "moonshine spells trouble." Sam's invention of a pet kangaroo who is visiting her mermaid mother on Blue Rock nearly results in disaster for her small, believing friend, Thomas, who bicycles off to see the wonder as the tide comes in and a storm breaks. The text is so cleverly wrought that a young reader will be left with the impression—for just a frightening moment—that both Bangs, the pet cat, and Thomas have been drowned. The scare shakes Sam out of her dependence on moonshine, and she makes the distinction between reality and fantasy; the reader feels that she will depend on reality in the future. An exceptionally satisfactory ending is provided when the father gives Sam a tiny African animal which resembles a kangaroo, and she, in turn, presents it to Thomas. In this unusually creative story the fantasy in which many, many children indulge is presented in a realistic and sympathetic context. The illustrations in ink and pale color wash (mustard, grayish-aqua) have a touching realism too. This is an outstanding book and one that no library will want to miss.

> Evelyn Geller and Eric Moon, in a review of "Sam, Bangs & Moonshine," in School Library Journal, an appendix to Library Journal (reprinted from the October, 1966 issue of School Library Journal, published by R. R. Bowker Co./ A Xerox Corporation; copyright © 1966), Vol. 13, No. 2, October, 1966, p. 218.

[Sam, Bangs & Moonshine is a] literate and convincing little story. . . .

Miss Ness handles an overly fanciful tale with a good deal of down-to-earth realism. The language is mercifully devoid of frills, and her story builds up just the right kind of momentum. Her illustrations are excellent. Handsomely composed on the page, they make their point with a minimum of extraneous detail and a maximum of visual interest.

> John Gruen, "Fancy Free," in Book Week—World Journal Tribune (© 1966, The Washington Post), October 30, 1966, p. 5.*

[In the following article, Ann Durell recounts her experiences as Ness's editor for Sam, Bangs & Moonshine. She begins with her reactions to receiving the finished manuscript.]

Morning came. Radiant sunlight flooded the room. Norio sat up and looked straight into the bright, merry eyes of Saru as she squatted beside him. Perched on her nose were Norio's glasses. She reached out and patted his face, then she took his hand and led him outdoors.

From A Double Discovery, *written and illustrated by Evaline Ness.*

I settled back to savor, realizing that Eve had reached a new level as a writer; her style was fully developed, distinctively her own—tight as a cablegram; freshly flavorful as a child's way of speech. I told her so, but I don't think she really listened. She was already worrying about the pictures.

I went over to her apartment again and we discussed them. I had the curiously familiar sensation of discussing with Eve a book by another author that we had asked her to illustrate. She was as analytical as if she had seen the story for the first time.

She pulled out sketches from a drawer. "I think lots of drawing with this one. Houses, architectural shapes; look at these done at the shore. Marvelous houses, lots of detail. I want to do line, lots of line, with wash. Something different. What do you think?"

"Something different." Here I was on familiar ground. Every Evaline Ness book displays a different technique because she never stands still.

Since she is a highly skilled craftsman, one of those rare people who are so adept with their hands that they can master any technique of visual expression from tapestry to woodcuts, she has made the physical techniques into part of her creative success as an artist. Rather than imposing limitations, the techniques with which she is always experimenting open new dimensions because she is always completely in control of them.

It is a rich and heady education in graphic arts to work with her on a book.

"And Sam's a fisherman's daughter so the shore is right. I'm going to Portugal next month, and I think I'll sketch and sketch there. The book has to be set nowhere; somewhere is too limiting, all wrong. But I can see her father as a Mediterranean type, very strong—and the shapes of boats and nets and a little port will be right."

"Right" was of course too weak a word. And Portugal was only part of the total experience that flowed into the pictures. The illustrations, like the text, were "everywhere"—a child pretending she had a mother when she did not and a cat who talked and gave her the total acceptance the real world did not accord her. A child whose genesis was the picture of another child who was denied home, family, and security by the world's wars, but who smiled and wore her crude cast-off clothing with a certain flair.

Sam, Bangs & Moonshine was always to me a universal book, and I have been pleased, but not surprised, to watch the enthusiastic reception it has already received abroad. And I must admit I am very pleased to have this opportunity to praise without rebuttal an author-illustrator who deserves every word of it, but whose invariable reaction to editorial pats on the back is "Do you *really* think so? Now I was thinking the next time . . ."

Well, of course, we are all looking forward to "the next time." But in the meantime, and the forever time, I, for one, shall cherish Sam. (pp. 108-09)

> Ann Durell, "Evaline Ness," in School Library Journal, an appendix to Library Journal (reprinted from the March, 1967 issue of School Library Journal, published by R. R. Bowker Co./ A Xerox Corporation; copyright ©1967), Vol. 13, No. 7, March, 1967, pp. 108-09.

[Sam, Bangs and Moonshine is a] calculated and developed work of art, sophisticated too. . . . [The story's] working out is satisfactory. The pictures are interesting for their texture rather than their draughtsmanship, and may appeal more to adults and to older children with a taste for art than to the small children for whom the book was presumably designed. A clever book, certainly; perhaps too clever.

> A review of "Sam, Bangs and Moonshine," in The Junior Bookshelf, Vol. 31, No. 6, December, 1967, p. 373.

[Sam, Bangs and Moonshine] is a tribute to the writing and illustrating genius of Evaline Ness. The story may appear humorous and flighty on the surface, but in reality it penetrates deeply into the behavior of many children. . . . The character of Sam is so convincingly drawn that although one does not believe her, one is able to understand her and identify with her. The illustrations are done in a style that contributes to the Moonshine that Sam talks and the fantasies she creates.

> Bernard J. Lonsdale and Helen K. Mackintosh, "Picture-Story Books: 'Sam, Bangs and Moonshine'," in their Children Experience Literature (copyright © 1973 by Random House, Inc.; reprinted by permission of the publisher), Random House, 1973, p. 248.

LONG, BROAD AND QUICKEYE (1969)

Evaline Ness, for anybody's money, can do no wrong. Now she has done right again by this Bohemian fairy tale with its traditional cast of a handsome prince, a beautiful princess, a wicked sorcerer, and with the three characters of the title who must have captured her fancy in the same way that the tale of "Tom Tit Tot" . . . must have. From a long time admirer, a heart-felt request to Evaline Ness: next time around, write the story you illustrate? This picture book is a charmer, but it's been much too long since "Sam, Bangs and Moonshine".

> A review of "Long, Broad & Quickeye," in Publishers Weekly (reprinted from the April 21, 1969 issue of Publishers Weekly, published by R. R. Bowker Company, a Xerox company; copyright © 1969 by Xerox Corporation), Vol. 195, No. 16, April 21, 1969, p. 65.

[In Long, Broad & Quickeye], Evaline Ness has made use of a Bohemian tale from Andrew Lang's Grey Fairy Book, [and interpreted it] with striking results. . . . Her mixed-media illustrations have brilliance of design, sharp characterization, and a humor and grotesquerie related to the medieval setting. (p. 7)

> Virginia Haviland, "Catching Essences with Pictures and Words," in Book World—The Washington Post (© 1969 Postrib Corp.; reprinted by permission of Chicago Tribune and The Washington Post), May 4, 1969, pp. 6-7.*

There should be music to the retelling of that Bohemian favorite, "Long, Broad and Quickeye" . . . and the illustrating, one might expect a symphony. Alas, the melody is muted. The colors of the woodcuts are drab; the tone of the text understated.

> Jane Yolen, in a review of "Long, Broad and Quickeye," in The New York Times Book Review (© 1969 by The New York Times Company; reprinted by permission), May 4, 1969, p. 50.

This is a thoroughly satisfactory tale of mystery and enchantment, and Evaline Ness's spacious, magical woodcuts are, as always, a delight, using a minute range of colour to create an impression of great richness and variety.

> "Of Mice and Men," in The Times Literary Supplement (© Times Newspapers Ltd. (London) 1971; reproduced from The Times Literary Supplement by permission), No. 3634, October 22, 1971, p. 1324.*

[Evaline Ness's] slightly voluble version tells the story of the prince who goes to find his bride with the aid of a servant who can stretch, one who can spread and one whose glance shatters mountains. With this aid the odds are heavily in his favour, but there is still sufficient tension to hold the interest. In one strange and haunting episode the prince goes to a gallery in his father's castle and sees the living portraits of his potential brides. Evaline Ness draws this scene with her characteristic formality and restraint. The stiff conventions of her drawing are not for all tastes and children today expect more colour than she will give them. Here nevertheless is a major book-artist of the day. Her strange, mannered designs are always conceived in terms of the printed page, and they give this book a convincing unity. A book for connoisseurs, among whom can confidently be numbered many children.

> Marcus Crouch, in a review of "Long, Broad and Quickeye," in The Junior Bookshelf, Vol. 36, No. 1, February, 1972, p. 36.

THE GIRL AND THE GOATHERD; OR, THIS AND THAT AND THUS AND SO (1970)

It will come as no surprise that, among the outstanding books by outstanding artists reviewed this week, Evaline Ness's name should lead the list. She is a charter member of that exclusive club, The Individualists: she is her own woman, her work is her own work, never to be mistaken for anybody else's. She celebrates the eccentrics, bless her astringent, wild heart. In her latest story, the eccentric is an ugly girl, who discovers from this and that (a witch and a goatherd) that thus and so is true (true character and true love.) Evaline Ness at her best. And that's the best news today.

> A review of "The Girl and the Goatherd; or, This and That and Thus and So," in Publishers Weekly (reprinted from the September 14, 1970 issue of Publishers Weekly, published by R. R. Bowker Company, a Xerox company; copyright © 1970 by Xerox Corporation), Vol. 198, No. 11, September 14, 1970, p. 59.

Evaline Ness has spun a curiously monotone tale about a girl who was ugly, "got uglier as she got older, and when it came time for her to marry, no man except the goatherd would look at her." Not much romance there! Thus, the reader sympathizes when the heroine turns him down and thinks of "nought else except to be beautiful." Kate Millett, of course, might legit-

From Sam, Bangs and Moonshine, *written and illustrated by Evaline Ness.*

imately lament the poverty of the maiden's societally-sanctioned goal. Be that as it may, girl meets witch and gains heart's desire only to find that flawless beauty provides cold comfort. A patient goatherd ultimately wins a wiser girl.

Though Miss Ness makes her subtle point in a mildly-droll backwoods voice ("Hark you now . . . stop your nattering," etc.) and her illustrations have both wit and polish, the whole is oddly impersonal, even lifeless. Like the ugly girl turned perfect beauty, the book can be admired yet not loved. It [does not have] the heart of her Caldecott winner, **"Sam, Bangs and Moonshine."** . . .

> *Selma G. Lanes, in a review of "The Girl and the Goatherd; or, This and That and Thus and So," in The New York Times Book Review (© 1970 by The New York Times Company; reprinted by permission), October 23, 1970, p. 38.*

[The] cadence of the prose and the offbeat vocabulary (an author's note indicates that the "colloquial tone" of the tale derives from the speech of Virginia hill people) make this original story a nice addition to American folklore collections. The sophisticated, stylized illustrations . . . will strike adults as lovely but may fail to capture children's imaginations: they have a static quality, and the design elements tend to obscure the human.

> *Mary E. Ballou, in a review of "The Girl and the Goatherd; or, This and That and Thus and So," in*

School Library Journal, *an appendix to* Library Journal *(reprinted from the November, 1970 issue of* School Library Journal, *published by R. R. Bowker Co./ A Xerox Corporation; copyright © 1970), Vol. 17, No. 3, November, 1970, p. 102.*

Books by Evaline Ness are widely enjoyed both by children and adults who like fine design and highly original multimedia illustrations which capture the comic and grotesque as well as the lovable human qualities of characters. [In *The Girl and the Goatherd*], . . . Miss Ness uses bold pen-and-ink drawings over woodcuts and many-textured surfaces bright with blues, browns, blacks and oranges. . . . There's sly humor and great satisfaction in watching the girl discover that being beautiful isn't half as nice as being homely and living happily with the goatherd ever after.

> *Martha Bennett King, "Comic, Grotesque and Lovable," in Book World—The Washington Post, Part II (© 1970 Postrib Corp.; reprinted by permission of Chicago Tribune and The Washington Post), November 8, 1970, p. 24.**

Told in a light and flavorful style, a story that follows a familiar pattern: suitor spurned, selfishly used, and wed after a twist in the tale. . . . [After the heroine becomes beautiful, she] finds herself installed in pomp by the king—but nobody will speak to her, touch her, or smile at her. (This is the weak point of the story. Why? "They thought, you know, she was more

From Long, Broad and Quickeye, *adapted and illustrated by Evaline Ness.*

gold than girl''.) So the goatherd comes into his own. There is no reference to this in the text, but the girl appears, in the illustrations, to regain her ugliness at the close. The illustrations are delightful, the style good, the plot adequate.

> Zena Sutherland, in a review of ''The Girl and the Goatherd; or, This and That and Thus and So,'' in Bulletin of the Center for Children's Books (reprinted by permission of The University of Chicago Press; ©1971 by The University of Chicago), Vol. 24, No. 9, May, 1971, p. 142.

DO YOU HAVE THE TIME, LYDIA? (1971)

Characteristically impressive illustrations—dramatic, expressive, distinctively patterned—enliven this story of a girl who never has time to finish her projects or to help her little brother. When she does agree to convert a lobster trap into a racing car for him, she is distracted by so many other half-finished tasks that the race is over before the car is finished. Lydia of course learns her lesson. . . . The cautionary theme is not as inventively developed as was Sam's problem with lying in *Sam, Bangs and Moonshine* . . . but it's just as congenially resolved. The sweeping pink and yellow pictures clinch the characterization of Lydia and vivify her [tropical island] world. . . .

> A review of ''Do You Have the Time, Lydia?'' in Kirkus Reviews (copyright © 1971 The Kirkus Ser-

vice, Inc.), Vol. XXXIX, No. 18, September 15, 1971, p. 1010.

As in the author's *Sam, Bangs and Moonshine,* . . . many familiar details drawn from daily child life contribute to the believability of the characters and situations. . . . The personalities of the children emerge from the expressive ink drawings shaded with pencil and highlighted in sunny shades of pink, orange, and yellow.

> Willa M. Levy, in a review of ''Do You Have the Time, Lydia?'' in School Library Journal, an appendix to Library Journal (reprinted from the January, 1972 issue of School Library Journal, published by R. R. Bowker Co./ A Xerox Corporation; copyright © 1972), Vol. 18, No. 5, January, 1972, p. 52.

The tropical setting adds appeal to the pictures, and the theme of procrastination is interesting, but the protagonist's about-face is too sudden to indicate that any real change has taken place.

> Zena Sutherland, in a review of ''Do You Have the Time, Lydia?'' in Bulletin of the Center for Children's Books (reprinted by permission of The University of Chicago Press; © 1972 by The University of Chicago), Vol. 25, No. 6, February, 1972, p. 95.

How [Lydia] learned the wisdom of her father's comment, '' 'If you *take* time you can *have* time,' '' is presented through a combination of explicit childlike text with sun-drenched illustrations . . . suggesting the flamboyant beauty of a "tropical island in the middle of a warm and noisy sea." Although Lydia lives in this exotic setting, her problem is a universal one—learning to discriminate between what is essential and what is merely inviting, when both seem equally intriguing and equally important. Suitable as it is for reading aloud, the book would be most effective when used with small groups or with an individual child; for the illustrations which present brown-skinned Dr. Arnold as an important minor character are an extension and enlargement of the text in the best tradition of the picture-story. (pp. 135-36)

> *Mary M. Burns, in a review of "Do You Have the Time, Lydia?" in* The Horn Book Magazine *(copyright © 1972 by The Horn Book, Inc., Boston), Vol. XLVIII, No. 2, April, 1972, pp. 135-36.*

Evaline Ness has a gift for elevating the ordinary on to a new and interesting plane. The setting of **Do You Have the Time, Lydia?** is exotic—. . . a happy pretext for rich pink and golden landscapes—but the story itself is one that could happen anywhere. . . . The story of how [Lydia] learns to organize her many activities is convincingly told, and illustrated by its author in her customary spare, satisfactory style.

> *"Pictures Worth Looking at Twice," in* The Times Literary Supplement *(© Times Newspapers Ltd. (London) 1972; reproduced from* The Times Literary Supplement *by permission), No. 3687, November 3, 1972, p. 1326.**

YECK ECK (1974)

[Ness] is at her best in this new book which she says is an evoction of her own childhood yearnings. . . . The author has obviously had a wonderful time with her quirky story and its merry pictures; so will her readers.

> *A review of "Yeck Eck," in* Publishers Weekly *(reprinted from the September 16, 1974 issue of* Publishers Weekly, *published by R. R. Bowker Company, a Xerox company; copyright © 1974 by Xerox Corporation), Vol. 206, No. 12, September 16, 1974, p. 60.*

Ness' brown, orange, and black woodcuts are delightfully expressive. Her text is smooth with many touches of humor, but the story, as a whole, doesn't jibe. What starts out as a realistic situation—many kids would like to buy a baby—abruptly changes to wish fulfillment fantasy. The net result is confusing and jarring.

> *Judith S. Kronick, in a review of "Yeck Eck," in* School Library Journal, *an appendix to* Library Journal *(reprinted from the November, 1974 issue of* School Library Journal, *published by R. R. Bowker Co./ A Xerox Corporation; copyright © 1974), Vol. 21, No. 3, November, 1974, p. 50.*

["Yeck Eck" is] Evaline Ness's nicest book in a while. . . .

Miss Ness understands fantasy too well to explain where pretend begins and ends in this story, nor will most children need to be told. Her woodcut illustrations are characteristically deft and humorous, although perhaps too subtle for 4-8-year-olds. But there's plenty here to amuse small children, with the sophisticated bits a bonus for adult storytellers.

> *Jennifer Farley Smith, in a review of "Yeck Eck," in* The Christian Science Monitor *(reprinted by permission from* The Christian Science Monitor; © 1974 *The Christian Science Publishing Society; all rights reserved), November 6, 1974, p. 12.*

Not a trace of sweetness or sentimentality can be detected in the freewheeling, unpredictable, somewhat tall tale or in the pictures (as amusing as any the artist has ever done) of energetic, determined babies.

> *Ethel L. Heins, in a review of "Yeck Eck," in* The Horn Book Magazine *(copyright © 1974 by The Horn Book, Inc., Boston), Vol. L, No. 6, December, 1974, p. 685.*

AMERICAN COLONIAL PAPER HOUSE: TO CUT OUT AND COLOR (1975)

Authentic and handsome reproductions of early American rooms, furniture and accessories appear in a production which can become a dollhouse in little more than the twinkling of an eye. Ms. Ness, whose prose is as attractive as her illustrations, gives a short history of colonial housekeeping and offers a clue to color coordinations on the front and back covers. She stresses, however, the value of the young readers using their own tastes in painting and assembling the house. You could hardly find a more welcome Christmas present than this, for boy or girl, especially in our Bicentennial year. The book could also provide the impetus for a family or schoolroom activity.

> *A review of "American Colonial Paper House: To Cut Out and Color," in* Publishers Weekly *(reprinted from the November 10, 1975 issue of* Publishers Weekly, *published by R. R. Bowker Company, a Xerox company; copyright © 1975 by Xerox Corporation), Vol. 208, No. 19, November 10, 1975, p. 54.*

FOUR ROOMS FROM THE METROPOLITAN MUSEUM OF ART (1977)

A can't-miss gift for children who like to use their hands and their imaginations. . . . Like her two previous works in this line (one a colonial house and the other a palace), the new book is spiral-bound and opens to make the walls of classic rooms which Ness has reproduced in collaboration with the Museum's curators. Readers get her guidance in cutting out and coloring the miniatures of French, Syrian, Venetian and Spanish rooms on display at the Metropolitan. . . . [The book] can be a worthwhile project for the whole family.

> *A review of "Four Rooms from the Metropolitan Museum of Art," in* Publishers Weekly *(reprinted from the October 24, 1977 issue of* Publishers Weekly, *published by R. R. Bowker Company, a Xerox company; copyright © 1977 by Xerox Corporation), Vol. 212, No. 17, October 24, 1977, p. 77.*

MARCELLA'S GUARDIAN ANGEL (1979)

Nag, nag, nag; that's all little Marcella's Guardian Angel does. . . . At last, the girl tells her implacable foe to get lost for good and Angel agrees, if Marcella will turn herself inside out. "Impossible," says the child; "Easy," declares the Guardian. The secret is a game, Flip-Flop. So Marcella goes at it: the rule is contrasting bad-good, polite-rude, messy-neat, stingy-generous and ''a zillion others.'' An ace at depicting tempestuously naughty small females, Caldecott Medalist Ness also tells this vigorous story perfectly and her etchings (in color) jump with excitement. It certainly is refreshing to discover a moral encapsulated in so much fun.

> *A review of ''Marcella's Guardian Angel,'' in* Publishers Weekly *(reprinted from the January 29, 1979 issue of* Publishers Weekly, *published by R. R. Bowker Company, a Xerox company; copyright © 1979 by Xerox Corporation), Vol. 215, No. 5, January 29, 1979, p. 115.*

No doubt Ness means well, but turning [inner restraint] into a game doesn't make will power into child's play. Self-discipline isn't a sometime thing (with lapses O.K. or not O.K. depending on the day), and the difficulty of developing it is sold short. Behavior mod with a fictional coating, slick woodcuts, and the flavor of a chewable vitamin.

> *Pamela D. Pollack, in a review of ''Marcella's Guardian Angel,'' in* School Library Journal *(reprinted from the March, 1979 issue of* School Library Journal, *published by R. R. Bowker Co./ A Xerox Corporation; copyright © 1979), Vol. 25, No. 7, March, 1979, p. 128.*

Guardian angels, in my limited experience, are supposed to be benevolent creatures who protect us from bad luck and the consequences of our own misdeeds. Marcella's guardian angel is a different breed; in fact, she sounds suspiciously like the Voice of Conscience, a known spoilsport. . . . Followed literally, the rules of the game would lead Marcella into some bizarre situations, but Evaline Ness, who has created delightfully raffish and perverse heroines in the past, never lets Marcella enjoy the slapstick possibilities. Instruct the average girl to act contrary and I guarantee you she will not react by cleaning up her room; nor will the average child be so easily tricked into thinking that virtue is fun. Marcella and her guardian angel deserve each other.

> *Joyce Milton, in a review of ''Marcella's Guardian Angel,'' in* The New York Times Book Review *(© 1979 by The New York Times Company; reprinted by permission), April 8, 1979, p. 32.*

SHAKER PAPER HOUSE: TO CUT OUT AND COLOR (1979)

Author-illustrator Ness, winner of enviable awards, presents an addition to her extremely popular activity books on memorable period houses. This thoroughly researched and carefully executed volume on the Shakers opens with a history of the austere sect whose members came to America with their leader, Mother Ann, in 1747. Readers will understand the reasons for the functional beauty of Shaker furnishings: anything perfect

had to answer its purpose perfectly—with no gimmicks. There are easily understood instructions for cutting out and setting up the four rooms included and coloring them according to suggestions in the photo on the front cover.

> *A review of ''Shaker Paper House: To Cut Out and Color,'' in* Publishers Weekly *(reprinted from the September 24, 1979 issue of* Publishers Weekly, *published by R. R. Bowker Company, a Xerox company; copyright © 1979 by Xerox Corporation), Vol. 216, No. 13, September 24, 1979, p. 106.*

FIERCE: THE LION (1980)

The Caldecott Medalist's singular artistry and buoyant sense of humor make her new book another of her not-to-be-missed creations. Ness illustrates the story of Isobel, an old-fashioned child of the circus, with vivacious etchings in predominantly strawberry-pink and olive-green tones. Isobel's best friend, Fierce the lion, is a magnificent beast you believe in wholly. . . . The story's ending is joyful but Ness's inspired coda is even more fun.

> *A review of ''Fierce: The Lion,'' in* Publishers Weekly *(reprinted from the August 8, 1980 issue of* Publishers Weekly, *published by R. R. Bowker Company, a Xerox company; copyright © 1980 by Xerox Corporation), Vol. 218, No. 6, August 8, 1980, p. 83.*

Ness' fine-tuned language gives panache and other enduring qualities to a story with a simple plot. . . . Everything about this book is satisfying and self-satisfied. Ness' characteristic multitextured illustrations place the story in a turn-of-the-century setting and give it no small measure of additional flavor.

> *Judith Goldberger, in a review of ''Fierce: The Lion,'' in* Booklist *(reprinted by permission of the American Library Association; copyright © 1980 by the American Library Association), Vol. 77, No. 6, November 15, 1980, p. 460.*

A lion who'd rather be loved than feared is easy to sympathize with. . . . But a circus lion whom all the other performers (human, too) are jealous of, who weeps as a consequence, who'd rather [give rides to children], *and* who gets such a job at the zoo is, from first to last, a fabrication. And that's not the whole of it: this lion, yclept Fierce, is the pet of a little girl (whose parents are the circus lion-trainers); it's the tricks he learns from her that make him a star; and it's she who attests to his loving kindness and so secures him the job giving rides at the zoo. Oh yes—she also learns ''lion-roar talk,'' while he masters ''girl-giggly talk.'' All this is presumably meant to be adorable—the hairbows-and-highbutton-shoes pictures included—but it all comes across as an act.

> *A review of ''Fierce: The Lion,'' in* Kirkus Reviews *(copyright © 1981 The Kirkus Service, Inc.), Vol. XLIX, No. 2, January 15, 1981, p. 73.*

Mary Norton

1903-

British author of fiction and drama and journalist.

Norton is often regarded as the best contemporary writer of fantasy for children. She is well-known for her series on "The Borrowers," a family of six-inch high people who live in hiding in the houses of human beings. *The Borrowers* and its sequels describe a complete miniature world which conforms to the natural laws of reality. Norton is praised for creating a unique, absorbing fantasy which is amazingly believable in spite of its focus. She achieves this realistic atmosphere through her portrayal of the borrowers and their lifestyle and by consistent attention to detail in the development of her characters and settings. Critics also approve of Norton's original themes and lifelike characterizations in her other fantasies.

Norton was an actress in the prestigious Old Vic Theatre Company until she married Robert C. Norton, a member of a well-known ship-owning family in Portugal. Her stories began as entertainment for her four children while she was living there in isolation, but she did not start writing professionally until her husband went bankrupt. When he joined the British Navy, she took the family to New York and began writing short stories and articles for adults. When she returned to England she wrote her first book, *The Magic Bed-knob*, which was later combined with *Bonfires and Broomstick* as *Bed-knob and Broomstick. The Magic Bed-knob* was immediately recognized as a potential classic. It was compared to the books of E. Nesbit for its logical use of magic and to P. L. Travers's *Mary Poppins* for its wry humor and memorable witch, Miss Price. After nearly forty years, *Bed-knob and Broomstick* is still widely popular.

The Borrowers, a somewhat less magical story, is believed to be Norton's finest work. She applies her writing talents to depict the Clock family—Pod, Homily, and Arrietty—who creatively use small items that big people usually think they have misplaced. Norton explores varying aspects of behavior in both the borrowers and the human characters, adding the implications of the borrowers's dependence upon humans and the emotional struggles and conflicts such circumstances cause. Critics commend nearly every aspect of *The Borrowers;* its sequels are largely considered as good as the first book. Reviewers cite the originality of Norton's idea and her descriptions of how the borrowers survive. The books are also noted as especially good for reading aloud. In fact, they are structured as oral narratives: in most tales a person who has seen the borrowers tells the story to a girl named Kate. This technique adds to the credence of the existence of the borrowers and helps the stories seem like genuine family history.

After a ten year lapse, Norton published *Poor Stainless,* a short story that differs from the other tales in being told by a borrower and focusing on the Overmantel family rather than the Clocks. It was often called unsuccessful by critics, but *The Borrowers Avenged* was greeted as a pleasant surprise when it was published in 1982. Although some reviewers say it does not equal Norton's previous works in plot and character development, most applaud her use of suspense and detail and look forward to future episodes. With *Are All the Giants Dead?* Norton profiles a world in which familiar

story characters live "happily ever after." Critics find this book relevant to today's children because of its characterization of scientific, practical-minded James, who makes a skeptical journey to fairy land and returns with his childhood faith restored. Although this story departs from her previous work, Norton's style is consistently inventive and witty. By applying this style to her themes she has created fantasies which are undoubtedly modern children's classics. She received the Carnegie Medal in 1952 and the Lewis Carroll Shelf Award in 1953, both for *The Borrowers.*

(See also *Something about the Author*, Vol. 18 and *Contemporary Authors*, Vols. 97-100.)

AUTHOR'S COMMENTARY

I think the first idea—or first feeling—of the Borrowers came through my being short-sighted: when others saw the far hills, the distant woods, the soaring pheasant, I, as a child, would turn sideways to the close bank, the tree roots and the tangled grasses. Moss, fern-stalks, sorrel stems, created the *mise en scène* for a jungle drama, lacking in those days its dramatis personae. But one invented the characters—small, fearful people picking their way through miniature undergrowth; one saw smooth places where they might sit and rest: branched stems which might invite them to climb: sandy holes into which they might creep for shelter.

All childhood has its lonely periods—the brisk 'run-out-and-play' of harassed grown-ups: the 'stay-there-till-we-come-for-you' of elder brothers: and it was later I invented, for the sake of companionship, a way to people this tiny Eden. In those days before the First World War, one could buy small, china dolls with movable arms and flaxen hair, naked except for shoes and socks which were painted on. They stood about three or four inches high and were on sale among the lollipops in every village shop. It took no time at all to dress and disguise these and to assign to each its role. Water-colour, silver paint, odd pieces of coloured silk, tufts of black fur from a hearth rug—and here were one's puppets made. Infinitely docile, they played out great dramas for a child's entertainment. . . . (pp. 68-9)

On the days when one was confined to the house, imagined excursions took place among the chair-legs and across the deep pile of the carpets. Here, the hazards were even greater: hearth and fire-irons for these tiny people took on almost nightmare properties. The sideboard, too, with its gleaming slippery silver, was rather frightening. No wonder they took to mouse-holes and the wainscot, creating their own small safety.

Children nowadays are encouraged to invent, but still in ways devised by adults. 'Clear-up-that-mess' has destroyed many a secret world. As the Borrowers' house was destroyed by Mrs. Driver. This particular incident, oddly enough, worries grown-ups far more than it does children. Children are used to repeated small destructions—in the name of punctuality or tidiness—and have learned to accept them. If the raw materials are there to hand, they simply build again. Grown-ups, faced with equivalent disaster, make far more fuss. Sometimes, perhaps, we should think about this. . . . (p. 69)

> *Mary Norton, "About Borrowers," in* Chosen for Children: An Account of the Books Which Have Been Awarded the Library Association Carnegie Medal, 1936-1975, *edited by Marcus Crouch and Alec Ellis (© Marcus Crouch and Alec Ellis, 1977), third edition, The Library Association, 1977, pp. 68-9.*

GENERAL COMMENTARY

It is not always the case that unusual juvenile titles are recognized as being of fine quality and gain a deserved place in children's literature as quickly as these two books of Mary Norton's [**The Borrowers** and **The Borrowers Afield**] have assumed theirs. . . .

And I do not consider **The Borrowers Afield** as just a sequel—it is part and parcel of the first book and all that has been said appreciatively about the one can be applied to the other. (p. 69)

[Be] assured that Mrs. Norton is one of those artists who weaves into her stories such minute and satisfying detail, who develops her books so consistently and who makes her characters so much a piece of the people we meet every day that the engrossed reader "believes"—well, at least believes while engrossed. In fact, some readers are almost irritated while reading **The Borrowers** to have the author leave the way open for doubters to wonder whether this "might have happened." 'Tis something of a relief, as the borrowers are later forced afield, to have everyone, author included, assuming the realness of the situation.

In an article which Mrs. Norton wrote for *Woman's Day* (June, 1954), she mentions that some authors

> lack the spark which turns the simplest
> home-spun story into magic or makes the
> wildest flights of fantasy seem real.

Of this particular kind of creative spark, Mrs. Norton has an abundance. (p. 70)

Homily, perhaps because she is part and parcel of so many good souls in this world, is the first to emerge as a real character. Bustling, talkative, worrisome, a bit tart and something of a gossip, Homily has to be admonished now and then by her family not to "take on." Taking on is apt to occur when her nerves are "all of a piece." As the situation calls for it, Homily can become, in turn, the stricken martyr or the courageous helpmate, and when there is need she can be completely winning. (After all, it takes some special effort to get Pod to change his deliberate British mind.) Both Pod and Arrietty realize that Homily is truly a wonderful woman and when "put to it" can face up to any situation.

It is so easy to visualize an angry Homily seizing the broom to work off her ruffled feelings, to understand how she almost becomes "house proud" when borrowing is suddenly too easy, and to sense her indignation when she is caught with her hair up in curlers and the supper washing-up not yet done. Something within the understanding reader pauses to smile, as Homily pushes back her untidy hair and smooths down her apron when she hears Pod returning. And, there is almost an ache for her when, out of doors for the first time, she sees a flower. (pp. 71-2)

Homily's life is made up of love, work, and worry, and to the living of it she brings real wisdom. As for all of us, so with Homily, little things help; in fact, there's nothing like a cup of tea to brighten her up. And, when faced with having to go back to drinking her tea from a common acorn cup she does so cheerful, even as she mourns for lost riches and remembers, "But it's once you've *had* a teacup, if you see what I mean."

[Pod] emerges more slowly as a person. But then one can expect little else, for Pod would be inconsistent if he was anything other than deliberate. Like most men, he does not come into his own, as it were, in everyday home life. But when an emergency arises, thank goodness he is at hand to take charge . . . and the most dreaded of all emergencies comes as the Clocks are not only "seen" but are hunted and forced to emigrate. Pod is a bulwark of strength, utterly practical and completely stubborn. Because he has been out in the world (the place of Victorian borrowing ladies is definitely in the home), he knows something of the dangers and vicissitudes his family must meet as they start out to try to find Uncle Hendreary, Aunt Lupy, and another home.

Now Homily may, at times, enveigle Pod into moving the furniture from room to room by the hour, but he *is* the man of the house, the undisputed master, when the well-being of his family is threatened. When Homily starts to moan, a quick and firm "Have done" from Pod is enough to set her aright and "We want none of that now" can stem an imminent flow of tears. Pod may be a bit stolid and ponderous in his thinking, but none can doubt his courage nor his practicality. (p. 72)

Those who, when they feel cooped-up, hemmed-in, and lonely, frequently go from window to window seeking some escape, will recognize in Arrietty a kindred spirit. Her family has tried in many ways to keep her happy and contented. She has a charming room. The ladies on the cigar box lid, which makes its ceiling, are delightful to look at while she falls asleep at night and Homily tries to keep her busy all through the day. Arrietty has been taught to read and write and Pod has borrowed Tom Thumb editions for her bookshelf as well as a Diary and Proverb Book. By writing just one line each evening, Arrietty hopes to make the diary last at least twenty years.

But the events of the day are too often recorded simply by making ditto marks and lonely Arrietty turns longingly toward the grating through which she can glimpse a "bit of path, a few flowers and once in a while a bird flying by." (pp. 72-3)

Homily finally realizes that Arrietty must explore a wider world for she can't stand being "cooped-up . . . day after day . . . year after year. . . ." So Pod takes her through the hall of the big house, to the out of doors, and there Arrietty dances joyously into adventure . . . is "seen" and even talks to the boy. This, of course, finally leads to the emigration and though Homily never ceases to bewail her lost treasures, and Pod faces many a problem, Arrietty is always glad that they have escaped—glad "no matter what."

And so, you come to picture Arrietty as a part of joyous and adventurous youth. She is dainty, but proves her durability as she adjusts easily to new and complex ways of life. She is at times fearful, but curiosity often overcomes caution. (p. 73)

You cannot long doubt the depth of Mrs. Norton's insight nor the keenness of her powers of observation. Arrietty, when she doesn't want to help with the household tasks, knows that it is safe to be writing, for "Homily liked her to write." Pod warns his wife or daughter against becoming fussed because it makes one silly and "that's when accidents happen." Arrietty is really disturbed when for the first time, her parents agree with her!

> Oh, no—it shocked her to be right. Parents were right, not children. Children could say anything, Arrietty knew, and enjoyed saying it—knowing always they were safe and wrong.

The books are not always easy reading for our boys and girls, for some of the words used are definitely British in flavor and others, too, are relatively new, but as the author says . . . "Words have color and feeling, as well as sense," and somehow children who are enjoying the stories can capture enough of the feel and meaning that the strangeness of the vocabulary does not disturb their reading.

The rather dry bits of humor tucked unexpectedly into paragraphs are such fun. A chessman has been taken from upstairs and graces the Clocks living room and "lent that air . . . which only statuary can give." . . .

The vision of Uncle Hendreary in all his stuffiness standing by the cupid on the mantel and being dusted brings forth many a giggle. . . . And the idea of Homily, in all of her plainness and fussiness, longing for a "palm in a pot" is just too much for some listeners.

And listeners there should be. The books are better when they are read aloud and shared. The only other way of even thinking of reading them is to go through each one swiftly and then reread, slowly taking the needed time to savor them fully. The first reading has to be swift—otherwise the suspense is just too much. By going slowly on the second reading, you can see the leeches like "blobs of expanding velvet" and you can feel the "sharp-edged leaves, deceptively sappy and swaying, which cut their hands."

Swiftly or slowly, it isn't until you read the books aloud, that you realize the full enchantment of those halcyon days when Arrietty read aloud to the boy. . . . (pp. 74-5)

I have never known a boy or girl who has listened to either book as it was read aloud, who has not been caught by its magic. (p. 75)

Mary Harbage, "The Borrowers at Home and Afield," (copyright © 1956 by the National Council of Teachers of English; reprinted by permission of the publisher and the author), in Elementary English, *Vol. XXXIII, No. 2, February, 1956, pp. 67-75.*

Occasionally one comes across an author who seems to have a special genius and a special concern for childhood. An author whose views of life and unique means of expression colour his writings, so that none may be labelled "for children only". Mary Norton belongs in this category. She, like Lewis Carroll and Kenneth Grahame, Hans Andersen and Arthur Ransome, gives the impression of being keenly aware of the wonders of life and the riches of the earth. Behind each of her stories, one is conscious of a mind richly stored with the kind of imagination that adds colour and dimension to a plot. . . .

["**The Magic Bedknob**"] introduced an immortal character in Miss Price, a very prim and ladylike music teacher, who secretly studied, by correspondence course, to become a witch. This exquisitely funny and fantastic little tale, unquestionably established its author as a genuine writer of comedy.

It was not, however, from reading "**The Magic Bedknob**", that I was first introduced to Mrs. Norton's works. My introduction was so charged with delightful nostalgic qualities, that I could wish every adult might experience a similar one. As a child I read with a sense of wonder and delight at the magic and adventure enclosed between the covers of a book. . . .

Gradually the magic disappeared as magic must, and, like adults the world over, I resigned myself to becoming slightly disenchanted. . . . Never again would I plunge eagerly and wholeheartedly into the world of fantasy. Then one day I opened "**The Borrowers**". . . . (p. 207)

The shadowy world in which the Borrowers live is created with wisdom and understanding out of a perfection of small and consistent details. Children will love it, especially those who find pleasure in creating secret worlds of their own. . . .

Mary Norton has that creative ability which enables her readers to share, in an intensely personal way, in the fortunes of her characters. The authentic quality of her writing allows us to enter into their lives, to the extent that we try to imagine beyond the last page of a story. Surely one of the best tests of a good book. (p. 208)

Jean de Temple, "The Magic of Mary Norton," in Ontario Library Review, *Vol. XLII, No. 4, November, 1958, pp. 207-08.*

Mary Norton's *Bed Knob and Broomstick* starts . . . on a very ordinary note. Miss Price lives in the Bedfordshire village where Carey, Charles and Paul go to stay with an aunt. . . . When Paul first sees her lurching past his bedroom window on her broomstick, he thinks what an inefficient witch she is; in fact, being too ladylike to ride astride, she is often in difficulties, and it is because the children help her home after a fall that she confides to them her plans for study. She even does an advanced spell for them, and with the help of Paul's bed-knob they journey to distant places and distant periods, escaping from cannibals, from the police, and finally from Restoration London after the Great Fire. It is on this last journey that they meet, and bring back to their own times, the lugubrious necromancer Emelius Jones, whose neglected appearance rouses Miss Price's maternal instincts. If there is plenty of humour in these two eccentric characters, there is far more in Mary Norton's comments on the technique of witchcraft. No child could resist the description of Miss Price's workroom, or her explanation to Carey who wonders why she can't make money. . . . (p. 103)

Mary Norton makes her comic points so well because of her close attention to detail. In her three stories about the Borrowers, everything depends on incongruity—on creatures of another race behaving like humans—but this time humour is merged into tenderness and poetry. . . . To us, as we read, the Borrowers are not miniature humans; they are *reminders* of what humans are like.

The first of three books about these little people sounds a note of pathos. We are told that the race is dwindling, that Pod, Homily and Arrietty, who live under the kitchen floor of an old house in Bedfordshire, have long ago said goodbye to the Harpsichord family and the Overmantels, and it is a long time since they saw their relations the well-to-do Clocks. For the moment, however, the family is safe, so long as they are not 'seen'. (p. 104)

Mary Norton has said that they will find the [model village they believe is the perfect home] and settle down, in a fourth book. How passionately she makes her readers hope that they will. This is not only because her Borrowers remind us of all the dispossessed, the small and valiant and under-privileged people of this world and of all worlds. The books must be read with this in mind, but, as with Tolkien, it is an idea, not a moral. These are fairy stories, and they make their impression as much by their style as by their story.

Mary Norton is a most skilful story-teller. First, she is absolutely consistent. She is herself short-sighted, and she has a sure, sharp vision of small things. She can see *exactly* how half a pair of embroidery scissors would be used by the Borrowers, or a knob of sealing-wax or a button. . . . Secondly, this magical world (only a few inches away from our own world of chairs and teacups) is reached by a roundabout route. These are stories within stories. At first we listen to old Mrs May telling young Kate about her brother and *his* tales about the Borrowers. Old Tom Goodenough, in the gamekeeper's cottage, Mrs Driver the cook, the gardener Crampfurl who abetted her in getting rid of the 'mice dressed up', all add their mite of detail and authenticity to the story.

But if there were still any doubt of the existence of the Borrowers, it would be dispelled by their personalities. Arrietty, bright as a button, chronicler and enthusiast; Homily keeping her integrity as a housewife through danger and misfortune (when she arrives, dishevelled and dirty, at Aunt Lupy's gracious home, she refuses to be patronized: 'Poor dear Lupy', she was saying, glancing wearily about, 'What a lot of furniture. Whoever helps you with the dusting?'); and Pod, brave as a lion, common in speech, full of sensible philosophy—('There's a lot of worse food, when you care to think of it, than a piping-hot, savoury stew made of corn-fed field-mouse.'). They are as real as many characters we or our children will meet in real life, and just as real is the setting of the stories—the dirty world under the floorboards, the damp hedge with its safe corners, Spiller's kettle, the pile of sticks in the water where they hide from Mild-Eye the Gypsy, and the spread of Midland landscape, whole and real and touched with poetry. (pp. 106, 108)

Margery Fisher, "The Conversation of Witches: Humour and Character in Fairy-Tales," in her Intent Upon Reading: A Critical Appraisal of Modern Fiction for Children *(copyright © 1961 by Margery*

Fisher), Hodder & Stoughton Children's Books (formerly Brockhampton Press), 1961, pp. 97-115.*

The idea of the little people who live under the floor and behind the skirting, who 'borrow' from humans all those small objects which disappear so mysteriously and put them to strange and ingenious uses in their perpetual struggle for existence, is indeed a startlingly original and satisfying invention and has added a new and convincing bit of folk-lore to the nursery. It is as if we always knew that the Borrowers were there, but had forgotten the fact until Mary Norton reminded us of it and began to chronicle the adventures of a particular family of them. . . . (pp. 275-76)

Roger Lancelyn Green, "New Wonderlands," in his Tellers of Tales *(copyright 1946, 1953, 1956, © 1965 by Edmund Ward (Publishers) Ltd; reprinted by permission of Kaye and Ward Ltd), revised edition, Franklin Watts, Inc., 1965 (and reprinted by Kaye and Ward, Ltd, 1969), pp. 269-79.*

'Supposing,' the boy said, 'you saw a little man, about as tall as a pencil, with a blue patch in his trousers, half-way up a window curtain, carrying a doll's tea-cup—would you say it was a fairy?'

'No,' said Arrietty. 'I'd say it was my father.'

This kind of writing is good enough for anyone. . . . I prefer the first [book in the **Borrowers** series] in which the family live snug under the floorboards and are very bourgeois and calm; when they become pioneers, making do in an old boot or kettle, they are less credible. There is also rather too much chat of the Archers variety [and] too many sympathetic human beans take over. . . . But I'd warmly recommend Miss Norton to any child—from, say, seven and a half to 11¾—who has a few minutes to spare between finishing off the model railway and cooking a four-course meal. (pp. 707-08)

Penelope Mortimer, "Thoughts Concerning Children's Books," in New Statesman *(© 1966 The Statesman & Nation Publishing Co. Ltd.), Vol. 72, No. 1861, November 11, 1966, pp. 707-08.*

The fundamental idea behind ['**The Borrowers**'] books is admittedly a marvellous one. Mrs. May, a wise old lady, is led by the circumstance that things are continually disappearing without trace to tell a child the story of the Borrowers, the little underground beings who live in a world of their own under the floor-boards and who improve their standard of living with all these vanished things. Mrs. May's story becomes imperceptibly the history of these subterranean folk with a great deal of traditional fairy-tale wisdom worked into it. Figures like the little humpy man of the nursery rhyme, Rumpel-Stilt-skin, the dwarfs and hop-o'-my thumbs of fairy tales are again brought to life for the child. As a modern interpretation of ancient dwarf-lore coupled with the secrets of the underground life this has certainly helped to make these books into fascinating stories and they have enjoyed an enormous popularity among English children. A world where safety-pins become giant tools, where cotton-reels become stools, and chess-men classical statues has a glamour of its own, regardless of any profounder readings which can be made of this nether-nether land. As a modern story it has taken over elements mostly from fairy stories and especially from those of the dwarfs. It is most remarkable how the life of these people under the floor is brought into a relationship with that of human beings. There is something sinister and spooky, indeed occasionally malicious about it all. But to children reading the story it will come as a pleasure that a small boy is the only person to reach an understanding with these 'little people', as the author calls them, and to know them well. Here again we find a child who, like Peter Pan, understands the language of those who live beyond the boundaries of the visible, everyday world. (p. 80)

> *Bettina Hürlimann, "Fantasy and Reality," in her* Three Centuries of Children's Books in Europe, *edited and translated by Brian W. Alderson (translation © Oxford University Press 1967; reprinted by permission; originally published as* Europäische Kinderbücher in drei Jahrhunderten, *Atlantis Verlag, 1959), Oxford University Press, Oxford, 1967, pp. 76-92.**

It is for her stories about the Borrowers . . . that Mrs. Norton's place in literature is secure. The logical development of a completely original idea, the conviction of characterizations of both Borrowers and human beings, and the clean, beautiful strength of her style make the books as nearly perfect literary creations as have been produced for children in the English language within the past fifteen years. (p. 460)

> *Ruth Hill Viguers, "Worlds without Boundaries," in* A Critical History of Children's Literature *by Cornelia Meigs, Anne Thaxter Eaton, Elizabeth Nesbitt, and Ruth Hill Viguers, edited by Cornelia Meigs (reprinted with permission of Macmillan Publishing Company; copyright © 1953, 1969 by Macmillan Publishing Company), revised edition, Macmillan, 1969, pp. 446-83.**

[*In this essay Eleanor Cameron discusses the differences between a fairy tale in which the laws of nature are transcended and a fantasy in which magic is used in a realistic setting.*]

But, it appears, there is a kind of fairy tale other than the traditional sort, for what of Mary Norton's *Borrower* stories? *If* the borrowers have been in hiding all these years and are a normal part of our everyday world, then magic isn't *beginning* to happen and Mrs. May's brother didn't step *into* a world of magic at Firbank Hall, because it was always there. Or one might say the borrowers aren't magic at all; they simply are, as you and I are. And yet no one outside of Mrs. May's brother and Miss Menzies and Mrs. Driver and the gypsy Mild Eye, and the Platters has ever seen borrowers any more than he has seen elves or hobbits, and it must be admitted they are fantastical. Therefore the *Borrower* stories are assuredly a kind of fairy tale. . . . (pp. 11-12)

In *The Borrowers*, the fantasy of their smallness is the limit of fantasticality, which is quite a different matter from that of *Alice*. If all at once, near the end of the book, the borrowers had been allowed by Mary Norton to eat little cakes so that they could shoot up to giant size and crush and annihilate Mrs. Driver, rather than shout for joy, we would have been filled with disappointment, for the premise would have been shattered, the boundary lines changed, and all would have been spoiled by this use of a device which would so easily—and unfairly, given the discipline we understood in the beginning—solve the borrowers' dilemma, a device which actually increased Alice's. We would have put the book aside with a sharp sense of letdown, feeling, ''Oh, well, then—anything goes—is that it?'' In good fantasy, anything does *not* go. Magic is not rife, ready to be called upon at anytime by anyone who needs it. The whole delight of the tales of the fragile little borrowers is that they must constantly pit their tiny, nimble

wits, under the most discouraging circumstances, against cruel and clumsy giants, just as Molly Whuppie did and Jack the Giant Killer in the old fairy tales. They have no special drinks, no little cakes. Just their wits. (pp. 17-18)

Mary Norton has said that when she was a child she was fascinated by all things minute [see excerpt above]. She would crouch in the grass, her nose a few inches above the earth, watching by the hour the comings and goings of all those tiny creatures of the undergrowth that most people look at with indifference or with positive dislike from a distance: beetles and ants and crickets and snails going slowly or energetically about their own private business. And, having become a woman with a luminous imagination, she has given us the privilege of sharing the intense dramas of her own small beings, transformed from the beetles and ants and crickets she had watched once upon a time into a new and enchanting race of humans quite capable of becoming lost in a forest of grass blades. (p. 264)

> *Eleanor Cameron, "The Unforgettable Glimpse," and "The Dearest Freshness Deep Down Things," in her* The Green and Burning Tree: On the Writing and Enjoyment of Children's Books *(copyright © 1962, 1964, 1966, 1969 by Eleanor Cameron; reprinted by permission of Little, Brown and Company in association with The Atlantic Monthly Press), Atlantic-Little, Brown, 1969, pp. 3-47, 258-74.**

[*The Borrowers* is] the best of the series in this writer's opinion. . . . Owning nothing of their own does not prevent Borrowers from being touchy, conceited, and firm in the belief that they own the world. . . . A dwindling race, they had grown smaller and smaller, according to Boy who first told another human about them, because they were so frightened. . . . Borrowers are not human beings; they are reminders of what humans are like. These tiny creatures do not steal from human beings. They take only what is necessary for survival and a modicum of comfort. Arrietty tells Boy: ''Human beans are for Borrowers like bread's for butter.'' . . . This point, reiterated over and over, has a ring of pathos later on. In *The Borrowers Afloat* Arrietty tells her parents that the cottage to which they have emigrated will be abandoned by its human occupants. Pod is horrified, for Borrowers need humans even if they cannot be trusted. ''No food, no fire, no clothes, no heat, no water, chanted Homily, almost as if she were quoting.'' (pp. 185-86)

Mary Norton's world of fantasy is entered by a roundabout route in each of the books. Human beings are involved in the life of the Borrowers, representing both good and evil. Elderly Mrs. May tells young Kate how her brother first saw the little creatures and what he knew of their adventures. When Kate and Mrs. May later on visit a cottage the latter has inherited, Kate meets Old Tom Goodenough, the gatekeeper. He recognizes a kindred spirit in Kate and recounts other events in the lives of Pod and his family. Tom gives little Kate Arrietty's *Diary and Proverb Book*. Finally, it is Kate, having grown up and raised her own family, who decides to record the latest adventures of the Borrowers for posterity.

Like any qualified writer of fantasy Mary Norton has more than one story. . . . She . . . points out that greed can lead to unhappiness, even tragedy, and it is not confined to humans. In *The Borrowers* Homily finally but reluctantly, accepts Boy's friendship, and a new world opens up as he brings all kinds of trinkets and gadgets, accepted with gusto by Homily. Pod, the philosopher, is a little saddened by all these riches and wonders if they were really happier with these gifts. And, indeed, the wide-scale borrowing by Boy arouses Driver's suspicions and ultimately forces the little family to emigrate.

Pod and Homily insist that despite their dependence, "No good never really came to no one from any human bean." . . . Driver, Mild Eye, Mr. Platter, and others support Pod and Homily's contention. But as Arrietty would contend, Boy, Tom Goodenough, and Miss Menzies were not enemies of Borrowers even if they could not always save them from the vicissitudes of life. It is Miss Menzies, further, who, observing that the Borrowers do not trust humans despite their need of them, shrewdly comments: "They're quite right I suppose. One has only to read the paper."

The observation and delineation of character—human and Borrower—constitutes one of Mary Norton's major qualities as a writer. She is eminently aware of the complexity of personality and conveys this to her readers in a manner within the grasp of understanding by children.

Homily is fussy, distracted, and sensible by turn, she must maintain her integrity as a housewife at any cost; easily upset by misfortune she nonetheless can face up to it as well as the others.

Pod's qualities come through best in an emergency. Although a bit laconic, he knows what life is all about. He is absolutely fearless when necessary to save his family but is sensibly wary of needless risks. His practicality and courage are mainstays to his women-folk.

Arrietty is the extremely bright, dreamy child who has learned to read and keeps a diary. She represents the longing in all of us to explore a broader world. Some of Mary Norton's best writing can be found in passages describing Arrietty's responses to the world of nature when she leaves her parents to go exploring. And, throughout, Arrietty cannot share her parents' distrust of humans.

In keeping with her personality it is Spiller's gypsy qualities which first attract Arrietty to him. For a long time he is less acceptable to her parents, Homily especially. It is apparent, at first, that Spiller sees no need for "family" and the gentilities so important to Homily. Gradually, however, he quietly becomes devoted to them, and, as noted, rescues them several occasions. Ultimately, Homily is as dependent upon him as the others. Pod's quiet observations about Spiller's qualities and explanations of his attitudes towards life help, too.

Characterizations of human beings also show the author's perceptivity. Miss Norton conveys the pomposity of the lawyer, Mr. Beguid; the greed of the Platters; the gentle patience of Mr. Pott who likes Miss Menzies even though she was a "talker" like his late wife; the elegance of the bed-ridden Great Aunt Sophy, etc.

This same acute quality of observation accounts for the strength of Mary Norton's writing style. Whether portraying a character, describing the homes of the Borrowers or the Hendrearys . . . , the exact method of escape down the drain, or the construction of the balloon, Mary Norton writes with meticulous attention to detail. Ordinarily, one would expect this to make children shy away from her books as being "wordy." Indeed, her vocabulary does make demands upon upper-elementary age children, but the descriptions are of things that capture their fancy. And the prose is rich enough for reading aloud.

Rereading the books in preparation for this article one realizes that the plots after *The Borrowers* are a bit spun out, with

narration of day-to-day events, comments on personality, and detailed explanations of various operations the major content. E. Nesbit earlier recognized that children love details if based upon things of interest to them. But the plots of *Five Children and It, The Story of the Amulet,* and *The Phoenix and the Carpet* are more tightly constructed, over-all, with one engrossing episode following close upon another. In the writer's opinion, *The Borrowers Afield* and *The Borrowers Afloat* might have been combined.

Further, although her books recognize the conflict between good and evil they lack the heightened confrontation found in other writers of fantasy such as de la Mare's *Three Royal Monkeys,* J.R.R. Tolkien's *The Hobbit,* Carol Kendall's *The Gammage Cup,* C. S. Lewis's Narnia stories, and some of Lucy Boston's Green Knowe books. Admittedly, these are more demanding books for children. Mary Norton has given them a delightful family. They represent a good step to others written on a more comprehensive scale. (pp. 188-89)

> *Barbara V. Olson, "Mary Norton and the Borrowers," (copyright © 1970 by the National Council of Teachers of English; reprinted by permission of the publisher and the author), in* Elementary English, *Vol. XLIII, No. 2, February, 1970, pp. 185-89.*

My contention is that Mary Norton is one of the two or three most satisfying and rewarding writers for children of the last twenty years. She has been relatively neglected in favour, generally, of more flamboyant and ostentatious authors, but when the sifting has been done I think she will be found to be more fully satisfying than all but perhaps one or two of her contemporaries. Not only that, but it seems to me that if we are to give an account of what has happened in writing for children in the last twenty or thirty years—in terms of the relationship between literature and society—then *The Borrowers,* deceptively simple as the four books are, must be a principal point of reference. . . .

[Although] *The Borrowers* is truly a work for children, necessarily restricting itself to a fairly narrow range of experience (in fact this too is deceptive as the range is wider than that of many 'adult' novels!), it is relevant to the experience of anyone living in the 'technologico-benthamite society'.

But to begin with, at the level at which most reviewers of children's literature seem to respond—story, plot, humour, characterization—*The Borrowers* challenges comparison with the most successful work in the field. (p. 38)

In achieving [unity of tone and] complete absorption in her subject, Mary Norton has solved a major problem of the children's author as successfully, it seems to me, as anyone in the contemporary field. The problem is that insofar as the characters of the children's author are either children or fantasy figures, there will almost inevitably be a disjunction between the author's narrative style and whatever language he makes his characters speak. It is a problem of relationship, the upshot of which is usually that the characters have the air of being presented, or as it were flashed up on a screen by the author. (One way of avoiding the problem is to use the autobiographical convention. But this brings its own difficulties, and in any case is rarely feasible with a protagonist below the age of, say, Jim Hawkins.) William Mayne seems to me to have solved the problem as convincingly as anyone; the quirky indirectness of his narrative is at one with the elusive childish logic of his dialogue. And as with Mary Norton, this essential fusion indicates the completeness of the author's engagement with his characters. But in William Mayne's case this almost unique success turns into a limitation, for in the end he becomes trapped in the child's world, he is unable to transcend it, to give his work a wider frame of reference. There is a lot to be said for a writer who can identify with and realize the child's world so sympathetically, but the very finest children's literature measures itself implicitly against a more complete world thereby, in the end, rendering childhood a greater service.

One of the ways Mary Norton transcends the immediate realm of childhood or fantasy is through the conception of the Borrowers themselves. In one way the Borrowers are children—diminutive, inhabiting a mental world of their own, surrounded by a larger and often menacing environment upon which, however, they are dependent for their existence and about which they consequently have highly ambivalent feelings. Children can identify with all this, realized as it is so concretely by Mary Norton. On the other hand, the three central characters are a very ordinary and human family and Pod and Homily are adults and parents. Whereas the characters in most fantasies face many exotic varieties of danger, the Borrowers are preoccupied with essentially ordinary needs and problems—creating a home, bringing up a daughter, obtaining food, struggling for a little privacy and security.

It is Mary Norton's achievement to have transformed these central human concerns, rather than the exotic and fabulous, into one of the most exciting and compelling stories we have. It means that the drama is never mere theatre, the narrative never just suspense; the fiction is always rooted in a search for secure and healthy conditions of life.

The result of this subtle blending of childhood and adult experience is not only that the Borrowers are fascinating and original characters, but that the author can conduct a debate with her young readers as to what it means to grow up and become adult and responsible, in terms which they can understand. (There is room also for some subtle insights into the intimate relationships—the continuity—between adult and child psychology, in particular how adult and child anxieties are connected, and how this relates to invasions of privacy.) Though the conventions which provide security for the young reader against too overwhelming and direct a confrontation with adult anxieties are always present, and handled with unfailing tact by Mary Norton, the issues are nevertheless urgent, and powerfully if humorously presented. (pp. 40-1)

From time to time Mary Norton's essential preoccupations emerge explicitly through dialogue and narrative. One such preoccupation is the meaning of freedom and its relationship to security, especially in the life of a growing girl:

> She slid out from between her sleeping parents and, just as she was, with bare feet and in her vest and petticoat, she ventured out of doors. It was a glorious day, sunlit and rain-washed—the earth breathing out its scents. 'This,' Arrietty thought, 'is what I have longed for; what I have imagined; what I knew existed—what I knew we'd have!'
>
> She pushed through the grasses and soft drops fell on her benignly, warmed by the sun. Downhill a little way she went, towards the hedge, out of the jungle of higher grass, into the shallow ditch where, last night, the rain and darkness had combined to scare her. . . .
>
> She climbed the bank—leisurely and happily, feeling the warm sun through her vest, her bare

feet picking their way more delicately than clumsy human feet. . . . From this bank she could see across the field. . . . She thought of her mother's fear of open spaces. 'But I could cross this field,' she thought, 'I could go anywhere . . .' Was this perhaps what Eggletina had thought? Eggletina—Uncle Hendreary's child—who, they said, had been eaten by the cat. Did enterprise, Arrietty wondered, always meet with disaster? Was it really better, as her parents had always taught her, to live in secret darkness underneath the floor?

The subtle notation by which Mary Norton charts Arrietty's development from timorous longing for a freer life to an increasingly spontaneous independence modulates occasionally towards reflective generality, but the generality is always precisely rooted in the situation, in Arrietty's meditative reaching out towards new possibilities of life. We are not, of course, given the conventionalized adolescent self-assertion, or the unrealities of children 'making out' on their own which are, today, two of the staples of fiction for and about children; what we have is an honest and delicately observed imaginative testing of experience, within the security and continuity of the family, which leads to growth. Consider, in the passage above, how Arrietty's mind opens responsively to the life around her (the parts of this passage omitted in the quotation give this effect in sensuous detail); how the fears of the night before are implicitly placed; how she tests her own feelings against those of her mother, and against the ominous story of Eggletina which hangs ambiguously over the earlier part of the whole series.

In the last sentence in the quotation the subtly interrelated issues of growth, security and freedom modulate into an even more urgent question—what sort of a life do I want to grow up into, what are the possibilities and limitations? It is a very remarkable achievement by Mary Norton to have embodied these questions so honestly, delicately and responsibly in a fiction that can be readily understood by an eleven year old. (pp. 43-4)

But Pod too develops through the four books, and after all their scrapes, indignities, false solutions to the problem of safety and comfort, he can say:

> 'No Homily, it isn't taps and switches that count. Nor dressers and eiderdowns neither. You can pay too high for a bit of soft living, as we found out that time with Lupy. It's making your own way that counts and being easy in your mind, and I wouldn't never be easy here. . . .'

Pod's conclusion does not encompass the whole communication of the books. Though he develops more than the class-bound and anxious Homily, the essential limitations of his character, increasingly strong and purposeful as it becomes, are illuminated by contrast with Arrietty's spontaneity. Another way of putting it is to say that the freely-creative imagination is a strongly felt value in the whole work, and that this value 'places' Pod's overly domestic and restricted outlook. But the matter is more complicated than that, for Pod is a craftsman. His ability to transmute bits and bobs of human left-overs into machines for living is a creative activity, for all its utilitarian practicality. It seems to me, in fact, that to look closely at the Borrowers' craftsmanship is to see one of the most original things that has been done in children's literature for very many years. The term 'fantasy' is misleading when applied to these novels. It usually connotes the fabulous, magical, supernatural, something external to the characters. Apart from the fact of the Borrowers themselves, there is no such element in their story. Fantasy as an atmosphere or a world with its own rules has been translated back into the creative imagination by which we in fact all live. The Borrowers live by their ability to conceive new possibilities for objects, things, places—*to transform their own environment*. Thus the fantasy is not a more or less arbitrarily conceived world in which the characters are placed, but it becomes in *The Borrowers* a continual process of living, a creative act on the part of central characters themselves. In this way fantasy or creative imagination is seen as the essential human faculty for making or invention. Imagination has been rehabilitated: fantasy, with its inevitable connotations of the unreal, becomes the means by which human beings create the world they live in.

Though never explicit as a theme, as freedom, security and the ethics of 'borrowing' occasionally are, creativity is powerfully embodied in the characters and the drama. It is presented with different emphases through Spiller, Pod, Miss Menzies, Mr Pott, and the Platters; it is also present in Mary Norton's style:

> As villas fell vacant and funerals became scarcer, Mr Platter (who is an undertaker) had time on his hands. He had never liked spare time. In order to get rid of it he took up gardening. All Mr Platter's flowers were kept like captives—firmly tied to stakes: the slightest sway or wriggle was swiftly punished—a lop here or a cut there. Very soon the plants gave in—uncomplaining as guardsmen they would stand to attention in rows. . . .

Metaphor and simile are fairly sparse in *The Borrowers*, but there is a sustained metaphorical energy in the transformations of objects and environments made by the Borrowers themselves.

The irony in this passage is that Mr Platter's attempt to manipulate and exploit life has its corollary in the increasing emptiness of significance in his own life, so that *time* becomes the dominant value. It serves to show that by a kind of literary tact, Mary Norton uses the insights of, and draws strength from, the major tradition in English literature, re-creating her own fresh little version of the theme in a delicate and subtle miniature. (pp. 45-6)

Mr Pott is obviously the antithesis of the Platters. He is not a commercial exploiter, but a craftsman, with the craftsman's painstaking responsibility to his skill. He is also significantly like Pod, for skill and inventiveness is in a very important sense what each of them lives by. But for Mr Pott his creativity has an unconsciously healing function. No longer able to work in the railway, which has been his whole life, because of an accident which was the result of an attempt to save the life of a badger, his model-making enables him still to relate to what he was before the accident, and in exercising his craft and imagination he still finds and creates meaning and order in his life.

Miss Menzies embodies another aspect of this affirmation and analytic illustration of the uses of imagination:

> Miss Menzies was very useful to Pott, she designed Christmas cards for a living, wrote children's books and her hobbies were wood-carving, handweaving and barbola waxwork.

She has also been the victim of an unhappy love affair and has an intense capacity for sympathetic identification with little creatures like the Borrowers. The relationship between the frustrated love and the intensely sympathetic imagination ('sublimation') is conveyed with characteristic tact and delicacy, in such a way that the young reader can grasp the essentials intuitively. Miss Menzies' imaginative sympathy contrasts with Mr Pott's stolid lack of perception of others—they are two versions of the 'creative' life, illuminating each other's limitations. In addition, startlingly enough, Mary Norton seems to be placing the creativity of the children's author within the context of the book.

Also, there is Spiller. . . . (pp. 48-9)

Spiller's stunted growth is shown clearly enough against Arrietty's untrammelled spontaneity; but the comparison is not quite so simple, for in a dangerous and lonely world Spiller's dogged survival is also a triumph of courage and imagination. Here also is another example of the author's subtle art of blending—on the one hand Spiller is shy and unimaginative, an embarrassed and engaging little boy; on the other the romantic hero, living a wandering, 'natural' life, rescuing the Borrowers at exciting moments and destined to marry the heroine.

No sooner have the Borrowers escaped (sometimes with Spiller's help) from one danger than they fall into another. The periods of tension and crises are balanced by times of recuperation and renewal, when the family, touchingly, asserts itself as a living thing and they attempt to settle down to a normal pattern of family life. But not for long! It is in her treatment of the family as a group that Mary Norton shows her sensitivity to the situation of the child in contemporary society. Bearing in mind that the first book of the series came out in 1952, the note struck in these passages is startling. Here the note is first struck:

> 'The child is right,' (Homily) announced firmly. Arrietty's eyes grew big. 'Oh, no' she began. It shocked her to be right. Parents were right, not children. Children could say anything, Arrietty knew, and enjoy saying it—knowing always they were safe and wrong.

(p. 50)

We have heard all about the dissolution of the family and of traditional codes and values, and of how the young are now dictating to their elders the style of life appropriate to the technological society. These tensions are present . . . throughout *The Borrowers*. Unlikely as it may seem at first sight, a number of well-known concomitants of the symptoms already mentioned are equally firmly delineated in this fantasy—above all there is the Borrowers' anxiety which, we may easily infer, is the product not only of highly objective danger, but of a rootless and insecure way of life; the dissolution of the class structure (see especially the first volume for some neat and economical social history in 'borrower' terms!); an existence in which even this last strategy of withdrawal threatens failure; in short, the pains of social mobility in a technological society! As Pod remarks, answering Arrietty's question about danger . . . : 'It's everywhere. . . . Before and Behind, Above and Below.'

It is clearly more than an awareness of objective dangers: anxiety is a pervasive aspect of their consciousness. Of course, Arrietty gradually grows beyond this to psychological freedom, and it is in the character of Homily by contrast, that we are shown the dangers of petulance and regression. Her anxiety is registered with very considerable psychological accuracy. . . .

[She retreats], which everyone has noticed at times of stress, into obsessively repeated everyday action ('opening drawers and shutting them'), and the attempt to shut out anxiety by reasserting the known and everyday world—curling her hair. But how the spilled out contents of the drawers suggest the unrelated disorder of Homily's emotions! At times the withdrawal becomes more pathological:

> Arrietty felt very bruised and shaken: she glanced at her mother, who lay back limply, in her long white nightgown, her eyes still doggedly closed, and knew that, for the present, Homily had given up.

And of course this morbid reaction acts as a foil for Arrietty's outgoing spontaneity, her delightful capacity for a full and courageous response to life. . . . (pp. 51-2)

Class and the use of defensive roles come together in this delightful scene:

> None of their clothes had been washed for weeks, nor, for some days, had their hands and faces. Pod's trousers had a tear in one knee and Homily's hair hung down in snakes. And here was Aunt Lupy, plump and polite, begging Homily please to take off her things in the kind of voice Arrietty imagined usually reserved for feather boas, opera cloaks, and freshly cleaned white kid gloves.
>
> But Homily, who back at home had so dreaded being 'caught out' in a soiled apron, knew one worth of that. She had, Pod and Arrietty noticed with pride, adopted her woman-tried-beyond-endurance role backed up by one called yes-I've-suffered-but-don't-let's-speak-of-it-now; she had invented a new smile, wan but brave, and had—in the same good cause—plucked the two last hairpins out of her dust-filled hair. 'Poor dear Lupy,' she was saying, glancing wearily about, 'what a lot of furniture! Whoever helps you with the dusting?' And swaying a little, she sank on a chair.
>
> They rushed to support her, as she hoped they might.

(Actually, in the phrase 'adopted her . . . role' I think that for one brief and rare moment Mary Norton takes her eye off the child reader: but how rare this is, considering the complexity of the material.)

Though the tone is light enough, we can see here the essentially aggressive nature of the two women's strategies. And notice how in this very trying situation Pod and Arrietty line up behind Homily—Mary Norton is a realist!

However Homily is capable of generous recognitions:

> 'This boy,' went on Homily in ringing tones, 'this—well, anyway, there he stands!' and she threw an arm out towards Spiller. . . .
>
> 'He saved her life,' went on Homily, throaty with gratitude, 'at the expense of his own!'
>
> 'Not expense,' Pod pointed out. . . . 'I mean he's here, isn't he?'

But even this, of course, is a dramatization, essentially an avoidance of full response, for fear of the other recognitions which such a response entails. Later she can say: 'He's not our kind really . . . even if he did save our lives.' The inconsistency goes with the unpredictable outbursts of temper and panic, all clearly enough springing from an intense and unresolved anxiety.

Through the character of Homily Mary Norton registers some of the tensions of life in a mobile and technological society, with all its uncertainties and loss of traditional bearings; and with great economy she shows what unproductive strategies it can generate. But what finally seems to me so strong in *The Borrowers* is this: though Mary Norton sees and registers firmly all the disorientations and dissolutions, she does not give us any of the fashionable sentimental solutions. We are not, in the end, invited into a conspiracy to 'knock' Homily, still less Pod; to demolish the image of parenthood altogether because it has become tarnished and because we are, children and adults, frustrated at this. Nor are we invited to imagine that the child Arrietty can make her own way, defiantly perhaps, to a free and spontaneous life. Mary Norton holds the circle; affirms, amidst all the difficulties, the continuity of life. For all the amazing adventures, Arrietty experiences a steady rhythm of family life, renewing itself after each crisis; and it is these moments of happy certainty of love and security, that are the conditions of her growth to spontaneity and freedom. (pp. 53-5)

Nigel Hand, "Mary Norton and 'The Borrowers'," in Children's literature in education *(© 1972 Agathon Press, Inc.; reprinted by permission of the publisher), No. 7 (March), 1972, pp. 38-55 [the excerpts of the author's works included here were taken from* The Borrowers Afield *(© copyright, 1955, by Mary Norton; reprinted by permission of Harcourt Brace Jovanovich, Inc.), Harcourt Brace Jovanovich, 1955;* The Borrowers Aloft *(© 1961 by Mary Norton; reprinted by permission of Harcourt Brace Jovanovich, Inc.), Harcourt Brace Jovanovich, 1961;* The Borrowers *(copyright, 1953, by Mary Norton; reprinted by permission of Harcourt Brace Jovanovich, Inc.), Harcourt Brace Jovanovich, 1953].*

[In *The Magic Bedknob*] Mary Norton introduced a witch of modest attainments into English village society; much of the fun of this book—which is very much more than a comic novel—comes from this basic incongruity. Miss Price could pass for a member of the Women's Institute—indeed she is ideal for the office of Honorary Secretary although she lacks the indefinable quality which would make her a good President—but she is a witch. (p. 107)

Barbara Sleigh's witch [in *Carbonel*] is a malicious creature. Even in retirement, when she runs a sweet-shop, she cannot refrain from giving her customers stomach-ache. Miss Price is a witch of quite another school. In Mary Norton's expert hands Miss Price is wonderfully real and complex. She rides into *The Magic Bedknob* . . . on a high bicycle, visiting the sick and teaching the piano. 'In all the village there was none so ladylike as Miss Price'. . . . Miss Price is a learner-witch. What she finds most difficult is wickedness, although she has her moments when the children notice how very long and yellow her teeth are. The adventures which follow when she gives the children the magical charge which makes their bed into a flying-machine are in the Nesbit manner, partly funny, partly terrifying. (pp. 115-16)

Mary Norton, as she proved conclusively a little later with her books of the Borrowers, is a master of detail. Not for her a half-imagined context. The two stories about Miss Price are exquisitely written, and the portrayal of character is done with tenderness and understanding, but what puts these books in a class apart is the actuality. In *The Magic Bedknob* Miss Price and the children go by flying bed on a visit to an uninhabited South Sea island. Unfortunately it *is* inhabited—by cannibals. In her deepest distress, with a savage's grip upon her, Carey sobs 'People should be careful what they write in encyclopaedias.' Miss Price and the local witch-doctor engage in a contest of skills. Miss Price wins a struggle to control the broomstick, but the witch-doctor thinks he can trump this ace with a knife. Miss Price then turns him into a frog. Mary Norton gives an eye-witness account of how she does it. (p. 116)

There is no room for two [Lucy] Bostons in children's literature; her only peer in the creation of little worlds is Mary Norton whose world is smaller still and, though not less perilous, is threatened not by pure evil but by natural hazard and foolish malice.

Originality is not in itself necessarily an important element in children's books. Most of the basic themes and forms had been devised by the end of the first decade of this century, and writers have, in general, been content to exercise their originality within an existing framework. Only rarely is a writer visited by an entirely new idea. There is nothing new in little people; folk-tales are full of them and Lilliput has appeared in literature many times since Gulliver first landed on its shores. But the idea of a miniature society living alongside and on our own came to Mary Norton out of the blue—or, as she says, out of her childhood memories of a myopic world seen at very close range.

'''There's rules, my lass, and you got to learn''', says Pod, and what makes *The Borrowers* . . . outstanding among fantasies is that Mary Norton knows her own rules and abides by them. The harshness in parts of the story, which distressed some readers, comes inevitably from this recognition that an author is responsible for his creation and cannot take short cuts or easy ways out. The Borrowers, as the boy who discovers them sees prophetically, are doomed. (p. 140)

Disaster comes because they break the rules. On her first borrowing expedition Arrietty is 'seen' by a small boy who befriends the tiny people and, during a brief golden age, supplies them with all their needs and more. It is magnificent, but it is not borrowing. Pride of possession goes to all their heads, and they overreach themselves. The Borrowers are 'seen' not by kindly boys or drunken old ladies but by the stupidly malicious housekeeper. The exquisite life that they have built up with so much labour is destroyed. And the Borrowers . . .? In a brilliant coda Mary Norton leaves their fate in doubt.

Unfortunately the book was so vastly successful that the writer had to go on with a string of sequels, following the escaping Borrowers into new out-door adventures. There are excellent inventions in these books, and no one would grudge Arrietty's hard-won bliss with the virile and resourceful Spiller, but the original book, with its finely conceived introduction and conclusion, is perfect and needs no appendages. There is no magic in *The Borrowers*. Once the basic thesis is accepted, the book follows its self-imposed rules logically and with no concessions to sentimentality. It may not be strictly a fantasy at all; it certainly possesses in a high degree all the essentials—concept, development, character, environment, social criticism—of the novel. (p. 141)

Marcus Crouch, "Laughter" and "Magic Casements," in his The Nesbit Tradition: The Children's Novel in England 1945-1970 (© Marcus Crouch 1972), Ernest Benn, 1972, pp. 101-11, 112-41.*

[Mary Norton's *The Borrowers* is] a brilliant feat of imagination. Her conception of the little people who live under the

floorboards on odds and ends borrowed from humans, is not only almost perfectly conceived to delight the mind of a small child, but it has the inspired logic of the best fantasies, for it seems to fit so well with the thoughts that even adults have about the mysterious way in which small things disappear. (p. 117)

Mary Norton wrote three other books about her family of Borrowers, Pod, Homily and Arrietty: *The Borrowers Afield, The Borrowers Afloat* and *The Borrowers Aloft* and, surprisingly, though the original book remains the best, she contrived to sustain the reality, humour and brilliant inventiveness of her story to the end. Of all the contemporary fantasies for younger children *The Borrowers* is probably the most successful—and enjoyable. (p. 118)

Frank Eyre, "Fiction for Children," in his British Children's Books in the Twentieth Century (copyright © 1971 by Frank Eyre; reprinted by permission of the publishers, E. P. Dutton, Inc.; in Canada by Penguin Books Ltd.), Longman Books, 1971 (and reprinted by Dutton, 1973), pp. 76-156.*

Mary Norton's five books about the Borrowers almost convince you that the tiny people who live in the small spaces under the floor and behind the wall really do exist. They're "as like to humans as makes no matter," says one adult as he describes them to a curious child in *The Borrowers Afield*. (pp. 203-04)

Paralleling the travail of the Borrowers is an emerging theme of human belief and disbelief in their existence. . . . Human characters who believe in the Borrowers are presented as empathic to all nonhuman, fanciful creatures, while the nonbelievers are the practical, pragmatic skeptics in our midst. Mrs. Driver, the mean housekeeper who actually sees the Borrowers, denies their existence. Her orderly world, designed to be controlled for her own purposes, simply won't permit that belief. The fantasy has a serious core within its literary device for credibility: empathy includes reaching out to the unknown and caring about its existence.

In these stories there is a touching alliance between the young and the elderly. Children learn of the Clock family's existence through the tipsy, bedridden Great-Aunt Sophy, a "some kind of relation" oldster named Mrs. May, senile Old Tom, one-legged Mr. Pott, and others like them. Perhaps the implication is that only the old and the young have the time and the will to "see." (pp. 204-05)

Sam Leaton Sebesta and William J. Iverson, "Fanciful Fiction," in their Literature for Thursday's Child (© 1975, Science Research Associates, Inc.; reprinted by permission of the publisher), Science Research Associates, 1975, pp. 177-214.*

THE MAGIC BED-KNOB; OR, HOW TO BECOME A WITCH IN TEN EASY LESSONS (1943)

Mary Poppins would have known immediately what Miss Price was up to—and would have approved, we feel sure. . . .

No one can tell for certain when a classic is born—but this story has all the makings of one. There is a lovely, glancing humor in the characterization of Miss Price—a kind of Lolly Willowes for children—and of Paul, as real a little boy as was ever bullied by older brother and sister. Real, too, seems the magic for its all-too-brief duration. . . . So exactly right is the story that one almost fears to ask for a sequel. . . .

Ellen Lewis Buell, in a review of "The Magic Bed-Knob; or, How to Become a Witch in Ten Easy Lessons," in The New York Times Book Review (© *1944 by The New York Times Company; reprinted by permission), March 12, 1944, p. 6.*

"Carey was about your age, Charles a little younger, and Paul was only six," begins this convincing tale of how to be a witch in ten easy lessons. . . . Funny, crisp, unexpected, keeping as strictly as E. Nesbit's stories to the good old laws of magic, the book affords refreshing laughter not only at first sight but on readings often repeated.

May L. Becker, in a review of "The Magic Bed-Knob," in New York Herald Tribune Weekly Book Review (© *I.H.T. Corporation; reprinted by permission), June 4, 1944, p. 9.*

Somewhat in the Mary Poppins tradition of wry, British, whimsical humor, but a wonderful tale in its own right, is this story of the eccentric Miss Price, who is learning how to be a witch. . . . The story is what matters here. . . .

A review of "The Magic Bed-Knob; or, How to Become a Witch in Ten Easy Lessons," in The New Yorker (© *1944 by The New Yorker Magazine, Inc.), Vol. XX, No. 21, July 8, 1944, p. 56.*

THE BORROWERS (1952)

I missed Mary Norton's earlier books so this came as a delightful surprise—delightful up to the last two chapters. The life of tiny Tom Thumb-ish creatures under the floor boards, incompletely reflecting our own daily life, is imagined with humour and exquisite inventiveness. How children will love it, specially those who are still allowed to be a little solitary, to think their own thoughts, and imagine their own play! It describes a world which would have delighted Beatrix Potter in her lonely nursery days when she too watched a mouse hole in the wainscot. Indeed, it is a delicious piece of fantasy, light and perfect (except for the ending) as a soap bubble safely blown and floating in the air before our eyes in all its perfection of iridescent colour and form. Alas that the author could not resist the destructive child's trick of thrusting a finger into that beauty and destroying it. She has made a cruel ending, one which will come as a shock to children made vulnerable by the spell of the rest and by their own imaginative response to it. She brings the miniature world to an end at the hands of a spiteful woman, and the horror of the tearing up of floor boards, the vicious smashing of the treasures in the tiny rooms, the introduction of the rat catcher, the apparatus to smoke the little creatures out, is unbearable after the early loveliness. I wish more than I can say that the last chapters could have been left out. (pp. 211-12)

A review of "The Borrowers," in The Junior Bookshelf, *Vol. 16, No. 4, November, 1952, pp. 211-12.*

The Victorian house, which engendered so many Victorian novels, is the source of *The Borrowers*—a remarkable book; really, a brilliant piece of invention. Perhaps a still better story is lost after the opening pages, when an old lady sits in her firelit room, and tells her strange tale to the child. It is an enchanting beginning. . . .

These little creatures, only to be found now in old houses deep in the country where their borrowing would not be disturbed, created from odds and ends a parallel life to that of the humans

who supplied them. The queer analogy of the two homes, the meeting of human and Borrower's child, the wit of the detail, and of the conclusion itself—all this leaves a disturbing impression that is not to be quickly dispelled.

Naomi Lewis, "The Wonderful Nursemaid," in The New Statesman & Nation (© *1952 The Statesman & Nation Publishing Co. Ltd.), Vol. XLIV, No. 1135, December 6, 1952, pp. 692, 694.**

[It] seems to me that a gold star for the most unusual juvenile should go to *The Borrowers*. . . . In the first place the idea is distinctive. . . .

The book is a specialized sort of thing in style as well as in theme. While some children might be delighted by it, others might think it silly. In other words, it has an *Alice in Wonderland* quality that puts it in a class by itself.

Margaret Ford Kieran, in a review of "The Borrowers," in The Atlantic Monthly (copyright © *1953, by The Atlantic Monthly Company, Boston, Mass.; reprinted with permission), Vol. 192, No. 6, December, 1953, p. 98.*

In *The Borrowers*, the Carnegie Medal recognized that rarest of all books, one which is firmly in its tradition and at the same time highly original in theme and treatment. The minute world of the Borrowers was conceived in exquisite detail and worked out in terms of dispassionate naturalism. Of all the winners of the Carnegie Medal, it is the one book of unquestioned, timeless genius. (pp. 184-85)

Marcus Crouch, "Salute to Children's Literature and Its Creators: 21st Birthday for Carnegie Medal," in Top of the News (reprinted by permission of the American Library Association), Vol. 14, No. 4, 1958 (and reprinted in Readings about Children's Literature, edited by Evelyn Rose Robinson, David McKay Co. Inc., 1966, pp. 183-87).*

As British as tea for breakfast, but with action, suspense, and characters of universal appeal, *The Borrowers* . . . was immediately popular in the United States as well as in Great Britain. (p. 224)

This book can give children some ideas about the characteristics of fantasy. Most important, it can generate strong emotional response. Children are intrigued with the lives of the tiny people; they share the Borrowers' fear of discovery and they enjoy the clever uses the Borrowers have for items we "lose." The stories are so intriguing that more than one child has remarked that it almost seems possible there could be little people behind the walls. Children can also respond to literary aspects of the story. They begin to appreciate the use of point of view to create an effect and it is rather a surprise when they realize that the "human beans" described by the tiny Borrowers in this story are very much like themselves. With some guidance, children can also see that the author has used manipulation of characters in a clever way to create this fantasy. For in this story it is the characters who make it a fantasy. They are not talking animals as in Russell Hoban's *A Bargain for Frances*, nor are they people from another planet. They are tiny people who look and talk and feel just like us. The setting is realistic; only the characters have been manipulated to produce the fantasy. (pp. 554-55)

Zena Sutherland, Dianne L. Monson, and May Hill Arbuthnot, "Modern Fantasy" and "Introducing Literature to Children," in their Children & Books (copyright © 1981, 1977, 1972, 1964, 1957, 1947 by Scott, Foresman and Company; reprinted by permission), sixth edition, Scott, Foresman, 1981, pp. 213-54, 543-63.*

THE BORROWERS AFIELD (1955)

Some favourite childhood characters bring their own worlds with them, complete worlds of the imagination only a mirror's depth, it seems, from the real. The Borrowers and Worzel Gummidge are examples of these. In *The Borrowers Afield* . . . Miss Norton continues the saga of Pod, Homily and Arrietty, begun, and so frighteningly broken off at the end of the first volume when they are hounded from their home under the floorboards of the big house. This new instalment covers their trek across country to a new home in the wall of an old cottage. Their adventures in the open, living for a time in an old boot in a ditch, surviving the new dangers of the wild, are more enthralling than ever. To write of a Thumbelina world of people less high than dandelions and not become fussy and over-detailed needs a most delicate touch. Miss Norton has it. She is no Gulliver peering clumsily down at Lilliputians between her feet. She writes from a Borrower's angle. Irresistible it is to read how they boiled their water over a candle flame in the lid of an aspirin bottle, how they caught huge cobnuts in their aprons and dragged heavily home a few ears of wheat; how they woke to see the world powdered with the first frost as though every trunklike grassblade were weighted down with sugar grains.

Borrowers are not only interesting because they are small; as characters, as themselves, they are delightful. Pod is still the hardworking, responsible father, Homily is still the struggling housewife even in the boot, still thin and anxious and expecting the worst, and Arrietty, their daughter, is a miniature of all youthful excitement as she daringly explores the new wide world that she has always longed to see. For just long enough we are given a mouse-eye view of field and hedgerow where a trickle in a ditch is a river and a bumble bee is the size of a turkey.

The fact that the Borrowers' experiences are told looking backwards through the mind of an old man who remembers, and then through a listening child, adds depth and strangeness to Miss Norton's telling. Her new book is that rare thing, an entirely successful sequel.

> *"Round the Corner," in* The Times Literary Supplement *(© Times Newspapers Ltd. (London) 1955; reproduced from* The Times Literary Supplement *by permission), No. 2801, November 4, 1955, p. iii.**

Sound the trumpets! It is something of a miracle to find the quality of a first book so well sustained in its sequel. The Borrowers are back to continue their adventures and their miniature view of the world in a story as completely delightful and satisfying as the first one. . . .

Either book about the Borrowers is a story complete in itself, but no family should deprive itself of the pleasure of reading both aloud. Children accept the premise of the Borrowers' existence with unquestioning delight and adults become so fascinated in the detailed description of the problems encountered by these six-inch people living in an over-sized world that they, too, slip into the same faith unconsciously. After only a few paragraphs they will recognize in these books the same rare, indescribable quality that made "Alice in Wonderland" and "The Wind in the Willows" the great inheritance of all childhood.

> *Anne Izard, in a review of "The Borrowers Afield," in* New York Herald Tribune Book Review *(© I.H.T. Corporation; reprinted by permission), November 13, 1955, p. 5.*

Sequels are usually tricky affairs and readers who found Mary Norton's **"The Borrowers"** just about perfect may approach this one with the nervous premonition that it couldn't possibly be as good. It is, though and in some ways even better. . . .

She takes the reader down to the dimension of the borrowers and makes him feel at home there. The plot is less diffuse than in the first story and . . . one hardly sees how this book could be better.

> *Jane Cobb, in a review of "The Borrowers Afield," in* The New York Times Book Review *(© 1955 by The New York Times Company; reprinted by permission), November 13, 1955, p. 30.*

The book, like its predecessor, is a lovely thing, with the logic and exactness of true fantasy; the Borrowers are fascinating not just because they are tiny creatures in a large world, but because they are people and personalities. However, I do worry about Tom. An independent old man and friend of Borrowers would hate an almshouse, and we're never told what becomes of him. Perhaps another book will settle this; the children would welcome it.

> *Heloise P. Mailloux, in a review of "The Borrowers Afield," in* The Horn Book Magazine *(copyrighted, 1955, by The Horn Book, Inc., Boston), Vol. XXXI, No. 6, December, 1955, p. 455.*

The close of *The Borrowers* suggested that Pod, Homily and Arrietty found very snug quarters indeed after escaping from the cook's assault on their home under the kitchen floor, a fact ignored by many reviewers in their horror at the assault. This horror was at once a tribute to Mary Norton's ability to make the reader accept her Borrowers as real beings, and an odd reflection on the times, as violence attractively displayed is usually accepted with little comment, particularly if it is shown taking place in the past when men were men and only women cringed at the sight of blood and destruction. But destruction, looting and pillaging are ugly things, and it is no small part of *The Borrowers'* merit that their ugliness is revealed, before the countryside residence is brought in to round off the story happily. (p. 335)

Those shocked by their narrow escape in the kitchen may object to their near-starvation and frightening encounter with the gipsy Mild Eye, but children are made of tougher stuff and those who may object may skip these episodes in later re-readings. For the book is one to be re-read often, to relish again Arrietty's delight in the outdoor world, enjoyed for the first time and from so near the ground, and Homily's characteristic reaction to the trials and new experiences (and to Aunt Lupy) and Pod's inventions and quiet fortitude, the mysterious Spiller, and the author's uncanny knowledge of just what might be encountered by such miniature individuals.

This is real creation, and it is achieved with writing of high quality. The Borrowers are not merely miniature humans but a separate order, entirely credible, and their story contains more drama, humour and imagination than many novels of human activities, and sends the reader off to look at his own world with freshened appreciation. (pp. 335-36)

A review of "The Borrowers Afield," in The Junior Bookshelf, *Vol. 19, No. 6, December, 1955, pp. 335-36.*

BED-KNOB AND BROOMSTICK   (1957; British edition as *Bedknob and Broomstick*)

The *Magic Bed-Knob* enchanted a few—very few—readers with its story and depressed us with its format. . . . The text is its own best advocate, as it regales the reader with entertaining adventures for Carey, Charles and Paul when they spend an enchanted summer with an old aunt in Bedfordshire, and encounter prim-Miss Price in her garden. . . . In the capricious days that follow, the children become part of the experiment with the acquisition of a magic bed-knob, and are allowed to participate in an off-beat romance between Witch Price and Necromancer Emelius. Here's enchantment realistically experienced, whimsy that has elements of sophistication. . . . A story too good to miss.

A review of "Bed-Knob and Broomstick," in Virginia Kirkus' Service, *Vol. XXV, No. 17, September 1, 1957, p. 638.*

The old war-time edition (in two columns of very small print) of **"The Magic Bed-knob, or How to Become a Witch in Ten Easy Lessons,"** looking a bit bedraggled because it has been read aloud so many times, has a place on our shelf of favorite fantasies with Alice, The Wind in the Willows, Nils, The Three Mulla Mulgars, Mary Poppins, The Enchanted Castle, Pooh, The Hobbit, Mistress Masham's Repose, The Wind on the Moon, Stuart Little, the Children of Green Knowe and Mary Norton's later books about the Borrowers. It is splendidly real, this story of the Wilson children and Miss Price. . . .

There is an extra joy to the book now. The sequel, **"Bonfires and Broomsticks,"** is bound with it. This story is new to us and most satisfactory. The children find the magic bed-knob, visit Miss Price for a summer holiday and experiment with visiting the past in a very convincing manner. Miss Price is just as conscientious and fussy, the children as natural and sensible and the inventions as logical and interesting as before. The ending is especially clever and satisfying. This is a treasure every one will want, the tens on to read to themselves, and all families as a read-aloud story for younger children.

Margaret Sherwood Libby, in a review of "Bed-Knob and Broomstick," in New York Herald Tribune Book Review (© *I.H.T. Corporation; reprinted by permission), October 20, 1957, p. 10.*

[*Bedknob and Broomstick* is a story instinct with the magic of literary craftsmanship.] Miss Norton has indeed, "an infinite capacity for taking pains" over detail—she seems never at a loss for just the right touch to make a room, a landscape or a conversation real. With this essentially poetic gift she imparts truth and solidity to the most improbable situations. That three more or less ordinary children should discover an elderly piano-teaching spinster called Miss Price in the act of practising witchcraft is thus the most natural thing in the world. Equally reasonable are the impossible adventures which follow. This matter-of-factness in fantasy is something which Miss Norton might have caught from Swift or Defoe, who were never at a loss for circumstantial corroboration for the most thumping lie. This faculty is no mere power of invention: it springs from a loving instinct for treasuring the very observations, moods and feelings of childhood itself, and re-creating them in the most

artlessly studied language imaginable. Humour and intelligence light up this fantasy like spring sunshine.

"The Taste for Magic," in The Times Literary Supplement (© *Times Newspapers Ltd. (London) 1957; reproduced from* The Times Literary Supplement *by permission), No. 2907, November 15, 1957, p. iii.**

As one reads of [the children's] bed landing them on a South Sea island and later back into seventeenth-century London, it becomes clear that the book will be enjoyed by the child who likes the Eager and the Nesbit combinations of magic and reality. The make-believe has humor and originality in its inventions, conversations, and unexpected twists of plot; the child characters are convincing in their relationships.

Virginia Haviland, in a review of "Bed-Knob and Broomstick," in The Horn Book Magazine (*copyright, 1957, by The Horn Book, Inc., Boston), Vol. XXXIII, No. 6, December, 1957, p. 489.*

THE BORROWERS AFLOAT   (1959)

By now, the borrowers . . . are well established in the world of fantasy. . . . Mary Norton, in her earlier books, masterfully created a miniature world which is sustained in this latest sequel. Every aspect of it is sharply defined, and the borrowers continue to contain, within their diminutive forms, that concentrated essence of personality which makes them, if less than life size, somewhat more than human.

A review of "The Borrowers Afloat," in Virginia Kirkus' Service, *Vol. XXVI, No. 24, December 15, 1958, p. 906.*

This is the third book about the borrowers and it is a pleasure to report that it is just as good as the earlier ones. . . . Once a reader has been introduced to [the borrowers] they become as much a part of his literary life as Mary Poppins or Rat and Mole.

It is not mere extravagance that has prompted comparisons of these books with "The Wind in the Willows" and "Alice in Wonderland," for, like the great writers of fantasy, Mary Norton is truly original (no important fantasy is ever like anyone else's) and persuasive. We are sure this is the way these people actually lived—in every detail. . . .

And, also like the great makers of fantasy, Mrs. Norton writes on two levels. Even while we are fascinated by the details of this miniature life and by the borrowers' ingenuity, we are amused by their frailties or deeply moved by their courage. In the new book when Pod, Homily and Arrietty are once more uprooted, they are truly philosophic—they have learned to let go and to begin again. As they journey down a drain, live briefly in a teakettle beside a river, are swept away in a flood and are hunted by their old enemy, Mild Eye the gypsy, each meets the ever-recurring dangers with his or her own brand of fortitude. And, in the end, as they float serenely—in a wooden knife-box—toward a new haven, we are sure that they'll make it all right. Obviously there will be another story about that new home and that's as it should be.

Ellen Lewis Buell, in a review of "The Borrowers Afloat," in The New York Times Book Review (© *1959 by The New York Times Company; reprinted by permission), February 22, 1959, p. 30.*

When Mary Norton wrote **The Borrowers** she created and set in motion a complete small world. The result is that no story about the "borrowers" can come to an actual end, and each of the books following the first has been no mere "sequel." Each is, rather, an opportunity to step again into that world of Mrs. Norton's creation, to identify with appealing characters, experience unique adventures, meet new problems with philosophy and fortitude, and in addition, to enjoy fresh aspects of living and some of the best writing that has appeared in recent years for "human beans" of any age. . . . I expect that for generations to come children will be reading about the "borrowers," perhaps in a thick volume containing many adventures, for this book belongs as much with the other two as *Through the Looking Glass* belongs with *Alice*.

> *Ruth Hill Viguers, in a review of "The Borrowers Afloat," in* The Horn Book Magazine *(copyright, 1959, by The Horn Book, Inc., Boston), Vol. XXXV, No. 2, April, 1959, p. 132.*

The charmed pen of Mary Norton has created further adventures of Pod, Homily, and Arrietty, that miniature family which "borrows" its livelihood from the world of humans. . . . The fresh and harrowing adventures which assail them as they travel down the river in a leaky teakettle in hopes of reaching Little Fordham will entrance all readers.

The author's ability to depict the miniature world of the Borrowers in such realistic detail is amazing, for somehow she never loses her perspective on this world-within-a-world. The only things that are never undersized are the crises that beset the Borrowers and their ability to meet them all in man-sized fashion.

> *Alice Brooks McGuire, in a review of "The Borrowers Afloat," in* Saturday Review *(© 1959 Saturday Review Magazine Co.; reprinted by permission), Vol. XLII, No. 19, May 9, 1959, p. 44.*

Thousands who have read with delight of Pod, Homily and Arrietty will find ["**The Borrowers Afloat**"] not a whit less interesting than the others. It begins at exactly the point where "**The Borrowers Afield**" left off, even weaving a few pages of the old book very cleverly into the beginning of the new. . . . Old friends of the Borrowers of Firbank Hall and fields beyond will be delighted to meet the other family for the first time. . . .

It is all as real as ever, the characters as unforgettable as those of Dickens, sharp-tongued Homily, tender, valiant, loyal, thrifty, her shy enterprising young daughter Arrietty and Pod, courageous, dependable, philosophic, sure there's always a way to manage. The reader shrinks to their six inches and shares breathlessly in their adventures.

Mrs. Norton never lets drama wait on description. There is the terrible moment when the bathwater flood (smelling of sandalwood) threatens to drown them as they wade down the drain, the frightful lurching trip in a leaking teakettle on the flood-swollen river and the moment when Mild Eye spots them and casts skilfully for them with his poaching fishhook. We sigh with relief as we watch them sailing with Spiller in his wooden knifebox, small garments flying from the knitting needle masthead, but we can hardly wait to discover what the miniature village of Little Fordham will offer them. In the meantime, "To all three valiant souls, good luck and good borrowing".

> *Margaret Sherwood Libby, in a review of "The Borrowers Afloat," in* New York Herald Tribune Book Review *(© I.H.T. Corporation; reprinted by permission), May 10, 1959, p. 3.*

Mary Norton's Borrowers are already an established myth. . . . With the woodland Spiller as guide they sail through the drain in a soap dish—a journey of anxious and detailed drama; then, changing their craft to an ancient kettle, continue down the stream. "Maybe," says poor Homily, voicing the book's philosophy, "there is always some way to manage. The trouble comes, like, or so it seems to me, in whether you hit on it." But while applauding the power of Miss Norton's invention— and this is an intensely moving story—a reader may sometimes query her obsession with disagreeables: old egg-shells, hairpins, the seepings of the drain. Does this rise from a Swiftian repulsion in the author or a happy insensibility? If the conception of the Borrowers demands this note, does the whole fairy tale belong with the allegories of life after all? (p. xiv)

> *"The Wisher and the Wish," in* The Times Literary Supplement *(© Times Newspapers Ltd. (London) 1959; reproduced from* The Times Literary Supplement *by permission), No. 3014, December 4, 1959, pp. xiv-xv.**

THE BORROWERS ALOFT (1961)

This story, in which the Borrowers are imprisoned by the proprietor of a model village, is somewhat more contrived than the previous Borrowers' adventures, but it is better than most of the season's output all the same.

> *A review of "The Borrowers Aloft," in* Publishers Weekly *(reprinted from the September 25, 1961 issue of* Publishers Weekly, *published by R. R. Bowker Company; copyright © 1961 by R. R. Bowker Company), Vol. 180, No. 13, September 25, 1961, p. 62.*

Here is indeed a remote and invisible yet sure and certain reality and a story that is all the more real because of the truth it expresses. Miss Norton has created another little world that fascinates and exercises the imagination whilst delighting and captivating the reader by its strange yet homely character. It is a perfect story for children. . . . (pp. 227-28)

> *A review of "The Borrowers Aloft," in* The Junior Bookshelf, *Vol. 25, No. 4, October, 1961, pp. 227-28.*

Educators tell us we should 'relate children's fiction to the modern world', but children delight in E. Nesbit's books even today. In much the same way they also delight, I am sure, in the world of Mary Norton's Borrowers, where fizzy drinks come in bottles stoppered by marbles, and motorists wear dust coats and goggles, and the *Illustrated London News* is full of information about balloons. . . . In *The Borrowers Aloft* [the Clock family is] stolen from the model village, to be exploited for commercial purposes by Mr and Mrs Platter (undertakers and builders—they specialise in houses for older folk). They escape, like Gambetta, by balloon (though I wish they hadn't filled it from the gas-fire, for surely that's heavier than air?) and at the end must move again, though Arrietty, who has made friends, as usual, with a human, wants to stay. 'They love us,' she says, and Pod replies:

> Maybe. Like they do their pets . . . Like your cousin Eggletina had that baby mouse, bringing it up by hand, teaching it tricks and such and rubbing its coat up with velvet. But it ran away in the end, back to the other mice. And your uncle Hendreary's second boy once had a cockroach. Fat as butter it grew, in a cage he made

out of a tea-strainer. But your mother never thought it was happy. Never a hungry moment that cockroach had, but the strainer was still a cage.

It is the same note of true seriousness. Children will be reading about the Borrowers in 50 years time, as they read about the Psammead today. (p. 698)

John Bowen, "Bags of Balloons," in New Statesman (© 1961 The Statesman & Nation Publishing Co. Ltd.), Vol. LXII, No. 1600, November 10, 1961, pp. 698, 702.*

We may as well say at the beginning what Mary Norton tells us at the end: this is the last book about the Borrowers. To leave Pod and Homily and Arrietty is a real wrench but Mrs. Norton is wise. She has been wonderfully consistent in portraying these tiny people in all their gallantry, ingenuity, and human foibles and it would be painful to see them suffer the attrition that comes to all good characters if they are presented too often in print.

In ["**The Borrowers Aloft**"] we see them still growing and changing yet remaining essentially themselves as they face the worst of all fates. . . .

During the long winter of their imprisonment Pod, the brave and ever-resourceful, almost gives way to despair. We watch him age. It is Arrietty, now growing out of little girlhood, who thinks of a way of escape. For the unhandy there may be just a little too much of the mechanics of building a balloon out of a strawberry box, a curtain ring, a toy balloon and other castoffs in their dreary attic prison but as the winter shortens and they work, ingeniously, patiently, the suspense is almost unbearable. Our admiration is boundless when, safe again in their own village, they realize that freedom, their own way of life, is better than the most benevolent protectorate. They are off again—with a few comfortable hints from the author to give us complete confidence in their future. This is a fitting end to a miniature saga of a family which captivated a generation. And, after all, one can always read their adventures again. That is even more fun.

Ellen Lewis Buell, "Kidnapped," in The New York Times Book Review (© 1961 by The New York Times Company; reprinted by permission), November 12, 1961, p. 38.

It is hard to know which to admire most, [the borrowers'] resourcefulness or Miss Norton's skill in involving the eight-year-olds and older in a how-to-improvise-a-balloon course. But then she makes us care tremendously about all that affects these lovable little people. Everything about her book is irresistible—the people, human and otherwise, the village, the storytelling atmosphere; and since this is the last story about the borrowers, we must be content reading and re-reading this and the two earlier books again.

Pamela Marsh, "The Land of the Unicorns," in The Christian Science Monitor (reprinted by permission from The Christian Science Monitor; © 1961 The Christian Science Publishing Society; all rights reserved), November 16, 1961, p. B4.*

The Borrowers Aloft [is] the latest and last of the series (one mourns, but respects a sensible austerity: enough is enough). Here again there are no sentimental evasions. . . .

By now we know what feats of ingenuity and heroic patience to expect from Borrowers, but this last book is reflective, making explicit what has only been implied before. As the Balloon sails far above the heads of the unaware Platter and others—

"Isn't there anything that hunts human beings?" Arrietty asked.

"Not that I know of", said Pod. "Might do 'em a bit of good if there were. Show 'em what it feels like, for once." He was silent for a moment, and then said: "Some say they hunt each other—"

"Oh no!" exclaimed Homily, shocked . . . "You shouldn't say such things, Pod—no kind of creature could be as bad as that!"

"I've heard it said", he persisted stodgily. "Sometimes singly and sometimes one lot against another lot!"

"All of them human beings?" Homily exclaimed incredulously.

Pod nodded.

No wonder that, finally, the Borrowers decide to leave even the good Mr. Pott and to live hidden lives again. Presumably we should not know as much as we do but for Miss Menzies, Mr. Pott's helper. Mary Norton draws shrewdly but sweetly the village spinster shy, fey, whose "days are *far* too full ever to be lonely"—full of watching natural things, of handloom weaving and barbola work and designing Christmas cards *and writing children's books*.

"The Highest Game: Imagination Held on a Tight Rein," in The Times Literary Supplement (© Times Newspapers Ltd. (London) 1961; reproduced from The Times Literary Supplement by permission), No. 3118, December 1, 1961, p. vii.*

POOR STAINLESS: A NEW STORY ABOUT THE BORROWERS (1971)

I believe in **"The Borrowers."** . . . Everybody who has read any of Mary Norton's four books about them *must* believe—their world is quite real and so are the characters. . . . (p. 34)

But here is more about their *past*, a slim chapter, a reminiscence told by Homily about the search for Poor Stainless, a mischievous boy Borrower lost on a foray to the scullery. His story, told from a distance, lacks the immediacy, drama and suspense of the other books. Nor can it stand alone as the previous books do—the atmosphere is not built up. Perhaps old fans who thirst for more of The Borrowers might enjoy **"Poor Stainless,"** but newcomers should be introduced to them through the four full-length books—immediately. (p. 35)

Alice Low, in a review of "Poor Stainless: A New Story about the Borrowers," in The New York Times Book Review (© 1971 by The New York Times Company; reprinted by permission), May 2, 1971, pp. 34-5.

A fragmentary story about the mysterious, busy, and brave creatures "with human tastes and almost human needs." . . . Children who have read the other books will pounce on this one with delight; but the brief story will only whet the appetite of those who have been longing for more news of the Borrowers.

Ethel L. Heins, in a review of "Poor Stainless: A New Story about the Borrowers," in The Horn Book Magazine *(copyright © 1971 by The Horn Book, Inc., Boston), Vol. XLVII, No. 3, June, 1971, p. 289.*

The brevity of this adventure about the long-popular small-scale people is its only disappointment. That very shortness, however, could whet the appetites of some reluctant readers.

Anne Weaver, in a review of "Poor Stainless," in Childhood Education *(reprinted by permission of the Association for Childhood Education International, 3615 Wisconsin Ave., N.W., Washington, DC 20016; copyright © 1971 by the Association), Vol. 48, No. 1 (October, 1971), p. 34.*

It is a pleasure to find this tale of Poor Stainless and his wicked ways in a separate publication. It was originally written for Eleanor Farjeon as a birthday gift and in 1966 included in *The Eleanor Farjeon Book*, which meant that many devotees of **The Borrowers** missed it.

The timeless stories of the Borrowers have become a modern classic and although the idea has been pirated by more recent authors they have never been and never could be so successful.

This very talented and imaginative author, whose originality and artistry speak for themselves has created a world that children immediately recognise, perhaps have even seen? A parody of a world which adults will recognise even though they may pretend it no longer exists.

The 'Overmantels', that rather snobbish and obnoxious branch of the Borrowers who lived in the drawing room come into their own in this story. In the other collections they have only been glimpsed like shadowy figures on the mantelpiece in a half-darkened room of one's mind. . . .

A book whose production will appeal to the adult book collector, lacking the immediate impact necessary for many of today's children; nevertheless I have no doubt that this new edition will reach its true audience.

Vivien Jennings, in a review of "Poor Stainless," in Children's Book Review *(© 1972 by Five Owls Press Ltd.; all rights reserved), Vol. II, No. 2, April, 1972, p. 40.*

ARE ALL THE GIANTS DEAD? (1975)

Fairy-tale is sympathetically and humorously prolonged in *Are all the giants dead?* If they are not dead, it is because of the particular gifts of Mildred, a society reporter who has conceived it her duty to visit (through her own inventive powers as well as those of the author) such noble characters as Beauty and the Beast (known to their friends as Boofy and Beau), entertaining their aristocratic middle-age with Tatler-style magazines and informing herself of their well-being. For Mildred these people *are* fairy-tale; other inhabitants of this "Land of Cockayne", like "shepherds and goatherds and swineherds and woodcutters and charcoal-burners and all sorts" are not very interesting, "At least, not to write about". But for young James, who has evidently been privileged to accompany her on earlier journeys, this one has real possibilities. It is true that he prefers science fiction to fairy-tale, but he has a proper curiosity about giants, witches, wolves and other traditional denizens of the fairy world, and while Mildred is away reporting a royal wedding, he sets himself, with considerable courage and common sense, to help the little Princess Dulcibel, who will have to marry the toad in the palace well unless a certain magic female frog can be found. From the inn kept by two Jacks, of Beanstalk and Giant-killing fame, James embarks on his strange adventure. Strange, but totally believable. For James himself, sturdy and practical, is no more four-square-real to the reader than the errant red shoes, the gnarled old retired witch Hecubenna, the elegant royal ladies. . . . (p. 2687)

This is one of those rare stories which combine ease and grace of manner with an extreme economy of effect. Every word counts, every piece of talk or description deserves close and renewed attention, however simple it may appear. . . . How many people must have wondered what kind of book could possibly follow the tales of the Borrowers. The one that has followed is unexpected, but as brilliant, beguiling and original as one could possibly wish. (pp. 2687-88)

Margery Fisher, in a review of "Are All the Giants Dead?" in her Growing Point, *Vol. 14, No. 3, September, 1975, pp. 2687-88.**

There are difficulties inherent in success. For a writer, one of them is the problem of the next book. . . . [Admirers] of Mary Norton's work will be glad to know that the new book has been well worth waiting for; it is original, witty and excellently plotted. Although so different, it has the same consistency and attention to detail of the earlier books. . . .

The tone is light and ironical and there is plenty to amuse the adult reader, but this is in no way a satire on traditional fairy-tales. It is a loving contemporary exploitation of their rich possibilities.

Ann Thwaite, "Fey, Fi, Fo, Fum," in The Times Literary Supplement *(© Times Newspapers Ltd. (London) 1975; reproduced from* The Times Literary Supplement *by permission), No. 3836, September 19, 1975, p. 1053.**

The fanciful journey through the land of fairy tales is a disappointing addition to the author's earlier works. . . . James is an attractive hero, brave and thoughtful, and the plot is neatly worked out; but there are too many shortcomings in the book: the unexplained identity of Mildred (who is she supposed to represent?), the arch use of folk tale characters, and the sadly outmoded tone of whimsy.

Ann A. Flowers, in a review of "Are All the Giants Dead?" in The Horn Book Magazine *(copyright © 1975 by The Horn Book, Inc., Boston), Vol. LI, No. 5, October, 1975, p. 465.*

"Are All the Giants Dead?" could have been cute enough to cause acne. It is instead amusing, affecting and provocative. Mrs. Norton has gotten the fairy tale down and, rather than breaking its arm, has tickled it. Hers is a bemused meditation on the rules of the story, its necessary furnishings, its symbology.

And in James she has fashioned the perfect anchor for such a meditation. He is impatient with some of the elements of the tale. For instance, he isn't as fatalistic as most of the people he meets, and he wants them to get on with their business. But he is not a cynic. He is willing to enter into their logic, as though it were an unfamiliar game by whose rules he agrees to play insofar as he grasps them. When the game is over, he goes home, having enjoyed himself. His next dream, Mrs. Norton tells us, will be about cosmonauts.

"Are All the Giants Dead?" is a good story, nicely told; it is also a story *about* stories—very clever. (p. 38)

> *John Leonard, in a review of "Are All the Giants Dead?" in* The New York Times Book Review (© *1975 by The New York Times Company; reprinted by permission), November 16, 1975, pp. 29, 38.*

Mary Norton is assured of a place in the history of children's literature by **The Borrowers**. It will not be immediately evident to the young that the theme of her new book is an extension of the old. She has caught in her writing the sophistication of the pert child of the seventies who has to sort out the traditional world of faery, here ageing but still spellbinding, from the unlikely but real world of cosmonauts that provides his inner fictions. Mary Norton still writes some of the best dialogue ever penned for the young. . . . [Her] tale can be read aloud with great success. This is the best way in for the less sophisticated.

> *Margaret Meek, in a review of "Are All the Giants Dead?" in* The School Librarian, *Vol. 24, No. 1, March, 1976, p. 45.*

[In *Are All the Giants Dead?* Norton] takes readers on a self-conscious tour of the fairy-tale world of the old stories which strips away the veils of timeless enchantment to reveal sadly aging and disillusioned folklore characters. (p. 123)

Eventually Norton reaffirms the power and magnitude of the tales. After his adventures in this retirement home for fairy-tale characters, James returns to his own world a more mature individual, with greater compassion and courage, having experienced adventure, love, jealousy, loss, and a rediscovery of childhood faith. Norton's lucid writing style is enhanced by her lively, quicksilver storytelling; brisk, entertaining dialogue; and offhand, dry wit which satirizes adult nostalgia for lost childhood innocence while remaining true to the bittersweet human need for an eternal return to the archetypal paradisical time of legend and fairy tale. But Norton has a final adult laugh: "These people belong to no particular period: they belong—as one might say—to Time Immemorial. They were more or less what they like. In some cases, of course, they go by the illustrator."

This wit is the identifying mark of light fantasy, which often mildly pokes fun at its very substance and structure. Whether the humor is broadly cartoonlike, child-simple, or sophisticatedly adult, its presence removes the stories from the threatening struggles and tragic themes of serious fantasy. Rather, the sharp parody or good thunderous fun of much of the writing almost makes it a separate genre in children's literature. (p. 124)

> *Sheila A. Egoff, "The New Fantasy," in her* Thursday's Child: Trends and Patterns in Contemporary Children's Literature *(copyright © 1981 by the American Library Association), American Library Association, 1981, pp. 80-129.**

THE BORROWERS AVENGED (1982)

One or two short stories published since 1961 suggested that Mary Norton had not entirely turned her back on her miniature people, but nothing really prepared us for the tremendous vitality of the new book and the immensely satisfying, subtle way the characters have developed—not only Arrietty, who

was obviously going to learn from experience, but also the enigmatic Spiller and disagreeable Lupy, two minor actors with important parts to play. As the title of the new book suggests the main line of the plot concerns the way the Platters set about hunting for their lost victims; there are some agonising moments of danger before the greed of the unattractive couple betrays them and forces them to leave the district, while Pod, Homily and Arrietty settle down safely in the Old Rectory. (p. 3970)

With Peagreen (whose real name is Peregrine Overmantel) we come to one of the most fascinating aspects of the book. The tantalising glimpses of Borrower hierarchies in the earlier books is now filled out a little. The Rectory Overmantels, clearly a branch of the stuck-up family Homily criticised at their first home, Firbank Hall, had to leave when a tenant decided to introduce *art nouveau* into the Tudor Rectory; unfortunate Peregrine, then a small child, fell off the shattered overmantel and was left behind, to be nursed by the humbler but kinder Wainscots until he could look after himself. We learn, too, from one of Homily's typical remarks, that the first husband of her sister-in-law Lupy was a Harpsichord, though Lupy was 'only a Rainpipe from the stables'. Homily, in fact, is surprised to find that she likes young Peagreen, even if his voice sounds affected, and Arrietty is well able to stand up to his moments of intellectual snobbery (as he says, the Overmantels had always been educated, through listening to generations of children having lessons in the library, 'and the books were always left on the table'.) These minutiae, and the constant delight of the personal idiom through which each character is revealed, account for some of the attraction of the new book. Then, too, there is the entrancing detail we expect, born originally, as Mary Norton has said, as part of an early fantasy in the life of a very short-sighted child, 'before it was known that she needed glasses'. Domestic matters are viewed as though through diminishing lenses, with irresistible exactness. (pp. 3970-71)

Each and every detail has its place because of the Borrowers. We see through their eyes. . . . The Clock family are perfectly realised as the focal points of the book. Pod upholds what one could call the moral code of Borrowers: 'Improvisation' is their breath of life, and human beings are not there to be used except in emergencies. Homily, the home-maker, has her own sense of values, her own courage, behind a nervous disposition. Arrietty—dauntless, eager for adventure, warm-hearted—stands for the imagination without which no child, and no story, can hope to be complete. (p. 3971)

> *Margery Fisher, in a review of "The Borrowers Avenged," in her* Growing Point, *Vol. 21, No. 4, November, 1982, pp. 3970-71.*

As in the previous Borrowers books, there is much attention to the mechanics of functioning in a giants' world—not cute thimbles-and-mushrooms arrangements but real practical difficulties, solved with an ingenuity that is usually 99 percent perspiration. There is also Norton's fond observation of her typically British characters. And there is always the hovering menace from the likes of the Platters—whose pursuit of little cousin Timmis in the church makes for a grand conclusion.

> *A review of "The Borrowers Avenged," in* Kirkus Reviews *(copyright © 1982 The Kirkus Service, Inc.), Vol. L, No. 22, November 15, 1982, p. 1236.*

Our delight in the borrowers is part active, part passive. We long, like the kind Miss Menzies, to protect and house them and to preserve them against a disbelieving and mercenary world; we also long to be them, to re-explore our disbelieving world from their Lilliputian vantage, to clamber into and reinhabit the deserted interstices of our elephantine and abused environment. It's a hard life being four inches tall, but because it stimulates invention and imagination we feel sure it must be a good one. "Improvisation is the breath of life to borrowers", Mary Norton assures us, and as improvisers they take their place in the oldest British comic tradition of eccentrics, making do, crazily re-exploiting, in their hopelessly disadvantaged way, anything that comes to hand. They see the useful potential, the alternative significance, of the mundanities that are overlooked by human beans.

As fictional characters, though, they are at odds with the children's world in which they are cast. For while other tiny creatures, like fairies and gnomes, are palpably supernatural, the borrowers are substantially real; they don't come and go in puffs of smoke, live in icy caves or anything like that. The essence of borrowing is in its practicality, and we can legitimately ask and be satisfied, as we cannot with most homunculi, about their eating habits, their natural resources, their toilet training and their view of the afterlife. The borrowers are entirely human in their attributes—Pod plodding, paternal and patient, Homily homely, houseproud and huffy, Arrietty artful, articulate and ardent. When we spend a long time among them we think of them, with their errands, worries and small pleasures, as humans, and forget we are looking down the wrong end of the telescope; we forget the quality which alone makes them truly interesting—that they are, in the fullest sense, a minority.

The calculating, cryptic, improvisatory genius of the minority is the touchstone of borrowing survival. There is danger and they must not be seen. . . . The exploration of the adult world from an innocent viewpoint can lead to Martian ingenuities, like "the black thing they have in the hall. They turn a handle and tell it things. They grind the handle round and round, like, and tell it where they're going and this and that . . .". And such rediscoveries are refreshingly derived from a practical need to put inordinate things to use, like the Clocks' legible newsprint wallpaper or their new kitchen-door made from the cover of the *Essays of Emerson*. The further determining oddness of there being so few of them is that they are entirely innocent of money; to Arrietty a bank is merely a slope covered in grass.

This financial innocence is what sets them apart from profiteering human beans in **The Borrowers Avenged,** especially from Mr Platter, the cold-hearted undertaker . . . , who wants to trap them and exhibit them to the public. It also points to a curious limitation which is imposed on these books by their being conceived, unlike *Gulliver's Travels,* for children. For the satirical potency of the little people, their paradoxical identification with and yet absurd distance from, big people, is

never really developed. This last, late sequel, too, is sadly unequal in its handling—there is very little plot, an ungainly degree of contrivance which parodies the ingenuity of the borrowers themselves (the climactic device of church bells being left *up* will only be understood by unusually campanological children) and much inert time-killing dialogue along the lines of "Whatever shall we do now?" "Oh we'll think of something". This can with no trouble at all be seen as an inner dialogue of the author faced with the task of reanimating her offspring, long since devolved, and regrettably (for she has given us so much pleasure) never looking likely to succeed.

Alan Hollinghurst, "A Tiny Minority," in The Times Literary Supplement *(© Times Newspapers Ltd. (London) 1982; reproduced from* The Times Literary Supplement *by permission), No. 4156, November 26, 1982, p. 1307.*

The story is at its exciting best whenever the evil Platters are on the scene. A cozier mood prevails as the Clock family settles into their new home. There's an interesting dichotomy here—sometimes Norton's writing, which painstakingly chronicles the borrowers' doings, is fascinating, but often the reader feels overwhelmed by minutiae (in every sense of the word). Editing would have helped immensely here, as would a less abrupt end. There's a lot to enjoy however, and readers who have followed the borrowers will overlook some flaws in the pleasures of pursuing more of their escapades.

Ilene Cooper, in a review of "The Borrowers Avenged," in Booklist *(reprinted by permission of the American Library Association), Vol. 79, No. 8, December 15, 1982, p. 566.*

Mrs. Norton herself has said 'stories never really end', and there was always room for another, even if the hope has faded over the years. However, here at last it is, not a revamping of an old idea but a genuine new chapter in the matchless story. . . .

The exciting climax is as good and convincing a big scene as Mrs. Norton has ever given us. As always, the story is open-ended. Are we to have another sequel? After another twenty-one years? We can hope. On the evidence of this book the author is at the height of her powers still.

There is little more to be said, except that, if you like high adventure, fine detail and total integrity in writing, this book is not to be missed. All the Norton ingredients are here: the characters continue to grow, in themselves and in their relationships within their miniature society, every detail is worked out realistically, the story is beautifully constructed, the pervading humour is, as always, tinged with sadness.

Marcus Crouch, in a review of "The Borrowers Avenged," in The Junior Bookshelf, *Vol. 47, No. 1, February, 1983, p. 30.*

Jan Pieńkowski

1936-

Polish-born English author/illustrator and illustrator of fiction and nonfiction.

Pieńkowski is one of the most popular contemporary creators of picture books. He is credited with reviving the pop-up book, a popular nineteenth century toy book designed so that certain parts of its illustrations become three-dimensional when the book is opened. Pieńkowski's illustrations are characterized by bright colors, silhouettes against marbled backgrounds, thick black lines, and flat hues. He notes his Central European heritage and a fascination with comic strip art as important influences on his style. Pieńkowski especially admires the emphatic visual effect of dialogue balloons used in comic strips, a device he utilizes in the *Meg and Mog* books. Written with Helen Nicoll, these simple stories about a little witch and her cat are usually considered good for beginning readers, although the illustrations excite some reviewers more than the texts. Pieńkowski is also the creator of a group of concept books—*Numbers, Shapes, Sizes, Colors, ABC, Time, Weather,* and others—which use brightly colored illustrations to represent each principle. Critics cite simplicity and clarity as reasons for their success among young children.

Perhaps Pieńkowski's most popular work is *Haunted House,* his first pop-up book. Although the text is again considered secondary to the illustrations, *Haunted House* is consistently praised for its ingenuity and engineering, and even the youngest children are attracted to it. Besides two other well-received pop-up books, *Robot* and *Dinnertime,* Pieńkowski has illustrated books for other authors. He won the Kate Greenaway Medal in 1972 for Joan Aiken's *The Kingdom Under the Sea* and in 1980 for *Haunted House.*

(See also *Something about the Author,* Vol. 6 and *Contemporary Authors,* Vols. 65-68.)

GENERAL COMMENTARY

Meg, a skinny, scraggly witch with an appealing personality, and Mog, her striped cat, are the main characters in these funny, simple witch stories [*Meg and Mog* and *Meg's Eggs*], where spells and chants abound. . . . The text [of *Meg and Mog*] is minimal; pre-schoolers will enjoy having it read to them and beginning readers will be able to handle it themselves.

Meg's Eggs is not up to the quality of the first story. . . . However, both books are enhanced by simple, brightly colored pictures which will appeal to children.

> *Shirley Wayland, in a review of "Meg and Mog" and "Meg's Eggs," in* School Library Journal, *an appendix to* Library Journal *(reprinted from the May, 1973 issue of* School Library Journal, *published by R. R. Bowker Co./ A Xerox Corporation; copyright © 1973), Vol. 19, No. 9, May, 1973, p. 65.*

[*Meg at Sea* and *Meg on the Moon* are two] bright, bold, witty stories about the scraggy witch, Meg, and her scrawny cat, Mog, who adventure through worlds of intense, clean, exciting colour. A boon for bedtime-reading, scurrying Mums (and Dads of course) who want a short story where the pictures do

most of the work. Ideal for leaving around in cots and for beginner readers to begin on.

> *Robert Walker, in a review of "Meg at Sea" and "Meg on the Moon," in* Children's Book Review (© *1974 Five Owls Press Ltd.; all rights reserved), Vol. IV, No. 1, Spring, 1974, p. 12.*

There have been times in the development of children's book publishing when, perhaps by happy coincidence, a specific demand has suddenly been met by the appearance of an author or illustrator particularly suited to satisfy that need. With the advent of pre-school playgroups and an increasing demand for picture and story books at pre-school level, Dick Bruna emerged, to be followed by a succession of illustrators catering for the needs of infant children. Some of them had already established a name in other fields of book illustration, among them Jan Pieńkowski, the winner of the 1972 Kate Greenaway Medal, who has now produced the first four of a new series of small pre-school picture books [*Colours, Numbers, Shapes,* and *Sizes*]. Like Bruna, Pieńkowski uses large patches of bright colour with simple, bold outlines, combined with a short text line in large (in this case 'handwritten') type using the minimum of words. The books offer a gay, attractive introduction to the concepts of Colour, Number etc., for young children and their small format makes them easy to handle. (pp. 14-15)

Edward Hudson, in a review of ''Colours,'' ''Numbers,'' ''Shapes,'' and ''Sizes,'' in Children's Book Review (© 1975 Five Owls Press Ltd.; all rights reserved), *Vol. V, No. 1, Spring, 1975, pp. 14-15.*

[In *Shapes* and *Sizes* Jan Pieńkowski] uses bold, unshaded colour to show . . . familiar objects. Contrast is the basis of *Sizes*—a tree and a flower juxtaposed, a fat woman and a small boy, for example. In *Shapes* he exhibits a simple geometrical shape and places examples beside it (a door and a picture beside a rectangle, a bracken frond beside a spiral and so on). The impact of his gay, fluent style is likely to be considerable.

Margery Fisher, in a review of ''Shapes'' and ''Sizes,'' in her Growing Point, *Vol. 13, No. 9, April, 1975, p. 2594.*

Those little books [*Sizes* and *Shapes*] are wholly admirable, because Jan Pieńkowski sticks to illustration, at which he excels, and does not aspire to be academic and all-embracing. *Sizes* demonstrates, in simple, clear, amusing pictures of figures, animals and objects, the difference between ''big'' and ''little''. *Shapes* shows in turn each basic shape and follows it with a humorous illustration in which that shape is to be found. As may be expected, the books are beautifully designed, in vivid colours.

Mary Hobbs, in a review of ''Sizes'' and ''Shapes,'' in The Junior Bookshelf, *Vol. 39, No. 2, April, 1975, p. 99.*

This set of four concept books [*Colors, Numbers, Shapes,* and *Sizes*] should wow the pre-school set. In each the hand-lettered text acts in combination with brightly colored, eye-grabbing illustrations. Stressing simplicity in format and design, the books attempt to teach young children the most basic concepts using 10 easily recognizable objects as examples and following them with an appropriate question.

In *Colors,* the most successful of the four, the illustrations are the boldest and most striking. The electrifying black cat and the grinning green frog almost leap off the page.

Shapes are appealingly presented from a mermaid sitting on ocean waves combing her wavy hair to an owl startled by a zig-zag flash of lightning in a forest of zig-zaggy pine trees. Children will delight in noticing not only a circle in the shape of a farmer's tractor wheels but in the shape of the sun as well.

Introducing the concept of big and little, *Sizes* sticks to the narrowest conception possible. Thus a very big elephant and a very small mouse are presented with no attempt to portray a mouse as big when compared to, for example, a mosquito.

The illustrations in *Numbers* are cluttered. Not only are objects named in the one through ten sequence but they are depicted twice on adjoining pages so that, at first glance, one leopard looks like two leopards and so forth. It's also puzzling that after showing 10 apples on a tree the next spread poses the question ''how many?'' in reference to 20 peas on a plate. (pp. 40-1)

Gemma S. DeVinney, in a review of ''Colors,'' ''Numbers,'' ''Shapes,'' and ''Sizes,'' in School Library Journal *(reprinted from the February, 1976 issue of* School Library Journal, *published by R. R. Bowker Co./A Xerox Corporation; copyright © 1976), Vol. 22, No. 6, February, 1976, pp. 40-1.*

Among the many books offering an extended list of familiar objects and concepts to the very young, Pieńkowski's [*Weather* and *Homes*] will make their impact partly by his broad, mannered illustrations with their bold, eccentric shapes and positive colour, and partly by the implicit humour with which he enlivens the commonplace—showing a watchful cat beside the goldfish bowl that illustrates one of many homes and emphasising the nature of hail as it bounces off a tortoise's back. Each tiny scene is dramatic and active in spite of the chunky, static nature of the objects and animals that are shown.

Margery Fisher, in a review of ''Weather'' and ''Homes,'' in her Growing Point, *Vol. 18, No. 3, September, 1979, p. 3584.*

[*Homes* and *Weather* are two] more colourful, distinctive picture books in the series which gave us *Shapes, Numbers, Colours* and *Sizes*. Simplicity of design and boldness of colour are the keynotes of these concept books which do have an immediate appeal to young children. As a first picture book to buy for a baby they are to be highly recommended and are worth the money. Each opening of *Homes* is vividly coloured with just one word in large black fat letters—kennel, castle, house; and on the facing page a full colour picture of the type of home. Admirers of Jan Pieńkowski's '**Meg and Mog**' books will recognise the style. . . .

On each left hand page of *Weather* a window shows the— clouds, rainbow, sun—which is then colourfully pictured on the facing page.

As children begin to identify letters and words the books will be read proudly alone, and should be firm favourites.

A review of ''Homes'' and ''Weather,'' in Books for Your Children *(© Books for Your Children 1979), Vol. 14, No. 4, Autumn, 1979, p. 5.*

Always original, Jan Pieńkowski has livened up his *ABC* with unusual examples (jigsaw, robot, dice) and with the emphatic exaggerations and dazzling colours typical of his art-work. *Time* is illustrated by clocks marking hours from five in the morning to midnight and here again there is visual humour to enforce the point (a scarred knee pokes out of bath water at six o'clock, a cat yowls at midnight). Two useful books for the very youngest, striking and direct.

Margery Fisher, in a review of ''ABC'' and ''Time,'' in her Growing Point, *Vol. 19, No. 5, January, 1981, p. 3822.*

''A is for apple, B is for bird and C is for Mog''. The two year old spoke with conviction. A devoted fan of Meg and Mog she instantly recognized Jan Pieńkowski's distinctive illustrations employed here in an explicitly educational series.

ABC introduces the alphabet in the simplest way; the letters, upper and lower case, are established with an appropriate illustration. There is an acceptable balance between traditional examples—the oft-invoked apple—and more intriguing ones— an x-ray, a zig-zag; though I had hoped for more of Y than the inevitable yacht. This book is worth considering for ages two to five.

Time is presented less effectively. It opens at 5 o'clock with a cock crowing. The bird is splendid but the example rather literary. Subsequent clock positions seem arbitrarily chosen to illustrate a day in the life of a yellow-headed lad. There are touches of diverting humour which unfortunately tend to divert from the concept. The teaching of time requires a more systematic presentation. By the time a child is able to deal with this quite difficult concept he would find these illustrations over-simplified. Perhaps the author sensed these short-comings. We abandon the yellow-headed lad in a shop stuffed with clocks of all designs. Is it a coincidence that his hand is straying to the only digital?

> Lesley Wood, "C Is for Mog," in The Times Educational Supplement (© Times Newspapers Ltd. (London) 1981; reproduced from The Times Educational Supplement by permission), No. 3369, January 16, 1981, p. 34.

COLOURS (1974; U.S. edition as Colors)

This little book consists of left-hand pages of a named solid colour facing right-hand pages with an eye-catching different coloured background and a central picture in the named colour. Most small children when turning the pages of a picture book for themselves look first at the right-hand page. It is therefore not immediately apparent to them which colour is being featured as, for example, when a left-hand white page faces a white mouse on a vivid blue background. Adult help is essential to familiarise the child with the method and then the attractive simple drawings will prove a happy aid to colour recognition.

> E. E. Ashworth, in a review of "Colours," in The School Librarian, Vol. 23, No. 2, June, 1975, p. 129.

MOG'S MUMPS (with Helen Nicoll, 1977)

Once again this outstanding team have come up with zany humorous pictures, matched by a sparkling text in which every word counts. Every three or four year old ought to be introduced to Meg the witch and Mog her cat, and once they have made that acquaintance their book will become very well thumbed indeed.

> A review of "Mog's Mumps," in Books for Your Children (© Books for Your Children 1981), Vol. 16, No. 1, Spring, 1981, p. 8.

WEATHER (1979)

This picture book for the very young in strong colour, has a symbol, a simple lively picture, and a single word for each different kind of weather. Rain symbol has a bright duck image. The sun symbol has a sand castle. At the end a questionnaire reproduction of the symbols tests whether the child has associated word, picture and symbol.

A well-produced book. . . .

> A. Thatcher, in a review of "Weather," in The Junior Bookshelf, Vol. 43, No. 6, December, 1979, p. 320.

Picture books with labels are quite useful introductions to reading, especially when they are used as talking points. Pieńkowski manages to get more movement into simple line-drawn, primary block-coloured illustrations than a dozen Brunas could ever manage. Weather . . . will need discussion with young children even after a weather-focused introduction. One approach would be to point out that the type of weather is indicated in the window on each left-hand page. Even then 'fog' is difficult (plain grey window) and might have been better

with a vague car-headlight shape in the grey mass of the 'picture'; and the colours of 'cloud' and 'sun' do not correspond across the pages. There is a good deal of confusion for the unwary, but Weather will still seduce young eyes.

> Cliff Moon, in a review of "Weather," in The School Librarian, Vol. 28, No. 1, March, 1980, p. 32.

A newcomer to Pieńkowski's wee books for wee folk, this one is almost wordless, like others in the series (on the alphabet, homes, shapes, numbers, sizes and time). There is a caption for each of the extravagantly inventive paintings in the artist's unmistakable style, in colors so loud they shriek. . . . One boffo picture shows an octopus, struggling with giant waves and dodging lightning during a raging storm.

> A review of "Weather," in Publishers Weekly (reprinted from the April 29, 1983 issue of Publishers Weekly, published by R. R. Bowker Company, a Xerox company; copyright © 1983 by Xerox Corporation), Vol. 223, No. 17, April 29, 1983, p. 52.

HAUNTED HOUSE (1979)

"Let yourself in," says a notice above the handle of the door that forms the cover of Jan Pieńkowski's book; but a nasty-looking tentacle protrudes from the letter-box, ivy proves that the door has been unopened for some time, and the book is called Haunted House, so we should clearly be prepared for some of the contents—though not all. For this three-dimensional pop-up has a surprise on every page, plus more when you pull arrows or twiddle a disc in the direction indicated, and the result is like one of those rides on a ghost train at a fun fair, where you meet all the Nasties of your imagination but in a form that enables you to laugh even while you shudder. Suffice it to say that as much danger lurks in the kitchen sink as in the attic, and that by the end of the book aural stimulus is added to visual as Something attempts to saw its way out of a packing case. A wonderful book, full of fun, and the ideal for the Christmas ghost story.

> Ursula Robertshaw, "Choice for Children," in The Illustrated London News (© 1979 The Illustrated London News & Sketch Ltd.), Vol. 267, No. 6977, December, 1979, p. 141.*

It is not surprising that Haunted House credits a "paper engineer"; this must indeed be the apotheosis of the picture book with moving parts. Eyes flash, ghosts pop out or lurk, monsters show their teeth and a sinister black cat with restless eyes is under and behind every other surface and—on the final spread—a bat flaps its wings while a saw scrapes noisily in sympathy. The story line is minimal and superfluous; there is more than enough without it in this book to delight children of any age over four for many a sleepless night.

> Heather Neil, "Pop Up and See Me," in The Times Educational Supplement (© Times Newspapers Ltd. (London) 1979; reproduced from The Times Educational Supplement by permission), No. 3313, December 7, 1979, p. 25.*

Not much is left to the imagination in Jan Pieńkowski's Haunted House. Horrible creatures spring out at you as you turn the page; a ghost or skeleton appears at the pull of a tab. Eyes roll, flames flicker and clock hands move at the touch of another; cupboard doors open like some parody of those Advent

Mary Hobbs, in a review of "Haunted House," in The Junior Bookshelf, *Vol. 44, No. 2, April, 1980, p. 64.*

From Haunted House, *written and illustrated by Jan Pieńkowski.*

calendars to reveal further horrors. A do-it-yourself ghost story in fact, with plenty for the reader to do on every page.

If reader is the right word, since there is hardly any text. The long-suffering inhabitant of the house, understandably not on peak form, has summoned the doctor and is describing symptoms (loss of appetite, difficulty in sleeping and who can wonder?). It is a pretext for the pictures, and anyone looking for a good read will have to look elsewhere.

We find it grotesque, but we can also be sure that many people—and children in particular—will not agree. A lot of children will thoroughly enjoy it. Certainly it is well constructed—the tabs do work smoothly and the creatures spring out as they are meant to do without getting entangled: and it gives the impression (welcome or not) of being strong enough to withstand a fair amount of handling.

Caroline Copnall, "Popping Up," in The Times Literary Supplement *(© Times Newspapers Ltd. (London) 1979; reproduced from* The Times Literary Supplement *by permission), No. 4004, December 14, 1979, p. 131.**

Children have strong nerves but they also have strong fingers and however much the attendant adult may shrink from pop-out skeletons or unfolding bats, he or she should be at hand to make sure that the various ingenious devices in the book are not ruined by over-enthusiastic handling. A book as clever, as artistically accomplished and as diverting as this really deserves to have a long life.

Margery Fisher, in a review of "Haunted House," in her Growing Point, *Vol. 18, No. 6, March, 1980, p. 3660.*

Meggendorfer rides again! The colour and indeed the cheerfully gruesome humour is less subtle, but will delight young readers, with so many flaps and tabs to pull, revealing monsters, ghouls, dangling spiders, skeletons, and a splendid crocodile in the bath. These are linked by a thread of monologue with sinister double meanings. The covers of the book are the doors of the house; a note on the door invites the doctor in to hear why the elderly owner feels unwell or in need of help—but by the end, there is no doctor! It is hard to stop playing with this ingenious toy book.

Approximately one hundred years ago, the children's book publishing world found itself in the midst of the Golden Age of pop-up books, or movable books to be more precise. Artists like Lothar Meggendorfer and Ernest Nister were turning out some of the most elaborate and beautifully illustrated movable books ever to be invented. The publishing world, like the education world, tends to move in recurring cycles, and in 1982, quality movable books are not only being published again, but many of these books are so outstanding that the 1980s may well be the second Golden Age of movable books and children and teachers may be the chief beneficiaries of such a rebirth. The best of these new pop-up books serve to motivate youngsters to read and to show them that experiences with books can be enjoyable. The books also serve as unique stimuli for creative writing and original art work.

Jan Pieńkowski's **Haunted House** is one of the best examples of the new movable book. In this book, monsters spring forth from almost every page. Alligators come out of the bathtub, while ghosts and skeletons appear and disappear at the reader's will. The art work is outstanding. Indeed, **Haunted House** won the Kate Greenaway Medal for the most distinguished work in the illustration of children's books published in the United Kingdom in 1979. For a pop-up to receive England's equivalent to our Caldecott Medal is some indication of just how beautiful these new movables are. Filled with monsters, spiders, and bats, Pieńkowski's book has guaranteed popularity with young readers. The seven sentences of text are not particularly interesting or scary, but it is the text's shortcomings that provide the boon for language arts teachers. Once students have had the pleasure of manipulating the book, teachers can challenge young readers to write a better storyline. The pictures provide the basic structure for the story and young authors get a chance to unlease their unique, ghoulish story. (p. 342)

Richard F. Abrahamson and Robert Stewart, "Movable Books—A New Golden Age" (copyright © 1982 by the National Council of Teachers of English; reprinted by permission of the publisher and the author), in Language Arts, *Vol. 59, No. 4, April, 1982, pp. 342-47.**

DINNER TIME (1981)

Pieńkowski's lauded **"Haunted House"** . . . is more ambitious than his new, mad pop-up, but this slim volume packs plenty of punch. A clue to the scary laughs appears in the red-splattered title. Opening the pages keeps pace with creatures opening their mouths and snapping them shut on what makes their "dinner time." Frog is catching flies when Vulture swoops down and finishes off the croaker with one huge bite. Gorilla makes a meal of Vulture, and so on, until Shark closes its gory teeth on Crocodile. The full-color paintings of the predators and their prey are joltingly real yet very funny. It doesn't matter that the artist has resorted to poetic license, putting Tiger in an alien habitat or, for that matter, getting Croc into the deep where Shark operates.

A review of "Dinner Time," in Publishers Weekly *(reprinted from the May 29, 1981 issue of* Publishers Weekly, *published by R. R. Bowker Company, a Xerox company; copyright © 1981 by Xerox Corporation), Vol. 219, No. 22, May 29, 1981, p. 43.*

Watching a seven and a half month-old baby with Jan Pień-kowski's **Dinnertime** . . . , fingers clutching, whole body pulsating, panting with excitement . . . and seeing the page playfully held back by the mother to get her peering under the curve of it, head on one side, so eager to see what's next . . . I think for the hundredth time how extraordinarily we underestimate babies, limiting them to our theories. . . . Many books, like this one, are a vivid success with children far younger than those they are "intended for"—particularly perhaps if there are older children in the family, as in this baby's case. . . .

> *Leila Berg, "Knowing the Story," in* The Times Educational Supplement *(© Times Newspapers Ltd. (London) 1981; reproduced from* The Times Educational Supplement *by permission), No. 3396, July 24, 1981, p. 26.**

Dinner Time—which might be subtitled 'Food Chain'—is the most successful of modern pop-up books. This is largely due to Pieńkowski's genius, but the paper engineers—who for once get a credit on the cover—have played their part too. Never were there such jaw-snapping openings, calculated to produce howls, of laughter or fear according to temperament. The trouble with most pop-ups is that they quickly fall to pieces, but this is not only artistically miles ahead but exceedingly robust. Many heavy-handed children and adults have already proved that it will stand up to harsh treatment. Lovely!

> *Marcus Crouch, in a review of "Dinner Time," in* The Junior Bookshelf, *Vol. 45, No. 6, December, 1981, p. 244.*

ROBOT (1981)

Pieńkowski's new **Robot** with its increasingly astonishing machines which burst out of every opening adds a new dimension to the concept of "turning the page". Some might argue that any book a book-hating child actually wants to open is worth buying. But the contemptible truth is that it's the combination of mere ingenuity and sheer ephemerality that makes pop-up books so pleasurable. At the pull of a paper tab, one of Pieńkowski's robots stands up, lifts a pair of dumb-bells over his head and sees his trousers fall down. On the next page, a grandfather robot struggles with yards of poisonously coloured snakes. On another, a spaceship blasts into the sky as the distant earth turns serenely—or rather, as the reader makes it turn serenely—on its axis. The devices are so complicated, so varied and at the same time so vulnerable that they cock a decadent snook at the simple-and-sturdy ethic of the nursery school.

> *Jeremy Treglown, "The Movable Element," in* The Times Literary Supplement *(© Times Newspapers Ltd. (London) 1981; reproduced from* The Times Literary Supplement *by permission), No. 4103, November 20, 1981, p. 1360.**

Pieńkowski's new pop-up is an absolute wonder. It takes the form of a robot's letter home. The views of that "home" are unbelievable. . . . There are hilarious little details hidden in the backgrounds. The paper is sturdy, and the pop-ups work smoothly. This would be a marvelous gift.

> *Nelda Mohr, in a review of "Robot," in* Children's Book Review Service *(copyright © 1981 Children's Book Review Service Inc.), Vol. 10, No. 4, December, 1981, p. 33.*

Robot is another amazing book-experience from the hands that constructed **The Haunted House.** Rockets fly out, robots comb their hair, washing-machines revolve. One snag with these book-toys is that they have more built-in obsolescence than a toilet roll. . . .

> *Michael Rosen, in a review of "Robot," in* New Statesman *(© 1981 The Statesman & Nation Publishing Co. Ltd.), Vol. 102, No. 2646, December 4, 1981, p. 18.*

The Worst Children's Books of 1981: **Robot** by Jan Pieńkowski . . . , like most of this year's worst children's books, is a negative enchantment. Its high point is when the Robot's rocket pops out—this is another infernal pop-out book—Freudian fashion into space.

> *John Horder, in a review of "Robot," in* Punch *(© 1981 by Punch Publications Ltd.; all rights reserved; may not be reprinted without permission), Vol. 281, December 16, 1981, p. 1121.*

The pop-up boom won't last forever but **Robot** is its star performer, closely followed by the same artist's **Haunted House.** . . . It even has a storyline, not that anyone with tabs to pull that make gigantic Dad lift a mighty weight, rise from the page, collapse again in exhaustion, will bother. Alternative delights: Robot's Sis stroking her lipstick back and forth before going out with 'that Neanderthal'; Robot's rocket soaring into Outer Space. (pp. 21-2)

> *Elaine Moss, in a review of "Robot," in her* Picture Books for Young People 9-13 *(copyright © 1981 Elaine Moss),* Thimble Press, *1981, pp. 21-2.*

Humanised animals are one thing, humanised robots quite another, and technically ingenious though Jan Pieńkowski's new pop-up book is, one's immediate reaction is that the complications over-reach themselves. I find the comparatively logical sequence of **The Haunted House** more pleasing, despite the consistent position held by the newcomer at the top of the

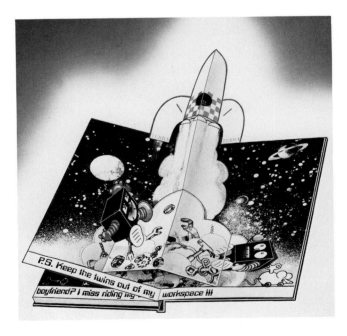

From Robot, *written and illustrated by Jan Pieńkowski.*

Times charts. However, in this realm between book and toy, it may be argued that the more there is to play with, the more successful the pop-up! The thoughts in a robot-astronaut's letter home (the actual letter is in Mother Robot's apron pocket) are illustrated line by line. . . . A good time will be had by all recipients of the book—including particularly, I suspect, the adults.

> *Mary Hobbs, in a review of "Robot," in* The Junior Bookshelf, *Vol. 46, No. 1, February, 1982, p. 22.*

ABC (1981)

Pieńkowski presents a book entirely different from what one expects from the ingenious creator of the bestselling popups **"Haunted House"** and **"Robot."** This and ["**Numbers,**" "**Colors,**" and "**Shapes**"] are sure-fire attractions for toddlers since they are very like the popular works of Dick Bruna, with similar bold graphics, shapes and colors.

> *A review of "ABC," in* Publishers Weekly *(reprinted from the January 8, 1982 issue of* Publishers Weekly, *published by R. R. Bowker Company, a Xerox company; copyright © 1982 by Xerox Corporation), Vol. 221, No. 2, January 8, 1982, p. 83.*

The illustrations are bright and bold, and should appeal to the very young. Then, on the last page, twenty-five colorfully shirted children—and one smiling green creature—sport letters on their chests, making further letter identification possible. It's an alphabet book with a twist.

> *Margo Showstack, in a review of "ABC," in* Children's Book Review Service *(copyright © 1982 Children's Book Review Service Inc.), Vol. 10, No. 10, May, 1982, p. 93.*

MOG AT THE ZOO (with Helen Nicoll, 1983)

Another stunning, eye catching book from Jan Pieńkowski with poor old Mog getting into and out of a series of scrapes with zoo keepers, crocodiles and Meg. Lots of strong colours and shapes which will stimulate a lot of activity in youngsters. I can see them wanting to crayon or paint just like this.

> *A review of "Mog at the Zoo," in* Books for Your Children *(© Books for Your Children 1983), Vol. 18, No. 1, Spring, 1983, p. 9.*

Thomas Rockwell

1933-

American author of fiction, poetry, and drama.

Like his artist father, Norman, Rockwell is usually considered a talented depicter of childhood. His appeal lies in his childlike sensibility and a humor which focuses on subjects that many adults find disgusting and most preteens find terrifically funny. Rockwell ventures into various kinds of fiction, but his most popular book is *How to Eat Fried Worms*, which has received numerous child-selected awards.

Rockwell's initial work, *Rackety-Bang and Other Verses* is among the first informal poetry books for children. It covers such themes as a child who refuses to blow her nose, the disgusting birth name of Xerxes Xenophon Gort (which is worse than having warts), and various encounters with such animals as a skunk, an aardvark, and a rhinoceros. While some critics find the poems unpleasant nonsense, others praise Rockwell's ability to stimulate reading pleasure through humorous poetry. Critics observe that some of Rockwell's books have a scatological quality that middle-grade children enjoy. One of these is *The Portmanteau Book*, a mixture of short stories, games and puzzles, and poetry. The index, which is a story and spoof in itself, is a feature readers especially like. *How to Eat Fried Worms*, however, may best represent Rockwell's qualities as a humorist. Rarely has a book captured the readership of so many children, putting Rockwell in the select company of such popular authors as Judy Blume and Beverly Cleary. The story centers on the creative cookery of worms and Billy's effort to eat one a day for fifteen days in order to win a minibike. Critics applaud the originality of the plot and the natural quality of the characters and their relationships. *Worms* is one of the few Rockwell books to be appreciated by both reviewers and children.

Rockwell also writes books of a more serious nature. Like his approach to humor, his dramatic stories highlight some of the unpleasant aspects of life. *Hiding Out* concerns a child's adjustment to his mother's remarriage. Critics note the story's realism—particularly the incident when Billy kills a squirrel for food—and its topical theme. While Rockwell's works are not unanimously acclaimed, most critics agree that he knows how to delight and entertain his intended audience. He won the Young Reader Medal and the Mark Twain Award in 1975, the Massachusetts Children's Book Award, the Nene Award, the South Carolina Children's Book Award, and the Sequoyah Children's Book Award in 1976, the Young Hoosier Award in 1977, and the Iowa Children's Choice Award in 1979, all selected by children for *How to Eat Fried Worms*. Rockwell was given the Golden Archer Award for his body of work in 1975.

(See also *Something about the Author*, Vol. 7 and *Contemporary Authors*, Vols. 29-32, rev. ed.)

AUTHOR'S COMMENTARY

Most people act as if *How To Eat Fried Worms* isn't a serious book, I'm sorry to say. But look at all the problems there are in the world—unemployment, inflation, pollution, next week's arithmetic test, who's going to sit in the front seat the next

Photograph by Arax-Serjan Studios; courtesy of Thomas Rockwell

time your family drives to Tulsa, the food shortage. You don't think I'd write a funny book in the face of all that? No, I was serious. Eating a worm is no joke. If you don't believe that, try it when you're going home this afternoon. Stop by the side of the road, dig up a worm, lay it out on a paper plate, and then think about eating it. You'll begin to feel serious. It won't look like a joke.

While I was writing the book, at the part where Billy wakes up in the middle of the night imagining that he's poisoned himself by eating the worms, it suddenly occurred to me: suppose worms really would poison somebody? I didn't know whether they would or not. And then I remembered something that had happened years before. An old folksong about a boy who puts peas up his nose had become popular. But so many kids were trying it and ending up in hospitals with teams of doctors removing the world's record number of peas from their noses, that the folksong was finally taken off the radio. I could just see my book all of a sudden being removed from libraries and bookstores, a wormy menace to the health of the children of the United States. So I asked a doctor. "On the contrary," he said, "worms are **good** for you: seventy per cent protein, low in calories, full of minerals." (p. 4)

I got the idea for *How To Eat Fried Worms* while driving home from New York City one day. I had been to see an editor about

234

another story I'd written. She hadn't liked it. So I was depressed, there was a nasty taste in my mouth, as if she had just been making me eat a cold liver and spinach sandwich. At the same time I was trying to think of an idea for another book. She had suggested that I write something more realistic. The trees and guardrails flashed by. And then, I suppose, the nasty taste in my mouth, as if I'd just been eating mud, and my half-hearted search for an idea all of a sudden collided in my mind, and I thought: how about a book about a boy who eats worms?

I have often wondered why I was immediately delighted by the idea. A book about a boy who eats worms? Probably it was the outrageousness of the idea which delighted me. That's a ridiculous, weird, yucky thing to do—eat worms. It's such an outrageous thing to do, it's almost heroic. Other kids would point you out to their friends half in derision, half in awe. You've done something nobody else will, sort of thumbed your nose at the whole conventional everyday world of school, grown-ups, clean socks, no-elbows-on-the-table-eat-your-peas, dear.

This quality of outrageousness, ridiculousness, runs through most of my books. (p. 5)

I suppose one of the reasons I write books for children is because I feel I can be more outrageous than if I were writing for adults. But it wasn't the reason I started writing for children. When my son Barnaby was three or four years old . . . , someone gave him a copy of the **Oxford Nursery Rhyme Book.** Reading it to him so delighted me, the poems were so varied and wonderful . . . that I began to try to write some myself. And that, in turn, brought me back to children's literature, a whole world which had once been very important to me but which I had since forgotten. My mother read aloud to my brothers and me a great deal, wrote stories for us, took us to the library, encouraged us to write ourselves, brought us books she thought we'd like.

Sometimes when people learn that I write childrens' books, they ask me if I don't feel restricted, limited. Can I write about the things I'm interested in? In certain areas—outrageousness for one—I feel less restricted. And then there are other things about being a child, certain attitudes, which I seem to share: the sense of being an underdog, for instance, of living in a world controlled by others.

But all this is in a sense a long way from writing. Why one writes a particular kind of book doesn't really have very much to do with writing it. After I'd got the idea for **How To Eat Fried Worms,** there was still everything to do. **Why** would a boy eat worms? A bet. Okay. What kind of a bet? What kind of a boy? Where would he live? How many worms would he eat? That was a delicate question. After Billy has eaten two or three worms, just the eating of another worm isn't disgusting, outrageous, exciting, even interesting. But of course, if he eats only a few worms, the bet is too easy. So I compromised on fifteen worms but hurried over the actual eating of the later worms, concentrating instead on the complications and difficulties created by Alan and Joe—the worm made of beans, the fake letter from the doctor.

The ending of the book was a problem, too. In my first draft, after Billy had eaten the twelfth and thirteenth worm, Alan and Joe conceded the bet, and all four boys became involved in very complicated maneuverings to trick Alan's parents into giving him the fifty dollars to pay Billy. For instance, they staged a fake burglary of Alan's room. But that ending wasn't right. It was about as exciting as a rotten orange. So I worried

about it, tried rewriting parts of it, and finally realized that the book should focus all the way through on the bet and end as Billy wins it by eating the fifteenth worm.

After that there was lots of polishing to do. I revise a great deal. I imagine a scene in my mind—for instance, four boys talking on the stoop of a house. But I can't describe everything in the scene—the trees, the weather, what each boy looks like, the house, how each boy feels at every moment. The scene would be pages and pages too long. Instead, I have to select a few details which will suggest the rest. Then I have to put all this into words so that a reader will see the scene in the same way I do, so that a reader will feel as if he has just crossed the street and is actually watching and listening to the four boys. All this, I find, takes care and revision after revision.

But after going over a manuscript four or five or six times, it's difficult to tell if the words are conveying anything. If the first draft is like a lively green frog croaking and splashing about in a stream, the fifth or sixth draft is like a gray dead frog floating limply in a jar of formaldehyde. A joke, for instance, is never very funny the fifth or sixth time you hear it.

So when I finally send a manuscript off, I am not really sure if it's good . . . or bad . . . I hope it's passable at least. Of course, it's encouraging when a publisher buys the book. But then the copy editor throws out all my punctuation; the editor asks for more revisions. I begin to be doubtful of the book again. Finally the book is published. A few reviews. . . . And then . . . silence. Sometimes publishing a book is like dropping a rock down a well and waiting to hear the splash . . . and waiting . . . and waiting . . . and waiting . . . and finally going back to my typewriter for another, bigger rock. (pp. 5-6, 15)

Thomas Rockwell, "Sequoyah Award Acceptance Speech 1976" (originally a speech delivered at the Sequoyah Children's Book Awards on March 27, 1976), in Oklahoma Librarian, *Vol. 26, No. 3, July, 1976, pp. 4-6, 15.*

RACKETY-BANG, AND OTHER VERSES (1969)

Hilaire Belloc said that children's verse should have "terseness, simplicity, improbability and finality as to theme, strongly emphasized lilt—something indelible for the memory." It is sad to say that although more books of poetry for the young are being published now than ever before, few, if any of them, have these characteristics. . . . It is rather a relief to come on a book like **Rackety-Bang and Other Verses,** in which there is a lot going on, most of it unpleasant. . . . The rackety, raucous nonsense of this volume is intended to be wild and hair-raising, and, I take it, riotously funny. The level of humor and verbal felicity, however, is illustrated by **"The Excursion"**:

> When I was a little boy
> I went to New York
> and dined with the mayor
> on cabbage and pork.
>
> But the cabbage was sour,
> the pork was fat,
> I'd rather eat spinach
> with smelly Sam Knapp.

I am certain that children are sick of verses by lady poets about sweetness and light, but it would be too bad if this were all they could find in the way of stronger fare. This bang unfortunately ends in a whimper.

> *William Jay Smith, "Poems with Something Indelible for the Memory," in* Book World—The Washington Post *(© 1969 Postrib Corp.; reprinted by permission of* Chicago Tribune *and* The Washington Post*), May, 1969, p. 24 [the excerpt of Thomas Rockwell's poetry used here was originally published in his* Rackety-Bang, and Other Verses *(reprinted by permission of Pantheon Books, a division of Random House, Inc.), Pantheon Books, 1969].**

Writing verse is like any other craft. There are rules and if you violate them—well you have to violate them consistently enough to justify a new set of rules. One example, most of the rhymes in the poem called **"An Alphabet"** are sour or at least effective, but "F is for Fran / who lives in a clan" made me wince (why not "can"?).

So it goes in almost all the poems, and that's a pity because Thomas Rockwell does write good, and a little editing would have gone a long way.

> *Selden Rodman, in a review of "Rackety-Bang," in* The New York Times Book Review, Part II *(© 1969 by The New York Times Company; reprinted by permission), May 4, 1969, p. 46.*

Unconventional in choice of subjects and in style, these verses . . . are more stimulating than a shot of B-12. And the pleasure of reading them will last a lot longer. Don't let any of your young poets miss the fresh flavor of these verses.

> *A review of "Rackety-Bang," in* Publishers Weekly *(reprinted from the May 26, 1969 issue of* Publishers Weekly, *published by R. R. Bowker Company, a Xerox company; copyright © 1969 by Xerox Corporation), Vol. 195, No. 21, May 26, 1969, p. 55.*

The author's fertile imagination and sharp wit combine to produce an extraordinary, varied collection of poems for, as well as about, children. The characters are unforgettable. . . . This is not a placid, run-of-the-mill collection; some of the selections, notably **"The Punishment"** and **"Drips,"** might seem distasteful and out-of-sorts. But these two, for example, comically illuminate the commonplace experiences of punishing a child, and of a child refusing to blow her nose. Utilizing expressive imagery and economy of language, Thomas Rockwell has certainly contributed something of quality to a collection area glutted with sugary drivel.

> *Barbara Gibson, in a review of "Rackety-Bang," in* School Library Journal, *an appendix to* Library Journal *(reprinted from the October, 1969 issue of* School Library Journal, *published by R. R. Bowker Co./A Xerox Corporation; copyright © 1969), Vol. 16, No. 2, October, 1969, p. 143.*

SQUAWWK! (1972)

*Squawwk*ing its way across the page of Billy's schoolbook, a black blotch comes to life and begins growing into an electric-blue, furniture-eating roc "as big as Yankee Stadium." . . . Somewhere along the way the roc gets away from the author . . . and becomes neither joke nor parable nor horror monster but just a blight on the landscape, and the notion which seemed so clever in the first few chapters assumes unmanageable proportions long before *Squawwk* flies away.

> *A review of "Squawwk!" in* Kirkus Reviews *(copyright © 1972 The Kirkus Service, Inc.), Vol. XL, No. 17, September 1, 1972, p. 1028.*

An unsuccessful combination of fantasy and social message. . . . The message is that when adults are confronted with a threat to the status quo they react with force. . . . The story is confusing, and the message forced.

> *Jean C. Holloway, in a review of "Squawwk!" in* School Library Journal, *an appendix to* Library Journal *(reprinted from the January, 1973 issue of* School Library Journal, *published by R. R. Bowker Co./A Xerox Corporation; copyright © 1973), Vol. 19, No. 5, January, 1973, p. 70.*

Does the Roc escape? Of course, but not before the author has said a few choice things about the ignorance of adults and the wisdom of kids.

Nothing very subtle about this story, but it involves the kind of uproar upper-elementary kids thrive on. It will brighten everyone's March. (p. 111)

> *Judith Higgins, "Some Most Unusual Stories," in* Teacher *(copyright © 1974 by Macmillan Professional Magazines, Inc.; used by permission of The Instructor Publications, Inc.), Vol. 91, No. 7, March, 1974, pp. 110-11.**

HOW TO EAT FRIED WORMS (1973)

Even fried with ketchup, mustard and horseradish sauce or baked as "Alsatian Smothered Worm" with onions and sour cream by Billy's supportive Mother, fifteen nightcrawlers are still a lot of worms to eat. Having made a fifty dollar bet, Billy persists in his one-a-day regimen. . . . The person who comes off best here is Billy's mother, who after a quick call to the doctor accepts the plan with perfect equanimity, but Rockwell's sensibilities (if that's the word) are so uncannily close to those of the average ten year-old boy that one begins to admire Billy as a really sharp operator.

> *A review of "How to Eat Fried Worms," in* Kirkus Reviews *(copyright © 1973 The Kirkus Service, Inc.), Vol. XLI, No. 16, August 15, 1973, p. 883.*

Readers will enjoy this book, particularly the culinary art displayed in the preparation of each fried worm and the very nonchalant manner Billy displays in fulfilling his part of the wager. . . . Let's hope that we will have more humorous books like this.

> *Margaret M. Nichols, in a review of "How to Eat Fried Worms," in* Children's Book Review Service *(copyright © 1973 Children's Book Review Service Inc.), Vol. 2, No. 3, November, 1973, p. 21.*

A hilarious story that will revolt and delight bumptious, unreachable, intermediate-grade boys and any other less particular mortals that read or listen to it. Billy and Alan stumble into making a $50 bet on whether Billy will eat 15 worms in 15 days—Alan's money against Billy's digestive system. The chapters march briefly and irresistably on, worm by worm, with the circumstances surrounding the ingestion of each becoming more bizarre as the boys and their dualing seconds tense toward a climactic ending. The characters and their families and activities are natural to a T, and this juxtaposed against the uncommon plot, makes for some colorful, original writing in a much-needed comic vein.

> *A review of "How to Eat Fried Worms," in* The Booklist *(reprinted by permission of the American Library Association; copyright © 1973 by the American Library Association), Vol. 70, No. 6, November 15, 1973, p. 342.*

Not for the nervous parent: there is a bit of risk of readers attempting to better Billy's record. . . . These four boys have to be among the most lively and believable in recent fiction, and the very chaptering of the book bespeaks originality and fun. A good bet for reluctant readers.

> *Patricia Tonkin, in a review of "How to Eat Fried Worms," in* Childhood Education *(reprinted by permission of the Association for Childhood Education International, 3615 Wisconsin Ave., N.W., Washington, DC 20016; copyright © 1974 by the Association), Vol. 50, No. 5 (March, 1974), p. 294.*

The principle prank offered for our delight . . . certainly has a touch of originality, and, indeed, incredibility.

Eating worms is not a richly comic theme to sustain 120 pages, and Mr. Rockwell's characters provide little help. Their early forbears may be Tom Sawyer and Huck Finn, but Disney diluted that strain, and Billy and his friends are close relatives of the wide-eyed, lovable-beneath-the-freckles androids of American television. Billy's efforts to eat the worms, and his friends' attempts to divert him, are told in a strenuous hey-get-this welter of CAPITAL LETTERS. . . .

The proof of this pudding, as it were, was that I did not care at all whether Billy ate the worms, did not eat the worms, got poisoned, vomited continuously, or what he did.

> *Geoff Fox, "Whatever Makes You Laugh," in* The Times Educational Supplement *(© Times Newspapers Ltd. (London) 1978; reproduced from* The Times Educational Supplement *by permission), No. 3296, September 1, 1978, p. 15.**

THE NEON MOTORCYCLE   (1973)

Personally we'd be happy to leave such ROARRRing frenzy to TV, but we must admit that Rockwell . . . [packs] as much zap into Sam's wild ride on a runaway Harley as hard covers can be expected to contain. . . . Rockwell slips in a few nice phrases (we like "flamboyant with pigeons") between the THWONKs and the SPRONGs. . . .

> *A review of "The Neon Motorcycle," in* Kirkus Reviews *(copyright © 1973 The Kirkus Service, Inc.), Vol. XLI, No. 17, September 1, 1973, p. 963.*

Thrill along with young Sam Waterhouse who amazingly falls out of his window onto the seat of an idling Harley-Davidson motorcycle. . . . Second and third grade boys who read this book agreed that it was "Neat!" "Funny! Funny!" and they hoped that we would get the book for our library.

> *Margaret M. Nichols, in a review of "The Neon Motorcycle," in* Children's Book Review Service *(copyright © 1973 Children's Book Review Service Inc.), Vol. 2, No. 2, October, 1973, p. 12.*

["The Neon Motorcycle"] is as unconventional as long hair or blue jeans. The story . . . begins in a slightly hysterical gear

and doesn't slow down for 40 pages. . . . Instead of leaving one breathless with excitement the airbrushed Thwonks, Sprongs and Frums become, like any steady roar, monotonous.

> *Karla Kuskin, in a review of "The Neon Motorcycle," in* The New York Times Book Review *(© 1973 by The New York Times Company; reprinted by permission), November 4, 1973, p. 60.*

Zooming through neighbors' houses, an A & P, and a circus on a huge Harley Davidson motorcycle, Sam Waterhouse enjoys a hectic ride until he is safely catapulted from the bike onto a passing train. Although Rockwell uses action words and plenty of "ROAAR's" and "SCREECH's" to hold readers' interest, the story is frantic rather than fun. Moreover, the vocabulary is often beyond the comprehension of second or third graders, e.g., "labyrinthine," "flamboyant." . . . All in all, this seems to be an adult's idea of what a hip kid's book should be and not a story that children will enjoy.

> *Sharon Rinkhoff, in a review of "The Neon Motorcycle," in* School Library Journal, *an appendix to* Library Journal *(reprinted from the December, 1973 issue of* School Library Journal, *published by R. R. Bowker Co./A Xerox Corporation; copyright © 1973), Vol. 20, No. 4, December, 1973, p. 45.*

THE PORTMANTEAU BOOK   (1974)

An irreverent montage of short stories, poems, puzzles, nonsense quizzes, and other assorted oddities that are ostensibly to be savored while traveling, though the parodistic humor will appeal to anyone with a taste for *Mad* magazine wit. The writings range from straightforward tales of pranks (**"Hot I: Nakedness"**) and localized happenings (**"The Great Duck Rescue"**) to somewhat sophisticated, tongue-in-cheek mocks like **"Breaking Loose,"** a pseudo-epic that readers acquainted with modern poetry will get the most out of. The diversity of content and levels of meaning defy pigeonholing in one age group or readership: Rockwell himself humorously anticipates a blank-look reaction (huh?) to the book in a satiric closing report on the results of a poll taken of young people who allegedly read advance copies of the book. Droll farce for a select audience.

> *A review of "The Portmanteau Book," in* The Booklist *(reprinted by permission of the American Library Association; copyright © 1974 by the American Library Association), Vol. 71, No. 5, November 1, 1974, p. 294.*

["The Portmanteau Book"] is rather like Jack and Jill magazine written by an only partially civilized Huck Finn. Some of the humor is scatological at a youngster's level (no, Miss Prim from the local decency group, I do not mean dirty), such as the story called **"Toilet Paper,"** about a little boy who is trapped in the Girl's Room. There is shivery terror (as in the story about a group of boys cooped up in an empty factory with Crazy Tom), fantasy (Jack Mears decides, in the middle of January, that it is June and school's out), icky things (the recipe for "entomological soup"), [and] satire. . . . All very knockabout, irreverent and boyish—though there are girls' stories too—and I think [close] to the real contents of the childish id. Dr. Freud would have a field-day with **"The Portmanteau Book"**—and I mean that as a compliment. (p. 40)

> *Richard R. Lingeman, "The Sound of Laughter," in* The New York Times Book Review *(© 1974 by The*

New York Times Company; reprinted by permission), November 3, 1974, pp. 39-40.*

"I like *The Portmanteau Book* because . . . I hit Edward Watkins in the stomach with it and he threw up all over the lawn." Probably no one over twelve can really get a good yuck out of this testimonial—or, for that matter, appreciate the subversive, sub-scatological humor of a story called "Toiletpaper". . . . But Rockwell (remember "How to Eat Fried Worms") doesn't intend to please grownups; in fact, his readiness to offend them is the basis of his appeal. Yet we still have to admit that there's a lot of really good stuff here. . . . Rockwell is something different—maybe a little of Carl Sandburg and Alfred E. Neuman mixed together. [Even] the index is funny. . . . Rise to the occasion.

> *A review of "The Portmanteau Book," in* Kirkus Reviews *(copyright © 1974 The Kirkus Service, Inc.), Vol. XLII, No. 22, November 15, 1974, p. 1205.*

The "6½" stories are truly funny: four may be read in sequence: and "Underwear" is the best. "The Great Duck Rescue" and "Loony Bin" (about what happens to a substitute teacher) should be especially appealing to the age group. The poetry is also immensely readable and funny. Some of the contributions, however, are inane: the mystery page (just a full page of dots) and "A Star Spangled Contest" in which readers select answers to "I like the Portmanteau Book because—" stretch the off-the-walls humor of the collection too far. Still Rockwell has put together a treasury that has flair and built-in audience appeal (e.g., kids will have great fun zigzagging through the cross-references of the index which details a bank robbery and doles out other bits of daffy information).

> *Margaret Blue, in a review of "The Portmanteau Book," in* School Library Journal *(reprinted from the March, 1975 issue of* School Library Journal, *published by R. R. Bowker Co./A Xerox Corporation; copyright © 1975), Vol. 21, No. 7, March, 1975, p. 100.*

HIDING OUT   (1974)

Details of Billy's wilderness survival project give some needed heft to this version of the adjustment-to-a-new-stepparent theme. . . . A tame, carefully guided and too easily abandoned experiment, but the incidental realism (for example, his difficulties and eventual triumph in skinning, cooking and eating his first squirrel) make Billy accessible and sympathetic.

> *A review of "Hiding Out," in* Kirkus Reviews *(copyright © 1975 The Kirkus Service, Inc.), Vol. XLIII, No. 1, January 1, 1975, p. 19.*

The story of [Billy's] exploits—particularly his reactions when he has to shoot, skin and roast a squirrel—is beautifully understated by the author. . . . A really satisfying story for the 8-10 age group, not always taken into consideration by publishers.

> *A review of "Hiding Out," in* Publishers Weekly *(reprinted from the January 20, 1975 issue of* Publishers Weekly, *published by R. R. Bowker Company, a Xerox company; copyright © 1975 by Xerox Corporation), Vol. 207, No. 3, January 20, 1975, p. 77.*

When Billy's widowed mother decides to marry a neighbor with children of his own, Billy's sense of security is badly jarred. Believing his worst fantasy—that his mother thinks only of herself in allowing strangers to disrupt the family—Billy engages the aid of a friend to build the perfect hideout in the woods. . . . Smooth writing for the age level, a touch of humor, and a theme with general appeal will make this fit snugly and naturally its intended readership. (pp. 620-21)

> *A review of "Hiding Out," in* The Booklist *(reprinted by permission of the American Library Association; copyright © 1975 by the American Library Association), Vol. 71, No. 12, February 15, 1975, pp. 620-21.*

Although the relationship between mother and son has been pictured as laconic and stoic, the flat tone of the final scene is disappointing; the whole story is almost too low-keyed although convincing and adequately written. While there is appeal in the boy-against-the-elements episode, . . . the early episode, in which the two boys go hunting for sport rather than food, may disturb some readers. (pp. 154-55)

> *Zena Sutherland, in a review of "Hiding Out," in* Bulletin of the Center for Children's Books *(reprinted by permission of The University of Chicago Press; © 1975 by The University of Chicago), Vol. 28, No. 9, May, 1975, pp. 154-55.*

TIN CANS   (1975)

A strange, stark, surreal adventure, with a background of flames and darkness and the stench of garbage, about a magic Campbell's soup can that David, visiting his aunt, finds at the town dump where a girl named Jane, a welfare foster child, is engaged in her habitual scrounging. . . . A blazing but baffling orgy of acquisition.

> *A review of "Tin Cans," in* Kirkus Reviews *(copyright © 1975 The Kirkus Service, Inc.), Vol. XLIII, No. 13, July 1, 1975, p. 714.*

This story is unsuccessful both as a fantasy and as an examination of the ethical dilemma of choosing between want and thievery. In this brief volume, Rockwell hasn't allowed himself enough time to develop characters or theme. The action is so fast paced that the chase scenes are hard to follow. It's really too bad since the idea is intriguing. (pp. 4-5)

> *Nelda Mohr, in a review of "Tin Cans," in* Children's Book Review Service *(copyright © 1975 Children's Book Review Service Inc.), Vol. 4, No. 1, September, 1975, pp. 4-5.*

A city dump yields unusual treasure for 10-year-old David and Jane who stumble upon a Campbell's soup can which has the ability to siphon goods from whatever direction it is pointed. . . . After a close brush with police, Jane and David disagree as to what course to take: David, a product of a middle-class environment, trusts the authorities to believe that he and Jane have made an honest mistake if they will only give up the can; Jane, a welfare child who does not trust anybody, wants to cling to the can, even if they can no longer use it, as a symbol of escape from her limited, stifling existence. Sparsely and suspensefully told, this smooth fantasy moves to a credible conclusion. . . . [*Tin Cans*] reveals yet another facet of Rockwell's talent.

Carolyn Johnson, in a review of "Tin Cans," in
School Library Journal (reprinted from the October,
1975 issue of School Library Journal, published by
R. R. Bowker Co./A Xerox Corporation; copyright
© 1975), Vol. 22, No. 2, October, 1975, p. 101.

A magical Campbell's soup can, turned up out of the waste-heaps of a smoldering city dump, is the catalyst for an obscure fantasy that probes the dynamics of a power struggle between two children of differing circumstance and values. . . . Rockwell's prose, though simple, is intense and demands the reader's involvement. The desolation of the wasteland setting underscores the bleak sentiments throughout; this is one for special readers to ponder. (p. 241)

Denise M. Wilms, in a review of "Tin Cans," in
The Booklist (reprinted by permission of the American Library Association; copyright © 1975 by the
American Library Association), Vol. 72, No. 3, October 1, 1975, pp. 240-41.

THE THIEF (1977)

A young boy must face the fact that his only neighborhood friend is a thief, and the reckoning comes hard. . . . Rockwell's study is poignant and accurate in terms of family lifestyles. Moreover, he probes the psychological reverberations for Tim, who wonders if things would have been different had Dwayne been confronted about his behavior. Moving in its way, and a good starting point for discussion. (pp. 483-84)

Denise M. Wilms, in a review of "The Thief," in
Booklist (reprinted by permission of the American
Library Association; copyright © 1977 by the American Library Association), Vol. 74, No. 5, November
1, 1977, pp. 483-84.

The uncertainty of how and what other people think is Tim's problem. . . . This is a short book, but in it Tim finds out how he feels about wrongdoing and its consequences; the questions about Dwayne are never answered. It is a fast-paced novel with which boys will probably be able to identify, but it is not as good as the author's earlier books.

Linda Worden, in a review of "The Thief," in Children's Book Review Service (copyright © 1977 Children's Book Review Service Inc.), Vol. 6, No. 4,
December, 1977, p. 35.

Picked on by his older brothers, nine-year-old Tim is mildly grateful for the daily visits of the new, poor kid next door. . . . Then the family begins to suspect Dwayne of stealing . . . and soon after, Dwayne inveigles Tim into an old man's shack which Dwayne proceeds to mess up. That's enough for Tim, who doesn't mind when he's forbidden to play with Dwayne; still, it bothers him that his understanding, reasonable parents care more about how the old man feels than about how Dwayne feels. This last alleviates the general air of middle-class complacency, but it doesn't dispel the stereotypes. A competent but thin problem piece.

A review of "The Thief," in Kirkus Reviews (copyright © 1977 The Kirkus Service, Inc.), Vol. XLV,
No. 24, December 15, 1977, p. 1321.

Certainly there is a need for short novels with active boy characters—but not this shallow and didactic treatment of friendship, loyalty, and disillusionment. . . . Connecting class with morality; poverty with theft, neglect, and poor training, the story descends into unfortunate stereotypes. Worst of all, the inconsistency of Tim's parents' morality—they ignore the brutal behavior of his big brothers who gang up on him to steal his gum yet punish Tim for vandalism—is not explored and young readers will see Dwayne as the only "bad" boy in the story. (pp. 90-1)

Christine McDonnell, in a review of "The Thief,"
in School Library Journal (reprinted from the January, 1978 issue of School Library Journal, published
by R. R. Bowker Co./A Xerox Corporation; copyright
© 1978), Vol. 24, No. 5, January, 1978, pp. 90-1.

Rockwell draws a believable enough picture of a young delinquent, giving clues as to the contributing factors in Dwayne's home environment, but the story seems to reach no conclusion; Tim ponders the problem, wonders why nobody has taken any action to help or to discipline Dwayne. The only result, for Tim, is that he has become interested in setting animal traps as Dwayne's father does—and there the story ends. The writing style is adequate, the characterization slight.

Zena Sutherland, in a review of "The Thief," in
Bulletin of the Center for Children's Books (reprinted by permission of The University of Chicago
Press; © 1978 by The University of Chicago), Vol.
31, No. 8, April, 1978, p. 134.

HOW TO EAT FRIED WORMS, AND OTHER PLAYS (1980)

Although this reviewer felt squirmy by the end, the grade school set will relish the plot. The other plays call for large casts and fairly elaborate props; these may not be possible for the average grade-school dramatic productions, but they make for enjoyable reading.

Barbara Baker, in a review of "How to Eat Fried
Worms and Other Plays," in Children's Book Review Service (copyright © 1980 Children's Book
Review Service Inc.), Vol. 8, No. 9, April, 1980, p.
90.

Though the combination of slapstick humor and ghoulish silliness in these four plays is a winning one, the zaniness often lapses into sheer hysteria. The title play . . . is also the most successful, as the worm eating episodes reach new and revolting heights. The least successful is **"Myron Mere,"** a slight effort in which the villainous Mere captures a queen and turns her into a butterfly. . . . The overworked plots are subordinate to the highjinks that Rockwell is adept at manufacturing. He manages, though, to keep the productions and props fairly simple and easily assembled for this age level. For some reason, however, Rockwell has chosen to give all the villains thick Eastern European accents—a disturbing stereotype.

Susan H. Roth, in a review of "How to Eat Fried
Worms," in School Library Journal (reprinted from
the August, 1980 issue of School Library Journal,
published by R. R. Bowker Co./A Xerox Corporation; copyright © 1980), Vol. 26, No. 10, August,
1980, p. 70.

The three original plays that Rockwell has concocted to accompany the dramatization of his 1973 comic novel are mere curtain-raisers by comparison—brief burlesques of fantasy genres complete with characters who speak in dialect and elaborate stage effects (for which instructions are provided). The wilder they're played, the funnier they'll be, and kids on either side of the footlights will have a great time. But the play that will really give youngsters a chance to act and react variously is of course **"How to Eat Fried Worms"** (and win a $50 dare), which Rockwell has adroitly scripted and staged—with attention, in the program notes, to everything from advertising . . . to casting the adult parts. . . . They're all theater-wise, but **"How to Eat Fried Worms"** could be a community treat.

> *A review of "How to Eat Fried Worms and Other Plays," in* Kirkus Reviews *(copyright © 1980 The Kirkus Service, Inc.), Vol. XLVIII, No. 18, September 15, 1980, p. 1234.*

HEY, LOVER BOY **(1981)**

Rockwell does some artful crafting in his jolting story of a seventh-grade boy who is oblivious to his insensitivity even as a "slam" book concocted by two girls spells out some particulars. The book shocks Paul, who has been trying to figure out how to handle the advances of one of its writers, a girl named Margaret, whose play he disrupted as a joke. Paul's cruel public reactions to Margaret are shaped in part by his fogginess over what to do about sex and girls but are also consistent with a general boorishness that's quietly displayed in his relationships with others. There's scarcely any authorial judgment on Paul: it's up to readers to imagine the effects of his casual callousness, and also to ponder whether Margaret's shoving "some of his own moldy nasty oil down his own throat" is warranted. The evocation of Paul's consciousness is nearly brilliant; the only false note is the caliber of play writing attributed to Paul and classmates in their seventh-grade dramatic English class. Very strong stuff.

> *Denise M. Wilms, in a review of "Hey, Lover Boy," in* Booklist *(reprinted by permission of the American Library Association; copyright © 1981 by the American Library Association), Vol. 77, No. 20, June 15, 1981, p. 1348.*

Thirteen-year-old Paul Nesbit is a cut-up, and this begins with a series of ridiculous classroom take-offs on well-known plays and genres—burlesques in which sometimes Paul, sometimes Rockwell himself, is mocking the 7th-grade student script writers. There's much funny stuff here, but it gets tiresome. However, that might be the point. For it turns out that some of Paul's classmates have become fed up with his jokes at others' expense. . . . [When he realizes Margaret has set him up], the joke's on Paul, and the whole school laughs. There's a method, then, to the nonsense, but not too heavy a moral. First, the Margaret action is interspersed with Paul's hilarious downtown odyssey to find out about sex—he believes he can avoid having his own play produced if he makes it pornographic, but he's not quite sure just what goes on in pornography. Finally, in the last scene, Paul gets back at the whole class with his slyly soft-porn science-fiction sendup. It's a funny story, told with clipped, shotgun timing, a smattering of innocent, seventh-grade-level raunch, and a real awareness of the intensities and overwhelming uncertainties of early adolescence.

> *A review of "Hey, Lover Boy,' in* Kirkus Reviews *(copyright © 1981 The Kirkus Service, Inc.), Vol. XLIX, No. 17, September 1, 1981, p. 1087.*

Rockwell, in *How to Eat Fried Worms* . . . , wrote a believable story. In his new book he has lost his way. The writing is disjointed and uneven; at times you can lose all track of who's who. The thin plot revolves around a 13-year-old boy who is out to find the answer to THE question. How he does find answers to his questions about sex is never made clear, but they seem to have been found in a massage parlor. As luck would have it, there are many such places in his small New England town. The book is too silly and simple for most at a junior-high level, and younger readers may have trouble keeping up with the writing style. Adults may find some of the language offensive.

> *Mark Singer, in a review of "Hey, Lover Boy," in* School Library Journal *(reprinted from the November, 1981 issue of* School Library Journal, *published by R. R. Bowker Co./A Xerox Corporation; copyright © 1981), Vol. 28, No. 3, November, 1981, p. 110.*

Paul Showers

1910-

American author of nonfiction.

Showers is noted for writing good introductions to a wide variety of topics. Memories of his children struggling with uninteresting beginning readers prompted him to write books a young audience could enjoy and read comfortably. Many of Showers's works deal with the body and its functions and needs, such as the heart and blood, the brain, the senses, sleep, and the biological beginnings of life. Part of a series called "Let's Read and Find Out," his books also center on Indian festivals, family trees, space, and new siblings. Showers occasionally presents his information in verse, often in picture book format.

Showers contends that young people can comprehend much more than their reading levels indicate, and he spends a great deal of time researching his subjects and talking to children to assure the accuracy and readability of his books. Critics are quick to note that Showers retains a simple style while dealing with complex subjects, but he is sometimes criticized for failing to treat his subjects with the necessary depth. However, Showers is usually credited with creating well-structured books that successfully instruct and entertain their inquisitive readers.

(See also *Something about the Author*, Vol. 21; *Contemporary Authors New Revision Series*, Vol. 4; and *Contemporary Authors*, Vols. 1-4, rev. ed.)

GENERAL COMMENTARY

["**Find Out by Touching**" and "**In the Night**"] are particularly suited for children of 6 or younger. The first book helps a child to realize the importance of the sense of touch by suggesting that he feel a variety of objects and making comparisons of their differences. To be most effective, the book should be read with adult supervision and is well suited for classroom use. "**In the Night**" describes objects a child sees after the lights are out and his eyes have become accustomed to the dark. An emphasis on the sameness of the room in daylight or darkness will comfort the child plagued by nighttime fears. Mr. Showers turns the theme into a delightful before-bed volume with [his] verses. . . .

> *Carolyn A. Lavender, "Beginners' Introductions to the Wonders of the World," in* The New York Times Book Review, *Part II (© 1961 by The New York Times Company; reprinted by permission), May 14, 1961, p. 31.*

Showers gives accurate information in the very simplest language, chooses important facts, and tells them in logical sequence, so that the child can read the books alone or the adult can use them as a springboard for discussion. (p. 459)

> *Zena Sutherland, Dianne L. Monson, and May Hill Arbuthnot, "Informational Books: Paul and Kay Showers," in their* Children and Books *(copyright © 1981, 1977, 1972, 1964, 1957, 1947 by Scott, Foresman and Company; reprinted by permission), sixth edition, Scott, Foresman, 1981, pp. 459-60.*

FIND OUT BY TOUCHING (1961)

Encouraging an awareness of the sense of touch, the child is invited to put many things of wood, cloth or metal into a box, close his eyes and tell what he has fished out and how it feels. An excellent subject choice for this age group.

> *A review of "Find Out by Touching," in* Virginia Kirkus' Service, *Vol. XXIV, No. 4, February 15, 1961, p. 159.*

[Here] the text suggests identification of different kinds of objects by tactile sense. The demonstration seems unnecessary for the child who is old enough to read the book himself, and the use of direct address makes the text obtrusive if it is read aloud. . . . The material in the book is, in contrast to previous books in the series, familiar; children who read the book may be reminded that identification can often be made by touch alone, and they may be stimulated to try guessing the nature of a collection of objects (as the book suggests they do), but it seems improbable that the reader will learn any new scientific principle or fact from the book.

> *Zena Sutherland, in a review of "Find Out by Touching," in* Bulletin of the Center for Children's Books *(reprinted by permission of The University of Chi-*

cago Press; copyright 1961 by The University of Chicago), Vol. 15, No. 1, September, 1961, p. 17.

THE LISTENING WALK (1961)

"**The Listening Walk**" sketches imaginatively . . . a boy's perception of ordinary sounds. Excellent independent reading on 2nd-grade level, it is also a fine read-aloud for younger ones where group participation in the suggested sounds will be fun.

> *May H. Edmonds, in a review of "The Listening Walk," in* School Library Journal, *an appendix to* Library Journal *(reprinted from the October, 1961 issue of* School Library Journal, *published by R.R. Bowker Co./ A Xerox Corporation; copyright © 1961), Vol. 8, No. 2, October, 1961, p. 153.*

[*The Listening Walk*] will charm the 5 to 7 age group. New words are here, too. The *z-z-z-z-z-zzzzoooommmmm* of a power mower, the *hmmmm* of a shiny new car, and the *rak, rawk, rak, rawk* of roller skates. . . . [Any] youthful reader will turn the last page with a new sensitivity to the world around him.

> *June Johnson, in a review of "The Listening Walk" (reprinted by permission of The Literary Estate of June Johnson), in* Chicago Tribune, *November 12, 1961, p. 22.*

HOW MANY TEETH? (1962)

A child who's intrigued by newly-lost teeth will find this cheerful little book amusing even though the subject matter is so limited it can hardly maintain interest through many readings. This mother regrets that some junior-size dental care and diet concern wasn't included: it certainly wouldn't have spoiled the gaiety of the story and would have entitled it to a respectable place in a family library.

> *Carolyn H. Lavender, in a review of "How Many Teeth?" in* The New York Times Book Review, *Part II (© 1962 by The New York Times Company; reprinted by permission), November 11, 1962, p. 51.*

This is a delightful addition to an extremely popular series with which many young children have extended their horizons. My daughters aged eight and ten read it for me and were most enthusiastic in commending it to infants [for] . . . the information. Indeed, the information on our first teeth is presented in a most fascinating way, with its short pithy sentences conveying the basic essentials with a touch of humour. This jolly book is a must for the infants' classrooms and for lower juniors too.

> *Eric Linfield, in a review of "How Many Teeth?" in* The School Librarian, *Vol. 18, No. 1, March, 1970, p. 121.*

LOOK AT YOUR EYES (1962)

A first science book for beginning readers, and an unusual one. It is lucid in explaining basic facts about eyes, it does not cover too much material, and the writing is not any more stilted than a book for beginning independent readers must be. It is unusual, also, in the simplicity with which the text and the illustrations show the speaker to be a Negro child; he is quite matter-of-fact about brown eyes, quite matter-of-fact about his friends, whose eyes may be blue or brown.

> *Zena Sutherland, in a review of "Look at Your Eyes," in* Bulletin of the Center for Children's Books *(reprinted by permission of The University of Chicago Press; copyright 1963 by The University of Chicago), Vol. 16, No. 3, November, 1963, p. 48.*

[The] child is given very little physiological information but is rather encouraged to think about eyes and their function. This aim seems reasonable and valid, though possibly a little more explanation could have been given. However, the function of this type of book is to encourage the child to observe first, then question his environment, and not to give explanations. In this respect the [book succeeds] admirably.

> *Janet Leach, in a review of "Look at Your Eyes," in* The School Librarian, *Vol. 18, No. 2, June, 1970, p. 247.*

YOUR SKIN AND MINE (1965)

[Paul Showers's "**Your Skin and Mine**"] supplies a smattering of information about the skin, and is rather commendable as a simple explanation of differences of skin color for inquisitive children of our racially-conscious society.

> *Carolyn H. Lavender, in a review of "Your Skin and Mine," in* The New York Times Book Review, *Part II (© 1965 by The New York Times Company; reprinted by permission), November 7, 1965, p. 56.*

Scrambled facts concerning the human integument, its pigmentation, hair, fingernails and toenails, fingerprints and footprints, sweat glands and the sense of touch, are presented in this slight, beginning-to-read book. Information and diagrams are lacking on the cellular composition of the epidermis, and on the nerves and blood supply. Such details are essential to a truly scientific presentation of the subject and are not too advanced for the young reader.

> *A review of "Your Skin and Mine," in* Science Books *(copyright 1965 by the American Association for the Advancement of Science), Vol. 1, No. 3, December, 1965, p. 167.*

HOW YOU TALK (1966)

This simple science book will interest and inform the young child. Mr. Showers points out that the growth of language ability is slow and must be encouraged and tolerated. In very easy steps, he introduces the reader to the way humans make sounds using the lungs, lips, tongue, and so forth. The little "experiments" are readily performed with no equipment. The book, though presenting the normal growth of normal speech, would be particularly valuable to the parent or child in touch with speech problems.

> *John Graham, in a review of "How You Talk," in* School Library Journal, *an appendix to* Library Journal *(reprinted from the April, 1967 issue of* School Library Journal, *published by R. R. Bowker Co./ A Xerox Corporation; copyright © 1967), Vol. 13, No. 8, April, 1967, p. 64.*

As always, Paul Showers writes very simply, very clearly, and quite briefly; his text covers the subject in just enough depth for the very young reader.

Zena Sutherland, in a review of "How You Talk," in Bulletin of the Center for Children's Books (reprinted by permission of The University of Chicago Press; copyright 1967 by The University of Chicago), Vol. 20, No. 9, May, 1967, p. 147.

The problem [with the Let's-Read-and-Find-Out-Science-Books series] is that either the book has a vocabulary which is so difficult that the average six-year-old has to depend on an adult to hear it read, or it has a vocabulary which is within his capacity but new concepts have to be introduced through a very restricted medium.

How you talk succeeds in doing the latter well. Good readers of six and average readers of seven to eight will read for themselves and will make a first venture into a study of linguistics. They will discover how sounds are produced and will be encouraged to assess their quality and analyse their content.

S. W. Allen, in a review of "How You Talk," in The School Librarian, Vol. 17, No. 2, June, 1969, p. 217.

A DROP OF BLOOD (1967)

The greatest difficulty—one not overcome in this book—in writing science material for the elementary level lies in attempting to deal with concepts too complex for reduction to the vocabulary and experience of a primary grade audience. This book attempts to explain the chief functions of blood in the human body. Although some of the information, such as how a scab forms, will surely be of interest to beginning readers . . . , much of the text will probably leave readers more confused than enlightened. Such words as fluid, intestines, lungs, and cells receive cursory explanations or none at all. The condescending jogging verses that begin and end the book add insult to the dignity of inquiring second graders.

Janet French, in a review of "A Drop of Blood," in School Library Journal, an appendix to Library Journal (reprinted from the November, 1967 issue of School Library Journal, published by R. R. Bowker Co./ A Xerox Corporation; copyright © 1967), Vol. 14, No. 2, November, 1967, p. 62.

In very simple language . . . Mr. Showers introduces youngsters to some of the elementary concepts of the blood and its functions. The notion of the red cell as the carrier of oxygen necessary for metabolism is introduced, although the word "metabolism" is not used. White cells are noted to be capable of engulfing bacteria, and platelets are described as necessary for stanching the flow of blood from a cut. All this is told in the most basic and direct manner. This little book will generate many questions and lead to lively discussions, as evidenced by the reactions of the reviewer's own children. (pp. 252-53)

A review of "A Drop of Blood," in Science Books (copyright 1967 by the American Association for the Advancement of Science), Vol. 3, No. 3, December, 1967, pp. 252-53.

Crisp, straightforward writing and gay, cartoon-like illustrations [by Don Madden] combine to make this introduction to the topic of human blood clear, simple, and accurate. The author describes circulation and the protective powers of the blood, the types of cells of which blood is composed, and the reassuring fact that there is constant replenishment of the blood supply—although the details of this process are not given.

Zena Sutherland, in a review of "A Drop of Blood," in Bulletin of the Center for Children's Books (reprinted by permission of The University of Chicago Press; copyright 1968 by The University of Chicago), Vol. 21, No. 5, January, 1968, p. 85.

Generally, this book is simple and informative, but it has several puzzling omissions which detract from its value. Although a schematic diagram is presented with the suggestion that the heart is involved in the circulation of the blood, not even one sentence in the text makes it clear that the heart is the driving force. There is another significant omission, of the fact discovered by Harvey that blood moves in a closed circulation: nowhere is it stated that after passing through the tissues, the blood returns to the heart to begin the cycle again. If the author had limited his discussion to the constituents of the blood, as the title suggests, these omissions would not have been so critical.

Ronald T. Rozett, in a review of "A Drop of Blood," in Appraisal: Children's Science Books (copyright © 1968 by the Children's Science Book Review Committee), Vol. 1, No. 3, Fall, 1968, p. 21.

HEAR YOUR HEART (1968)

Good things often come in small portions, and this is a good rule for children's science books. In other words, don't cover too much territory, and what you do encompass in a book, deal with it expertly and adequately. In this successful effort, Mr. Showers has explained the basic principles of the human heart, tells the young reader how he may hear heartbeat by using a cardboard tube as a stethoscope (encouraging scientific observation); that the heartbeat of babies is more rapid than that of children, and children's heartbeat is more rapid than adults (encouraging comparison). Small animals have more rapid hearts than large ones, the reader is told (inference). The anatomical description of the heart and the diagrams are very rudimentary, and adequate for the purpose, although labelling of the major blood vessels would have been helpful for the occasional child who wants more detail.

A review of "Hear Your Heart," in Science Books (copyright 1968 by the American Association for the Advancement of Science), Vol. 4, No. 1, May, 1968, p. 55.

This book starts with youngsters listening to each other's and their own heart beats. Appropriate terms enhance the description, for example, "pumpum"—child's heart beat; "ka dum" adult's (slower), "tuppa tuppa tuppa" baby's (faster). . . . Text and illustrations vividly tell how these processes take place, but fail to touch on why. This latter point is the only criticism of an otherwise worthwhile book.

A review of "Hear Your Heart," in The New York Times Book Review, Part II (© 1968 by The New York Times Company; reprinted by permission), May 5, 1968, p. 52.

In his usual competent fashion, Mr. Showers gives basic facts about the heart and its operation, adding no extraneous material and explaining lucidly the details of heart action. The fact that the blood moves through the lungs is omitted in the interest of simplification, for example. The diagrams follow the text closely, so that the complexity of the illustrations grows as does that of the text. Other parts of the circulatory system are described briefly, enough to round out the picture without detracting from the real topic. (pp. 33-4)

> *Zena Sutherland, in a review of "Hear Your Heart,"* in Bulletin of the Center for Children's Books *(reprinted by permission of The University of Chicago Press; copyright 1968 by The University of Chicago), Vol. 22, No. 2, October, 1968, pp. 33-4.*

Easily read by eight-year-olds. . . . A clear account of the heart as a pump is neatly pinned to [the listening experiment], although pulse-taking by light touch perhaps comes less easily to children than is made out. The tone is pleasant and thoughtful throughout.

> *Philip Morrison and Phylis Morrison, in a review of "Hear Your Heart,"* in Scientific American *(copyright © 1968 by Scientific American, Inc.; all rights reserved), Vol. 219, No. 6, December, 1968, p. 128.*

No one needs to listen to the condescending tone of this book. I object to statements such as: "A heart is something like this inside: It is divided down the middle into two halves. Each half has. . . ." It is not necessary to belittle a four-year-old.

> *Althea L. Phillips, in a review of "Hear Your Heart,"* in Appraisal: Children's Science Books *(copyright © 1969 by the Children's Science Book Review Committee), Vol. 2, No. 1, Winter, 1969, p. 19.*

The author has written a commendable book. . . . It is flawed only by a rather difficult section on the action of four cardiac valves which, I think, will be incomprehensible to most children. The most exciting aspect of the book is the author's emphasis on the variations in cardiac function which occur in different age groups, in the two sexes, and with changes in physical activity. These variations are, as the author demonstrates, easily heard and felt.

> *Ronald T. Rozett, in a review of "Hear Your Heart,"* in Appraisal: Children's Science Books *(copyright © 1969 by the Children's Science Book Review Committee), Vol. 2, No. 1, Winter, 1969, p. 19.*

BEFORE YOU WERE A BABY (with Kay Sperry Showers; 1968)

Let's read and find out indeed—and in full. . . . [The] text is simple and succinct rather than clinically detailed. Nevertheless the only word for this presentation *in toto* is *graphic*—albeit sensibly and tastefully graphic—and the value, and virtue, of such a very young revelation you'll have to decide for yourself.

> *A review of "Before You Were a Baby,"* in Kirkus Service *(copyright © 1968 The Kirkus Service, Inc.), Vol. XXXVI, No. 20, October 15, 1968, p. 1172.*

Without fanfare, mystery, coyness, or superfluous information, this gives the facts about conception, gestation, and birth in a format that is attractive and in language that is clear and simple. . . . [The] writing is lucid and matter-of-fact, happily combining exact terminology and a sense of respectful wonder at the marvelous process of human reproduction. Simple enough to be read aloud to younger children, but primarily for independent reading. (pp. 46, 64)

> *Zena Sutherland, in a review of "Before You Were a Baby,"* in Saturday Review *(© 1968 Saturday Review Magazine Co.; reprinted by permission), Vol. LI, No. 45, November 9, 1968, pp. 46, 64.*

Basic physical facts about human conception, gestation, and birth are related in language that is simple enough for seven- and eight-year-olds to read and understand. A tasteful book, the text is rhythmic and imaginative. . . . The strength of the book is its straightforward approach; it does not circumvent the subject by resorting to animal analogies. Its limitation is that sex is treated as a purely physical function of the human body. . . . [It does] convey a sense of wonder about the physical miracle of life. For the age level, it is the clearest and most sensitive handling of the subject encountered by this reviewer.

> *Diane Farrell, in a review of "Before You Were a Baby,"* in The Horn Book Magazine *(copyright © 1969 by The Horn Book, Inc., Boston), Vol. XLV, No. 2, April, 1969, p. 185.*

I am not sure that the picture book age child will be spontaneously interested in the subject, but certainly it would be a useful book for parents to use if needed. We tested this book with three classes of kindergarten children and found them completely uninterested and bored.

> *Beryl B. Beatley, in a review of "Before You Were a Baby,"* in Appraisal: Children's Science Books *(copyright © 1970 by the Children's Science Book Review Committee), Vol. 3, No. 1, Winter, 1970, p. 29.*

Though accurate in its information, this book seems to neglect children's most often asked questions: those concerning sexual intercourse. The physiological descriptions, statements on anatomy, and ideas about embryonic development are concise and well presented. (pp. 29-30)

> *A. Harris Stone, in a review of "Before You Were a Baby,"* in Appraisal: Children's Science Books *(copyright © 1970 by the Children's Science Book Review Committee), Vol. 3, No. 1, Winter, 1970, pp. 29-30.*

A BABY STARTS TO GROW (1969)

In the author's preceding book, **Before You Were a Baby,** the lucid text described conception and reproduction with simplicity and dignity. . . . The text is clear and useful, but there is so little real difference between the books that this would seem to have value only where additional material was needed.

> *Zena Sutherland, in a review of "A Baby Starts to Grow,"* in Bulletin of the Center for Children's Books *(reprinted by permission of The University of Chicago Press; © 1969 by The University of Chicago), Vol. 22, No. 11, July-August, 1969, p. 182.*

[This] book describes the development of a human embryo from a single cell to birth without reference to the particulars of conception which were included in [**Before You Were a Baby**] . . . [presented] in clear and simple language suitable for use with very young children and for independent reading by third graders.

> *A review of "A Baby Starts to Grow,"* in The Booklist *(reprinted by permission of the American Library Association; copyright © 1969 by the American Library Association), Vol. 66, No. 2, September 15, 1969, p. 140.*

The material is very basic and much simplified, the format definitely juvenile, making this unsuitable for use beyond the second grade. But it's a good companion volume to the author's earlier book and a helpful lead-up to . . . other juvenile sex education books. . . .

> *Lois F. Ruby, in a review of "A Baby Starts to Grow,"* in School Library Journal, *an appendix to* Library Journal *(reprinted from the January, 1970 issue of* School Library Journal, *published by R. R. Bowker Co./ A Xerox Corporation; copyright © 1970), Vol. 16, No. 5, January, 1970, p. 52.*

Detailed account of the development of a baby inside the uterus. Clear and factual. . . . The book focuses on the baby and on the mother. Only a brief mention that sperm comes from the father gives any indication that the mother is not the only adult involved.

> *Masha Kabakow Rudman, "Sex: 'A Baby Starts to Grow',"* in her Children's Literature: An Issues Approach *(copyright © 1976 by D. C. Heath and Company), Heath, 1976, p. 169.*

INDIAN FESTIVALS (1969)

Brief as this is, it could not be an ethnological study or an extensive catalog of customs; but its focus, in any case, is on representative ceremonies and celebrations *today*, mostly sacred [but some secular]. . . . Indicative of the author's understanding, his concern to legitimatize what might seem alien, is the reference to "the tribe's priest, who is called the Medicine Man." Informative to the extent that it describes the observances listed, this is also educational in the larger sense of keeping them alive.

> *A review of "Indian Festivals,"* in Kirkus Reviews *(copyright © 1969 The Kirkus Service, Inc.), Vol. XXXII, No. 17, September 15, 1969, p. 1006.*

A worthy addition to [the Holiday Book] series, geared for younger children who have been conditioned by controlled vocabularies. . . . He points up the distinction between those affairs which welcome tourists and the ceremonies which remain private to the tribe. Transitions are occasionally abrupt, but the text is clear and non-fictionalized.

> *Eleanor C. Trimble, in a review of "Indian Festivals,"* in School Library Journal, *an appendix to* Library Journal *(reprinted from the January, 1970 issue of* School Library Journal, *published by R. R. Bowker Co./ A Xerox Corporation; copyright © 1970), Vol. 16, No. 5, January, 1970, p. 53.*

WHAT HAPPENS TO A HAMBURGER (1970)

What Happens to a Hamburger is a tract on digestion reduced to bite size and in terms that are easy to visualize (the "soupy food" squeezed into the small intenstine from the stomach). Scientific terminology is not scanted, however—saliva is spit or what pours into your mouth when "you say your mouth is watering"—though a simpler word may be preferred over its identified equivalent (e.g. gullet instead of esophagus). Altogether it's a clear, animated depiction of the process. . . .

> *A review of "What Happens to a Hamburger,"* in Kirkus Reviews *(copyright © 1970 The Kirkus Service, Inc.), Vol. XXXVIII, No. 22, November 15, 1970, p. 1253.*

A simple but quite adequate explanation of the digestive process. . . . The text does not give all the facts or terms (there is no mention of enzymes) and it does, in some instances, move into peripheral areas, but on the whole it is a competent, simplified treatment of a phenomenon about which most children are curious.

> *Zena Sutherland, in a review of "What Happens to a Hamburger,"* in Bulletin of the Center for Children's Books *(reprinted by permission of The University of Chicago Press; © 1971 by The University of Chicago), Vol. 24, No. 8, April, 1971, p. 129.*

[*What happens to a hamburger*] neglects the important role of taste in food acceptance but emphasizes the breakdown of solids into fluids and then into their molecular components, some of which are absorbed into the blood, and that the unusable portion is eliminated. . . . [Some] of the words used may not be familiar to the child [of the advanced elementary grades]. For example, it is written "another name for esophagus is gullet." Is the gullet more familiar to the child than the word esophagus? There is no mention of the kidney and its role in digestion even though it may be as important as the intestine. In spite of its limitations, this book is good reading for the child.

> *A review of "What Happens to a Hamburger,"* in Science Books *(copyright 1971 by the American Association for the Advancement of Science), Vol. VII, No. 1, May, 1971, p. 70.*

USE YOUR BRAIN (1971)

Lively, cheerful, and broad in scope, **Use Your Brain** . . . tells how a brain operates, with its nerve-messengers, to keep human beings safe, sensitive and running. . . . A suggestion of the damage "mind-blowing" drugs (including alcohol) can do is an important but unobtrusive part of the account. (pp. 69-70)

> *Eleanor C. Trimble, in a review of "Use Your Brain,"* in School Library Journal, *an appendix to* Library Journal *(reprinted from the December, 1971 issue of* School Library Journal, *published by R. R. Bowker Co./ A Xerox Corporation; copyright © 1971), Vol. 18, No. 4, December, 1971, pp. 69-70.*

A good introduction for the young reader, not going into too much much detail but giving facts about the structure and function of the brain and some information about the rest of the nervous system. The text explains very simply the response to stimuli and the role of nerves. . . . Only one part of the text seems tangential for the scope of the book: several pages are devoted to the effect of drugs on the efficiency of the nervous system.

> *Zena Sutherland, in a review of "Use Your Brain,"* in Bulletin of the Center for Children's Books *(reprinted by permission of The University of Chicago Press; © 1972 by The University of Chicago), Vol. 25, No. 5, January, 1972, p. 80.*

WHERE DOES THE GARBAGE GO? (1974)

An easily understood survey that makes its ecological point without being heavy-handed. The little girl who narrates this book . . . tends to talk in choppy prose, but guides us deftly. . . . The spirit of resource conservation has the last word as our heroine retrieves a cast-off yo-yo and makes it good as new.

A review of "Where Does the Garbage Go?" in The Booklist *(reprinted by permission of the American Library Association; copyright © 1974 by the American Library Association), Vol. 70, No. 20, June 15, 1974, p. 1155.*

Problems of sanitation, conservation, and recycling are seen from the child's viewpoint. "Everything goes in the garbage pail in our house," the text begins. The child points out that it's different in the country: garbage goes to the pigs and trash is buried. After discussing the problems of the mess and the vermin of city dumps, the pollution of water from garbage, and the possibilities of separating garbage components for recycling, the text comes back to the child's viewpoint. . . . Very simple [and] quite succinct. . . . (pp. 16-17)

Zena Sutherland, in a review of "Where Does the Garbage Go?" in Bulletin of the Center for Children's Books *(reprinted by permission of The University of Chicago Press; © 1974 by The University of Chicago), Vol. 28, No. 1, September, 1974, pp. 16-17.*

Since the author intended to make this book an introduction for the four- to seven-year old, he did not explore pollution problems in depth; the reader of this book may well come away with the idea that recycling of all used materials either occurs now or will soon be occurring on a widespread basis and that this alone will solve our solid waste pollution problems. . . . It is regrettable that nowhere in this book is the amount of garbage and trash we as a people discard seriously questioned. Furthermore, only household waste is referred to, and no distinction is made between re-usable and non-reusable, or biodegradable and nonbiodegradable materials. An injustice is done to youngsters by oversimplifying the issues which are part of this complex and grave problem.

Diane Holzheimer, in a review of "Where Does the Garbage Go?" in Appraisal: Children's Science Books *(copyright © 1975 by the Children's Science Book Review Committee), Vol. 8, No. 3, Fall, 1975, p. 30.*

SLEEP IS FOR EVERYONE　　(1974)

Some mild observations on the importance of sleep for people and animals are filled out by low-priority comments and asides. The most interesting part of this easy-reader describes an experiment by an undesignated group of scientists testing their tolerance for staying awake. An undemanding introduction. . . .

A review of "Sleep Is for Everyone," in The Booklist *(reprinted by permission of the American Library Association; copyright © 1974 by the American Library Association), Vol. 71, No. 1, September 1, 1974, p. 47.*

One of the most adept and dependable contributors to a series notable for the succinct treatment of limited areas of information, Paul Showers writes with simplicity and smoothness about an intricate subject. . . . Nicely done.

Zena Sutherland, in a review of "Sleep Is for Everyone," in Bulletin of the Center for Children's Books *(reprinted by permission of the University of Chicago Press; © 1974 by The University of Chicago), Vol. 28, No. 4, December, 1974, p. 70.*

Children are often apprehensive about sleep. They fight it because it keeps them from play. They fear it because of imagined monsters and scary dreams. This book explains in an interesting manner the nature of sleep and why we need it. It is accurate, well written, . . . and should appeal to both preschoolers and primary grade children.

Herbert J. Stolze, in a review of "Sleep Is for Everyone," in Appraisal: Children's Science Books *(copyright © 1975 by the Children's Science Book Review Committee), Vol. 8, No. 1, Winter, 1975, p. 34.*

Sleep is so much a part of life that it is refreshing to come across a book which makes the reader stop and think about its universal necessity. [The] limited reading matter [is] most suitably selected for the younger reader. The sentences are short, the vocabulary simple. Starting from facts about sleep it progresses to a scientific experiment and ends with a delightful description of a child falling asleep. (pp. 220, 223)

Joan C. Walker, in a review of "Sleep Is for Everyone," in The School Librarian, *Vol. 23, No. 3, May, 1975, pp. 220, 223.*

THE BIRD AND THE STARS　　(1975)

From the tidy, topiary-dressed lawn and stylized, smiling sun to the constantly recurring rhythm, this seems overcalculated. Yet (shades of Stephen Daedalus) the concept is one which children often discover to their own fascination so this prim little repetition game can be expected to catch on with some.

A review of "The Bird and the Stars," in Kirkus Reviews *(copyright © 1975 The Kirkus Service, Inc.), Vol. XLIII, No. 5, March 1, 1975, p. 237.*

[*The Bird and the Stars*] follows the traditional form of the accumulative folk verse, "The House That Jack Built." But that's where the resemblance ends! Simply and cleverly, Showers' verse tale begins with a bird's egg on a branch, then deftly moves through various spatial relationships—from tree to earth to space, beyond and back again—to give the reader a basic understanding of what a map is all about. (pp. 29-30)

Lee Bennett Hopkins, "The Poetry Peg Grows and Grows," in Teacher *(copyright © 1975 by Macmillan Professional Magazines, Inc.; used by permission of The Instructor Publications, Inc.), Vol. 92, No. 8, April, 1975, pp. 29-30, 32.**

Both the text and the illustrations cumulate in a picture book that can give children support for concepts of place and space. The end is a bit abrupt, but the verse is bouncy and both the concept and the cumulation are appealing. . . .

Zena Sutherland, in a review of "The Bird and the Stars," in Bulletin of the Center for Children's Books *(reprinted by permission of The University of Chicago Press; © 1975 by The University of Chicago), Vol. 28, No. 10, June, 1975, p. 167.*

[This] cumulative tale telescopes from microcosm to macrocosm. . . . [It] brings an awareness of relationships as well as a basic understanding of maps. Some of the vocabulary will be difficult for the intended audience (turret, fertile, etc.), but the concepts still come across clearly.

Joan G. Reamer, in a review of "The Bird and the Stars," in School Library Journal *(reprinted from the November, 1976 issue of* School Library Journal, *published by R. R. Bowker Co./ A Xerox Corporation; copyright © 1976), Vol. 23, No. 3, November, 1976, p. 51.*

THE MOON WALKER (1975)

After comparing new baby Christopher to the astronauts seen on TV who had to learn how to walk in the new lunar environment, an older sister describes the baby's homecoming, notes all the things that he can't yet do. . . . Though the youngest might have trouble grasping the "moon walker" analogy, and we could do without those cute little metaphors from Daddy, Showers channels siblings' attention in a new, solidly positive (as opposed to falsely harmonious) direction. . . .

A review of "The Moon Walker," in Kirkus Reviews *(copyright © 1975 The Kirkus Service, Inc.), Vol. XLIII, No. 15, August 1, 1975, p. 845.*

Here is a clever approach to the "We have a new baby" theme. . . . The narrator watches as Christopher develops in a year from infancy to toddlerhood. It is not just a "Today he smiled at me, now he is trying to walk" type of description, but rather a close look at the ups and downs of each stage, from the focusing of visual attention to the first staggering steps. Christopher's parents believe in letting him progress at his own pace and insist on nonintervention by the visiting friends and relations who are often in attendance. . . . This book also describes a very personal relationship between a young girl and her new brother as she watches him learn "how to live on earth." A must for any small child awaiting a new addition to the family. (pp. 172-73)

Barbara Dill, in a review of "The Moon Walker," in Wilson Library Bulletin *(copyright © 1975 by the H. W. Wilson Company), Vol. 50, No. 2, October, 1975, pp. 172-73.*

If this book is any indication, outer space has replaced the stork as the deliverer of new life on earth. . . .

Daddy's comments, which a four-year-old might find amusing, may be a bit too much for adult out-loud readers. "He doesn't know how to work his telephone" replies Dad to sister when she comments, "I think he wants to talk to me." "He doesn't know how to turn off the water," he explains when she asks about the diapers. (p. 67)

"Christopher is learning how to live on earth" concludes the text. Yes, indeed he is—under optimum conditions that do not prevail in the majority of America's homes. To non-affluent youngsters, Christopher's surroundings might seem like being on the moon. (pp. 67-8)

"The Analyses: 'The Moon Walker'," in Human—And Anti-Human—Values in Children's Books: A Content Rating Instrument for Educators and Concerned Parents, *edited by the Council on Interracial Books for Children, Inc. (copyright © 1976 by the Council on Interracial Books for Children, Inc.), Racism and Sexism Resource Center for Educators, 1976, pp. 67-8.*

A BOOK OF SCARY THINGS (1977)

Everyone is afraid of something some of the time, and sometimes it's good to be a little afraid of certain things. So much for generalizations; this is mostly just a list of the predictable things that "I" am afraid of (monsters in the night, upstairs at the country house); the more peculiar fears of others ("My sister Peggy is afraid of cows, . . . the man next door is afraid of cats, . . . and dog Murphy is afraid of thunder"); and some things that should put anyone on guard (traffic, tornados, wild animals). It sounds dull, but with [illustrator] Susan Perl on hand it isn't. You can't look at [the faces and action of the characters] without appreciating their terrors—and Showers' points.

A review of "A Book of Scary Things," in Kirkus Reviews *(copyright © 1977 The Kirkus Service, Inc.), Vol. XLV, No. 14, July 15, 1977, p. 725.*

While it's nice to get fears out into the open, this seems an odd melange of irrational fears and those that have a more logical base. "A spider is scary because it has too many legs" is not on a par with fear of lightning or fear of working on a tall ladder. The first is mentioned in passing, the second is corroborated by stern warnings about the dangers of lightning and instructions about safety measures. A small boy rambles on about these and other fears . . . that he has or that are held by people he knows.

Zena Sutherland, in a review of "A Book of Scary Things," in Bulletin of the Center for Children's Books *(reprinted by permission of The University of Chicago Press; © 1977 by The University of Chicago), Vol. 31, No. 4, December, 1977, p. 69.*

ME AND MY FAMILY TREE (1978)

[Showers spends] over half the book just introducing and counting the young narrator's many ancestors. . . . If devoting a book to this one scratch-on-the-surface will open the way to learning about genetics, okay; but as set down here . . . all those great-great-greats tend mainly to generate clutter. Marginal.

A review of "Me and My Family Tree," in Kirkus Reviews *(copyright © 1978 The Kirkus Service, Inc.), Vol. XLVI, No. 24, December 15, 1978, p. 1361.*

[Explaining the principles of family genetics and heredity] is accomplished nicely by the author . . . in a manner that would allow a young reader to generalize to his/her own family. Moreover, in the spirit of science, the reading promotes questioning by the child in regard to his/her own genetic background. Showers' attempt to relate to the pea plant experiments of Gregor Mendel, the pioneer of heredity research, to why children have certain physical characteristics falls slightly short. A quick transition is made from a discussion of third generation pea plants to why the young girl has red hair, which is likely to leave many a young child a bit confused.

Jim Palmer, in a review of "Me and My Family Tree," in Appraisal: Children's Science Books *(copyright © 1979 by the Children's Science Book Review Committee), Vol. 12, No. 1, Winter, 1979, p. 58.*

This basic introduction on the process of heredity should help unravel the often confusing concept of ancestral relationships for young readers. Showers uses a lively tone to discuss what a family tree is and how genetic traits are inherited.

Barbara Elleman, in a review of "Me and My Family Tree," in Booklist *(reprinted by permission of the American Library Association; copyright © 1979 by the American Library Association), Vol. 75, No. 9, January 1, 1979, p. 752.*

Showers introduces several simple concepts relating to genetics and heredity by focusing on one child's red hair and the red hair of several of her ancestors. Thus Showers explains traits and the idea that they are "passed down" from one generation to the next. . . . There are several other books available on this subject, but most get bogged down in discussing terminology; young children will be able to follow Showers' text and gain a basic understanding in the process.

> *Kathryn Weisman, in a review of "Me and My Family Tree," in* School Library Journal *(reprinted from the February, 1979 issue of* School Library Journal, *published by R. R. Bowker Co./ A Xerox Corporation; copyright © 1979), Vol. 25, No. 6, February, 1979, p. 47.*

Showers, in his usual direct and informal style, reinforces an explanation of family generations. . . . Showers doesn't go into dominant and recessive traits or the role of the gene, but describes clearly the facts about inheriting ancestral traits and notes that all living things are governed by the laws of heredity.

> *Zena Sutherland, in a review of "Me and My Family Tree," in* Bulletin of the Center for Children's Books *(reprinted by permission of The University of Chicago Press; © 1979 by The University of Chicago), Vol. 32, No. 8, April, 1979, p. 143.*

NO MEASLES, NO MUMPS FOR ME   (1980)

The minimal amount of scientific vocabulary (virus, bacteria, white and red blood cells, antibodies) is used straightforwardly and is quite clearly defined in context. . . . The tone is friendly; this is a useful, basic introduction that is original in its combination of family story and information. (p. 1210)

> *Denise M. Wilms, in a review of "No Measles, No Mumps for Me," in* Booklist *(reprinted by permission of the American Library Association; copyright © 1980 by the American Library Association), Vol. 76, No. 16, April 15, 1980, pp. 1208, 1210.*

As is usual . . . , there is no extraneous material; Showers describes, in a direct and casual writing style, how preventive medicine can confer immunity against common childhood diseases. He discusses the way in which bacteria and viruses multiply, and how the leucocytes of the human body manufacture antibodies to attack the invaders when, in weakened form, they have been ingested by, or injected into, people. Sensible in approach, the book is in the first person; it is useful information that is nicely gauged for the beginning independent reader.

> *Zena Sutherland, in a review of "No Measles, No Mumps for Me," in* Bulletin of the Center for Children's Books *(reprinted by permission of The University of Chicago Press; © 1980 by The University of Chicago), Vol. 33, No. 10, June, 1980, p. 201.*

A simple, accurate account of how immunization fights disease, how antibodies form and how they protect against infection. . . . Though the use of a child narrator is awkward, the text gives good concise information on a complex topic.

> *Anne McKeithen-Boes, in a review of "No Measles, No Mumps for Me," in* School Library Journal *(reprinted from the August, 1980 issue of* School Library

Journal, published by R. R. Bowker Co./ A Xerox Corporation; copyright © 1980), Vol. 26, No. 10, August, 1980, p. 56.

This is a scientifically accurate book. . . . The scientific concepts have been simplified and written in language that the child will understand. Children who have this book read to them will no longer fear their "shots" and will understand what they do for them. (pp. 56-7)

> *Herbert J. Stolze, in a review of "No Measles, No Mumps for Me," in* Appraisal: Science Books for Young People *(copyright © 1981 by the Children's Science Book Review Committee), Vol. 14, No. 1, Winter, 1981, pp. 56-7.*

Showers explains the basic ideas of immunity, using childhood diseases that were prevalent in the past and that are preventable by immunization today. The topic is a good one, and the text and explanations are appropriately written for the level of the reader. Unfortunately, some of the facts presented are not entirely correct. For example, whooping cough vaccine is made from killed cells, not weakened ones as stated. The author gives the impression that antibodies are formed immediately on administration of a vaccine. When discussing the mechanism of immunity to polio, he mentions the action of "killer cells" alone (I assume referring to phagocytic leucocytes) and nothing about antibody production. There are other serious errors, mostly by omission of related facts. The clever, accurate and informative illustrations [by Harriet Barton] are the best feature of the book.

> *Lucia Anderson, in a review of "No Measles, No Mumps for Me," in* Science Books & Films *(copyright 1981 by the American Association for the Advancement of Science), Vol. 16, No. 3, January-February, 1981, p. 158.*

YOU CAN'T MAKE A MOVE WITHOUT YOUR MUSCLES   (1982)

"STOP! Before you do another thing: 1. Make a funny face. 2. Hop up and down on one foot five times. 3. Scratch your head with one hand and pat your stomach with the other. Now, turn the page." When you've turned the page, you're told that you used cheek, leg, hand, and arm muscles to perform these actions. Showers' simple explanations of biceps and triceps and skeletal muscles are similarly introduced. ("TRY THIS. . . .") Once he's got kids involved in relating his anatomy lesson to their own actions, Showers explains the difference between skeletal and smooth muscles, notes that "your heart" is a third kind of muscle, and reminds readers that exercising is good for skeletal muscles. It's a well structured first lesson. . . .

> *A review of "You Can't Make a Move without Your Muscles," in* Kirkus Reviews *(copyright © 1982 The Kirkus Service, Inc.), Vol. L, No. 12, June 15, 1982, p. 680.*

As with other books in this outstanding series, this has plenty of white space, large type and not too much of it per page, and a crisp, direct style. In other words, everything the very young reader needs to facilitate the reading experience. . . . The text explains the musculature of the human body with just enough detail to make the material clear but not so much that it will overwhelm the primary grades reader. (pp. 77-8)

Zena Sutherland, in a review of "You Can't Make a Move without Your Muscles," in Bulletin of the Center for Children's Books *(reprinted by permission of The University of Chicago Press; © 1982 by The University of Chicago), Vol. 36, No. 4, December, 1982, pp. 77-8.*

A book on muscles may seem overspecialized, but by reading it youngsters may actually pick up a fine understanding. Children should relate quickly [to the text and its opening]. . . . Eighteen pages of text . . . should give a child a mental image of the hundreds of muscles in his body and an understanding of a key principle—that they work in pairs. The reader also sees that stomach, heart, and arm muscles represent three types and learns that when unused, muscles become weak. [Harriet Barton's] drawings often help by juxtaposing a part of the body as seen on the surface with the same part seen with its muscles. Skeletal muscles typically attach to a tendon, which attaches to bone; therefore, muscle ends are not shown in color as are muscles in the diagrams. Since no mention is made of tendons in the text, this incomplete-looking muscle might seem slightly puzzling. Still, there is much information in the brief book.

Sarah Gagné, in a review of "You Can't Make a Move without Your Muscles," in The Horn Book Magazine *(copyright ©1983 by The Horn Book, Inc., Boston), Vol. LIX, No. 1, February, 1983, p. 83.*

A catchy title and engaging activities draw readers in from the very first page. . . . Five to nine year olds will enjoy this cheerful introduction to the muscular system. . . . Most material on the muscular system is geared toward the intermediate grades, so this book should fill a need.

Diane Holzheimer, in a review of "You Can't Make a Move without Your Muscles," in School Library Journal *(reprinted from the February, 1983 issue of* School Library Journal, *published by R. R. Bowker Co./ A Xerox Corporation; copyright © 1983), Vol. 29, No. 6, February, 1983, p. 71.*

Yoshiko Uchida

1921-

American author of fiction and nonfiction and author/illustrator of fiction.

A versatile writer of picture books, folk tales, historical fiction, and contemporary fiction for children, Uchida attempts to advance an understanding of Japanese life and increase the pride of Japanese-Americans in their heritage. Set in Japan and the western United States, her books are described as simple, charming, and smoothly written. Her stories treat such universal topics as interacting with parents and friends, assuming responsibility, and gaining in self-confidence. They generally include some suspense and humor and portray well-behaved children as protagonists.

During World War II, Uchida and her family suffered the humiliation of being interned by the United States government in a Japanese relocation center in Utah. She draws on this experience in *Journey to Topaz* and *Journey Home* where, without rancour, she portrays the injustices suffered by her people. Critics find these works weak in characterization, but nonetheless moving. In 1952, a Ford Foundation research fellowship enabled her to visit Japan for two years to collect material for her writing and study native folk arts. Subsequently, Uchida wrote three collections of Japanese folk tales, which critics see as adapted in simple, flowing English. *The Magic Listening Cap: More Folk Tales from Japan* is her only self-illustrated book done for major publication.

Uchida is well-known for her *Sumi* books, which reviewers regard as accurate reflections of contemporary Japanese village life. Warm relationships between adults and children and traditional reverence for the elderly appear in such stories as *Sumi's Special Happening* and *The Rooster Who Understood Japanese*, while family loyalty helps the Sukanes adjust to adverse circumstances in the *Journey* books. Assumption of responsibility is the theme of *Mik and the Prowler, Takao and Grandfather's Sword*, and *In-Between Miya*. Critics note that the latter book effectively reveals the contrasts between the new and the old, the rich and the poor. Considering the success of her books and the longevity of her writing career, it is clear that Uchida has effectively portrayed Japanese culture and Japanese-American society. Her awards include the *New York Herald Tribune* Children's Spring Book Festival honor award in 1955 for *The Magic Listening Cap*, an ALA Notable Book designation in 1972 for *Journey to Topaz*, the Commonwealth Club of California Medal in 1972 for *Samurai of Gold Hill*, and an Award of Merit in 1973 from the California Association of Teachers of English.

(See also *Something about the Author*, Vol. 1; *Contemporary Authors New Revision Series*, Vol. 6; *Contemporary Authors*, Vols. 13-16, rev. ed.)

THE DANCING KETTLE, AND OTHER JAPANESE FOLK TALES (1949)

[Uchida has retold these tales] with suitable adaptations, based upon genuine understanding of the tastes of American children. The stories possess dramatic quality, humor and a gently insinuated doctrine of human kindness and generosity. They are

Photograph by George Fry for Addison-Wesley Publishing Company; courtesy of Yoshiko Uchida

told with directness and economy in good storytelling style. Their imagery is concerned with humble and with royal beings, with monsters and with gods that walked the earth like men. A few stories picture the rulers, palaces and kingdom of the sea, reflecting the natural inventions of an island people.

American children's books have in the past offered scant variety of folk literature from Japan. Older collections once in print contained a few of these selections. "**The Wedding of the Mouse**" and "**The Tongue-Cut Sparrow**" will be remembered. Others new to the English language bear Japanese resemblances to such familiar folk tales as "Tom Thumb," "Peachling" and "Thumbelina."

> *Irene Smith, "From Japan," in* The New York Times Book Review *(© 1949 by The New York Times Company; reprinted by permission), April 24, 1949, p. 34.*

If one remembers stories for over forty years, there must be something special about them. So I have remembered "**Momotaro: the Peach Boy**" and "**The Tongue Cut Sparrow**" and "**The Princess of the Sea.**" . . . Here they are again, with others as good, ably adapted for American reading or telling by a Japanese-American who heard them in her childhood. The amusing "**Dancing Kettle,**" the tricky "**Rabbit and Crocodile,**" the "**Old Man with a Bump**" could come from peasant people anywhere in the world. The rest have the overtones of old Japan, with hints, here minimized, of unknown gods and ogres, of princes and places stranger than those of our more accustomed fairy books. The tales are well chosen for points clear to children, all with happy endings for the good and justice for the wicked. . . .

In the author's hope that these tales will help toward "one world," she joins Dr. Northrop's theory of the possible meeting of East and West through mutual understanding of cultural heritages.

> *Louise S. Bechtel, "Fairy Stories," in* New York Herald Tribune Weekly Book Review *(© I.H.T. Corporation), May 8, 1949, p. 13.*

[This book] retells folktales some of which are familiar to American boys and girls in an earlier translation. "**The Dancing Kettle**," "**Momotaro**," and "**The Tongue-Cut Sparrow**" have been favorites for many years. Others are less well-known and one or two are completely unfamiliar to this reviewer. They are told simply, in an easy, flowing English that has in it a glint of humor. Atmosphere and background are subordinate to the story. This and their smooth continuity will make them a good choice for a storyteller. Because almost all of the older collections of Japanese folktales are now out of print this is an important book. (pp. 37-8)

> *Merritt P. Allen, in a review of "The Dancing Kettle and Other Japanese Folk Tales," in* The Saturday Review of Literature *(© 1949, copyright renewed © 1977, Saturday Review Magazine Co.; reprinted by permission), Vol. XXXII, No. 21, May 21, 1949, pp. 37-8.*

NEW FRIENDS FOR SUSAN (1951)

A mild, slow-moving little story about a young Japanese American girl, her family, friends, and dress-up occasions. . . . A quiet, mannerly account of a little girl's third-grade ups and downs, perhaps a bit too soft-toned in episode for sectional easy reading.

> *A review of "New Friends for Susan," in* Virginia Kirkus' Bookshop Service, *Vol. XIX, No. 19, October 1, 1951, p. 579.*

[Susan's] Japanese ancestry gives her and her Caucasian school friends only pleasure, for she can share with them the delightful custom of the Doll Festival, as well as the beautiful silk kimonos in her mother's trunk for dress-up in her new school's spring festival. The Berkeley background is woven in subtly and deftly by the author who grew up there.

The wartime experiences of the Japanese-Americans on the West Coast are not touched upon, nor is there the faintest plea for racial tolerance. A good story for little girls who have just learned to read well.

> *Gladys Crofoot Castor, "Japanese Heritage," in* The New York Times *(© 1951 by The New York Times Company; reprinted by permission), November 4, 1951, p. 42.*

THE MAGIC LISTENING CAP: MORE FOLK TALES FROM JAPAN (1955)

Yoshiko Uchida's second volume of Japanese folk tales retold maintains the lively straightforwardness of the first, *The Danc-*

ing Kettle. . . . There are fourteen tales in all and a sampling of their themes illustrates a universality that will make them appeal to children everywhere. In "**The Magic Listening Cap**" a poor man is endowed with the power to understand animals and thus is enabled to save a life and earn a secure future; "**The Fox and the Bear**" adds Oriental spice to a familiar dish; through his faith in Buddha, another poor man becomes rich in "**The Wrestling Match of the Two Buddhas**," and so on. Black and white drawings by the author have the simplicity of Japanese art.

> *A review of "The Magic Listening Cap," in* Virginia Kirkus' *Bookshop Service, Vol. XXII, No. 24, December 15, 1954, p. 809.*

Children's librarians who have found Miss Uchida's **Dancing Kettle** a good source for storytelling will be glad to know that the folk tales in this new collection have the same simplicity and directness. A few are variants of familiar tales; all are easy to tell and fun for children to read themselves.

> *Jennie D. Lindquist, in a review of "The Magic Listening Cap," in* The Horn Book Magazine *(copyrighted, 1955, by The Horn Book, Inc., Boston), Vol. XXXI, No. 2, April, 1955, p. 112.*

The fourteen folk tales in this collection show a fine feeling for the countryside and country folk of Japan. However, they are not on a par with the stories in *The Dancing Kettle,* by the same author, for they are told in a flat uninspired style and the

From The Magic Listening Cap: More Folk Tales from Japan, *written and illustrated by Yoshiko Uchida.*

author's illustrations are often simple to the point of crudity. The small print limits the book's use to the storyteller and to ages ranging from fifth grade up.

> *Carol S. Rathore, in a review of "The Magic Listening Cap: More Folk Tales from Japan," in* Junior Libraries, *an appendix to* Library Journal *(reprinted from the April, 1955 issue of* Junior Libraries, *published by R. R. Bowker Co./ A Xerox Corporation, copyright © 1955), Vol. 80, No. 8, April, 1955, p. 1005.*

In the preface to this second collection of Japanese folk tales the reteller expresses the hope that as the children of Tokyo and Kyoto and Osaka read and listen to these stories, so will the children of San Francisco and New York. There is no reason to doubt the fruition of this hope. The fourteen tales included offer the same general appeal, the same fundamental folk quality as do the stories in **"The Dancing Kettle."** They are pervaded by a recognition of the decency and dignity of simple, average people, and by a sound moral contrast between generosity and greed, wisdom and folly. The unpretentious, respectful tone of the retelling lays delicate emphasis upon these qualities, and enlivens the stories with appropriate touches of humor. Three of the stories have their counterparts in Sugimoto's "Japanese Holiday Picture Tales," but the versions differ.

Storytellers will welcome this collection. There are refreshing variants on familiar themes and motifs. All the stories are essentially tellable, and none needs adaptation. A glossary of Japanese words is included.

> *Elizabeth Nesbitt, "Five Honor Books, Humor and Fantasy at Its Best: 'The Magic Listening Cap: More Folk Tales from Japan','' in* New York Herald Tribune Book Review *(© I.H.T. Corporation; reprinted by permission), May 15, 1955, p. 7.*

Like the stories in the first collection, these are told with charm and humor and display those universal elements of folk lore that will give them wide appeal. Several of the stories have counterparts in other folk lore. The stories are suitable for reading aloud, or for telling, and will also be of interest to students of comparative folk lore.

> *A review of "The Magic Listening Cap: More Folk Tales from Japan," in* Bulletin of the Children's Book Center *(reprinted by permission of The University of Chicago Press), Vol. 9, No. 1, September, 1955, p. 13.*

TAKAO AND GRANDFATHER'S SWORD   (1958)

A very well-written book which combines a great deal of information about Japanese life with a good story which could have been set almost anywhere. The book is . . . an excellent piece of merchandise for the middle-age group.

> *A review of "Takao and Grandfather's Sword," in* Publishers Weekly *(reprinted from the February 3, 1958 issue of* Publishers Weekly, *published by R. R. Bowker Company; copyright © 1958 by R. R. Bowker Company), Vol. 173, No. 5, February 3, 1958, p. 82.*

In **"Takao and Grandfather's Sword,"** Yoshiko Uchida has not only told a delightful and fast-moving story about a Japanese boy of 10 but has described how a young Asian today

may differ from and resemble his counterpart in the United States. Like many American boys his age, Takao squabbles with his younger sister, is impatient to do grown-up things and boasts of imaginary exploits to impress a best friend who does everything just a little better than he. At the same time, Miss Uchida shows us how much less luxurious a Japanese potter's home is than that of almost any American; and how much Japanese children still respect their elders and generally pay homage to courtesy and good manners.

Miss Uchida's plot, characterization and style are excellent. It is quibbling, perhaps, . . . to wish that authors would either forego using foreign words (geta, tatami, samurai) or would footnote them at the bottom of each page instead of making readers scramble for a glossary at the back of the book.

> *Peggy Durdin, "Potter's Son," in* The New York Times *(© 1958 by The New York Times Company; reprinted by permission), March 9, 1958, p. 34.*

In **"The Dancing Kettle"** and **"The Magic Listening Cap,"** Yoshiko Uchida gave us fresh and charming collections of Japanese folk tales. Now she uses her story-telling gifts to introduce a little modern Japanese boy. . . . A quiet, restrained little story, this makes the reader share the wise and warm family life of the Yamakas, the anxious efforts to earn a living in the competitive modern world when one is pushed to produce too many articles in too great a rush and "it is not wise to hurry the making of a beautiful thing," and above all their pride in their pottery. . . .

> *"Intrepid Boys and a Seafaring Cat," in* New York Herald Tribune Book Review *(© I.H.T. Corporation; reprinted by permission), May 11, 1958, p. 18.*

THE PROMISED YEAR   (1959)

The story line [of Keiko's discovery that her stern uncle is really very kind] is enlivened by a lost kitten, the hazards of operating a greenhouse, and the long-lost son of a Japanese friend who is happily reunited with his mother. Written in smooth and easy style, with warm and realistic people in relationships that are seldom static.

> *Zena Sutherland, in a review of "The Promised Year," in* Bulletin of the Center for Children's Books *(reprinted by permission of The University of Chicago Press), Vol. 13, No. 1, September, 1959, p. 23.*

Adjustment to the life of a Japanese-American household and to an American community, interesting sidelights on the carnation industry, unusually real characters—all these are part of a story that only someone completely at home in the two cultures could have written with so much humor and verve.

> *Ruth Hill Viguers, in a review of "The Promised Year," in* The Horn Book Magazine *(copyright, 1959, by The Horn Book, Inc., Boston), Vol. XXXV, No. 5, October, 1959, p. 385.*

The plot is excellent, with enough zigs and zags to absorb the reader. Miss Uchida expressively chronicles the blending of the ways of East and West as Keiko grows emotionally, learning to love, understand and respect those in her new American home.

> *Olga Hoyt, "Keiko and Tama," in* The New York Times Book Review *(© 1959 by The New York Times*

Company; reprinted by permission), November 1, 1959, p. 50.

Ten-year-old Keiko arrives from Japan to live for a year with her Aunt Emi and Uncle Henry in California. Her reception by relatives at the airport marks the beginning of Keiko's somewhat uncomfortable relationship with Uncle Henry over her newly acquired pet cat. Later, at her relative's apartment, Keiko is welcomed by their Japanese American friends, at which point one wonders why no one has thought to introduce Keiko to other children her age.

When the cat disappears, Keiko privately believes her Uncle Henry has turned it loose. But, lo and behold, a friend appears to help her with her troubles—a white boy, Mike Michaelson, whose mother works in Uncle Henry's flower shop (Keiko's mother also runs a flower shop in Japan—an occupational stereotype). And who should come to Uncle Henry's aid when Aunt Emi is hospitalized, but Mrs. Michaelson? With the exception of Keiko's friend, Auntie Kobe, one wonders where the Japanese American friends are in these times of need. Like so many other books about minorities, this story employs the stereotype of understanding persons from the majority culture rescuing minority characters from adversity.

Another negative chord is struck when someone is described as sitting "cross-legged . . . like an old Indian chief.". . .

Although *The Promised Year* ends happily with Uncle Henry and Keiko resolving their differences, the story fails to deal realistically with any of the difficulties a young girl might have adjusting to life in a new country. No problems or cultural barriers of any kind impede Keiko's entrance into American society. These omissions strongly promote the image of Keiko as the model minority type—sweet, charming and resourceful.

> *A review of "The Promised Year," in* Interracial Books for Children Bulletin *(reprinted by permission of* Interracial Books for Children Bulletin, *1841 Broadway, New York, NY 10023), Vol. 7, Nos. 2 & 3, 1976, p. 18.*

MIK AND THE PROWLER (1960)

A cheerful story about a boy of ten, Mik Watanabe, who wanted very much to be thought reliable and therefore was delighted when a neighbor asked him to look after her plants and her cats while she was away. All went well until the cats were accused of eating the pet birds of the grouchy man next door—and some mysterious prowler got in and ravaged the pantry. . . . The book gives a pleasant picture of a family of Japanese background—ordinary people—with no obtrusion of intergroup problems. The family relationships are excellent, the book being somewhat weakened by the characterization of some of the adults: the grouchy Mr. Potts who thaws completely, the friendly ice cream man, the owner of the cats, Mrs. Whipple, who is rather stereotyped with her cats, rag rugs, garden, and a zeal for feeding cake or cookies to hungry boys.

> *Zena Sutherland, in a review of "Mik and the Prowler," in* Bulletin of the Center for Children's Books *(reprinted by permission of The University of Chicago Press; copyright 1960 by The University of Chicago), Vol. 14, No. 4, December, 1960, p. 67.*

Another of the author's Japanese-American family stories with setting in California. Not so well-paced as **"The Promised**

Year,"** but with enough suspense to maintain interest. Moralizing is successfully avoided, and boys will identify their problems with Mik's, while girls will gleefully approve of clever Tamiko.

> *Ruby Ewing, in a review of "Mik and the Prowler," in* Junior Libraries, *an appendix to* Library Journal *(reprinted from the December, 1960 issue of* Junior Libraries, *published by R. R. Bowker Co./ A Xerox Corporation; copyright © 1960), Vol. 85, No. 22, December, 1960, p. 4571.*

Miss Uchida is an excellent writer. In **"Mik and the Prowler"** she has told a good story about a real boy, but I miss the special charm of her previous books, **"The Promised Year"** and **"Takao and Grandfather's Sword."** Mik is so Americanized that there is no place for the expressive oriental flavor which Miss Uchida can impart so skillfully. This will not, however, bother other American boys, and girls, who will rate this story highly.

> *Olga Hoyt, "Things Went Wrong," in* The New York Times Book Review *(© 1961 by The New York Times Company; reprinted by permission), January 22, 1961, p. 28.*

This is more ordinary than the author's other writing—only mildly suspenseful as a mystery, with a few of the characters merely types—yet it is completely real and appealing in its interpretation of a boy's outlook and his development of a sense of responsibility, and in its picture of a happy Japanese-American family in California.

> *Virginia Haviland, in a review of "Mik and the Prowler," in* The Horn Book Magazine *(copyright, 1961, by The Horn Book, Inc., Boston), Vol. XXXVII, No. 1, February, 1961, p. 52.*

THE FOREVER CHRISTMAS TREE (1963)

A simple childlike Christmas story with unusual freshness and charm. Quiet in its two colors when compared with other Christmas books, but we hope it will not be overlooked on this account.

> *A review of "The Forever Christmas Tree," in* Publishers Weekly *(reprinted from the October 14, 1963 issue of* Publishers Weekly, *published by R. R. Bowker Company; copyright © 1963 by R. R. Bowker Company), Vol. 184, No. 16, October 14, 1963, p. 56.*

This is an unusual story which shows how the contagious spirit of Christmas enables children to bring happiness to an old man. American children will be interested in discovering that children of another country who do not worship in the Christian manner can still appreciate the spirit of its most meaningful holiday. . . . Recommended.

> *Patricia H. Allen, in a review of "The Forever Christmas Tree," in* School Library Journal, *an appendix to* Library Journal *(reprinted from the November, 1963 issue of* School Library Journal, *published by R. R. Bowker Co./A Xerox Corporation; copyright © 1963), Vol. 10, No. 3, November, 1963, p. 59.*

SUMI'S PRIZE (1964)

The title more or less gives the show away. The appealing heroine, Sumi, moves through a story that is contrived, even though the contrivances are decorated after the fashion of Japan. Information on Japanese family life and custom bolster the plot and may help the book to find its way to the foreign study unit fiction lists in early grades. . . . [Sumi's] decision to make an all-out effort for the kite and kite flying prize allows a discussion of the methods of building a traditional kite and the varieties of shape and decor.

> *A review of "Sumi's Prize," in* Virginia Kirkus' Service, *Vol. XXXII, No. 17, September 1, 1964, p. 893.*

How Sumi sets about to earn "the best prize there ever was" (which proves to be rather an unusual one) makes a winsome, buoyant tale of modern-day Japan. Yoshiko Uchida gives a lift to the story with the enthusiasm of gentle humor and unobtrusive details of Japanese life and customs. (pp. 18-19)

> *Margaret F. O'Connell, in a review of "Sumi's Prize," in* The New York Times Book Review *(© 1965 by The New York Times Company; reprinted by permission), January 3, 1965, pp. 18-19.*

THE SEA OF GOLD, AND OTHER TALES FROM JAPAN (1965)

Filled with delicate magic and humor, these Japanese fairy tales are told in the gentle manner that characterizes Miss Uchida's other collections. Familiar elements appear, such as a Japanese Rumplestiltskin and a nose that grows, but the sea of gold, hats for the statues, and the terrible black snake are more uncommon. [This is] a delightful book. . . .

> *Charlotte A. Gallant, in a review of "The Sea of Gold and Other Tales from Japan," in* School Library Journal, *an appendix to* Library Journal *(reprinted from the October, 1965 issue of* School Library Journal, *published by R. R. Bowker Co./ A Xerox Corporation; copyright © 1965), Vol. 90, No. 18, October, 1965, p. 4623.*

In folk tales the heroes are usually common people caught in uncommon circumstances, and their very innocence is their attraction for us. Thus, all the heroes in these 12 tales inhabit a homely world into which the miraculous enters. A supernatural being appears; a challenge is posed—and the peddler, farmer, or woodcutter succeeds or fails according to his goodness of heart. In one story, a poor weaver, unable to sell his reed hats on a snowy New Year's eve, places them on six statues—only to find the statues showering him with gifts. In another, a scoundrel who has found a way of making noses grow short or long is trapped in his own magic and grows the longest nose in the world. Yoshiko Uchida has retold these ancient tales quite beautifully, and each has a different lesson to teach from a body of traditional wisdom that is nationless in its simplicity, universal in its laughter.

> *Barbara Wersba, in a review of "The Sea of Gold and Other Tales from Japan," in* The New York Times Book Review, *Part II (© 1965 by The New York Times Company; reprinted by permission), November 7, 1965, p. 40.*

The combination of original sources and authenticity of presentation . . . makes this new collection from the Japanese-American compiler as acceptable as her earlier volumes. While the twelve tales have considerable variety in characters and folk motifs, they are distinctively Japanese in their unusual, sometimes somber, elements. Some themes, however, are universal: honesty pays, as does kindness to animals; poverty has its own reward in happy contentment; name-guessing spares the winner a dreadful end. (pp. 55-6)

> *Virginia Haviland, in a review of "The Sea of Gold and Other Tales from Japan," in* The Horn Book Magazine *(copyright © 1966, by The Horn Book, Inc., Boston), Vol. XLII, No. 1, February, 1966, pp. 55-6.*

Here are a dozen Japanese folk tales retold in a simple, quiet style. The tales have the folk appeal of universality, but they have a gentle, almost somber, quality that is distinctive. (p. 410)

> *A review of "The Sea of Gold and Other Tales from Japan," in* The Best in Children's Books: The University of Chicago Guide to Children's Literature: 1966-1972, *edited by Zena Sutherland (reprinted by permission of The University of Chicago Press; © 1973 by The University of Chicago), University of Chicago Press, 1973, pp. 409-10.*

SUMI'S SPECIAL HAPPENING (1966)

[*Sumi's Prize*] introduced an appealing little girl of modern rural Japan. This time Sumi's problem is to find the perfect gift for Ojii Chan. He was going to be ninety-nine and Sumi wanted it to be the birthday he'd never forget. . . . The story reveals the silent detachment of old age, the gestures which replace words. . . . Story and text complement each other and provide a reasonable, readable idea of present day country and village life in the Far East.

> *A review of "Sumi's Special Happening," in* Virginia Kirkus' Service *(copyright © 1966 Virginia Kirkus' Service, Inc.), Vol. XXXIV, No. 18, September 15, 1966, p. 979.*

Simple but original story. . . . Sumi is a definite individual; her village, with its people shown wearing a mixture of Japanese and Western clothing, is very convincing. Traditional respect for age is expressed in presenting the warm feeling that is possible between very old and very young. For all its humorous and breezy style, this is a moving story. The few Japanese words used are not defined but their meanings emerge clearly from the context.

> *Patricia Alice McKenzie, in a review of "Sumi's Special Happening," in* School Library Journal, *an appendix to* Library Journal *(reprinted from the October, 1966 issue of* School Library Journal, *published by R. R. Bowker Co./A Xerox Corporation: copyright © 1966), Vol. 13, No. 2, October, 1966, p. 219.*

A most engaging story. . . . The story gives a charming picture of a small girl and a small town anywhere; it is particularly enjoyable because it is written with a light touch and because it reflects the Japanese reverence for the elderly.

> *Zena Sutherland, in a review of "Sumi's Special Happening," in* Bulletin of the Center for Children's Books *(reprinted by permission of The University of Chicago Press; copyright 1967 by The University of Chicago), Vol. 20, No. 5, January, 1967, p. 82.*

IN-BETWEEN MIYA (1967)

[Miya] might be any country girl in awe of the big city—or at least she might be if the contrasts between simple village life and Western-style affluence weren't so pronounced in Japan. This particularity gives an edge to an otherwise pleasantly affecting story. . . . [Without] denying her desire for refrigerator and car, Miya sees that self-respect comes first. A familiar theme is built upon an accretion of lively, sometimes amusing incidents, and even the coincidences (Miya lost in a giant department store, found by her elderly friend from the train) have a credible core. In-between Miya is not only the middle child (a minor aspect) but also a stout-hearted link between old and new allegiances.

> A review of "In-Between Miya," in Kirkus Service (copyright © 1967 Virginia Kirkus' Service, Inc.), Vol. XXXV, No. 20, October 15, 1967, p. 1272.

Yoshiko Uchida well understands the universal pain and dissatisfaction, the restless frustration of a 12-year-old—especially a poor one who has been given a taste of the good life. Besides Miya, there are some splendid people in the story: the father, a wise priest-teacher; the sister, a modern Japanese working girl; a perfectly marvelous plump grandmother person who saves the day on more than one occasion; and even a greasy Japanese con-man.

> Elinore Standard, in a review of "In-Between Miya," in Book World—The Washington Post (© 1967 Postrib Corp.; reprinted by permission of Chicago Tribune and The Washington Post), November 5, 1967, p. 45.

So natural is Miya in her relationships with her family . . . , her contemporaries, and the kind old lady she meets on the train that readers will identify with her, sympathizing with her uncertainties and her joys, experiencing Japanese life with its sharp contrast between old and new, poor and rich. Young readers who are friends of Sumi, another memorable character of Miss Uchida's, will want to become acquainted with Miya. (p. 756)

> Helen B. Crenshaw, in a review of "In-Between Miya," in The Horn Book Magazine (copyright © 1967, by The Horn Book, Inc., Boston), Vol. XLIII, No. 6, December, 1967, pp. 755-56.

This story for girls aged eight up is unusual in its vivid detail of Japanese life and customs in both town and country early in the 1960s, and outstanding for its sincere attempt to grapple with problems not only Japanese, but universal. In-between Miya's life fairly bristles with problems connected with her family, friends, and also with the materialistic pressures from the Western world. This book makes a firm stand for worthwhile values which cannot be over-emphasized in an increasingly materialistic society. Readers will sympathize with Miya's struggles to accept her ulterior motives for a visit to her relatives in Tokyo, her sense of failure about being sent home, and her feelings of shame about her simple home, which she feels cannot be acceptable to her wealthy friend from Tokyo. Grown-ups are often shadowy figures in children's books, but here parents, relatives, and adult friends play an integral part in Miya's story.

> A. Ellis, in a review of "In-Between Miya," in Children's Book News (copyright © 1968 by Baker Book Services Ltd.), Vol. 3, No. 5, September-October, 1968, p. 265.

[In Prudence Andrew's *Dog!*, the] details are convincing, the boy's devotion compelling, the minor characters etched surely so that one realizes with pleasure that the trammels of formula fiction have been transcended.

This is also the case in **In-between Miya,** a tender, thoughtful tale. . . . Miya fails because the task is beyond her, but she learns much about coming to terms with life, and the reader is entranced by the descriptions of a strange culture, where the basic problems are the same, the family conflicts as intense.

> "Independence Days," in The Times Literary Supplement (© Times Newspapers Ltd. (London) 1968; reproduced from The Times Literary Supplement by permission), No. 3475, October 3, 1968, p. 1121.*

The disarming domestic tone of **In-between Miya** is just right for girls around nine or ten, who will find the perplexities of this Japanese girl not much unlike their own. . . . Without pressing too much detail into service the author makes the Japanese way of life very vivid and with her firm hold on characters, young or old, she ensures that her story will be relevant to girls everywhere.

> Margery Fisher, in a review of "In-Between Miya," in her Growing Point, Vol. 7, No. 4, October, 1968, p. 1183.

HISAKO'S MYSTERIES (1969)

Hisako's mysteries—who sent the 1000 *yen* note for her birthday? who is household helper Hana's artist friend?—are unmistakably linked to Grandmother's and Grandfather's discomfiture at mention of Hisako's "dead" father—and youngsters who catch on quicker than Hisako will find this a less satisfying story than **In-between Miya**. . . . But that's not all there is to it: like Miya, Hisako is both a reflection of Japanese life today (she's a daredevil on a bike, dutiful at home) and a distinct personality. . . . [She acknowledges] that she'd rather stay with Grandfather and Grandmother and finish school than return with [her father] to a Paris studio. He's engineered her about-face via an amusing preview of *la vie Boheme* and there are other sharp glimpses of village mores (e.g. the civic responsibility of street-sprinkling) and of Grandmother and Grandfather mating old and new. . . . It could be better but it couldn't be nicer.

> A review of "Hisako's Mysteries," in Kirkus Reviews (copyright © 1969 The Kirkus Service, Inc.), Vol. XXXVII, No. 5, March 1, 1969, p. 239.

Hisako is engagingly real; and her hopes, impatience, and problems are universal. But of great interest, too, is the authentic presentation of a land and a people feeling the impact of merging cultures.

> Ethel L. Heins, in a review of "Hisako's Mysteries," in The Horn Book Magazine (copyright © 1969 by The Horn Book, Inc., Boston), Vol. XLV, No. 3, June, 1969, p. 309.

Since there has already been a broad hint that a mysterious present had come from Hisako's father, . . . few readers will be surprised when he turns up at his daughter's hospital bedside in Kyoto after she has a bicycling accident. There is some awkwardness in this "mystery" but the book is otherwise very well written and is interesting both because Hisako is so ordinary and universal a thirteen-year-old and because it gives a vivid picture of life in Japan today. (pp. 19-20)

> *Zena Sutherland, in a review of "Hisako's Myster-ies," in* Bulletin of the Center for Children's Books *(reprinted by permission of The University of Chi-cago Press; © 1969 by The University of Chicago), Vol. 23, No. 1, September, 1969, pp. 19-20.*

SUMI AND THE GOAT AND THE TOKYO EXPRESS (1969)

[The] high-speed Tokyo train to run on the new tracks "will never, never stop at Sugi Village" [according to Sumi's class-mate, Ayako]. . . . Until one day, instead of the usual *Whinnnnnng*, there's a soft *Whuuuuuuf* sound: Mr. Oda's goat Miki, wearing Sumi's old red hat, has stopped the Tokyo Ex-press. There'll be a chance for the children to marvel at the interior, and for Sumi to share Miki's acclaim, but it's the blithe way this is carried off that makes it, like its predecessors, a thorough delight.

> *A review of "Sumi & the Goat & the Tokyo Express," in* Kirkus Reviews *(copyright © 1969 The Kirkus Service, Inc.), Vol. XXXVII, No. 21, November 1, 1969, p. 1149.*

Just as Sumi charmed readers in earlier books about her . . . , so is she likely to do it in this title. . . . Kazue Mizumura's drawings reflect the warm humor and the very human qualities of the story, which will appeal to young independent readers and make a good read-aloud.

> *Eleanor Glaser, in a review of "Sumi and the Goat and the Tokyo Express," in* School Library Journal, *an appendix to* Library Journal *(reprinted from the April, 1970 issue of* School Library Journal, *pub-lished by R. R. Bowker Co./A Xerox Corporation; copyright © 1970), Vol. 16, No. 8, April, 1970, p. 112.*

[This is] a sequel that maintains the standards and appeal of *Sumi's Prize* and *Sumi's Special Happening*. . . . The satis-factions and yearnings Sumi has are common to children ev-erywhere, the thrill of the occasion is crystal-clear, and the touches that are uniquely Japanese . . . add to the book's charm.

> *Zena Sutherland, in a review of "Sumi and the Goat and the Tokyo Express," in* Bulletin of the Center for Children's Books *(reprinted by permission of The University of Chicago Press; © 1970 by The Uni-versity of Chicago), Vol. 23, No. 9, May, 1970, p. 153.*

MAKOTO, THE SMALLEST BOY: A STORY OF JAPAN (1970)

Makoto was not only the smallest in the third grade, he was the slowest, and an all-round loser on Field Day. . . . Cham-pion potter Mr. Imai sets him to thinking, and to sketching, and eventually to painting . . . a temple scene that rates BEST IN CLASS in the school-wide Hobby Show. This is the stan-dard juvenile ego-booster (as usual for the poor-at-sports) with the standard assumption that everyone can excel at something. But talents not being distributed that evenly, it's not necessarily so—or a healthy solution. Better Mr. Imai's initial emphasis on doing what you like diligently; and better anyhow the visits to Father's workshop (he's a potter too), to Mr. Imai's for tea and bean-paste cakes, the shopping jaunt with Mother. . . . Qua story it's slightly lethargic as well as more than slightly

specious but as Japan turned-out it has integrity plus a pleasant glow. . . .

> *A review of "Makoto, the Smallest Boy," in* Kirkus Reviews *(copyright © 1970 The Kirkus Service, Inc.), Vol. XXXVIII, No. 11, June 1, 1970, p. 600.*

It is unfortunate that the interesting facts included about life in Japan were not presented in a straightforward, informational book rather than disguised as they are here in a story that is not good enough to stand on its own. (pp. 133-34)

> *Florence M. Heath, in a review of "Makoto, the Smallest Boy: A Story of Japan," in* School Library Journal, *an appendix to* Library Journal *(reprinted from the October, 1970 issue of* School Library Jour-nal, *published by R. R. Bowker Co./A Xerox Cor-poration; copyright © 1970), Vol. 17, No. 2, Oc-tober, 1970, pp. 133-34.*

[Pleasantly] told; the Japanese background is kept in good proportion to the universality of the theme and the individual emphasis of the story. It *is* a bit unfortunate to have the pro-tagonist, in so many such stories, seem always to be getting a consolation prize for not being able to achieve in the important arena of athletics.

> *Zena Sutherland, in a review of "Makoto, the Small-est Boy," in* Bulletin of the Center for Children's Books *(reprinted by permission of The University of Chicago Press; © 1970 by The University of Chi-cago), Vol. 24, No. 3, November, 1970, p. 50.*

JOURNEY TO TOPAZ: A STORY OF THE JAPANESE-AMERICAN EVACUATION (1971)

What was it like to be a Japanese-American living in California after the attack on Pearl Harbor? Drawing upon similar events in her own life, author Yoshiko Uchida relates her experiences through the eyes of 11-year-old Yuki. . . . **"Journey to To-paz"** is the story of a spirited family adjusting to a new life; it also presents a different picture of American attitudes during wartime. The result is a story that will thoroughly satisfy the reader.

> *A review of "Journey to Topaz," in* Publishers Weekly *(reprinted from the September 6, 1971 issue of* Pub-lishers Weekly, *published by R. R. Bowker Com-pany, a Xerox company; copyright © 1971 by Xerox Corporation), Vol. 200, No. 10, September 6, 1971, p. 51.*

It is probably unreasonable to be disappointed in a gentle un-assuming story for little girls because it is not a more substantial book. But if the author is Japanese-American and the story a fictionalized account of the year her family spent as "enemy aliens" . . . , comparison with other based-on-fact family sto-ries is inevitable. . . .

At first the circumstances of the evacuation are so overwhelm-ing—for a while the Sakane family must live in a horse stall—that the narrative is carried by the sheer force of the events. But the characters are overshadowed by the situation; they all seem to be holding their breath until the terrible mistake that deprived them of their homes has been rectified and they can once more take up their lives as American citizens. Whatever the reason, their lack of depth makes the book seem predictable and flat compared to Esther Hautzig's "The Endless Steppe" or Laura Ingalls Wilder's "The Long Winter"—or even the author's earlier **"In-Between Miya."**

> *Sidney Long, in a review of "Journey to Topaz," in* The New York Times Book Review *(© 1972 by The New York Times Company; reprinted by permission), March 12, 1972, p. 8.*

Miss Uchida's book is largely autobiographical and this makes her statement all the more significant. She knows well what she is writing about and makes it very clear how painful it was for families to be taken from their homes and sent to camps far away.

That family life not only maintained itself but even became closer and more unified is not easy for many to understand. But through Yuki, her major character, the author shows how Japanese-American families displayed tremendous courage and strength at a time when it would have been so easy to express only utter disappointment and sorrow.

Young Japanese-Americans could benefit considerably from reading this work for it would enable them to come to grips with an experience their parents, grandparents, and others in their families lived through. Others, neither Japanese-American nor young, should find Miss Uchida's work a moving experience.

> *Laurence E. Smardan, in a review of "Journey to Topaz," in* Journal of Home Economics *(copyright © by the American Home Economics Association 1972), Vol. 64, No. 9, December, 1972, p. 54.*

Much of the novel is moving, sad and painful, but it is written from a perspective that accepts and does not protest the circumstances that produced the Topazes, the Tule Lakes and the Manzanars. Instead, the author justifies the internment of 110,000 Americans as an act attributable to war hysteria. An emotionally laden historic injustice becomes bland and colorless.

> *A review of "Journey to Topaz," in* Interracial Books for Children Bulletin *(reprinted by permission of Interracial Books for Children Bulletin, 1841 Broadway, New York, NY 10023), Vol. 7, Nos. 2 & 3, 1976, p. 21.*

SAMURAI OF GOLD HILL (1972)

Based on the few available scraps of information on the Wakamatsu Colony—founded at Gold Hill, California by members of a Japanese clan defeated along with the Shogun—this is notable for its sharply realized 1869 backgrounds (both Japan and California) and for its sympathetic inside view of one boy's adaptation to a new life. Raised to follow his father as a samurai, Koichi has mixed feelings about crossing the ocean to become a silk and tea farmer, but demonstrates his manhood in the end not by using his grandfather's magnificent sword but by selling it to feed the impoverished colony. A bigoted California miner . . . adds a note of rather melodramatic but needed tension to the plot. . . .

> *A review of "Samurai of Gold Hill," in* Kirkus Reviews *(copyright © 1972 The Kirkus Service, Inc.), Vol. XL, No. 21, November 1, 1972, p. 1241.*

This well-written and researched historical fiction about the first Japanese immigrants to the United States easily allows the reader to identify with Koichi and his people. . . . Though

a delightful story, a good background in Japanese history is necessary in order to fully understand the conflicts he faces.

> *A review of "Samurai of Gold Hill," in* Children's Book Review Service *(copyright © 1973 Children's Book Review Service, Inc.), Vol. 1, No. 5, January, 1973, p. 32.*

An author well known for her stories of Japanese life in Japan and in the United States artfully chronicles the experiences of the ill-fated Wakamatsu Colony. . . . [The] story of the group's high hopes for the future and their gradual disillusionment and failure as a result of natural catastrophes, prejudice, and villainy comprises a moving narrative of courage and patience in the face of adversity. Author's note on the factual background of the story and a glossary are included.

> *A review of "Samurai of Gold Hill," in* The Booklist *(reprinted by permission of the American Library Association; copyright © 1973 by the American Library Association), Vol. 69, No. 12, February 15, 1973, p. 575.*

The author gives a balanced picture: some of the neighbors are very helpful, and Koichi is befriended by an Indian; the writing flows smoothly, the characters are well-defined, the period details unobtrusively incorporated. Above this, the story has a brisk pace and a warmth in its relationships, especially in Koichi's growing understanding of his father and the other colonists.

> *Zena Sutherland, in a review of "Samurai of Gold Hill," in* Bulletin of the Center for Children's Books *(reprinted by permission of The University of Chicago Press; © 1973 by The University of Chicago), Vol. 26, No. 9, May, 1973, p. 147.*

Both Japanese and white characters are warmly depicted—except, of course, for the few townspeople who make life difficult for the colony. But although few records of the Wakamatsu Colony are left, it would seem that the difficulties, sacrifice, disappointments, spirit and resourcefulness and despair of its workers could have been conveyed by the author with a little more intensity.

> *[Lyla Hoffman], in a review of "Samurai of Gold Hill," in* Interracial Books for Children Bulletin *(reprinted by permission of Interracial Books for Children Bulletin, 1841 Broadway, New York, NY 10023), Vol. 7, Nos. 2 & 3, 1976, p. 18.*

THE BIRTHDAY VISITOR (1975)

[Emi] gets the bad news that a minister is arriving, on the day when she'll be seven, to spoil her birthday. It turns out, however, to be the best birthday Emi has ever had, thanks to the special qualities of the guest. The author presents some engagingly subtle bits of information about life among Japanese-Americans and some Japanese phrases. . . . A *nice* book.

> *A review of "The Birthday Visitor," in* Publishers Weekly *(reprinted from the April 14, 1975 issue of* Publishers Weekly, *published by R. R. Bowker Company, a Xerox company; copyright © 1975 by Xerox Corporation), Vol. 207, No. 15, April 14, 1975, p. 54.*

There is always, in Uchida's books, a happy blend of verisimilar details that evoke vividly Japanese or Japanese-American life and a universality that speaks for and to all children. . . . The story . . . is appealing both because of the ever-entrancing subject of birthdays and because of the familiarity of the situation of boring (or potentially boring) adult visitors—but it also has the subtler appeal of being imbued with the gently firm, loving discipline that is so characteristic of Japanese family life.

> *Zena Sutherland, in a review of "The Birthday Visitor," in* Bulletin of the Center for Children's Books *(reprinted by permission of The University of Chicago Press; © 1976 by The University of Chicago), Vol. 29, No. 5, January, 1976, p. 87.*

Yoshiko Uchida's heroines are model children who possess common sense, self-confidence, humor and modesty. . . .

Orderliness and serenity permeate this book, and the conflict [between Emi and her parents] is calmly resolved. The story takes place in a never-never land of non-materialistic, middle-class comfort and stability which would seem rare in the U.S. today. Could one consider this other-worldliness, this peace and feeling of unity a typically Japanese characteristic? If so, is it possible within the American societal setting? Furthermore, although the traits themselves are positive, don't they perpetuate certain myths about cool, collected, unemotional "Orientals"?

> *[Lyla Hoffman], in a review of "The Birthday Visitor," in* Interracial Books for Children Bulletin *(reprinted by permission of* Interracial Books for Children Bulletin, *1841 Broadway, New York, NY 10023), Vol. 7, Nos. 2 & 3, 1976, p. 15.*

THE ROOSTER WHO UNDERSTOOD JAPANESE (1976)

Mrs. Kitamura, a babysitter, is fond of animals and maintains a bilingual menagerie named for heroes of American history. When Mrs. K. must give up her rooster, Mr. Lincoln . . . , little third grader Miyo finds a new home for her babysitter's pet. . . . [Unlike] many elderly characters in children's fiction, Mrs. K is a strong individual and a free spirit by her own admission. . . . [The] story is slight but presents a very positive view of middle class Japanese-American culture. As in the author's **The Birthday Visitor** . . . , this emphasizes affection and understanding between child and adult.

> *Dora Jean Young, in a review of "The Rooster Who Understood Japanese," in* School Library Journal *(reprinted from the November, 1976 issue of* School Library Journal, *published by R. R. Bowker Co./A Xerox Corporation; copyright © 1976), Vol. 23, No. 3, November, 1976, p. 52.*

Completely spontaneous is the relationship between little Miyo and Mrs. Kitamura. . . . Miyo's notice in her class newspaper for a "NICE HOME FOR A FRIENDLY, INTELLIGENT, DIGNIFIED ROOSTER. P.S. HE UNDERSTANDS JAPANESE" typifies the story's vivacity. Presented as normal instead of problematic is the situation of an only child whose father is dead and whose mother works long hours in a hospital; the story is written with spicy humor.

> *Virginia Haviland, in a review of "The Rooster Who Understood Japanese," in* The Horn Book Magazine *(copyright © 1976 by The Horn Book, Inc., Boston), Vol. LII, No. 6, December, 1976, p. 622.*

[The story has] a direct simplicity and warmth in this guileless book. . . . The solution is quite credible and satisfies everybody; the plot has just enough suspense and pace to appeal to children's love of action, but its real charm is in the gentle humor of the writing and the pervasive aura of neighborly affection and concern. This is also a good choice for reading aloud to younger children.

> *Zena Sutherland, in a review of "The Rooster Who Understood Japanese," in* Bulletin of the Center for Children's Books *(reprinted by permission of The University of Chicago Press; © 1977 by The University of Chicago), Vol. 30, No. 5, January, 1977, p. 84.*

JOURNEY HOME (1978)

Twelve-year-old Yuki Sakane still dreams of the awful time she and her family spent in Topaz, a U.S. concentration camp for Japanese during World War II. Still, the Sakanes are lucky to have been released, although anti-Japanese feeling makes earning a living nearly impossible. In this aura of hostility the Sakanes return to Berkeley and eventually go into partnership with other Japanese-Americans to set up a grocery store. For Yuki, adjustments include watching her veteran brother go through postbattle emotional agonies and accepting the fact that her environment won't return readily to its prewar ideal. Though one wishes that relationships and characters were more fully explored and developed, there are many sensitive touches and interesting glimpses into a largely ignored but important historical episode.

> *Judith Goldberger, in a review of "Journey Home," in* Booklist *(reprinted by permission of the American Library Association; copyright © 1978 by the American Library Association), Vol. 75, No. 8, December 15, 1978, p. 691.*

As in other Uchida books, including the one to which this is a sequel, **Journey to Topaz** . . . , family tradition and loyalty overcome all problems. This book fills a great need in describing the cruel treatment inflicted upon Japanese-Americans during World War II by their fellow Americans.

> *Dora Jean Young, in a review of "Journey Home," in* School Library Journal *(reprinted from the January, 1979 issue of* School Library Journal, *published by R. R. Bowker Co. / A Xerox Corporation; copyright © 1979), Vol. 25, No. 5, January, 1979, p. 58.*

Commendably blunt about the wartime misfortunes of the West-Coast Japanese, this is also hearteningly even-handed in treating of its outcome: it's staunch old-neighbor Mrs. Jamieson who best responds to Mr. Oka's grief when the atom bomb, obliterating Hiroshima, wipes out his kin. Uchida is not suggesting that many small rights—gestures or words—undo a monstrous wrong, only that each individual and each act counts. (pp. 6-7)

> *A review of "Journey Home," in* Kirkus Reviews *(copyright © 1979 The Kirkus Service, Inc.), Vol. XLVII, No. 1, January 1, 1979, pp. 6-7.*

This sequel to **Journey to Topaz** offers a realistic picture of the domestic cruelty governments and people—including the American—have been capable of in wartime. The persecution of the Nisei during the 1940s will open the eyes of many young readers.

> *Sharon Spredemann Dreyer, in a review of "Journey Home," in her* The Bookfinder: A Guide to Children's Literature about the Needs and Problems of Youth Aged 2-15: Annotations of Books Published 1975 through 1978, Vol. 2 *(© 1981 American Guidance Service, Inc),* American Guidance Service, Inc., *1981, No. 657.*

A JAR OF DREAMS (1981)

Packed into this novel are themes and plot enough to keep a TV series going for years. Unfortunately, the story has the depth and style of most TV shows, too. In the first person, 11-year-old Rinko Tsujimura describes the catalytic effect on her family of Aunt Waka's visit to California from Japan in 1935. Waka's reaction to the prejudice she sees (including the family dog being killed to scare them out of a competitive laundry business) and her questioning of the status quo prod disillusioned family members to open a garage (Papa's dream), continue in the laundry business (Mama) and pursue an education (brother Cal, who felt no one would hire a Japanese engineer). So much for the "jar of dreams" aspect; the second theme, heavily underlined, is the virtue of being true to one's self; in the end, Rinko is "almost look[ing] forward" to school in the fall, though "'Before Aunt Waka'" she loathed being different and was snubbed and insulted there. There is little characterization but a mundane modern vernacular and an irritating tendency to ponder pimples and peel hangnails.

> *Sally Holmes Holtze, in a review of "A Jar of Dreams," in* School Library Journal *(reprinted from the August, 1981 issue of* School Library Journal, *published by R. R. Bowker Co. / A Xerox Corporation; copyright © 1981), Vol. 27, No. 10, August, 1981, p. 72.*

In addition to the jar in which she's saving college money, Rinko plans a "jar of dreams," a fund that can be used to visit Japan, now that she is no longer too embarrassed to acknowledge her Japanese heritage. Smoothly written, smoothly structured, this gives a picture of a time, a culture, and a child that is moving and is realistic in the extent of the change and development in Rinko and her family.

> *Zena Sutherland, in a review of "A Jar of Dreams," in* Bulletin of the Center for Children's Books *(reprinted by permission of The University of Chicago*

Press; *© 1981 by The University of Chicago), Vol. 35, No. 1, September, 1981, p. 18.*

The sparkle Uchida brought to everyday doings in Japan (*Sumi's Prize* et al.) is joined, now, to an ugly American situation—but not, as in *Journey Home,* a historic injustice. Eleven-year-old Rinko's situation, in 1935 Berkeley, is more ordinary—hence, more universally applicable. . . . The family—kidding each other, helping each other—[discovers] its own Japanese-American resources. An affecting, spirited coming-to-terms. (pp. 1345-46)

> *A review of "A Jar of Dreams," in* Kirkus Reviews *(copyright © 1981 The Kirkus Service, Inc.), Vol. XLIX, No. 21, November 1, 1981, pp. 1345-46.*

[*A Jar of Dreams* is told with an] ingenuous simplicity and grace. . . . Compared with the many worldly-wise contemporary book heroines, Rinko in her guilelessness is genuine and refreshing, and her worries and concerns seem wholly natural, honest, and convincing.

> *Ethel L. Heins, in a review of "A Jar of Dreams," in* The Horn Book Magazine *(copyright © 1981 by The Horn Book, Inc., Boston), Vol. LVII, No. 6, December, 1981, p. 666.*

The author raises several issues about being Japanese American—Japanese values, looking different, reactions to being different and discrimination. These issues are resolved in ways which promote a healthy and positive self-concept about being Japanese American. In addition, stereotypes of Asian Americans, especially Japanese Americans, are dispelled. The characters are not passive, submissive nor "inscrutable." They are individuals with feelings and unique personalities who initiate and react to situations.

Although *A Jar of Dreams* takes place during the Depression, its messages are still relevant. However, it should be pointed out that the story focuses on what happens within a family in terms of its interpersonal relationships. The racism against Asian Americans, especially those of Japanese ancestry, that pervaded California prior to World War II is not discussed. Although individual family members do learn to confront others, their impact on institutional racism is highly questionable. (pp. 27-8)

> *Gloria Kumagai, in a review of "A Jar of Dreams," in* Interracial Books for Children *(reprinted by permission of Interracial Books for Children Bulletin, 1841 Broadway, New York, NY 10023), Vol. 13, Nos. 3 & 4, 1982, pp. 27-8.*

Alki Zei

1928-

Greek author of fiction.

Zei's war novels for children present a sympathetic view of the pain of civil strife as perceived particularly by the young. They receive praise both for their literary and moral value. Three of her books, in English translation by Edward Fenton, are applauded for their exciting and absorbing narratives and for presenting realistic characters of varying ages and political beliefs.

Zei was deeply affected by the changes which took place in her homeland following Mussolini's attack on Greece in 1940. It is evident from the vivid descriptions and subtle treatment of a child's naive examination of war in her first two books that the impact of this experience is fresh in Zei's memory. *Wildcat under Glass* and *Petros' War* are set in Greece, the former during the political climate which prevailed when Zei was the age of her protagonist. *The Sound of the Dragon's Feet*, set in czarist Russia, is noted for the depth and variety of Zei's characters, who are compared to those of Chekhov and Turgenev. Some reviewers feel that this book will not be appreciated by large numbers of children and recommend it for the special reader. Zei's novels bring forth an inspiring plea for peace through skillfully written, enjoyable reading for children. *Wildcat under Glass* received an ALA Notable Book selection in 1968, a *Horn Book* Honor List selection in 1969, and the Mildred Batchelder Award in 1970; *Petros' War* received an ALA Notable Book selection in 1972, a *Horn Book* Honor List selection in 1973, and the Mildred Batchelder Award in 1974; *The Sound of the Dragon's Feet* received a *Horn Book* Honor List selection and the Mildred Batchelder Award in 1980.

(See also *Something about the Author*, Vol. 24 and *Contemporary Authors*, Vols. 77-80.)

TO KAPLANI TIS VITRINAS [WILDCAT UNDER GLASS] (1963)

In the light of recent events in Greece, this is a stunning and important book. Though the story is set in the 1930's, its theme is timeless, as Zei shows accurately a nation's reactions to a Fascist takeover in the microcosm of passionate family strife. The narrator is the puzzled youngest, Melissa; the family is representative: Father is a petty bureaucrat afraid to speak out for fear of losing his job at the bank; Mother is scarcely more than a girl, so her feelings are discounted; Great-aunt Despina is a relic of more stylish times when monarchy meant class; Grandfather is a classics professor devoted to that man whose name is synonymous with democracy, Pericles. Melissa's older sister Myrto is apolitical, thus becoming for a time a willing tool of the Fascist flunkies. Spearhead for the book is Niko, the cousin who belongs to the underground; he leaves clandestine notes in the stuffed wildcat of the title; his life is in danger because he is a spy. All of this is related in a wonderfully understated, understanding manner, which will allow readers to sort out the truth as the book's young heroine does. One hopes Alki Zei is in a safe place and extends thanks to [translator] Edward Fenton for bringing the book to Americans.

Courtesy of E. P. Dutton, Inc.

Jean C. Thomson, in a review of "Wildcat under Glass," in School Library Journal, *an appendix to* Library Journal *(reprinted from the April, 1968 issue of* School Library Journal, *published by R. R. Bowker Co./A Xerox Corporation; copyright © 1968), Vol. 14, No. 8, April, 1968, p. 134.*

The wildcat under glass of the title held a place of honor in the family parlor and, in this memorable tale, comes to symbolize the spirit of freedom that was kept alive in Greece after a Fascist dictatorship took over shortly before World War II. . . . In an unforgettable scene, Grandfather's books are burned as "harmful" in the town square. Friends are arrested and taken away.

In a swiftly moving story, very real characters and the anxieties and problems that beset them create excitement, suspense and often pathos. No reader can fail to respond to the underlying theme: the historic longing of the Greek people for liberty and human dignity. A book with deep meaning for young people today.

Polly Goodwin, in a review of "Wildcat under Glass," in Book World—The Washington Post *(© 1968 Postrib Corp.; reprinted by permission of* Chicago Tribune *and* The Washington Post*), July 28, 1968, p. 14.*

[*Wildcat Under Glass*] vividly reveals the subtle and overt ways in which a dictatorial government imposes its will on young and old. . . . The narrative, based on the author's childhood experiences, is distinguished by an artless spontaneity that gives vitality to characters and poignancy to events. (pp. 117-18)

> *"Easy and Picture Books: 'Wildcat under Glass',"* in Books for Children, 1967-1968 (copyright © 1968 by the American Library Association), American Library Association, 1968, pp. 117-18.

It is sad that the beginning of this sensitive and delicate story . . . is so slow and quiet. Although this is a deliberate contrast to the later part, some readers may not survive the first two chapters. It is well worth persevering however. . . . The reader experiences the effect of the sudden confrontation with brutality, arrests, suspicion and fear. Even the narrator's sister is drawn by personal vanity to become active in the fascist youth organisation. . . . The characters are beautifully drawn: the loyal servant, the country children with their different domestic tragedies, the conflicting personalities at the school stay in the mind.

> *A review of "Wildcat under Glass,"* in The Junior Bookshelf, Vol. 33, No. 3, June, 1969, p. 196.

The effects [of a Fascist regime] on the children, particularly of the founding of the National Youth Organization, and their resistance to indoctrination when they realize that the new ideas are alien and repugnant, are very poignantly conveyed. The stuffed wildcat in the glass case in the parlour becomes in their minds a symbol of the spirit of freedom and it plays its part in the drama in an intriguing and effective way. As a lesson in human values, the book will prove of great value, and the experience of reading it a moving and thought-provoking one.

> *Robert Bell, in a review of "Wildcat under Glass,"* in The School Librarian, Vol. 17, No. 2, June, 1969, p. 201.

The book is particularly effective in showing the reactions of the very young and the very old to the abrasive imposition of a Fascist Government. Although the story is set in the 1930's, its local atmosphere is more important than the period. Well written, deftly translated, and—despite the fact that the children in the story seem quite young, while the subtler concepts and theories are suitable for rather older children—an absorbing story. (pp. 434-35)

> *Zena Sutherland, in a review of "Wildcat under Glass,"* in The Best in Children's Books: The University of Chicago Guide to Children's Literature, 1966-1972, edited by Zena Sutherland (reprinted by permission of The University of Chicago Press; © 1973 by The University of Chicago), University of Chicago Press, 1973, pp. 434-35.

HO MEGALOS PERIPATOS TOU PETROU [PETROS' WAR] (1971)

The time is October, 1940, in Athens, Greece. War has been declared against Italy and 10-year-old Petros begins what he terms an unheroic involvement with the Resistance. Through Petros' eyes we witness the tragic consequences of defeat, the pressures of German occupation and one small boy's dreams of glory contrasted against a collapsing familiar world. Alki Zei and Edward Fenton have brought to this new story the outstanding qualities of their highly acclaimed **"Wildcat Under Glass."** This is a rich, glorious tapestry of human emotions under stress.

> *A review of "Petros' War,"* in Publishers Weekly (reprinted from the May 15, 1972 issue of Publishers Weekly, published by R. R. Bowker Company; copyright © 1972 by R. R. Bowker Company), Vol. 201, No. 20, May 15, 1972, p. 54.

The story describes, in vivid . . . style, the privation and ignominy of living under occupation, the tenacious resistance of the Athenians, and the dangers and small satisfactions that came to Petros in his work with the Underground. . . . The characters are sharply etched, the story well paced and filled with action and drama.

> *Zena Sutherland, in a review of "Petros' War,"* (originally published in Bulletin of the Center for Children's Books, Vol. 26, No. 3, November, 1972), in The Best in Children's Books: The University of Chicago Guide to Children's Literature, 1966-1972, edited by Zena Sutherland (reprinted by permission of The University of Chicago Press; © 1972 by The University of Chicago), University of Chicago Press, 1973, p. 434.

Perhaps the education of the heart can be effected as much through emotion as by the anguish of wartime and enemy occupation, but as one reads **Petros' War** by Alki Zei, beside one's extreme pleasure there runs a feeling of shame: it is as though one has been complaining of a twisted ankle to someone who has lost a leg. Not that Petros or any of his Greek friends or family would see it that way, for self-pity is entirely absent from their tale.

Told with matter-of-fact simplicity, Petros's story needs no elaboration, for the events of the wartime occupation of Greece speak for themselves: the vanishing bread, the slow onset of hunger with its different and quirky effects on the characters, the shoes that grow ever tighter, the clothes more worn and inadequate. Theodore, the pet tortoise who goes under to the Nazis; the English dog. The excitement of the small boys when they help the freedom fighters, the futile deaths of the girl who aided them, and that of Sotiris, Petros's cocky friend. The well-fed smugness of the trinket-laden "Little Czarinas", whose father is a profiteer in flour, the gradual change in Petros's sister Antigone, with the sixty-four curling rags which she puts nightly in her hair. Here are pleasure and sorrow, courage and cowardice, grandeur and pettiness, all shown with a Chaucerian humour, through the lively family and friends of one sublimely ordinary boy, who still unbelievably translates horror into terms of his childhood ("Hit it right in the heart", the girl at the fairground shooting-range had said to Uncle Angelos, so long ago), who still dreams in hunger (oh, that insidious shame again!) of white bread and English marmalade. For pure enjoyment, and so very much more besides, this is a book which every child should read.

> *"Hearts Growing Older,"* in The Times Literary Supplement (© Times Newspapers Ltd. (London) 1972; reproduced from The Times Literary Supplement by permission), No. 3687, November 3, 1972, p. 1319.*

Though it records much suffering, this story of the Italian/German occupation of Greece during World War II salutes the human spirit. . . . The prose has a naive quality—perhaps because the protagonist is so young. Nevertheless, the resilience and energy of the small hero come through admirably, and

Alki Zei again provides a vivid, authentic picture of a proud, oppressed people.

> *Jean C. Thomson, in a review of "Petros' War," in* School Library Journal, *an appendix to* Library Journal *(reprinted from the January, 1973 issue of* School Library Journal, *published by R. R. Bowker Co./A Xerox Corporation; copyright © 1973), Vol. 19, No. 5, January, 1973, p. 73.*

Unlike some fictional heroes, ten-year-old Petros wins no wars where armies have failed, solves no crime that has defeated Interpol, rescues no heroines from dangers that have defied the bravest of men. His battlefield is Athens under Italian and German occupation: his contribution to victory nothing more spectacular than rescuing a dog, scattering nails on the road or daubing slogans on walls. So he emerges as a convincing character, firmly set in a besieged, sad city which itself is realistically brought to life (or death?) through such episodes as a woman eating garbage, Sortiris' grandmother dying of hunger, Petros' grandfather turning professional beggar, Antigone's dress made from a tablecloth, Drossoula's death in a demonstration, the execution of Antonis—a disturbing novel that makes its impact by uncovering the stark, shattering cruelties of war and their effect on a variety of sufferers, a moving reminder of bad old days that still keep turning up in somebody's calendar. (pp. 64-5)

> *George Bott, in a review of "Petros' War," in* The Junior Bookshelf, *Vol. 37, No. 1, February, 1973, pp. 64-5.*

A novel which portrays both the indiscriminate atrocities spawned by war and the individual heroism performed by ordinary people is Alki Zei's **Petros' War.** This book does not come from one of the major combatant countries, but from Greece, an area considered, if we may judge from the scant news stories of the time, a minor war theater. Zei shows, however, that no suffering or courage is minor. In 1940, Petros is an animal-loving and game-playing boy, much like boys of other places and other times. Then foreign invasion and occupation bring cold and hunger, which sap not only physical health, but also moral strength. Revolted at first by his grandfather's begging and petty stealing, Petros comes to understand the old man, who is obsessed with fear of becoming another of the streetside cadavers. Inspired by the beautiful and beauty-loving Drossoula, Petros assists her freedom-fighter group and matures into manhood by the time of liberation in 1944. But the cost of courage is great: both Drossoula and Petros's neighbor, the urchin-saboteur Sotiris, are shot down.

The novel includes a sympathetic portrayal of an enemy deserter and realistically develops his relationship to the family. Petros—and the reader—learn that "Garibaldi's" fear is not simple cowardice and his submission to drudgery not abject when it helps heal the chilblained hands and shrunken spirit of Petros's mother. Amid the horrors of hunger, death, and fear, Zei has depicted the Greek resistant and resilient spirit. Petros grows to exhibit a courage like that of Alexios, the hero of his boyhood stories. (pp. 203-04)

> *Joan Stidham Nist, "Perspective on World War II," in* Children's Literature: Annual of the Modern Language Association Group on Children's Literature and the Children's Literature Association, *Vol. 9, edited by Francelia Butler (copyright © by Children's Literature An International Journal, Inc.), Yale University Press, 1981, pp. 203-09.**

KONTA STIS RAGIES [THE SOUND OF THE DRAGON'S FEET] (1977)

In this unusual story, set in 1894 in a Russian town near the Polish-Lithuanian border, 10-year-old Sasha opens her eyes to the great differences between the rich and the poor around her and begins to question the injustices she observes. . . . The action and the large cast of Chekovian characters are seen from Sasha's perspective so that readers, identifying with her, should assimilate some of the atmosphere of pre-Revolutionary Russia.

> *Matilda R. Kornfeld, in a review of "The Sound of the Dragon's Feet," in* School Library Journal *(reprinted from the September, 1979 issue of* School Library Journal, *published by R. R. Bowker Co./A Xerox Corporation; copyright © 1979), Vol. 26, No. 1, September, 1979, p. 151.*

[Sasha Velitsanskaya] tells her first-person story in the present tense. The ten-year-old girl . . . was close to her father and bombarded him daily with questions—some of them unanswerable. "'Do people positively have to die?'"; "'What happens to the flies in winter?'"; "'Why did my uncle who got engaged want his bride to give him her hand?'" In the course of the narrative, however, the social climate of Russia at the turn of the nineteenth century is casually re-created, and the people who stimulate Sasha's curiosity suggest similar characters in the fiction of Turgeniev and Chekhov: the cook, who has "two smoked-up icons set on a little shelf beside her cauldrons and her frying pans"; the old woman who sells rolls on the street; and Sasha's beloved tutor, a revolutionary student, who has spent three years in Siberia. Never didactic or doctrinaire, the story, with its episodic but subtly woven plot, is filled with the faint, distant rumblings of the Russian Revolution, while the richly varied characters are refracted through the momentary but urgent experiences—pleasurable as well as, thought-provoking—of an alert young child. [**The Sound of the Dragon's Feet** is] a work significant for its humanity and for its skillfully balanced art.

> *Paul Hines, in a review of "The Sound of the Dragon's Feet," in* The Horn Book Magazine *(copyright © 1979 by The Horn Book, Inc., Boston), Vol. LV, No. 5, October, 1979, p. 538.*

[At first Sasha] is portrayed with an emphasis on that cute innocence which appeals more to adults than to other children; even so, she will probably manage to captivate most readers by the time she announces to her new French tutor: "Mademoiselle Pauline, when I grow up I am going to be a wild animal tamer or an agitator." (The tutor's response: "Sashenka, I think I have begun to love you very much.") It's another tutor, revolutionary Pavel Grigorevitch, a former medical student and Siberian prisoner, who becomes the focus of the story when he is arrested for instigating a strike. This upsets Sasha's household, grieving even the maid who keeps icons in the kitchen and had earlier threatened to resign in protest against the "jailbird's" presence. And by the time that Father has traded his life-saving treatment of the Colonel's wife for the tutor's freedom (conditional, alas for Sasha, on his departure from town), Sasha has learned something about real bravery, and her childhood perception has grown to take in the injustice and heroism she sees around her. Zei, who doesn't overdo the growth in awareness, gives us an engaging portrait of an outgoing, observant little girl—and a skillfully distilled and filtered one of pre-Revolutionary Russia. (pp. 1327-28)

A review of "The Sound of the Dragon's Feet," in Kirkus Reviews *(copyright © 1979 The Kirkus Service, Inc.), Vol. XLVII, No. 22, November 15, 1979, pp. 1327-28.*

[A] whole cast of distinctly drawn characters, reminiscent of those in a Chekhov drama, touches [Sasha's] life in a series of occurrences that are imbued with pathos, drama, and bits of humor. More quiet and reflective (with less clear allusions to the historical references) than Zei's *Wildcat under Glass* . . . , the story has subtle qualities that will nevertheless hold interest for special readers, who will be seeing prerevolutionary Russia through Sasha's naive viewpoint and child-toned interpretations.

Barbara Elleman, in a review of "The Sound of the Dragon's Feet," in Booklist *(reprinted by permission of the American Library Association; copyright © 1979 by the American Library Association), Vol. 76, No. 7, December 1, 1979, p. 563.*

[A] story that is imbued with concern for social conditions and reform is told by ten-year-old Sasha. . . . A tract? No. Zei is too skilled a storyteller to let her message overburden her medium. Skillfully translated, the book has a lively flow and balanced treatment, as the curious, sympathetic, and intelligent Sasha quizzes her father, pokes gentle fun at the household staff, enjoys the unorthodox and effective teaching methods of her tutor, and delights in the small pleasures of a ten-year-old's life.

Zena Sutherland, in a review of "The Sound of the Dragon's Feet," in Bulletin of the Center for Children's Books *(reprinted by permission of The University of Chicago Press; © 1980 by The University of Chicago), Vol. 33, No. 6, February, 1980, p. 124.*

APPENDIX

THE EXCERPTS IN CLR, VOLUME 6, WERE REPRINTED FROM THE FOLLOWING PERIODICALS:

American Artist
American Association for the Advancement
  of Science
American Libraries
The American Scandinavian Review
The American Scholar
Appraisal: Children's Science Books
Appraisal: Science Books for Young People
The Athenaeum
The Atlantic Monthly
The Babbling Bookworm
Blackwood's Edinburgh Magazine
Book Week—New York Herald Tribune
Book Week—The Sunday Herald Tribune
Book Week—World Journal Tribune
Book Window
Book World
Book World—Washington Post
Book World—The Washington Post
Booklist
The Booklist
The Booklist and Subscription Books
  Bulletin
The Bookman, London
Books
Books for Your Children
Bulletin of the Center for Children's Books
Bulletin of the Children's Book Center
Canadian Children's Literature: A Journal of
  Criticism and Review
Catholic Library World
Chicago Tribune
Childhood Education
Children's Book News
Children's Book Review
Children's Book Review Service
Children's Literature: Annual of The
  Modern Language Association Seminar
  on Children's Literature and The
  Children's Literature Association

Children's Literature Association Quarterly
Children's literature in education
Choice
The Christian Science Monitor
The Critic
Curriculum Review
Design
The Dublin University Magazine
Ebony
The Economist
Elementary English
Growing Point
The Horn Book Magazine
The Illustrated London News
Instructor
The International Review
Interracial Books for Children Bulletin
Journal of Home Economics
The Junior Bookshelf
Junior Libraries
Kirkus Reviews
Kirkus Service
Kliatt Young Adult Paperback Book Guide
Language Arts
Library Journal
The Lion and the Unicorn
The Listener
The Living Age
Los Angeles Times
The Nation
The National Magazine
The National Observer
The New Republic
New Statesman
The New Statesman & Nation
New York Herald Tribune Book Review
New York Herald Tribune Books
New York Herald Tribune Weekly Book
  Review

The New York Times
The New York Times Book Review
The New Yorker
Newsweek
Notes
Oklahoma Librarian
Ontario Library Review
Orbis Litterarum
Poetry
Publishers Weekly
Punch
The Reading Teacher
Saturday Review
The Saturday Review, New York
The Saturday Review of Literature
The School Librarian
The School Librarian and School Library
  Review
School Library Journal
Science Books
Science Books & Films
Science Fiction & Fantasy Book Review
Science Fiction Review
Scientific American
Signal
The Spectator
Studio International
Teacher
Temple Bar
Time
The Times Educational Supplement
The Times Literary Supplement
Top of the News
Virginia Kirkus' Bookshop Service
Virginia Kirkus' Service
Voice of Youth Advocates
Wilson Library Bulletin

THE EXCERPTS IN CLR, VOLUME 6, WERE REPRINTED FROM THE FOLLOWING BOOKS:

Amis, Kingsley. What Became of Jane Austen? and Other Questions. *Jonathan Cape, 1970, Harcourt, 1971.*

Arbuthnot, May Hill, and Sutherland, Zena. Children and Books. *4th ed. Scott, Foresman, 1972.*

Auden, W. H. Forewords and Afterwords. *Edited by Edward Mendelson. Random House, 1973.*

Bader, Barbara. American Picturebooks from Noah's Ark to the Beast Within. *Macmillan, 1976.*

Bain, R. Nisbet. Hans Christian Andersen: A Biography. *Dodd, Mead & Company, 1895.*

Baskin, Barbara H., and Harris, Karen H. Notes from a Different Drummer: A Guide to Juvenile Fiction Portraying the Handicapped. *Bowker, 1977.*

Belloc, Hilaire. On Anything. *Dutton, 1910.*

Böök, Frederick. Hans Andersen: A Biography. *University of Oklahoma Press, 1962.*

Books for Children, 1967-68. *American Library Association, 1968.*

Boyesen, Hjalmar Hjorth. Essays on Scandinavian Literature. *Charles Scribner's Sons, 1895.*

Bracken, Jeanne; Wigutoff, Sharon; and Baker, Ilene. Books for Today's Young Readers: An Annotated Bibliography of Recommended Fiction for Ages 10-14. *Feminist Press, 1981.*

Brandes, Georg. Eminent Authors of the Nineteenth Century: Literary Portraits. *Translated by Rasmus B. Anderson. Thomas Y. Crowell Co., Inc., 1886.*

Bredsdorff, Elias. Hans Christian Andersen: The Story of His Life and Work, 1805-75. *Charles Scribner's Sons, 1975.*

Cameron, Eleanor. The Green and Burning Tree: On the Writing and Enjoyment of Children's Books. *Atlantic-Little, Brown, 1969.*

Cianciolo, Patricia. Illustrations in Children's Books. *2nd ed. Brown, 1976.*

Couperie, Pierre; Horn, Maurice C.; Destefanis, Proto; François, Edouard; Moliterni, Claude; and Gassiot-Talabot, Gérald. A History of the Comic Strip. *Translated by Eileen B. Hennessy. Crown, 1967.*

Crouch, Marcus. The Nesbit Tradition: The Children's Novel in England 1945-1970. *Ernest Benn, 1972.*

Crouch, Marcus, and Ellis, Alec, eds. Chosen for Children: An Account of the Books Which Have Been Awarded the Library Association Carnegie Medal, 1936-1975. *3rd ed. The Library Association, 1977.*

Cullinan, Bernice E.; Karrer, Mary K.; and Pillar, Arlene M. Literature and the Child. *Harcourt Brace Jovanovich, 1981.*

Darton, F. J. Harvey. Children's Books in England: Five Centuries of Social Life. *2nd ed. Cambridge at the University Press, 1958.*

Dixon, Bob. Catching Them Young 1: Sex, Race and Class in Children's Fiction. *Pluto Press, 1977.*

Dreyer, Sharon Spredemann. The Bookfinder: A Guide to Children's Literature about the Needs and Problems of Youth Aged 2-15. *American Guidance Service, Inc., 1977.*

Duff, Annis. "Bequest of Wings": A Family's Pleasures with Books. *The Viking Press, 1944.*

Eakin, Mary K., ed. Good Books for Children: A Selection of Outstanding Children's Books Published, 1950-65. *Third edition. University of Chicago Press, 1966.*

Eaton, Anne Thaxter. Reading with Children. *Viking Press, 1940.*

Egoff, Sheila. Thursday's Child: Trends and Patterns in Contemporary Children's Literature. *American Library Association, 1981.*

Eyre, Frank. British Children's Books in the Twentieth Century. *Longman Books, 1971, Dutton, 1973.*

Fisher, Margery. Intent Upon Reading: A Critical Appraisal of Modern Fiction for Children. *Hodder & Stoughton Children's Books, 1961.*

Fisher, Margery. Who's Who in Children's Books: A Treasury of the Familiar Characters of Childhood. *Holt, Rinehart and Winston, Weidenfeld & Nicolson, 1975.*

Godden, Rumer. Hans Christian Andersen: A Great Life in Brief. *Knopf, 1955.*

Green, Roger Lancelyn. Tellers of Tales. *Rev. ed. Franklin Watts, Inc., 1965, Kaye and Ward, Ltd, 1969.*

Grønbech, Bo. Hans Christian Andersen. *Twayne, 1980.*

Haviland, Virginia, and Smith, William Jay, eds. Children & Poetry: A Selective Annotated Bibliography. *The Library of Congress, 1969.*

Hazard, Paul. Books, Children and Men. *4th ed. Translated by Marguerite Mitchell. Horn Book, 1960.*

Hotchkiss, Jeanette. African-Asian Reading Guide for Children and Young Adults. *The Scarecrow Press, Inc., 1976.*

Huck, Charlotte S., and Kuhn, Doris Young. Children's Literature in the Elementary School. *2nd ed. Holt, Rinehart and Winston, 1968.*

Human—and Anti-Human—Values in Children's Books: A Content Rating Instrument for Educators and Concerned Parents. *Racism and Sexism Resource Center for Educators, 1976.*

Hürlimann, Bettina. Three Centuries of Children's Books in Europe. *Edited and translated by Brian W. Alderson. Oxford University Press, 1967.*

James, M. R. Preface to Forty-Two Stories, *by Hans Andersen. Translated by M. R. James. Faber and Faber, 1968.*

Jan, Isabelle. On Children's Literature. *Edited by Catherine Storr. Schocken, 1974.*

Jarrell, Mary von S. "Notes," *taken from the phonograph record album cover for* Randall Jarrell: The Bat-Poet. *Caedmon Records, 1972.*

Lanes, Selma G. Down the Rabbit Hole: Adventures and Misadventures in the Realm of Children's Literature. *Atheneum, 1972.*

LeShan, Eda J. In Search of Myself—And Other Children. *M. Evans and Company, Inc., 1976.*

Livsey, Rosemary E., & others, eds. Notable Children's Books: 1940-1959. *American Library Association, 1966.*

Lonsdale, Bernard J., and Mackintosh, Helen K. Children Experience Literature. *Random House, 1973.*

MacCann, Donnarae, and Richard, Olga. The Child's First Books: A Critical Study of Pictures and Texts. *Wilson, 1973.*

Meigs, Cornelia; Eaton, Anne Thaxter; Nesbitt, Elizabeth; and Viguers, Ruth Hill. A Critical History of Children's Literature. *Rev. ed. Edited by Cornelia Meigs. Macmillan, 1969.*

Moore, Anne Carroll. A Century of Kate Greenaway. *Warne, 1946.*

Moss, Elaine. Picture Books for Young People: 9-13. *The Thimble Press, 1981.*

Moss, Elaine, ed. Children's Books of the Year: 1974. *Hamish Hamilton, 1975.*

Muir, Percy. Victorian Illustrated Books. *B. T. Batsford Ltd, 1971.*

Ord, Priscilla A., ed. The Child and the Story: An Exploration of Narrative Forms. *Children's Literature Association, 1983.*

Peterson, Linda Kauffman, and Solt, Marilyn Leathers. Newbery and Caldecott Medal and Honor Books: An Annotated Bibliography. *G. K. Hall & Co., 1982.*

Printed for Children: World Children's Book Exhibition. *Saur, 1978.*

Reumert, Elith. Hans Andersen the Man. *Translated by Jessie Brochner. Methuen & Company, Limited, 1927, Tower Books, 1971.*

Robinson, Evelyn Rose, ed. Readings about Children's Literature. *McKay, 1966.*

Root, Jr., Shelton L., & others, eds. Adventuring with Books: 2,400 Titles for Pre-K-Grade 8. *Citation Press, 1973.*

Rudman, Masha Kabakow. Children's Literature: An Issues Approach. *D. C. Heath and Company, 1976.*

Sale, Roger. Fairy Tales and After: From Snow White to E. B. White. *Harvard University Press, 1978.*

Salway, Lance, ed. A Peculiar Gift: Nineteenth Century Writings on Books for Children. *Kestrel Books, 1976.*

Scudder, Horace E. Childhood in Literature and Art. *Houghton Mifflin, 1894.*

Sebesta, Sam Leaton, and Iverson, William J. Literature for Thursday's Child. *Science Research Associates, 1975.*

Smaridge, Norah. Famous Author-Illustrators for Young People. *Dodd, Mead, 1973.*

Smith, Irene. A History of the Newbery and Caldecott Medals. *The Viking Press, 1957.*

Smith, Janet Adam. Children's Illustrated Books. *Collins, 1948.*

Smith, Lillian H. The Unreluctant Years: A Critical Approach to Children's Literature. *American Library Association, 1953.*

Spielmann, M. H., and Layard, G. S. Kate Greenaway. *Putnam's, 1905.*

Sutherland, Zena; Monson, Dianne L.; and Arbuthnot, May Hill. Children and Books. *6th ed. Scott, Foresman, 1981.*

Sutherland, Zena, ed. The Best in Children's Books: The University of Chicago Guide to Children's Literature, 1966-1972. *University of Chicago Press, 1973.*

Thwaite, M. F. From Primer to Pleasure: An Introduction to the History of Children's Books in England, from the Invention of Printing to 1900. *The Library Association, 1963.*

Townsend, John Rowe. Written for Children: An Outline of English-Language Children's Literature. *Revised edition. Lippincott, 1974.*

Townsend, John Rowe. A Sounding of Storytellers: New and Revised Essays on Contemporary Writers for Children. *J. B. Lippincott, 1979.*

Viguers, Ruth Hill. Introduction to The Kate Greenaway Treasury: An Anthology of the Illustrations and Writings of Kate Greenaway, *edited by Edward Ernest with Patricia Tracy Lowe. World Publishing Co., 1967.*

CUMULATIVE INDEX TO AUTHORS

Author Index

Author Index

CUMULATIVE INDEX TO TITLES

Title Index

CUMULATIVE INDEX TO NATIONALITIES